Routledge Revivals

The Swahili Coast

First published in 1971, *The Swahili Coast* deals with a sixty-year period in which Arabs from Oman in Arabia extended their influence over the East African coast from Mogadishu in the north to Cape Delgado in the South. This region had a culture and a way of life quite distinct from that of the interior and had always been an area of great maritime activity. For hundreds of years, Arabs had come down on the monsoon winds to trade there, and for two centuries, the Portuguese had controlled the region.

In the course of the period covered by this book the ruler of the Omani Arabs transferred his seat of government from Arabia to Zanzibar. This involved him in delicate relationships with the Western powers who developed strategic and commercial interests in the area, and in conflicts with the local inhabitants of the East African littoral. Based on many original and hitherto unpublished materials, this book illuminates the reasons for this extension of Arab influence in the western part of the Indian Ocean, and shows the growing involvement of Western powers with the politics of the Sultanate of Zanzibar. Attention is also focused on the development of trade on the Swahili coast, as well as the reaction of the local populace to Arab and Western pressures. This study will be particularly useful for advanced students of African history, African Studies and anyone interested in political, social, and economic development of East Africa.

The Swahili Coast

Politics, Diplomacy and Trade on the East African Littoral, 1798-1856

C. S. Nicholls

First published in 1971
by George Allen & Unwin Ltd.

This edition first published in 2024 by Routledge
4 Park Square, Milton Park, Abingdon, Oxon, OX14 4RN

and by Routledge
605 Third Avenue, New York, NY 10017

Routledge is an imprint of the Taylor & Francis Group, an informa business

© George Allen & Unwin Ltd, 1971

All rights reserved. No part of this book may be reprinted or reproduced or utilised in any form or by any electronic, mechanical, or other means, now known or hereafter invented, including photocopying and recording, or in any information storage or retrieval system, without permission in writing from the publishers.

Publisher's Note
The publisher has gone to great lengths to ensure the quality of this reprint but points out that some imperfections in the original copies may be apparent.

Disclaimer
The publisher has made every effort to trace copyright holders and welcomes correspondence from those they have been unable to contact.

A Library of Congress record exists under ISBN: 0049670026

ISBN: 978-1-032-81911-2 (hbk)
ISBN: 978-1-003-50199-2 (ebk)
ISBN: 978-1-032-81912-9 (pbk)

Book DOI 10.4324/9781003501992

THE SWAHILI COAST

POLITICS, DIPLOMACY AND TRADE
ON THE EAST AFRICAN LITTORAL
1798-1856

BY

C. S. NICHOLLS

LONDON
GEORGE ALLEN & UNWIN LTD
RUSKIN HOUSE   MUSEUM STREET

First published in 1971

This book is copyright under the Berne Convention. All rights are reserved. Apart from any fair dealing for the purpose of private study, research, criticism or review, as permitted under the Copyright Act, 1956, no part of this publication may be reproduced, stored in a retrieval system, or transmitted, in any form or by any means, electronic, electrical, chemical, mechanical, optical, photocopying, recording or otherwise, without the prior permission of the copyright owner. Enquiries should be addressed to the publishers.

© *George Allen & Unwin Ltd 1971*

ISBN 0 04 967002 6

Printed in Great Britain
in 11 on 12 pt. Fournier type
by T. & A. Constable Ltd
Edinburgh

To Alexander

CONTENTS

	page
Preface	11
Note on use of plurals	12
Abbreviations	13
Maps	15
I. Society and politics on the southern Swahili Coast at the beginning of the nineteenth century	19
II. Society and politics on the northern Swahili Coast at the beginning of the nineteenth century	45
III. Trade and commerce on the Swahili Coast at the beginning of the nineteenth century	74
IV. The prelude to Omani expansion in East Africa: the growth of Muscat and its relations with Great Britain and France	101
V. The expansion of Omani interests on the Swahili Coast	119
VI. Saiyid Saʻid and the Western powers, 1819-1839	134
VII. Saiyid Saʻid and the Western powers, 1839-1856	163
VIII. The Slave Trade on the Swahili Coast	197
IX. Attempts to suppress the Swahili Coast Slave Trade and their effect	218
X. Zanzibar: the consolidation of Omani authority	246
XI. The Swahili Coast: the consolidation of Omani authority and local reactions to it	295
XII. The economic development of the Swahili Coast	324
Conclusion	376
APPENDIX	
I The Mazrui governors of Mombasa	380
II Sources	381
Bibliography	390
Index	401

The cover illustration showing a Swahili family is taken from a lithograph made from a daguerreotype taken during Guillain's voyage along the Swahili Coast 1846-9. The lithograph is to be found in the album which accompanies Guillain's *Voyage à la côte orientale d'Afrique*.

MAPS

1. Mombasa
2. The Lamu Archipelago
3. The Swahili Coast
4. Zanzibar Island
5. Oman and the Persian Gulf
6. The Indian Ocean

PREFACE

In this book I have attempted to describe the impact of an aggressive maritime group, the Omani Arabs, on the peoples of the Swahili Coast in the first half of the nineteenth century. I have tried to illustrate the way in which the Omanis reacted to and benefited from the interests of Western powers and Western merchants in this area during the same period. My researches have led me from the Swahili Coast itself to the archives of the East India Company in London and the records of French ministries in Paris. Despite the fascinating implications of the French, British, American and German interests in this region, I have tried to focus my attention mainly upon the Swahili Coast itself and upon the reaction of its peoples to the various intruders with whose threats and blandishments they had to contend.

In writing this book I have received much valuable help and encouragement. It is impossible to name all those to whom I am indebted. However, I do wish to record my thanks to Dr R. D. Bathurst and Dr J. C. Wilkinson for the assistance which they gave me in matters connected with Oman. I am particularly grateful to the late Sir John Gray for his help and advice. I should also like to express my gratitude to St Antony's College, Oxford, and the Institute of Commonwealth Studies, London University, for financing my research. Finally I should like to thank my husband for his constant encouragement.

NOTE ON THE PLURALS OF PROPER NAMES AND OTHER NOUNS

I have anglicized the plurals of a number of Arabic and Swahili words where this is already common practice and where the Arabic or Swahili plurals might confuse the reader – for example, Al Bu Saʻidis, Mazruis, Swahilis, and *qadhis*. In some other cases I have felt it necessary to leave some words in their singular form even when used in a plural sense. For example, the Swahili plural for *jumbe* is *majumbe*, but this might confuse the reader; on the other hand, an anglicized plural would not be satisfactory. Three Swahili plurals, which have a collective meaning, are in fact used – *vijana, watu wakuu,* and *waẓee*.

ABBREVIATIONS USED IN FOOTNOTES

Amer.N.A., Zanz.   American National archives at Washington. Inwards from Zanzibar.

A.N.   Archives Nationales, Paris.

A.E.   Archives of Ministère des Affaires Étrangères, Quai d'Orsay, Paris.

M.O.   Ministère d'Outremer, Paris.

Aff.Etr.   Affaires Étrangères – a series in the Archives Nationales.

O.I.   Océan Indien – a series in the Ministère d'Outremer.

Z.A.   Zanzibar Archives (previously in the Peace Memorial Museum and the Secretariat, Zanzibar).

P.R.O. Adm.   Public Record Office, London, Admiralty records.

F.O.   Public Record Office, London. Foreign Office records. Also Foreign Office.

C.O.   Public Record Office, London. Colonial Office records.

P.L.B.   Bombay Political Letters Received. India Office Library, London.

E.S.L.B.   Enclosures to Secret Letters from Bombay, India Office Library, London.

S.L.B.   Secret Letters from Bombay, India Office Library, London.

L.R.B.   Letters Received from Bombay (a series which preceded the division into Political Letters Received and Secret Letters Received).

Beng.S.P.C.   Bengal Secret and Political Consultations.

B.C.   Board's Collections, India Office Library, London (the enclosures to Political letters from India were filed with the drafts of the replies from London in Board's Collections). The 'Dr.' following 'B.C.' indicates the draft number of the replying letter.

B.P.C.   Bombay Political Consultations, India Office Library, London (the deliberations of the Bombay Council).

B.Pub.P.   Bombay Public Proceedings, India Office Library.

B.S.C.	Bombay Secret Consultations, India Office Library, London (deliberations of the Bombay Council).
B.P.S.P.	Bombay Political and Secret Proceedings, India Office Library, London.
Proc.	Proceedings (follows the above letters).
Ministry of F.A.	Ministry of Foreign Affairs, Paris.
T.N.R.	*Tanganyika Notes and Records.* (Now *Tanzania Notes and Records.*)
J.R.G.S.	*Journal of the Royal Geographical Society.*
R.G.S.	Royal Geographical Society.
E.I.C.	East India Company (British).
I.O.L.	India Office Library, London.
L/Mil.	A series in the military records in the India Office Library, London.
C. of Ds.	Court of Directors of the East India Company, London.
Sec. of State	Secretary of State.
Madag.	Madagascar (a series in the Ministère d'Outremer).
C.P. and C.C.	Correspondance politique and correspondance commerciale (series in the Ministère des Affaires Étrangères).

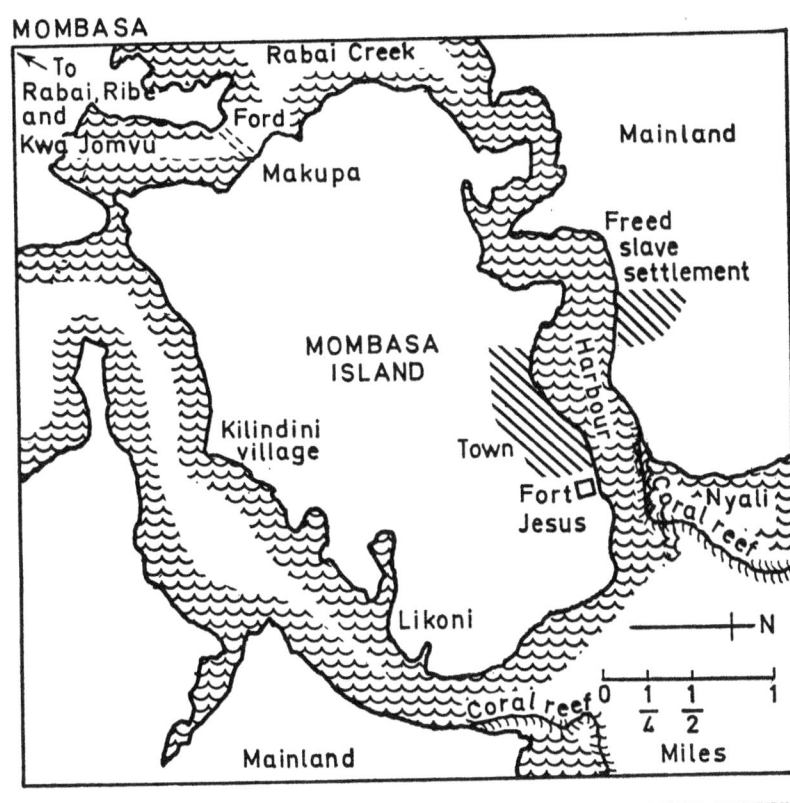

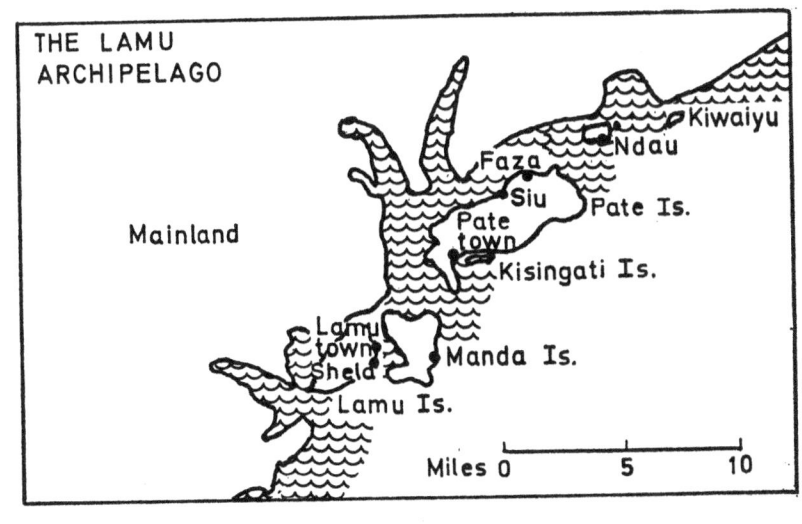

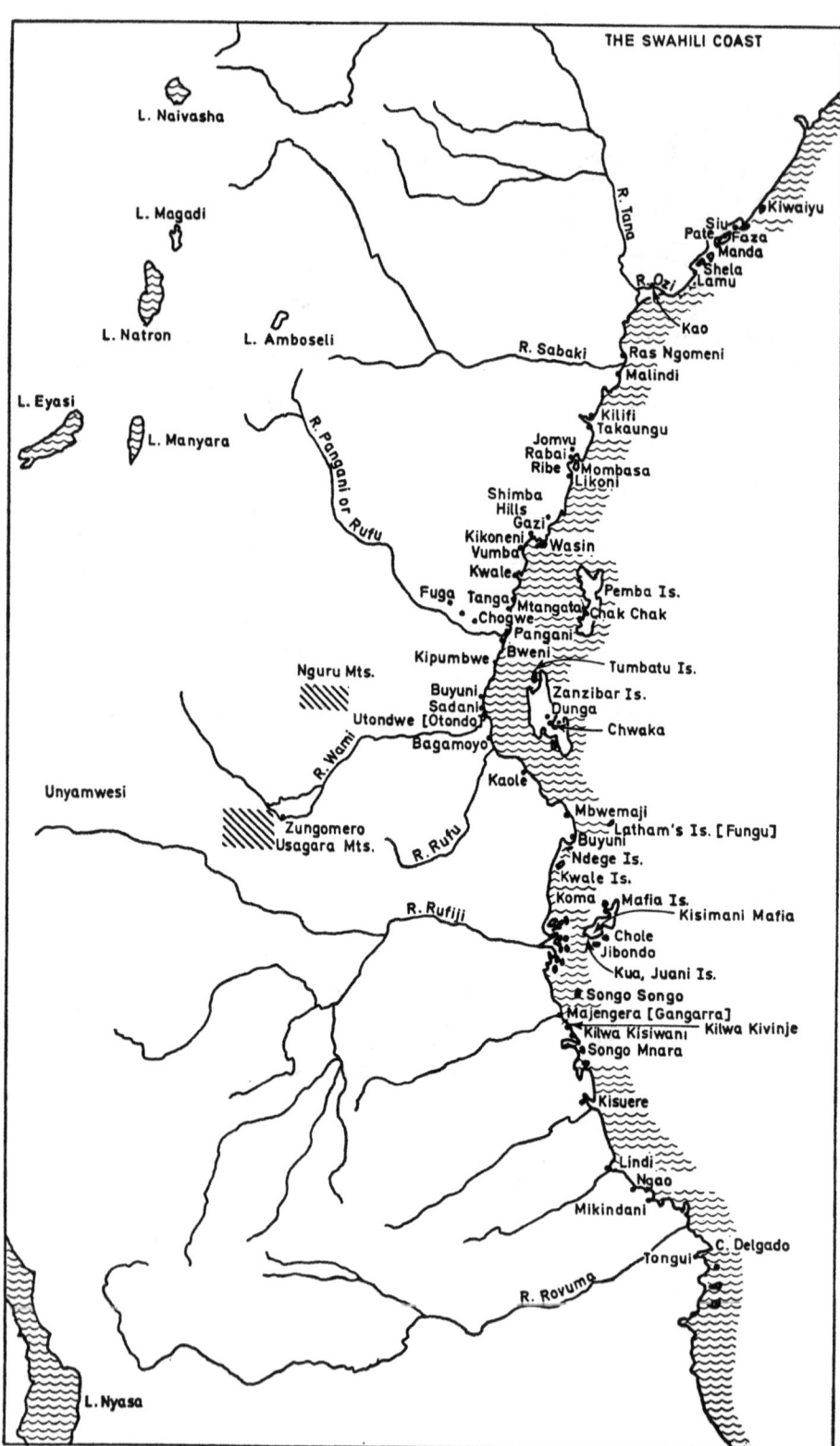

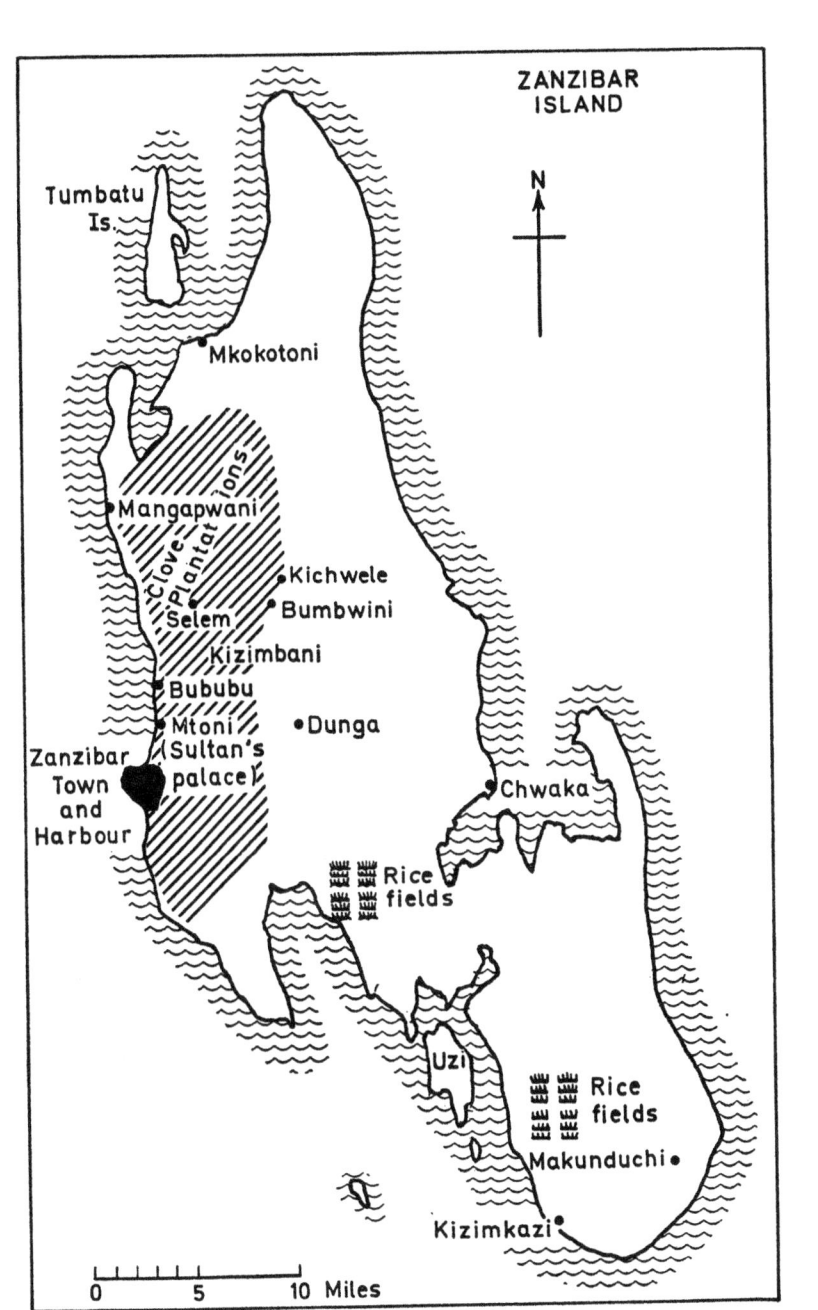

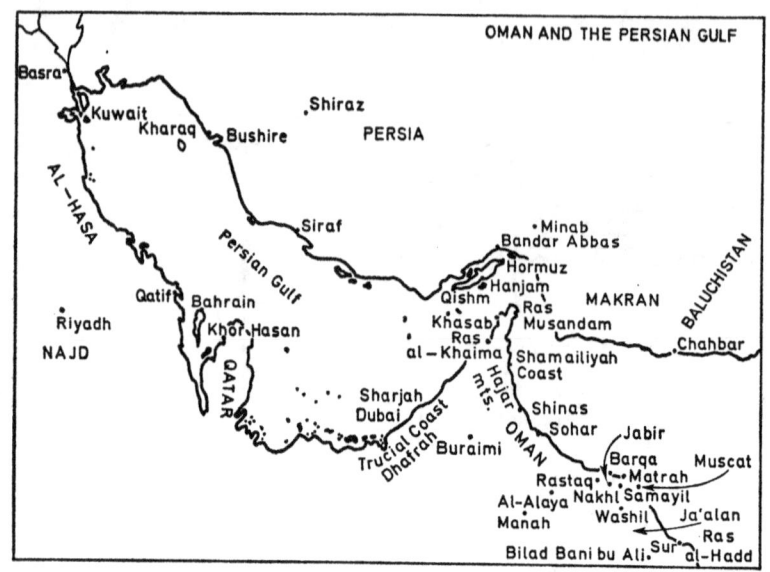

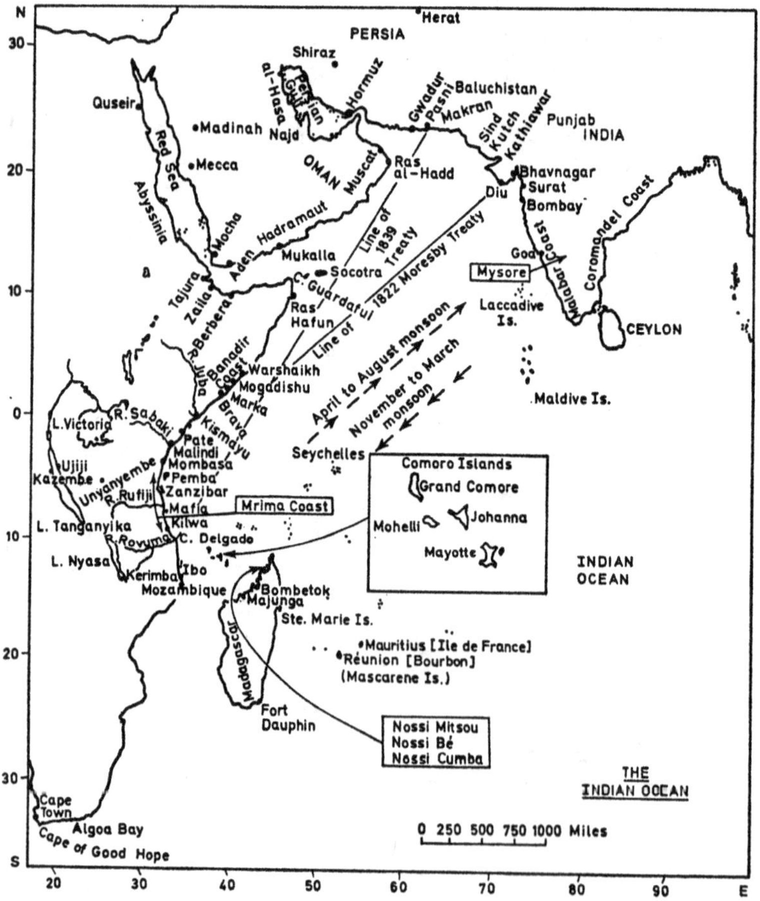

CHAPTER I

SOCIETY AND POLITICS ON THE SOUTHERN SWAHILI COAST

AT THE BEGINNING OF THE NINETEENTH CENTURY

In the Arabic language the word 'Swahili' simply means 'belonging to the coast', but by the beginning of the nineteenth century some Arabs were using it to describe a specific group of people: those who inhabited the East African coast from the mouth of the River Juba in the north to Cape Delgado in the south.[1] In this sense it had more than a merely geographical meaning, and carried with it cultural and political implications. It is not known when this particular definition of the word came into common usage or when the inhabitants of the East African coast began to apply it to themselves.

'Swahili' was indeed an apt name for these people, since they owed their cultural and economic identity to the opportunities afforded them by their position on the coast. The products of the African interior were inaccessible to visiting traders without their co-operation,

[1] Although there is evidence that the Swahili language was in existence before the eighteenth century, the name 'Swahili' does not appear to have been applied to either the people of the East African coast or their region. An exception is the use of the word in 1331 by Ibn Batuta to describe what is probably the coast of present-day Tanzania and its inhabitants – translation by G. S. P. Freeman-Grenville, *The East African Coast – Select Documents* (London, 1962), p. 31 (hereafter cited as *Select Documents*). The word 'Swahili' is not found in Portuguese sources – see Justus Strandes, *The Portuguese Period in East Africa* (Nairobi, 1961), p. 162. No maps of this period bear the word. In 1802, however, the Omani Arabs were calling the East African coast 'Sawahil' – Seton to Bombay, 9 July 1802, Proc. 27 Aug., B.P.S.P. 381/33. Soon the word was being commonly used to describe the people of the region; for example, Lt Smee, visiting East Africa in 1811, said that people called 'Soowilees' inhabited the littoral region from the Equator to Cape Delgado, and he also compiled a list of 'Soowilee' words – Smee's log, entry for 13 Feb. 1811, I.O.L., Marine Records Miscellaneous 586.

and likewise the peoples of the interior could obtain goods from overseas only through their medium. Foreign traders came to East Africa to buy goods highly desirable in their own countries: ivory, gold, amber, and tortoise-shell were among the most exotic of their purchases. East Africa also provided the cowry shells used for currency in India and the rhino-horn which was so popular as an aphrodisiac. More mundane exports were skins, gum, and wood. Finally, the traders who came to East Africa indulged in the traffic in human lives, for that region was a major source of slaves.

It is not within the scope of this book to trace the historical development of the distinctive Swahili way of life which existed on the East African coast at the beginning of the nineteenth century. All that can be said here is that at various stages during the preceding centuries the coastal inhabitants had been greatly affected by their political and commercial contacts with the diverse peoples who had visited their homeland. Their traditions and practices showed evidence of their association with peoples of the hinterland and interior of Africa. They had also been influenced by the merchants from the Persian Gulf, Arabia, and India, who had been able to voyage regularly to East Africa because of the existence of the monsoon winds. Throughout the centuries many of these traders had settled temporarily or permanently on the East African coast, leaving their mark on the way of life there. Under their influence the inhabitants of the East African littoral region had become Muslim.

Later, European influences had reached the East African coast. By 1508, ten years after their discovery of a new route to India round the Cape of Good Hope, the Portuguese conquered all the important towns on the East African coast from Mozambique to Brava. For two centuries the Portuguese remained the major political influence in that region. They were then superseded by Arabs from Oman. By the beginning of the nineteenth century these Omani Arabs had maintained a close political association with the towns of the East African coast for more than a hundred years.

In order to understand Swahili society at the beginning of the nineteenth century it is therefore necessary to examine the impact of the Omanis on Swahili life. Before the latter half of the seventeenth century the links between Oman and East Africa had been mainly commercial. The Omanis had become great maritime traders because they possessed ports which occupied very favourable positions in the trade routes of the Indian Ocean. For centuries they had sailed their

SOUTHERN SWAHILI SOCIETY AND POLITICS, CIRCA 1800

ships to India and to the East coast of Africa, as far south as Mozambique.[1] As early as the tenth century, East African ivory destined for the markets of India and China was routed through Oman.[2] Some of the Omanis who went to East Africa to trade had stayed there permanently. At the beginning of the sixteenth century the Omanis' contacts with East Africa had assumed a more significant aspect when their own coastline, like that of East Africa, had been conquered by the Portuguese. Already sharing a common commercial interest, the Omanis and the inhabitants of the East African littoral now faced a common enemy. In 1650 the Omanis were able to recapture Muscat, their major seaport, from the Portuguese. At the same time they seized some Portuguese ships which gave them the nucleus of a naval force. As more vessels were added in succeeding years the Omanis were able to carry their fight against the Portuguese into more distant waters. In 1668 they attacked Diu on the coast of India, and the following year they took their fleet even further, to Mozambique in East Africa. Skirmishes at such a distance had only limited success, but nearer home the Omanis were far more effective. With the aid of the Dutch they pushed the Portuguese out of the Persian Gulf.[3]

Having achieved victory over the Portuguese in home waters, the Omanis were able to turn their attention to Swahili rebellion against Portuguese rule. Although they were 2,200 miles from the East African coast their fleet enabled them to offer the East Africans effective help. The Omanis had two major motives when encouraging Swahili resistance to the Portuguese. Firstly, they feared that the Portuguese, having only recently been ejected from the Persian Gulf, might be tempted to launch a counter-attack from East Africa. Secondly, they hoped that, by driving the Portuguese from the Swahili Coast, they would free Omani ships from the tolls and commercial restrictions which had been imposed upon them. The Omanis therefore laid siege to Fort Jesus in Mombasa, the bastion of Portuguese rule on the Swahili Coast. In 1698 it fell to them, and this event ushered in a period of Omani influence.

The maintenance of this influence throughout the eighteenth century

[1] George Hourani, *Arab Seafaring in the Indian Ocean in Ancient and Mediaeval Times* (Beirut, 1963), p. 80.
[2] Translation of extracts from Al-Masudi in Freeman-Grenville, *Select Documents*, pp. 14-17.
[3] For this period of Omani history see R. D. Bathurst, 'The Ya'rubi dynasty of Oman', D.Phil. thesis, University of Oxford, 1967.

and its impact on the Swahili towns was partly determined by the politics of Oman itself and the power struggles there. The inhabitants of the Omani peninsula were provided with a limited form of political unity by their allegiance to their Imam. The office of Imam had been politico-religious in origin, having been established in the eighth century in opposition to the Caliphate by a movement which had previously splintered from the main body of Islam. This breakaway Muslim sect became known as Ibadhi. The political unity of the Omani peninsula was only limited because not all its inhabitants were Ibadhi, and those who were often refused allegiance to particular Imams. Succession to the Imamate, although supposed to be elective, tended to become dynastic, a development which encouraged factionalism. In the early eighteenth century, discontent aroused by a disputed succession initiated a civil war which split the Omanis into two factions – the Hinawi and Ghafiri. The domestic upheaval continued until Ahmad ibn Sa'id, of the Al Bu Sa'idi clan, became Imam of Oman in the 1740s. He was able to maintain his authority as Imam for about forty years but his son, Sa'id, who succeeded him in the 1780s, was not so adroit. Although Sa'id retained the title of Imam, he lost a great deal of his political importance. In Muscat and the littoral ports real authority was exercised by his son, Hamad. The fact was that the new situation created by commercial expansion and contact with the West presented problems which could not be effectively tackled by a leader whose office was hedged about by a rigid set of religious doctrines.

The Omanis needed leaders who would both encourage their maritime trade and manage the consequent relations with foreigners. To meet these requirements the Imamate would have had to have altered its nature. However, the pace of political and economic change on the coast was too rapid for it, and it lost its political influence. The new leaders of the maritime section of the Omanis based themselves on Muscat and required no religious sanction. For a while the Imamate continued to exist side by side with the new secular authorities, but its worthlessness was acknowledged when Sa'id ibn Ahmad died and no new Imam was elected to the post.[1]

The disorganization within Oman inevitably confused the Omani governors on the East African coast. The Swahili towns became directly involved in the internal struggles of Oman when their

[1] Sa'id died sometime between 1811 and 1821 – note by Badger, p. 342, in Salil ibn Ruzayq (or Razik), *History of the Imams and Seyyids of Oman*, ed. G. P. Badger (Hakluyt Society, 1871).

governors took sides in the faction fighting. Each time a new ruler acceded to power in Oman he had to make desperate efforts to secure the allegiance of the overseas territories before they drifted away or rivals acquired them. New leaders, therefore, tried to appoint as governors men on whose loyalty they could rely. This constant change in personnel prevented the development of a system in which governors of outlying possessions felt a sense of responsibility towards the central authority rather than towards individual holders of that authority. Insecurity of tenure also tended to provoke the Omani governors on the Swahili Coast to declare their 'independence' of the central power. In practice this meant that they ceased to send revenue to Oman. The governors of different towns also quarrelled among themselves about the legitimacy of individual claims to the Imamate and put themselves forward as supporters of rival candidates. An Imam might therefore be faced not only with a loss of revenue from Oman's overseas possessions but also with the possibility that such places might become bases of rebellion against him.

By the beginning of the nineteenth century the Swahilis' involvement with the Omanis had affected them in a number of ways. It is not possible to generalize about the impact of the Omanis on the Swahili towns. This is because these towns, despite their cultural similarities, were politically independent of one another. Each town or island had a separate, although similar, political structure. Such fragmentation had been determined in part by topographical factors, which discouraged the formation of larger political units. For reasons of defence some towns were situated on offshore islands. Many, it is true, were on the mainland itself, but even these had difficulty in establishing a territorial domain of any size. Along much of the coast the fertile littoral strip was backed by a drier hinterland whose inhabitants, of necessity, adopted a way of life very different from that of the coast dwellers. Consequently coastal settlements had no territorial backing. Political combination between the towns along the coast, which was an alternative, was hindered by the thick scrub bush of the land and the seasonal contrary winds and currents of the sea. The political isolation of the Swahili towns was further encouraged by their economic rivalry. Since all places offered much the same commodities for sale, each would compete with its neighbours in trying to entice interior peoples and maritime traders to its own market. The parochialism which resulted was aggravated by the consequent importance of local leaders who were determined to retain their positions. The long subjection of the towns of the Swahili Coast to the Portuguese had encouraged their political isolation. The domination of the Europeans had prevented individual towns from extending their authority beyond their own boundaries. Indeed, when the Omanis began to expand along the East African coast they discovered that it was not enough to conquer one township or subject one ruler to their authority: each community had to be reduced separately if it were to be brought under Omani control. If we are to understand the impact of the Omanis on the Swahili Coast, it will therefore be necessary to examine each township separately.

However, before embarking on this description of individual Swahili settlements, the terminology which will be employed when describing the different elements in the coastal population must be explained. In the eighteenth century some French visitors to the Swahili Coast placed its inhabitants in three categories: Arabs, Moors, and Africans.[1] The group they called 'Arab' included residents who had recently come from Oman, and the floating commercial population from the Red Sea, Arabia, and the Persian Gulf. In this book the word 'Arab' will apply to precisely these people. The French visitors based their distinctions between Moors and Africans on what they supposed to be differences in racial origin or social status. In fact, they often exaggerated such differences and on closer examination the use of these terms is seen to be unjustified. In this book those whom the French named as Moors and Africans will all be called Swahilis.

By the beginning of the nineteenth century, at some of the towns of the Swahili Coast a distinction could be made between Swahilis with property and those who lived at virtually subsistence level. There were instances when some of the former were reported to have lighter skins than the latter, but this was by no means universally the case. Propertied Swahilis occupied positions of importance in the political structure of the towns, and in this context they maintained strong clan loyalties. Despite the political isolation of the various settlements, there were clan connexions and frequent intermarriages between prominent Swahili families of different towns. There is evidence that some clans of propertied Swahilis called themselves 'Shirazi', tracing

---

[1] In particular Morice and others in writings contained in a manuscript book entitled 'Projet d'un établissement', now kept in Rhodes House Library, Oxford. For this source, see Appendix II. This manuscript has been translated by G. S. P. Freeman-Grenville and published in his *The French at Kilwa Island* (Oxford, 1965).

SOUTHERN SWAHILI SOCIETY AND POLITICS, CIRCA 1800

their origin to Shiraz in Persia. This was, however, more of a status symbol than an accurate description of their origin. The propertied Swahilis were also dominant in the economic sphere. They were both merchants and landowners, organizing the trade of the Swahili Coast and possessing estates which were cultivated by their slaves.

In contrast, there were those who pursued a simpler way of life: the fishermen, sailors, smallholders, and craftsmen. They spoke the same language as the propertied Swahilis. In general it was these people whom the French called Africans. In this book, however, the word African will refer not to these non-propertied Swahilis but to the non-Muslim, non-Swahili-speaking peoples of the hinterland and interior. People in this category will also be given group, or 'tribal', names when appropriate. It must be remembered that the distinctions between all these categories are blurred, and that it was possible for people to pass from one category to another. For example, second-generation Arabs often looked like, and spoke the same language as, the Swahilis.

By 1800 the centre of Omani power on the Swahili Coast was Zanzibar. Originally, however, the Omanis regarded Mombasa as their major base. After taking that town from the Portuguese in 1698, they also established garrisons at Kilwa, Zanzibar, and Pemba.[1] In the 1720s Zanzibar was still of only limited importance to the Omanis. When in that decade the Portuguese launched a serious and long-awaited counter-attack against the Omanis on the Swahili Coast, Zanzibar apparently played no important part in the conflict.

The Portuguese had been encouraged to reassert themselves both by a group of deposed Swahili notables living in Goa and by inhabitants of Swahili towns who were dissatisfied with the Omani presence. In 1727 they recaptured a number of Swahili towns, including the most important, Mombasa.[2] Their position was, however, very unstable, and two years later the Omanis were able to retake the Swahili towns.[3] Thereafter it became increasingly obvious that the Portuguese would confine their activities to the Mozambique section of the East African coast, from which they had never been ousted.

---

[1] Report of a Portuguese observer sent from Mozambique, 1710, quoted in Strandes, *op. cit.*, pp. 275-6.

[2] Strandes, *op. cit.*, pp. 277-87; and Guillain, *Documents sur l'histoire, la géographie et le commerce de la côte orientale d'Afrique*, 3 vols and album (Paris, 1856), I, 530-1 (hereafter cited as *Documents*).

[3] Strandes, *ibid.*, pp. 290 and 294; and Guillain, *ibid.*, I, 533.

THE SWAHILI COAST

As the Portuguese threat diminished, there arose a new challenge to the Omani position in East Africa. This time the difficulties stemmed from within Oman itself. When Ahmad ibn Sa'id became Imam in the 1740s he was not accepted by all Oman's outlying possessions. Mombasa, the Imamate's major base in East Africa, refused allegiance.[1] As a result Ahmad ibn Sa'id began to regard Zanzibar as an alternative centre. He appointed as governor of that island one of his kinsmen, Abdullah ibn Jad, and provided him with a force of soldiers.[2]

Mombasa's action in the 1740s illustrated the ease with which Omani establishments along the Swahili Coast could be used as bases for rebellion against the ruling authority in Oman. This danger revealed itself once again in the 1780s. Sa'id ibn Ahmad's succession to the Imamate displeased his brother Saif who departed for East Africa to raise rebellion and establish his own domain. He appealed to the French for aid, and even when this was refused he remained a dangerous source of opposition to the Imamate. Sa'id had to send a force to remove him. During this conflict the governor of Zanzibar remained loyal to the Imamate, a fact which would have encouraged the Omani rulers to concentrate on that island rather than Mombasa.[3]

As the Omani rulers strengthened their position in Zanzibar, so they improved that town's defences. Zanzibar fort was able to resist an attack from the Mombasans in 1754, and twenty years later Morice described it as a formidable obstacle to any Swahili assault.[4] The fort would not, however, have been able to withstand bombardment from armed vessels: in 1811 Lt Smee of the Bombay Marine said a single ship of war would find little difficulty in battering it down.[5] As Zanzibar became the centre of Omani authority on the Swahili Coast its governors were more carefully chosen. In 1799 the ruler of Muscat appointed a kinsman as governor.[6] Shortly afterwards the position

---

[1] See Chapter II, p. 48.

[2] Guillain, *Documents*, I, 547, and Mazrui MS., p. 22. For Mazrui MS. see Appendix II.

[3] Report by J. Crassons de Medeuil, 1784/5, printed in Freeman-Grenville, *Select Documents*, pp. 194-5. See also Guillain, *Documents*, I, 556, and Ibn Ruzayq, *op. cit.*, p. 205.

[4] For the 1754 incident, Guillain, *Documents*, I, 549-50, and Mazrui MS., p. 23. For Morice, 'Projet d'un établissement', p. 68.

[5] Smee's Description of the island of Zanzibar, I.O.L., Marine Records Miscellaneous 586.

[6] Saif ibn Muhammad to Bombay, 15 Dec. 1799, Proc. 7 Jan. 1800, B.P.S.P. 381/9.

was given to Yaqut, an Abyssinian eunuch and freed slave with large estates in Oman which were regarded as a guarantee of his loyalty.[1]

Even though by the beginning of the nineteenth century there were only about 300 Omanis in Zanzibar, their presence inevitably affected the indigenous inhabitants.[2] In the town of Zanzibar there existed a propertied class of Swahilis who called themselves 'Shirazi'.[3] They had kinship connexions with other dominant families elsewhere on the Swahili Coast: in the 1840s Swahilis at Mafia had family links with former notables of Zanzibar.[4] The distinction between the propertied classes and the other inhabitants of Zanzibar was noticed by Ruschenberger in 1834, when he described the former as 'Swahilis' and the latter as 'free negroes'.[5] This was the same type of division as Morice earlier had made between Moors and Africans.

It is not clear what happened to the propertied families of Zanzibar when the Omani governors were appointed at the beginning of the eighteenth century. If Loarer, writing in the 1840s, is correct, many of them left for the islands in the Mafia archipelago.[6] What became of the ruler of Zanzibar, who came from one such propertied family, is also unknown. This local ruler was at first exiled from Zanzibar by the Omanis, but was allowed to return sometime before 1710.[7] It is difficult to tell whether the position of ruler of Zanzibar continued to exist in the eighteenth century, or, if it did, whether the office was kept in one family. In the 1840s some Swahilis at Mafia claimed that their family had formerly provided the rulers of Zanzibar, but this may have been before the coming of the Omanis.[8] Despite the presence of Omani governors some individual Swahilis certainly did play a leading role in Zanzibar during the eighteenth century. Guillain, writing in the 1840s, named some who co-operated extensively with the Omani

[1] Dallons to the Captain-General, Ile de France, 1804, Mauritius Archives GA 11, no. 119 (hereafter cited as 'Dallons, 1804'), printed in Freeman-Grenville, *Select Documents*, pp. 197-201.

[2] Morice, 'Projet d'un établissement', p. 50.

[3] R. F. Burton, *Zanzibar, City, Island, and Coast*, 2 vols (London, 1872), I, 411 (hereafter cited as 'Burton, *Zanzibar*').

[4] Loarer's Report, Part II, 1849, M.O., O.I. 2/10. Loarer was a commercial adviser who accompanied the Frenchman, Guillain, in his exploration of the East African coast in the late 1840s.

[5] S. W. Ruschenberger, *Voyage Round the World*, 2 vols (Philadelphia, 1838), I, 64.

[6] Loarer's Report, Part II, 1849, M.O., O.I. 2/10.

[7] Strandes, *op. cit.*, p. 275.

[8] Loarer's Report, Part II, 1849, M.O., O.I. 2/10.

Imamate.[1] It is possible that these men were the successors to the rulership of Zanzibar which had existed in Portuguese times. Such an office did exist in 1828, because an American visitor then distinguished between the 'king' of Zanzibar with his 'princes' and the Omani governor of the island.[2] The existence in the eighteenth century of the office of ruler of Zanzibar is supported by the endurance of regalia, consisting of two drums and two carved wooden horns, which in the 1840s and afterwards belonged to the dignitary known as the *mwenyi mkuu*.[3] However, the office might not have been occupied continuously. Indeed, shortly after the opening of the nineteenth century a claimant to the office appeared to be living on the mainland rather than in Zanzibar.[4]

It is probable that the office of ruler of Zanzibar did continue in existence because it was the practice of the Imamate to retain local leaders. The Omanis were interested in local administration only in so far as it affected maritime trade, relations with foreigners, and collection of revenue. Such matters were attended to by governors appointed by the Imamate and were thereby removed from the sphere of local leaders, although the latter might be encouraged to co-operate, particularly in such matters as the collection of revenue. There may in fact have been some arrangement between the local ruler of Zanzibar and the Omanis about sharing the revenue.[5]

The effect of the coming of the Omanis on the non-propertied Swahilis of Zanzibar cannot be assessed with any accuracy. These local people were called the Hadimu and Tumbatu by the Omanis. Although these names do not appear in written sources until 1811 they were probably first applied in the eighteenth century in order to distinguish the indigenous peoples who were engaged primarily in agricultural and maritime activities from both the prosperous town-dwelling Swahilis and the newly arrived Arabs.[6] The Tumbatu were

[1] Guillain, *Documents*, II, 76-7.

[2] Sir John Gray, *History of Zanzibar* (London, 1962), p. 160, quoting letters of Edmund Roberts to Senator Levi Woodbury, 19 and 26 Dec. 1828.

[3] For a description of the regalia, F. B. Pearce, *Zanzibar, the Island Metropolis of Eastern Africa* (London, 1920), pp. 175-6. For the *mwenyi mkuu*, see Chapter X, pp. 281-3.

[4] W. H. Ingrams, *Zanzibar, its History and Peoples* (London, 1931), p. 149.

[5] For a discussion of this system and its origin, see Chapter X, p. 281.

[6] The first use of 'Hadimu' in a written source appears to be in Hardy's Report on Zanzibar, 1811, I.O.L., Marine Records Miscellaneous 586, where

SOUTHERN SWAHILI SOCIETY AND POLITICS, CIRCA 1800

from a small island of the same name near Zanzibar. Their dependence on Zanzibar for fresh water gave them close connexions with the larger island, and some of them went to live there.[1] As for the name Hadimu, this may derive from the Arabic word *khadim*, meaning 'slave'. Alternatively, and this is the view of those to whom the name was applied, it may come from the Swahili word *ahadi*, which means 'promise' or 'covenant'. The Hadimu claim that they were given their name when they allowed foreigners on to their island in return for promises that they should be left to themselves.[2]

The coming of the Omanis may have influenced the indigenous peoples to alter their way of life or their places of habitation, but the evidence is extremely difficult to evaluate. The land to the north and east of Zanzibar town is the most fertile part of the island and it would have been extraordinary had the indigenous peoples not used it. However, by the middle of the nineteenth century they were occupying other parts of the island, where the land was coral rock interspersed with small pockets of good soil. They also had settlements along the east coast, the largest of which was Chwaka.[3] By that time the Omanis had established their plantations in the fertile western area. It may have been that the indigenous agriculturalists were pushed from the fertile area by the foreigners, or indeed earlier by propertied Swahilis.

The takeover of the fertile area for landed estates is not easy to date. Such estates certainly existed prior to the planting of cloves in the nineteenth century. In 1811 Smee said that the middle region of Zanzibar island, where the land rises into hills, was cultivated, and he further remarked that some inhabitants of Zanzibar town owned

the 'Macauduns' are mentioned as 'the aboriginal inhabitants of Zanzibar'. The next source to use the word is Hamerton to Mauritius, no. 11, 15 Feb. 1845, Z.A.: 'In Zanzibar there is a race of people who are never sold called the Mokhadim, who pay a poll tax to the Imam. They are aborigines of the island.' Guillain, *Documents*, II, 76, written a few years later, also uses the word.

[1] Burton, *Zanzibar*, I, 24.
[2] Ingrams, *op. cit.*, pp. 30-1. Ingrams records many local traditions. See also Chapter X, p. 284.
[3] Burton, *Zanzibar*, I, 432-3; Report on Zanzibar, 1860, by C. P. Rigby, printed in C. E. B. Russell, *General Rigby, Zanzibar and the Slave Trade* (London, 1935) – hereafter cited as 'Rigby's Report, 1860'. See also Alfred Belleville, 'A trip round the southern end of Zanzibar island', 1875, R.G.S., Collection no.: Africa 3; and Oskar Baumann, 'Der Sansibar Archipel', p. 30, Part III of *Wissenschaftliche Veröffentlichungen des Vereins für Erdkunde zu Leipzig* (Leipzig, 1899), for a detailed picture of Hadimu settlements in the 1870s and 1890s.

estates.[1] These estates supported fruits, rice, sugar, and coconuts. At the beginning of the nineteenth century the only one of these products which was exported from Zanzibar on a large scale was the coconut, mainly in the form of coir.[2] It is therefore likely that by that date there had been only limited acquisition of land. Assuming that the local agriculturalists had been living in the fertile part of the island, they might have been deprived of only part of their land. Because Zanzibar did not export foodstuffs, they required only enough land for their own subsistence and for some surplus sales in the town of Zanzibar.

The numbers of the local agriculturalists indicate that pressure on land would not have been very great. In the 1770s Morice estimated that the total population of Zanzibar, including the non-agricultural town dwellers, numbered 40,000; and in 1834 Ruschenberger calculated that the non-town dwellers numbered 17,000.[3] In 1856 Burton, basing his calculation on the tax paid by each household head, said there were 10,000 to 12,000 households.[4] Such an estimate must be treated with caution since there may have been tax avoidance. Taking these estimates into account, and remembering that Zanzibar island consists of 375,000 acres, about half of which are fertile, it would appear that there was little land hunger among the indigenous agriculturalists.

Another important point to be borne in mind is that the indigenous people may have occupied themselves more with fishing than cultivation. The fishing grounds off the east of Zanzibar are better than those off the west, so many of the local people may have been living there from preference rather than from pressure. This does not, however, accord with a tradition held by the people of Chwaka in the 1930s: that their ancestors had been spread throughout the bush, occupying themselves in cultivation, but that succeeding generations had taken more to fishing.[5]

Although it is not easy to establish whether or when the indigenous peoples of Zanzibar had to alter their places of habitation or methods of gaining a livelihood, there was one direct side-effect of the establishment of landed estates: the imposition of taxation and of a *corvée*. This too, cannot be dated, but it is unlikely to have preceded the era

[1] Smee's Report on Zanzibar, I.O.L., Marine Records Miscellaneous 586.
[2] See Chapter III, p. 83.
[3] Morice, 'Projet d'un établissement', p. 50; and Ruschenberger, *op. cit.*, I, 64.
[4] Burton, *Zanzibar*, I, 414.
[5] R. H. W. Pakenham, *Land Tenure among the Wahadimu of Chwaka, Zanzibar Island* (Zanzibar, government printer, 1947), p. 3.

SOUTHERN SWAHILI SOCIETY AND POLITICS, CIRCA 1800

of the plantations.[1] In the nineteenth century the *mwenyi mkuu* was responsible for organizing the *corvée*. He was assisted in doing so by local headmen. It is possible that the structure needed to fulfil the requirements for the *corvée* was one of the factors which encouraged the development of a corporate identity among the Hadimu which was later apparent to observers.[2] Such feelings of common identity would also have been stimulated if local agriculturalists had needed to uproot themselves and settle in different parts of the island.

By the beginning of the nineteenth century the Omanis were exercising only a limited authority over the people of Zanzibar. The role they played on other parts of the Swahili Coast was even more restricted. On the southern section of the coast the only place, apart from Zanzibar, where they established control was Kilwa Kisiwani. Close to the mainland, Kilwa Kisiwani was an island about three miles long and two wide – far smaller than Zanzibar. Kilwa Kisiwani was the most important Swahili settlement near that section of the East African coast still retained by the Portuguese. Consequently, even though the Omani position there was precarious, it was necessary for the Imamate to retain its hold on Kilwa. In 1710 there was an Omani garrison on the island, but by 1726 it had been expelled by the local sultan with the aid of the Portuguese.[3] However, the Omanis probably regained Kilwa when they recaptured other Swahili towns from the Portuguese in 1729.

In Kilwa, as in Zanzibar, Omani influence fluctuated as a result of events within Oman itself. Although the Kilwa Omanis, unlike those of Mombasa, accepted Ahmad ibn Sa'id as Imam in the 1740s, the local inhabitants probably took advantage of the unstable position of the new Imam, for in the 1770s there was no longer an Omani governor and garrison on Kilwa and the local leader, known as the sultan, had regained his authority.[4] The Omani political troubles of the 1780s,

---

[1] For the tax, which amounted to 4,000 dollars annually in grain etc. (in 1811), see Hardy's Report on Zanzibar, I.O.L., Marine Records Miscellaneous 586. For the *corvée*, Ruschenberger, *op. cit.*, I, 64, and Guillain, *Documents*, II, 77. See also Chapter X, p. 282.
[2] Observers such as A. Werner, 'The Wahadimu of Zanzibar', *Journal of the African Society* (July 1916), vol. 15, no. LX, pp. 356-60; and Pakenham, *op. cit.*
[3] Strandes, *op. cit.*, pp. 275, 277-8.
[4] Morice, in 'Projet d'un établissement', p. 142, says the governor was removed in 1771. For the title of '*sultan*' for the overall ruler of Kilwa and of '*mfalme*' for the prominent members of his family, see Princes of Kilwa to Commander of Bourbon, 12 Mch. 1819, M.O., Réunion 72/472.

which as usual had repercussions in East Africa, encouraged the Imamate to reimpose a governor on Kilwa. The Imam's brother, Saif ibn Ahmad, had tried to raise rebellion in Kilwa, an action which demonstrated that, despite the disappearance of the Portuguese threat, it was dangerous to leave that port unattended.[1] In any case, the Imam's interest in Kilwa had been revived by the new prosperity which had come to the island with the sale of slaves to Frenchmen from Bourbon and Ile de France.[2] In 1785 the Imam forcibly re-established a garrison at Kilwa.[3] It appears that in doing so he had to compromise with that part of his family which had disapproved of his accession, because he appointed as governor Saif ibn Ahmad's son.[4]

An attempt must be made to define the limits of the Omani governor's authority in Kilwa. There are various difficulties in doing so due not only to a lack of historical sources but also to the amorphous nature of Omani rule. From the Omani point of view the governor's main function was to collect revenue and ensure that Kilwa did not become positively disloyal to the Imamate. He was supported in doing so by a garrison of between twelve and twenty men who dwelt in a fort defended by three cannon.[5] This force by itself was hardly enough to repress the local population, had it wished to overthrow the Omanis. The fact was that the Omanis had little interest in domestic administration of the island. If they were faced with serious revolt they could always call in additional reinforcements from Zanzibar and Oman. The casual nature of their authority is demonstrated by the fact that,

[1] Report by J. Crassons de Medeuil, 1784/5, printed in Freeman-Grenville, *Select Documents*, p. 194.

[2] James Prior, *Voyage of the Frigate Nisus* (London, 1819), p. 68. The *Nisus* visited Kilwa in 1811. See also Chapter V, p. 121.

[3] For the date, inscription over the gate of the fort at Kilwa Kisiwani. Albrand, a Frenchman who visited Kilwa in 1819, was given by Sausse an eyewitness report of what was probably the same incident – Albrand to Milius, 1 June 1819, M.O., Réunion 72/472 (hereafter cited as 'Albrand's Report, 1819').

[4] Prior, *op. cit.*, pp. 68 and 71. Prior names the man as Ali and says he was Saiyid Sa'id's brother. In fact he was Sa'id's uncle and he died shortly before 1819 – Albrand's Report, as above. He must have been Ali ibn Saif, the brother of Sa'id's wife (see Chapter X, p. 280) and the son of Saif ibn Ahmad mentioned in the text above – see *Aulad el Imam*, a genealogy of members of Zanzibar's Sultanate family, prepared by Philip Pullicino (Zanzibar, 1954), table IV.

[5] Prior, *op. cit.*, p. 71, giving the number as twenty, and W. H. Smyth, *The Life and Services of Captain Philip Beaver, Late of H.M. Ship Nisus* (London, 1829), p. 277, giving the number as twelve. Smyth prints the diary of Beaver, the captain of the *Nisus* on its visit to Kilwa in 1811.

SOUTHERN SWAHILI SOCIETY AND POLITICS, CIRCA 1800

on both occasions of recorded European visits to Kilwa in the early nineteenth century, there was no Omani governor on the island.[1] However weak the physical presence of the Omanis in Kilwa, they were nevertheless able to carry out their most important function, which was the raising of revenue. This was done mainly by the control of customs duties which were farmed out to an agent. Some of the duties still went to the local sultan because, upon the arrival of the Omanis at Kilwa, they had made an agreement with the sultan that he should retain his title and one-fifth of the customs dues.[2]

Despite the presence of an Omani governor, therefore, the Kilwans retained their traditional political system. Frenchmen who visited Kilwa to purchase slaves in the 1770s and 1780s have provided us with a picture of its sultanate and society, and it is not unreasonable to use their descriptions as a guide to the situation at the beginning of the nineteenth century. As in many Swahili towns, in Kilwa the sultanate remained in one clan which regarded itself as 'Shirazi'.[3] The succession to this office was affected by the wishes of previous sultans, the influence of notables from both Kilwa itself and nearby mainland villages, and the ability of alternative candidates to depose the holder of the position.[4]

In most of the towns of the Swahili Coast, the traditional rulers were advised by prominent people who were often given special titles. The success of a ruler would partly depend on his ability to retain the allegiance of his counsellors who were themselves prominent members of important clans.[5] The most powerful of such men at Kilwa in the 1770s was an official whom the French slaver, Morice, called the *malindane* or 'vizier'.[6] It is likely that this man led a group of inhabitants who had emigrated from Malindi in some former period and who,

---

[1] Prior, *op. cit.*, p. 70 (the governor was absent on a visit to Zanzibar), and Albrand's Report, 1819, M.O., Réunion 72/472 (the governor had recently died).

[2] Albrand's Report, as *ibid.*

[3] For 'Shirazi', treaty between Morice and the sultan of Kilwa, 'Projet d'un établissement', p. 59. For the office remaining in the same clan, Prior, *op. cit.*, p. 68; Smyth, *op. cit.*, p. 276; and Princes of Kilwa to Commander of Bourbon, 12 Mch. 1819, M.O., Réunion 72/472.

[4] For examples of deposition, see Morice, 'Projet d'un établissement', p. 54; for influence of mainland chiefs, Albrand's Report, 1819, M.O., Réunion 72/472.

[5] Morice, 'Projet d'un établissement', p. 197; and Prior, *op. cit.*, p. 70.

[6] Morice, *ibid.*, p. 55; and Morice's Memoir concerning the East Coast of Africa, 15 June and 26 Sept. 1777, A.N., Colonies C4/42.

according to traditional history, were allowed to have their own leaders.[1] In 1811 neither of two British visitors, Prior and Beaver, mentioned any such notable, but in 1819 the Frenchman Albrand met a man called 'Moïndani' who was 'un vieux serviteur . . . [du] Prince'.[2]

It was the nature of the authority of the traditional government of Kilwa rather than the structure of that government which was affected by the appointment of an Omani governor. Prior made a good summary of the position when he said of the sultan:

'The Arabs save him the trouble of collecting the revenues, otherwise he is so far independent as to have the honour and trouble of a kingdom without the substantial profits attached to it.'[3]

Whether the sultan received his portion of the revenue provided for by the original agreement is unknown, but Prior was of the opinion that he had little other emolument than what he could earn from his own trading ventures.[4] The fact that the traditional rulers had lost one of their essential powers must have affected their authority. Evidence from other Swahili towns, which will be considered later, indicates how important it was for leaders to possess the financial means to coerce and conciliate their subjects.

Despite losing their control over the island's revenues, the sultans of Kilwa appear to have had far more authority than the Swahili leaders of Zanzibar. When Prior and Beaver visited Kilwa in 1811 it was the principal Swahilis who met them and negotiated the sale of spars.[5] It is true that the Omani governor was absent, but no deputy or garrison representative had dealings with the visitors. A similar situation occurred in 1819 when foreigners again carried on negotiations with the sultanate clan, apparently without any Omani intervention.[6]

The sultanate of Kilwa also had some influence over nearby mainland villages. In 1777 it was claimed that this extended from the Ndege islands in the north to Mikindani in the south.[7] This may have meant, among other things, that the sultan's views were taken into account when chiefs were appointed in this area.[8] The sultanate retained its

[1] A traditional history of Kilwa Kisiwani, printed in C. Velten, *Prosa und Poesie der Suaheli* (Berlin, 1907), pp. 243-52 (hereafter cited as *Prosa und Poesie*).
[2] Albrand's Report, 1819, M.O., Réunion 72/472.
[3] Prior, *op. cit.*, p. 68. [4] *Idem.*
[5] *Ibid.*, p. 70. For the visit, see Chapter V, p. 121.
[6] Albrand's Report, 1819, M.O., Réunion 72/472.
[7] Morice, 'Projet d'un établissement', pp. 113, 118-19.
[8] Morice states that this was done, *ibid.*, p. 113.

SOUTHERN SWAHILI SOCIETY AND POLITICS, CIRCA 1800

influence on the mainland after the appointment of an Omani governor, which may have been due to the fact that the Omanis as yet had no wish to levy customs duties at all the village ports. When Prior visited Kilwa its sultan was at Mongallo (Ngao?) 'where he had been for some months regulating the government'.[1]

On the whole, the relationship between the sultanate and the Omani occupiers was one of uneasy coexistence. The sultan was too cautious to risk an open confrontation with the Omanis, even though the temptation presented by the small Omani garrison must at times have seemed very great. Although he had no soldiers, the sultan surreptitiously collected cannon, arms, and powder, which he concealed in his house.[2] He was careful to let night fall before he landed the muskets and ammunition which Beaver gave him in 1811.[3] But the sultans of Kilwa would not have acted without stimulus and assistance from outside. On many occasions they discussed with Europeans the removal of the Omanis.[4] Yet, so long as no practical assistance was provided, they did nothing themselves to make their hopes a reality.

If during this period the sultans of Kilwa were able to maintain themselves fairly effectively, the rest of the population was, on the whole, less fortunate. As in most of the towns of the East African coast, in Kilwa there were two broad groups of inhabitants: the propertied Swahilis who were land-owners, slave-dealers, and merchants, and the poorer people who were engaged in agricultural and maritime pursuits and who lived mostly at subsistence level.[5] The livelihood of all these people was affected by the rise of Zanzibar as the commercial centre of the Swahili Coast and the diminution in sales of slaves to the French.[6] They also suffered raids by parties of Sakalava from northern Madagascar.[7] Many sources comment on Kilwa's declining prosperity during these years and there is a striking contrast between descriptions of the

---

[1] Prior, *op. cit.*, p. 70. Mongallo was between Lindi and Cape Delgado. It had previously been a place of some importance (it occurs on most European maps of the period), but by the 1840s, if it can be identified with 'Ngao', it had declined – Loarer's Report, Part II, 1849, M.O., O.I. 2/10.

[2] Smyth, *op. cit.*, p. 279.

[3] *Idem*, and Prior, *op. cit.*, p. 75.

[4] Smyth, *op. cit.*, p. 279; Prior, *op. cit.*, p. 79; Sausse to Minister of Marine, 15 Nov. 1817, and Albrand's Report, 1819, M.O., Réunion 72/472.

[5] For the castes, classes, and occupations of the Kilwans, Morice, 'Projet d'un établissement', pp. 176, 180.

[6] See Chapter III, pp. 84-5.

[7] Albrand's Report, 1819, M.O., Réunion 72/472.

island made in the 1770s and those of 1819.[1] At the earlier date all Kilwa island was cultivated and covered with dwellings, but by 1819 much of the land had been overrun by forest.[2] Nevertheless, by 1811 there had not been any dramatic emigration from Kilwa, because in that year the population was estimated to be between 2,000 and 3,000, which was the same figure given in the 1770s.[3]

On the mainland close to Kilwa there were a number of important settlements: Lindi, Mongallo, and Gangarra (Majengera). Prior was of the opinion that these each had more than twice as many inhabitants as Kilwa island.[4] Despite the size of these places no Omani governors had been appointed to them by the beginning of the nineteenth century. This can be explained by the fact that the sultans of Kilwa had more extensive authority than other leaders of the region and it was therefore important for the Omanis to control their island.

The Omanis did, however, have some authority at another point near Kilwa – in the Mafia group of islands. This group consists of the large island of Mafia, and the smaller ones of Chole, Juani, Jibondo, Songo Songo, Kwale, and Koma. The main settlements were Kisimani Mafia on Mafia island, Chole town on the island of the same name, and Kua on Juani island. During the eighteenth century the Mafians had some role in the interplay between the Swahilis, Omanis and Portuguese. Although originally the Omanis do not appear to have placed a garrison on Mafia, in the 1720s the inhabitants became involved in the disturbances during which the Portuguese regained their position on the Swahili Coast.[5] The Mafians also played a part in the upheaval of the 1740s which followed the accession of Ahmad ibn Sa'id as Imam.[6] Later on they were sympathetic with the Kilwans when the latter removed their Omani governor.[7] This support cost the Mafians their independence because they were attacked by the Omanis in the mid-1780s when Kilwa was retaken.[8] The Mafians did not, however, have

---

[1] For the reasons for Kilwa's declining prosperity, see Chapter III.

[2] Morice, 'Projet d'un établissement', p. 174; and Pommier, 'Topographie medicale de l'isle de Quiloa', encl. in Kenaudren to Jubelin, 1 Mch. 1820, M.O., O.I. 15/62.

[3] Morice, 'Projet d'un établissement', p. 176; and Prior, *op. cit.*, p. 69.

[4] Prior, *op. cit.*, p. 69.

[5] Mafia was not among the places named as having Omani garrisons in 1710 – Strandes, *op. cit.*, pp. 275-6. For the events of the 1720s, *ibid.*, p. 293.

[6] Freeman-Grenville, *The French at Kilwa Island*, pp. 40-1.

[7] Morice, 'Projet d'un établissement', p. 142.

[8] Prior, *op. cit.*, p. 68.

any Omani soldiers stationed on their islands. Apparently the Omanis thought that it was sufficient to have a governor at Kilwa, and Mafia was put under his charge.¹ The Omani hold on the Mafia islands was therefore slight, but it was effective enough for its purpose: the control of the revenues there.²

The notables and ruling family of Mafia seem to have fared better than those of some other Swahili towns under Omani authority; indeed, Mafia became a kind of refuge for rich and influential families from other places, particularly Zanzibar, who felt that their position was being eroded by the Omanis. In the 1840s a French visitor to Mafia was told that at the beginning of the eighteenth century 20,000 Swahili families had fled thither from Zanzibar as a result of the exactions of the Omani governors. Chole town had consequently grown in size and prosperity.³ The Frenchman met one Saiyid Bakr ibn Abdullah al-Shatri, who claimed to be a descendant of a former Swahili ruler of Zanzibar, and also four other people who maintained that their ancestors were 'sultans' at places on the Swahili Coast between Lamu and Tongui.

Very little is known about the society and government of the Mafia islands at the beginning of the nineteenth century. It is likely that the Mafian towns were similar to other Swahili settlements in that they drew their leaders from one particular clan. That they had the same type of social divisions as elsewhere on the Swahili Coast is evident from a French visitor's observation in the 1840s that propertied Swahilis were lighter skinned than other inhabitants.⁴ At that date the most prominent clan among the propertied Swahilis was the al-Shatri and, if twentieth-century sources are to be believed, this had also been the case at the beginning of the nineteenth century. In 1936 the Mafia al-Shatri were claiming that their ancestors had settled there at least two centuries earlier.⁵

Apart from the propertied Swahilis and their slaves, there was a second group of Mafia inhabitants. In the 1770s this was described as a kind of caste of free Africans who lived in the woods and were distinguishable from the Moors (the propertied Swahilis). They were

¹ *Idem.*   ² *Idem.*

³ Loarer's Report, Part II, 1849, M.O., O.I. 2/10. Loarer says these events occurred in the time of one Saiyid Saif – this was probably Saif ibn Sultan, Imam of Oman from 1692/3 to 1711.

⁴ Loarer, *idem.*

⁵ A tradition quoted by T. M. Revington, 'Some notes on the Mafia Island group', *Tanganyika Notes and Records* (hereafter *T.N.R.*), no. 1, Mch. 1936, pp. 34-7, here p. 34.

more numerous than the propertied Swahilis and pursued a separate existence.[1] They may have owned some of the cattle for whose export Mafia was famous.[2] By the end of the nineteenth century, members of this group were called Mbwera, a name which also belongs to a village on the mainland opposite Kisimani Mafia.[3]

The Omanis were more reluctant to establish themselves at mainland villages than on offshore islands, and the littoral between Mombasa and Kilwa remained free of their governors and soldiers during the eighteenth century. There were numerous Swahili settlements on this part of the coast, the most important of which were Wasin, Tanga, Mtangata, Pangani, Bweni, Kipumbwe, Sadani, Otondo, and Mbwemaji.[4] Since the Omanis did not yet control the customs dues of these places they caused little disturbance to their societies and systems of government, which are therefore good examples of the Swahili way of life.[5] Since the evidence available for a description of the structure of authority in the settlements on this part of the Swahili Coast is more extensive than for other areas, it will be convenient to describe the system there in some detail. It should be remembered that these settlements themselves were not particularly impressive as regards size or importance. However, they can be taken to exemplify a system of authority which existed – if with important variations – along the whole of the Swahili Coast.

The villages in this region were administered by leaders who were called, in different places, *jumbe*, *diwani*, or *shomwi*,[6] and by other men subordinate to these, called *shaha*, *waziri*, *mwenyi mkuu*, *mwenyi mkubwa*, and *amiri*. The position of the overall leader (who for convenience will be called the *jumbe* in spite of the different nomenclature at different places) was formalized both by the process of acceptance he had to undergo when he stated his candidature and the regalia which came into his possession. The succession was determined, as in most Swahili towns, by a combination of heredity and consensus.

[1] Morice, 'Projet d'un établissement', pp. 173-4.
[2] For Mafia's livestock, Morice, *ibid.*, p. 80, and Loarer's Report, Part II, M.O., O.I. 2/10.
[3] Baumann, *op. cit.*, p. 13.
[4] Hardy's 'Account of the different rivers on the coast from Qualiffe towards Mozambique', I.O.L., Marine Records Miscellaneous 586.
[5] For no Omani control of customs dues, *idem*.
[6] C. Velten, 'Sitten und Gebräuche der Suaheli', in *Mitteilungen des Seminars für Orientalische Sprachen* (Berlin, 1898), vol. I, pp. 9-85, here p. 77 (hereafter cited as *Sitten und Gebräuche*).

SOUTHERN SWAHILI SOCIETY AND POLITICS, CIRCA 1800

In this region the heredity factor appeared to be more precise than in other Swahili towns because, if late nineteenth-century sources can be trusted, the succession to the position of *jumbe* was strictly patrilineal, whereas in towns such as Kilwa, Pate, and Lamu, succession to the leadership was merely cognatic.[1] An aspiring *jumbe* had to undergo a formal process to acquire the consensus he needed to succeed in his ambition. Having announced his candidature, letters were despatched throughout his own district and also, in some cases, to neighbouring districts which had close ties with his own. These were addressed not only to the lesser officials – the *shaha*, *mwenyi mkuu*, *waziri*, and *mwenyi mkubwa* – but also to the young men in the warrior age-group – the *vijana* – and to less important people.

All these people then met together and the candidate distributed money and wares among them.[2] Presumably at this point a candidate could be challenged and, were the opposition strong enough, rejected. The refusal of the people of Kikoneni to accept Hasan as *diwani* of Wasin in 1744/5 and Shaikh as *diwani* of the same place in 1802 are examples of this procedure.[3] However, in neither of these cases did the protest hinder the accession. Seven days after the distribution of money the candidate was proclaimed *jumbe*. At this stage the *jumbe*'s electors were once again asked whether they would accept him, but this seems to have been a mere formality.[4] In addition to these ceremonies of acceptance, the *jumbe* possessed some indispensable symbols of office. These were the traditional horn, umbrella, and drums which the *jumbe* generally took with him wherever he went.[5] In all the towns of the Swahili Coast the acquisition and retention of these objects was of prime importance in the rise and survival of leaders.

As the highest authority the *jumbe*'s main task was to settle disputes. After listening to the case of disputant parties he would pronounce judgment, which had to be followed except when blood had been shed. He could impose imprisonment and fines, being allowed to keep a

---

[1] For the succession of *jumbe*, Velten, *ibid.*, p. 78.

[2] *Idem*, and C. Velten, *Desturi za Wasuaheli* (Göttingen, 1903), p. 222 (hereafter cited as *Desturi*).

[3] Sir A. C. Hollis, 'Notes on the History of Vumba', *Journal of the Royal Anthropological Institute*, vol. XXX (London, 1900), pp. 275-97, here pp. 287 and 289.

[4] Velten, *Sitten und Gebräuche*, p. 79.

[5] *Ibid.*, pp. 79-80; Velten, *Desturi*, p. 222; and J. L. Krapf, *Travels, Researches and Missionary Labours during an Eighteen Years' Residence in Eastern Africa* (London, 1860), p. 417.

quarter portion of the latter.¹ It appears that a *jumbe's* judgment had to take into account traditions which were partly Islamic and partly customary.² An example of the latter was the practice that a plaintiff's representatives, if dissatisfied with the judgment of a *jumbe* in a case of bloodshed, could fight the representatives of the defendant in the *jumbe's* presence. The *jumbe's* writ extended only to those living in the region in which he had authority; in the case of a complaint being made by one of his own men against one from another district, the plaintiff would have to apply to the defendant's chief for judgment.³

The *jumbe's* authority to carry out such duties was bolstered by his traditional privileges. On the one hand he had the sole right to wear certain trappings of office, such as special sandals and a special turban.⁴ On the other hand he possessed certain financial privileges. When a cow was slaughtered he received its hump, and if a particularly large fish was caught he had the right to take part of it. He could also claim a portion of any cargo retrieved from wrecks, and part of the redemption fee for runaway slaves.⁵ To him went the annual rent payable by outsiders who came to live in his district, and the presents – called *magubiko* – with which peoples from inland bought permission to trade. He could also obtain, without charge, certain articles for his own consumption from foreign merchants living in his district.⁶ These financial rights helped the *jumbe* to buy and distribute the presents without which he would have had difficulty in maintaining his authority.⁷

In the exercise of his authority a *jumbe* relied heavily on his ability to sustain the loyalty of his subordinate officials – the *shaha, waziri, mwenyi mkuu, mwenyi mkubwa,* and *amiri*. It is not clear whether these dignitaries, who were drawn from the propertied clans, were actually appointed by the *jumbe* himself.⁸ Descriptions of their role in the election of a new *jumbe* indicate that they retained their positions at least for some time after a previous *jumbe* had died.⁹ In practice probably the most able or influential among them were retained by the new *jumbe* and the less successful ones were replaced. However they attained their position, these men limited the *jumbe's* authority. Their chief function

---

¹ Velten, *Desturi*, p. 303. ² *Idem.*
³ *Ibid.*, pp. 306 and 309.
⁴ Krapf, *op. cit.*, p. 417; and Burton, *Zanzibar*, II, 124.
⁵ Velten, *Desturi*, pp. 227–8.
⁶ Velten, *Sitten und Gebräuche*, pp. 81 and 82.
⁷ For the common practice of giving presents, *ibid.*, pp. 78–9.
⁸ For the propertied clans, *ibid.*, p. 78, note 2.
⁹ For such descriptions, *ibid.*, pp. 78–91 and Velten, *Desturi*, pp. 222–3.

was to decide matters of importance and proclaim their opinion, without which a *jumbe* generally would not act. There is some evidence to suggest that the *mwenyi mkuu* and *mwenyi mkubwa*, of whom there may have been several, met in formal council under the chairmanship of the *waziri*. The *shaha* would also have been present at the meetings. It is not possible to define the functions of these dignitaries in any precise way. They did, it is true, perform specific ceremonial duties, but otherwise their function depended on influence which it is difficult to categorize. The *amiri* is perhaps an exception in that his duties, which were concerned with the organization of men for battle, gave him a more defined position.[1]

The structure of authority in the villages of this particular region is typical of that all along the Swahili Coast. There was, however, one rather striking difference. Most of the important towns of the Swahili Coast had an overall leader, but the villages in this region appear to have had more than one *jumbe* in each. In 1856 there were as many as six in some villages.[2] Vumba and Wasin were exceptions in that they retained sole leaders, a fact which may in part be due to their anxiety to avoid domination by Mombasa.[3] The plurality of *jumbe* in each settlement does not appear to have affected the substructure of authority, because each *jumbe* had a defined territorial jurisdiction within the village, and so the Swahili system of government was merely reproduced in smaller units than usual.[4] The existence of smaller units did, however, affect the relationship of one unit to another. There was a greater need for co-operation, particularly when there were several *jumbe* to a village. Later on there were three confederacies of units centred on Tanga, Mtangata, and Pangani, and this may also have been the case earlier.[5] Such co-operation was a result not only of close kinship ties between leaders of different units – the genealogies of the *diwani* of Vumba, for example, show that intermarriage was common between members of prominent Swahili families not only from neighbouring villages but also from all along the Swahili Coast – but also of the need for defensive arrangements against peoples of the hinterland.[6]

[1] Velten, *Desturi*, pp. 124 and 226.   [2] Burton, *Zanzibar*, II, 124.
[3] Hollis, *op. cit., passim*; and see Chapter II, pp. 59-60.
[4] Burton, *Zanzibar*, II, 124.
[5] J. L. Krapf, *Reisen in Ost-Afrika* (Stuttgart, 1858), 2 vols, II, 276-81. This is the original, and longer, version of the *Travels* already quoted, but, unless otherwise indicated, it will be the English version that is used in references.
[6] For the genealogies, Hollis, *op. cit.*, and E. C. Baker, 'Notes on the Shirazi of East Africa', *T.N.R.*, no. 11 (Apr. 1941), pp. 1-11.

THE SWAHILI COAST

The danger from hinterland peoples was far more real to these villages, situated as they were on the mainland, than to the island settlements. It was particularly important for the coast dwellers to live at peace with their non-Swahili neighbours because their economic prosperity largely depended on their function as middlemen who dealt in goods brought by peoples from the hinterland and interior. Any restrictions imposed by such peoples on goods passing through their lands would have seriously affected the coastal villages. Behind the Swahilis, ranging from north to south, were the Digo, Segeju, Shambala, Zigua, Zaramo, and Doe peoples. There seem to have been definite attempts by the Swahilis to co-operate with some of the hinterland peoples; for example, there existed an *utani* relationship, which implied assistance in wartime, between the *diwani* of Vumba and the Segeju.[1] This alliance brought practical benefits to the Swahilis when in 1754/5 the *diwani* gathered Segeju and Digo warriors to assist the Mombasans fight Zanzibar.[2]

Relations between the Swahilis and non-Swahilis extended so far as the consultation of the hinterland peoples when a new *jumbe* was to be appointed at a coastal village. There is evidence that this happened at Wasin, where the Digo and Segeju participated in the enthronement ceremonies of *diwani*.[3] Later in the nineteenth century the chiefs of the Zaramo were also consulted by the coastal villages nearest to them, and this may have been the case earlier.[4] The chiefs of the Shambala, with their seat inland at Fuga, were particularly influential in the appointment of Swahili leaders on the coast.[5] That it was wise to heed the wishes of the non-Swahili peoples was evident in 1802 when the Digo supported the people of Kikoneni in their opposition to the candidature of Shaikh for the position of *diwani* of Wasin. In general, at the beginning of the nineteenth century relations between the Swahilis and the hinterland peoples were good enough to allow trade to pass fairly freely to and from the

---

[1] E. C. Baker, 'Notes on the history of the Wasegeju', *T.N.R.*, no. 27 (June 1949), pp. 16-39, here p. 31.

[2] Mazrui MS., pp. 23 and 25.

[3] Hollis, *op. cit.*, p. 279.

[4] Velten, *Desturi*, pp. 222-3.

[5] Krapf, *op. cit.*, p. 416. For the rise of the chieftainship of Fuga, see Abdallah Bin Hemedi 'L Ajjemy, *The Kilindi*, ed. by J. W. T. Allen and others (Nairobi, 1963).

African interior.¹ Only the Doe were recorded as putting hindrances in the way of trade.²

The political systems of the Swahili settlements on the mainland opposite Zanzibar have been described in some detail because they have features typical of the Swahili system of government as a whole. In addition, the systems seen elsewhere had already been affected by the coming of the Omanis. The first half of the nineteenth century was to see a gradual extension of this Omani presence. In summary, the Omani expansion to the Swahili Coast during the eighteenth century had had three stages of development: first, an expansion encouraged by an initial impulse and unity in Oman; then the collapse of this unity and the reflection of the troubles at home on East Africa; and, finally, the efforts of the winning side in Oman to strengthen the authority that was left to it in East Africa. This laid the basis for the much more decisive control of the Swahili Coast in the first half of the nineteenth century by the Omani leader, Saiyid Sa'id, and it provided him with a good foundation on which to build.

That the Omanis had been able to establish themselves on the Swahili Coast was due, in the main, to the nature of their authority there, which was slight and indefinite. The Omanis and Swahilis were both maritime peoples, and had had trading, and consequently cultural, contact for centuries. The Swahilis did not, therefore, look upon the Omanis as dangerous newcomers as they would have regarded non-Muslim Europeans. The Omanis' light hold made them even more acceptable. Except in the collection of customs dues, the governors and garrisons imposed by the Omanis exercised little formal control in the Swahili towns. They allowed local leaders to remain in office with only slight diminution of function. It was only very gradually that the political system of the Swahilis was eroded, and by the beginning of the nineteenth century such an erosion had not been perceptible enough to have caused serious rebellion. The number of soldiers the Omanis maintained on the Swahili Coast were so small that it is difficult to believe that they could not have been expelled had the desire to do so been strong enough.

The fact was, however, that Omani control, provided it was light, was acceptable because the advantages it brought almost outweighed the disadvantages. The political system of the Swahilis was essentially

¹ See Chapter VIII, p. 208.
² Hardy's 'Account of the different rivers on the coast from Qualiffe towards Mozambique', I.O.L., Marine Records Miscellaneous 586.

a fragmented one, where the concept of subjugation of one settlement to another was undeveloped. Each town had its own separate structure of authority. A feature of this system, in which disputes between villages were bound to arise, was the preference of leaders and putant leaders to turn to outsiders for help and a willingness to accept the authority of such outsiders, provided it remained slight, rather than to be dominated by local rivals. How those outsiders gradually extended their authority, and what effects this had on the Swahili peoples, is the story to be told in this book.

CHAPTER II

SOCIETY AND POLITICS ON THE NORTHERN SWAHILI COAST

AT THE BEGINNING OF THE NINETEENTH CENTURY

The towns of the northern section of the Swahili Coast had much in common with those of the southern. Each settlement on the littoral between Mombasa and the River Juba, where the Swahili culture shaded into the Somali, had its own rulers and hierarchy of officials. In contrast to the situation in the southern region, the rulers on this section of the coast had not had officials appointed by the authorities in Oman imposed upon them. Instead, a breakaway group of Omanis – the Mazruis – had established a preponderant influence not only at Mombasa, their base, but also to the north and south of that town and, to a certain extent, in the Lamu archipelago. In many respects the reactions of the inhabitants of the northern region to these alien rulers was the same as those of the southern littoral to the 'legitimate' Omani representatives. But, because the Mazruis had to make a special effort to maintain their irregular position, the society over which they had influence was affected in many ways. In particular, the Swahili peoples became caught up in the struggles between the Omani authorities and their former compatriots.

Mombasa was the best fortified town of the northern region, and, indeed, of the whole Swahili Coast. When the Omani Imamate first developed a political interest in East Africa, Mombasa was the primary object of its ambition for it was both the Portuguese administrative capital and the most impregnable town on the coast. Mombasa town lay on an island which was close to the mainland but separated from it by sufficient depth of water to discourage invasion from that quarter. It had two places suitable for anchorage – on its north and south-west sides – but the northern harbour, alongside which lay Mombasa town, was that used by commercial vessels. Access to this harbour lay through a narrow strait dominated by a formidable fort of Portuguese construction. It was therefore easy to deny entrance to unwelcome visitors. There were also hindrances to attacks on the town mounted from the south-west anchorage. Such assaults depended upon the willingness of the inhabitants of Kilindini village to allow the assailants to land and to march uninterrupted across the island. Mombasa's defensive position was further strengthened by the difficulties of mounting a blockade. Blockade tactics, assisted, it is true, by the narrowness of the harbour's entrance, were greatly hindered by the monsoon winds. Vessels could only maintain a blockade for the duration of one monsoon or forfeit their freedom to return to their home port.

Mombasa was therefore the most coveted prize on the Swahili Coast. In 1698, after a struggle of two and a half years' duration, the Omanis succeeded in capturing the town from the Portuguese. Thereafter the Omanis regarded Mombasa as their most important possession on the Swahili Coast. They found, however, that it was very difficult to control from Arabia, for the factors which made it a desirable prize also led it to be a troublesome client. Mombasa was both the obvious target for attack from outside and a most dangerous breeding-ground for rebellion from within. It was a combination of these which first rocked the Omanis' hold on Mombasa. In 1727 internal discontent in the town prompted the Portuguese to counter-attack on the Swahili Coast.[1] They retook Mombasa, but further internal dissension, which this time operated in favour of the Omanis, led to their expulsion and the re-establishment of an Omani governor and garrison.[2] Mombasa was thereafter a model of the difficulties faced by the Omani political authorities in their attempts to retain control of outlying posts.

In the first place, the governorship of Mombasa, which was such an important political prize, came to be regarded by one Omani clan – the Mazrui – as its own monopoly. The Mazruis formed themselves into a tightly-knit group which was determined to retain its hold on Mombasa and exclude the appointment of governors from Oman.[3] In

[1] Strandes, *op. cit.*, pp. 278-98; Guillain, *Documents*, I, 529; and *Mombasa Chronicle*. The *Mombasa Chronicle* was acquired at Mombasa in 1824 by Lt Emery and was printed in W. F. Owen, *Narrative of Voyages to Explore the Eastern Shores of Africa*, 2 vols (London, 1833), I, 414-22. For other versions, see Appendix II.

[2] *Mombasa Chronicle*, and Mazrui MS., p. 15.

[3] In order to avoid confusion, the word 'Mazrui' will be put into the plural by adding an 's'. This is not the correct Arabic plural.

NORTHERN SWAHILI SOCIETY AND POLITICS, CIRCA 1800

Oman itself the Mazrui clan had not been particularly powerful or well-known. It was probably a section of the Bani Jabir, a large group inhabiting the valley of Jabir and the hilly district to the east.[1] The Mazruis appear to have lived in various parts of Oman, but most of them congregated in Rastaq and Samayil.[2] A clan of the same name which forms a section of the Bani Yas in the Dhafrah area is probably unconnected with the Mazruis of eastern Oman, and Krapf's statement that the Mazruis were of Persian origin is mistaken.[3]

It is not clear how the governorship of Mombasa came to be a Mazrui monopoly. Some members of the clan participated in the original capture of Mombasa from the Portuguese and it is possible, though all sources do not agree about this, that the first governor appointed by the Imam in 1698 was a Mazrui.[4] It is more certain that in 1727, when Mombasa was lost to the Portuguese, its governor was a Mazrui – Nasir ibn Abdullah.[5] After regaining the town in 1729 the Omanis appointed two successive non-Mazrui governors. At this point there were internal disturbances at Mombasa and the Omani authorities thought the situation might be calmed if Nasir ibn Abdullah al-Mazrui, by now back in Oman, were re-appointed governor.[6] Being

[1] Notes on the Tribes of Oman, by S. B. Miles, in *Report on the Administration of the Persian Gulf Political Residency and Muscat Political Agency* (Calcutta, 1880/1), p. 30.
[2] S. B. Miles, *The Countries and Tribes of the Persian Gulf*, 2 vols (London, 1919, new edn in one vol., 1965), p. 432 – (hereafter cited as *Persian Gulf*). See also Al-Siyabi, *Is'af al-'a'yan fi ansab ahl 'Uman* (Beirut, 1964), pp. 79-80 for Mazruis in the province of Shinas, in lower Samayil, and in Burj al-Mazari'ah at Rastaq. See also Mazrui MS., p. 4, basing its information on legal documents, for the Mazruis in Manah, Samayil, and Washil, and for their having their own fortified town of Al-Alaya in Rastaq.
[3] For this group, see J. B. Kelly, *Eastern Arabian Frontiers* (London, 1964), pp. 36-8, and *Selections from the Records of the Bombay Government* (Bombay, 1856), XXIV, p. 462 (hereafter the latter will be cited as *Bombay Selections XXIV*). For Krapf, see his *op. cit.*, p. 119.
[4] For different views about who was appointed, Mazrui MS., pp. 11-12; *Mombasa Chronicle*; Shihabuddin Chiraqdin, *Shaikh Mbaruk bin Rashid bin Salim bin Hemed al-Mazrui*, Makerere College Arts Research Essay Prize, 1953/4; and *Pate Chronicle*, p. 55, printed in C. H. Stigand, *The Land of Zinj* (London, 1913) – this will be the version of the Pate Chronicle quoted in this book. For other versions, see bibliography.
[5] *Mombasa Chronicle*; Strandes, *op. cit.*, p. 282; and Guillain, *Documents*, I, 529.
[6] *Mombasa Chronicle*, and Mazrui MS., p. 16.

47

married to the sister of one of the leading Swahili notables of Mombasa, he might have sufficient influence to settle the disputes.[1] When he was approached, however, Nasir excused himself from reassuming the office on the grounds of his age and suggested in his stead a kinsman, Muhammad ibn Uthman al-Mazrui. In 1730/1 this man was in fact appointed governor of Mombasa.[2]

From that date the governorship of Mombasa remained in the Mazrui family. There is a tradition that this was because a bargain was struck between the Omani authorities and the Mazruis to the effect that the latter could retain control of Mombasa provided the town caused Oman no expense.[3] One version of the story maintains that Muhammad ibn Uthman rented Mombasa from the Omani *amiri* there, one Sahdad ibn Sahdi, a Baluchi, who wanted to reduce the cost of the town to Oman.[4] It is surprising that this tradition, which could be designed to absolve the Mazruis from accusations of dynasticism and deliberate retention of the governorship, occurs in two sources which lack any interest in presenting a favourable picture of that clan. Indeed one of them, the Pate Chronicle, is often highly critical of the Mazruis. Two other local sources also maintain that this Sahdad appointed Muhammad ibn Uthman governor of Mombasa, but they do not say that this was done for financial reasons.[5]

Whatever the facts, one of the main reasons why the Mazruis kept the governorship of Mombasa was the failure of the Ya'rubi clan to remain as Imams of Oman and the resultant Mazrui disapproval of their successors, the Al Bu Sa'idis. During the civil war the Mazruis in Oman probably sympathized with the Ghafiri group, whereas the Al Bu Sa'idis belonged to the Hinawi faction.[6] In the 1740s the governor of Mombasa refused to accept the authority of the new Imam, Ahmad ibn Sa'id Al Bu Sa'idi. In practical terms this probably meant that the

[1] For the marriage, see Mazrui MS., p. 16.

[2] *Ibid.*, p. 17, and *Mombasa Chronicle*. Guillain, *Documents*, I, 535, gives 1739 as the date of Muhammad's appointment.

[3] *Pate Chronicle*, p. 56, and *Kitab al-Zunuj*, p. 276. The latter is published with an Italian translation by Cerulli in *Somalia, scritti vari editi ed inediti* (Rome, 1957), I, 233-92. The page nos. quoted are those of Cerulli's translation.

[4] *Kitab al-Zunuj*.

[5] Omari bin Stamboul, An early history of Mombasa and Tanga, p. 33, translated by E. C. Baker, *T.N.R.*, no. 31 (July 1951), pp. 32-6; and *Asili ya Mvita*, printed in *Swahili* (the journal of the East African Swahili Committee), vol. 34/2 (1964), pp. 21-4.

[6] Miles, *Persian Gulf*, p. 432. Guillain, *Documents*, I, 587, says the Mazruis were Hinawi, but this is probably a mistake.

governor ceased to send any money to Oman.¹ Aware of the danger of having an Omani family embattled in the most important stronghold on the East Africa coast, Ahmad ibn Saʻid tried to regain the allegiance of Mombasa by sending a group of men to assassinate Muhammed ibn Uthman al-Mazrui.² Although the deed was successfully performed, the Mazruis soon re-established themselves as governors of Mombasa.

The Mazruis then consolidated their position by attacking the Omani authorities at Zanzibar in 1753/4.³ Although this venture failed, the fact that the Mazruis had been able to organize such an expedition demonstrated their strength. It may have discouraged Ahmad ibn Saʻid from taking further action against Mombasa because there is no record of any subsequent harassment of the Mazruis from Oman during his Imamate. But the dangers inherent in having fellow-countrymen as governors of 'independent' towns once again revealed themselves when Ahmad ibn Saʻid died. The new Imam feared that his rebellious brother might seek help from Mombasa. One of the leaders of a force he despatched to East Africa to deal with the situation called at Mombasa and obtained a document from the Mazrui governor stating that the fort belonged to the Omanis. The governor afterwards claimed he had agreed to say this because the Omani commander had surprised him by entering the fort in the guise of a simple trader. He explained his conduct with these words:

'For that reason I gave him a piece of paper so as to avoid the evil of that hour. If they come again wanting to take the fort, we are grown-up men and each man has his weapons.'⁴

That the governor regarded his submission as meaningless is also borne out by French sources. Shortly afterwards the French were considering lending assistance to the Imam 'pour faire rentrer sous sa domination les rebelles qui y [à Mombasa] sont établis'.⁵ Although the Imamate had managed to re-establish its authority at Kilwa in 1785, it had not succeeded in doing so at Mombasa.

At the beginning of the nineteenth century the Mazruis were firmly

¹ For the Mazrui attitude, Mazrui MS., p. 18; *Mombasa Chronicle*; *Pate Chronicle*, p. 79; and Guillain, *Documents*, I, 543. For the cessation of monetary contributions, Mazrui MS., p. 17.   ² *Ibid.*

³ Mazrui MS., p. 23; *Mombasa Chronicle*; *Pate Chronicle*, p. 60; and Guillain, *Documents*, I, 550.

⁴ *Pate Chronicle*, pp. 80-1. See also Chapter I, p. 26.

⁵ Report by Le Brasseur on the 1785 expedition of the frigate *Venus*, n.d. (but clearly *c.* 1786), A.N., Colonies C4/72.

entrenched as governors of Mombasa. By that date considerable numbers of them were settled at Mombasa because, during the eighteenth century, fourteen Mazrui families had gone thither from Oman.[1] The Mazrui possession of Mombasa compelled the Imamate to develop Zanzibar as its main base in East Africa. As time passed, the continued presence of a rebellious Omani clan in one of the most important towns of the Swahili Coast forced the Omani authorities to analyse their true intentions in East Africa. For the first three decades of the nineteenth century their policy was shaped by the insecurity they felt in the face of the Mazrui position on the Swahili Coast. The corresponding insecurity of the Mazruis aggravated the rivalry because they drew closely together in order to maintain their position and prevent the Omani authorities from interfering with them.

One feature of Mazrui solidarity was the relatively smooth succession to the governorship of Mombasa, a characteristic which denied the Omani authorities an opportunity to collaborate with dissatisfied parties. In 1744 Muhammad ibn Uthman was succeeded by his brother, Ali, and on Ali's death in 1754/5 Ma'sud, son of the first Mazrui governor, Nasir ibn Abdullah, succeeded. This may have been because none of Ali ibn Uthman's descendants were old enough to assume office. In 1779 Ma'sud was followed by Abdullah, and in 1782 Ahmad succeeded. Both these latter governors were sons of Muhammad ibn Uthman. On Abdullah's death the sons of Ma'sud had claimed that the succession should pass alternately between the families of Nasir ibn Abdullah and Muhammad ibn Uthman, and therefore it was the turn of one of them to become governor. Their rebellion was, however, suppressed. The governorship remained in the same family when in 1814 Ahmad was succeeded by his son, Abdullah. However, on Abdullah's death in 1823 there was another dispute over the succession, and a compromise candidate was found in Sulaiman, son of Ali ibn Uthman, who had been governor seventy years earlier.[2] On only one occasion, therefore – when Abdullah ibn Muhammad died – did the Mazruis divide into warring factions. It appears that the succession was usually settled by discussions among the leading members of the Mazrui families.[3] For example, when dissatisfaction was expressed with the rule of the Governor Sulaiman in 1825, some Mazrui notables, among

[1] Mazrui MS., pp. 1 and 17.
[2] For these dates and incidents, see Mazrui MS., and Guillain, *Documents*, I. See also Mazrui family tree, Appendix I.
[3] Mazrui MS., *passim*.

them Salim and Mubarak, who were both sons of Ahmad, the previous governor, combined to dethrone him. But it was a peaceful incident: Sulaiman was merely informed that he no longer had the support of the leading Mazruis, so he moved out of the fort and went to live in Mombasa town. A council of Arabs and Swahilis then agreed that Salim should become the new governor.[1] The importance of the amicable nature of these arrangements concerning the succession to the governorship of Mombasa became evident in the 1830s when there arose serious quarrels over the matter, and the Mazruis divided into factions. Outsiders were quick to take advantage of Mazrui disunity.

A further source of Mazrui strength was their ability to raise adequate revenue from the region which they dominated. The taxes they levied may have existed before their arrival, or may have been newly instituted by them. One of these was a tax of twelve *kila* (each *kila* weighed about 2·75 kilograms) of millet for each slave owned. The cultivator could, however, opt to pay an alternative levy of one *kikanda* (i.e. 45 *kila*) of his crop for each *mlia* (800 × 200 paces) of cultivated land.[2] This tax on produce also applied to the island of Pemba and to some towns to the north and south of Mombasa.[3] In addition, the Mazrui governor levied a tax on fishing and could compel vessels belonging to the local inhabitants to fill half their cargo space with his cargo without any other cost to him than that of providing the crews' food for the voyage.[4] The governor could also insist on prior right of purchase, but when in 1825 one governor wanted to extend this privilege and acquire without payment half of a local dhow's cargo of rice, there was an outcry. The governor maintained that his claim was customary but this was denied by Mombasa's leading men.[5] The Mazruis' revenue would have been augmented by the lands they owned around Mombasa.[6]

The presence of the Mazruis as governors of Mombasa must have had a marked effect on the life of the Swahili peoples there. The relationship which developed between the indigenous inhabitants and the alien rulers is of great importance in explaining the success of the Mazruis in

[1] 'A Journal of the British Establishment at Mombasa from 1824 to 1826', by Lt J. B. Emery, P.R.O. Adm. 52/3940, entries for 16 Aug., 29 Sept., and 15 Oct. 1825 (hereafter this will be cited as 'Emery's Journal').

[2] Guillain, *Documents*, III, 259; and Emery's Journal, entry for 16 Feb. 1825 (the latter gives no details).

[3] Emery's Journal, *idem*, specifically mentioning Mtwapa and Mtangata. For Pemba, Guillain, *Documents*, III, 260.   [4] Guillain, *idem*.

[5] Emery's Journal, entry for 2 Jan. 1825.   [6] *Ibid.*, entry for 16 Nov. 1824.

avoiding subjection to the Omani authorities. But, first, what sort of Swahili society existed at Mombasa? As in other towns, 'Shirazi' ancestry was claimed by the prominent lineages of the Mombasa Swahilis.[1] A local history states that the last truly 'Shirazi' ruler of the town was Sham ibn Misham, who may have held office in the sixteenth century.[2] A clue to the origin of the claims of the East African coastal dwellers to be 'Shirazi' may be provided by the Mombasa Swahilis, many of whom came from the Tana River area to the north.[3] That region could well have been a dispersal point for peoples later found all along the Swahili Coast.

That the Mombasa peoples came from the north is supported by the names of their different groups. A particular feature of the Mombasa Swahilis at the beginning of the nineteenth century was their division into twelve tribes (*taifa* or *mji*), nine of which combined into one unit and the remaining three into another. Sources from the later nineteenth century generally name the Three Tribes as the Kilindini, Changamwe, and Tangana, giving this unit the overall name of Kilindini, and the Nine Tribes as the Mvita, Kilifi, Pate, Mtwapa, Shaka, Paza, Katwa, Bajun, and Jomvu, known overall as the Mvita. In the 1840s, however, Guillain included two tribes called the Malindi and Ozi in the Nine Tribe unit, while he did not name the Mvita and Katwa.[4] Confusion of nomenclature could well arise from the fact that within each tribe there were several clans (*mbari*); for example, the Malindi are a clan of the Mvita. The tribal divisions may have developed as a result of individual groups arriving at different times, having halted at different places on their way, and settling in separate parts of Mombasa and its environs. The names of the tribes, which are mostly place names, support this theory.

Most probably the presence of the Mazruis as governors of Mombasa actually emphasized and consolidated the tribal divisions of the Swahilis. Since no evidence is available to describe the situation before the nineteenth century, it may be that some of the divisions in fact arose under Mazrui governance. The Mazruis certainly exploited the divisions among the Mombasa Swahilis, particularly those between the two larger units. When Muhammad ibn Uthman became governor he was careful to

---

[1] Guillain, *Documents*, III, 246.   [2] *Mombasa Chronicle*.
[3] For a discussion of this, see F. J. Berg, 'The Swahili Community of Mombasa, 1500-1900', *Journal of African History* (London, 1968), vol. IX, no. 1, pp. 35-56.
[4] Guillain, *Documents*, III, 237 and 599.

develop a favourable relationship with the Three Tribes, who thereafter lent the Mazruis their support.¹ During the governorship of Abdullah ibn Muhammad (1779-81) they signed a treaty binding themselves 'not to kill the Mazruis'.² It was possibly the championship of the Mazruis by the Three Tribes which led the Nine Tribes to be ill-disposed towards the alien governors. When Muhammad ibn Uthman refused to remit his land tax to the first Al Bu Sa'idi Imam, the shaikhs of the Kilifi, one of the Nine Tribes, immediately informed the new Imam and aided the men subsequently sent from Oman to assassinate Muhammad.³ Later the Bani Kibanda section of the Kilifi encouraged the people of Pate to raid Mombasa.⁴ Members of the Kilifi tribe caused further trouble by encouraging the sons of Ma'sud to rebel against the governor Ahmad ibn Muhammad (1782–1814).⁵ On this occasion the Mazrui governor might have been in grave difficulties had he not been assisted by the Changamwe, of the Three Tribes. In the Mazrui rise to power and retention of position, manipulation of the Swahili divisions played an important role. When they lost the support of both the Three and Nine Tribes in the 1830s the Mazruis were in serious trouble. Like so many other parvenu rulers they depended for their position on the use they made of the strains already existing in their new domain. As for the Swahilis themselves, they were prepared to tolerate the position because they preferred to be dominated by outsiders than by rival groups of their own people. Indeed, when the Portuguese left Mombasa in 1729 the Swahilis, unable to agree among themselves about the governance of the town, sent a delegation to Oman to ask that an Omani governor be appointed.⁶

Apart from making use of tribal divisions, the new rulers also utilized the existing structure of leadership in Mombasa. This meant accepting the assistance of traditional Swahili leaders, and in particular of the dominant Swahili family – the Malindi. This arrangement was mutually beneficial. The Malindi retained their status as the chief subordinates of the new rulers – a position they had already enjoyed under the Portuguese. At the same time other Swahili leaders benefited from Mazrui rule because it was an alternative to dissension among themselves. As for the Mazruis, they had the advantage of taking over a ready-made system of social control which enabled them to establish their authority without great difficulty.

The Mazrui/Swahili political organization must be examined in more

[1] *Mombasa Chronicle.*   [2] Mazrui MS., p. 37.   [3] *Ibid.*, p. 18.
[4] *Ibid.*, p. 27.   [5] *Ibid.*, p. 37.   [6] *Ibid.*, p. 15, and *Mombasa Chronicle.*

detail. Each Swahili tribe had at least one shaikh (*shaha* or *shehe* in Swahili), many of whom acted in a consultative capacity to the governor, often being present at Mazrui councils, which took place regularly.[1] On several occasions in the 1820s Emery, a British naval officer, attended these councils of 'the Arab and Swahili chiefs' at Mombasa fort.[2] There is little evidence to indicate what sort of influence the Swahili leaders exercised in Mazrui councils, but one instance of Swahili participation occured in 1825 when the governor Sulaiman called a meeting of Swahilis in order to appoint a governor for the coastline south of Mombasa.[3]

It appears that a single Swahili leader was selected as an overall representative for the indigenous inhabitants of Mombasa. It is unclear whether the Swahilis could freely choose their representative, or whether the Mazrui governors appointed the holder of the office. It is likely that there was no established system and on occasion the Mazruis may have influenced the choice. In that case, however, they probably would have appointed men who had already emerged as leaders. It is known that on one occasion at least they removed the holder of the office: when the Mazrui governor heard that the sons of Ma'sud had been aided in a rebellion by Sharif Sa'id ibn Umar of the Nine Tribes, he

'therefore discharged him from the shaikhdom and took it from the Nine Tribes and asked them to choose a leader who belonged to other groups. They chose Ahmad ibn Shaikh al-Malindi. . . and the governor gave him the post of the shaikh of the people of Mombasa.'[4]

The Mazrui MS. calls this overall leader *shehe* but an earlier source describes him as vizier (i.e. *waziri*).[5] It is difficult to define what influence this overall representative had in Mazrui councils. When Ahmad ibn Shaikh al-Malindi held the post he had considerable power, but this may have been untypical and due to his particularly forceful personality. 'His countenance', wrote a visiting naval officer, 'was strongly expressive of activity, penetration, and a vivacity which even sixty years could not entirely repress.'[6] The officer remarked that a

[1] Emery's Journal, entries for 17 Feb. and 2 Mch. 1825, and 22 July 1826. Also Mazrui MS., pp. 37-8, and Thomas Boteler, *Narrative of a Voyage of Discovery to Africa and Arabia* (London, 1835), 2 vols, II, 7.
[2] Emery's Journal, as above.　　[3] *Ibid.*, 17 Feb. and 2 Mch. 1825.
[4] Mazrui MS., pp. 37-8.　　[5] Guillain, *Documents*, III, 259.
[6] Boteler, *op. cit.*, II, 8. In 1825 Emery said Hammud ben Shia, who was doubtless the same person, was chief of the Swahilis – Emery's Journal, entry for 3 July 1825.

conference he had with the Mazrui leaders was delayed to await the arrival of Ahmad ibn Shaikh, 'without whose sanction nothing could be finally adjusted'.

Apart from these advisers there was also another official belonging to the political structure of Mombasa: the *amiri*. The *amiri*, who was probably drawn from among the Mazruis, was responsible for raising and organizing troops in time of need.[1] This task he appears to have performed effectively on several occasions: Mombasan troops attacked Zanzibar in 1754/5 and shortly afterwards a number of them were sent to Pate.[2] At a later date the governor Ahmad ibn Muhammad took a force of Mombasans to Pate and left there a garrison of 500 men.[3] During a subsequent dispute the Mombasans provided a considerable number of men – it is said between 5,000 and 6,000 but this figure may be exaggerated – to fight in the battle of Shela (c. 1814).[4] Apart from raising these large numbers of troops for specific occasions, the *amiri* also controlled the few regular soldiers who garrisoned Mombasa fort. There was only a limited number of these: indeed in 1824 Emery had great difficulty in obtaining more than fifteen or twenty soldiers from the Mazrui governor to defend the newly formed British Establishment at Mombasa. The governor used the harvest season as an excuse for providing only a small number of men.[5]

The political system of Mombasa did not entirely exclude the non-Swahili peoples of the hinterland. These peoples relied for their influence on their good relations with the Mombasans rather than on any formal participation in the town's politics. Their relationship certainly contributed to Mombasa's ability to maintain its independence, for it was particularly important for that town, making a stand against the Omani authorities, to co-operate with its more numerous non-Swahili and non-Muslim neighbours. It is clear from the fact that Swahilis actually lived among the hinterland peoples that relations were particularly amicable: for example, Jomvu, on the mainland, was a Swahili village.[6] The hinterland peoples were agricultural and pastoral in occupation and were called 'Nyika' by the Mombasans. *Nyika* is a common Swahili noun meaning 'wilderness' or 'barren area', and as such is applied to the

[1] Guillain, *Documents*, III, 259.   [2] *Ibid.*, I, 551; and Mazrui MS., p. 26.

[3] Guillain, *Documents*, I, 568; *Pate Chronicle*, p. 74; and Mazrui MS., p. 35. The Mazrui MS. gives the figure.

[4] *Kitab al-Zunuj*, p. 282.

[5] Emery's Journal, entries for 11 Sept. and 5 Oct. 1824. For the British Establishment, see Chapter V, p. 132.

[6] Boteler, *op. cit.*, II, 179; and Krapf, *op. cit.*, p. 181.

plains of the Mombasa hinterland. The people who were called 'Nyika' did not actually inhabit that bush-scrub region but rather the fertile strip lying between it and the sea. Peoples with cultural and social features similar to those of the peoples of Mombasa's immediate hinterland also inhabited the littoral region from Takaungu to Wasin, and these will all be called 'Nyika'. The Nyika divided themselves into groups, the most commonly distinguished of which were the Digo, Duruma, Rabai, Giriama, Kauma, Chonyi, Jibana, Kambe, and Ribe.[1] Non-Nyika groups of the area were, to the north the Galla and Pokomo, to the west the Kwavi and Kamba, and to the south-west and south the Bondei, Shambala, and Segeju.

The relationship of the Swahilis and the Nyika was based on a system of patronage, in which different Swahili groups were the 'patrons' of different Nyika groups. Writing in the 1840s, Guillain was of the opinion that this system had arisen because the Nyika had reached the region after the arrival of the Swahilis:

'En arrivant dans le pays, ils devaient nécessairement accepter le patronage des Souhhéli qui leur etaient supérieures en nombre ... et, tant que ceux-ci furent maîtres du littoral, ce patronage dut être une suzeraineté réelle. Quand, plus tard, une autre autorité domina à Mombase, ils devinrent les intermédiaires naturels entre les représentants de l'autorité nouvelle et les populations qui relevaient d'eux depuis longtemps. De la cette espèce de suprématie, ou plutot d'influence exercée, encore aujourd'hui, par les sheikhs souhhéli dans tels ou tels villages environnants.'[2]

Guillain listed the affiliations of the Nyika and the Twelve Tribes thus: Giriama – Mvita; Chonyi – Mtwapa; Kambe, Ribe, and Kauma – Kilifi; Rabai – Jomvu and Malindi; all others – Kilindini.[3]

The connexions of the Swahilis with the Nyika groups were of mutual benefit, for the Swahilis were thereby guaranteed a peaceful hinterland and a supply of manpower for purposes of war. The Nyika could be persuaded, with the aid of presents of cloth, to participate in Mombasa's battles: on more than one occasion the Digo contributed fighting men.[4] In their turn the Nyika were given military aid by the

---

[1] Krapf (German edition), II, 91 and 95, also adds the Lungo, Mtawe, Mtawe-Shimba, and Tiwi. Other lists add several other groups, most of which are village names – e.g. Guillain, *Documents*, III, 244; *Mombasa Chronicle*; and an almost indecipherable list given in Emery's Journal, entries for 14 and 15 Oct. 1825.
[2] Guillain, *Documents*, III, 244.   [3] *Idem*.   [4] *Idem*, and see Chapter I, p. 42.

NORTHERN SWAHILI SOCIETY AND POLITICS, CIRCA 1800

Swahilis: when the Galla threatened to attack the Nyika in 1824, the Mombasans offered to help their allies.[1] The bonds between the Nyika and the Swahilis were strengthened by their commercial interdependence; the Nyika provided Mombasa with much of its food supply and they were also middlemen between the Mombasans and the peoples of the interior.[2] Of course the relationship was not one of uninterrupted calm, but the ruptures that occurred seem to have been speedily healed. There was, for example, some trouble at Jomvu in July 1825 and the Swahilis flocked out of Mombasa with arms and ammunition to fight the Nyika. Ultimately, however, the matter was settled peacefully.[3]

Part of the success of the Mombasans in retaining the friendship of the Nyika lay in their willingness to allow the hinterland peoples a small voice in the political affairs of Mombasa. In 1729 the Nyika were among those who sent representatives to Oman to ask that an Omani governor be appointed to Mombasa.[4] The Nyika were generally invited to give their consent to the succession of new governors.[5] According to one observer, when they visited Mombasa on public business they received subsistence from the governor.[6] They could freely enter the town and went there in large numbers at certain times of the year to sell their produce.[7] That it was important for the ruling authorities in Mombasa to preserve good relations with the Nyika was demonstrated in Ahmad ibn Muhammad's governorship, when the Rabai Nyika supported a group of dissident Mazruis.[8]

The relationship of the Mombasans and the Nyika made outsiders think that the former had substantial authority in both the immediate and the further environs of Mombasa. Whatever the true facts, such an impression evoked respect for the Mombasans and the Mazruis. Their prestige was further bolstered by their authority, which in some places was more apparent than in others, over the non-Nyika peoples and towns to the north and south of Mombasa. One of Mombasa's most important acquisitions was the island of Pemba, to the north of

[1] Emery's Journal, entry for 9 Oct. 1824.
[2] See Chapter III, pp. 88-9.
[3] Emery's Journal, entries for 12, 13, 22, and 31 July 1825.
[4] *Mombasa Chronicle.*
[5] Emery's Journal, entries for 14 and 15 Oct. 1825.
[6] Boteler, *op. cit.*, II, 207.
[7] Emery's Journal, entries for 3 Sept., 4 Oct., 6 Dec. 1824, and 18 Feb., 23 Mch., 14, 18, 24, 28 Apr., 21, 25 June, 5, 11, 17 July, 3, 22 Aug., 14, 15 Oct. 1825.
[8] Mazrui MS., p. 36.

Zanzibar. Exactly when and how Mombasa obtained governance of that island is obscure. Before the Omanis came to East Africa in the 1690s the local ruler of Mombasa, who was tolerated by the Portuguese, had also controlled the government of Pemba. On their arrival the Omanis established a garrison at Pemba but three decades later the Portuguese, having recaptured Mombasa, arranged a treaty with Pate which gave the latter some sort of stake in Pemba.[1] When the Portuguese were expelled shortly afterwards, Pate may have kept its hold on Pemba or it may have been taken by the Omani governor of Zanzibar. According to Guillain, Pate controlled Pemba until Ali ibn Uthman was governor of Mombasa. By that time the Pate agent had made himself so unpopular with the people of Pemba that they offered to put themselves under the rule of Mombasa, whereupon Ali ibn Uthman ousted the Pate agent and established a Mazrui in his stead.[2] The Mazrui MS. supports the view that Ali ibn Uthman took Pemba, but it omits to say from whom. If it was Pate whom Ali ousted from Pemba, circumstances soon led to a reinstatement. Ali's successor, Ma'sud, gave Pate a share in Pemba in return for a treaty of mutual aid, defence, and non-aggression. This agreement allowed Pate to place a garrison in one part of Pemba and the Mazruis to put one in Pate.[3] A similar arrangement is noted by the Pate Chronicle, although it is given an earlier date: 'Bwana Mkuu made friends with the Mazaru'i and they divided the taxes from the island of Pemba, each taking half'.[4] However it originated, the alliance was later destroyed when the Mazrui agent in Pate was killed: in retaliation the Mazruis expelled the Pate garrison from Pemba.[5] Some other sources give different accounts of Pemba's position. For example, in the 1770s Morice reported that the Imam of Oman held Pemba, and in 1811 Prior observed that part of the island was subject to Muscat, part to Mombasa, and a third part was independent.[6] Mombasa certainly had a garrison in Pemba in 1821.[7]

There is little evidence to explain the nature and effect of the rule of outsiders in Pemba. The people of Pemba, of mixed origin similar to that of the peoples of Zanzibar, probably lacked a local overall leader like the *mwenyi mkuu* of Zanzibar; rather their political system approximated to that of the opposite mainland coast, for they had

---

[1] Strandes, op. cit., pp. 276 and 287.   [2] Guillain, *Documents*, I, 548.
[3] Mazrui MS., p. 26.   [4] *Pate Chronicle*, p. 56.
[5] Mazrui MS., p. 28, which dates this incident c. 1776.
[6] Morice, 'Projet d'un établissement', p. 62; and Prior, op. cit., p. 81.
[7] See Chapter V, pp. 177-8.

NORTHERN SWAHILI SOCIETY AND POLITICS, CIRCA 1800

several leaders called *diwani*. That the people of Pemba were to some extent dissatisfied with the presence of the Mazruis may be observed by the action of two of these *diwani* in 1822, when they went to Oman to ask for help against the Mombasans.[1]

To observers Mombasa also seemed powerful because it appeared to have influence on the mainland coast for a certain distance to the north and south. In Portuguese times the towns and villages as far south as the Pangani River had had close relations with Mombasa. When the Portuguese recaptured Mombasa in 1727, among the leaders who came to give homage to them were those of Wasin, Vumba, Pangani, Mtangata, and Tanga.[2] According to Guillain in 1729 Wasin, Tanga, and Mtangata were 'dépendantes de Mombase'.[3] When they took over as governors of Mombasa the Mazruis reaffirmed this relationship. The Mazrui MS. claims that the Mazruis allowed the local rulers of these towns to retain their positions but at the same time placed their own governors (*wali*) at all the littoral towns between Ras Ngomeni near Malindi and Pangani, south of Mombasa.[4] There are some specific examples of Mazrui agents being present at some towns. For example, it is known that there was a Mazrui governor at Tanga when Ahmad ibn Muhammad was governor of Mombasa, because the ruler of Tanga rebelled against him.[5]

The Mazruis also established some influence over the *diwani* of Vumba and Wasin and consequently could make use of Digo and Segeju as fighting men.[6] They did not acquire this influence without opposition. At the beginning of the eighteenth century the *diwani* of Vumba, named Ruga, held authority, the exact nature of which is unclear, from Kwale, ten miles north of Tanga, to Likoni, on the mainland beside Mombasa island. Mombasa soon began to challenge this authority and Ruga, in an attempt to evade subjection, moved from Vumba to the island of Wasin. Ruga's successors, however, were unable to escape Mombasan influence, and they appear to have accepted the situation: Qasim, Ruga's son, accompanied the governor of Mombasa in his attack on Zanzibar in 1754/5 and *Diwani* Shaikh's daughter was actually married to Abdullah ibn Ahmad al-Mazrui, who became governor of Mombasa in 1814.[7] At some stage between 1780

---

[1] Ingrams, *op. cit.*, p. 155; and see Chapter V, p. 127.
[2] Strandes, *op. cit.*, p. 285. [3] Guillain, *Documents*, I, 533.
[4] Mazrui MS., pp. 5 and 30. [5] *Ibid.*, p. 30.
[6] See Chapter I, p. 42.
[7] Information about Vumba and Wasin from Hollis, *op. cit.*

and 1814 Mombasa sent an agent to reside at Wasin.[1] It may have been he who was responsible for the whole of the coastline south of Mombasa over which Mombasa had influence, or that duty may have been performed by another official. Such a post existed in 1825 because in that year a council was held at Mombasa in order to appoint a governor for the littoral to the south.[2] As for the coastline to the north of Mombasa, the Mazruis had some sort of influence as far north as Ras Ngomeni. Both the Mazrui MS. and the Pate Chronicle agree that point was the northern limit of Mazrui influence, and Guillain was informed of a similar boundary – the River Kilifi.[3]

It is claimed by the Mazrui MS. that the Mazruis also had authority over the Galla in the Malindi area, the Zigua, Shambala, and Bondei. As the manuscript specifies no dates for this, it may be referring to a later period when the Mazrui group who moved to Takaungu in the nineteenth century had some relationship with the Galla. It is unlikely that any such connexion existed in the eighteenth century: in fact, in 1824 Emery said that there was an old law existing 'that obliges all Arabs to pay a fee on all grain grown to the northward, which fee goes to the Gallas to keep them from making war and plundering'.[4] This may, however, have been a fabrication by the Mazruis to avoid having to pay duty on grain recently imposed by the British. The Mazrui MS. may also be referring to a much later period when stating that the Mazruis had influence over the Shambala and Bondei.[5] At the end of the nineteenth century some Mazruis led a rising in the area inhabited by those peoples. It is not unlikely, however, that in the eighteenth century Mombasa had friendly relations with the Zigua, Shambala, and Bondei through its connexions with the littoral towns fronting the territory of these peoples.

The Mazrui domain was one of influence rather than defined territory. As a centre of power the governor of Mombasa would have been recognized by towns and villages along the littoral for a certain distance north and south of Mombasa, and by the inhabitants of the Mombasa hinterland. At the coastal towns the governors or agents appointed by the Mazruis probably had only a light authority: their duties would have been to remit the grain taxes to Mombasa and to act in an advisory capacity to the local rulers, who retained their posts. The position of

---

[1] Information about Vumba and Wasin from Hollis, *op. cit.*, p. 285, and Mazrui MS., p. 30. [2] See note 1, p. 54.
[3] *Pate Chronicle*, p. 56; and Guillain, *Documents*, III, 235.
[4] Emery's Journal, entry for 29 Sept. 1824. [5] Mazrui MS., p. 30.

NORTHERN SWAHILI SOCIETY AND POLITICS, CIRCA 1800

the Mazruis was therefore strong. In fact, in many ways they were better placed on the Swahili Coast than the authorities of Oman. The latter had less opportunity than the Mazruis to recruit soldiers locally in East Africa and also appeared to be more alien overlords because, unlike the Mazruis, they remained oriented towards Oman. At the beginning of the nineteenth century, however, there was still a balance between the positions of the Mazrui and Omani authorities in East Africa. But, apart from the Mazrui and Omani domains, there was a third important region on the Swahili Coast. If either side obtained control of that area the balance between them would be upset. What had formerly been an uneasy tolerance of each other could develop into a struggle for ascendancy. That region was the Lamu archipelago.

The Lamu archipelago, to the north of Mombasa, consists of the three islands of Lamu, Manda, and Pate, together with some smaller islands. On Lamu island the most important settlements were the town of Lamu and the village of Shela; on Pate island the largest settlements were those of Pate, Siu, and Faza. As for Manda island, by the beginning of the nineteenth century it was uninhabited. The people who lived on the islands of the Lamu archipelago could rightly be called Swahili because they were descended from Arabs, peoples of the Persian Gulf, and mainland Africans. They could be divided into three rough categories: townsmen who called themselves 'Arabs' but more correctly should be called Swahili; a less prosperous group who were called Bajun; and slaves and their descendants who may have been freed. The largest group was the Bajun, who were called the 'Watikuu' by the other people of Pate.[1] Originally this group may have been a mixture of south Arabians who had come to the Banadir coast (the coast of the present-day Republic of Somalia) and Somali peoples.[2] According to the Pate Chronicle, which cannot be regarded as accurate, they settled first at Siu and later spread throughout the archipelago. In many ways they remained a distinct group: at the end of the nineteenth century they were still distinguishable from the Swahili townspeople of both the higher and lower classes.[3]

At the opening of the nineteenth century, Pate town was the most powerful of the settlements of the Lamu archipelago. Its inhabitants

---

[1] *Pate Chronicle*, p. 35; and Stigand, *The Land of Zinj*, pp. 165-8. 'Watikuu' literally means 'people of the mainland' – i.e. '*wa nti* (local dialect for *nchi*) *kuu*'.

[2] Stigand, *ibid.*, p. 168; and W. W. A. Fitzgerald, *Travels in East Africa, Zanzibar, and Pemba* (London, 1898), p. 382.

[3] Fitzgerald, *idem.*

were mainly Swahilis who possessed many 'native slaves', but there were also a few Galla and other mainland peoples including presumably, the Bajun.[1] Like Swahilis elsewhere, the people of Pate were divided into a number of clans. The most prominent of these was the Nabhani. Tradition has it that the Nabhani came to Pate from Oman as early as the seventh century A.D., but recently it has been suggested that they did not arrive before the seventeenth century.[2] If the latter is the case they very soon established their predominance because throughout the eighteenth century that clan provided the rulers of Pate.

It is important to study briefly the system of government in Pate town because political instability there in the late eighteenth century was to have far-reaching effects on both the Lamu archipelago and the whole Swahili Coast. The system was similar to that of other Swahili towns. There was an overall ruler, locally called the *mfalme*, who relied for support and advice on lesser officials, elders, and notables (the *watu wakuu*, *amiri*, and *waziri*).[3]

The rulers of Pate seem to have been inept in their management of this system. They were subject to continous disloyalty and challenge from their advisers and their kinsmen. Their difficulties appear to have stemmed in part from the absence of clear rules of succession to the rulership. This meant that when a ruler died the succession was decided by a trial of strength between members of the Nabhani clan, each of whom solicited the support of notables. Factionalism flourished and, even when a successor did emerge, his tenure of office seldom escaped intermittent challenge from the defeated factions. No ruler of the last half of the eighteenth century avoided agitation by a rival claimant or other rebellious forces.[4] Circumstances were therefore favourable for alien interference; not only was united opposition to outsiders unlikely but local peoples often invited foreigners to assist them in domestic struggles.

Whether a ruler of Pate could maintain his position depended to a large degree on how many fighting men he could raise. The fact that Fumomadi was supported by several men bearing arms was put forward as an argument that he should succeed to the office.[5] The poem

---

[1] Smee's log, entry for 13 Feb. 1811, I.O.L., Marine Records Miscellaneous 586.

[2] *Pate Chronicle*, p. 30. For new interpretation, N. Chittick, 'A new look at the history of Pate', *Journal of African History* (London, 1969), vol. X, no. 3, pp. 375-91).

[3] *Pate Chronicle*, pp. 67 and 69.   [4] *Ibid., passim.*   [5] *Ibid.*, p. 64.

NORTHERN SWAHILI SOCIETY AND POLITICS, CIRCA 1800

Al-Inkishafi tells us that rulers kept a few regular soldiers, but of as great importance as the possession of troops was the ability of men holding or hoping to hold office to persuade ordinary people to fight for them.[1] The Bajun and people from the mainland were often enlisted as troops: Sultan Omari, defeated by Mwana Khadija's forces, fled to the Bajun at Faza, and then went to Brava to obtain support before returning to Pate. Rival candidates for the rulership would try to enlist the support of Ozi (on the mainland at the mouth of the River Tana), Siu, Faza, and Lamu. Fumomadi is remembered as having killed many soldiers from Pate, Lamu, Siu, and Ozi who opposed him.[2]

Another important measure of any ruler's authority was whether he could levy taxes. The available sources do not say if customs duties were paid to the rulers of Pate, but it is likely that such dues existed. More certain is the existence of a crop tax, called the *kikanda*. This was paid to the ruler of Pate by both the people of Pate and those of Lamu, but whether the inhabitants of Siu and Faza also contributed is unknown. That there were methods of enforcing payment of this tax is evident from what happened to one Abdullah ibn Hafithi, a Lamu notable, when he refused to provide Fumomadi with his dues of three loads of produce. Fumomadi despatched a captain and twelve soldiers to the man's house and exacted 1,000 dollars as a fine.[3] Regular tax receipts would have been very important to a ruler's ability to maintain an adequate number of soldiers. Sultan Ahmad ran into trouble about his finances and as a result pressed a British officer to give him money to pay his troops.[4]

A ruler of Pate had more chance of retaining his position if he kept possession of the royal regalia which consisted of a horn (*siwa*) and a chair. The chair was a high, fixed one and appeared to be the only raised seat in the residence of the ruler.[5] A candidate for the high office probably had more chance of success if he managed to acquire the horn. This is borne out by the example of Sultan Abubakr's daughter, who felt that her son had been deprived of his opportunity to become ruler and so had her own rival ivory horn carved in a bid to revive

[1] W. Hichens (ed. and trans.), *Al-Inkishafi* (Medstead, 1926). For other versions of this poem, see bibliography.
[2] *Pate Chronicle*, p. 66.   [3] *Ibid.*, pp. 67-9.
[4] Smee's log, entry for 8 Feb. 1811, I.O.L., Marine Records Miscellaneous 586.
[5] *Idem.*

his candidature.¹ Fumomadi also tried to ensure his own succession after Fumoluti's death by ordering the crier to beat (*sic*) the horn in the town and proclaim that he had taken up office.²

These prerequisites for a successful tenure of office were seldom all present for the late eighteenth-century rulers of Pate. Their position was made more difficult by alliances and rivalries between Pate town and its neighbouring settlements. There were close connexions between the Lamu archipelago and the mainland because the islands were dependent on mainland crops for their food supply.³ It is not likely, however, that the island rulers exerted any political control on the mainland, although they may have had a certain influence. A clause of a treaty of 1637 which the Portuguese arranged between the rulers of Pate, Faza, Siu, and Manda indicates that at that date the Galla of the mainland supported Pate while the Bajun and Marakatos were closer to Siu, Faza, Manda, and Lamu.⁴ In 1811 a British naval officer described the coast between the River Juba and the Lamu archipelago as 'subject' to Pate, but this was probably his own interpretation of the fact that the mainland settlements to the south of the River Juba traded more with Pate than did those north of the river, where the Swahili way of life and language shaded into that of the Somali, and trade links were more with the Banadir coast.⁵ The dubious claim made in the Pate Chronicle that a ruler of Pate and the Mazrui governor of Mombasa made the Sabaki River a frontier between their lands in the eighteenth century is more likely to refer to a delineation of spheres of influence than to a division of territorial control.⁶ The Pate Chronicle does not mention that any rulers of Pate appointed governors to mainland settlements; in fact the geographical extent of the ruler of Pate's authority was as ill-defined as that of local potentates elsewhere on the Swahili Coast.

As regards the relationship between Pate town and Siu and Faza, the two other towns on Pate island, this, too, was ill-defined. A description of the relationship is made even more difficult by the lack of information about Siu and Faza. As has been seen, both these towns were involved in opposition to Fumomadi and thus cannot have been isolated from Pate's affairs. In fact, in the 1890s Hardinge obtained the information that during the eighteenth century the aggressions of the Nabhani

---

¹ *Pate Chronicle*, p. 53.   ² *Ibid.*, p. 65.   ³ See Chapter III, pp. 91–2.
⁴ Strandes, *op. cit.*, p. 214. The Marakatos may have been Somalis.
⁵ Report by Lt Hardy, I.O.L., Marine Records Miscellaneous 586.
⁶ *Pate Chronicle*, p. 56.

NORTHERN SWAHILI SOCIETY AND POLITICS, CIRCA 1800

rulers of Pate upon Siu became so formidable that its inhabitants appealed to the Somalis on the opposite mainland to protect them, promising them half their town and an equal share in their government if they succeeded in repelling the enemy.[1]

Lamu's relationship with Pate was more amicable than that of Siu. In the eighteenth century it had close ties with Pate town but at the same time retained its own political system. Lamu's political organization displayed characteristics typical of the Swahili system of government. There was an overall leader, known as the *mngwana wa yumbe*, and a number of prominent clans, such as the Famao, Wayunbili, and Kinamte, who were headed by a chief elder (*mkubwa wa wazee*) and whose members acted as the ruler's advisers (*watu wakuu*).[2] As at Pate, the clan element encouraged factionalism to develop. Two main factions emerged in Lamu, calling themselves the Zena and Su'udi parties. Such a division must have facilitated intervention by outsiders, particularly nearby Pate, in the politics of Lamu.[3]

Lamu's proximity to Pate made connexions and rivalries between the two towns inevitable. Lamu was constantly involved in the disputes which arose over the succession to the rulership of Pate. One eighteenth century ruler of Pate, Bwana Bakari wa Bwana Mkuu, married a Lamu woman, and when their child was later offered as a candidate for the rulership war broke out between Lamu and Pate; the Lamu people wanted their countryman to become ruler of Pate whereas Pate's inhabitants preferred a candidate of pure Pate birth.[4] One ruler of Pate, Bwana Mkuu, actually chose Lamu as his place of residence, making it the main harbour for vessels coming to trade in the archipelago.[5] Bwana Bakari of Pate also lived at Lamu, and his successor, Sultan Ahmad, was approved by both Pate and Lamu. Relations were not always so

---

[1] Sir Arthur Hardinge, *Report on the condition and progress of the East Africa Protectorate* (Parliamentary Command Paper 8683, 1898), p. 14.

[2] Shaikh Faraji ibn Hamad al-Bakarij al-Lamuy, 'The Chronicle of Lamu', pp. 12 and 20, ed. by W. Hichens, in *Bantu Studies* (Johannesburg, 1938), XXI, pp. 3-33 (hereafter this will be cited as *Lamu Chronicle*). See also *Pate Chronicle*, p. 69.

[3] *Pate Chronicle*, p. 73; Mazrui MS., pp. 34-5; and *Lamu Chronicle*, p. 26. The *Lamu Chronicle* uses the word *safu* of these groups, which generally means 'party', but Hitchens translates it as 'regiments'. Prins, basing his information on fieldwork in Lamu, says the parties had a territorial basis, and the heads of each occupied alternately the position of ruler of Lamu – A. H. J. Prins, *The Swahili-speaking peoples of Zanzibar and the East African Coast* (London, 1961), p. 100 – (hereafter cited as *Swahili-speaking Peoples*).

[4] *Lamu Chronicle*, p. 18, and *Pate Chronicle*, p. 81. [5] *Pate Chronicle*, p. 56.

amicable: Bwana Tamu the Younger had to fight twice with the people of Lamu, and towards the end of Fumomadi's tenure of office the chief elder of Lamu informed the ruler of Pate that his people no longer wanted to be 'governed' by Pate. Fumomadi had to exert his position by force, and he began to construct a fort at Lamu.[1]

Pate's intermittent dominance over Lamu and its influence on the mainland indicate that its rulers, despite their difficulties, were more powerful than other local potentates. This impression is strengthened by the Swahili poem, *Al-Inkishafi*, which describes the glories of Pate in a period which is most likely to be the eighteenth century. It talks of men of wealth with many servants, of mansions and banquetings, of trappings such as rich canopies and Chinese celadon ware, and of viziers surrounded by soldiers.[2] The poem's purpose is didactic, praising the values of the spiritual world in contrast to those of the ephemeral material world, and consequently it would be expected to employ poetic licence when describing former glories which have vanished. There is also the possibility that it refers to a period earlier than the eighteenth century, but archaeological evidence does not support this view. The coral-block palace and town wall date from the seventeenth or eighteenth century, as possibly do the remainder of the coral ruins.[3] Within the walls there were about twenty-three quarters in the town; since each quarter contained from twenty to sixty houses, the total number of dwellings in Pate town was between 1,000 and 1,250.[4] Pate was therefore a settlement of considerable size in the eighteenth century.

As the nineteenth century opened, however, Pate entered upon a decline. By 1811 Smee said the town consisted merely of mud huts. Its inhabitants dared not venture out for fear of attack from the party supporting a deposed ruler, and, because of the troubled state of affairs, vessels preferred to anchor at Lamu.[5] By 1824 the only substantial coral building in the town was the palace, and even that was in ruins. The remainder of the dwellings were constructed of stakes, reeds, and mud.[6] It is possible, however, that, rather than having suffered a decline, Pate town had continued much the same. Sources dealing with early nineteenth-century Pate are more trustworthy than those referring to the

[1] *Pate Chronicle*, pp. 57, 59, 60, and 70.
[2] *Al-Inkishafi*, pp. 68, 70, and 89.
[3] J. S. Kirkman, *Men and Monuments on the East African Coast* (London, 1964), p. 64 – (hereafter cited as *Men and Monuments*).
[4] Stigand, *The Land of Zinj*, pp. 161-2, basing his observations on the ruins.
[5] Smee's log, entry for 13 Feb. 1811, I.O.L., Marine Records Miscellaneous 586.
[6] Boteler, *op. cit.*, I, 375.

eighteenth century. The latter may be providing an inaccurate impression of Pate's power and prosperity. In addition, as the nineteenth century progresses, we begin to hear more about Lamu, Siu, and Faza, about which information for the period of the eighteenth century is almost entirely non-existent. Standing in comparison with these places, therefore, Pate begins to be judged in its true light. From the topographical point of view it is odd that Pate assumed the importance that is claimed for it because it had a particularly bad harbour. Long-distance trading vessels were more likely to put in at Lamu harbour than that of Pate. However, if Pate had some control over Lamu, as the chronicles indicate, this difficulty could be overcome.

On balance it does seem that Pate was the dominant town in the Lamu archipelago in the eighteenth century, and that it was losing this position at the opening of the nineteenth. The repeated struggles over the succession to the rulership must have played some part in the waning influence of Pate. Outsiders found opportunities in the internal confusion to interfere in Pate's political affairs. At various times different factions in Pate invited both the Mazruis of Mombasa and the Omanis to help them. Once these foreigners had accepted these invitations they quickly observed the opportunities offered by the region and the dangers of letting the other party monopolize them. The Lamu archipelago thus became the site of the struggle for ascendance on the Swahili Coast between the Mazruis and the Omanis.

If Alexander Hamilton, writing in 1727 and in good position to hear reports of British and Indian visits to East Africa, is to be believed, the Omanis obtained control of Pate before they captured Mombasa in 1698. He claims that the Omanis, jealous of British, Indian, and Portuguese trade with Pate, sent 'a colony' to that island in 1692 and prohibited its commerce with all other nations.[1] In 1710, however, the Omanis had no garrison at Pate.[2] But succession disputes soon drew the Omanis back into Pate's affairs. In 1727 one faction in Pate solicited the aid of the Omani garrison in Zanzibar, and another appealed to the Portuguese.[3] It is likely that the authorities in Oman took advantage of the situation to order the murder of the ruler,

[1] Alexander Hamilton, *A New Account of the East Indies* (London, 1727), 2 vols, I, 18.
[2] Strandes, *op. cit.*, p. 275. Nor does Ibn Ruzayq, *op. cit.*, p. 92, include them in his list of places taken by Oman.
[3] Strandes, *op. cit.*, p. 281.

Bwana Tamu the Younger, and to place a garrison in Pate.[1] After this incident, however, there is no further mention of Omani soldiers being present in Pate in the eighteenth century, and the archipelago probably remained free of Omani interference.

It did not, however, escape Mazrui intervention. After their break with the Al Bu Sa'idi Imamate in the 1740s, the Mazruis seem to have tried to strengthen their position by seeking allies in the Lamu archipelago. Their first recorded participation in the affairs of that region was in the role of mediator between Pate and discontented elders from Lamu.[2] They established a more definite position when Bwana Tamu the Younger was murdered:

'... the Mazrui had become very powerful and they had entered Pate in friendship, but had become more powerful than the Nabahans.... They wanted to seize Pate and Amu [Lamu] and to take the kingdom of the Nabahans, but they were unable. So they lived with them in friendship and in guile, thinking, "if we get the chance we will take their kingdom".'[3]

When Mwana Khadija ruled they actively encouraged opposition to her, and one of their protegés, Sultan Omari, was set up as a rival ruler in Pate. On Mwana Khadija's death another Mazrui candidate, Fumoluti, acceded to office. The Pate Chronicle mentions a Mazrui 'governor' in Pate during Fumoluti's reign, but it is more likely that the Mazruis merely maintained a representative or an agent there.[4] Such an agent may, however, have exercised considerable influence. Both the Pate Chronicle and the Mazrui MS. claim that the Mazrui-Nabhani alliance was mutually planned and intended to be a joint opposition to Al Bu Sa'idi influence on the Swahili Coast.[5]

As the eighteenth century drew to its end the Mazruis were unable to maintain their influence in Pate, probably because their interference became too marked. Fumoluti was killed by the people of Pate and his successor, Fumomadi, turned out the Mazruis: 'Since they had come to Pate no one had been able to govern any more without their aid, but Sultan Fumomadi put an end to this state of affairs.'[6] The Mazruis reappeared in the early nineteenth century, when their activities encouraged the Omanis to establish direct control of the Lamu archipelago.

---

[1] *Pate Chronicle*, p. 57. However, Werner's version of the Chronicle, p. 288, says the Omani expedition to Pate failed.
[2] *Ibid.*, p. 59. [3] *Ibid.*, pp. 60-1. [4] *Ibid.*, pp. 61 and 63.
[5] *Ibid.*, p. 79; and Mazrui MS., p. 26. [6] *Pate Chronicle*, p. 67.

NORTHERN SWAHILI SOCIETY AND POLITICS, CIRCA 1800

* * *

An adequate picture of the Swahili Coast at the beginning of the nineteenth century cannot be obtained merely by a study of political systems and events. Although this book is not primarily concerned with the social aspects of Swahili life, a brief description of them must be given because they provide many clues both to the reaction of the Swahilis to the coming of the Omanis and to the nature and extent of Omani settlement. One of the most important factors in the success of this settlement on the Swahili Coast was a feature the Swahilis and Omanis had in common: both were Muslim in their religious beliefs. Since Islam penetrates all levels and practices of society the Swahilis and Omanis therefore had a great deal in common, even though they belonged to different sects, the former being Shafi'i and the latter Ibadhi.[1]

In general the Swahili townspeople, being in regular contact with Arab traders from the north, inclined to more orthodox Shafi'i beliefs whereas the inhabitants of the smaller and more remote villages held certain beliefs peculiar to themselves and were more inclined to incorporate animistic substrata. The animism of the Swahilis has been used as evidence of their divergence from Islam, but in actuality animism is a common feature of Islam, particularly that of peasant or rural peoples. Like other Muslims the Swahilis believed in the evil eye and spirits, against which they protected themselves with talismans and Koranic verses.[2] The Omanis did likewise. When the British consul, Hamerton, was ill, Saiyid Sa'id sent for a shaikh well known for his writings, and with a silver nail attached a sheet of the man's work to the door of Hamerton's sickroom in order to exclude evil spirits and the ghost of Napier, who had died there.[3] In the 1820s Emery watched the Arabs and Swahilis of Mombasa together making a great noise around the town trying to expel the devil who had, they said, been there for the past three weeks.[4] The spirits against which such measures were taken inhabited the sea, ruins, and other isolated parts. Like other Muslims, the Swahilis were not image worshippers. They did, however, differ from their co-religionists in their emphasis upon the powers of medicine-men (*mganga*).[5] It is true that other Muslims had similar

[1] Guillain, *Documents*, II, 95; and Burton, *Zanzibar*, I, 421. It is most likely that Albrand was mistaken when he said the people of Kilwa were Shi'a in their beliefs – Albrand's Report, 1819, M.O., Réunion 72/472.
[2] Guillain, *Documents*, II, 97-8; and Burton, *Zanzibar*, I, 86, and 422-3.
[3] Burton, *Zanzibar*, II, 304-5.
[4] Emery's Journal, entry for 14 July 1825.
[5] Burton, *Zanzibar*, I, 422 and II, 30.

practitioners of magic, but no such elaborate ceremonial and ritual beliefs accompanied their doings. The town, and sometimes the village Swahilis kept the usual Islamic feasts and fasted at Ramadhan.[1] For example, the inhabitants of Zanzibar were fasting when Commodore Blankett visited the town in 1798.[2] Some Swahilis were not strict in their fasting and religious observances, particularly those from the lower classes.[3]

There was, therefore, a great deal in common between the religious beliefs and practices of the Swahilis and Omanis, and this must have contributed to the success of the latter in establishing themselves on the Swahili Coast. The two groups did not, however, worship together, but there was tolerance on either side of the other's differences of belief. The Omanis did not try to convert the Swahilis to their own way of thinking. They worshipped in different mosques and had their own separate religious leaders and officials.[4] This religious toleration can be explained partly by the fact that the Omanis who came to the Swahili Coast were in the main seafarers and merchants.

Islam penetrated many facets of Swahili society, and in particular that of education, which, as with other Muslims, was Koranic. In the towns education reached a large number of boys, but in the smaller villages and country areas boys were less likely to attend school. At the age of seven, boys were sent to schools run by *qadhis* (judges of Koranic law) where they spent one to three years perfecting their *khitmah* (knowledge of the Koran), after which they returned to their fathers.[5] In the 1820s there were four such schools at Lamu, which all the boys of the town attended.[6] In the 1840s there were three schools in Zanzibar, but ten years later the number had increased to fifteen or sixteen, some of which were Ibadhi and some Shafi'i.[7]

Although the boys learnt to read the Koran in these schools, few obtained any proficiency in writing. The script used was, of course, the Arabic: there was no Swahili alphabet. There was, however, little

[1] Burton, *Zanzibar*, I, 390; and Guillain, *Documents*, II, 106.
[2] A. Bissell, *A Voyage from England to the Red Sea* (London, 1806), p. 36.
[3] Burton, *Zanzibar*, I, 421. Prior, *op. cit.*, p. 80, found the people of Kilwa casual in their religious observances.
[4] Guillain, *Documents*, II, 95 and 105; Burton, *Zanzibar*, I, 307 and 396; and Krapf, *op. cit.*, pp. 124 and 419.
[5] Boteler, *op. cit.*, I, 385; Burton, *Zanzibar*, I, 406 and 424; and Guillain, *Documents*, II, 115.
[6] Boteler, *op. cit.*, I, 384.
[7] Guillain, *Documents*, II, 115; and Burton, *Zanzibar*, I, 405.

NORTHERN SWAHILI SOCIETY AND POLITICS, CIRCA 1800

incentive for Swahili boys to become good writers of either the Arabic language or script, since Arabic was not the language they used, and its script conveyed but poorly the sounds of the Swahili language. In 1819 Arabic was spoken at Zanzibar only by Omanis and Indians, and when they first arrived in that town Arabs had to use interpreters to communicate with the local people.[1] The influx of the Omanis before the 1840s did not alter the situation, and by then few of the Arabs even knew Arabic. That language was used only in the official relations of the Sultan with his subjects or with foreigners.[2]

It was said in 1856 that Swahili *ulama* (learned men) were capable of reading the Koran but generally unable to write Arabic.[3] There were, however, some exceptions. In the 1840s Krapf was assisted in his translation of the first book of Moses into Swahili by the Swahili shaikh Ali ibn Muhyi al-Din, then a *qadhi* at Mombasa. Shaikh Ali had, however, come from Brava.[4] In the same period Kimwere, chief of the Shambala, always had a Swahili scribe with him to write his letters, and his two sons had learnt to read and write.[5] A learned Swahili at Zanzibar was Muhyi al-Din, who originated from Lamu. The Mazrui MS. mentions his writings several times, and it was he who compiled the Kilwa Chronicle from previous manuscripts.[6] At Mombasa there were several learned Mazruis, although these, being more recent immigrants, had a better knowledge of Arabic. For example, there was Abdullah ibn Nafi' al-Mazrui, who spent nine years at Mecca, where he came into contact with many scholars. His son, Ahmad, was the author of works on syntax and jurisprudence, and another son also wrote many booklets and commentaries.[7] In general, however, Swahili culture tended to have an oral emphasis. There existed many proverbial sayings, riddles, legends, songs, poems, and eulogies of the brave. Among the most famous were the poems of *Liongo* and *Al-Inkishafi*.[8]

In several of their cultural and social practices the Swahilis differed from Islamic societies, but in many respects their usages were typically Islamic. As with other Islamic societies the pedigree (*nisba*) based on the patrilineal line was important, particularly among the higher-class

[1] Albrand's Report, 1819, M.O., Réunion 72/472. For a similar situation in 1834, Ruschenberger, *op. cit.*, I, 64.
[2] Guillain, *Documents*, II, 94.   [3] Burton, *Zanzibar*, I, 423.
[4] Krapf, *op. cit.*, p. 131.   [5] *Ibid.*, p. 279.
[6] Burton, *Zanzibar*, I, 263 and 423. In 1861 Muhyi al-Din gave the Kilwa Chronicle to Kirk, who donated it to the British Museum in 1883.
[7] Mazrui MS., p. 2. These works remained in manuscript.
[8] Hichens, *Al-Inkishafi*, and E. Steere, *Swahili Tales* (London, 1870).

Swahilis. Among the most important and respected Swahili lineages were the Alawi, Shatri, Nabhani, and Harthi.[1] As in Islamic practice elsewhere, ancestor cults existed among the Swahilis. In some cases, however, patrilineage was modified: in Zanzibar, for example, children of lower-class Swahilis belonged not to their parents, but to their mother's brother.[2] Neither did the Swahilis adhere to endogamous marriage with the same strictness as upper-class Arabs.[3] None the less members of notable Swahili families would generally marry members of other notable families. Following Islamic practice, polygamy was practised by the Swahilis, but very often there was only one wife.[4] Swahili women were less closeted and heavily veiled than in usual Islamic society; indeed, none of the women of the notable Swahili families of Mafia were veiled.[5] Swahili women tended to play an active part in social, and sometimes political, life. Sometimes women succeeded to positions of leadership: for example, in 1652, and again in 1698, the ruler of Zanzibar was a woman; in eighteenth-century Pate Mwana Khadija became ruler, and Mwana Darini played a large part in politics; and in the nineteenth century a woman was a *sheha* in Tumbatu.[6]

Absent from usual Islamic societies were the Swahili practices of swearing brotherhood (*kuchanjana*), of abusing corpses, and of initiation ceremonies.[7] As regards the last, all girls had a steadmother (*kungwi*) who attended at the first ablution at puberty, instructed in sexual matters, and sat on the couch at the wedding.[8] Boys were circumcised from nine to fourteen years old in contradistinction to the Islamic practice of from up to five years old, and then they entered a lodge for instruction.

The Swahilis used their own solar calendar rather than the Islamic lunar calendar, and indeed the natural cycle of seed-time and harvest was more useful to them than the lunar year. The Swahilis added ten to twelve days to the Islamic year and thus made the seasons recur at the same time every year. Originally their calendar was totally different

---

[1] Burton, *Zanzibar*, I, 410; Loarer's Report, Part II, 1849, M.O., O.I., 2/10; Albrand's Report, 1819, M.O., Réunion 72/472; and Dallons, 1804, printed in Freeman-Grenville, *Select Documents*, p. 199.

[2] Burton, *Zanzibar*, II, 437.   [3] *Ibid.*, I, 394.   [4] Boteler, *op. cit.*, I, 383.

[5] Loarer's Report, Part II, 1849, M.O., O.I. 2/10.

[6] Strandes, *op. cit.*, pp. 228 and 276; *Pate Chronicle*, pp. 53 and 61; and Ingrams, *op. cit.*, p. 150.

[7] Burton, *Zanzibar*, I, 23, 420, and II, 428-9. These were more prevalent among the lower classes.

[8] *Ibid.*, I, 420.

NORTHERN SWAHILI SOCIETY AND POLITICS, CIRCA 1800

from the Islamic but it soon absorbed certain Islamic features. The Swahilis did not, however, begin their year with the first Islamic month (*Muharram*) but commenced with the ninth lunar month (*Shawwal*), which they called *Mfunguo Mosi*. The Swahili almanac was kept by a sage who, in the 1850s, lived at Tumbatu. He found the solar new year's day by looking at the sun, tracing figures on the ground, and comparing the results with the Islamic calendar. The new year's day, called *siku kuu ya mwaka*, was a great festival for the Swahilis. Their week began on a Saturday, and the day began at sunset – the first hour.[1]

The Swahili way of life possessed some characteristics which were derivative from typical Islamic practices and others which were distinct. It was affected by many disparate elements, for in it were reflected the influences of Persian Gulf peoples, Arabs, Indians, and inhabitants of the hinterland and interior of East Africa. These several influences had coalesced into a system which was common to all the littoral and island settlements between the River Juba and Cape Delgado, a fact which justifies the description of all these places as 'Swahili'. However due to geographical factors and the presence of a multiplicity of political entities, at the beginning of the nineteenth century the Swahilis were not yet conscious of their corporate identity. This, among other things, made easier the Omani expansion into their lands, a development which was in any case facilitated by common religious beliefs. The Omanis did, however, meet with some opposition, as the story of their expansion will reveal.

[1] *Ibid.*, I, 170-4; and Guillain, *Documents*, II, 107.

CHAPTER III

TRADE AND COMMERCE ON THE SWAHILI COAST

AT THE BEGINNING OF THE NINETEENTH CENTURY

In the days before the advent of steam propulsion, ports which lay in the path of good sailing winds enjoyed an important commercial advantage. The ports which bordered the Indian Ocean were especially fortunate in this respect because ships which sailed to them with a following wind in one season could return straight to their home ports later in the year, when the wind assumed an opposite direction. Predictable and constant, the monsoon winds drew the lands skirting the Indian Ocean into a trading unit. The East African coast was an integral member of this unit for it provided and accepted articles essential to the pattern of exchange.

The north-east monsoon, covering the Indian Ocean as far south as Madagascar, starts to blow at the beginning of November, is at its most forceful between December and March, and peters out as March closes. Gentle, variable breezes then occur until the middle of April when the south-west monsoon tentatively sets in. That wind is at its strongest from June to September, waning towards the end of the month. Until the north-east monsoon begins the cycle again there are light and variable breezes. These monsoons made it possible for vessels to travel the 2,200 miles from the Persian Gulf and India to East Africa in as few as twenty-five days.[1] From the Red Sea and southern India the journey took even less time. Speed depended on catching the wind at its most suitable strength for one's vessel and destination. Ships began to leave East Africa for the north from the beginning of April. They had to depart by the middle of September except in special cases. Vessels could not be certain to reach Bombay if they left East Africa

[1] Smee's journey of thirty days from Muscat was average – Smee's log, 5 Mch. 1811, I.O.L., Marine Records Miscellaneous 586

after 15 September, but boats for Kutch could depart after that date, although not after 5 October.[1] It was not possible to defy the regime of the monsoons: in 1841 boats which left Zanzibar for Bombay too late in the season had to return after spending eighty to ninety days at sea without nearing their destination.[2] Ignorant of the strength of a contrary monsoon, in 1798 Commodore Blankett spent weeks trying to beat up the East African coast towards the Red Sea in order to intercept an anticipated Napoleonic invasion of India.[3]

During the north-east monsoon the first arrivals to East Africa from the north were Zanzibar boats which had transported grain to Arabia; they arrived home at the end of November or in the first days of December. Shortly afterwards some of the larger northern vessels started to come in, many of them having stopped on their way at Ras Hafun, Warshaikh, Marka, Brava, and the ports of the Lamu archipelago. Most of the Omani vessels did not leave their home ports until the first fortnight in January, and arrived in East Africa during the course of February. Vessels from Bombay, Kutch, and other Indian ports, tended to leave at the end of December, arriving towards the end of January. Vessels from the Red Sea and southern India, having a shorter distance to travel, usually chose the end of January as the time of their departure.[4]

The commerce of the Swahili Coast was dependent on these Arabian and Indian ships because the boats built by the Swahilis were generally too small to cross the ocean.[5] The larger vessels were dhows, baghlas, and ganjas. The dhow, distinctive because of its pointed and projecting prow and stern, had a single forward-sloping mast which employed a square matting sail. The baghlas and ganjas, which came mainly from Kutch, had large square sterns, high poops, long prows, and either one or two masts. Smaller Indian vessels were the ghurabs and batelas. Descriptions given in the first half of the nineteenth century vary in their estimation of the tonnage of dhows, baghlas, and ganjas. We hear from one source that dhows ranged from 30 to 50 tons, whereas baghlas and ganjas had an average tonnage of 50 to 60, but they occasionally reached 160.[6] A different source maintained that dhows

[1] *Ibid.*, 28 Mch. 1811; and Report by Guillain in Guillain to Ministry of Marine, 23 June 1849, A.N., Marine BB4/1036. The latter will hereafter be cited as 'Guillain's Report, 1849'.
[2] Hamerton to Bombay, no. 52, 28 Sept. 1842, Z.A.
[3] Bissell, *op. cit.*   [4] Guillain's Report, 1849, A.N., Marine BB4/1036.
[5] Morice, 'Projet d'un établissement', p. 163.
[6] Guillain's Report, 1849, A.N., Marine BB4/1036.

ranged from 50 to 500 tons, and yet another that the ships from Surat which visited East Africa were of 300 to 400 tons.[1] Another writer said the large vessels which came from Muscat were called 'shalingas' and had a maximum tonnage of 250.[2] Since these sources are all European, these discrepancies may be explained by the different meanings of the word 'ton' in European shipping. Those who reported a high tonnage may have been referring to gross displacement tonnage (the weight of the cargo and the vessel), while those who gave lesser figures may have been using as their measure deadweight tons (the weight of the cargo only). Alternatively, the high figures may refer to deadweight tons and the lower to volumetric tons (the capacity of the cargo space in a ship, one ton equalling 100 cubic feet of space).

All the commerce of the Swahili Coast was geared towards ensuring that the articles to be sold to these vessels were in readiness at the correct time of year. In the early nineteenth century the organization required to achieve this was reasonably developed, but would not have borne any real increase in the volume of commerce without improvement and extension. Many of the Swahili Coast's exports originated in the East African interior and were taken to the coast either by caravans or by a relay system.[3] Commercial and maritime activity on the coast was affected by the time at which these caravans arrived, and that, in turn, was dependent on the rainy seasons. Caravans could only travel when they could be sure of getting water on the way, but, at the same time, they must not be faced by floods. This was particularly important for caravans in what is now Tanzania because more than 90 per cent of that region possessed no permanent surface streams. In the dry season the Rivers Pangani, Wami, Rufu, Rufiji, and Rovuma almost dried up in their middle and lower courses. The caravans from Unyamwesi arrived at the coast in June and July; those from the interior behind Kilwa arrived in August. The caravans organized by the Kamba reached the villages behind Mombasa in June and July, but those to the Banadir coast, having a shorter distance to travel, reached the coast in February and March.[4]

The arrival at the coast of the articles which the caravans brought for sale therefore coincided with the presence of the northern vessels. Because those ships had to leave in September, the organization of the

---

[1] Burton, *Zanzibar*, I, 75; and Morice, 'Projet d'un établissement', p. 65.
[2] Boteler, *op. cit.*, I, 385-6.
[3] For the development of caravans, see Chapter VIII, p. 208.
[4] Guillain's Report, 1849, A.N., Marine BB4/1036.

SWAHILI TRADE AND COMMERCE, CIRCA 1800

sale of the articles had to be efficient. Consequently the period of most activity on the coast was from June to September. In those months Swahili and Indian middlemen bought the export articles prior to their sale to merchants from the north. There was much coasting trade at this time of year, as the exports were transported for sale to other Swahili towns. The practice grew of taking goods from the littoral ports to Zanzibar, a town which began to serve as an entrepot for larger shipments to the north. Most of this coastal transport was in the hands of the Swahilis who were able to combine it with their middlemen activities. They used small locally-built vessels called *mtepe*, which varied from 12 to 20 tons, and were about 36 feet long and 9 broad, with matting sails and six oars or poles.[1] They coasted or poled inside the reefs for much of their journey and consequently were less dependent on monsoon winds than larger vessels. However, winds and currents were useful to them; they often travelled at the end of a monsoon so as to be able to return with the first of the opposite winds.[2] And, whereas it was possible to get from Zanzibar to Lamu in the month of October, during the period of variable winds, it was not easy to make the journey once the north-east monsoon had set in. The ports to the north of Zanzibar had an advantage over those to the south. Not only could vessels from the north put in at them to make purchases on their way down to the main entrepot, but it was also easy for small local vessels at those places to take articles recently acquired from caravans down to Zanzibar for sale before the large vessels left for their home ports. This was in contrast to the situation to the south of Zanzibar. Since caravans arrived at Kilwa in August, its merchants had only a month to get their goods to Zanzibar before the northern vessels left. This was not altogether disastrous because the monsoon was in their favour at this time, and often ships lying at Zanzibar would wait for the Kilwa cargoes.[3]

Least dependent of all on the wind was the traffic between Zanzibar and the opposite mainland coast, and this may well have been a prominent factor in the success of Zanzibar in emerging as the main entrepot of the Swahili Coast. This traffic continued all the year round even in the slackest season of October and November, and consequently

---

[1] Morice, 'Projet d'un établissement', p. 163; and Emery to Cooley, 18 Dec. 1835, R.G.S., Emery Correspondence Block 1834-40.

[2] Emery, *idem*.

[3] Guillain's Report, 1849, A.N., Marine BB4/1036; and Smee's log, 28 Mch. 1811, I.O.L., Marine Records Miscellaneous 586.

Zanzibar could have a good stock of articles to offer the first-comers from the north in December. As Zanzibar became the entrepot for the whole coast it may have stimulated the exploitation of the African interior opposite. Articles from the mainland opposite Zanzibar could be stockpiled in Zanzibar at a time when it was far less easy for goods from Kilwa to reach that port because the northward wind had ceased.

The coastal traffic was swollen by non-local vessels which were small enough to participate. These 15 to 20 ton boats, called *bedeni*, were mainly from Sur, to the south of Muscat. They were equipped for fishing, and carried a large load of salt. They began to fish at Ras al-Hadd and continued to do so as far as Warshaikh on their southward journey. They then sold their salted fish at the Banadir and Swahili ports. Those which waited to return home until the end of the south-west monsoon employed themselves meanwhile in the local coasting trade. Excellent sailors, they had an advantage over other coastal traders.[1] Other, larger, northern vessels which were reluctant to remain idle while they waited for the monsoon to change also indulged in coastal trade where they could.[2]

The actual transport of trading articles was largely in the hands of Swahilis and recently arrived Omanis who owned boats and manned them with local people and slaves, but many of the middleman activities were performed by Indians. Indians had been able to enter East African commerce because Indian cloth was a staple article of barter in East Africa. For centuries Indian ships, particularly those of Kutch and Surat, had traded to the Swahili Coast; in fact, much of that coast's commerce had been in Indian hands in pre-Portuguese times.[3] It is most likely that firms in Kutch and Surat established agents on the Swahili Coast in order to facilitate their dealings there. These agents would barter at coast towns for goods from the interior and store their purchases at littoral ports or in Zanzibar until their own firms' vessels came from India or they could sell to other merchants from the north.

The residence of the Indians on the Swahili Coast was seasonal; before the nineteenth century they do not appear to have spent long periods of time there. Morice, writing in the 1770s, does not describe any Indian commercial community at the Swahili ports, although he notices that there was extensive trade with India.[4] By 1804, however, the Zanzibar customs collection was farmed out to an Indian, and by 1811 'a considerable number' of Indians resided in Zanzibar, 'many of

[1] Guillain's Report, 1849, as above.   [2] *Idem*.   [3] Strandes, *op. cit.*, pp. 92-3.
[4] Morice, 'Projet d'un établissement', p. 163.

whom appear to be wealthy and to hold the best part of the trade in their hands'.[1] This last statement was not entirely true because another contemporary observer said that the trade was chiefly in the hands of 'the Arabs from Muscat, Mukalla, etc., and a few adventurers from Kutch and the Coast of Sinde'.[2] The first estimate of the number of Indians is that of 214 given by Albrand in 1819. The Indians had to pay for permission to live and trade in Zanzibar and were not altogether welcome.[3] They were, however, accepted because they provided indispensable services such as banking and money-lending; in 1811 Lt Hardy was loaned 786 dollars at 25 per cent.[4] Indians also owned the vessels which came to East Africa from India. They were skilled navigators; in fact most vessels, including those belonging to Arabs, had Indian navigators, who practised lunar observations and possessed excellent chronometers and navigation manuals.[5] Most of the ordinary members of crew were slaves.

It remains to examine the nature of the commercial activity conducted at each of the more important ports on the Swahili Coast. By the beginning of the nineteenth century Zanzibar was pre-eminent among these. This had not always been the case; indeed it was only in the last half of the eighteenth century that Zanzibar rose to commercial importance. The primary reason for this was the determination of the Omani Arabs to establish it as their main base on the Swahili Coast. Zanzibar was well suited to their intention, for it had a spacious harbour which was sheltered by islands and banks and was safe throughout the year.[6] Zanzibar was also fortunate in its lack of dependence on the monsoon winds for communication with the opposite mainland. As a neighbour to Pemba it could draw upon that island for the extra provisions it required, and it was self-sufficient as regards drinking water.[7]

[1] Dallons, 1804, in Freeman-Grenville, *Select Documents*, p. 198, and Smee's Description of the island of Zanzibar, 1811, I.O.L., Marine Records Miscellaneous 586.

[2] Hardy's Report, 1811, I.O.L., Marine Records Miscellaneous 586.

[3] Albrand's Report, 1819, M.O., Réunion 72/472.

[4] Hardy's Report, 1811, I.O.L., Marine Records Miscellaneous 586.

[5] Emery to Cooley, 18 Dec. 1835, R.G.S., Emery Correspondence Block 1834-1840; and E. Roberts to Louis McLane, 14 May 1834, printed in N. R. Bennett and G. E. Brooks, *New England Merchants in Africa* (Boston, 1965), p. 157.

[6] For the harbour at that date, Burton, *Zanzibar*, I, 144; and Smee's log, 7 Apr. 1811, I.O.L., Marine Records Miscellaneous 586.

[7] Smee's Description of the island of Zanzibar, 1811, I.O.L., as above.

The tendency to centre the trade of the Swahili Coast on Zanzibar had begun by the 1770s: Morice said that it was to Zanzibar that the ships from India preferred to go in order to unload their cargoes for distribution along the coast.[1] In the opinion of one European, this was because the Arabs of Zanzibar were richer and more business-like than the Swahilis and consequently had almost entirely attracted the trade of the coast to their island.[2]

A side-effect of the promotion of Zanzibar to be the main Omani base, and one which contributed to that island's emergence as the entrepot for the Swahili Coast, was the development of certain commercial restrictions. These probably had their origin in the desire of the governors of Zanzibar to enrich themselves rather than as a result of a deliberate policy formulated by the authorities within Oman. In 1804 Dallons said the governor of Zanzibar forbade anyone other than himself to trade with the French and generally committed 'atrocious and revolting extortions'.[3] In the opinion of American merchants the governors resorted to 'the most nefarious practises to accumulate wealth'.[4] Europeans and Americans could only trade by buying from the governor the right to do so.[5] One could almost conclude, and indeed this was Dallons' opinion, that the East African Arabs wanted to keep Europeans and Americans out of their trade, but it is more likely that the Omanis, aware of the desire for and rarity of their main export, slaves, tried to get maximum profit from prices and impositions. The governor of Zanzibar monopolized trade with Europeans and Americans not only by refusing to let anyone else sell to them before he had had first opportunity, but also by prohibiting these foreigners from visiting the mainland coast opposite Zanzibar, known as the 'Mrima'. If foreigners had been able to go to the Mrima to make their purchases, they could have avoided the heavy restrictions and impositions to which they were subjected at Zanzibar. The Omanis had learnt the value of such a prohibition when Kilwa, freed from their yoke, grew rich from selling slaves to the French. By 1804 the governor of Zanzibar was trying to prevent a recurrence of such a situation by

[1] Morice, 'Projet d'un établissement', pp. 56-7.
[2] Morice's 'Memoir concerning the East Coast of Africa', 15 June and 26 Sept. 1777, A.N., Colonies C4/42.
[3] Dallons, 1804, printed in Freeman-Grenville, *Select Documents*, p. 198.
[4] E. Roberts to L. McLane, 14 May 1834, printed in Bennett and Brooks, *op. cit.*, p. 158.
[5] *Idem*; Dallons, as above; and Smee's Description of the island of Zanzibar, I.O.L., Marine Records Miscellaneous 586.

prohibiting European contact with the continent, and this was a policy which continued for several decades.[1]

Indians, too, were subject to restrictions and impositions. Unlike the Omanis, who paid regular duties of 5 per cent, they faced arbitrary exactions.[2] There seems to have been considerable justification in the complaints which Indians from a Surat vessel at Zanzibar made to a British visitor in 1811 about the treatment they suffered.[3]

The monopoly exercised by the governor of Zanzibar is unlikely to have applied to Omani traders except in certain articles, such as cattle, sheep, goats and grain, the importation of which the governor reserved to himself. As these articles were cheap and numerous on the mainland, the governor could make a vast profit by selling them at four times the price they would have fetched had their import been open to anyone.[4] There is a possibility that Arab merchants were also subject to the Mrima prohibition; certainly this was claimed thirty years later, when the Sultan of Zanzibar said that Arabs had faced restrictions on trade with the Mrima for seventy or eighty years, being allowed to indulge in commercial activity there only with the permission of the customs master at Zanzibar.[5] This could, however, have been a distortion of the true state of affairs, put forward only to reinforce an attempt to keep Europeans and Americans from the region; at the beginning of the nineteenth century the Omani authorities did not have the administrative machinery to enforce such a restriction on Arab merchants.

The monopolies and restrictions imposed by the governor of Zanzibar may well have assisted Zanzibar's emergence as the entrepot of the Swahili Coast. By 1811 that island was described as 'the great depôt of the Imaum's colonial commerce and power'.[6] More than a hundred large vessels from Arabia and India arrived there every year.[7]

[1] For the governor's monopoly and the Mrima restrictions, Dallons, as above; Bissell, op. cit., p. 35; Hardy's Report, 1811, I.O.L., as above; Prior, op. cit., p. 81; Owen, op. cit., I, 317.

[2] Smee's log, 1 Apr. 1811, Hardy's Report, and Smee's Description of the island of Zanzibar, I.O.L., Marine Records Miscellaneous 586.

[3] Smee's log, 20 Mch. 1811, I.O.L., as above.

[4] Smee's Description of the island of Zanzibar, as above.

[5] Saiyid Sa'id to President of the USA, n.d. (but end of 1842), Amer.N.A., Zanz. 1; and Saiyid Sa'id to Palmerston, 2 June 1839, F.O. 54/3.

[6] Prior, op. cit., p. 81.

[7] Hardy's Report, 1811, I.O.L., Marine Records Miscellaneous 586.

When Smee was at Zanzibar he actually observed fifty vessels lying in the harbour.[1] These ships brought goods to a value of twelve *lakhs* of rupees (about 60,000 dollars) annually, among them beads, sugar, rice, grain, ghee, fish, dates, iron bars and, most important of all, Surat cloth. In payment for these Zanzibar exported ivory and slaves, coconuts, coir, and copal, wax, cowry shells and turtle-shells, and the hides and horns of rhinoceros.[2] Apart from the products of the coconut palm, all these articles were brought to Zanzibar from other ports on the Swahili Coast.

Omanis who had come to Zanzibar in the course of the eighteenth century grew prosperous from this entrepot trade, and so they were able to diversify their activities. At the beginning of the nineteenth century there was an attempt to develop Zanzibar as a producer in its own right, both industrially and agriculturally. By 1811 sugar cane was being cultivated extensively in Zanzibar, but sugar was not as yet being produced.[3] An attempt had been made to remedy this by 1819 with the setting up of two sugar factories, one of which belonged to the governor, but these produced only a small amount of dirty sugar.[4] The Omanis also experimented with other export crops, such as cloves, cinnamon, coffee, and nutmeg.[5] The most important of these was cloves. It is not certain exactly when these were first introduced to Zanzibar. There is a tradition that at the end of the eighteenth century an Arab, called Haramili ibn Salih, took a few clove seeds and plants to Zanzibar from the island of Bourbon, where the French were trying to cultivate them.[6] In 1819 a Frenchman, Albrand, said that a French merchant named Sausse had introduced cloves into Zanzibar from the French islands seven years previously.[7] By 1822 the clove trees were already 15 feet high and they were soon to make a deep impact on the economy of Zanzibar.[8]

An important development was therefore taking place at the beginning of the nineteenth century. Omani Arabs, having achieved a dominant position in the entrepot trade, were now diversifying their

---

[1] Smee's Description of the island of Zanzibar, 1811, I.O.L., as above.
[2] *Idem*; and Hardy's Report, as above.
[3] Smee's Description of the island of Zanzibar, as above.
[4] Albrand's Report, 1819, M.O., Réunion 72/472.
[5] Massieu to Freycinet, 9 Oct. 1822, M.O., Réunion 72/473.
[6] Fitzgerald, *op. cit.*, p. 554.
[7] Albrand's Report, 1819, M.O., Réunion 72/472. See also Guillain, *Documents*, II, 49, for the introduction of cloves to Zanzibar.
[8] Massieu to Freycinet, 9 Oct. 1822, M.O., Réunion 72/473.

economic activities and setting up plantations in Zanzibar.[1] They were well suited to this new activity, familiar as they were with plantation economics from their experience of date cultivation in Oman. The acquisition by the Omanis in Zanzibar of landed estates was to have important social and economic effects on the Swahili inhabitants of that island. The Swahilis were gradually ousted from their former position and forced to concentrate on small-scale agriculture, fishing, and the coastal carrying trade. It was they who produced most of the foodstuffs, such as fruit, manioc, and rice, which were consumed in Zanzibar.[2]

As well as acquiring landed estates, the Arabs also experimented with small-scale industry. Apart from the sugar manufacture already mentioned, Zanzibar also produced for export coir rope and mats made from coconut fibre and oil from the coconut itself.[3] There was a boat-building industry, mainly in the hands of Swahilis, which constructed the vessels of up to 25 tons used in the local coasting trade. By 1819 Arab enterprise was affecting this industry and an attempt was being made to build a much larger dhow than usual in Zanzibar.[4] But boat-building and other industries did not flourish, because Zanzibar had few raw materials for building purposes. All metal and good-quality stone had to be brought from India, and at that date there was of course little knowledge of machinery. There may have been further discouragement from the Omani authorities themselves: one source mentions that the ruler of Muscat wanted to prevent the establishment of any industry in Zanzibar in order to keep that island dependent on Muscat.[5]

The eighteenth-century growth of Zanzibar under the impact of the Omanis was at the expense of other Swahili ports. Most important among these had been Kilwa Kisiwani, Mombasa, and the towns of the Lamu archipelago. Kilwa Kisiwani (called merely 'Kilwa' in the eighteenth and early nineteenth century, as there was then no need to distinguish it from Kilwa Kivinje) was an island separated from the mainland by a narrow stretch of water, which at low tide was only one fathom deep. It had two harbours; that on the north-west side was twelve to thirty fathoms deep, and that on the south side eight to

[1] See Chapter I, pp. 29-30, and Chapter X, pp. 283-7.
[2] Smee's Description of Zanzibar and Hardy's Report, in I.O.L., Marine Records Miscellaneous 586; and Dallons, 1804, printed in Freeman-Grenville, *Select Documents*, p. 198.
[3] Hardy's Report, as above; and Albrand's Report, 1819, M.O., Réunion 72/472.
[4] Albrand, *idem*.   [5] *Idem*.

twenty fathoms. Kilwa was easy of access from the sea, but the journey down the Mrima coast had to be negotiated with care, for there were many islands, reefs, and shoals on the way, the most dangerous of which was the partially submerged Latham's Island (locally known as 'Fungu').

Kilwa Kisiwani had its great days of prosperity in the 1770s and 1780s when Frenchmen from Ile de France and Bourbon went there to buy large numbers of slaves. At that date Kilwa was the central market for slaves on the Swahili Coast, particularly as the governor of Zanzibar had quarrelled with European buyers and forbidden them to acquire their cargo in his own town.[1] Already, however, other markets had superseded Kilwa for the exchange of other trading articles: indeed, the merchants of Kilwa themselves travelled to Zanzibar to sell their wares to northern vessels.[2] The trend away from Kilwa was aggravated by the recapture of that town by the Omanis in 1785, an action which better enabled the Omanis to centralize trade in Zanzibar. The Omanis also settled their differences with French slavers who began to obtain more of their cargo at Zanzibar.[3]

Apart from slaves, Kilwa also offered for sale on a fairly large scale ivory, hippo teeth, tortoise-shell, and cowries. It exported on a smaller scale, and mainly to Swahili ports, various foodstuffs, including molasses (made from sugar-cane), millet, rice, maize, coconuts, bananas, ghee, fish, yams, and plantains. Also exported for local Swahili use were timber and cotton, but Kilwa's wax, pyrites, gum, and indigo went further afield, to India and Arabia. In payment for these exports Kilwa accepted cloth, hardware, dates, beef from Mafia, salt, and – always welcome – arms, ammunition, and money.[4]

Most of the articles which Kilwa exported were obtained locally, but ivory and slaves were brought to the coast from the interior. The people of the littoral did not themselves go far inland to acquire them; according to Morice, writing in the 1770s, the Africans would not allow the Swahilis and Arabs to go inland, just as the island inhabitants

---

[1] Journal of the voyage of *Le Gracieux* to Kilwa, entry for 11 Sept. 1776, encl. in Feray and Massieu to Mistral, 1 Feb. 1778, M.O., O.I. 15/61.

[2] Morice, 'Projet d'un établissement', p. 57.

[3] Dallons, 1804, printed in Freeman-Grenville, *Select Documents*, p. 199; and Smee's Description of the island of Zanzibar, 1811, I.O.L., Marine Records Miscellaneous 586.

[4] Morice, 'Projet d'un établissement', pp. 57, 65, 67, 69, 80, 81, 84, 93; Report by J. Crassons de Medeuil, 1784-5, printed in Freeman-Grenville, *Select Documents*, p. 196; Prior, op. cit., pp. 67, 69, 80; and Smyth, op. cit., p. 278.

SWAHILI TRADE AND COMMERCE, CIRCA 1800

refused to let Africans come to their villages.[1] Exchanges therefore took place at the mainland littoral settlements, whence the goods were taken to Kilwa or Zanzibar. Although trade was increasingly centred at Zanzibar, northern vessels did continue to come to Kilwa in reduced numbers. Some indication of the volume of Kilwa's trade at the beginning of the nineteenth century, when sales of slaves to the French were diminishing, can be obtained by looking at the amount of the customs dues. In 1804 the Omani governor remitted 6,000 dollars to the ruler of Muscat, a sum which had risen to 12,000-20,000 dollars in 1810.[2] These figures are only a rough guide because the latter figure includes remittances from Mafia and because they represent the amount of the customs rental rather than the receipts. They are, however, of some use since the receipts and the rental were usually proportionate. They may be compared with the 40,000 dollars which Zanzibar remitted to Muscat in 1804.[3]

Trade at Kilwa was in the hands of Swahili, Indian, and Arab merchants, but the last two groups were in the main only seasonal residents.[4] Apart from their trading activities, the Swahilis also engaged in agriculture and produced, with the help of slave labour, most of the food consumed on the island. In the 1770s most of Kilwa island was cultivated, as were parts of the opposite mainland.[5] The Kilwans may also have woven the cotton they grew.[6]

At the beginning of the nineteenth century, Kilwa Kisiwani was not a commercial backwater, despite the rise of Zanzibar. But it was soon to become one: in 1811 it was already being described as a 'petty village'.[7] Kilwa's decline was due not only to the rise of Zanzibar as a commercial centre and the restrictions which the British began to impose on the sale of slaves to Europeans, but also to the increased commercial importance of a village seventeen miles to its northward – Kilwa Kivinje. Kilwa Kivinje had a harbour inferior to that of its southern neighbour, but it was more fortunate in its geographical position.

[1] Morice, 'Projet d'un établissement', pp. 68-9, and Prior, *op. cit.*, p. 80.
[2] Dallons, 1804, printed in Freeman-Grenville, *Select Documents*, p. 200; and Prior, *op. cit.*, p. 68.
[3] Dallons, as above, p. 198.
[4] Morice, Prior, and Beaver (in Smyth) mention no Indian residents.
[5] Morice, 'Projet d'un établissement', p. 174.
[6] Morice (*ibid.*, p. 164) says there was no weaving, but bobbins have been found at Kilwa – note 2, p. 163, in Freeman-Grenville, *The French at Kilwa Island*.
[7] Prior, *op. cit.*, p. 66.

Since it was situated on the mainland, caravans from the interior could go directly to it. Kilwa Kivinje's harbour, with a depth of only five or six fathoms, was two miles north of the town inside some reefs. Landing there was difficult, except at high water. None the less Kilwa Kivinje began to usurp Kilwa Kisiwani's commercial position in the region. Very little information about how this happened is available. Morice merely mentions Kilwa Kivinje as a village north of Kilwa Kisiwani, and Prior and Beaver do not even note its existence.[1] The Omanis, however, recognized its potential, because they placed a governor there by 1819.[2] By that date it must already have begun to supersede Kilwa Kisiwani, but its true expansion came in the following two decades.

Northwards from Kilwa Kivinje lay a number of littoral settlements, most of which received goods from peoples of the interior and transported them to Zanzibar for sale. As Zanzibar became more prosperous, the villages on the opposite mainland, and in particular Bagamoyo, Buyuni, and Mbwemaji, experienced a parallel commercial expansion. These villages were not generally visited by large vessels, their topography being more suited to their participation in the coasting trade.

The islands of Mafia and Pemba were also omitted from the ports of call of most of the large northern ships. Pemba was the most fertile place on the whole Swahili Coast, but it never became a flourishing commercial centre because its coastline, with numerous deep inlets, provided inadequate anchorages, and Chak Chak, the main port, was at the end of a muddy creek from which the sea drained out at low tide. Pemba was only twenty-eight miles from Zanzibar, but its physical features differed from those of its neighbour because it had separated from the mainland in the Miocene age, whereas Zanzibar remained a mainland promontory until late Pleistocene times. Pemba is covered with dense vegetation, for its undulating hills give pools and lakelets more chance to form than on Zanzibar, which has the same rainfall – fifty inches a year. Pemba could therefore grow successfully rice, sugar, and manioc, and it could also maintain cattle.[3] Its abundant provisions were much sought after by other Swahili towns, particularly Mombasa and Zanzibar, and consequently it was a coveted political prize. Emery's

---

[1] Morice, 'Projet d'un établissement', p. 62.
[2] Albrand's Report, 1819, M.O., Réunion 72/472.
[3] Owen, *op. cit.*, I, 316; Vandries to Philibert, Feb. 1822, M.O., O.I. 17/89; and Loarer's Report, Part II, 1849, M.O., O.I. 2/10.

Journal has a wealth of references to small vessels plying between Mombasa and Pemba carrying grain.

Eighty miles from Pemba lay Mombasa, which in Portuguese times had been the most important port on the Swahili Coast, but as the eighteenth century progressed it was overtaken commercially by Zanzibar. This did not mean that northern vessels ceased to visit Mombasa, but rather that export articles from the Mrima, which formerly were brought to Mombasa for sale, were now taken to Zanzibar. Mombasa was unable to replace this curtailed supply by exploiting her own hinterland because that region did not provide the great numbers of slaves and the particular quality of ivory which were available from the Unyamwesi and Lake Nyasa areas to the southward.

Mombasa therefore had to concentrate on offering for sale local products, and as much ivory as it could obtain. Among its numerous exports were gum, honey, beeswax, grain, rice, rhino-horn and skins, calumba root, cattle, sheep, goats, fowls, cowries, ghee, sugar-cane, coconuts, betel-nuts, and sesame.[1] Most of the foods among these would have gone to other littoral towns. In return for its exports Mombasa accepted provisions which were non-existent or in short supply – particularly, at certain times of year, grain – and, cloth, beads, and wire, for use in exchange with peoples of the interior.[2]

A tentative estimate of the volume of Mombasa's trade can be made from the number of vessels entering the port and the amount of dues paid. According to Emery, about 150 vessels visited Mombasa annually, but unfortunately he made no distinction between large northern ships and the smaller local coasting vessels.[3] Emery also observed that in one year – probably 1825 – dues paid amounted to 11,060 dollars in cash and 5,044 dollars in kind. These figures appear to refer to import dues. Emery lived at Mombasa for two years and gave an impression of a lively port with flourishing trade, but Boteler, a contemporary of his, said trade was languishing, poverty was rife, and 60,000 dollars worth of goods would overstock the market for six to eight months.[4] Boteler claimed that an embargo on Omanis trading to Mombasa issued by the ruler of Muscat was seriously affecting its trade, but Emery never

[1] Boteler, op. cit., II, 17; and J. G. Emery, 'A Short Account of Mombas and the neighbouring Coast of Africa', *Journal of the Royal Geographical Society* (hereafter *J.R.G.S.*), vol. III (1833), pp. 280-3.

[2] Emery, idem.

[3] Emery to Cooley, 19 May and 18 Dec. 1835, R.G.S., Emery Correspondence Block 1834-1840.

[4] Boteler, op. cit., II, 206.

mentioned the existence of any such prohibition. Indeed, throughout his stay in Mombasa he reported the daily arrival of an assortment of vessels from Kutch, Sur, Muscat, and the Banadir coast. Some of these were on their way to Zanzibar. He also described instances of vessels putting in at Mombasa on their return journey northwards from Zanzibar, and ships belonging to Mombasans themselves sailing northwards for Oman and India. It is true that his journal contains more references to local coasting vessels than to larger ships, but this is because the former were more numerous than the latter. The local vessels transported goods between Mombasa and Ozi, Lamu, Pate, Siu, Faza, Pemba, and settlements on the Mrima such as Lindi and Mikindani. There are also references to local vessels plying between Mombasa and Zanzibar, a traffic which would have been unlikely had any effective embargo been in operation.[1]

The mechanism of Mombasa's commerce was similar to that of other Swahili ports. Not having access to large numbers of slaves from its hinterland, Mombasa had to import slaves from elsewhere.[2] Mombasa did, however, export ivory in some quantity, and this had to be procured from the interior. Prominent in the business of providing Mombasa with ivory were the Kamba, who organized caravans to transport it to the Nyika villages. The Nyika purchased the ivory and re-sold it at Mombasa. In order to keep the profits they made as middlemen and the dues they charged Mombasans they were anxious to prevent Mombasan merchants having direct contact with the Kamba. As well as ivory, from the Kamba the Nyika bought cattle and rhinohorn and skins, which they then sold to Mombasans.[3] The intercourse between Nyika and Mombasans took place mainly at an annual fair held at Jomvu, a mainland village eight miles from Mombasa. Arab and Indian merchants sent agents thither to barter.[4] It has been suggested that, in addition to the Kamba caravans, coastal peoples – both the Nyika and the Mazruis – organized caravans which went inland. The Nyika are said to have despatched caravans mainly to the north and north-west, and to have tried to make a treaty with the Galla so that they could push more directly across into the Kamba region.[5]

[1] Emery's Journal, *passim*.   [2] *Ibid.*, entry for 25 Sept. 1824.
[3] Emery's 'Short Account of Mombas', as above; and Boteler, *op. cit.*, II, 187.
[4] *Ibid.*
[5] J. L. Lamphear, 'The Kamba and the Northern Mrima Coast', p. 78, in R. Gray and D. Birmingham (eds), *Pre-colonial African Trade: Essays on trade in Central and Eastern Africa before 1900* (London, 1969), pp. 75-101.

SWAHILI TRADE AND COMMERCE, CIRCA 1800

Early missionary journals also hint that the Mazruis themselves organized caravans, but had to forgo this enterprise because of political unrest and the incursion of warlike peoples.[1]

The Nyika were not solely middlemen: they also engaged in agriculture and cattle-raising and sold their products to Mombasa. At certain times of the year they flooded into Mombasa to sell their grain.[2] The Swahilis, too, engaged in agriculture and copal-gathering. The poorer of them performed these activities personally, but the richer used slave labour. Several Swahilis appear to have owned land around and to the north of Mombasa, because on several occasions Emery noted canoes arriving in Mombasa with grain originating from such plots.[3] Richer Swahilis bought vessels and entered the carrying trade. Most of the shipowners were, however, Arab and Indian.[4] Swahilis were also the masons and mechanics, the boat builders, timber-hewers, fishermen, and collectors of cowries.[5]

The Indian inhabitants of Mombasa were less prolific in their activities than the Swahilis. Like Indians elsewhere on the Swahili Coast, they had come to Mombasa originally as the representatives of Indian firms. It is clear that by the beginning of the nineteenth century some of them had settled at Mombasa and had set themselves up as moneylenders. Like the Indians at Zanzibar, they were not always well treated by the Arab merchants – in this case, the Mazruis. One Mazrui governor died owing Indians 12,000 dollars, a sum which, in Emery's opinion, they would never recover. When an Indian refused credit to the successor of the defaulting governor, he was jailed.[6] The Indian merchants were hindered in their commercial activities by restrictions imposed by the Mazrui governors, measures which, like those of the governors of Zanzibar, were probably designed to raise revenue rather than to squeeze competitors out of the market. It is probable that Arab and Swahili traders were also subject to the restrictions. There was, for example, the privilege claimed by the governor of pre-emption of ivory, which prohibited any merchant from entering Jomvu before the governor had made his choice.[7] But Emery succeeded in putting an end

[1] *Ibid.*, p. 77. [2] Emery's Journal, *passim*; and Boteler, *op. cit.*, II, 23.
[3] Emery's Journal, *passim*, e.g. 6 Nov. 1824.
[4] *Ibid.*, entries for 8 and 19 Sept. and 25 Oct. 1824.
[5] Emery's 'Short Account of Mombas', *J.R.G.S.*, vol. III (1833), pp. 280-3; Emery to Cooley, 20 Dec. 1833 and 18 Dec. 1835, R.G.S., Emery MS. File and Emery Correspondence Block 1834-40, respectively.
[6] Emery's Journal, entry for 17 Oct. 1824; and Boteler, *op. cit.*, II, 206.
[7] Boteler, *idem*; and Emery to Cooley, 18 Dec. 1835, as above.

to this restriction, and merchants were thereafter allowed free access to mainland villages and the inland peoples free ingress to Mombasa. In compensation the governor received half a dollar on every *frasela* of ivory brought into Mombasa. This development must have had a deleterious effect on the position of the Nyika as middlemen, and it may also have stimulated the commercial activities of the Kamba, who began to establish colonies within the Nyika area.[1]

At the beginning of the nineteenth century, therefore, Mombasa was a flourishing port, which was regularly visited by vessels from the north and from other Swahili ports. Unlike Kilwa and Zanzibar, Mombasa was seldom visited by European ships, mainly because it did not offer slaves for sale. Boteler's view of the poverty of the merchants of Mombasa in the 1820s is contradicted by the witness of Lt Emery. The Omanis therefore had good reason to be apprehensive about the economic, and with it the political, strength of Mombasa.

North of Mombasa as far as the Lamu archipelago there were no settlements which conducted extensive commerce. The littoral villages of this region took their products to the larger commercial centres. Malindi, formerly an important port, had fallen into ruin by the beginning of the nineteenth century.[2] The towns of the Lamu archipelago, in spite of their topographical disadvantages, did not suffer a similar fate. Navigation among the islands of that archipelago was made difficult by the strong currents and frequent shallows. Currents made it dangerous to anchor at Manda bay.[3] Lamu bay, on the southwest of Lamu island, gave partial shelter during the north-east monsoon, but it was only approachable by a narrow channel and at high tide. None the less Lamu was the best harbour in the archipelago. Pate town was also only accessible at high tide, for it was situated at the end of a creek overgrown with mangroves, half a mile from the sea. In 1811 a British ship found that the nearest it could get to Pate at low water was one and a half miles.[4] Siu was also at the head of a creek. The third settlement of Pate island – Faza – was the most accessible. Even so, it could only be reached by a half-hour walk on sand from the anchorage at the creek mouth. Although the inaccessibility of the harbours of the Lamu archipelago was a hindrance to commercial vessels, it did mean that the settlements had a certain security. All the towns were difficult to

[1] Lamphear, *op. cit.*, pp. 82-3; and Krapf, *op. cit.*, p. 144.
[2] Boteler, *op. cit.*, I, 396; and Krapf, *op. cit.*, p. 152.
[3] A. H. J. Prins, *Sailing from Lamu* (Assen, 1965), pp. 20 and 46.
[4] Smee's log, 8 Feb. 1811, I.O.L., Marine Records Miscellaneous 586.

SWAHILI TRADE AND COMMERCE, CIRCA 1800

surprise or attack, and it was possible actually to block the creek which led to Siu.

Further commercial disadvantages suffered by the towns of the Lamu archipelago were the scarcity of sweet water and the infertility of the soil. The only place where fresh water could be obtained was Lamu island; elsewhere the wells were brackish.[1] All the islands were formed of coral on which grew thick thorn scrub. The soil was poor and unsuitable for growing any crop except coconuts, although in places it was able to provide poor grazing for a few cattle. There was a great deal of sand on the island surfaces, particularly on Lamu. There sand-dunes, blown up by the monsoon winds, encroached on buildings. In 1884 the town of Shela near Lamu was in the process of being covered with sand, and by 1903 the old town of Lamu had been completely buried.[2]

Despite its disadvantages, the Lamu archipelago produced some coveted export articles. Its strong currents made it an excellent fishing ground and a favoured home for cowry shells, and in the inlets and creeks mangroves grew in abundance. Among its exports were coconuts, cowries, dried fish, and mangrove poles, the last of which was an essential building material for Swahili dwellings.[3] Cowries could be obtained in larger quantities in the Lamu archipelago than at any other place on the Swahili Coast. In the 1770s two to three hundred tons a year were taken thence to India.[4]

Like other Swahili towns, the settlements of the Lamu archipelago were able to augment their commerce by acting as middlemen for northern traders and interior peoples. The archipelago also faced a fertile mainland whose products, particularly those of grain and cattle, it could both consume itself and sell to others.[5] From the mainland also came calumba roots and hides; an American merchant bought 900 *frasela* of the former at the end of 1831.[6] But the most valuable mainland product was ivory, brought to the coast by the Galla.[7] The Galla

---

[1] *Ibid.*, 13 Feb. 1811; and Boteler, *op. cit.*, I, 372.

[2] Sir Frederick Jackson, *Early Days in East Africa* (London, 1930), p. 7; and Stigand, *The Land of Zinj*, p. 151.

[3] Boteler, *op. cit.*, I, 385-6.

[4] Morice, 'Projet d'un établissement', p. 86.

[5] Boteler, *op. cit.*, I, 376 and 385; Smee's log, 13 Feb. 1811 and Report by Lt Hardy, I.O.L., Marine Records Miscellaneous 586.

[6] Nathaniel Isaacs, *Travels and Adventures in Eastern Africa* (London, 1836), 2 vols, II, 323.

[7] Boteler, *op. cit.*, I, 387.

would not allow the littoral peoples to go inland to get ivory: on one occasion they attacked and plundered a party of Swahilis engaged in a commercial speculation to the interior.[1] As at Mombasa, the hinterland peoples of this region did not provide the coast with slaves, and as a result the slave trade in the Lamu archipelago was inconsiderable.

The exports were either sold directly to northern vessels which put in at the Lamu archipelago on their way down to Zanzibar, or were taken by the local inhabitants to Zanzibar and other commercial centres, including Mozambique and Johanna.[2] It was a common practice for northern ships to leave an agent in the Lamu archipelago on their way southward, and to pick up him and his purchases on their homeward journey.[3] Unfortunately it is not possible to make an estimate of the volume of the trade of these islands at this period, because no figures are available.

The commercial personnel of the Lamu archipelago was similar to that of other Swahili towns. There were the usual Indian merchants, but most of the commerce was in Swahili hands.[4] Swahilis also pursued maritime activities such as coastal transport, shell-collecting, fishing, and boat-building. The boat-building facilities in the Lamu archipelago seem to have been particularly good, for an American crew was able to overhaul and repair its vessel there.[5] Swahilis also owned land on the opposite mainland, which they used for agricultural purposes.[6] Many Swahilis actually dwelt on the mainland, particularly at nearby Ozi. Although the people of Ozi traded with the Galla and Pokomo, it was not possible for their town to develop as a large commercial centre because the entrance to the River Tana, upon which it stood, was very shallow.[7]

The Lamu archipelago had trading links with the neighbouring Banadir coast, a region which should be treated briefly because of the ruler of Muscat's later activities there. The three main towns of the Banadir coast – Mogadishu, Marka, and Brava – were all open to the sea, unsheltered by reefs. Consequently, during the south-west monsoon from April to September, it was excessively difficult to anchor

---

[1] Boteler, *op. cit.*, I, pp. 388 and 394.
[2] *Ibid.*, p. 385; Isaacs, *op. cit.*, II, 320; and Morice, 'Projet d'un établissement', p. 71.
[3] Isaacs, *op. cit.*, II, 323.   [4] *Idem.*   [5] *Ibid.*, p. 321.
[6] Smee's log, 13 Feb. 1811, I.O.L. Marine Records Miscellaneous 586.
[7] Boteler, *op. cit.*, I, 392 and 393.

there.[1] Conditions improved in the north-east monsoon, and ships from the north on their way down to Zanzibar often put in at the Banadir ports. They purchased ivory, cattle, grain, amber, butter, ghee, goats, and hides, but their major requirement was the Somali slaves which were more highly prized than those of Bantu origin.[2] The people of the Banadir coast also took their goods southwards to the Swahili Coast; when Smee was at Zanzibar in 1811 he was visited by two Somali merchants who had gone there to transact business.[3]

This survey of the commerce of the Swahili Coast can provide only a hazy picture of the true state of affairs because of the lack of evidence relating to the beginning of the nineteenth century. However, it is obvious that East Africa had great economic potential. Not only were its several ports traditionally oriented towards middleman activities but they also had many articles which they themselves produced for sale. With their country fronting an enormous area of Africa, the merchants of the Swahili Coast cannot have remained blind to the possibilities which would ensue from an expansion of the slave and ivory trades. What was needed to effect this was further organization and capital. Omani Arabs and Indians were beginning to provide these two essentials, and Europeans were also tentatively entering the market. At the same time a parallel economic development was progressing – Zanzibar was beginning to be transformed into a plantation island.

By the beginning of the nineteenth century the merchants who were going to exploit East Africa to a far greater extent than had the Swahilis – the Arabs, Indians, and Europeans – had only begun to make advances. In order to understand fully the future development of these interests these beginnings must be described. Part of the reluctance of the Europeans to trade with the Swahili Coast in the eighteenth century, after the Portuguese had departed from the region, was due to the inadequacy of their geographical knowledge. Maps were scarce and inaccurate, and the few descriptions that existed portrayed the Swahili Coast as a hostile and dangerous region. It was not until 1811 that the first nautical survey of the East African coast was performed. The expedition was despatched by the Indian Navy (then

[1] Guillain, *Documents*, II, 547; and Journal of Lt Christopher, 1843, encl. in Bombay to Secret Committee, no. 54, 18 July 1843, E.S.L.B. 60.

[2] Christopher's Journal, as above; Isaacs, *op. cit.*, II, 315-17; and Report by Lt Hardy, 1811, I.O.L., Marine Records Miscellaneous 586.

[3] Smee's log, 20 Mch. 1811, I.O.L., as above.

called the Bombay Marine) under the command of Thomas Smee. Previous to that date French knowledge of the region was more extensive than British. D'Après de Mannevillette published his *Neptune Oriental* in Paris in 1745, and subsequent maps he produced were improved by incorporating information derived from Morice and other Frenchmen who were visiting East Africa. The Portuguese of course had the most extensive knowledge of the region, but this only became widely available to sailors of other nationalities when Manoel Pimentel published his *Arte de Navegar* in 1762.[1] For the first half of the eighteenth century the British had had to rely on Alexander Hamilton's *A New Account of the East Indies*, printed in 1727, which, although useful, discouraged potential merchants with such remarks as 'the Elephants of this Country are very large and so are the Men, who are all Barbarians'.[2] The situation for British sailors was a good deal improved in 1772 when Dalrymple, the cartographer of the East India Company, published his *General Collection of Nautical Publications*. This drew together information obtained from French, British, Portuguese, and Dutch sources, using the maps of Gerard and Jan van Keulen, D'Après, Bento d'Almedoe, and Pimentel, together with facts derived from British sailors and geographers, such as Captain Kempthorne, who travelled several times to India, and Captain William Smith, the surveyor of the Royal African Company.[3] British knowledge of the Swahili Coast was augmented by information given by the participants in Blankett's voyage of 1798/9.[4] Horsburgh's *The India Directory*, first published in 1809, relied heavily on Blankett's voyage – an unhappy reliance from the point of view of British commerce, since that expedition's experiences were far from felicitous.[5]

The India Directory became the general handbook of all naval and merchant vessels in the Indian seas and, although it was given periodic revisions, some of the most discouraging remarks contained in the first edition were kept for several decades. At Kilwa 'the natives have in general been considered unfriendly to strangers', and at Mafia 'great care is requisite in approaching the southern part of the island, on

[1] Manoel Pimentel, *Arte de Navegar* (Lisbon, 1762).

[2] Alexander Hamilton, *op. cit.*, I, 18.

[3] Alexander Dalrymple, *General Collection of Nautical Publications*, 9 vols (London, 1772). Most of the sources for this are in the British Museum – e.g. Van Keulen, 'A Collection of Charts of Various parts of the World'. Kempthorne's drawings and logs are in B. M. Sloane MS. 3665, 1688-90.

[4] Log of *Leopard*, P.R.O. Adm. 51/1312; and Bissell, *op. cit.*

[5] Horsburgh, *The India Directory* (London, 1809), 2 vols.

account of the extensive and steep coral reefs'. As for Pemba, its 'shore is in general rocky, and the natives not to be trusted', whereas Mombasa

'... is rather difficult of access, on account of the extensive reefs, and the natives are said to be inimical to Europeans. Since the Arabs and natives expelled the Portuguese from the ports on this part of the coast, few European vessels touch at any of them, more particularly at Mombasa where the government has in general endeavoured to allure and seize the European ships that touched here for refreshments.'

The coast between Mombasa and Malindi was 'very imperfectly known, being delineated on the charts clear, without islands and dangers, whereas several of both exist'. All the channels to Pate were 'intricate and dangerous; there is generally a high surf beating against the reefs'. At the entrance to the River Juba 'the perfidy of the natives should exclude European ships from touching at this place', for some sailors from the *Daedalus* had been killed there in 1798. Likewise the inhabitants of Mogadishu and Brava 'may be considered hostile to Europeans'.[1]

Any merchant hoping to exploit the Swahili Coast as a new region for his commercial enterprise would have had second thoughts on reading Horsburgh. The erroneous impression of the area which that book gives was slightly alleviated by the survey expedition led by Smee which was despatched from India in 1811. Smee's new information was not, however, made available to merchant vessels until the 1840s.[2] It was Owen's surveying expedition of 1824 which finally gave British sailors the detailed information they required about the coast of East Africa. It was of great service in encouraging British, French, and American vessels to trade with that region.[3]

The absence of correct information had meant that there had been very infrequent British trade with East Africa during the eighteenth century. Early that century it was reported that British ships from India formerly had traded with Pate, but that the exchange had been abandoned in 1692 when the Omanis took Pate.[4] But the British trade with Pate must have continued in a desultory way, because in the 1770s we

[1] *Ibid.*, pp. 181-6.
[2] The account was printed as 'Voyage to the Eastern Shores of Africa, 1811', in *Transactions of the Bombay Geographical Society*, vol. VI (1844).
[3] For example, the Americans were using Owen's charts as early as 1827 – log and East India Marine Society Journal of the brig *Ann* of Salem, 1827, printed in Bennett and Brooks, *op. cit.*, pp. 147-51.
[4] Hamilton, *op. cit.*, I, 18.

hear that British ships from India were going to Pate to purchase cowries, although they did not visit other parts of the coast.[1] This fact was confirmed in 1809.[2]

By the beginning of the nineteenth century, French trade with the Swahili Coast was far more extensive than that of the British. They were frequent visitors to Kilwa and Zanzibar, and by 1811 even had a broker and a 'factory', from which flew the French flag, at the latter place.[3] The main object of their interest was the purchase of slaves, a trade which will be considered in detail in Chapter VIII. The French seldom visited Mombasa and Pate. Their vessels had made themselves very unpopular in the Lamu archipelago in the 1770s by raiding canoes and stealing their crews for slaves. The ruler of Pate was therefore reluctant to engage in commercial exchange with them, and on one occasion chartered two vessels in order to prevent Morice entering Pate port. Although Pate changed its mind and wrote to the governor of Bourbon asking that French ships once again visit the archipelago, the French behaviour was not forgotten: in the 1820s Boteler reckoned memories of it gave rise to his unfriendly reception.[4]

At the beginning of the nineteenth century, European trade with the Swahili Coast, a trade which was later to have a deep effect on the economic growth of the region, was hindered not only by inadequate topographical knowledge but also by the restrictions and impositions which were encountered. Chief among these were the prohibitive and arbitrary duties already discussed. Not until the removal of such impositions could trade with Europeans truly expand.

Although it had not yet occurred to Omani officials that they were likely to obtain greater profit from the expansion of European and American commerce which would follow if they allowed favourable terms of trade, they did not fail to expand their own trading connexions with the Swahili Coast. It is now necessary to look in some detail at Omani trade, particularly that conducted with the Swahili Coast, because in it lie many clues to subsequent Omani political expansion. Omani trade in general will first be considered, so that the branch of commerce with the Swahili Coast can be placed in its context.

At the end of the eighteenth century there was a considerable

[1] Morice, 'Projet d'un établissement', p. 86.
[2] Horsburgh, op. cit., p. 184.
[3] Smee's log, 25 Feb. 1811, I.O.L., Marine Records Miscellaneous 586.
[4] Morice, 'Projet d'un établissement', p. 187, and Boteler, op. cit., I, 371.

expansion of Omani commerce. This was largely due to the outbreak of the Napoleonic Wars, during which the Omanis, sailing under a neutral flag, were able to capture a large proportion of the carrying trade in the Indian seas.[1] The Omanis also derived benefit from the efforts of British merchants who traded to the Persian Gulf to keep the trade closed. British officials at Surat had monopolized the trade of that port by preventing Arabs from buying direct from the manufacturer. This was most advantageous to British merchants, but they nevertheless protested against a 2 per cent tax on capital. As a result the government abandoned its protection and threw the trade open. The Arabs then took over the buying and freighting because their charges for the latter were less than those of British merchants. To counter the increase in Arab commercial activity a 2 per cent tax was imposed on exports to the Persian Gulf, but by then the damage had been done and Arabs merely took their trade to ports other than Surat.[2] A third factor which contributed to the commercial expansion of Muscat was the active encouragement given by the local ruler, Sultan. Several Indian and Persian shipowners settled at Muscat because of the protection and encouragement afforded by the government, the moderate duties, and the expedition and despatch in transacting business and clearing the customs house.[3] They paid a 5 per cent *ad valorem* import duty but no export duty. Arabs and other Muslims, however, paid only 2 to $2\frac{1}{2}$ per cent duty.[4] Sultan further assisted his merchants by negotiating trading agreements with the British. He used the fact that he had consented to a political concession in 1798 as a lever to obtain the privileges of exemption from pilotage and of free wooding and watering for one of his ships annually resorting to Bombay and two to Bengal, and he got permission for each Arab ship to import 1,000 *maunds* (a *maund* equals about 3 lbs.) of salt annually to Calcutta and for two of his own ships to import 5,000 *maunds*.[5] When the British blocked this business one season on a technicality over incorrect papers, Sultan vigorously

[1] J. S. Buckingham, 'Voyage from Bushire to Muscat', p. 89, *Oriental Herald*, vol. XXII (Sept. 1829), pp. 79-103.
[2] Seton to Bombay, n.d., Proc. 21 Aug. 1804, B.Pub.P. 343/14.
[3] *Idem*.
[4] Seton to Bombay, 9 July 1802, Proc. 27 Aug., B.P.S.P. 381/33; and Buckingham, *op. cit.*, p. 87.
[5] Bombay to ruler of Muscat, 30 May 1799, Proc. 31 May, B.P.S.P. 381/3; same to same, 28 Jan. 1800, Proc. 28 Jan., and Bogle to Bombay, 12 Mch. 1800, Proc. 21 Mch., B.P.S.P. 381/9; Saif ibn Muhammad to Mehdi Ali Khan, 22 May 1800, Proc. 30 Sept., B.P.S.P. 381/16.

protected his merchants and elicited an apology.¹ Sultan also had commercial agreements with Shiraz, Abyssinia, Sind, and Batavia.²

In the furtherance of his commercial ambitions Sultan conceived a plan for all trade in the Persian Gulf to be carried in Omani vessels. This idea was stimulated by the practice of Indian merchants leaving goods destined for Qatif and Al-Hasa at Muscat because piracy made it too dangerous to pass through the Straits of Musandam. Omani ships then carried the goods to their destination.³

Muscat therefore became a great entrepot, being the exchange centre for articles from Surat, Bhavnagar, Bombay, the Malabar and Coromandel coasts, Makran, Sind, Punjab, Kutch, Bengal, Batavia and the Malay islands, East Africa and the Mascarene islands, and, of course, the countries bordering the Persian Gulf.⁴ Omani shipowners prospered and bought new vessels. By 1802 there were at Muscat fifteen ships from 400 to 700 tons, three brigs, fifty dhows, and fifty large dinghies; at Sur and Ja'alan there were 250 dhows and baghlas.⁵ In 1803 the Omanis built ships at Bombay and repaired old ones to the amount of five *lakhs* of rupees, and by 1804 they possessed from 40,000 to 50,000 tons of shipping.⁶ 'It is ... notorious', reported some European merchants at Bombay, 'that the present shipping of the subjects of the Imam, including domiciled Arabs of our own settlements, exceeds the British tonnage of this port.'⁷ They went on to complain that in 1803 the Omanis had made a profit of five *lakhs* of rupees on the carrying trade they had taken from the Bombay merchants. 'We shall soon find', they said, invoking the Navigation Laws, 'the Arab shipping to be to our Indian commerce what the Dutch was to our European till the Act of 26 George III destroyed its ascendancy.' They feared that the Omanis would capture the China trade and prophesied the decline of the British Empire in the East unless their rivals were restricted in their commercial activities. The British Resident at Muscat pointed out that it was partly

---

¹ Bombay to Mehdi Ali Khan, 30 Sept. 1800, Proc. 30 Sept., B.P.S.P. 381/16.
² Seton to Bombay, 19 May 1802, Proc. 27 May, B.P.S.P. 381/31; same to same, 9 July 1802, Proc. 27 Aug., B.P.S.P. 381/33; same to same, n.d., Proc. 21 Aug. 1804, B.Pub.P. 343/14.
³ Seton to Bombay, n.d., Proc. 21 Aug. 1804, B.Pub.P. 343/14.
⁴ Seton to Bombay, 9 July 1802, Proc. 27 Aug., B.P.S.P. 381/33.
⁵ *Idem.*
⁶ Seton to Bombay, n.d., Proc. 21 Aug. 1804, B.Pub.P. 343/14; and European merchants (Bruce Farrell & Co., Forbes & Co., Alexander Adamson) to Bombay, 4 July 1804, Proc. 13 July, B.Pub.P. 343/14.
⁷ European merchants, *idem.*

the fault of the British merchants themselves that they had lost the carrying trade: the British were unwilling to do short trips, which the Omanis were not. For example, no British merchants had attempted to take the place of the former Mogul vessels from Surat in the Mocha trade because the shortness of the trip did not give a high enough freight return to compensate for delays attending payment for the cargo.[1]

What was the relevance of this general expansion of Omani trade at the opening of the nineteenth century to events in East Africa? Its most obvious effect was to strengthen the position of the ruler of Muscat who, as a result, would be more able to look even further afield and contemplate exploiting another country. As a merchant-prince, the ruler of Muscat would be alive to the economic potential of a region like the Swahili Coast. So also would be the prosperous merchants and shipowners of Muscat, who could have been an effective pressure-group. Many of the powerful men who are noted in documents of this time were merchants; there were, for example, Saif ibn Muhammad whom Sultan appointed as regent while he was campaigning in the Persian Gulf, and the sons of Khalfan, who competed to gain control of Sultan's fleet when he died.[2] Many of the merchants would have had links with the Swahili Coast because that region provided two vital articles which it was difficult to obtain elsewhere – ivory and slaves.

The carrying trade gave Muscat a prosperity independent of its commercial links with the Swahili Coast. None the less the East African commerce was far from being an unimportant element in the Omani economy. It provided the ruler of Muscat with a considerable proportion of his revenue. In 1802 it was calculated that the ruler of Muscat received 40,000 dollars a year from the Swahili Coast, a figure corroborated in another source two years later.[3] In 1811 the sum was put at 60,000 dollars from Zanzibar and about 12,000 from Kilwa and Mafia.[4] This revenue was derived from farming out the customs dues, but the ruler of Muscat also made arbitrary levies when occasion demanded. While Smee was at Zanzibar a ship arrived from Muscat with a demand for 25,000 dollars to assist Saiyid Sa'id in opposing the

[1] Seton to Bombay, n.d., Proc. 21 Aug. 1804, B.Pub.P. 343/14.
[2] Malcolm's Journal, entry for 10 Jan. 1800, Proc. 4 Feb., B.P.S.P. 381/9; and Bombay to Calcutta, 2 Feb. 1805, Proc. 9 Feb., B.P.S.P. 382/3.
[3] Seton to Bombay 9 July 1802, Proc. 27 Aug., B.P.S.P. 381/33; and Dallons, 1804, printed in Freeman-Grenville, *Select Documents*, p. 198.
[4] Prior, *op. cit.*, p. 80; and Smee's Description of the island of Zanzibar, I.O.L., Marine Records Miscellaneous 586.

Wahhabis. An additional tax was immediately imposed, and the chief men of the districts were ordered to collect it. The Surat traders were called upon to contribute a quota of 3,500 dollars.[1] Apart from this official revenue, the ruler of Muscat also derived profit from the Swahili Coast by trading there privately. In the 1770s he was every year sending thither his own ship of 400 tons laden with various goods which were exchanged for ivory.[2] The value of the East African connexion to the ruler of Muscat becomes evident if the revenues derived from the Swahili Coast and Muscat are compared. In 1802 Muscat was providing him annually with 112,500 dollars and East Africa with 40,000.[3]

A proportion such as this makes it clear to see why in the next few years the authorities in Muscat found it easy to bow to the compulsion of political events and extend their sway on the Swahili Coast. The Omanis had already to a limited extent exploited the commercial opportunities of the region; soon they were to expand their activities and make the profits from East Africa rival those from Oman.

[1] Smee, *idem*.
[2] Morice, 'Projet d'un établissement', p. 181.
[3] Seton to Bombay, 9 July 1802, Proc. 27 Aug., B.P.S.P. 381/33.

CHAPTER IV

THE PRELUDE TO OMANI EXPANSION IN EAST AFRICA

THE GROWTH OF MUSCAT AND ITS RELATIONS WITH GREAT BRITAIN AND FRANCE

It is not within the scope of this book to examine in detail the reasons why the Imamate of Oman lost its power and was replaced by the rulership of Muscat. None the less the development must be kept in mind because it had a direct relevance to events in East Africa. Those who acceded to power in Muscat were known to their countrymen as 'saiyid', which has a generalized meaning of 'lord'. The Europeans, however, ignorant of the intricacies of the situation, continued to use the title 'Imam'.[1]

The first Saiyid of Muscat to assume powers formerly held by the Imam was Sultan, who manœuvred himself into a position of authority in 1796.[2] By 1802 he had acquired a regular force consisting of 300 slaves, 1,700 Sindis, Baluchis and Arabs, 300 horses and 12,000 camels. In time of need he could muster about 20,000 more men.[3] Sultan also controlled a large fleet.[4] These forces he employed in engagements both at home and in the Persian Gulf. He obtained Hormuz, Qishm, and Hanjam in the Gulf, Gwadur and Chahbar on the Makran coast,

---

[1] The British used 'Imam' until their mistake was pointed out to them in 1839; they then employed the term 'Sultan', which was afterwards adopted by the inhabitants of Muscat and Zanzibar themselves. This title of 'Sultan' had been used occasionally when Sultan ibn Ahmad was in control of Muscat because foreigners wrongly assumed that his name was actually a title.

[2] Skinner to Manesty, 3 Oct. 1796, Proc. 18 Nov., B.P.S.P. E/11; and Beauchamp to *Ministère des Relations Extérieures*, 12 Brumaire, an 6 (2 Nov. 1797), A.E., Muscat C.C.1.

[3] Ibn Ruzayq, *op. cit.*, p. 219; and Seton to Bombay, 9 July 1802, Proc. 27 Aug., B.P.S.P. 381/33.

[4] Skinner to Superintendent of Marine, 18 Aug. 1796, Proc. 30 Sept., B.P.S.P. E/11; and Sultan to Bombay, 24 Dec. 1799, Proc. 5 Mch. 1800, B.P.S.P. 381/10.

Bandar Abbas and Minab on the Persian coast, and the fort of Khasab on Cape Musandam. He also made repeated attempts to acquire Bahrain. Despite his successful expansion abroad, Sultan was experiencing difficulties at home. His shipping was harassed by the Qawasim, who inhabited the western coast of the Omani peninsula. This was a group over which the Saiyid of Muscat had no authority. Being Sunni rather than Ibadhi in religious belief, they had no tradition of recognition for the Imamate or the subsequent secular authorities. In 1799 Sultan attacked Ras al-Khaima, one of their main ports, but they continued to be troublesome, finding an ally in the Wahhabis, a powerful religious sect from Najd. The Wahhabis had pushed across Arabia to Oman and the Persian Gulf, capturing the Buraimi oasis in 1795.[1] Buraimi was a position of great strategic importance, from which it would be possible to sweep down towards Muscat. Concerned about this threat, Sultan moved up to oppose the Wahhabis, but they had acquired the support of most of the tribes to the west of the Hajar mountains and so were able to force him to make a truce. Later Sultan made a further agreement to pay the Wahhabis an annual sum of 12,000 dollars and to receive one of their agents in Muscat. He was given a respite from the Wahhabi threat when their leader, Abdul Aziz, was murdered in 1803.[2] These political difficulties kept Sultan's attention fixed on his position in Oman and the Persian Gulf. Problems arising in the distant region of the Swahili Coast were for the time being shelved.

It was not long, however, before the ruler of Muscat felt secure enough at home to turn his attention to East Africa. This security was to a great degree due to European support. Sultan was assisted in establishing his position by his relationships with France and Great Britain. These connexions at once raised his status among his fellow-countrymen and afforded him direct aid. Observing the rivalry between the two powers, he seized his chance to enlist their assistance and obtain certain concessions. It was a rivalry which was inflamed by the French Revolutionary Wars. As these wars proceeded the British in India were apprehensive of a French attack, which they thought might come from the area of the Persian Gulf. The Gulf could be used as a military route to India, or could provide bases within striking distance of that subcontinent. It was also the route which the British used for the

[1] Sultan to Hajji Ibrahim, 16 Nov. 1799, Proc. 17 Dec., B.P.S.P. 381/7; and Bogle to Bombay, 30 Jan. 1800, Proc. 15 Feb., B.P.S.P. 381/9.
[2] *Bombay Selections XXIV*, p. 431, and Ibn Ruzayq, *op. cit.*, p. 230.

EUROPEANS AND THE BEGINNINGS OF OMANI EXPANSION

transmission of political despatches, and therefore had to be kept clear of obstruction in time of war.[1] Factors such as these made the British recognize how important it was to obtain the friendship of Muscat, which dominated the straits of Cape Musandam and therefore commanded the entrance to the Persian Gulf.

The French were likewise alive to the importance of courting Muscat. Their association with Oman had originated in the 1740s, with the commercial contacts between the Arabs and the French factories in India. The Imams of Oman had maintained a correspondence with Paris, through the agency of the French Residents at Basra, the main subject of which was the seizure of an Omani vessel by a French privateer.[2] The Omanis and the French also came into contact through their possessions south of the Equator. Merchants from Ile de France who bought slaves on the East African coast made representations to the Imam to regularize the duties they had to pay, and in 1785 Rosilly was sent to Muscat to negotiate an agreement.[3] Since the governor of Ile de France was pondering the wisdom of establishing a trading centre at Muscat, Rosilly was accompanied by a commercial agent, Comarmond, with orders to review the trading possibilities.[4] The French obtained permission to found a factory at Muscat, and a French agent was appointed to reside there.[5] The Omanis began to employ French commanders and navigators for their ships, while the Imam himself appointed a Frenchman as his doctor.[6]

When the Revolutionary Wars broke out, the French strengthened their connexion with Oman. The country was brought to their notice when another vessel was seized by a French ship and repeated protests

---

[1] For the preference at this time for the Persian Gulf route over the Red Sea route, Bombay to C. of Ds., 6 Mch. 1798, L.R.B. 15; and Holden Furber, 'The Overland Route to India', *Journal of Indian History* (Aug. 1951), pp. 106-33.

[2] Rousseau to Versailles, Aug. 1783; the Imam to the King of France, 1784/5, A.E., Muscat C.C.l.

[3] Rosilly to de Castries, n.d., c. 1785, A.N., Marine B4/276.

[4] Comarmond to Governor of Ile de France, 20 June 1789, A.N., Colonies C4/85.

[5] Sa'id ibn Imam Ahmad to Rosilly, 8 Sept. 1785; de Souillac to the Imam, 20 Nov. 1786 – both A.N., Colonies C4/83; and Rousseau to de Castries, 26 Nov. and 27 Dec. 1787, A.N., Aff.Etr. B1/177. Moustier was appointed – Moustier to Chaillon, 2 Mch. 1788, A.N., Aff.Etr. B1/197. His arrival in Muscat – the Imam to Rousseau, 1788, A.E., Muscat C.C.1.

[6] Rousseau to de Castries, 26 Dec. 1786, A.N., Aff.Etr. B1/176; and Miles, *Persian Gulf*, p. 289.

from Muscat were placed before the Revolutionary Council in Paris.[1] When considering the memoranda about this matter, the Council became aware of the strategic and commercial importance of Muscat for the French, and particularly for Ile de France. It decided to send to Muscat as consul the Abbé Beauchamp, who was conversant with Near Eastern affairs. As a nephew of the Bishop of Babylon, he had travelled widely in the Near East and had become proficient in Arabic and Turkish.[2] Aware of these developments, in 1796 the British sent Lt Skinner to Muscat to capture the French consul, but the plan was frustrated because Beauchamp, having heard rumours of the dangers he would face, did not proceed to his destination.[3] Skinner had to be content with exacting a promise from the authorities in Muscat that they would not harbour Frenchmen.[4]

In 1798 the French landed in Egypt and British fears of an invasion of India increased. The Bombay Council, which dealt with Persian Gulf affairs on behalf of the British Government in India, had reason to suppose that the Saiyid of Muscat was not keeping his promise to exclude the French, because a vessel manned by Frenchmen, but with the Saiyid's seal, had arrived in Bombay from Muscat in August 1797.[5] It had also been revealed that Sultan's French doctor was the agent for two small vessels which passed continually between Muscat and Ile de France.[6] British suspicions that the Omanis were provisioning Ile de France were correct: in 1794 Guirard had gone to Muscat to arrange

[1] Shaikh Khalfan ibn Abdullah to Rousseau, n.d. (c. 1791/2), A.E., Muscat C.C.1; Rousseau to Minister of Marine, no. 105, 18 Feb. 1792, A.E., Baghdad C.C.104; Guirard to Rousseau, 25 Sept. 1794, Report to *Bureau des Relations Extérieures*, 11 Ventôse, an 3 (1 Mch. 1795), Questions asked and Note on Muscat, 18 Ventôse, an 3 (8 Mch. 1795), Report to Committee of Public Safety, n.d., *Commission de la Marine et des Colonies* to *Commission des Relations Extérieures*, 23 Germinal, an 3 (12 Apr. 1795) – all from A.E., Muscat C.C.1.

[2] *Mémoire* for Instructions to Beauchamp, 1 Prairial, an 3 (12 May 1795), A.E., Muscat C.C.1, and Bishop of Babylon to Versailles, 22 Aug. 1778, A.N., Aff.Etr. B1/176, and various correspondence in A.N., Aff.Etr. B1/177 and 197.

[3] Instructions to Skinner, Proc. 1 July 1796, B.P.S.P. E/10; and Beauchamp to Ministry of *Relations Extérieures*, 26 Messidor, an 6 (14 July 1798), A.E., Muscat C.C.1. Beauchamp died in Egypt shortly afterwards.

[4] Saiyid of Muscat to Bombay, n.d., recd. 18 Nov. 1796, Proc. 18 Nov. 1796, B.P.S.P. E/10.

[5] Bombay to Khalfan, 1 Sept. 1797, Proc. 5 Sept., B.P.S.P. E./10.

[6] Instructions to Mehdi Ali Khan, Proc. 4 Sept. 1798, B.P.S.P. 380/71.

just such a matter.[1] The Bombay Council decided to take further steps: it ordered Mehdi Ali Khan to call at Muscat and remind Sultan of his promise. He was also to offer him a British replacement for his French doctor and to request permission for the establishment of a British factory at Muscat.[2] Although there was no mention of a written treaty in Mehdi Ali Khan's instructions, he caused the agreement he made to be put in writing.[3]

The agreement stipulated that Sultan was to dismiss a 'certain person of the French nation' from his employment, and prohibit French vessels from entering Muscat cove (although there was nothing to say they could not provision and water outside). Sultan was not to take part in the hostilities on the high seas, but must actively assist with his army, navy and people if there was fighting between the French and British at Muscat. Sultan also promised that, as long as the war continued, the French and Dutch should never be allowed, throughout all his territories, 'a place to fix or seat themselves in, nor shall they ever get ground to stand upon, within this state'. Finally, it was stipulated that 'the friend of that *Sirkar* [the East India Company] is the friend of this [Oman]; and in the same way the enemy of this is to be the enemy of that'. The agreement was ambiguous on more than one point, which is not surprising since the envoy himself drafted it. In particular the 'friends and enemies' clause was to cause trouble later. Whereas Muscat regarded it as merely a point of etiquette, Bombay was far more formal in its interpretation.

The Muscat authorities were well aware of what they were doing when they negotiated this engagement. They were wise to make concessions because in 1796 Bombay had threatened to terminate the Omanis' free access to British ports in India.[4] In actuality Muscat forfeited little by the agreement, for it contained nothing specific about putting an end to trade with the French and Dutch, Bombay, however, later claimed that this was covered by the 'friends and enemies' clause.

[1] Guirard to Rousseau, 25 Sept. 1794, and Rousseau to Descorches 30 Vendémiaire, an 3 (21 Oct. 1794), A.E., Muscat C.C.1.
[2] Bombay to Mehdi Ali Khan, 4 Sept. 1798, Proc. 4 Sept., B.P.S.P. 380/71.
[3] Text of the engagement, dated 12 Oct. 1798, enclosed in Mehdi Ali Khan to Bombay, 14 Oct. 1798, Proc. 30 Oct., B.P.S.P. 380/72. Also printed in C. U. Aitchison, *A Collection of Treaties, Engagements and Sanads Relating to India and Neighbouring Countries* (Delhi, 1933), 12 vols, XI, p. 287, and in *Bombay Selections XXIV*, p. 248.
[4] Bombay to Muscat, 1 July 1796, Proc. 1 July, B.P.S.P. E/10.

THE SWAHILI COAST

In their concern that the terms of the engagement be fulfilled, the British developed their relationship with Muscat. A connexion which had been stimulated originally by strategic and defensive considerations, expanded into other fields. In 1799 the British offered commercial concessions to the Omanis in a further bid to wean them from French influence.[1] None the less the Omanis continued to be obstructive, unwilling as they were to come down on one side or the other until they saw who was winning. When accused of continuing to consort with the French, Sultan said that his people could not distinguish who was a Frenchman and who was not, a claim which was probably true. He said that some Frenchmen had been employed in the East for years and knew nothing of events at home.[2]

A catalogue of Omani misdemeanours was drawn up by Bombay: a British vessel had been attacked in the Persian Gulf by a French privateer which then put into Muscat and sold the cargo of its prize; the Omani governor in Zanzibar had mistreated Commodore Blankett on his way to the Red Sea; Sultan himself was freighting a ship bound for Ile de France with large quantities of grain and brimstone; he had passed on presents from Tipu Sultan of Mysore to Baba Khan, Shah of Persia, when he knew that the East India Company was at war with Mysore; and a suspicious correspondence had taken place between dissident elements in Bengal and some principal Arabs of Muscat.[3] It is probably true that the Omanis were giving the French considerable assistance: forty years later the French still remembered their aid with gratitude, saying it had been the reason for Ile de France's long stand against the British in the Revolutionary Wars.[4]

In view of all this, the British attitude towards Muscat hardened. They decided to withdraw Sultan's commercial privileges, and to send him a British doctor who could check on his activities 'by possessing and being able to exert such a share of local influence as shall be equal to prevent the Imam from continuing his intercourse with the French, and to induce that chieftain to abide more fully and more strictly by

---

[1] See Chapter III, p. 97.

[2] Mehdi Ali Khan to Bombay, 21 Apr., and Dobinson to Bombay, 11 May 1799, Proc. 17 May, B.P.S.P. 380/3.

[3] Deposition of Baboo Ram, Lascar of the *Pearl*, 25 Nov. 1799, Bombay to Rainier, 8 May 1799, and Instructions to Malcolm, Proc. 3 Dec. 1799, B.P.S.P. 381/7.

[4] Ministry of Agriculture and Commerce to Ministry of F.A., 18 Mch. 1844, A.F., Zanz. C.C.1.

EUROPEANS AND THE BEGINNINGS OF OMANI EXPANSION

the tenor of his Cowlnamah [*qaulnamah*, i.e. written engagement]'.[1] Archibald H. Bogle, the doctor selected for the post, was to confine himself outwardly to medical duties, but was also to endeavour 'by every secret means' to obtain information.[2]

In actual fact there was no need for secrecy, because Sultan accepted Bogle in a political capacity and at the same time confirmed the 1798 agreement.[3] His opinion of the French had been temporarily revised when he heard that they had been repulsed from Acre and that Tipu Sultan had been defeated. Omani interests had also been materially changed when the whole coast of Malabar fell into the hands of the British, a development which gave the Company possession of every port at which a vessel could anchor from Surat to Calcutta.[4] In addition, the French had fallen from grace by their seizure of an Omani ship in the China Seas.[5] Nevertheless Sultan would not commit himself totally to the British. He was unwilling to dismiss the remaining Frenchmen from his employment unless British gunners were sent to replace them.[6] He replied to Bombay's complaints against him, and in answer to an accusation that his excuses were 'specious' he wrote a proud, sharp letter, abandoning the usual compliments:

'I am Ruler of my own country and sovereign over it and the inhabitants thereof, and independent of everyone. The course I observe therefore with the French proceeds from the necessity I am under not to put an entire stop to the trade by sea of my subjects, a consideration which obliged me to keep fair with them in appearance.'[7]

He then shrewdly offered to join the British in the war against the French provided they bore all his expenses, an offer which he must have known would be refused. He thus manœuvred Bombay into tacitly accepting the continuance of his connexion with the French.

None the less the British would have been astounded had they known that in 1803 Sultan sent an envoy to Ile de France to ask for a French agent at Muscat and to complain of the vexations he had suffered from

---

[1] Bombay to Sultan, 28 Jan. 1800, Proc. 28 Jan., B.P.S.P. 381/9, and Bombay to Malcolm, 3 Dec. 1799, Proc. 3 Dec., B.P.S.P. 381/7.
[2] Malcolm's instructions to Bogle, 8 Jan. 1800, Proc. 31 Jan., B.P.S.P. 381/9.
[3] Malcolm's Journal written at Muscat, Jan. 1800, Proc. 4 Feb., B.P.S.P. 381/9.
[4] Malcolm to Bombay, 4 Feb. 1800, Proc. 5 Mch., B.P.S.P. 381/10.
[5] Malcolm's Journal, as above, entry for 10 Jan. 1800.
[6] Malcolm to Bombay, 4 Feb. 1800, as above.
[7] Sultan to Bombay, n.d., recd. 12 May 1800, Proc. 30 Sept., B.P.S.P. 381/16, and Instructions to Malcolm, Proc. 3 Dec. 1799, B.P.S.P. 381/7.

the British.[1] As this occurred at a time of Franco-British truce, Sultan may have felt that he could risk British displeasure. He may also have hoped that the move would put a stop to piratical depredations on his countrymen's vessels by French ships; indeed this may have been the true reason for his overture because the envoy demanded compensation for the French prizes.[2] The French greeted Sultan's approach favourably, despatching Cavaignac to Muscat as consul.[3] He was to have the same rank as Seton, the British agent who had been appointed in 1802. But there was a sudden change of heart on Muscat's part: when Cavaignac arrived he was forbidden to live ashore and was kept waiting almost a month for an audience with Sultan. Recognizing that he was unwelcome, the French consul left Muscat.[4] Sultan's *volte-face* about a French consul is most likely to have been due to the resumption of hostilities by France and Great Britain. Although in peacetime he would openly protest his friendship to the French, in time of war he had to be more careful lest he endanger his trade with India.

By 1803, then, the Revolutionary Wars had thrust Muscat into European attention. The British maintained an agent there, and the French had twice failed to establish a consulate. The British regarded Muscat as the key to the Persian Gulf, and their alliance with her as vital to their security in India; the French saw Muscat as a source of provisions for Ile de France and a useful base for depredations on British shipping. As for Muscat itself, its contacts with the Europeans heightened its prestige among Arabs of the Omani peninsula and the rest of the Persian Gulf, and bolstered the authority within Oman of those who executed the negotiations. The contact with the Europeans assisted the division between the secular and religious power, and was a contributory factor in the decline of the office of Imam and the increase in importance of the ruler of Muscat.

The Saiyid of Muscat's equivocation towards the French had made

---

[1] Magallon Lamortière to Ministry of Marine, no. 198, 20 Pluviose, an 11 (9 Feb. 1803), A.N., Colonies, C4/117; and Decaen to General Decrès, Minister of Marine and Colonies, no. 64, 30 Fructidor, an 11 (17 Sept. 1803), A.N., Colonies, C4/118.

[2] *Ibid.* Decaen's view was that the prime purpose of the envoy had been to get reparation for the captured vessels.

[3] Instructions to Cavaignac, 5 Vendémiaire an 11 (27 Sept. 1802), and Report to First Consul from Ministry of *Relations Extérieures*, 12 Vendémiaire, an 11 (4 Dec. 1802), A.E., Muscat C.C.1.

[4] Cavaignac to Decaen, 15 Frimaire, an 12 (7 Dec. 1803), and extract from the Journal of *L'Atalante* during her voyage to Muscat A.N., Colonies C4/118.

EUROPEANS AND THE BEGINNINGS OF OMANI EXPANSION

the British emphasize the necessity of maintaining friendly relations with Oman. Since they were dealing with a region where the political institutions were loosely defined, they were reliant on the goodwill of a particular leader, to whom it would be wise to lend their support lest a successor be less co-operative. When the man with whom they had negotiated died, the British hoped that, by supporting his son or a close relation in the struggle for the succession they would be able to maintain the relationship which had been so carefully constructed. This continual British support for the rulers of Muscat was an important factor in those leaders' ability to maintain their own position and expand their country's frontiers.

Sultan died in 1804.[1] There followed a struggle for power, the contenders for which were the Imam Sa'id, his brother Qais, a nephew Badr, and Salim and Sa'id, two of the late Saiyid's sons.[2] Badr and the brothers Salim and Sa'id threw their lot together, forming a combination which acquired the support of two important groups – the Wahhabis and Qawasim.[3] At the beginning of the nineteenth century, Persian Gulf shipping was being seriously harassed by the Qawasim. Ships of all nationalities fell prey to them, but it was the British who were in the strongest position to protest. The British suspected that Qawasim depredations were encouraged by Wahhabi pressure because the two groups had formed an alliance when the Wahhabis, lacking ships themselves, recognized the importance of commanding the seas.[4] The Qawasim used Sultan's death as an opportunity to assert themselves further in the Persian Gulf, and within a month they had captured two British vessels.[5] This made more immediate the prospect of direct or

[1] Seton to Bombay, 28 Feb. 1805, Proc. 6 Mch., B.P.S.P. 382/3.
[2]

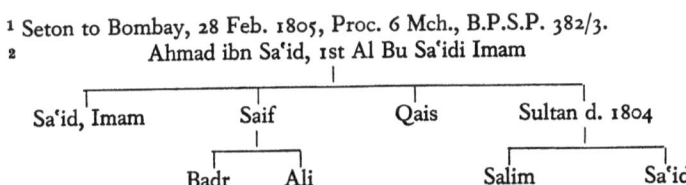

[3] Seton to Bombay, 16 Nov. 1805, and Sa'ud ibn Abdul Aziz to Badr, n.d., Proc. 13 Dec. 1805, B.P.S.P. 382/10. Badr had fled to the Wahhabis in 1803 – Bombay to C. of Ds., 22 Feb. 1806, L.R.B. 19. Ibn Ruzayq, *op. cit.*, p. 274, says he got the help of 200 Wahhabis.
[4] See R. Bayly Winder, *Saudi Arabia in the Nineteenth Century* (London, 1965), for the Wahhabis and their arrangement of a treaty with the Qawasim. See also Kelly, *Persian Gulf*, Chapter 3.
[5] William Bruce, Resident at Bushire, to Calcutta, 17 Dec. 1804, Proc. 9 Feb. 1805, B.P.S.P. 382/3.

109

indirect Wahhabi control of the Persian Gulf, a situation in which the Ottoman Empire, to the support of which the British were committed, would be threatened from the rear.[1] In addition, the agglomeration of petty shaikhs in the Gulf provided a situation in which the British could interfere if they wished, and therefore they wanted to prevent the aggrandizement of any one power. Since the connexion with Muscat was one of the bases of this informal British influence in the Gulf, it was decided to support her by sea against the Qawasim, while the candidate for the succession turned all his attention to dealing with the Wahhabis on land.

There was, however, a problem: which candidate should the British support, and how should they justify interference in the succession? Calcutta, the seat of supreme British authority in India, found the excuse in the existing engagements between the British and Muscat, which

> 'do not impose upon the former any obligation to support the succession of the sons of the late Imam to the rights and power of their father, but ... justify the interference of the British Government in support of that candidate whose pretensions shall appear to be founded on justice, provided that support can be afforded without the hazard of involving the British Government in hostilities with the state of Muscat.'[2]

Calcutta added that 'every degree of countenance and support' should be given to the sons of Sultan, but if they did not prevail, friendship should be cultivated with the successful candidate. The partiality of the British for the sons of Sultan arose not only from the misconception that there was patrilineal succession, but also from a hope that, since Sultan had co-operated with the British, so might his sons. The importance of British influence emerges from the attempts of both the main candidates for the succession to solicit British goodwill. One of them, Badr, thought a formal acceptance of Sultan's engagements with Bombay and a mention that a French frigate had been in the vicinity would win the British to his side.[3] The other, Qais, tried to gain

---

[1] Seton to Bombay, 16 Nov. 1805, Proc. 13 Dec., B.P.S.P. 382/10.
[2] Bombay to Seton, quoting a letter from Calcutta, 3 Mch. 1805, Proc. 6 Mch, B.P.S.P. 382/3.
[3] Badr to Bombay, n.d., and same to same, 4 Oct. 1805, Proc. 13 Dec., B.P.S.P. 382/10.

EUROPEANS AND THE BEGINNINGS OF OMANI EXPANSION

British support by telling them that Badr was preparing two ships to go to Ile de France, and had also called in the Wahhabis.[1]

Bombay did not interfere in the early manœuvres over the succession but once Badr, and his allies, the sons of Sultan, had prevailed, they considered aiding them by sea.[2] Meanwhile the British agent at Muscat managed to negotiate a truce with the Qawasim, which relieved the Omanis of considerable pressure.[3] Badr did not long survive: within a year he was dead, but his successor, Sa'id, less worried by opposition from the sea, was able to establish his position more quickly. Again Bombay did not interfere in the actual succession – in fact, the British agent was not in Muscat at the time.[4] They were also wary of recognizing Sa'id because they knew he had murdered Badr and they were afraid faction fighting would develop.[5] They did not write to him until they heard that he had firmly established his position. In the troubled years 1804–6 the British were not, therefore, king-makers in Muscat, but, having waited to see who would emerge from the struggles, they backed the leaders who prevailed. Had the Gulf not been pacified by the truce with the Qawasim organized by the British, it is possible that Badr and Sa'id would have been unable to resist the combined force of the Wahhabis and Qawasim.

Sa'id had a long struggle to establish himself in a position of real power, for he had few of the necessary bases of authority which had enabled his father, Sultan, to maintain his position. According to the British agent at Muscat, in 1808 Sa'id had lost much of the influence his father had possessed, and held only the sea coast. He had direct control of only Muscat, Matrah, and Barqa.[6] He began to remedy this by calling on the European powers for assistance. The British were still relying on Muscat to support them against the French. They had a chance of succeeding in their courtship because the French, indignant at the treatment of Cavaignac, were making sporadic attacks on Omani shipping – an unofficial but effective method of diplomacy. But Sa'id, like his father, was unwilling to commit himself totally to the British.

[1] Qais to Bombay, n.d., Proc. 13 Dec. 1805, B.P.S.P. 382/10.
[2] Bombay to the Governor-General, 2 Feb. 1805, Proc. 9 Feb., B.P.S.P. 382/3.
[3] Seton's Journal of his expedition to sign a truce, Proc. 21 Mch. 1806, B.P.S.P. 382/16.
[4] Bombay to Secret Committee, 11 July 1806, L.R.B. 18.
[5] Bombay to Secret Committee, 12 Aug. 1806, L.R.B. 21.
[6] *Bombay Selections XXIV*, p. 178, quoting Seton to Bombay, 16 Jan. 1808; and Ibn Ruzayq, *op. cit.*, p. 318.

When in December 1806 a French ship was taken by a British cruiser just outside Muscat cove, Sa'id thought this was an unjust violation of the neutrality of his port. Anxious lest it provoke more French reprisals on his shipping, he sent an envoy to Ile de France to exculpate himself from blame and to conciliate the French. However, the governor of Ile de France was firm: Sa'id was to request the return of the ship and its crew. Sa'id did as he was asked, making it clear to Bombay that his shipping would have to be protected by the British if he were to continue his hostility to the French. He suggested that his ships be conveyed by British vessels to Calcutta, that a British man-of-war be permanently stationed at Muscat, and that he be given proper assistance in troops, money and vessels.[1]

These extensive and peremptory demands were the first real contact the British had had with the new ruler of Muscat. They forced Bombay to re-examine the British connexion with Muscat, and to consider under what conditions it was worth maintaining. They could appreciate that attacks on the Omanis' shipping struck at the mainstay of their livelihood. It was obvious that the almost complete severance of relations with the French which had been required of Muscat by the Bombay authorities in 1799 could no longer be demanded unless the British give Muscat direct support. Calcutta came to the conclusion that the protection of Omani shipping was not worth the difficulty and expense it would involve. It was decided that, although the 1798 and 1800 agreements with Muscat had made the Omanis pro-British benevolent neutrals, before 1803 the Omanis had in fact acted as mere neutrals and they should be allowed to pursue this course again.[2] They should now be permitted to trade openly with the French. However, neither the French nor the British should violate the neutrality of Muscat port. This was a definite departure from the 1798 agreement. So, nine years after the beginning of their connexion with Muscat, the policy of the British had turned a full circle. Instead of demanding the complete cessation of Omani relations with the French, Calcutta was now suggesting that the Omanis should not run the risk of being so harassed by the French that they might have to sever their relations with the British in self-defence. The connexion which had originated in the British need to exclude all French influence was now regarded

---

[1] Sa'id's envoy to Bombay, 21 Dec. and Bombay to Sa'id, 22 Dec. 1806, Proc. 23 Dec. B.P.S.P. 382/23; and Sa'id to Bombay, 15 Jan. 1807, Proc. 6 Feb., B.P.S.P. 382/26.

[2] Calcutta to Bombay, 23 Apr. 1807, Proc. 17 May, B.P.S.P. 382/29.

as too valuable to jeopardize by insistence on Muscat's enmity towards France.

Sa'id, only sixteen years old and with 'the warmth of disposition incident to youth', had emerged triumphant from his first contact with the British, and he eagerly exploited his new opportunities.[1] He concluded a treaty with Ile de France on 16 June 1807.[2] Both the Omanis and the French were to have most favoured nation privileges in matters of commerce and navigation. Both were allowed free access to each other's ports for merchant ships, privateers, and prizes. The French could confiscate contraband of war if found in Omani ships destined for a port of an enemy of France and any property of those ships if found in enemy vessels. Omani ships were permitted to visit enemy ports, but not to trade between two such ports, and French commercial agents were to be allowed to reside at Muscat or at other dependencies of Sa'id. It had thus taken Sa'id only a year to persuade the British to lift restrictions harmful to Omani commerce, and to arrange a favourable commercial treaty with the French.

The British might not have been so willing to grant the concessions to Muscat had they foreseen subsequent events. There had been hints of renewed French interest in India in 1806, and there was a menacing growth of France's influence in Egypt, now controlled by Muhammad Ali. The British suspected the French were trying to establish a permanent settlement in the Red Sea. Even more serious was Napoleon's attempt to make a triple alliance of France, the Porte, and Persia, aimed against Russia, which resulted in a treaty of alliance between France and Persia in May 1807, in which Persia ceded Bandar Abbas and Kharaq in the Persian Gulf to France.[3] The British were alarmed. For many years they had sought to keep the Gulf a sphere of British influence. For nine months of the year Bandar Abbas was but fifteen days from the Malabar coast. The British reaction was swift: sterner measures were to be taken with Muscat, which was no longer to be allowed to have dealings with the French. The British agent at Muscat was ordered to persuade Sa'id to dismiss any Frenchmen from Muscat,

[1] Bombay to C. of Ds., quoting Seton, 25 Feb. 1807, L.R.B. 21. Sa'id was born in 1791/2 – Ibn Ruzayq, *op. cit.*, p. 259.

[2] Text of the convention, A.E., Muscat C.C.1. The treaty was not ratified in France, but Ile de France acted as if it had been. There were slight modifications to the convention in 1808 and 1809, requested by Omani envoys sent to Ile de France – Note of 17 June 1808, and Decrès to Ministry of F.A., 13 Feb. 1809, A.E., Muscat C.C.1.

[3] Seton to Bombay, 25 Sept. 1807, Proc. 25 Sept., B.P.S.P. 382/33.

and to remonstrate with him for lading ships bound for Ile de France with grain. To supply Ile de France with grain was apparently no longer consistent with Saʻid's friendship with the British, 'or even with neutrality'.[1] There had, therefore, been yet another shift of opinion about Muscat's precise obligations to the British. It is little wonder that the authorities at Muscat followed no consistent line either. At that time there were no decisions of international law which stipulated the role, restrictions and duties of a neutral, but the definition of Muscat's neutrality, and its implications, seemed to change in direct proportion to the British fear of French invasion of India.

The tension diminished as quickly as it had mounted, for Napoleon became preoccupied in Spain. By now, however, the British were committed to making their influence in the Persian Gulf supreme, and their relations with the ruler of Muscat were an important element in this policy. There must be no disruptive force which might upset British relationships with Gulf rulers, and British shipping must have complete freedom of movement in the Gulf.

British shipping, relationships with Gulf rulers, and the *status quo* in Muscat were alike menaced by the Qawasim and the Wahhabis, who were again troublesome. Saʻid made it appear that Muscat was in imminent danger of falling to the Wahhabis. Faced with the possibility of Saʻid's fall from power and Wahhabi control of Muscat, the British decided to act. The Wahhabis could be indirectly curbed by action against the Qawasim, who gave them most of their support by land and also a fifth of any plunder from the sea.[2]

Consequently the British planned an expedition against the Qawasim which left in September 1809.[3] Saʻid co-operated with his own troops and vessels. The expedition succeeded in destroying some forts and boats belonging to the Qawasim, but Saʻid's troops were left on land to face the Qawasim while the British sailed away, unaware of the danger he faced. In this vulnerable position, Saʻid applied to the British for

[1] Bombay to C. of Ds., 20 Feb. 1808, L.R.B. 22.

[2] Bombay to C. of Ds., 20 Feb. 1808 and 20 Jan. 1809, L.R.B. 22, and 14 June 1809, L.R.B. 23.

[3] Instructions to Capt. J. Wainwright commanding the sea force of the Persian Gulf expedition – *Précis of Correspondence regarding the affairs of the Persian Gulf 1801-1853* (Calcutta, 1906), quoting Political Dept. Diary, no. 339 of 1809 (this précis will hereafter be cited as *Précis of Persian Gulf Correspondence*). For detailed accounts of the expedition, see H. Moyse-Bartlett, *The Pirates of Trucial Oman* (London, 1966), Sir Charles Belgrave, *The Pirate Coast* (London, 1966), and Kelly, *Persian Gulf*.

further aid. He must have been astounded when the answer came back that he was to expect no more help, and the British did not wish to hear anything further about the Wahhabi threat.[1] The explanation lay partly in the fact that the British thought Sa'id was exaggerating his distress: 'Perhaps there may be as much of policy as real jeopardy in the distressed situation to which he represents himself to be reduced.'[2] It was difficult to obtain a correct appreciation of the Wahhabi threat because there was no longer a British agent at Muscat. After several agents died in quick succession, Bombay had decided not to appoint any more, and now relied upon a local inhabitant as their agent and informer.[3] Apart from their incorrect analysis of the situation, the British were also reluctant to give Sa'id further help because, having already undertaken an expedition against the Qawasim, they could no longer shelter under the excuse that they were performing such actions in order to secure their own commerce. They shunned becoming involved in hostilities on land and therefore would not openly help Sa'id repel the Wahhabis In addition to these considerations, the importance of the connexion with Muscat had diminished, for the French had suffered a major setback with the loss of Ile de France to the British in 1810.

Sa'id was left to carry on alone against the Wahhabis. He was forced to pay tribute to them, but finally they retreated because both their general, Mutlaq al-Mutairi, and their leader, Sa'ud, died, and because Muhammad Ali's Egyptian troops were approaching them from the west. Sa'id then enjoyed a period of relative peace during which, no longer on the defensive, he was able to strengthen his position in Oman. He took Nakhl in the interior and confirmed his authority at the ports along the coast.[4] It was at this time that he began to turn his attention to East Africa. Previously his attention had been too engaged by his difficulties at home to consider his territories further afield.

Although the Wahhabis had retreated, Sa'id still had the Qawasim as an irritant on his home front. They had been only temporarily suppressed by the 1809 expedition, and were beginning to harass British and

[1] Sa'id to Bombay, 26 Mch. 1810, recd. 2 Apr., B.S.C. 3; and Bombay to Sa'id, 13 Sept. 1810, Proc. 18 Sept., B.P.C. 383/19.
[2] Bombay to C. of Ds., 14 Apr. 1810, L.R.B. 24.
[3] Bombay to C. of Ds., 31 Jan. 1810, L.R.B. 24; Bombay to Calcutta, 13 Jan. 1810, Proc. 13 Jan., B.P.S.P. 383/13; and Smith to Bombay, 1 May 1810, quoted in *Précis of Persian Gulf Correspondence*, p. 81.
[4] Ibn Ruzayq, *op. cit.*, p. 332.

THE SWAHILI COAST

Omani shipping again. By 1817 the new Governor-General of India, Lord Hastings, was convinced of the 'absolute necessity of destroying the power of the pirates'.[1] During the discussions about another expedition, the aims and policies of the British in the Persian Gulf, and particularly towards Muscat, came under detailed review. The governor of Bombay felt that Muscat should be built up as the dominant power in the Gulf. 'The conduct of the Imam during the course of his connexion with us', he said, 'entitled him to our most favourable consideration', and 'I should see with extreme regret any line of policy adopted that would be adverse to his interests'.[2] But a member of the Bombay Council, Francis Warden, disagreed with the elevation of Sa'id to a position of power in the Gulf. He thought the growth of piracy was to be attributed in a large degree to the impolicy of Sa'id's proceedings towards some of the independent Gulf tribes.[3] There then succeeded a new governor at Bombay – Elphinstone – who was strongly influenced by Warden's opinions. It was decided that Sa'id should be told to consolidate his present possessions rather than weaken them by extension, and that another expedition against the Qawasim should be undertaken.[3] Early in December 1819 a force consisting of both British and Omani troops and vessels took Ras al-Khaima and destroyed other ports. Treaties were then arranged with the Gulf shaikhs.[4]

Thompson, the expedition's interpreter, called at Muscat on his return to Bombay because he had been ordered to investigate a report of piracy. It was discovered that the Bani Bu Ali tribe, south of Muscat, were the offenders, and a plan was made for Thompson and Sa'id to act jointly against them. Bombay was specific in its instructions: all boats belonging to the tribe were to be destroyed, but no troops were to be landed 'unless with the very strong prospect of striking some blow without going too far inland'. Thompson disobeyed his instructions and did go inland. In a battle with the Bani Bu Ali he lost 400 men. Bombay

[1] Calcutta to Bombay, 22 Feb. 1817, Proc. 21 July 1819, B.S.C. 41.

[2] Minutes by Nepean, Proc. 14 Apr. 1819, B.S.C. 40, and 31 July 1819, Proc. 31 July, B.S.C. 41.

[3] Minutes by Warden, 3 Apr. 1819, Proc. 14 Apr., and 12 Aug. 1819, Proc. 20 Sept., B.S.C. 40 and 41.

[4] Bombay to Calcutta, 15 Dec. 1819, Proc. 15 Dec., B.S.C. 43. For a detailed account of the expedition, see Moyse-Bartlett, *op. cit.*, Chapter 4, and Belgrave, *op. cit.*, Chapter 12. There were 3 British naval warships, 9 Company cruisers, 18 transports, 1,453 European troops, 1,294 Indian troops, 2 Omani frigates and 600 Omani men – Moyse-Bartlett, *op. cit.*, pp. 86–9. For the treaties, Keir to Bombay, 16 Jan. 1820, Proc. 16 Feb., B.S.C. 43.

court-martialled him, and sent an expedition of 2,500 troops to engage the Bani Bu Ali, who were heavily defeated.¹

The Bani Bu Ali expedition, although geographically remote from the Swahili Coast, was of fundamental importance to its history. Its significance lay in the effect it had upon Sa'id's view of the relations between the British and Muscat. Without authority, after his defeat Thompson had told Sa'id that he had no need to fear – the resources of the British Government would be everywhere at his disposal.² Bombay saw the danger in this: it 'must have led the Imam to suppose that our late misfortune had turned our occasional co-operation against the pirates into a general defensive alliance or a guarantee of his dominions – an opinion that it was imperative to remove at the earliest period'.³ But the despatch of the second expedition meant that it was virtually impossible to efface the impression. The campaign against the Bani Bu Ali, who had adopted Wahhabi tenets, was regarded by Sa'id as a confirmation of the British policy, which had also been demonstrated in 1809 and 1819, to uphold the integrity of his territory. Sa'id had soon recognized that the British were interested in the maintenance of his authority in Muscat. He had therefore used the Europeans to help free him from the dangers posed by the Wahhabis, Qawasim, and Bani Bu Ali, and in return he had offered the Europeans limited co-operation. He had used his position to extract useful commercial agreements from both the British and French. In this way both he and his father had strengthened their own political power and prestige. Their countrymen regarded them as their representatives in dealings with European powers, and there was little chance of a return to the old-style Imamate authority. During their negotiations with the Europeans, Sultan and Sa'id were careful not to forfeit their freedom of manœuvre. They had manipulated the Europeans against each other with a skill that had brought them benefits in the form of new security on the home front. In 1820 Sa'id could turn to a consideration of matters in East Africa which had been claiming attention for many years. Two years later he sent troops to East Africa to reduce some ports to obedience.

Despite their periodic policy revisions, the British had continued to uphold the position of Sa'id and, as he himself was well aware, they were likely to follow the same path in the future. Their connexion with Muscat had originated in their fear of Napoleon and the French threat

¹ Moyse-Bartlett, *op. cit.*, pp. 133, 137, and 160-6.
² *Ibid.*, p. 153, quoting Thompson to Adjutant-General.
³ Bombay to C. of Ds., 17 Jan. 1821, P.L.B. 7.

to India. It had been necessary at once to keep the Gulf free of the French and open for the transmission of political despatches. This had required securing the most strategic point – Muscat – and maintaining a tranquillity which allowed British influence to reign among the maritime shaikhs. The expeditions against the pirates had been undertaken to achieve these two interrelated purposes, as had been the support they afforded the Saiyids of Muscat. It was these British activities which to a large extent now enabled Saiyid Sa'id to pursue his ambitions outside Oman.

CHAPTER V

THE EXPANSION OF OMANI INTERESTS ON THE SWAHILI COAST

Omani expansion to the Swahili Coast was a continuous process from 1698, at some times pursued more energetically than at others and often subject to reversals of fortune. After the initial spur to their activities in the late 1690s the enthusiasm of the Omani authorities might have been expected to wane. That it did not was due in part to continuous irritants in the form of rival factions which were challenging the Imamate authority in Oman and trying to establish themselves in East Africa in an attempt to win support, or which retired to East Africa to seek their fortunes there. In addition, the interest of the Europeans in the Swahili Coast began to encourage the rulers of Oman to maintain and consolidate their own position in the region.

It was the French who posed the first direct threat to Omani authority on the Swahili Coast. In the 1770s and 1780s traders like Morice put forward schemes which ranged from mild proposals for commercial treaties with the Omanis to the annexation of the entire coast by the French.[1] De Cossigny, the governor of Ile de France, sympathized with the annexation plan, but there was little chance of it being accepted in France. Some traders had apprehensions about the idea, thinking its execution would jeopardize Ile de France's sugar trade with Muscat.[2] Their fears were unwarranted because the plans were forgotten when the Revolutionary Wars broke out between

---

[1] 'Projet d'un établissement', pp. 110-12; 'Observations sur le pays et les productions de l'Isle [sic] de Quiloa', by Massieu, 1 Feb. 1778, M.O., O.I. 15/61; and Comarmond's 'Mémoire sur la nécessité et les moyens de former un établissement françois à Mongallo sur la Côte Orientale d'Afrique, 1787', A.N., Colonies C4/85 (hereafter cited as 'Comarmond's Mémoire').

[2] Morice, 'Projet d'un établissement', pp. 88-9.

THE SWAHILI COAST

France and Great Britain. Although the authorities in Oman could hardly have known the details of Morice's plans, they may have had suspicions of them, because the French traded extensively with the Swahili Coast before 1810. It was probably no coincidence that the reinstatement of an Omani governor in Kilwa in 1785 occurred at the height of French activities.

It was the British rather than the French who made the Omanis tighten their hold on the Swahili Coast. They came to the area later than the French: in the eighteenth century they seldom visited East Africa.[1] An exception to this was the visit of a British vessel to Mombasa in 1744, and indeed the fact that the ship's captain was a good friend of the deposed governor of that town suggests that this was not his first visit.[2] The interest of the British in the Swahili Coast region quickened during the Revolutionary and Napoleonic Wars, when they insisted that the Saiyid of Muscat should prevent not only Oman but also its overseas possessions from trading with the French. The Saiyid was also reminded of his overseas domains when he was reprimanded by the British for the treatment which his governor at Zanzibar had afforded Commodore Blankett in 1799.[3] An incident which occurred in 1801 may also have focused the Saiyid's attention on East Africa: the ruler of Pate, Muhammad, asked the British for protection against the French, whom he suspected of having designs on his island. He was inspired to take this action by the example of Johanna, an island with which Pate had close relations. A delegation from Johanna had made a similar appeal to the British in 1799.[4] Muhammad sent two envoys to Bombay to propose that the British build a fort and defend Pate, in return for half the produce of that island.[5] Duncan, the governor of Bombay, was interested, but the project was dropped after it was sent to the Governor-General.[6] Sultan, the Saiyid of Muscat, may well have

---

[1] See Chapter III, pp. 94-6.

[2] *Mombasa Chronicle*; and Mazrui MS., p. 20.

[3] Log of the *Leopard*, P.R.O. Adm. 51/1312; Blankett to Bombay, 17 Apr. 1799, Proc. 7 June; and Bombay to Saiyid of Muscat, 20 June 1799, B.P.S.P. 381/4.

[4] Sultan of Johanna to Bombay, n.d., Proc. 14 July 1799, B.P.S.P. 381/4. Another Johanna delegation to Bombay called at Pate on its return to Johanna in 1804 – Bombay to C. of Ds., 10 Aug. 1804, L.R.B. 18.

[5] Sultan of Pate to Bombay, Sept. 1801; Amir of Pate or Mombasa [sic] (probably a Mazrui in Pate) to Bombay, 13 Sept. 1801; petition of Bwana Kanga and Ali ibn Ahmad, 3 Oct. 1801, I.O.L., Home Miscellaneous 478.

[6] Duncan to Wellesley, 11 Nov. 1801, I.O.L., Home Miscellaneous 478.

been informed of this incident and have been worried lest the British establish themselves in East Africa. When Sultan died in 1804 his successor, Badr, immediately sent reinforcements to the Swahili Coast.[1]

There were three British visits to East Africa between 1809 and 1811. In 1809 Lt Tomkinson was sent to investigate suspicions that the French had erected stores and magazines there.[2] In 1811 Captain Beaver called at Kilwa after being informed that he might be able to purchase wood for masts and spars. He found the Sultan of Kilwa ill-disposed towards the Omanis and anxious to purchase arms and powder.[3] This, too, may have come to the notice of Muscat. At the same time the Bombay Council was developing an interest in the East African coast. The activities of Henry Salt in Abyssinia and Mozambique, and Bruce's journeys in Abyssinia, had inspired in Bombay an interest in the economic possibilities of East Africa and also a determination to enquire into the whereabouts of the source of the Nile.[4] It seemed an ideal opportunity to despatch Captain Thomas Smee on a long voyage of research to the East African coast. Smee was a discredited officer of the Bombay Marine, the further employment of whom on active service against the French was an embarrassment.[5] Smee and his companion, Lt Hardy, made extensive enquiries into political and economic matters along the Swahili Coast and also assisted some Indians in difficulties with the governor of Zanzibar.[6] When reports of this interference reached the Saiyid of Muscat he might have been suspicious of British intentions.

The revenue derived from the Swahili Coast and the close economic connexions between Oman and that region influenced the inclination of the Saiyids of Muscat to exert a firmer authority there.[7] For some time, however, they were not in a position to concentrate on East Africa, and it was not until Saiyid Sa'id had achieved relatively peaceful

---

[1] Seton to Bombay, 26 Feb. 1805, Proc. 26 Feb., B.P.S.P. 382/3.

[2] Vice-Admiral Bertie to Tomkinson, 18 May 1809, printed in G. M. Theal, *Records of Cape Colony*, 34 vols (London, 1897-1905), VI, 504; and Tomkinson's report, 7 June 1809, printed in G. M. Theal, *Records of South Eastern Africa*, 9 vols (London, 1898-1903), IX, 1-3.

[3] W. H. Smyth, *op. cit.*, p. 273.

[4] Instructions to Smee, 31 Dec. 1810, and Report by Ibrahim Purkar, 26 Feb. 1809, I.O.L., Marine Records Miscellaneous 586.

[5] Judicial Dept., Bombay, to C. of Ds., 25 Feb. 1807, L.R.B. 21; Public Dept., Bombay, to C. of D., 16 Mch. 1807 and 31 Jan. 1810, L.R.B. 22 and 23.

[6] Smee's log, entry for 1 April 1811, Marine Records Miscellaneous 586.

[7] See Chapter III.

THE SWAHILI COAST

conditions at home that he began to send military expeditions thither. His intentions were confirmed by his growing realization that the British would uphold his authority in Muscat.

There were various political matters which claimed Sa'id's attention in East Africa. Firstly, there was his rivalry with the Mazruis in Mombasa which was exacerbated by the confused situation in the Lamu archipelago, where many factions manœuvred for power. The Mazruis seized their chance to exploit the situation in the archipelago. Whereas in the past they had tried merely to influence the succession in Pate when its ruler, Fumomadi, died about 1807, they played an especially large part in the subsequent disputes. In so far as the story can be reconstructed, the Mazruis were asked to arbitrate in the Pate succession dispute, but when they failed to settle matters they gave their support to one of the candidates, Ahmad, who was thus able to overcome another candidate, Fumoluti. Fumoluti was taken as a prisoner to Mombasa.[1] This must have happened in 1810 or 1811, for when Smee was near Lamu in 1811 he hailed a boat which informed him that Sultan Ahmad, with the assistance of the chief of Mombasa, had seized his elder cousin, who had been taken to Mombasa in confinement.[2] The Mazruis took the opportunity of the succession to the Pate rulership of a candidate favourable to their interests to re-establish their garrison in Pate, which Fumomadi had removed.[3] If the Mazrui MS. is correct in its assertion that the garrison numbered 500, thereafter the Mazruis must have had considerable influence in Pate.[4]

Fumoluti's supporters fled to Lamu. That island was then attacked by the Mazruis, who were thoroughly defeated at the battle of Shela. A faction in Lamu, possibly fearing that the Mazruis would take revenge for their defeat, called upon the Saiyid of Muscat for help. Saiyid Sa'id met this request by despatching a governor and garrison to Lamu, an action which gave him a foothold in the valuable Lamu archipelago.

Smee, Owen, the Pate Chronicle, the Mazrui MS. and the Kitab al-Zunuj, tell different versions of the story. The Pate Chronicle, probably justly, attributes the Mazruis with the ambition to control Pate and Lamu. It claims that they indulged in intrigues with both islands, playing off one faction against the other. Eventually the Lamu

---

[1] Guillain, *Documents*, I, 567-8.
[2] Smee's log, entry for 18 Feb. 1811, I.O.L., Marine Records Miscellaneous 586.
[3] Mazrui MS., p. 28; *Pate Chronicle*, pp. 66-7; and Guillain, *Documents*, I, 568.
[4] Mazrui MS., p. 28.

leader discovered the plots, and his people defeated the Mazruis at the battle of Shela.[1] The Mazrui MS. dismisses the idea that the Mazruis were plotting, and finds the cause of the battle of Shela in a treaty the Mazruis had made with Sultan Ahmad which enjoined them to assist him in adversity. Such a situation arose when the Lamu inhabitants rebelled against him because he had imposed a crop tax on them. A joint Mazrui-Nabhani army attacked Lamu, 'but they were completely shattered and routed and turned their backs in flight'. Three hundred of the Mazrui-Nabhani troops were killed.[2] The Kitab al-Zunuj also says that war broke out because the people of Lamu rebelled against the Nabhani controllers of their island. The Mazrui leader in Pate, Abdullah ibn Ahmad, offered to help the people of Lamu, but, as he was secretly connected with Pate, this was a mere ruse to obtain Lamu.[3]

Despite their different accounts, all sources except the Kitab al-Zunuj agree that the Mazruis had a garrison in Pate prior to the battle of Shela, and that a Lamu faction asked the Saiyid of Muscat for help after that battle. Saiyid Sa'id, who would have been aware of the strong Mazrui influence in Pate, faced some difficulty when confronted by this appeal from Lamu. The envoy from Lamu, Abd al-Rahman ibn Nur al-Din, probably presented Sa'id with clear-cut alternatives: either he help Lamu, or the Mazruis would establish an influence there as strong as that they exercised in Pate.[4] Sa'id would have had no means of knowing whether or not this was an exaggerated version of the position. He had to make his decision on the assumption that it was true. He may also have been reminded of the ruler of Pate's appeal to the British in 1801. He possibly feared that a strong Mazrui influence in the Lamu archipelago, together with their control of Mombasa and Pemba, would threaten his own position in Zanzibar. Sa'id was alive to the dangers of losing his authority in East Africa: it might be a prelude to the collapse of his own position in Oman. His move into Lamu, therefore, was essentially a defensive measure. However, it led on to further acquisitions of territory.

[1] The *Pate Chronicle*, p. 76, dates the battle in 1812, and the Mazrui MS., p. 35, favours this dating but says that the 'people of Lamu' date the battle in 1808/9. The Mazrui MS. obtained its account of the battle from 'the works of the Lamu historian Bwana Misham ibn Kombo'. Guillain, *Documents*, I, 568, dates the battle some time between 1807 and 1811.

[2] Mazrui MS., p. 34.

[3] *Kitab al-Zunuj*, pp. 280-2.

[4] For this name of the envoy, Guillain, *Documents*, I, 568. The *Kitab al-Zunuj*, p. 282, names the envoy as Muhammad ibn Hajji al-Sa'sai.

THE SWAHILI COAST

So bound up were the politics of the two islands of Lamu and Pate that the controllers of Lamu could not be really safe without holding Pate as well. It is difficult to obtain a clear picture of the events which led to Saiyid Saʿid's acquisition of Pate because of contradictory accounts given by various sources. A succession of events can, however, be postulated. During the pro-Mazrui Sultan Ahmad's tenure of office in Pate, a faction went to Muscat for help and Saiyid Saʿid sent some soldiers. Sultan Ahmad and his Mazrui supporters were overcome and one Fumoluti, who was pro-Omani, succeeded as ruler.[1] A slightly different version has it that Sultan Ahmad died and was succeeded by Fumoluti who, being less eager to co-operate with the Mazruis, offered Saiyid Saʿid the sovereignty of Pate.[2]

Omani influence at Pate was only insecure, and Mazrui rivalry remained dangerous. When, in 1822, the ruler of Pate died, another Fumoluti from Pate, who was living in Mombasa, organized an expedition to Pate. He was aided in this by the Mazruis. Mubarak, the ruler of Mombasa's brother, headed a force of Mombasan soldiers which invaded Pate.[3] The Mazruis and their ally found, however, that Pate was not easily pacified. A faction on the island led by Bwana Mkuu, the chief elder, opposed Fumoluti's succession, preferring that of Bwana Shaikh, his brother.[4] The Omanis also took steps to regain their position on the island. The Omani governor of Lamu, who had designs on Pate, offered Saiyid Saʿid 3,000 dollars and an annual tribute of several hundred dollars if he would assist in the conquest of Pate. Saʿid agreed, and in 1822 some troops, led by Hamad ibn Ahmad Al Bu Saʿidi, came down from Muscat and defeated Mubarak and Fumoluti in Pate.[5] Mubarak returned to Mombasa.[6] Saif ibn Abdullah then became the Omani governor of Pate, but possibly a local man

---

[1] Guillain, *Documents*, I, 571.

[2] Mazrui MS., p. 43. The *Pate Chronicle*, p. 86, gives a different version which has a Bwana Shaikh calling in the Omanis.

[3] Emery to Cooley, 19 May 1835, R.G.S., Emery MS. File. Emery's version is probably the most reliable because he heard the story two years after the event. Emery gives Fumoluti's name as Fumoluti ibn Shaikh, which corresponds with a name given by the *Pate Chronicle*, p. 86.

[4] The *Pate Chronicle*, p. 86, names the man as Bwana Shaikh, whereas Emery, letter cited, calls him Bwana ibn Shaikh. Both sources make the man Fumoluti's brother.

[5] Emery, as above, gives the date but does not name the commander. The Mazrui MS., p. 43, gives the date and names the commander, as does Guillain, *Documents*, I, 572-3 which, however, calls the ruler of Pate Bwana Kombo.

[6] Mazrui MS., p. 43, and Guillain, *Documents*, I, 573.

THE EXPANSION OF OMANI INTERESTS

remained as nominal ruler: Guillain names one Sultan Ahmad the Younger.[1]

Saiyid Saʻid's involvement with Lamu had drawn him inevitably into the affairs of Pate. Whatever the exact sequence of events in this confused period, it emerges that the Saiyid of Muscat despatched two expeditions to Pate: one soon after he had garrisoned Lamu and the other in 1822. By 1824 an Omani garrison was well established in Pate.[2] Various factors had contributed to this eventual success: the presence of an Omani governor and force in neighbouring Lamu; chronic difficulties over the Pate succession which stimulated the formation of factions; the tendency of these factions to seek support outside Pate and their willingness to try alternative champions when weary with previous ones or fearful of their domination; the close relationship between factions in Lamu and Pate; and the existence of three towns on Pate island which made it possible for factions defeated in one place to retire to another and rebuild support for themselves.

By 1824, therefore, Saiyid Saʻid had control of the Lamu archipelago, an acquisition which considerably strengthened his position on the Swahili Coast and made him aware of the true influence of the Mazruis in the region. It was now almost certain that the uneasy balance on the coast, with the Mazruis in control of Mombasa and Pemba and in an influential position in the Lamu archipelago, and the Omani authorities holding Zanzibar and Kilwa, would be upset by the new Omani moves. The events in the Lamu archipelago had brought to a head a conflict which had been pending for some time. Possibly the clash might have been averted had a desire for peace been strong enough on both sides, but at that time both the Omanis and the Mazruis had ambitious leaders.

In 1814 Abdullah ibn Ahmad had succeeded as governor of Mombasa.[3] He was particularly interested in the Lamu archipelago, having at one stage been in charge of the Mazrui garrison in Pate, and having also been the leader of the Mazrui-Nabhani army at the battle of Shela.[4] It would have been with resentment that he remembered his defeat in the battle and it is likely that he determined to avenge it and reinstate Mazrui influence in the Lamu archipelago. According to the Mazrui MS., his first action on becoming governor of Mombasa was to

---

[1] Guillain, *ibid.*, p. 574. For Saif ibn Abdullah, see Emery, as above.

[2] Boteler, *op. cit.*, I, 374.

[3] Guillain, *Documents*, I, 624, quoting the date from the tomb in the Mazrui cemetery in Mombasa.

[4] Mazrui MS., pp. 33 and 42; and *Kitab al-Zunuj*, p. 280.

strengthen the fighting force by preparing munitions and appointing trained officers.[1] He also fortified Mazrui authority by despatching governors to the outlying areas under Mazrui influence.

The relationship of Abdullah ibn Ahmad and Saiyid Saʻid had had inauspicious beginnings. The governor of Mombasa was deliberately antagonistic towards the Omani authorities. In order to demonstrate his independence from Muscat he sent Saʻid a coat of mail, a measure of capacity, some powder and musket balls, thereby intimating that Saʻid was welcome to come and fight. According to one source these insulting gifts were sent at the time of Abdullah's accession, but another has it that they were despatched later as a warning to Saʻid after Fumoluti of Pate had asked Muscat for help, and Saʻid had told Mombasa not to interfere in Pate's affairs.[2] In Guillain's opinion, Abdullah's action marked a declaration of independence by Mombasa from Oman, particularly since at that point the governor ceased to send annual presents to Muscat. Whether or not Guillain is correct in thinking that Mombasa sent such yearly presents or tribute to Muscat is important because, if this was the case, Saʻid would have had added reason to resent Mazrui power when such tribute ceased. Two local sources mention that Abdullah did cease to send annual tribute to Muscat, and there is also the statement in the Kitab al-Zunuj that in 1739/40 the Mazruis leased Mombasa from the Imam.[3] In 1826 an Arab account of Muscat claimed:

'... from the period of the invasion of the Persians Mombasa and those parts have not been in such complete subjection as before, yet never asserted their independence and were until lately accustomed to send a yearly tribute to the Imam.'[4]

On the other hand, in 1804 Dallons reported that Mombasa was not 'subject' to Oman, and this may possibly have meant that its governor sent no tribute.[5] This is borne out by an investigation made by Bombay

---

[1] Mazrui MS., p. 39.

[2] Guillain, *Documents*, I, 569; and Mazrui MS., p. 43. The latter does not appear to have obtained the story from the former, for it names the bearer of the articles.

[3] *Kitab al-Zunuj*, p. 276. The two local sources are 'A History of Africa' recorded by Shaikh Hemedi ibn Abdullah of Tangata in July 1914, printed in *T.N.R.*, no. 32 (Jan. 1952), pp. 65-82, and *Asili ya Mvita*.

[4] A translated account of the Muscat family received by the Persian Secretary, Proc. 5 Apr. 1826, B.P.C. 386/6.

[5] Report by Dallons printed in Freeman-Grenville, *Select Documents*, p. 198.

THE EXPANSION OF OMANI INTERESTS

in 1824 during which the Persian Secretary was told 'by someone who had visited the East African Coast twenty years ago' that Mombasa was an independent principality governed by a chief of its own who paid no tribute to Muscat.[1]

Saiyid Sa'id gradually came to the conclusion that he must limit Mazrui power. His most provocative action to attain this end was the Omani taking of Pemba, which seriously affected the political position of the Mazruis. The Omanis were encouraged to take Pemba when two notables of that island, Ngwachani and Athmani, visited Muscat to seek help against their Mazrui governor. Saiyid Sa'id agreed to their proposal for a compact. It was arranged that,

'if the Saiyid should expel the Mazruis, they will be his allies and will be of one accord with him; and that they will make their people pay dues to the Saiyid. . . .'[2]

Either Saiyid Sa'id then ordered the governor of Zanzibar to seize Pemba from the Mazruis, or the governor captured it on his own initiative. To do this he chose the moment of the Mazrui governor of Pemba's annual visit to Mombasa in 1822. Mubarak ibn Ahmad al-Mazrui, the governor of Pemba, immediately tried to retake the island, but he was forced to make terms and retire. Mombasa refused to accept defeat and despatched another expedition to Pemba, but by this time the commander of the Omani force which had come to attack Pate, having completed his task there, had arrived in Pemba with reinforcements.[3] The Omanis were aided while establishing themselves in Pemba by the collaboration of Nasir ibn Sulaiman, a powerful local notable, who doubtless had his eye on the governorship under the Omanis, and was, indeed, given it.[4]

The Pemba incident was severely distorted in the Omani reports to Bombay protesting against later British assistance to the Mazruis. In 1823 Saiyid Sa'id urged as evidence of the Mazrui rebellion against him the claim that the Mazruis had attacked Pemba, which belonged to him.

[1] Report by the Persian Secretary on the rights of Muscat to the allegiance of Mombasa, Proc. 1 Dec. 1824, B.P.C. 385/53.
[2] Ndagoni Chronicle III, written on 13 July 1851. Peace Memorial Museum, Zanzibar. It is also printed in *Swahili*, vol. XXX (1959), p. 32.
[3] Guillain, *Documents*, I, 574.
[4] Nasir ibn Sulaiman al-Maskari, 'élevé et enrichi par les bienfaits des M'zara [Mazrui], et qui, oubliant toute gratitude, avait contribué, par ses intelligences avec le chef de Zanzibar, à leur faire perdre cette île, fut, en récompense de sa défection, investi du gouvernement de Pemba.' – *Ibid.*, p. 575.

His story was that the people of Pate had asked for his aid in opposing the aggressions of the Mazruis; Mombasa boats had blockaded Pate and Lamu, but were compelled to retreat by the Omani forces; on the way back to Mombasa they fell on Pemba, plundered the island, killed several Omanis, and held possession until driven out by fresh forces from Muscat.[1] This misrepresentation of what had happened was designed to gain Bombay's sympathy. It was balanced by a Mazrui account given to Bombay. The Mazruis said that Saiyid Sa'id had occupied Lamu on its people's request, and had then demanded the surrender of Pate, which at that time they themselves held. The Mazruis refused to surrender Pate, and in the ensuing conflict many Mombasa boats were destroyed by the Omani ships. Saiyid Sa'id proposed that, if the Mazruis gave him Pate, he would desist from any operations against Mombasa itself. The Mazrui account added that this letter was at Mombasa with Saiyid Sa'id's seal upon it. But, as soon as the Mombasans retired, the Omanis took possession of Pemba, which belonged to Mombasa. Because of this treachery, the Mazruis had decided to seek the aid of the British.[2]

Both of these accounts are subject to bias, but there is other evidence which shows that the Mazruis were in possession of Pemba before it was taken by the Omanis. Saiyid Sa'id's claim that the Mazruis had plundered the island was a distortion of their expeditions, described by Guillain, to regain Pemba. The Omani capture of Pemba did not, however, mean that Mombasa's links with that island were severed. The regular trade between Pemba and Mombasa, particularly in grain, continued. Almost every day Emery recorded the arrival in or departure from Mombasa of vessels for Pemba.[3] The people of Mombasa complained that the grain and cattle they owned on Pemba had been taken from them by Saiyid Sa'id's people, but when Captain Owen went to investigate he reported that the Mombasans had been returned all their private property.[4] While the British maintained their Establishment at Mombasa they kept the peace between Mombasa and Pemba. Owen arranged that the Mombasans should be allowed free ingress and egress to and from Pemba and should be able to enjoy

[1] Saiyid Sa'id to Bombay, 29 Oct. 1824, Proc. 1 Dec., B.P.C. 385/53; and Report by the Persian Secretary on the rights of Muscat to the allegiance of Mombasa, Proc. 1 Dec. 1824, B.P.C. idem.

[2] Statement of Salim ibn Rashid al-Mazrui of Mombasa, B.P.C. 385/53.

[3] Emery's Journal, entries for, e.g. 14, 27 Sept., 5, 11 Oct., 4, 5, 26, 29 Nov., 7, 10 Dec. 1824.

[4] Ibid., entries for 24 Jan. and 9 Feb. 1825.

property and commerce there.¹ The governor of Pemba's wife, in confinement at Mombasa, was restored to him, and the British mediated when the cargo of a Pemba vessel was seized.² The Mombasans did, however, have certain cause for resentment in that they had to pay dues to the governor of Pemba and their vessels had to carry passes in order to trade there.³ Although the Mombasans suffered little commercially from their loss of Pemba, politically they were in a weaker position. In November 1825, some inhabitants of Mombasa, discontented with the political situation there, wrote to the governor of Pemba suggesting that this would be a good time to invade Mombasa.⁴

Was the capture of Pemba a cleverly planned strategic move by the Saiyid of Muscat? Although it had such happy results for him, it seems that the taking of Pemba was not directly ordered. The governor of Zanzibar made the initial moves, and he was then supported by the Omani commander who was at Pate. Guillain implies that the commander only went to Pemba when he had heard that the governor of Zanzibar had attacked the island.⁵ On the other hand, the Pemba delegation had been recently in Oman asking for help. Whether or not Saiyid Sa'id ordered the taking of Pemba is important; if he did, this might have represented a clear decision on his part to oust the Mazruis from their position of power on the East African coast and strengthen his own authority there.

Probably Sa'id gave general instructions to his commanders to reduce the Mazruis, and left them to work out the details as to how this was to be done, and to follow up opportunities as they arose. For example, the commander of some ships Sa'id despatched in 1823 to blockade Mombasa performed other activities on behalf of Saiyid Sa'id. On his way southwards the commander, Abdullah ibn Sulaiyim, anchored at Mogadishu and seized some men, later ransoming them at Zanzibar for 2,000 dollars.⁶

Brava and Marka had in fact submitted to Saiyid Sa'id in 1822 when Hamad ibn Ahmad, commander of the troops sent to fight Pate, had watered there and compelled the inhabitants to accept Muscat's authority.⁷ However, in 1823 at none of the three Banadir towns were

¹ *Ibid.*, entry for 16 Feb. 1825.
² *Ibid.*, entries for 24 Jan., 31 Mch., 18, 19 Apr., and 16 May 1825.
³ *Ibid.*, entries for 16 Feb. and 2 Sept. 1825.
⁴ *Ibid.*, entry for 6 Nov. 1825.
⁵ Guillain, *Documents*, I, 574-6.
⁶ *Ibid.*, I, 582; and Owen, *op. cit.*, I, 359. See also Chapter XI, p. 297.
⁷ Guillain, *Documents*, I, 572-3; and Owen, *op. cit.*, I, 355.

soldiers left or governors appointed. As yet Saʻid's interest in them was peripheral, for there were more important places to secure further southwards. At the same time as his troops were attacking Pate his influence was being extended along the Mrima coast. When Boteler surveyed this coast in 1824 he reported that Saiyid Saʻid's forces had been harassing Wasin and Tanga. The governor of Zanzibar took an active part in this, for it was he who originally attacked Wasin, robbing the inhabitants of their vessels, slaves and other property. When Saʻid's forces called at Wasin, they found it deserted but none the less sacked the town.[1] As the Mazruis had formerly exercised some control over Wasin, the activities of the governor of Zanzibar and the Omani forces may have been part of the general anti-Mazrui policy.

The sultan found it easier to control the coast south of Wasin than he did the northern part. There were close commercial connexions between the southern region and Zanzibar. In 1824 Boteler, surveying the coastline for eighty miles south of the River Pangani, reported that the many littoral villages waved their red flag (the Omani flag) as an invitation to land and that the inhabitants were 'subject to the Imaum's power'.[2] In return for a payment of 6,000 dollars a year, Saiyid Saʻid rented to an Arab the right of levying taxes along the coast from Kilwa to Kwale,[3] and he also maintained governors at Kilwa Kisiwani, Mafia, Kilwa Kivinje and Lindi.[4] It is not known when governors were appointed to the two latter places, but that of Kilwa Kivinje was already present in 1819.[5]

As governor of Mafia, Saiyid Saʻid appointed Muhammad ibn Jumʻah al-Barvani Al Harthi, a member of a powerful old-established Zanzibar family. By 1818 he had been succeeded by his son, Nasir.[6] That year Mafia was pillaged by the Betsimisaraka of Madagascar.[7] Many Mafians were killed and the rest fled to Zanzibar.[8] The governor

---

[1] Boteler, *op. cit.*, II, 178. See also Chapter XI, p. 313.

[2] *Ibid.*, II, 28; and Owen, *op. cit.*, I, 429. Owen has the word 'red' before 'flag', whereas Boteler does not. However, Owen's editor is quoting from Boteler's journal at this point because it was Boteler, and not Owen, who visited this region, and it is unlikely that the editor would have inserted the word.

[3] Loarer's Report, Part I, 1849, M.O., O.I. 5/23.

[4] Boteler, *op. cit.*, II, 48.

[5] Albrand's Report, 1819, M.O., Réunion 72/472.

[6] 'History and traditions of Mafia', collected by *qadhi* Amr Umar Saʻadi, printed in *T.N.R.*, no. 12 (Dec. 1941), pp. 23-7, here p. 25.

[7] *Ibid.*, giving no date for the incident; Loarer's Report, Part II, 1849, M.O., O.I. 2/10; and Owen, *op. cit.*, I, 372.   [8] Loarer, *idem.*

THE EXPANSION OF OMANI INTERESTS

of Zanzibar came to the assistance of the Mafians, despatching a force of Baluchis, Bajun, and Arabs from the Hadramaut, which defeated the invaders.[1] At the head of this relieving force was Abdullah ibn Jum'ah, the previous governor of Mafia's brother.[2] It is possible that Abdullah was himself governor of Zanzibar at this time.[3] In any case, this action to help the Mafians would have strengthened the Omani hold on Mafia, and the prestige of the Omanis on the coast as a whole.

Fairly secure on the southern section of the coastline, but still threatened by the Mazruis on the northern, Saiyid Sa'id had problems enough in East Africa without the intervention of the Europeans. During these years, however, European interest in the Swahili coastline increased. In 1819 the French, looking for a new naval base, arranged a treaty with the sultanate family of Kilwa Kisiwani.[4] Saiyid Sa'id was probably not unaware of these intrigues, particularly as the negotiators visited Zanzibar immediately afterwards and asked many questions about its history. He was probably also aware of danger from another source: Abdullah ibn Jum'ah al-Barvani Al Harthi, who had led the relief force to Mafia. Abdullah had been appointed governor of Zanzibar by Sa'id, probably in an attempt to draw the old families into the administration and thus prevent their alienation. Soon after his appointment Abdullah was removed by Sa'id because, according to the governor of Bourbon, his great riches and spirit of intrigue had given offence.[5] When Vandries, an inhabitant of Bourbon, visited Zanzibar in 1821, Abdullah, obviously hoping to regain his position, told him that he would be willing to see Zanzibar under French rule. Abdullah gave Vandries a letter to this effect to deliver to the governor of Bourbon.[6]

The possibility of Europeans lending assistance to his enemies would have seriously worried Saiyid Sa'id. His fears had substance because, shortly afterwards, the British came to the active help of the Mazruis. The occasion for this was the Mazruis' loss of Pemba, which left them in an awkward political position and caused them to fall back on the expedient of calling for outside aid. They made a tentative attempt to

[1] As note 7, p. 130.   [2] Amr Umar Sa'adi, op. cit.
[3] Freycinet to Ministry of Marine, 9 May 1821, M.O., Réunion 72/472.
[4] See Chapter VI, p. 135.
[5] As note 3. See also Chapter VI, p. 138.
[6] Idem; Vandries to Philibert, Deputy at Bourbon, Feb. 1822, M.O., O.I. 17/89; and Abdullah Al Harthi to governor of Bourbon, 3 Apr. 1821, M.O., Réunion 72/472.

THE SWAHILI COAST

obtain French help in 1822,[1] but their final choice of champion was influenced by a member of the Johanna royal family who happened to be passing through Mombasa on his way to Bombay.[2] For more than twenty years the Johanna rulers had been requesting the intervention of the British in their succession squabbles, and had sent numerous delegations to Bombay. Bombay, embarrassed, but not wanting to alienate Johanna because British ships sometimes watered there, had paid the expenses of the delegations' stays in Bombay and had politely shipped them home as soon as possible with tactful replies. Sa'id Umar, the late ruler of Johanna's nephew, obviously encouraged Mombasa to imitate his policy. Abdullah, the Mombasa governor, complained to Bombay that Saiyid Sa'id wanted to get possession of his country, but 'to him I will not give it, but to the king of England'.[3] He asked for a Union Jack to be sent to him to hoist. This request was shortly after followed by another, taken personally this time by a Mazrui delegation. Mombasa offered the British

'half the produce of this island, consisting of elephants' teeth, shells, chundroos wheat, cattle, sheep, jowaree, rice and other grain'.

They suggested an agent be despatched to Mombasa to accept the British share of the revenues.[4] The Bombay Council was used to dealing with such suggestions because of the Johanna model. Almost without a second thought, Elphinstone[5] gave the usual reply: it was contrary to the British policy to enter into such intimate connexions in Africa. But, coincidentally, a British naval ship was carrying out a survey of the East African coast, and what Sa'id had most feared did in fact occur—the Mazruis appealed to the captain, W. F. Owen, to take Mombasa under British protection. The Union Jack was raised above Mombasa fort.[6] The expedition Sa'id had sent to Mombasa to reduce it to allegiance could do nothing when it saw the British flag. For three years Sa'id protested to the British about this breach of faith. The British presence in Mombasa, and Sa'id's agitation against it, emphasized the Saiyid of Muscat's determination to strengthen his authority in East Africa.

---

[1] Vandries to Philibert, Feb. 1822, M.O., O.I. 17/89.

[2] Abdullah ibn Ahmad al-Mazrui, governor of Mombasa, to Elphinstone, 24 Apr. 1823, Proc. 1 Dec. 1824, B.P.C. 385/53.   [3] *Idem.*

[4] Sulaiman ibn Ali, governor of Mombasa, to Elphinstone, 18 Sept. 1823, Proc. 1 Dec. 1824, B.P.C. 385/53.

[5] Mountstuart Elphinstone had succeeded Sir Evan Nepean as governor of Bombay in 1819.

[6] See Chapter VI, pp. 139-42.

THE EXPANSION OF OMANI INTERESTS

The Omanis did not become suddenly interested in the East African coast. They had held Zanzibar for more than a century before any real attempt was made to expand their influence on the coast. That such an expansion occurred was due to Saiyid Sa'id's opinion that the political situation had changed on the coast and his suspicion that the change would adversely affect the Omani position there. It seemed important to oppose the supposed Mazrui aggrandizement, because East Africa played a prominent part in the Omani economic system, and because the area might become a base for opposition to the internal Omani regime. Lamu's request for help was the occasion for expansion. Saiyid Sa'id's granting of aid to Lamu was a defensive measure, but subsequent defensive measures, such as the taking of Pate and Pemba, evolved into the aggressive policy of removing the Mazruis from their position and expanding Omani influence up and down the coast. Once Sa'id and the Mazruis became suspicious of each other's intentions, both became more aggressive. It is unlikely that Sa'id originally made a definite decision to expand in East Africa. It is much more likely that, as the years went by, so his involvement with the Swahili Coast developed its own momentum, and that, combined with a feeling of growing security in Oman itself, this produced an ever-increasing interest and implication in the problems and opportunities of East Africa. By 1820 the Qawasim danger was over, and so was that from the Wahhabis. Sa'id was fairly confident that the British would uphold his regime in Muscat. It is significant that the following years of 1822 and 1823 were years of great activity on the Swahili Coast for Sa'id. Pate, Mogadishu, Brava, Marka, Pemba, Wasin, and Tanga all submitted to Sa'id in varying degrees. Shortly afterwards the interference of the Europeans confirmed Sa'id in a conclusion which he had been slowly reaching for some time: that he must subdue the Mazruis and further emphasize his authority on the Swahili Coast. It was but a short step to developing a policy of aggressive expansion and economic exploitation in the region.

CHAPTER VI

SAIYID SA'ID AND THE WESTERN POWERS, 1819-1839

The extent to which Saiyid Sa'id's interest in the Swahili Coast was initially stimulated by European activities has already been described in Chapter V. It is now necessary to examine how far the development of these European activities continued to influence him in his policy there. In addition, European interests in Oman and the Persian Gulf had a great effect on the shaping of Sa'id's East African policies.

After 1819 Saiyid Sa'id was worried by French interest in the Swahili Coast. Rebellious elements there sought French support against him, and initially it appeared that the rebels might receive such assistance. Even though Sa'id had indicated during the Napoleonic Wars that he would not exclude the French from his commercial activities nor treat them as enemies, at the end of the war the French did not at first look upon him as a possible ally. His position in East Africa blocked their ambitions there. Ile de France had not been returned to them in the Treaty of Paris, and Bourbon, which they did regain, had a harbour wholly inadequate in the hurricane season.[1] They therefore looked to East Africa for alternative harbours. They saw their chance when the sultan of Kilwa, in unwilling subjection to Saiyid Sa'id, told the French that the Omanis had seized Zanzibar from him. Should the French help him regain it from the usurpers, he promised to cede the island in all sovereignty to them. Sausse, the captain of a merchant ship from Bourbon, to whom this offer was made, relayed it to the governor of Bourbon and the Ministry of Marine, adding that Kilwa harbour could

---

[1] For example, in December 1818, during a great storm all the ships in Bourbon harbour had to hoist sail – Milius, governor of Bourbon, to Ministry of Marine, no. 240, 1 Feb. 1819, M.O., Réunion 72/472.

contain sixty ships, and Zanzibar 500.¹ The *Ministère de la Maison du Roi*, to whom the offer was passed, expressed guarded interest, but feared the British reaction:

'Voudront-ils que nous élevions la colonie de Zanzibar sur les ruines de l'île de France qui leur a fait tant de mal pendant la dernière guerre, et qu'ils ont mis tant d'importance à nous enlever?'²

He also thought it likely that the Portuguese would still claim this part of the coast.³ It was decided to send a naval vessel, *L'Amaranthe*, to Kilwa to make further enquiries. Aboard *L'Amaranthe* were Sausse and Albrand, a student of oriental languages.⁴ The sultan of Kilwa was to be given powder and guns and to be persuaded to arrange a treaty. On the arrival of the French vessel, the sultan who had made the offer to Sausse was found to have died, but his relations were no less willing to strike a blow at the Zanzibar Arabs. It was agreed that the King of France should deliver the sultan of Kilwa from the yoke of the Arabs and protect him henceforth against them. In return the sultan would give the king of France to enjoy, in all sovereignty and ownership, the islands of Zanzibar and Mafia, which were formerly subject to Kilwa, and as soon as the sultan of Kilwa became independent again he would allow the French exclusive commerce with all the countries in his power.⁵ There was also a verbal promise that a third island, Pemba, would be ceded to France.⁶ The original of the treaty, in Arabic,

---

[1] Sausse to Minister of Marine, 15 Nov. 1817, M.O., Réunion 72/472.

[2] Ministère de la Maison du Roi to Minister of Marine, 16 Mch. 1818, M.O., Réunion 72/472.

[3] *Idem*. The central government was amazingly ignorant about the East African coast. It seemed to be unaware of the suggestions of Morice and others in the 1770s and 1780s, and did not consult the documents pertaining to them.

[4] Milius, the governor of Bourbon, thought little of Sausse – he said he had received bad reports of his morality: Milius to Minister of Marine, 1 Feb. 1819, no. 240, M.O., Réunion 72/472. Before he came to Bourbon, Sausse had lived at Ile de France. On one of his voyages he put into the Seychelles with a ship full of slaves. They were taken from him but he stole them back and took them to Mauritius to sell. This was all done under the British flag. The governor of Mauritius demanded that Milius surrender Sausse, but Milius refused because Sausse held the secret of the Kilwa treaty – Report of Ministry of Marine and Colonies, 5 Jan. 1820, M.O., Réunion 72/472.

[5] Treaty between the princes of Kilwa, Sausse, and Albrand, 23 Mch. 1819, M.O., Réunion 72/472.

[6] Report to the *Conseil des Ministres*, Dec. 1819, M.O., Réunion 72/472.

remained in Sausse's hands. The princes of Kilwa were not allowed to retain a copy[1] – presumably for fear they would show it to the English.

From Kilwa *L'Amaranthe* went to Zanzibar, and discovered that the Arabs' claim to it was not as shallow as the Kilwans had made out. Albrand was nevertheless eager to carry out the original plan. A colony at Zanzibar, he maintained, would offer military and agricultural advantages. Zanzibar was situated at an equal distance from the Red Sea, the coast of Malabar, and the Mozambique channel. From this base, the French could cover the seas with corsairs and close the channel passage to British commerce. There they could gather stores of arms, and, at the first signal of war, could ravage Malabar. Provisions were obtainable from the mainland, and there was a good harbour which could provide shelter in storms. Zanzibar could also be a point of departure for scientific expeditions to the interior; until then, explorations into tropical Africa had all been carried out by the British from the west side of the continent – 'n'est-il pas de la gloire de la France de prendre enfin part à ces nobles et utiles tentatives?' The British, of course, might be a problem, but in his enthusiasm Albrand dismissed them. He said:

'Dépouillée de tous ses établissements dans l'Inde, il est juste, il est necessaire (et toute l'Europe le jugera ainsi) qu'elle [la France] se crée un Port dans les mers Orientales, et qu'elle assure un asyle à ses navires dans la mauvaise saison.'[2]

At first Milius, the governor of Bourbon, was equally enthusiastic:

'Je pense ... qu'elle ne pourra jamais saisir une plus belle occasion de fonder une nouvelle colonie que celle qui se présente aujourd'hui.'[3]

He even worked out the number of men and ships which would be needed.[4]

The plan was eventually abandoned for the very reason which had inspired Albrand – the British position in the Indian Ocean. The Ministry of Marine warned the *Conseil des Ministres*, who had to make the final decision, that the Arabs would apply for British protection.[5] They added that the project nevertheless presented great advantages.

[1] Report to the *Conseil des Ministres*, Dec. 1819, M.O., Réunion 72/472.
[2] Albrand to Milius, 1 June 1819, M.O., Réunion 72/472.
[3] Milius to Ministry of Marine, no. 468, June 1819, M.O., Réunion 72/472.
[4] *Idem.*
[5] Report to the *Conseil des Ministres*, Dec. 1819, M.O., Réunion 72/472.

SAIYID SA'ID AND THE WESTERN POWERS, 1819-1839

In any case Milius lost his original enthusiasm when it occurred to him that Saiyid Sa'id could be a more useful ally than an enemy in East Africa.¹ What had happened to make him change his mind? At the same time as *L'Amaranthe* had sailed to Kilwa and Zanzibar, *La Zelée* had been despatched to Muscat from Bourbon.² Milius intended *La Zelée* to open commercial relations: although he was at the time toying with the idea of taking Zanzibar from Sa'id, there was no reason why the commercial activities which had existed during the Napoleonic Wars should not be renewed. The Zanzibar plan might come to nothing. *La Zelée* got a most favourable reception at Muscat,³ and returned with animals and products of Oman which sold well at Bourbon.⁴ This, combined with the receipt of Albrand's report about the strong position of the Omanis at Zanzibar, must have led Milius to decide that it would be wiser to co-operate with Sa'id than to attack one of his possessions:

'Attendu nos relations amicales avec ce gouvernement [Muscat], on ne pourrait guère songer à s'emparer de vive force de pays que lui appartiennent.'⁵

It seems that Sa'id sent his brother Ahmad to Bourbon to negotiate a commercial arrangement at this time, and this must have further deterred any plans for an attack on Zanzibar.⁶ Moreover, the French had renewed their interest in Madagascar – a place which might provide the harbour they needed. In 1821 Sainte Marie was re-occupied, and a few men were sent to Fort Dauphin.⁷

¹ Note by Milius in Ministry of Marine and Colonies, 22 Nov. 1821. M.O., Réunion 72/472. Milius had returned to France by now and was being consulted on the project by the Ministry of Marine.
² Report to *Conseil des Ministres*, Dec. 1819, and Milius to Ministry of Marine, no. 240, Feb. 1819, M.O., Réunion 72/472.
³ Report to *Conseil des Ministres*, Dec. 1819, M.O., Réunion 72/472.
⁴ Guillain, *Documents*, II, 212.
⁵ Report to *Conseil des Ministres*, quoting Milius, Dec. 1819, M.O., Réunion 72/472.
⁶ For Ahmad's presence in Bourbon, see Freycinet to Ministry of Marine, 30 Sept. 1822, M.O., Réunion 72/472. Guillain (*Documents*, II, 212), says that in 1822 a treaty was signed between Muscat and Bourbon. Probably Ahmad negotiated this. In 1825 the British Resident in the Persian Gulf obtained a letter from the French Ministry of Marine to Saiyid Sa'id which said that Sa'id's brother had been to Bourbon to establish intimate relations between the two countries – Resident in the Persian Gulf to Bombay, 11 Dec. 1825, Proc. 11 Jan. 1826, B.P.C. 386/3.
⁷ Hubert Deschamps, *Histoire de Madagascar* (Paris, 1965), p. 156.

Milius' successor, Freycinet, decided that co-operation with Saiyid Sa'id was a wiser course than an attack on Zanzibar. When Sa'id deposed Abdullah ibn Jum'ah al-Barvani Al Harthi from his position as governor of Zanzibar, the fallen official offered to give the French Zanzibar if they would help him regain his post.[1] Freycinet was unwilling to consider the proposal.[2] This was probably not because he regarded Sa'id as too valuable an ally to lose, but, as he himself said, it would be unwise, considering the state of European politics at the time, for the French to take Zanzibar, which he thought the British wanted for themselves. Recently the British had bombarded Mocha after their agent was badly treated there. Freycinet saw this, as well as the 1819 attack on the Persian Gulf pirates, as evidence of a grand design by the British to link their possessions of Malabar with those of the Cape of Good Hope. Within a few years Muscat, Mocha, Zanzibar, Madagascar, Kilwa, Johanna, and Mozambique, would form 'cette jonction redoutable'.[3]

Bearing the opinions of Freycinet and Milius[4] in mind, the Ministry of Marine decided to abandon the Zanzibar project. They argued that since Zanzibar was the principal entrepot for slaves, doubtless the British wanted the island for themselves; and that in any case the new relationship with Saiyid Sa'id precluded an attack on one of his possessions. Nevertheless, the sultan of Kilwa and Abdullah Al Harthi should be encouraged in their favourable disposition towards the French.[5] In other words the French were not committing themselves either way, and in the future would be able to support the party which most suited them.

Saiyid Sa'id would not have been unaware of the likelihood of rebellious elements applying to the French for aid during these years, and he was probably apprehensive of the possible consequences of French interest in the Swahili Coast. It therefore would have been with some relief that he observed the French attempts to co-operate with him: he took full advantage of these by arranging the commercial treaty. It is significant that it was in these years that Sa'id began to consolidate his position on the Swahili Coast.

[1] Abdullah to governor of Bourbon, 3 Apr. 1821, M.O., Réunion 72/472.
[2] Freycinet to Ministry of Marine, 9 May 1821, M.O., Réunion 72/472.
[3] *Idem.*
[4] 'Projet de livrer l'île de Zanzibar au français', by Milius, M.O., Réunion 72/472.
[5] Decision by Ministry of Marine, 16 May 1822, M.O., Réunion 72/472.

SAIYID SAʻID AND THE WESTERN POWERS, 1819-1839

Saiyid Saʻid was further encouraged to extend his control on the Swahili Coast by the expansion of British activities in the region in the early 1820s and by active British pressures upon him. British attention was drawn to East Africa in these years, because it was the principal source for the Indian Ocean Slave Trade.[1] In 1821 Moresby was in Zanzibar waters investigating that trade, and the following year he went to Muscat to arrange a treaty with Saiyid Saʻid. The treaty helped to confirm Saʻid's authority on the East African coast by making him a contractual party for the area. At the same time it gave the British an interest in propping up their collaborator, because a replacement might not be so co-operative about the Slave Trade.

The British were therefore put into a quandary when Captain W. F. Owen, on a hydrographical survey of East African waters, took Mombasa under British protection. Owen's expedition had been despatched not, as has been suggested,[2] because there was new interest in East African commerce, but because accurate maps of East African waters were lacking. This was the great age of surveying by the Admiralty Hydrographical Department.[3] Barrow, the Second Secretary to the Admiralty, was very interested in East Africa because it was one of the gaps in geographical knowledge.[4] Owen's mission was merely designed to complete the systematic survey of all the coasts of Africa, and to continue the work of William Walker, of H.M.S. *Dispatch*, who in 1817-18 had surveyed the east coast from the Cape to Algoa Bay.[5]

Owen had first become aware of the political situation in East Africa when he went to Bombay to get letters of recommendation to the rulers whose lands he would visit. His arrival there coincided with the visit of a Mazrui delegation from Mombasa seeking British aid against Saiyid Saʻid. Owen, although he had no orders on the subject, took it on his own initiative to combine surveying with a personal campaign against the Slave Trade. He talked with the Mazrui delegation at

---

[1] For a detailed discussion of the Swahili Coast Slave Trade and the British campaign against it, see Chapters VIII and IX.

[2] For example, by M. V. Jackson Haight, *European Powers and South East Africa* (London, 1967), pp. 172-4 [this book is a revised edition of M. V. Jackson, *European Powers and South East Africa* (London, 1942).]

[3] See W. A. Spray, 'Surveying and Charting the Indian Ocean: the British contribution 1750-1838' (London University Ph.D. thesis, 1966).

[4] R. C. Bridges, 'The British Exploration of East Africa 1788-1885' (London University Ph.D. thesis, 1963), Chapter 2.

[5] Spray, *op. cit.*, p. 261.

THE SWAHILI COAST

Bombay, tried to get Elphinstone, the governor of Bombay, to agree to its suggestions, and, when he failed, determined to accede to Mombasa's request on his arrival there.¹ Perhaps he thought that if he presented Bombay with a *fait accompli*, it would not be able to repudiate his actions.

When Owen reached Mombasa in 1824, he did what he had planned.² The British flag was hoisted and Owen prepared plans to eliminate the trade in slaves. He appealed for support to the governor of Mauritius, Sir Lowry Cole, but Cole said he would have to refer the matter to England.³ He was embarrassed by Owen's bringing to Mauritius Mubarak, a former governor of Mombasa's son. Owen also went to Pemba and tried to bring about its return to the Mazruis, and he ordered the governor of Zanzibar to prohibit the Slave Trade entirely.⁴ Saiyid Sa'id had sent an expedition to attack Mombasa in 1823, but it could do nothing when it found the British had taken possession.⁵

Saiyid Sa'id was irate, particularly as he himself had given Owen recommendations of safe passage on the East African coast.⁶ He remonstrated severely with Bombay, giving an exaggerated account of Owen's actions. He claimed that Mombasa had always belonged to him:

'It is commonly notorious that the people of Bombasa [sic] are dependents of Oman, and that their *wali* derives his office from Oman, but for some time past we have winked at their acts, and this they ascribe to weakness on our part.'⁷

---

¹ Sir John Gray, *The British in Mombasa, 1824-1826* (London, 1957), p. 31. Owen's actions and the taking of Mombasa will not be described in detail because the incident has been considered at length in Gray's book. See also above, Chapter V, p. 132.

² Owen to Moorsom, 21 Feb. 1824, P.R.O. Adm. 1/69.

³ Sir Lowry Cole to Sulaiman ibn Ali, governor of Mombasa, July 1824, Proc. 1 Dec. 1824, B.P.C. 385/53.

⁴ Saiyid Sa'id to Bombay, 29 Oct. 1824, Proc. 1 Dec., B.P.C. 385/53; Owen, *op. cit.*, I, 364; Saiyid Sa'id to king of England, n.d., Proc. 19 Jan. 1825, B.P.C. 385/55; Resident, Persian Gulf, to Bombay, 14 May 1825, Proc. 8 June; Governor of Zanzibar to Saiyid Sa'id, n.d., Proc. 8 June; and Nasir ibn Sulaiman, governor of Pemba, to Saiyid Sa'id, 12 May 1825, Proc. 8 June – all from B.P.C. 385/60.

⁵ Saiyid Sa'id to Bombay, 29 Oct. 1824, Proc. 1 Dec., B.P.C. 385/53; Owen, *op. cit.*, I, 367.

⁶ Saiyid Sa'id to king of England, n.d., Proc. 19 Jan. 1825, B.P.C. 385/55; Owen, *op. cit.*, I, 343.

⁷ Saiyid Sa'id to Bombay, 29 Oct. 1824, Proc. 1 Dec., B.P.C. 385/53.

SAIYID SA'ID AND THE WESTERN POWERS, 1819-1839

Bombay had heard Mombasa's side of the argument from the reports of the recent Mazrui delegation, and the Presidency tried to make a fair judgment.[1] This prompted yet another enquiry into the nature of the connexion between the British and the Omanis, and their obligations towards each other. Elphinstone heard for the first time about the existence of the 1798 and 1800 agreements with Oman, and the 'friends and enemies' clause. He could not imagine any ground for entering into such an engagement; but he could not deny that the negotiations had been carried out by an authorized agent, and that they had been ratified. He had the effrontery to remark:

'it is not surprising, considering the inaccurate habits of his nation, that the Imam should have only a vague notion of the existence of this treaty'.[2]

Elphinstone read the 1798 agreement as meaning that Britain should help the Saiyid of Muscat by sea, though not by land, 'as the treaty never could have intended the Imam to send troops into the heart of India or us into the deserts of Arabia'. As usual, Warden, a member of the Bombay Council, was opposed to giving Sa'id any help. He used the 1807 argument that the treaty had never been fulfilled by Sa'id and therefore was not binding on the British Government.[3] Ultimately Elphinstone decided that the treaty was binding, but that it had a narrower sense than the Bombay Council had understood in 1807. None the less, even according to the narrowest sense of the treaty, it restrained the British from joining Sa'id's enemies against him. The claims Sa'id had on the British because 'he has always been our faithful and cordial ally' should also be borne in mind.[4]

---

[1] Statement by Salim ibn Rashid al-Mazrui, Proc. 1 Dec. 1824, B.P.C. 385/53.

[2] Minute by Elphinstone, 14 Jan. 1826, Proc. 15 Feb., B.P.C. 386/4.

[3] Minute by Warden, Proc. 15 Feb. 1826, B.P.C. 386/4. Warden told Elphinstone that the 1798 and 1800 engagements had not been entirely forgotten by the Bombay Council – he had alluded to them in the 1819 discussions concerning the pirates. Warden tried to argue that the treaty was invalid because Saiyid Sa'id had not openly confirmed it; indeed, he seemed to be unaware of its existence. Elphinstone disagreed – he said he had always wondered why Sa'id so invariably conformed to the wishes of the British, and his knowledge of the engagement, even though vague, must have been the reason. – Minute by Elphinstone, 30 Jan. 1826, Proc. 15 Feb., B.P.C. 386/4.

[4] Minute by Elphinstone, *idem*.

THE SWAHILI COAST

This opinion was transmitted to England, but the British Government by that time had decided to repudiate Owen's actions. They had already received a report from Captain Moorsom that the Mazruis had changed their minds and no longer wanted the British in Mombasa.[1] The Mazruis had not expected the commander of the British Establishment to interfere to such an extent as he did in the administration of the island, nor did they like sharing the customs dues with the British or the prohibition of the importation of slaves.[2] In addition, the Mazruis thought that an article of the convention which Owen had arranged[3] had not been fulfilled by the British: that the British would retrieve Mombasa's lost possessions for her. As far as London was concerned, the Swahili Coast offered little. No strategic importance was attached to the region, for the British had not known about the French plans of 1819. It is true that the area was of interest to the British as a source of the Slave Trade, but there were no plans to establish a base there from which to counter that trade. London was ignorant of the fact that the British Establishment at Mombasa had set up a colony for freed slaves.[4] An order to withdraw the Establishment was issued.

Saiyid Sa'id was bitterly resentful about the British Establishment at Mombasa, and the French were not slow to exploit his feelings. They followed up their commercial soundings of 1821/2. On his way to take up a post in India, M. le Vicomte Debassyns, the nephew of Villèle, put in at Muscat and delivered a letter from the Ministry of Marine, which was designed to encourage trade between Muscat and Bourbon.[5] The next year one of Sa'id's ships – the *Salih* – put in at Bourbon.[6] The captain, Murshid, must have had some success in disposing of his cargo, because Sa'id decided to send him to Bourbon once a year.[7] On his 1827 trip Murshid asked if the duties the Omanis paid at Bourbon on the export of cloves, which had been fixed in the 1822 ordinance

---

[1] Sir Lowry Cole to R. Wilmot Horton, 20 Nov. 1824, C.O. 167/73, and Moorsom to Nourse, 20 Mch. 1824, Adm. 1/69.

[2] Emery's Journal, *passim*, particularly entries for 1826.

[3] The convention is contained in Moorsom to Nourse, 20 Mch. 1824, Adm. 1/69. It was not ratified by the British Government.

[4] See Gray, *The British in Mombasa, 1824-1826*, Chapter IX.

[5] Ministry of Marine to Saiyid Sa'id, enclosed in Resident, Persian Gulf, to Bombay, 11 Dec. 1825, Proc. 11 Jan. 1826, B.P.C. 386/3.

[6] Saiyid Sa'id to Comte de Cheffontaines, the governor of Bourbon, 17 Feb. 1827, A.E., Zanz. C.C.1.

[7] *Idem.*

negotiated by Freycinet and Ahmad, might be reduced from 15 per cent to 4 per cent.¹ The Minister of Marine favoured a reduction of the duty:

'Although the commercial relations of Muscat and Bourbon do not seem to me to be liable to acquire great importance, my intention is to favour them as much as possible.'²

French motives for this may have been purely commercial. They may, however, have been influenced by a knowledge of British activities at Mombasa. Murshid may originally have been sent to Bourbon, not in response to the letter Debassyns brought, but to persuade the French not to aid the rebellious Mombasans. Certainly he brought this matter up in his discussions with the governor. Sa'id was probably correct in thinking that the Mombasans, dissatisfied with the British, would turn to the French for aid, or he may have foreseen the British withdrawal and the subsequent search by Mombasa for alternative allies. In September 1826 Commodore Christian at Mombasa reported that the Mazruis had offered to cede their island to the French.³ As an island fortress with an excellent harbour Mombasa would have been an ideal base for the French. However, if the proposal ever reached Bourbon, it was not accepted. The French had more than one reason for rejecting the idea: on the one hand they probably knew about the British Establishment at Mombasa but were as yet ignorant that orders had been issued for its withdrawal; on the other, this was an opportunity to step in as an alternative ally for Saiyid Sa'id. If they set themselves up in authority on the East African coast in opposition to the Sultan, he would be precipitated into the British camp. Consequently, when Murshid raised the question of French co-operation with Mombasa, the governor of Bourbon assured him he need have no fear of such a development. The governor reiterated this promise in a letter to Saiyid Sa'id.⁴

As for the British, they were aware of the commercial arrangements between Muscat and Bourbon because their Resident in the Persian Gulf had acquired the letter Debassyns took to Sa'id from the Ministry of Marine.⁵ None the less, they were apprehensive that the French

[1] Governor of Bourbon to Ministry of Marine, 22 Sept. 1827, and same to Saiyid Sa'id, 10 July 1827, A.E., Zanz. C.C.1.
[2] Minister of Marine to Minister of F.A., 3 Sept. 1828, A.E., Zanz. C.C.1.
[3] Christian to Bombay, 5 Sept. 1826, Proc. 18 Oct., B.P.C. 386/12.
[4] Governor of Bourbon to Ministry of Marine, 22 Sept. 1827, and governor of Bourbon to Saiyid Sa'id, 10 July 1827, A.E., Zanz. C.C.1.
[5] Persian Gulf Resident to Bombay, 11 Dec. 1825, Proc. 11 Jan. 1826, B.P.C. 386/3.

might abandon their connexion with Muscat and take Mombasa. Not wanting to possess Mombasa for themselves, they preferred the town to be held by the Omanis rather than the French. They therefore urged Saiyid Sa'id to adopt a conciliatory attitude towards the Mazruis in order to return them to their allegiance.[1]

Saiyid Sa'id did not hesitate to turn the Franco-British rivalry in the Indian Ocean to his own advantage and thereby both to maintain his position in Oman and consolidate his authority in East Africa. He knew he owed the security of his rule in Oman to the support he had received from the British; consequently he could not afford at any time to relinquish his relations with them. At the same time he had no desire to become simply their satellite, and he was eager to exploit any opportunity to benefit from the presence of other Western interests in the Persian Gulf and East Africa.

However, the possibility of using the French as an alternative means of support when the Napoleonic Wars were over and they were again making their presence felt in the Indian Ocean lessened Saiyid Sa'id's obligation to the British. His diminished reliance on them is evident from his forward policy in the Persian Gulf and East Africa between 1826 and 1830. Saiyid Sa'id planned to take action against Bushire, Basra and Bahrain, and consulted the British to sound out their reaction. Although they tried to restrain the Sultan, he went ahead with his projects.[2] In 1826 he assembled a force against Bushire and captured its shaikh, whom he claimed had insulted him; later he blockaded Basra in order to obtain arrears of tribute; and at the end of 1828 he made an unsuccessful attack on Bahrain.[3] Simultaneously Saiyid Sa'id adopted a more aggressive policy towards Mombasa. Having made half-hearted attempts to conciliate the Mazruis, in January 1828 he sent vessels carrying 6,000 men to attack Mombasa.[4] The following year he made a second attempt to capture the town.[5]

In his disregard of British views, Saiyid Sa'id showed a considerable measure of freedom of action in these years. He gambled on the probability that they would support him if he were really in trouble,

---

[1] Bombay to C. of Ds., 12 Feb. 1827, P.L.B. 10.

[2] Bombay to C. of Ds., 2 July 1825, P.L.B. 9, and Stannus to Bombay, 14 Apr. 1826, Proc. 10 May, B.S.C. 59.

[3] Bombay to C. of Ds., 7 June 1826 and 21 June 1827, P.L.B. 10; and no. 37, 16 Nov. 1831, P.L.B. 14.

[4] See Chapter XI, p. 305.

[5] See Chapter XI, pp. 306-7.

SAIYID SAʻID AND THE WESTERN POWERS, 1819-1839

as they had done previously. In fact, the likelihood of this support possibly made him feel more secure at home and therefore encouraged him to act more adventurously abroad. That Saʻid should take advantage of his security and act more independently was not what the British had intended. It was, however, too late for them to abandon him: they had become too involved in a policy of influence in the Persian Gulf, one of the props of which was the alliance with Muscat. In Bombay's opinion:

'The Sultan, though likely, unless controlled, to produce disorder in the Gulf by indulging his personal ambition, is yet sincerely determined to prevent the revival of the former piratical system.'[1]

Saʻid was also their chosen ally for the measures against the Slave Trade. Moreover, in 1828 the British abandoned their policy of directly supporting Persia against Russia and adopted an alternative plan to emphasize their supremacy in the Persian Gulf.[2] Consequently they did not want to lose their most important ally there.

It was, then, incumbent upon the British to step in when it appeared in 1830 that the Saiyid of Muscat was about to lose his position. During Saʻid's visit to East Africa in 1830 there was a wide insurrection against him in Oman. Wilson, the Persian Gulf Resident, feared that the Arab chiefs of the Gulf might seize this opportunity to attack Oman, and, as a preventive measure, he despatched a cruiser to the Arabian coast to ascertain their intentions and to intimate that if they aided the rebellion they would incur the displeasure of the British Government.[3] He also wrote to one of the rebels, Hamud ibn Azzan, telling him that the British wanted an immediate end to the disturbances and that if he persisted in making any move against Muscat, Wilson had orders to stop him.[4] Meanwhile Saʻid's deputy in Muscat, Muhammad ibn Salim,

---

[1] Bombay to C. of Ds., no. 37, 16 Nov. 1831, P.L.B. 14.
[2] M. E. Yapp, 'British Policy in Central Asia 1830-1843' (London University Ph.D. thesis, 1960), pp. 1, 51, 52.
[3] Wilson to Collinson, Senior Marine Officer in the Persian Gulf, 2 Feb. 1830, Proc. 10 Mch; Wilson to Sultan ibn Saqr, 23 Jan. 1830, Proc. 10 Mch; and same to same, 2 Feb. 1830, Proc. 10 Mch., B.P.C. 386/61.
[4] Wilson to Hamud ibn Azzan, 24 May 1830, Proc. 4 Aug., B.P.C. 387/2. Hamud replied to this letter thus: 'I did not go to war by way of experiment but have been led to what I have done by the irresistible decrees of Almighty God in which I am a passive agent' – Hamud to Wilson, 5 June 1830, Proc. 27 Oct., B.P.C. 387/4.

sent an envoy to Bombay to ask for help.[1] Bombay felt so far bound to their ally

'... as to prevent his ruin and downfall by every means in our power, and without considering it necessary that the Resident should interfere on account of any partial disorders in His Highness' territories, or absolutely prohibit warlike measures by any chiefs against him, we had no hesitation in authorizing and directing him to inform the several chieftains in the Gulf that we could not permit any act, calculated to annihilate or seriously and permanently to weaken the Imaum's power, and that their refusal to submit to the arbitration of the Resident would be treated as an act of hostility'.[2]

Wilson thought Bombay's aim was to block any external thrusts against Sa'id, while interfering as little as possible with the interior affairs of his government unless his downfall was threatened.[3] How far the British were prepared to go to prevent Sa'id's downfall is plain from Wilson's instructions to a cruiser he sent to Muscat. If the port was attacked, the commander was to act as he thought best in defending the place; however, he was not on any account to join in any offensive operations without further orders or in any way involve himself in any negotiations or political transactions whatsoever; finally, although he was not to give advice on anything but the defence of the town, if he obtained information that an attack was actually intended against Muscat, then, without waiting for further orders, he was to send all the force at his disposal to assist in its defence.[4]

Although Saiyid Sa'id hurried back from East Africa when he heard of the disturbances, the measures taken by Bombay and the Resident had stabilized matters. Possibly, had Sultan ibn Saqr, one of the disaffected shaikhs, not received Wilson's warning, he would have taken the opportunity to capture Dubai, which he had long coveted. British threats must also have helped to restrain Hamud. The British had saved Sa'id, but he was loath to admit it. On his return he immediately sent

---

[1] Muhammad ibn Salim, Regent at Muscat, to Bombay, 13 Mch. 1830, and Aga Muhammad Shoostry to Bombay, 2 Apr. 1830, Proc. 14 Apr. 1830, B.P.C. 386/63.
[2] Bombay to C. of Ds., no. 37, 16 Nov. 1831, P.B.L. 14; and Bombay to Wilson, 12 Apr. 1830, Proc. 14 Apr., B.P.C. 386/63.
[3] Wilson to Bombay, 25 May 1830, Proc. 4 Aug. 1830, B.P.C. 387/2.
[4] Wilson to Collinson, 24 May 1840, Proc. 4 Aug., B.P.C. 387/2.

away the British cruiser[1] and apologized to Bombay for Muhammad ibn Salim having applied for help:

'We blamed him much for having written such a letter because we have attached ourselves to you with a view to obtaining your assistance under pressure of weighty events and not for such trifling occurrences as these.'[2]

Sa'id wanted to minimize the seriousness of the rebellion, probably to disguise his real weakness or to eradicate the idea that he was reliant upon the British, and therefore under their influence. Despite his ingratitude, Bombay reckoned it worth while to support Sa'id:

'We could not but be sensible that it would be unwise to allow the power of this deserving prince and useful ally to be destroyed, and that of a combination of chiefs substituted in its place. The chiefs would be likely to turn their power to piratical ends.'[3]

The policy of upholding Sa'id's position in Oman continued throughout the next few years. At the end of 1831, when Sa'id had again departed for East Africa, troubles arose at home, and this time it was Sa'id's aunt who appealed for help.[4] Blane, the new Resident in the Gulf, sent his assistant to Muscat with two cruisers and warned the chiefs of the Gulf that the British would not suffer Sa'id's authority to be subverted.[5] This time, however, it was not only the Gulf chiefs who threatened Sa'id. The Wahhabis were enjoying a revival under their new leader, Turki. Sa'id, hoping to hold them back by co-operation, had concluded an offensive and defensive alliance with Turki.[6] The Wahhabis none the less advanced into Oman, and in 1833 the Persian Gulf Resident suggested British armed interference in support of Sa'id.[7] It was feared that the Wahhabis would spread across the Gulf into Persia – a dangerous situation for India. Persia had no fleet to defend

[1] J. Sawyer, Acting Commander of the *Tigris*, to Collinson, 15 June 1830, Proc. 27 Oct., B.P.C. 287/4.
[2] Saiyid Sa'id to Bombay, 24 Aug. 1830, Proc. 15 Sept., B.P.C. 387/3.
[3] Bombay to C. of Ds., no. 37, 16 Nov. 1831, P.L.B. 14.
[4] Sa'id's aunt to the Persian Gulf Resident, 9 Apr. 1832, Proc. 27 June, B.P.C. 387/27. Hilal, whom Sa'id had left in charge, also applied for help – Hilal to Bombay, 30 May 1832, Proc. 18 July, B.P.C. 387/28.
[5] Blane to Hennell, 7 May 1832. Proc. 27 June, B.P.C. 387/27; Bombay to C. of Ds., no. 31, 14 Aug. 1833, P.L.B. 16.
[6] Bombay to C. of Ds., no. 37, 16 Nov. 1831, P.L.B. 14.
[7] Bombay to C. of Ds., no. 39, 24 Dec. 1834, P.L.B. 17.

herself, and if the Wahhabis captured Sa'id's fleet, they would become disastrously powerful.[1] Bombay was therefore in favour of giving active support to Sa'id.

Calcutta, however, suddenly altered British policy towards Muscat:

'We are not prepared to sanction the employment of British arms for maintaining the integrity of the continental possessions of the Imaum of Muscat. If we were once to commit ourselves by a declaration of our intention to that ruler, this line of policy must be followed up at any expense, and it is impossible to set limits to the waste of blood and treasure that might ensue in consequence.... Our concern is only with the maritime commerce of the Gulf and as long as that is not molested, it matters not to us whether one power or another holds dominion on its shores.'[2]

This volte-face cannot be explained by changes of personnel – Bentinck was still Governor-General. The 1833 Act of Parliament abolishing the East India Company's commercial privileges as a trading company may have had some influence in the change of policy, because originally it had been the need to protect the maritime commerce of the Gulf which had encouraged the British to attack the pirates and establish their own influence in the Gulf. Perhaps, too, the relaxation of tension between Great Britain and Persia had some effect. In 1832 Abbas Mirza had laid siege to Khorasan, and there was a possibility that he would proceed to Herat and threaten the north-west frontier of India. However, he died in October 1833, and his son withdrew the Persian forces. Perhaps Calcutta's opinion arose from their recognition that it was one thing to defend Muscat from internal rebels and Gulf shaikhs who would come by sea, and quite another to protect it from the powerful Wahhabis who controlled all Najd and would sweep across by land.

Bombay disagreed with Calcutta's point of view: 'It now appears a contrary line of policy is approved.'[3] In their opinion, it mattered much whose dominion prevailed on the shores of the Gulf because it was only by having shaikhs who were prepared to co-operate there that maritime peace could be maintained. It had taken many years of patient negotiation to establish satisfactory relationships with the Gulf chiefs, and build up a system of influence. The system had its greatest success

[1] Bombay to C. of Ds., no. 39, 24 Dec. 1834, P.L.B. 17.
[2] Calcutta to Bombay, 1 Feb. 1834, Proc. 12 Mch. 1834, B.P.C. 387/55.
[3] Minute by Clare, governor of Bombay, 6 Mch. 1834, Proc. 12 Mch., B.P.C. 387/55.

SAIYID SAʻID AND THE WESTERN POWERS, 1819-1839

where a large number of petty shaikhs held authority in towns and forts along the Gulf littoral. A warship anchored opposite the towns commanded obedience because it had the power to destroy them, and with them, the bases of the shaikhs' power. It would have been far more difficult to maintain such a system of influence if the shore was occupied by one power whose territories extended far inland. After all, it had been the fear lest the Wahhabis should control the Gulf shores and reintroduce piracy that had made Bombay send the 1819 expedition.

It was fortunate for Saʻid that the change in British policy coincided with the murder of Turki, and the consequent weakening of Wahhabi power.[1] Saʻid did not seem to welcome British help. In 1831 he had sent away the British cruiser, and in 1832, when Hennell had been sent to Muscat with two cruisers, Saʻid wrote a letter which the Persian Gulf Resident described as

'not so expressive of satisfaction with the measures adopted for the protection of his capital and support for his authority during his absence as I had expected'.[2]

The Resident hopefully suggested that this might be an error of writing rather than a lack of gratitude. Nevertheless, it seems that Saʻid did expect help from the British in times of trouble, or, as he himself put it, 'under pressure of weighty events'. If Hilal is to be believed, Saʻid had told him to call upon the British if trouble arose.[3] Saʻid's outward reluctance to accept British help was due to his desire to maintain his freedom of action and decision while yet relying on another power to support him, as well as to his unwillingness to appear in the eyes of his countrymen as a British puppet. Consequently he found it difficult to admit that British support was ever really needed.

Meanwhile Saʻid had been developing relations with other Western powers. The Americans had become interested in the trading possibilities of Zanzibar in the mid 1820s.[4] The first American vessel to

---

[1] Bombay to C. of Ds., no. 39, 24 Dec. 1834, P.L.B. 17.
[2] Blane to Bombay, 29 Oct. 1832, Proc. 31 Dec., B.P.C. 387/34.
[3] Hilal to Bombay, 30 May 1832, Proc. 18 July, B.P.C. 387/28. Saʻid's aunt said Saʻid had told Hilal that if anyone molested him, he was to tell the Persian Gulf Resident – Saʻid's aunt to Resident, 9 Apr. 1832, Proc. 27 June, B.P.C. 387/27.
[4] This book will not treat American activities in great detail, because a great deal of work has been done on this, particularly by Norman R. Bennett. See his 'Americans in Zanzibar 1825-1845' in *Essex Institute Historical Collections* XCV (July 1959), pp. 239-62 (also in *T.N.R.* no. 56, Mch. 1961, pp. 93-108), and his 'Americans in Zanzibar 1845-1865' in *Essex Institute Historical Collections*

visit Zanzibar was probably the *Titus* in 1818.¹ Mauritius, Bourbon, and Madagascar – all places which were frequently visited by American ships – may have revealed the opportunities for trade at Zanzibar. One of these ships, the *Mary Ann*, had been chartered by Edmund Roberts.² He was enthusiastic about the trading possibilities at Zanzibar, but irritated by the impediments he met. The Americans had to pursue their dealings through agents of the Sultan, and could not bargain on their own account. Roberts complained to the Sultan of these hindrances, and Sa'id seized the opportunity to suggest that the Americans negotiate a commercial treaty with him.³ At this time he was trying to develop East Africa commercially, but he also had his mind open to the possibility that the Americans might give him military help. He was at the height of his expansive period. He had captured the shaikh of Bushire; he had completed a successful blockade of Basra and he was trying to overcome Mombasa. As we know from his answers to Elphinstone's 1826 request that he entirely abolish the Slave Trade, he had remote dreams of acquiring the Portuguese section of the East African coast.⁴ He now suggested to Roberts that the United States provide him with 'bombs' and 'shells' to use against the Portuguese.⁵ It fact it was probably Mombasa he had in mind. According to Miles, Bombay heard that Sa'id had agreed to allow the Americans to open factories on the East African coast provided they gave him armed aid against Mombasa.⁶ Without taking the suggestion of military aid seriously, Senator Levi Woodbury expressed great interest in Sa'id's proposals for a treaty.⁷ In 1832 another message arrived in America from Sa'id requesting a treaty,⁸ and the same year Edmund Roberts

XCVII (1961), pp. 31-56 (also in *T.N.R.* no. 57, 1961, pp. 121-38). See also his article in *Essex Institute Historical Collections* XCVIII (1962), pp. 36-61, and Bennett and Brooks, *op. cit*. See also Sir John Gray, 'Early Connections between the United States and East Africa', *T.N.R.* no. 22 (Dec. 1946) pp. 55-86, and Phillip Northway, 'Salem and the Zanzibar – East African Trade', *Essex Institute Historical Collections* XC (Apr. 1954).

¹ See Chapter XII, p. 326.
² Bennett, *T.N.R.* (Mch. 1961), p. 93.
³ *Ibid.*, p. 96. In his capacity as ruler of Zanzibar, Sa'id will be called the 'Sultan'. ⁴ See Chapter IX, p. 226.
⁵ Bennett, *T.N.R.* (Mch. 1961), p. 96, quoting E. Roberts to L. Woodbury, 26 Dec. 1828. ⁶ Miles, *Persian Gulf*, p. 335.
⁷ Bennett, *T.N.R.* (Mch. 1961), p. 96. Levi Woodbury was the Senator from New Hampshire and shortly afterwards became Secretary of the Navy.
⁸ It was brought by one of N. L. Rogers' ships – *ibid.*, p. 97. See also Agent at Muscat to Persian Gulf Resident, 18 Sept. 1833, mentioning that such a

left on the U.S.S. *Peacock* with instructions to arrange commercial treaties with the rulers of Muscat, Siam, and Cochin China.[1] The following year the treaty with Muscat was arranged without Sa'id having openly consulted Bombay. He did, however, send a private enquiry to the British local agent at Muscat as to whether the British would have any objection,[2] but he did not wait for a reply before signing the treaty.

The Americans were to be allowed to trade freely in all the Sultan's ports, and were to pay only 5 per cent import duty. There was to be no export duty. They could establish a consulate, and it would be the consul's duty to settle disputes. He was removable only by direct complaint to Washington. The Americans were not to sell firearms and powder to anyone at Zanzibar except the government.[3] As it was a long and detailed treaty, Sa'id possibly may have agreed to it without realizing its full implications. Certainly there were clauses which were to cause trouble in years to come. The treaty was arranged at Muscat and Captain Hasan, who often served as Sa'id's interpreter, was away at Zanzibar during the negotiations.[4] However, Sa'id ibn Khalfan, who also spoke English, was at Muscat. Although one or two of the subtleties of the treaty may have escaped Saiyid Sa'id, it is unlikely that he was unaware of what he was doing. He was by now experienced in diplomatic negotiations with Western powers.

To a large extent it was the rapid expansion of American trade with Zanzibar consequent upon this treaty which encouraged the commercial development of the Swahili Coast in the 1830s. East Africa became increasingly attractive to the Omanis, and it was in this period that Zanzibar town grew and Saiyid Sa'id really expanded his activities on the Swahili Coast. He finally defeated the Mazruis in Mombasa, which meant that his political position became more stable.[5] The attractions of developing the Swahili Coast may also have been partly due to the political difficulties which beset Saiyid Sa'id in Oman in the 1830s and

letter had been sent – encl. in Resident to Bombay, 3 Oct. 1833, Proc. 18 Dec., B.P.C. 387/51.

[1] See E. Roberts, *Embassy to the Eastern Courts of Cochin China, Siam, and Muscat 1832-4* (New York, 1837), for a detailed account of the mission. See also Ruschenberger, *op. cit.*

[2] Agent at Muscat to Resident, Persian Gulf, 6 Oct. 1833, encl. in Resident to Bombay, 31 Oct. 1833, Proc. 18 Dec., B.P.C. 387/51.

[3] The American treaty, Proc. 27 May 1834, B.P.C. 387/59.

[4] Hart's Report, Proc. 21 May 1834, B.P.C. 387/58.

[5] See Chapter XI, pp. 305-8.

his disenchantment with the position there. However, he had no intention of abandoning Oman: he spent the 1830s regularly travelling between Oman and East Africa.[1]

If Sa'id's failure to consult the British before signing the treaty with the Americans had been designed to prevent them obstructing it, he was correct in thinking they would be displeased. When the British heard about the treaty, Captain Hart was sent to Zanzibar to investigate.[2] Sa'id admitted he had signed the treaty, but tried to minimize its importance by claiming that it had no meaning and the Americans were nothing to him compared with the British. 'Mr Edmund Roberts', he said, 'was an old, fat blustering man, and I was glad to sign the treaty to get rid of him, as I did not think it of any importance.' He also said he had not consulted Bombay because it always took such a long time to get an answer. When he wrote to Bombay, he was referred to the Persian Gulf Resident, and when he wrote to the Resident, he was referred to Bombay, 'and so between the two stools I fall to the ground'.[3]

Sa'id minimized the part he had played in arranging the American treaty because, while he wanted to widen his relations with other countries and therefore to extend his political possibilities, he could not afford to antagonize the British. Consequently, he said that he would break the treaty if the British wished it. This was the same tactic as he had used in 1807 when his treaty with the French displeased the British. He knew that if he broke a treaty at the request of the British, this would place upon them the obligation of defending him against the wronged party. Hart made the Sultan promise that he would never again arrange a treaty with another power without first consulting the British. This made Sa'id reveal that the French, too, had made overtures for a treaty.[4] When the Governor-General, Bentinck, was informed of the American treaty, he said he much regretted it, but was unable to discover any tenable ground upon which English interference to annul or modify its provisions could be upheld.[5] Bentinck expressed this regret merely two months after he had said it was a matter of indifference to him whose power prevailed on the shores of the Persian Gulf. It seemed that such indifference was felt only as long as the powers of the Gulf were duly subordinate to British influence and did not indulge in international negotiations of their own.

[1] See Chapter X, p. 247. [2] Hart's Report, Proc. 21 May 1834, B.P.C. 387/58.
[3] *Idem.* [4] *Idem.*
[5] Bentinck to Vice-Admiral Sir John Gore, 13 Apr. 1834, Proc. 27 May, B.P.C. 387/59.

SAIYID SAʿID AND THE WESTERN POWERS, 1819-1839

Negotiations with the French, like those for the American treaty, had been begun by Saʿid himself. In July 1833 he sent an envoy to Bourbon in order to obtain skilled sugar planters to develop the sugar industry he planned for Zanzibar.[1] Bourbon was in particular difficulties at this time, because it was overpopulated and because the sterner measures against the Slave Trade introduced by the new July Monarchy had hit it hard.[2] The 1833 session of the *Conseil Général* at Bourbon[3] expressed the view that the local government should employ ships of state to explore the countries with which the colony could have advantageous relations. As this coincided with the Oman envoy's overtures, it was natural that the governor's attention should be drawn to East Africa. He despatched Captain Vailhen on *Le Madagascar* to obtain concessions at Zanzibar for the French to found agricultural establishments, and to sign a treaty. The true object was 'd'amener l'Iman à nous concéder une portion de cette île [Zanzibar] favorable à nos vues'.[4] The Sultan was to place at the disposal of the governor of Bourbon land suitable for the culture of colonial produce (Article 1); he was for ten years to exempt from all tax the products of these establishments, and the French factories and materials (Article 2); and he was to receive a French Residency exercising consular jurisdiction (Article 3). In return the governor of Bourbon would send planters to Zanzibar to work this land without any cost to the Sultan, he would free from duty cloves exported from Bourbon to the Sultan's territories and would reduce duties on other products, and he would protect, during their stay at Bourbon, all the Sultan's subjects who came to trade.[5]

These activities of the governor and the *Conseil Général* at Bourbon demonstrated the independence of French colonial governments.

[1] Governor of Bourbon to Ministry of Marine and Colonies, no. 199, 3 Apr. 1834, M.O., Réunion 86/569, and Instructions to Vailhen, Mch? 1834, *ibid*. The envoy is called 'Captain Calfuen' by the French, but he was probably Saʿid ibn Khalfan, who spoke French.

[2] A treaty with the British was arranged in 1831 which allowed a reciprocal right of search.

[3] In 1825 Villèle had introduced a more centralized form of government for the colonies, but at the same time had given the governors more powers. The *Conseil Général* had twelve members appointed by the king from a list presented by the municipal councils. It met twice a year and its chief function was to give advice on the colony's budget. It also made known the needs and views of the colony.

[4] Instructions to Vailhen, Mch? 1834, M.O., Réunion 86/569.

[5] The Treaty enclosed in governor of Bourbon to Ministry of Marine and Colonies, no. 199, 3 Apr. 1834, M.O., Réunion 86/569.

THE SWAHILI COAST

Without reference to Paris, the governor had despatched a ship to negotiate a treaty which might have far-reaching effects for France. He had a considerable degree of freedom because Bourbon was a naval station, and its governor had from five to ten vessels under his direct command. It often happened that he himself was an ex-captain of one of those ships. The governor could therefore pursue a forward policy without reference to his superiors in France. Of course he had to account for his actions, but in many cases it would have been difficult or embarrassing for the French to disavow them. The governor of Bourbon had, therefore, more freedom than the governor of Bombay, who had to consult the commander of the Bombay Marine (after 1834 the Indian Navy) before moving a single ship. Often the commander of the Marine said there was no ship available for a proposed project.

The Sultan agreed to Vailhen's propositions on condition that the Frenchmen who were granted land became his subjects.[1] He must have been aware of the dangers of ceding part of his land to foreigners, but at the same time he needed Western knowledge for his sugar factory. As he had promised Hart, Sa'id informed the British about the proposed French treaty,[2] but matters went no further because on his return from Zanzibar to Bourbon, Vailhen was attacked by a fatal fever and in a fit of delirium threw all his letters and papers overboard.[3]

Vailhen's death and the loss of his papers meant that the treaty was not ratified and never came into force. By the time the matter came under consideration again the French were becoming interested in a wider area. In 1838 Commander Guillain in *La Favorite* was sent on a

[1] We only have the Sultan's word for what happened in the negotiations and for the articles of the treaty he agreed to, because Guillain asked him about it in 1840. Apparently some land in the north-west of the island was granted to the French – Guillain to governor of Bourbon, 9 Jan. 1841, M.O., O.I. 10/45. Guillain got the land grant confirmed but the French never took advantage of it because by 1840 their interests were more commercial. Guillain to Ministry of Marine, 21 Oct. 1840, M.O., O.I. 10/45.

[2] Saiyid Sa'id to Aga Muhammad Shoostry, his agent at Bombay, 2 May 1834, Proc. 3 June, B.P.C. 387/59. Bombay referred the matter to Calcutta – Bombay to Persian Secretary, 30 May 1834, *ibid.* – but when nothing further was heard from Sa'id, the matter was dropped.

[3] Governor of Bourbon to Guillain, 18 May 1840, M.O., O.I. 10/45 – this merely says that Vailhen's papers were lost. The story of Vailhen's delirium was heard in 1840 by Hennell, who was at Muscat when Guillain went there to establish a French consul and brought up the matter of Vailhen's treaty – Hennell to Bombay, 5 Aug. 1840, encl. in Bombay to Secret Committee, no. 56, 22 Aug. 1840, E.S.L.B. 23.

voyage of investigation to the Red Sea and the East African coast. His object may have been to discover the truth of recent reports that the British were showing great interest in the Red Sea and had purchased Socotra.[1] Guillain returned with details of British activities, and further information was provided by Fontanier, the French consul in Basra, who at the time was residing in Bombay.[2] The French learnt that the British had taken Aden in pursuit of their plans for steam navigation in the Red Sea. As a result the French decided to play a more active role in the region. They had plans of their own for steam navigation and were also interested in providing Muhammad Ali of Egypt with support. Consequently, in 1839 the French Ministry of Marine despatched two expeditions, one to explore Abyssinia with a view to its colonization, and another to visit both the Red Sea and Muscat.[3] When calculating the advantages which should ensue from the latter mission, the Ministry mentioned the commercial benefits which could be derived from communication with Abyssinia and Arabia, and the advantages of a steam link between the Indian Ocean and the Mediterranean by the Red Sea. In conclusion, the Ministry stressed that the Red Sea deserved French attention because of the activities of the British there.[4] Persuaded by these arguments, Paris decided to establish an agent at Zaila.

It was not, however, regarded as sufficient for French activities to be confined to the Red Sea; the Persian Gulf was also to become familiar with the French flag, and a mission was to be sent to the Amirs of Sind to open up commercial relations.[5] The French also saw possibilities in yet another region – the East African coast. After his expedition of 1838, Guillain reported that the Sultan would welcome a French agent at Zanzibar.[6] The Ministry of Foreign Affairs decided to establish such a post and also to find out whether a French subject was required as an agent at Muscat, or whether the Arab agent the French had been using – Sa'id ibn Khalfan – would suffice.[7] Ibn Khalfan (as he was known to the French) had never been officially appointed as agent but had been

[1] Bombay to C. of Ds., no. 29, 29 July 1835, P.L.B. 18.
[2] Note sur la mission à remplir à Mascate et dans la mer rouge et sur les avantages qui doivent en résulter, M.O., O.I. 10/45.
[3] *Idem*, and T. E. Marston, *Britain's Imperial Role in the Red Sea Area 1800-1878* (Connecticut, 1961), p. 119.
[4] As note 2.
[5] Ministry of F.A. to Ministry of Marine, 25 Sept. 1839, M.O., O.I. 10/45.
[6] *Idem*.
[7] *Idem*, and Ministry of F.A. to Noel, consular agent for Zanzibar, 18 Sept. 1839, M.O., O.I. 10/45.

useful as an interpreter and commercial adviser for Frenchmen visiting Muscat. Guillain had recently reported adversely on his morality, but this claim was denied by Fontanier, who said that Guillain had been misled by people who had evil intentions against Ibn Khalfan.[1] As a result of the enquiries, Ibn Khalfan's position was confirmed and the French thereafter had an official agent at Muscat.

This expansion of French activities in the Indian Ocean in the late 1830s was a response to British movements in the Red Sea and a by-product of the diplomatic tension in the Middle East. It had been encouraged by Guillain's enthusiastic reports, but even before he made these, the merchants of Bourbon, who had been hard hit by sterner measures against the Slave Trade, were making efforts to expand their trade with Swahili ports. It was Bourbon which had made Paris aware of the advantages of relations with Muscat and the benefits which a consul at Zanzibar and possibly also one at Muscat would bring to France. Paris was willing to implement Bourbon's suggestions for East Africa, because the plans were very different from those put forward in the early 1820s. Now it was merely suggested that a consul should be appointed to Zanzibar and enquiries should be made about commercial opportunities on the rest of the East African coast,[2] whereas beforehand it had been the actual capture of Zanzibar from a prince known to be supported by the British which had been contemplated.

The French plans for a consular establishment at Zanzibar had been anticipated by the British. When Hart visited Zanzibar in 1834 to find out about the American treaty, the Sultan asked 'if he could have an English person always with him to guide him'.[3] This may well have been part of Sa'id's attempt to calm British apprehension about his dealings with other powers rather than a genuine request. Certainly he disliked having a British consul with him when he eventually got one. He seemed to regard promises to receive consuls as a point of etiquette. He acceded to Vailhen's proposal for one in 1834 (although the French did not yet know it), and to Guillain's in 1838. At the same time as he asked for a British consul, Sa'id sent one of his ships, the

---

[1] Ministry of F.A. to Ministry of Marine, 27 Jan. 1840, and Fontanier to Ministry of F.A., 28 Nov. 1839, M.O., O.I. 10/45.

[2] The coast of Mogadishu and Brava was to be explored for commercial opportunities – Ministry of F.A. to Ministry of Marine, 25 Sept. 1839, M.O., O.I. 10/45.

[3] Hart's Report, Proc. 21 May 1834, B.P.C. 387/58.

SAIYID SA'ID AND THE WESTERN POWERS, 1819-1839

Liverpool, as a present to the King of England. It was too large for his purposes, a mistake having been made in the specifications he had given to the shipbuilding yard at Bombay.[1] Obviously deciding that the British displeasure over the American treaty was an excellent opportunity to get rid of his 'magnificent encumbrance', Sa'id put the vessel to good use.[2] 'He is', said Bombay, ' . . . resolved to part with her for the highest price he can obtain for money if nothing better can be had, but if possible for the useful and powerful gratitude of His Britannic Majesty'.[3] The Sultan wanted Captain Robert Cogan, of the Indian Navy, to take the ship to England for him, and since Cogan was due to go on leave anyway, Bombay allowed him to do this.[4]

Before Cogan arrived in England with the ship, the Foreign Office's attention had already been drawn to Zanzibar. Except for the Owen incident of 1824-6, dealings with the Sultan had formerly been carried out by the East India Company and by Mauritius. Then, in July 1834, Khamis ibn Uthman, an inhabitant of Zanzibar, came to England on a ship belonging to Newman Hunt and Christopher, a firm which had begun trading at Zanzibar. Khamis was a Swahili born at Lamu and became headman of the drummers at Zanzibar and afterwards a slaver. In this latter capacity he had visited many different parts, and could converse in fourteen languages. It was after he had defrauded the Sultan of 18,000 dollars that he had been forced to leave Zanzibar in 1834. It was he who provided W. D. Cooley, of the Royal Geographical Society, with much information relating to the interior and lake regions of Africa. After his visit to England, Khamis returned to Zanzibar and was pardoned by Saiyid Sa'id, becoming the latter's general factotum. Khamis sent his son, Muhammad, to England to be educated.[5]

Khamis had acted as Owen's interpreter during the 1824-6 survey of the East African coast. After the withdrawal of the British Establishment at Mombasa in 1826, Owen had been sent to Fernando Po to start a settlement to counter the Slave Trade. In 1831, however, he had returned to England. Hearing of Khamis' arrival, he contacted his former interpreter and learnt from him that the Americans were displaying

---

[1] The *Liverpool* was unfit for any purpose but war, and Sa'id liked his ships to be practicable for both war and commerce. He told Hart the ship was too big for him – Hart's Report, Proc. 21 May 1834, B.P.C. 387/58.
[2] For 'magnificent encumbrance', Hart's Report, *idem*.
[3] Bombay to C. of Ds., no. 29, 29 July 1835, P.L.B. 18.
[4] *Idem*.   [5] Burton, *Zanzibar*, II, 286-7.

interest in Zanzibar. This revived Owen's dreams for East Africa: 'Shall we still refuse', he asked Palmerston, 'to reopen to our fair enterprise those countries which aforetime furnished even to Solomon his Ivory, his Pearls, and his Gold?'[1] He offered himself as consul-general for Eastern Africa and South Arabia. Meanwhile Khamis, claiming, erroneously, that he was an ambassador from the Sultan of Zanzibar, asked to see the King.[2] This was not possible, but he was granted an audience by Palmerston.[3]

Palmerston afterwards asked the India Board for its opinion about the suggestion Owen had made.[4] The India Board had recently been corresponding with the Secret Committee of the East India Company about Hart's mission to Zanzibar, of which they had been informed by the Admiralty. Ignorant of the details of the mission, the Secret Committee was displeased that it had been undertaken without, as they thought, reference to the Supreme Government. They quoted the Act of Parliament stipulating that there should be one supreme authority in India: 'No communication on general subjects of government shall be held with those states except through the Governor-General in Council.'[5] Because of this outburst from the Secret Committee, the India Board thought that the appointment of Owen, who would not be an officer of the Government of India and not under its control, would be undesirable.[6] Palmerston accepted this view and dropped the matter.[7]

The question of appointing a consul at Zanzibar was soon to be raised again. The British firm of Newman Hunt and Christopher had established a commercial agent in Zanzibar – Robert Brown Norsworthy.[8] Norsworthy had sold goods on credit to one Armear (Amir) ibn Sa'id who failed to make any payment. Appeals to the Sultan for recovery of the debt had been unavailing, so Norsworthy and his employer,

[1] Owen to Palmerston, 8 Sept. 1834, F.O. 54/1. A year later Owen went to Campobello Island. He entered politics and sat in the New Brunswick Assembly. He also began the definitive survey of the Bay of Fundy. He died in 1857 – P. G. Cornell, 'W. F. Owen, Naval Surveyor', in *Collections of the Nova Scotia Historical Society*, vol. XXXII (1959), pp. 169-82.
[2] Newman Hunt and Christopher to Palmerston, 10 July 1834, F.O. 54/1.
[3] Note by Palmerston, *c.* 17 July 1834, F.O. 54/1.
[4] F.O. to India Board, Sept. ? 1834, enclosing Owen's letter, F.O. 54/1.
[5] Peacock to Stuart Mackenzie, 27 Aug. 1834, F.O. 54/1.
[6] India Board to F.O., 27 Sept. 1834, F.O. 54/1.
[7] F.O. to Owen, n.d., but Sept. 1834, F.O. 54/1.
[8] For the commercial activities of this firm, see Chapter XII, pp. 325-6, 327-8, 335.

SAIYID SAʻID AND THE WESTERN POWERS, 1819-1839

Hunt, both appealed to Bombay.[1] Norsworthy said the British traders at Zanzibar were suffering badly from the lack of a consul, and compared their lot with that of the Americans, who did have a consul.[2] He asked whether a decision of the Muslim authority was binding on Europeans at Zanzibar. Hence Bombay sounded Calcutta about establishing a consulate at Zanzibar, and the Supreme Government raised no objection.[3] The Court of Directors had no objection either[4] – this was merely four years after they had been so jealous of their privileges of dealing with countries such as Zanzibar. The opinions of these various bodies were relayed to the Foreign Office by the India Board.[5]

By now Cogan had brought the *Liverpool* to England. The gift was accepted and renamed the *Imaum*.[6] Cogan was then sent back to Zanzibar with the yacht *Prince Regent* as a present for the Sultan,[7] and Saʻid appointed him his agent in London and Europe.[8] As Cogan had commercial plans of his own for Zanzibar, a treaty would have been much to his advantage. On Palmerston's suggestion, Cogan was consulted on the question of placing a consul at Zanzibar.[9] He reported in detail on the advantages a connexion with Zanzibar would bring Great Britain, and went as far as to suggest a Mr Francis Peters for the post of consul.[10] Before he was consulted about a consul, Cogan had already suggested that the British arrange a treaty with Zanzibar to offset American influence there,[11] and this plan had been forwarded to the

[1] Petition from R. N. Hunt, Proc. 20 Dec. 1837, and Petition from R. B. Norsworthy, 23 Nov. 1837, Proc. 20 Dec. 1837, B.P.C. 388/50.
[2] Norsworthy's Petition, *idem*. The Americans had sent Richard Waters as consul to Zanzibar.
[3] Calcutta to Bombay, 1 Jan. 1838, encl. in India Board to F.O., 31 May 1838, F.O. 54/2.
[4] C. of Ds. to India Board, n.d., encl. in India Board to F.O., 31 May 1838, F.O. 54/2.
[5] India Board to F.O., *idem*.
[6] Editor's footnote to extracts from Hart's Report, printed in *Bombay Selections* XXIV, p. 276.
[7] Saiyid Saʻid to Queen Victoria, 5 June 1837, F.O. 54/2, thanking her for the present. The Sultan disliked the yacht and, after consulting Bombay, gave it to one of the princes of India.
[8] Saiyid Saʻid to Queen Victoria, 5 June 1837, F.O. 54/2.
[9] F.O. to India Board, 6 June 1838, F.O. 54/2.
[10] Cogan to India Board, 9 June and 16 June 1838, F.O. 54/2.
[11] Cogan's memo, on the political relations existing between the Imam of Muscat and the British Government, 5 Jan. 1838, encl. in Carnac to Hobhouse, 3 Feb. 1838, F.O. 54/2.

Foreign Office in February 1838.[1] Palmerston had agreed to work for this treaty before deciding to appoint a consul.

Cogan argued that the Sultan's favour was solicited by France and America and indirectly by Russia, that American piece goods could be supplanted by British, that Muscat could be used as a coal depot, and that Egypt could be approached commercially by Great Britain through the Sultan, who had good relations there.[2] Sa'id seems to have completely deceived Cogan about the extent of his power and possessions.[3] Palmerston, if not as naïve as Cogan, was nevertheless inexperienced in dealing with Sa'id. He seems to have been convinced by the Sultan's protestations of friendship and by the advantages a treaty would bring. He may also have been influenced by an article in *The Times* of February 1838 which quoted a speech by the American President stressing the importance of the American alliance with the Sultan. Shortly afterwards he consulted the Board of Trade, the India Board, the Secret Committee and Cogan about the drafting of a treaty.[4]

Saiyid Sa'id had not himself suggested this treaty; he had gone no further than polite protestations of friendship towards the British. It was Cogan who had raised the question of a treaty, and Sa'id had agreed, provided its stipulations were reciprocal.[5] These events of the late 1830s, therefore, should not be seen as a deliberate attempt by the Sultan to strengthen his bonds with the British. His attitude had not changed, but he was drawn into the British net when the British feared they were being commercially outmanœuvred by the Americans. This was not a sharply defined fear, but Palmerston's decision to arrange a treaty was a direct result of the commercial ambitions of Norsworthy and Cogan, and their apprehension that the Americans had a superior position in Zanzibar as a result of their treaty and their consul. The ground had been prepared by Owen, and by the long-established connexion between the Sultan and Bombay. The British campaign

---

[1] F.O. to Board of Trade, 7 Feb. 1838, enclosing the papers – F.O. 54/2.

[2] Cogan to Carnac, 5 Jan. 1838, encl. in Carnac to Hobhouse, 3 Feb. 1838, F.O. 54/2.

[3] Questions asked of the Sultan by Cogan, and the Sultan's replies, encl. in Cogan to Carnac, 5 Jan. 1838, F.O. 54/2.

[4] F.O. to Board of Trade, 7 Feb., 2 May, and 20 June; Board of Trade to F.O., 20 Feb. and 23 July; F.O. to India Board, 28 Aug.; India Board to F.O., 17 Sept.; Secret Committee to India Board, 13 Sept.; Cogan to India Board, 5 Sept.; F.O. to India Board, 26 Sept. – all 1838, F.O. 54/2.

[5] Questions asked of the Sultan by Cogan, and the Sultan's replies, encl. in Cogan to Carnac, 5 Jan. 1838, F.O. 54/2.

SAIYID SAʿID AND THE WESTERN POWERS, 1819-1839

against the Slave Trade had little direct influence on the negotiation of the treaty or the appointment of a consul.

The treaty the Sultan signed with the British in 1839 was very similar to the one he had signed with the Americans. It stipulated a 5 per cent import duty and the reciprocal right of appointing consuls. Other clauses concerned deaths, bankruptcies, debts, disputes, crimes, land-holding, prevention of monopolies (except in certain areas and articles), trade in times of war, shipwrecks, and the Slave Trade.[1]

The appointment of a British consul consequent upon this treaty was, though the Sultan did not know it, to lead to the complete domination of Zanzibar by the British. The late 1820s and the 1830s had been the period when Saʿid had most freedom to manœuvre. He took advantage of the willingness of the British to uphold his position in Muscat to establish his authority more firmly in some territories and to expand into others, a policy which was against British wishes. He tried to maintain his freedom of action by dealing with powers other than the British. He did not want to collaborate with the British, but he realized that to do so on some matters was a distasteful necessity because he needed British support for his tottering power in Oman. The British were surprised that their ally was faithless enough to arrange treaties with other powers without consulting them, but there was little they could do about it. Slowly Bombay began to understand that the Sultan's protestations of eternal friendship and promises to overthrow every other ally were examples of empty etiquette. Indeed, they would have been amazed had they been able to see the letters Saʿid was simultaneously writing to the French and Americans which expressed exactly the same sentiments. The first British dilemma was how to maintain peace in the Persian Gulf without interfering in the internal affairs of the maritime states of its shores. Obviously there had to be some interference, particularly if the ruler who had co-operated in maintaining the maritime peace was about to be overthrown and replaced by someone who might not be so obliging. The second British dilemma was how to counter the Slave Trade when the slaves came from the country of their firm ally. The solution they tried was to work through that ally to end the trade. The ease with which Saʿid thought he could manœuvre the British encouraged him to make approaches to other powers. He thereby stimulated the interest of the

[1] The treaty was arranged by Cogan on 31 May 1839 – see F.O. 54/2. It is also printed in *Bombay Selections XXIV*, pp. 250-6.

French and Americans in East Africa. By the mid 1840s there were three consuls on the tiny island of Zanzibar.

As Zanzibar grew in importance in Western opinion, so did the region increasingly appeal to Saiyid Sa'id's ambitions. The treaties he had arranged with the Americans, French, and British led to a commercial development of the Swahili Coast which was closely followed by the strengthening of Sa'id's authority there. Because the system of rule was so personal, all arrangements with Western powers were initiated and negotiated by Saiyid Sa'id himself. Consequently he became the representative, both in the eyes of the Westerners and of his own countrymen, for the successful implementation of the treaties. His political position among his countrymen was therefore one of great strength in these years before the consuls sent by the Western powers began to encroach upon it.

CHAPTER VII

SAIYID SAʻID AND THE WESTERN POWERS, 1839-1856

SECTION 1. 1839-1841

Western interest in the Swahili Coast presented simultaneous opportunities and dangers to Saiyid Saʻid. So long as the Western powers were amenable to manipulation and their interests remained largely commercial, Saʻid could benefit from their presence. However, as soon as these interests developed strong political overtones and the Great Powers became suspicious of each other's intentions, local potentates like Saʻid were in danger of suffering loss of authority, influence, or territory.

In the 1830s there had been an Anglo-French balance in the Indian Ocean, but towards the end of that decade initiatives by both these powers began to upset it. During the Napoleonic Wars, when there had also been considerable rivalry between the French and British, Saiyid Saʻid had been able to maintain his independence by playing off one side against the other. But in the later period Western rivalries developed in such a way that the ruler of Muscat and Zanzibar began to be overwhelmed by the pressures exerted upon him. There was, however, a time lag before the Europeans developed direct territorial ambitions on the Swahili Coast, and the 1840s were therefore a period in which Saʻid, though increasingly subordinated to the whims and influence of Western Powers, could still extend his commercial and political ambitions in that region.

The British had tolerated French connexions with Saiyid Saʻid in the 1820s and 1830s because they regarded them as purely commercial. The international situation at the end of the 1830s made the British change their opinion and policy. Muhammad Ali, ruler of Egypt, who was supported by the French, was threatening the Ottoman Empire, which the British were committed to uphold. In July 1839 Khurshid

THE SWAHILI COAST

Pasha, commander of one of Muhammad Ali's armies, was advancing towards Oman and the Persian Gulf.[1] He informed the British that he intended to take Bahrain.[2] Bombay, thinking this was part of an Egyptian plan to attack the Ottoman Empire from the rear, through Basra and Baghdad,[3] fell back on their former policy of using Muscat as the basis of their control of the Persian Gulf.

The lukewarm attitude towards Saiyid Sa'id which had been apparent in 1833 was no longer detectable:

'The Imaum of Muscat is one of the oldest as he has ever been one of the most faithful of our Eastern allies, and each succeeding mail from England seems to mark more strongly than its predecessor the wish of Her Majesty's Government that the encroachment of the Pasha of Egypt on the shores of the Persian Gulf should be resisted.'[4]

Calcutta ordered Bombay to ascertain what naval support, stores, munitions, and military officers the Saiyid might require. It seemed even more important to contact Sa'id when the Persian Gulf Resident reminded Bombay that Muscat and the Egyptian Government had previously enjoyed close relations, and that Saiyid Sa'id was connected to Muhammad Ali by marriage.[5] The Resident thought that Sa'id might be prepared to co-operate against Muhammad Ali if British troops would help him both to overcome Hamud ibn Azzan, who persisted in causing trouble from Sohar, and to take Bahrain, which Sa'id still coveted.[6]

Saiyid Sa'id could not resist the opportunity to gain possession of Bahrain. When he returned to Muscat from East Africa in September 1839,[7] he said he wanted neither munitions nor officers, for it was useless to try to get the Arabs to combine against the Egyptians. Instead, an officer and a body of British troops should occupy Buraimi, the important citadel in the Omani interior, and the British should take

---

[1] Bombay to Secret Committee, no. 87, 16 July 1839, S.L.B., 1st series 9.
[2] Khurshid Pasha to Hennell, n.d., encl. in Hennell to Bombay, 2 Mch. 1839, encl. in Bombay to Secret Committee, no. 87, 16 July 1839, E.S.L.B. 12.
[3] Bombay to Secret Committee, no. 34, 25 Mch. 1839, S.L.B., 2nd series 6.
[4] Supreme Government to Bombay, 18 July 1839, encl. in Bombay to Secret Committee, no. 103, 10 Sept. 1839, E.S.L.B. 15.
[5] Bombay to Supreme Government, 7 Sept. 1839, encl. in no. 103, as above.
[6] Hennell to Bombay, 21 Aug. 1839, encl. in no. 103, as above.
[7] Saiyid Sa'id to Bombay, 7 Oct. 1839, encl. in Bombay to Secret Committee, no. 129, 28 Nov. 1839, E.S.L.B. 18.

SAIYID SA'ID AND THE WESTERN POWERS, 1839-1856

Bahrain.[1] Sa'id obviously hoped the island would then be passed on to him. He came near to achieving his ambition. In order to save the British from the embarrassing duty of capturing Bahrain, Bombay decided that the Saiyid of Muscat should be encouraged to take it himself, and perhaps be given discreet aid.[2] Even the Supreme Government, usually more restrained than the Bombay Council, envisaged active British support, but ruled it out until the naval force in the Persian Gulf was strengthened by the arrival of ships from England.[3] But because a great proportion of the army was detained in Afghanistan, Sa'id never received any active help.[4] Without it he was not prepared to attack Bahrain.

The situation in Afghanistan also precluded British troops from carrying out Sa'id's other suggestion – that of occupying Buraimi. Although this suggestion was not seriously considered, the British did send an agent to Buraimi to view the state of the fortifications and advise on how they could be strengthened.[5] The man chosen to carry out the mission was Atkins Hamerton, who later became the British consul in Zanzibar.

Hamerton, born in 1804, the son of a Clerk of Ships' Entries at Donneycarney, County Dublin,[6] was nominated a cadet for the Bombay Infantry by the East India Company Director John Morris, having been recommended by Major-General Atkins.[7] He arrived in Bombay in 1825, and was promoted to lieutenant the following year. He showed an aptitude for languages and qualified as an interpreter in Hindustani in 1831. In the same year he stood trial for being a second at a duel between Lts Tucker and Montgomery in which the latter was killed. Despite this he had by 1837 been promoted to Captain, and in May 1838 he was appointed interpreter to a Field

[1] Bombay to Secret Committee, no. 135, 31 Dec. 1839, S.L.B., 1st series 10.
[2] Bombay told Hennell not to put any impediment in Sa'id's way if he decided to take Bahrain – Bombay to Hennell, 14 July 1840, encl. in Bombay to Secret Committee, no. 56, 24 Aug. 1840, E.S.L.B. 23.
[3] Supreme Government to Bombay, 14 Sept. 1840, encl. in Bombay to Secret Committee, no. 90, 30 Oct. 1840, E.S.L.B. 26.
[4] Bombay to Supreme Government, 22 Aug. 1840, encl. in Bombay to Secret Committee, no. 56, 24 Aug. 1840, E.S.L.B. 23.
[5] Bombay gave the order for this before Sa'id made his suggestion – Hamerton to Resident, Persian Gulf, 7 Jan. 1840, encl. in Bombay to Secret Committee, no. 5, 31 Jan. 1840, E.S.L.B. 19.
[6] I.O.L., L/Mil./9/156, no. 123, 1824.
[7] I.O.L., L/Mil./9/262, p. 104 – Cadet Register 1821-4.

detachment of his regiment proceeding on service to the Persian Gulf.[1]

The dangerous international situation and consequent renewal of close relations between the British and Muscat meant that Bombay would have to persuade Saiyid Saʻid not to consider any possible French approaches. The British had been informed that in 1838 Guillain had had discussions with Saʻid about the appointment of a French consul and that there had been an attempt to set up Saʻid ibn Khalfan as French agent in Muscat.[2] Bombay, not wanting their influence to be supplanted by that of the French, advised Saʻid not to enter into any connexion with that nation.[3] But it was almost too late: Guillain's discussions were in fact followed up by the despatch by the French Ministry of Foreign Affairs of a consul to Zanzibar.[4] Guillain and Noel, the man appointed consul, arrived in Zanzibar in June 1840. Happily for the British, the Sultan was absent in Muscat and his son refused to accept the consul without his father's permission. Noel thought this action was due to the influence of Waters, the American consul in Zanzibar, who feared French commercial competition.[5]

Guillain and Noel then went to Muscat to consult Saiyid Saʻid. On their arrival they were astounded to find that the Sultan refused to accept a French consul. Saʻid put all sorts of obstructions in Noel's way, demanding conditions that the French could not meet. He said that he was surprised a consul had been sent without any previous official communication to find out his views on the subject, and that a consul could not reside in his dominions without the prior conclusion of a treaty. He would, however, accept Noel as an agent with no consular powers.[6] In vain did Guillain remind him that, during a visit to Zanzibar in 1838, the Sultan had expressed a desire for a French consul. Saʻid's interpreter obediently denied transmitting any such notion.[7] Guillain impatiently reminded the Sultan that it had not been the French who had demanded Saʻid should sacrifice 50–60,000 dollars a year and

[1] Bombay Service Army Lists, vol. III, p. 373 (I.O.L.).
[2] Khojah Reuben, British agent at Muscat, to Bombay, 29 Sept. 1838, encl. in Bombay to Secret Committee, no. 5, 31 Jan. 1840, E.S.L.B. 19.
[3] Bombay to Secret Committee, no. 5, 31 Jan. 1840, S.L.B., 1st series 11.
[4] Ministry of F.A. to Ministry of Marine, 25 Sept. 1839, and Instructions to Noel, 18 Sept. 1839, M.O., O.I. 10/45.
[5] Noel to Ministry of F.A., 12 Feb. 1841, A.E., Zanz. C.C.1.
[6] Guillain to Saʻid, 4 Aug. 1840, M.O., O.I. 10/45; and Noel to Ministry of F.A., 12 Feb. 1841, A.E., Zanz. C.C.1.
[7] Saʻid to Guillain, n.d., but c. 5 Aug. 1840, M.O., O.I. 10/45.

should make concessions over the Slave Trade, nor had it been they who had occupied Mombasa or signed independent treaties with the chiefs of the Qawasim in revolt against Sa'id's authority, or who had imposed navigation restrictions on Sa'id's subjects.[1] Sa'id would not budge: he said he would have to await confirmation from Paris that Noel was truly accredited as consul.[2] This was merely a delaying tactic, as Sa'id himself admitted to the British. Hennell, the Persian Gulf Resident, and Hamerton were both at Muscat at this time and Sa'id told them he would keep the French in play until he heard from the British Government.[3] In fact he already knew the opinion of the British, but what he wanted was a guarantee of their support should the French punish him in any way for his refusal. Sa'id wrote to Palmerston to ask for advice.[4]

What had made Saiyid Sa'id change his policy and now cease to try to manipulate the French and British against each other? Undoubtedly his hope that he would obtain Bahrain with British aid was a factor in his decision. But Sa'id was, in addition, very worried about recent French activities in East Africa. In 1839, De Hell, the governor of Bourbon, who, in common with most holders of his office, had ambitious designs on Madagascar, had sent Passot to explore the north-west region of that island. During his expedition Passot had also visited the neighbouring island of Nossi Bé, and his reports persuaded De Hell to take the island.[5] Its inhabitants, the Sakalava, were at odds with the Hova of Madagascar, and could possibly help the French in their designs on the larger island.[6]

Sa'id had cause for concern, because he thought he had some right to Nossi Bé himself. In 1838 the Sakalava of north-west Madagascar had sent a deputation to Sa'id in Zanzibar asking for aid against the Hova.[7] The Sultan sent his ship, the *Curlew*, to investigate, and its captain suggested the Sakalava put themselves under Sa'id's protection.[8]

---

[1] Guillain to Sa'id, no. 4, n.d., but c. 16 Aug. 1840, M.O., O.I. 10/45.

[2] Sa'id to Guillain, n.d., but c. 16 Aug. 1840, M.O., O.I. 10/45.

[3] Hennell to Bombay, 5 Aug. 1840, encl. in Bombay to Secret Committee, no. 56, 22 Aug. 1840, E.S.L.B. 23.

[4] Saiyid Sa'id to Palmerston, 31 July 1840, F.O. 54/3.

[5] See Raymond Decary, *L'Ile Nosy Bé de Madagascar* (Paris, 1960), p. 14 et seq.

[6] For the Sakalava/Hova rivalry, see Deschamps, *op. cit.*, *passim*.

[7] Guillain, *Documents sur l'histoire, la géographie, et le commerce de la partie occidentale de Madagascar* (Paris, 1845), p. 134.

[8] *Ibid.*, p. 135.

Sakalava representatives went to Zanzibar to arrange this, and they signed a convention which placed the Sakalava territory in north-west Madagascar under Saʻid's suzerainty, and which bound the Sakalava and Antakara peoples to pay a tax of one dollar a head per year to Saʻid. For his part, the Sultan promised to re-establish the authority of the Sakalava.¹ Saʻid sent a ship with forty-five soldiers, munitions, and materials with which to arm two forts, to north-west Madagascar. The forts were duly built and a Hova attack was repulsed, but the man Saʻid had appointed as governor, who was to follow in another ship, did not arrive. There was disagreement among the troops about what should be done, and they returned to Zanzibar. The Sakalava were then forced to flee to Nossi Bé.² Saiyid Saʻid therefore thought he had a claim to Nossi Bé because his convention with the Sakalava had placed their territory under his suzerainty.

Saʻid was further alarmed when the French appeared to have ambitious designs on territories even nearer the Swahili Coast. Guillain, following instructions from the governor of Bourbon, made enquiries at Zanzibar about establishing French factories at such places as Mogadishu and Brava on the Banadir coast. When Guillain continued these enquiries at Muscat,³ the Persian Gulf Resident, taking advantage of Saʻid's apprehension, told the Sultan that the French were likely to deprive him of all his possessions in Africa.⁴

The British had to decide whether to advise Saʻid to refuse to accept a French consul and what support to offer him. The Persian Gulf Resident thought that unless Saʻid was actively supported by the British he would have to accept a French consul.⁵ The international situation made it almost impossible at this particular time for the British to allow Saʻid to form a close connexion with the French. The Anglo-French balance in the Indian Ocean had been upset by forward moves from both parties. Such moves had been encouraged by the

---

¹ Guillain, *Documents sur l'histoire, la géographie, et le commerce de la partie occidentale de Madagascar* (Paris, 1845), pp. 135-6. The treaty is enclosed in Saiyid Saʻid to Palmerston, 1 May 1841, F.O. 54/4.

² Guillain, as above, p. 136; and British local agent at Muscat to Bombay, 12 Mch. 1839, encl. in Bombay to Secret Committee, no. 41, 13 Apr. 1839, E.S.L.B. 12

³ De Hell to Guillain, 18 May 1840, M.O., O.I. 10/45; and Hennell to Bombay, 5 Aug. 1840, encl. in Bombay to Secret Committee, no. 56, 22 Aug. 1840, E.S.L.B. 23.

⁴ Hennell to Bombay, *idem.*

⁵ Hennell to Secret Committee, 31 July 1840, encl. in no. 56, as above.

invention of the steam engine and by the political situation in the Near East. The desire of both the British and French for coaling points in the Red Sea coincided with their enmity in the Near East, where they were supporting opposing interests. Each side was suspicious of the other's intentions. The British took Aden; the French sent exploratory expeditions into Abyssinia and developed plans for East Africa. It was rumoured that the French had also established a settlement at Tajura in the Red Sea.[1] The situation was further complicated by the British fear of the Russians in central Asia and their anxiety to defend the north-west frontier of India. The situation in Afghanistan and the threat posed by Persia, with whom the British had broken relations, made it important that the Persian Gulf should remain a sphere of British influence and that the French should be kept out of it. In 1840 Muhammad Ali's threat to the Turks seemed about to precipitate a European war. In September of that year Bombay expected to hear of a declaration of war at any moment: they had heard that five French warships were shortly expected in the Red Sea.[2] The French could not be allowed to subvert British influence in Muscat. On receipt of Saiyid Sa'id's application for advice, Bombay commented, 'We do not view this question purely as a commercial one'.[3] The Foreign Office also saw the dangers of the situation, and this was the reply Palmerston gave to Sa'id's letter:

'The British Government recommend Your Highness to refuse to comply with any demands which the French nation may make upon you, and which may in your opinion be incompatible with your interests, but to rely upon the support of England, if circumstances should render it necessary for Your Highness to seek for assistance.'[4]

Sa'id had got the assurance he had been seeking.

The British had been particularly anxious to exclude French influence at Muscat because they themselves had just appointed a European agent there. In fact a provision for the appointment of a consul had been included in the 1839 treaty negotiated by Cogan. At that time Saiyid Sa'id had written to the Foreign Office, asking for a

[1] Bombay to Secret Committee, no 20, 30 Apr. 1840, S.L.B., 1st series 11.
[2] Haines, British agent at Aden, to Bombay, 30 Aug. 1840, and minute by the governor of Bombay, 14 Sept. 1840, encl. in Bombay to Secret Committee, no. 73, 25 Sept. 1840, E.S.L.B. 24.
[3] Bombay to Supreme Government, 13 Sept. 1840, encl. in Bombay to Secret Committee, no. 90, 30 Oct. 1840, E.S.L.B. 26.
[4] Palmerston to Saiyid Sa'id, 30 Sept. 1840, F.O. 54/3.

THE SWAHILI COAST

'genuine Englishman' to be sent.[1] He had done this because he feared the appointment of a local man, such as the unpopular Jew whom the British had appointed their agent in Muscat, or of one of his own people: both the French and Americans had tried to appoint the Omani Saʻid ibn Khalfan as their agent, but Saiyid Saʻid refused to ratify the appointment.[2] Saʻid's letter had prompted the Court of Directors to reconsider the question of a consul. They decided that 'very serious inconveniences and embarrassment' would arise from such an appointment, because dealings with the Saiyid of Muscat were carried on by the Government of India and depended on the delicate influence on the Saiyid exercised by the Resident in the Persian Gulf, an influence that could not continue if a representative of the British Crown was placed in direct communication with the Saiyid.[3] The Foreign Office had lost no time in informing the India Board that the Court of Directors had been consulted during the drafting of the treaty and had then made no objection to the establishment of a consulate.[4] The East India Company had had to admit this, and they had offered a compromise: the officer in question should be an agent of the Company; he should be appointed by the governor of Bombay and could be dismissed by him but he should also hold consular authority from the Crown, as did the agents at Quseir, Suez, and Mocha. He would be paid by the Government of India.[5] Palmerston had agreed, but had insisted that the officer also be removable by the Secretary of State.[6] The East India Company was directed to choose a suitable person.[7]

Bombay was not happy when ordered to make this appointment, since they had unearthed the following instruction from Lord Minto, the Governor-General in 1810:

'After the repeated proofs which we have had of the fatal and seemingly unavoidable effects of the climate of Muscat, it is not advisable to appoint any person to the perilous situation of Resident at that place.'[8]

[1] Saiyid Saʻid to Palmerston, 2 June 1839, F.O. 54/3.
[2] British local agent, Muscat, to Hennell, 29 Sept. 1838, encl. in Bombay to Secret Committee, no. 5, 31 Jan. 1840, S.L.B., 1st series 11; and Saʻid ibn Khalfan to Ministry of F.A., 23 June 1841, A.E., Zanz. C.C.1.
[3] India Board to Palmerston, 8 Feb. 1840, F.O. 54/3, reporting the opinion of the Court of Directors.   [4] F.O. to India Board, 24 Feb. 1840, F.O. 54/3.
[5] India Board to Palmerston, 14 Mch. 1840, F.O. 54/3.
[6] Note by Palmerston, c. 6 Mch. 1840, F.O. 54/3.
[7] F.O. to India Board, 6 Mch. 1840, F.O. 54/3.
[8] Minto to Bombay, 27 Jan. 1810, encl. in Bombay to Secret Committee, no. 10, 28 Feb. 1840, E.S.L.B. 19.

A list drawn up of all the European agents who had died at Muscat before 1810 was startlingly long.¹ However, Bombay had to carry out the order, but they stipulated that the agent should leave Muscat in the bad season.² Since Hamerton had completed his journey to Buraimi, he was the obvious choice for the position. Hennell was ordered to appoint him, but no mention was made of the consular nature of Hamerton's authority.³ As far as Hamerton knew, he was merely East India Company agent at Muscat. So the Foreign Office decision to appoint a consul at Zanzibar, a decision which had been made in response to complaints by British subjects that they were having commercial difficulties in East Africa, had been interpreted by the Bombay Residency as referring to the troubles in the Persian Gulf. Instead of a consul being sent to Zanzibar, an East India Company agent was appointed to Muscat.

There the agent might have stayed had not the French chosen this moment further to indulge their ambitions in the Madagascar region. The governor of Bourbon had sent troops to take the island of Nossi Bé and a fort and storerooms were built there.⁴ Saiyid Sa'id was informed of this by his son Khalid, whom he had left in charge at Zanzibar while he went to Oman.⁵ Sa'id, worried about these renewed French activities, wrote to the governor of Bourbon to protest,⁶ but he also felt he should be in East Africa in person to see what was happening. The British therefore had to decide whether their agent at Muscat should remain there or accompany Sa'id to Zanzibar. A few months earlier, when Sa'id had also been contemplating returning to the Swahili Coast, the Persian Gulf Resident thought that the British agent should go as well. Hamerton agreed, saying that Sa'id wanted to be accompanied, although the Sultan later denied this.⁷ In the opinion of the Persian Gulf Resident, since the advantages of Hamerton's appointment lay

---

¹ Governor of Bombay's minute, 8 Feb. 1840, encl. in no. 10, as above.
² Bombay to Hennell, 15 Feb. 1840, encl. in no. 10, as above.
³ *Idem*, and Hennell to Hamerton, 13 Apr. 1840, encl. in Bombay to Secret Committee, no. 26, 20 May 1840, E.S.L.B. 22. Hennell merely told Hamerton that he had been appointed to assume charge of 'our political relations with His Highness in Oman'. Bombay omitted to mention that Hamerton was to be consul, but this was probably not deliberate.
⁴ Noel's Report on the taking of Nossi Bé, 30 June 1841, A.E., Zanz. C.C.1.
⁵ Hennell to Bombay, 3 Nov. 1840, F.O. 54/4.
⁶ Saiyid Sa'id to the governor of Bourbon, 3 Nov. 1840, F.O. 54/4.
⁷ Hamerton to Bombay, 15 July 1840, encl. in Bombay to Secret Committee, no. 56, 24 Aug. 1840, E.S.L.B. 23.

in the personal influence which it was hoped he would acquire over Saʻid, he should keep close to the Sultan.¹ The Supreme Government, however, thought that Hamerton should stay at Muscat and watch over affairs in Oman.² As far as they were concerned, his job was to maintain British influence in that part of the Persian Gulf which was important to them.

Now the situation had to be reviewed in the light of the new French forward moves in Nossi Bé. In addition, Oman was in less danger from the armies of Muhammad Ali, led by Khurshid Pasha. The British Consul-General in Egypt had told Muhammad Ali that the British would not tolerate his designs in the Persian Gulf, with the result that the Egyptian leader ordered Khurshid to abandon his plans for Bahrain.³ The general also had difficulties with his army – his troops were fifty months in arrears of pay – which forced him to withdraw from central Arabia to Madinah.⁴ The British could therefore turn their attention to the investigation of French designs in East Africa. Bombay thought Hamerton should go to Zanzibar with Saʻid and see what was happening, and the Supreme Government now agreed.⁵ In London the Foreign Office was also concerned. Although 'all the enquiries which have been made with a view of ascertaining where the island of Nissbee [Nossi Bé] is situated have been fruitless', the Foreign Office none the less protested to the French.⁶ No answer was received.⁷

Saiyid Saʻid, with Palmerston's promise of aid to hand, determined to seek British assistance.⁸ An envoy he had sent to Nossi Bé returned with the information that a French general and 600 men were there, and an explanation from the queen of the Sakalava, with whom Saʻid had arranged the treaty in 1839, that she did not like the French presence, but was forced to submit to it because 'your people were not with us'.⁹ As far as the British were concerned, the situation was more compli-

¹ Hennell to Bombay, 15 Apr. 1840, encl. in Bombay to Secret Committee, no. 26, 20 May 1840, E.S.L.B. 22.
² Supreme Government to Bombay, 14 Sept. 1840, encl. in Bombay to Secret Committee, no. 90, 30 Oct. 1840, E.S.L.B. 26.
³ Bombay to Secret Committee, no. 37, 22 June 1840, S.L.B., 1st series 14.
⁴ Hamerton to Bombay, 13 Oct. 1840, encl. in Bombay to Secret Committee, no. 94, 31 Oct. 1840, E.S.L.B. 26.
⁵ Supreme Government to Secret Committee, 11 Jan. 1841, F.O. 54/4; and Bombay to Hamerton, 16 Jan. 1841, Z.A.
⁶ Note, n.d., and Palmerston to Granville, 5 Feb. 1841, F.O. 54/4.
⁷ Bulwer to Aberdeen, 24 Sept. 1841, F.O. 54/4.
⁸ Saiyid Saʻid to Palmerston, 1 May 1841, F.O. 54/4.
⁹ Queen Seneko to Saiyid Saʻid, 21 Mch. 1841, F.O. 54/4.

cated than it had been in 1840 when Sa'id had previously asked for advice and assistance. At that time the British had only to advise the Sultan to refuse the French request to establish a consulate and make undefined promises of help. Now, if they admitted Sa'id's claims to Nossi Bé, they would be more or less obliged to follow this up with active assistance against the French. Palmerston decided not to bind himself until he knew more about the basis of Sa'id's claims. He warned the Sultan that

'there is a material difference between territories which have for a length of time belonged to a sovereign and districts which have only recently tendered their submission to such a sovereign, and over which he has in fact never exercised any practical authority'.[1]

At the same time, however, the Admiralty was directed to send a ship to Nossi Bé to discover whether the French were interfering in territories over which Saiyid Sa'id had actual sovereignty and in which he formerly had administrative authority.[2] Commander J. J. Allen was duly despatched in the *Lily*. He returned with a comforting report that the British need not be apprehensive of the French settlement which had been decimated by disease.[3] Hamerton, now in Zanzibar,[4] also told the Foreign Office that the Sultan's claims to Nossi Bé were 'vague and groundless'.[5] Hence the British decided to hold out no prospect of help to Sa'id.

Such was Saiyid Sa'id's position when Melbourne was replaced as Prime Minister by Peel in September 1841, a change of government which was to lead to an alteration of British policy towards the ruler of Muscat and Zanzibar. It was in the years 1839–41 that the British laid the foundations of a closer association with Zanzibar. At the same time the French had begun to make active moves in the region. Each power stimulated the other into activity. Sa'id, still manœuvring, derived what benefit he could from the Western interests. These circumstances enabled the Swahilis to prosper during the next two decades; yet they

[1] Palmerston to Saiyid Sa'id, 13 Aug. 1841, F.O. 54/4.
[2] F.O. to Admiralty, 13 Aug. 1841, F.O. 54/4.
[3] Allen to governor of Mauritius, 3 Nov. 1841, F.O. 54/4.
[4] Hamerton was sent to Zanzibar with a writer and interpreter, and arrived there on 4 May 1841 – Bombay to Secret Committee, no. 67, 30 Aug. 1841, S.L.B., 1st series 14, and same to same, no. 13, Feb. 1841, S.L.B., 1st series 13.
[5] Hamerton's 'Report on the proceedings of the French with respect to their aggressions in part of the territory of the Imam of Muscat', n.d., F.O. 54/4.

also implied an ineluctable diminution of Swahili independence which was to culminate in the triumph of Western imperialism.

SECTION 2. 1841-1856

In the 1830s, Saiyid Sa'id was fairly independent of British influence, although he could generally rely on British support in times of trouble. Why did he lose this position? For the first few years of the 1840s he attempted to retain the old system, but circumstances had changed. The presence of a British agent was an irksome check on his manipulations.

Hamerton did not try to establish, as Hennell had envisaged, a discreet and subtle influence. A forthright, irritable and impatient man, he tended to treat the Sultan and his subjects as inferiors and children. Waters, the American consul, said that Hamerton was vain, proud, and haughty, and his conduct towards the Sultan was almost insolent – in fact, he treated him like a recalcitrant pupil.[1] 'He is', said Cogan, who had negotiated the 1839 treaty with the Sultan, 'considered quick-tempered and overbearing in his conduct towards the Prince and people of Zanzibar.'[2] In 1844 the Sultan complained of a sneering insult from Hamerton to his son, Khalid.[3] The governor of Bourbon thought Hamerton had the habits and conceits of an old-fashioned soldier.[4] Another Frenchman, Loarer, saw Hamerton as Cerberus, and regarded him as vain, foolish, crafty, proud, imperious, and 'as plotting as an Asiatic'.[5] Although Hamerton, when reprimanded for his attitude to the Sultan by the Foreign Office,[6] protested that he never behaved with disrespect towards the Sultan or his people,[7] his own words betray him. When a letter from the Foreign Office about the necessity of prohibiting the Slave Trade completely was given an adverse reception by the Sultan, Hamerton 'at once assumed a high tone with him, which is the only way to do business with him'.[8] Hamerton's attitude towards the Sultan probably stemmed from the fact that he viewed Sa'id as a

[1] Kerdudal to Bazoche, 3 May 1844, M.O., O.I. 15/49, reporting Waters' opinion.
[2] Cogan to Sir Charles Forbes, 28 Oct. 1842, F.O. 54/5.
[3] Cogan's Diary, entry for 16 Feb. 1844, F.O. 54/6.
[4] R. Desfossés to Ministry of F.A., 4 Feb. 1845, A.E., Zanz. C.C.1.
[5] Loarer's Report, Part I, 1849, M.O., O.I. 5/23.
[6] F.O. to Hamerton, 27 Nov. 1844, F.O. 54/6.
[7] Hamerton to F.O., no. 5, 24 Mch. 1845, F.O. 54/7.
[8] Hamerton to Secret Committee, 9 Feb. 1842, encl. in Bombay to Secret Committee, no. 56, 23 May 1842, E.S.L.B. 45.

usurper who had assassinated his predecessor.¹ He was also very conscious of a man's station. Waters, the American consul, he regarded as hopelessly inferior, because of his commercial operations and low-church beliefs.² Hamerton's drinking habits also boded ill for his relations both with the strict American consul and the Arabs. Almost all the French who visited Zanzibar described Hamerton as an 'ivrogne',³ and if the almost total lack of punctuation in his letters indicates anything, it is that he was intoxicated whilst writing them.⁴

Hamerton's habits and attitudes did not augur well for the establishment of a discreet British influence at Zanzibar. There were also other difficulties which led to a cooling of the Sultan's feeling for the British. The main problem was that Saʻid saw the East India Company and the Foreign Office as two different entities which he could manipulate against each other. He much preferred dealing with Whitehall, because he regarded the Company as the source of all his past troubles and embarrassments. The frequent changes in British policy had not gone unnoticed by him. He was also impressed with the idea of a powerful distant land. The treatment of the envoy he had sent to England in 1838, to congratulate the Queen on her accession, had been impressive. The envoy had been entertained at public expense, had dined with the Queen and had spent the night at Windsor. He had also discussed matters of state with Palmerston.⁵ Saʻid was wary of the Company because he thought it had ordered Hamerton to pick a quarrel with

¹ Kerdudal to Bazoche, 24 May 1843, M.O., O.I. 15/63.
² Same to same, 3 May 1844, M.O., O.I. 15/59. Presumably Hamerton, who came from Dublin, was a Roman Catholic. Waters belonged to the Temperance Sect and was a Republican. See also below, p. 194.
³ In 1843 the French ship *Messager* and the British ship *Isis* were in Zanzibar harbour at the same time. The captain of the French ship was most surprised to find Hamerton clambering aboard very early one morning, but gave him a good welcome and entertained him to breakfast. Later, when, as usual, drunk, Hamerton told the captain that he had mistaken the French ship for the British – Kerdudal to Bazoche, 24 May 1843, M.O., O.I. 15/63. When Broquant first arrived as French consul in Zanzibar in 1844, Hamerton paid a call on the *Berceau* when he was drunk – Broquant to Ministry of F.A., 4 Feb. 1845, A.E., Zanz. C.C.1.
⁴ Hamerton was more than once reprimanded by the Foreign Office for not numbering his despatches correctly – e.g. F.O. to Hamerton, 26 July 1848, F.O. 54/12. Even Bombay, who supported Hamerton in all matters, admitted that he conducted his correspondence in 'an imperfect manner' – Bombay to Secret Committee, no. 93, 26 Aug. 1846, S.L.B., 1st series 22.
⁵ Correspondence relating to the visit is in F.O. 54/2.

him.¹ When, in 1842, another envoy, Ali ibn Nasir, visited England, he told Palmerston that Sa'id regretted the Company's want of confidence in him.²

Perhaps Sa'id also felt that the Company had not fulfilled its obligations according to the 1798 and 1800 engagements. Sa'id may have been aware of these engagements, and in that case many of his expectations and requests for help can be explained. In 1844 Sa'id told Cogan that his son had asked for British advice when the Wahhabis were threatening Oman, and Bombay had declined to give it despite the 1800 engagement.³ Sa'id may, however, have been informed of, or reminded of, the engagements by Cogan himself because when Cogan was awaiting a boat to take him from Bombay to Zanzibar in order to negotiate the 1839 treaty, he had made himself thoroughly familiar with the previous engagements with Muscat.⁴

Both the American consul and Cogan also influenced Sa'id against the Company.⁵ The personal animosity between Hamerton and Cogan, who now had commercial interests in Zanzibar, is important in assessing Sa'id's reaction to Foreign Office and Company policies in these years. Sa'id erroneously regarded Cogan, whom he liked, as a representative of the Foreign Office, and Hamerton as a Company man. Cogan learnt that Hamerton, when he first came to Zanzibar, did not hold consular authority, but was merely East India Company agent. Cogan informed the Foreign Office but was mistaken in his hope that this would lead to the appointment of someone else as consul.⁶ The Foreign Office claimed it did not know who, if anyone, had been appointed by the East India Company to fill the post Palmerston had ordered to be created in 1840. It therefore merely told the East India Company to name an officer for the post of consul. The India Board told the Foreign Office that the latter had indeed been informed of Hamerton's appointment as Company agent and it was up to the Foreign Office to

¹ Cogan to Sir Charles Forbes, 28 Oct. 1842, F.O. 54/5.
² Ali ibn Nasir to Aberdeen, 23 Nov. 1842, F.O. 54/4.
³ Cogan's Diary, entry for 7 Mch. 1844, F.O. 54/6.
⁴ Cogan to Bombay, 7 Jan. 1839, and Bombay to Cogan, 16 Jan. 1839, Proc. 16 Jan., B.S.C. 126. See also Chapter VI, p. 141, note 3.
⁵ Hamerton to Secret Committee, 9 Feb. 1842, encl. in Bombay to Secret Committee, no. 58, 23 May 1842, E.S.L.B. 45.
⁶ Dickson to F.O., n.d., 1841, F.O. 54/4, and Cogan to C. of Ds., 5 Oct. 1844, F.O. 54/6, admitting that it was at his instance that Dickson wrote this letter.

name him consul.¹ This muddle was doubtless a result of the government change-over in 1841. Hamerton was quickly appointed consul, a fact which he discovered much to his surprise when he visited Bombay in May 1842.²

Cogan's opposition to Hamerton did not stem from the fact that he coveted the post of consul himself – he had been offered it in 1838, but had refused. Rather, the views of the two men were fundamentally incompatible. Hamerton held things Arab in contempt, whereas Cogan had some respect for the Sultan.³ Cogan also did very well out of his championship of Sa'id. He induced the Sultan to waive repayment of a large sum of money for which Sa'id's agent, Aga Muhammad Rakim Khan, had started proceedings against him, and he got Sa'id to grant him Latham's Island, rich in guano, to the south of Zanzibar.⁴ The disagreement between the British consul and the negotiator of the 1839 treaty was emphasized when the Company championed the former and the Foreign Office the latter. The Company was always jealous of Foreign Office interference in the affairs of the Sultan, which they regarded as their preserve. The Company refused to take any notice of letters from the Sultan brought to England by Cogan in 1844, because these had not come through the 'proper channels'.⁵ The Foreign Office, on the other hand, took notice of Cogan's complaints about Hamerton and regarded the Company as unnecessarily prejudiced against Cogan. Cogan had initially antagonized the Company in 1839, when he had some dealings with the rajah of Satara while he was at Bombay.⁶

¹ Note by Aberdeen, 31 Oct.; F.O. to India Board, 1 Nov.; and India Board to F.O., 5 Nov. 1841, F.O. 54/4.
² Hamerton to Superintendent of the Consular Service, F.O., 21 May 1842, F.O. 54/4.
³ Hamerton spoke to the captain of a French ship of 'la nationalité arabe dont le fanatisme est ennemi de toute civilisation' – Ministry of Marine to Ministry of F.A., 14 Oct. 1845, M.O., O.I. 15/65, quoting a letter from Captain Baudais.
⁴ Hamerton to Bombay, no. 39, 17 June 1842, encl. in Bombay to Secret Committee, no. 92, 26 Aug. 1842, E.S.L.B. 50; and Hamerton to F.O., no. 5, 24 Mch. 1845, F.O. 54/7.
⁵ East India Company to Cogan, 3 Oct. 1844, encl. in Cogan to Canning, 5 Oct. 1844, F.O. 54/6.
⁶ The correspondence relating to this is in F.O. 54/3 – in particular, Cogan to Backhouse, 15 Jan. 1840, explaining the whole situation. It seems there was some intrigue between Cogan and the rajah. Other dealings of Cogan's were also suspicious. It was suspected that a ship carrying cargo of his was deliberately wrecked in 1843, and another of his ships was wrecked in 1847 – Bombay to C. of Ds., no. 11, 25 Feb. 1843, P.L.B. 27, and same to same, no. 33, 12 Mch. 1847, P.L.B. 34. He also caused some trouble at Aden, where he was living

THE SWAHILI COAST

Cogan encouraged Sa'id in his prejudice against Hamerton. When Sa'id's envoy, Ali ibn Nasir, went to England in 1842 he complained about Hamerton,[1] and two years later the Sultan wrote to Aberdeen that he was constantly perplexed by petty annoyances from the consul.[2] According to the American consul, the Sultan 'appears much dissatisfied with the English Agent here and would like to have him recalled'.[3] Hamerton's position was altogether very difficult. The policies he had to carry out would have made him unpopular even had he been diplomatic in his negotiations. Apart from the constant pressure he had to exert about the Slave Trade, Hamerton antagonized the Zanzibaris over other matters. He insisted that a close commercial connexion between the customs master and the American consul be broken,[4] he refused to allow two Englishwomen who had returned with the *Sultana* (the Sultan's ship which went to London in 1842) into his house in Zanzibar,[5] and he forbade the selling of 'free labourers' to ships from Mauritius.[6] Another small matter which affected the Sultan's relations with the British was Hamerton's tactless display to Sa'id of an English journal which contained an article claiming that Sa'id had sent the *Sultana* to England to recruit white wives. Sa'id was so annoyed that he said he would write to Queen Victoria to protest, but there is no record of him having done so.[7]

In August 1841, Hamerton reported that British influence at Zanzibar was at a low ebb, and that there was a strong party in favour of French and American interests.[8] Undoubtedly the American consul had great influence among certain powerful people in Zanzibar, but the French seemed to offer a more feasible alternative to the British because they made their strength much more apparent than did the Americans. French warships were regular visitors to Zanzibar. Prominent among those in favour of the French were the Sultan's son, Khalid, who was

in 1847 – Haines, Resident at Aden, to Bombay, 5 Jan. 1847, Dr. 700, 5 Aug. 1847, B.C. 2203.

[1] Ali ibn Nasir to Aberdeen, 23 Nov. 1842, F.O. 54/4.
[2] Saiyid Sa'id to Aberdeen, 8 Apr. 1844, F.O. 54/6.
[3] R. P. Waters to J. G. Waters, 1 Jan. 1842, printed in Bennett and Brooks, *op. cit.*, p. 236.
[4] Hamerton to Aberdeen, 21 May 1842, F.O. 54/4.
[5] Hamerton to F.O., no. 5, 24 Mch. 1845, F.O. 54/7.
[6] Hamerton to Bombay, 20 Aug. 1841, encl. in India Board to Aberdeen, 12 Jan. 1842, F.O. 54/4.
[7] Kerdudal to Bazoche, 24 May 1843, M.O., O.I. 15/63.
[8] Hamerton to the governor of Mauritius, 17 Aug. 1841, F.O. 54/4.

SAIYID SAʿID AND THE WESTERN POWERS, 1839-1856

generally left in charge when Saʿid went to Muscat; Sulaiman, the governor of Zanzibar; Ahmad ibn Nahman, who sometimes acted as the Sultan's secretary; and Khamis ibn Uthman, who was, however, fickle in his alignments.[1] Hamerton suggested as an antidote the visit of a few British cruisers to Zanzibar.[2] Indeed the presence of naval vessels seems to have had a great effect on the authorities of Zanzibar. After the arrival of the *Lily* in August 1841, Hamerton said he had been able to induce the Sultan to treat the representations of British merchants with much more consideration than formerly.[3] Kerdudal, captain of *Le Messager*, claimed that his ship's visit had an excellent effect on the Arab population of Zanzibar.[4] The only American warships that had ever touched at Zanzibar were the *Peacock* in 1834, the *John Adams* in 1838, and the *Constitution* in 1842.[5] Consul Ward felt this absence of a show of force was a contributory factor in his adverse treatment by Saʿid. He suggested warships touch more regularly at Zanzibar so that Saʿid could get a true idea of the size and power of the American nation.[6] The *Susquehanna* consequently put in at Zanzibar.[7] A succeeding

[1] For Sulaiman, the governor of Zanzibar, being favourable to French interests – Noel to Ministry of F.A., 12 Feb. 1841, A.E., Zanz. C.C.1. For Sulaiman as chief devotee of the French party – Kerdudal to Bazoche, 24 May 1843, M.O., O.I. 15/63. For Khalid's alignment – Hamerton to Bombay, no. 11, 3 Mch. 1842, Z.A. On the other hand, Khalid refused to accept Noel as consul when his father was absent in 1840. For Ahmad ibn Nahman's leadership of a French party – Hamerton to the governor of Mauritius, 17 Aug. 1841, F.O. 54/4. Khamis ibn Uthman helped the French when they tried to establish Noel as consul and was imprisoned for his pains – Noel to Ministry of F.A., 12 Feb. 1841, A.E., Zanz. C.C.1. For Hamerton's opinion that Khamis ibn Uthman was trying to make terms to his own advantage with the French – Hamerton to Bombay, 1 May 1841, Z.A. In that letter Hamerton enclosed a letter from Noel, now in the Comoro islands, to Khamis ibn Uthman. For the existence of pro-French feeling at Zanzibar – Kerdudal to Bazoche, 3 May 1844, M.O., O.I. 15/59. See also above, Chapter VI, p. 157, for Khamis ibn Uthman.

[2] Hamerton to Rear-Admiral Sir E. D. King, C.-in-C., Cape of Good Hope station, 17 Aug. 1841, F.O. 54/4. Nine British naval ships visited Zanzibar between 1840 and 1850: information from various letters of Hamerton and the Admiralty.

[3] Hamerton to Comm. W. Smyth of *Grecian*, 5 Dec. 1841, Z.A.

[4] Kerdudal to Bazoche, 3 May 1844, M.O., O.I. 15/59.

[5] Introduction to Ruschenberger, *op. cit.*; Journal of R. P. Waters, entry for 11 Sept. 1838, printed in Bennett and Brooks, *op. cit.*, p. 208; and Ward to Abbot, 13 Mch. 1851, Amer.N.A., Zanz. 3.

[6] George J. Abbot, Consular Bureau, State Dept., to Webster, Sec. of State, Mch. 1851, Amer.N.A., Zanz. 3, reporting a conversation with Consul Ward.

[7] Commander Aulick to Webster, 8 Dec. 1851, Amer.N.A., Zanz. 3.

consul, McMullan, also asked for regular visits.[1] The French consul informed the American consul in 1851 that he found it impossible to transact any important business with Sa'id without the presence of a French ship of war.[2]

It would seem from Hamerton's strained relations with Sa'id that the Sultan was open to renewed proposals from the French for the establishment of a consulate. What had happened when Noel and Guillain had reported Sa'id's refusal to accept a consul? Guizot had been surprised at Sa'id's attitude, but ascribed it to the international situation and the Sultan's reluctance to defy the British at that particular moment. He answered Sa'id's letter, confirming that Noel had indeed been appointed from France.[3] All the French could do was to await Sa'id's reply to Guizot's letter which Captain Page of *La Favorite* was to take to the Sultan.[4] Page went to Muscat, found the Sultan was not there, and returned to Bourbon.[5] There had just been a change in the governorship of Bourbon, and this, combined with the crossing of some orders from France, led to a confusion in which Noel returned to France.[6] The Ministry of Foreign Affairs was irritated by the muddle and wondered why Page had not been ordered to take the letter to Zanzibar.[7]

Meanwhile the new governor of Bourbon had plans of his own for obtaining labour for his island. He sent Kerdudal to Kilwa to acquire 'free labourers'. When the mission failed Kerdudal was sent to Zanzibar four times in an attempt to negotiate the provision of 'free labourers'.[8] At first Sa'id agreed to the proposals but later bowed to pressure from Hamerton and sent Ahmad ibn Nahman to Bourbon to withdraw his consent.[9] Bazoche, the governor of Bourbon, decided to use Sa'id's retraction to press the matter of consuls.[10] Sa'id said he would have to wait for a reply to the letter he had sent to France: he had sent a boat to

---

[1] McMullan to Mancy, Sec. of State, no. 5, 7 Dec. 1853, Amer.N.A., Zanz. 3.
[2] Ward to Abbot, 13 Mch. 1851, Amer.N.A., Zanz. 3.
[3] Guizot to Ministry of Marine, 27 Apr. 1841, M.O., O.I. 10/45.
[4] Ministry of Marine to governor of Bourbon, 11 May 1841, M.O., O.I. 14/55.
[5] Ministry of Marine to Ministry of F.A., 17 June 1842, M.O., O.I. 14/55.
[6] Noel to Ministry of F.A., 12 Dec. 1842, A.E., Zanz. C.C. 1; and Ministry of Marine to governor of Bourbon, 10 May 1843, M.O., O.I. 14/55.
[7] Guizot to Ministry of Marine, 27 Feb. 1843, M.O., O.I. 14/55.
[8] Bazoche to Kerdudal, no. 25, 21 Feb. 1843, M.O., O.I. 15/63.
[9] Sa'id's instructions to Ahmad ibn Nahman, n.d., 1843, M.O., O.I. 15/63.
[10] Bazoche to Sa'id, 22 July 1843; Bazoche to Kerdudal, 22 July 1843; and Bazoche to Ministry of Marine, no. 384, 1 Aug. 1843, M.O., O.I. 15/63.

Bombay to see if the letter from Paris had arrived there.[1] But what he was really waiting for, and what the boat had gone to get, was the reply to a letter to the British Foreign Office, in which he had again asked what to do should the French press their demands. Ali ibn Nasir had raised the question of the French during his visit to England in 1842, but Aberdeen had avoided giving any opinion. Sa'id had therefore written to Aberdeen in February 1843, asking whether, should the French insist on a treaty and threaten force, he could rely on the British.[2] The British Foreign Secretary returned a discouraging answer. 'Her Majesty's Government', said Aberdeen, 'have no wish whatever to interfere in the stipulations of any commercial treaties which the Imam may conclude with other states.'[3] Sa'id need not have been surprised. It was yet another complete change of policy on the part of the British. It had happened before.

This confirmed a situation which had been impending all along. Since 1839 Sa'id had been waiting for the British to help him take Bahrain and to give him a guarantee of support against the French. He had temporarily abandoned his previous policy of manipulation, had accepted a British consul, a British treaty, and had made concessions over the Slave Trade – all to no avail. Hence he might as well revert to his original policy and accept a French consul and a French treaty. There was one snag, however – he must be sure that he was dealing with the highest authority in France, so that he received a treaty and consul of equivalent status to the British ones. He feared, rightly, that Kerdudal was not authorized from Paris. He told the French envoy that he wanted a consul, if possible less intractable than Hamerton, who was appointed by Paris, and that a treaty must be signed which embraced all the French possessions, and not just Bourbon.[4]

Saiyid Sa'id was in a very difficult situation in 1844. In the hope that he would be helped to capture Bahrain, he had made concessions and subjected himself to British influence from which it was now difficult to escape. Even though Hamerton was so disliked, Sa'id had none the less agreed to some of his demands while he waited for Aberdeen's reply to his letter of February 1843. In 1843 Kerdudal described Sa'id

[1] Kerdudal to Ministry of Marine, 20 Aug. 1843, M.O., O.I. 15/63; and Ministry of Marine to Ministry of F.A., 28 Nov. 1843, M.O., O.I. 15/59.
[2] Sa'id to Aberdeen, Feb. 1843, encl. in Hamerton to F.O., 14 Feb. 1843, F.O. 54/5.
[3] Aberdeen to Hamerton, 11 July 1843, F.O. 54/5.
[4] Sa'id to Kerdudal, 27 Feb. 1844, A.E., Zanz. C.C.1; and Kerdudal to Bazoche, 3 May 1844, M.O., O.I. 15/59.

as no more than an English governor. He added that Saʻid, unhappy at such a state of affairs, feared that the British would absorb all his possessions, and was corresponding with Muhammad Ali, who had the same problem. Kerdudal tried to influence Saʻid against the British by telling him they had designs on Oman, an action which led the Sultan to admit that he had much fear of England.[1] None the less Saʻid still needed the support of the British in Oman, and could not afford to break with them, however enticing that prospect seemed. Khurshid Pasha had retreated from the borders of the Gulf and of Oman, but he was replaced by a new danger – that of the newly insurgent Wahhabis under Faisal ibn Turki, the son of the Wahhabi ruler Turki who had caused Oman so much trouble in the 1830s.[2] In 1842 the British had abandoned their establishment at Kharaq in the Persian Gulf, a withdrawal which made the authorities at Muscat feel very insecure.[3] The usual request for aid was made to the British, but Bombay did not consider the Wahhabis as dangerous a threat as the Egyptians had been. The Supreme Government did not want to interfere.[4] If Paris did renew negotiations for a consul, therefore, Saʻid would have to be careful to keep open the possibility of help from the British on the Oman front.

It was not long before Paris renewed negotiations. The East African coast now appeared more important to the French than it had seemed in 1839, when they had first planned to establish a consulate. Paris had approved the taking of Nossi Bé in 1840 because the news arrived at a time when war with England was an imminent possibility.[5] Bourbon, encouraged, proceeded to take the nearby islands of Nossi Cumba and Nossi Mitsou, and concluded a treaty wherein the sultan of Mayotte declared his country ceded to France. The *Direction des Colonies* within the Ministry of Marine and Colonies approved this step, but the Council of Ministers reserved the question for discussion.[6]

Consequently the whole question of French expansion came under review. De Hell, the ex-governor of Bourbon, now back in France,

[1] Kerdudal to Bazoche, 24 May 1843, M.O., O.I. 15/63.
[2] Bombay to C. of Ds., no 58. 30 Sept. 1843, P.L.B. 28.
[3] Yapp, *op. cit.*, p. 415. For the final evacuation, Bombay to Secret Committee, no. 56, 21 May 1842, S.L.B., 1st series 16.
[4] Bombay to C. of Ds., no. 5, 31 Jan. 1844, P.L.B. 29. Hennell advised against interference – Bombay to C. of Ds., no. 90, 30 Dec. 1843, and no. 58, 30 Sept. 1843, P.L.B. 28.
[5] Christian Schefer, 'L'expansion française dans la monarchie de Juillet', in *Revue des Deux Mondes*, 6ᵉ période, no. 11 (1 Sept. 1912), p. 167.
[6] *Idem*.

convinced the Minister of Marine, Admiral Duperré, that the French must take Madagascar. Also in favour of this was Filleau Saint-Hilaire, who had been in charge of the *Direction des Colonies* continuously from 1826 to 1842. The Council of Ministers decided to systematize French expansion. Guizot disapproved of the forward group, saying that French policy was not to conquer large stretches of territory, but just to acquire a sufficient number of maritime establishments for French ships.¹ The Council, agreeing with him, decided on the immediate occupation of Mayotte, which was thought to have that excellent harbour for which the French had been searching for so long, but the Madagascar enterprise was to be abandoned.² However, the Ministry of Marine proceeded to make its own interpretation of the Council decision. The French must find points of call beyond the Cape of Good Hope 'd'où puisse rayonner et s'étendre l'influence française'. All French plans would be compromised 'si une puissance maritime contrebalancait notre action dans ces parages'.³ This meant that the Madagascar project should not be entirely abandoned. This was an interpretation for which the Minister of Marine was removed from his post, but by then the damage had been done because Bourbon never needed more than a little encouragement.⁴

French activities in Madagascar and the Comoro islands introduced a new aspect to the discussions about setting up a consulate in Zanzibar. De Lagiène, the captain of a French ship, told Guizot that since the taking of Mayotte, Zanzibar had assumed a new commercial and political importance in relation to the recent French establishments in the Mozambique channel.⁵ In particular, the Sultan had pretensions to several places in which the French were interested.⁶ It would be useful to have an agent with him who could deal with his complaints about French activities in the Comoro islands, complaints he was doubtless repeating to the British. The demand for a consul at Zanzibar was now far more politically motivated than it had been in 1839, when commercial arguments had predominated.

¹ *Ibid.*, p. 169.
² Ministry of Marine to Rang, Commander of Nossi Bé and dependencies, 19 Sept. 1843, M.O., O.I. 15/59.
³ *Idem.*
⁴ Schefer, *op. cit.*, p. 177.
⁵ De Lagiène to Guizot, 9 June 1844, A.E., Zanz. C.P.1.
⁶ Note for the Commission on the Budget, 11 Apr. 1843; Guizot to Louis Philippe, June 1844, A.E., Zanz. C.C.1; and Guizot to Ministry of Marine, 22 Jan. 1844, M.O., O.I. 15/59.

Guizot ordered that funds from the 1844 budget be allocated for the establishment of a consulate at Zanzibar.[1] A special mission was to be sent to Zanzibar with a consul, and a commercial treaty was to be arranged by Romain Desfossés, the governor of Bourbon.[2] The consul chosen was a ship's captain called Broquant. In 1838 and 1839 he had explored the west coast of Africa at the instigation of the Bordeaux Chamber of Commerce, and on his return had been made a *Chevalier* of the *Légion d'Honneur*. He had then explored the Red Sea and parts of the East African coast, where he had become acquainted with Saiyid Sa'id. Broquant was interested in French commercial expansion in the Indian Ocean, and saw the possibilities of trade with Zanzibar. Having asked to be appointed consul at Bombay in 1841, Broquant must have welcomed his new post.[3] As for the treaty to be arranged at Zanzibar, it was similar to that of the British, which the French had studied. However, the French were unwilling to be subject to the Mrima monopoly.[4]

The French mission reached Zanzibar on 9 November 1844, and was given a good reception.[5] This was the approach from Paris for which Sa'id had been waiting. Now there was little to stop him arranging the treaty and accepting a consul. He had Aberdeen's letter to hand, and he had also heard of the British refusal to help his son Thuwaini, left in charge at Muscat, against the Wahhabis. Thuwaini had merely been advised not to entangle himself with the Wahhabis as long as they abstained from challenging the rights of his father.[6] Since Sa'id's hopes for British aid had been dashed he no longer had to conciliate that

[1] Guizot to Ministry of Marine, 4 Dec. 1843, M.O., O.I., 15/59; and Note for the Commission on the Budget, 11 Apr. 1843, A.E., Zanz. C.C.1.
[2] Ministry of Marine to Ministry of F.A., no. 153, 6 Oct. 1843, and same to same, 26 Apr. 1844, M.O., O.I. 15/59.
[3] Guizot to Ministry of Marine, 5 Apr. 1844, M.O., O.I. 15/59; Ministry of F.A. to Broquant, no. 1, 30 May 1844, A.E., Zanz. C.C.1; Broquant to Ministry of F.A., 30 Dec. 1841, and note by Broquant, n.d., but *c.* the same date, A.E., Zanz. C.C.1. Noel had been asked to be consul but had refused – Noel to Ministry of F.A., 11 Apr. 1844, M.O., O.I. 15/59.
[4] Note by Ministry of Marine, 26 Apr. 1844, and Guizot to Ministry of Marine, 30 May 1844, M.O., O.I. 15/59. The original draft of the treaty is in Ministry of F.A. to R. Desfossés, May 1844, M.O., O.I. 15/59. There is much correspondence on this question in M.O., O.I. 15/59, and A.E., Zanz. C.C.1.
[5] Broquant to Henri Galos, 24 Nov. 1844, M.O., O.I. 15/59.
[6] Bombay to Secret Committee, no. 22, 29 Feb. 1844, S.L.B., 1st series 20, quoting Supreme Government to Thuwaini, 10 Jan. 1844. As yet the threat to Oman from Faisal was not thought to be very serious.

party. He wrote to Aberdeen saying he had delayed a treaty with the French for a long time until he knew the views of the British Government, but now he had no further reason to procrastinate.[1] The Sultan accepted the French treaty in principle, although he insisted the French be subject to the Mrima monopoly. He also wanted to abandon the previous commercial treaties with Bourbon, although by doing so he himself lost some advantages. Consequently the articles which incorporated the previous treaties were withdrawn.[2] After his experiences with Hamerton, he wanted the right to approve or disapprove of all persons sent as consuls, but the French refused to allow this.[3] Broquant was left as consul, and with much pomp and ceremony the French flag was raised.[4]

When the British looked carefully at the treaty, they were relieved to find that it was almost identical to their own. However, they disliked Article 17, a translation of which gave the French liberty to establish 'magazines' at Zanzibar or in any other part of the Sultan's territories. This was, in fact, a mistake. The French had wanted to establish 'stores' or 'warehouses', and had used the word 'magasins' in their own treaty. In the Arabic version this had become 'makhzin', from which the French word derives. 'Makhzin' means 'stores' in Arabic, but can also mean 'magazines', the meaning from which the English word derives. The British consul saw the Arabic version of the treaty in Zanzibar and translated 'makhzin' as 'magazines'. So concerned was the British Foreign Office that the French might be setting up secret stores of arms that it asked Guizot, the French Premier, precisely what French intentions were. Guizot assured the Foreign Office that his interests were purely commercial.[5]

This incident, and Aberdeen's letter to Sa'id, were typical of the attitude of both the British and French now that the crisis concerning Muhammad Ali was over. Improved relations between Great Britain and France meant that each could tolerate the commercial ventures of the other, provided that similar trading advantages were open to both. The Ministry of Marine's letter to the governor of Bourbon, telling him not to take possession of points on Madagascar but to ensure that no one else did so, illustrates this point. Similarly, at the end of the

[1] Saiyid Sa'id to Aberdeen, 26 Nov. 1844, F.O. 54/6.
[2] R. Desfossés to Ministry of F.A., 19 Nov. 1844, A.E., Zanz. C.C.1.
[3] *Idem.*
[4] Broquant to Ministry of F.A., 22 Nov. 1844, A.E., Zanz. C.C.1.
[5] F.O. to Hamerton, 7 Mch. and 2 Apr. 1845, F.O. 54/7.

Opium War, Guizot wanted the same commercial concessions for the French as the British got by the Treaty of Nanking. Commercial ventures, then, were permissible, but if matters went beyond commerce, vigorous protests were made. This was a time of continuous watchfulness and mutual suspicion. Events in the Red Sea, East Africa, Madagascar, and the Comoro islands provide excellent examples of this state of affairs. The French Ministry of Marine was in an expansionist state of mind, and provided the British Foreign Office, and indeed its own Foreign Ministry, with many conundrums.

French aims in the western Indian Ocean, although continually changing, had certain consistent features. Firstly, the French were interested in the commercial possibilities of East Africa and did not want to be out-traded by the British or Americans in that area. Secondly, they wanted to control the Mozambique channel, possibly prior to taking Madagascar. Thirdly, they wanted to establish steam communication between Bourbon and the Red Sea, and, later, to cut a canal through Suez. British aims were more negative – they wanted to maintain the position they already had in the Red Sea and Persian Gulf in 1840, and to block any French designs which would lead to undue French preponderance in those areas. They also wanted to maintain their influence over the ruler of Muscat and Zanzibar, and to prevent the French from acquiring points on the East African coast. Lastly, they wanted at all costs to stop the French taking Madagascar.

The second fundamental objective of French policy – control of the Mosambique channel – was firmly opposed by the British. In 1847 Saiyid Sa'id complained to them that the French were interfering in Johanna and Grand Comore, and at the same time he wrote a letter of protest to Guizot.[1] Although their investigations had revealed that the Comoro islands were not of much importance, the British were not prepared to allow any further French encroachment on these islands off north-west Madagascar, and decided to send a consul to Johanna.[2] Johanna had generally been more friendly to the British than to the French, and had sent numerous deputations to Bombay to request aid in times of trouble.[3] In 1846 four Johanna chiefs had arrived at Aden

[1] Sa'id to F.O., 19 Aug. 1847, F.O. 54/11, and Sa'id to Guizot, 18 Aug. 1847, M.O., Madag. 270/605.

[2] Note in Palmerston's handwriting, 12 Dec. 1847, and F.O. to Sa'id, 29 Jan. 1848, F.O. 54/11. See also G. S. Graham, *Great Britain in the Indian Ocean, 1810-1850* (London, 1967), pp. 86-95.

[3] See Chapter V, p. 132.

asking for help, and in June 1850 a treaty of friendship was signed between the British and the sultan of Johanna.[1]

Although French activities in East Africa were closely linked with their interests in the Red Sea and the Mozambique channel, they also viewed East Africa as a commercial proposition. Soon after his arrival in Zanzibar, the French consul, Broquant, was asked to report on the commercial possibilities of the East African coast. He came to the conclusion that French products could not easily be sold there because the British and Americans were firmly in control of the market.[2] As well as Broquant's enquiries, a French ship, *Le Voltigeur* (Captain Baudais), was sent to Zanzibar to get information on the political and commercial situation there, while at the same time looking for a French slaver.[3] Baudais heard that Sa'id had just suffered defeat in battle at Pate, and he got the impression (mainly from Hamerton) that his empire was very unstable.[4] The Ministry of Foreign Affairs, worried by Hamerton's hints to Baudais about what the British intended to do if Sa'id's position weakened, ordered their ambassador in London to ask Palmerston about British intentions. Guizot was assured that Great Britain had no projects hostile to France in the area,[5] an assurance which entirely coincided with the facts. Hamerton was wont to make wild statements about British intentions. 'From conversations I have had with the English consul', wrote Ward, the American consul, in 1851, 'it is the policy of the British Government to take possession of the East African Coast at no distant day.'[6]

The French Ministry of Marine and the governor of Bourbon were fascinated at the possibility of a collapse of Saiyid Sa'id's empire. In 1845 Guillain, who had carried out a voyage of research along the coast of Madagascar, suggested to the Ministry of Marine and Colonies that he make a similar voyage on the East African coast.[7] Since a successful voyage of exploration had just been completed by *La Malouine* along the West African coast, the Ministry agreed to Guillain's suggestion.[8] They were probably influenced by a proposal made in 1842 for the

[1] Bombay to Secret Committee, no. 106, 30 Sept. 1846, S.L.B., 1st series 22, and same to same, no. 56, 21 July 1851, S.L.B., 1st series, 28.
[2] Broquant to Ministry of F.A., no. 37, 10 Mch. 1845, M.O., O.I. 15/65.
[3] Ministry of Marine to Ministry of F.A., 14 Oct. 1845, M.O., O.I. 15/65.
[4] Baudais to R. Desfossés, n.d., 1845, M.O., O.I. 15/65.
[5] French ambassador in London to Guizot, 30 Oct. 1845, M.O., O.I. 15/65.
[6] Ward to Abbot, 13 Mch. 1851, Amer.N.A., Zanz. 3.
[7] Report in Ministry of Colonies, 8 July 1845, M.O., O.I. 2/10.
[8] Ministry of Marine to Ministry of F.A., 19 Dec. 1845, M.O., O.I. 2/10.

establishment of a Company to trade in Asia and on the East African coast.[1] The Ministry also had obviously been encouraged by Baudais' report of the instability of Sa'id's empire, because the instructions they gave Guillain included one to find out the degree of subjection or independence of the governors of the littoral, and to see if the chiefs at Pate and Mombasa had the power to found independent states.[2] The following year the Minister of Marine openly admitted his interest in 'l'hypothèse que vous [the governor of Bourbon] posez de la formation d'un état indépendant sur la côte'.[3]

Guillain was not in favour of asserting French influence at Zanzibar. Like Broquant, he thought that there was no real possibility for French commercial activity there. Rather he suggested that the French exploit their possession of the Comoro islands, and create an alternative entrepot to Zanzibar at Mayotte. They should attempt to draw to Mayotte all the trade that then flowed through Zanzibar. It was not much more difficult, he reckoned, for the inhabitants of East Africa to bring their goods to Mayotte rather than to Zanzibar.[4] On the question of the existence of independent areas on the coast, he found that a local chief in the interior behind the littoral towns of Mogadishu, Brava, and Marka, in fact controlled that region despite Saiyid Sa'id's nominal authority. Guillain advised the French to support this chief, Yusuf.[5] Loarer, who accompanied Guillain as commercial agent, suggested that the French go even further and take actual possession of various points on the coast, particularly Marka.[6] Some negotiations must have taken place along these lines because a messenger from Brava went to Zanzibar to report that the French were trying to buy Brava.[7]

The men on the spot were enthusiastic about these suggestions, but Guizot as usual was more conservative, and then the plans got shelved in the revolution of 1848. In 1849 the Ministry of Foreign Affairs said they would bear Loarer's suggestions in mind but at the moment circumstances were not favourable for carrying them out.[8] Guillain

---

[1] Propositions de M. Aubert Roche relatives au développement du commerce en Asie, et dans l'Afrique orientale', M.O., O.I. 15/60.
[2] R. Desfossés to Guillain, 30 Aug. 1846, M.O., Madag. 17/32.
[3] Ministry of Marine to governor of Bourbon, 15 Mch. 1847, M.O., O.I. 2/10.
[4] Guillain's Report, 1849, A.N., Marine BB4/1036.
[5] Guillain to Ministry of Marine, 24 Oct. 1847, M.O., O.I. 2/10.
[6] Ministry of F.A. to Ministry of Marine, 15 Feb. 1849, M.O., O.I. 2/10.
[7] Hamerton to Commander Brown of *Snake*, 2 Aug. 1847, and Rear-Admiral Dacres to Admiralty, 31 Dec. 1847, encl. in Admiralty to F.O., 2 Mch. 1848, F.O. 54/11.   [8] As note 6.

later complained that, when he returned from his voyage, 'la France et son gouvernement ne se souvenaient plus ni du voyageur ni de l'objet du voyage'.[1] However, the project of a French establishment on the Banadir coast was revived by the Commision on Factories and Commerce.[2] In practice, it was left to the French consuls at Zanzibar to exert what influence they could there.

The French consulate's relations with Saiyid Sa'id had had inauspicious beginnings. Shortly after Broquant's arrival in Zanzibar, Maizan, a French explorer attempting to penetrate the African interior opposite Zanzibar, was murdered at the start of his journey. Despite repeated requests that the murderer be apprehended, nothing much was done by Saiyid Sa'id.[3] A second point of dispute was the value of the five-franc piece which the consul thought was exchanged for Spanish and Maria Theresa dollars at too low a rate.[4] Thirdly, there was continual argument about whether or not the French could trade on the Mrima.[5]

Broquant did not attempt to establish any sort of influence with Saiyid Sa'id. One reason for this may have been his friendship with the British consul, an association which, considering the diplomatic situation, was remarkable for its intimacy. Hajji Dervish, who brought one of Sa'id's ships, the *Caroline*, to Marseilles in 1849, said that French influence at Zanzibar had suffered much because of the intimate relations of Hamerton and Broquant.[6] The Sultan said they were so close they were almost one man,[7] and Hamerton himself described Broquant as 'a sincere friend and most agreeable companion'.[8] Broquant's lack of influence was also due to his inability to speak Arabic, and the death of his interpreter, Dumont, after only a few months in Zanzibar.[9]

[1] Preface to Guillain, *Documents*, I.
[2] 'Rapport du Commission des Comptoirs et du Commerce des côtes d'Afrique', M.O., O.I. 10/43.
[3] R. Desfossés to Ministry of Marine, no. 64, 20 Jan. 1846; no. 8, 27 Feb. 1846; and no. 139, 19 Aug. 1846, M.O., Madag. 17/32; Broquant to Ministry of F.A., no. 5, 5 Aug. 1845, A.E., Zanz. C.C.1; Guillain to Sa'id, 5 Oct. 1846, and Sa'id to Guillain, 7 Oct. 1846, M.O., O.I. 2/10; Guillain to Ministry of Marine, 24 Oct, 1847, M.O., O.I. 15/65.
[4] See Chapter XII, p. 340.
[5] See Chapter XII, p. 362.
[6] Belligny to Ministry of F.A., 7 May 1849, A.E., Zanz. C.C.1, reporting a conversation with Hajji Dervish.
[7] Guillain to Ministry of F.A., 12 Oct. 1847, M.O., O.I. 14/55.
[8] Hamerton to Bombay, no. 16, 30 Apr. 1847, Z.A.
[9] Broquant to Ministry of F.A., no. 5, 5 Aug. 1845, A.E., Zanz. C.C.1.

Broquant then had to use the indiscreet Khamis ibn Uthman as an interpreter.[1] The French consul's stay at Zanzibar was short; he soon became ill with elephantiasis and died in May 1847.[2] There were suspicions that his death was not entirely due to his illness. Hajji Dervish suggested that Zevaco, a Frenchman living in Zanzibar who apparently coveted Broquant's post, had murdered him.[3] Belligny, the succeeding French consul, discovered that Broquant 'vivait avec M. Zevaco dans une certain intimité' and did not believe the rumour that Zevaco had poisoned the consul.[4] Zevaco's versions of the matter varied: he told Guillain that Broquant had been poisoned by someone, but informed the Ministry of Foreign Affairs, in a letter in which he suggested he should assume the position of consul, that Broquant had died of violent dysentery.[5]

After Broquant's death there was a gap of over three years before another French consul arrived in Zanzibar. Belligny and Kuhlmann, his vice-consul, landed in October 1849.[6] The new consul was more assertive than the former. He immediately insisted the Sultan lift the ban on the French trading on the Mrima and asked for a warship to come and impress the Arabs.[7] It was unfortunate for French influence in Zanzibar that the naval station at Bourbon, which had been the source of the French influence in the area and had enabled the French to show themselves regularly in Zanzibar waters, ceased to exist in 1852. The station was transferred to Indo-China, and French ships stopped appearing on the Swahili Coast. Belligny left Zanzibar in January 1855 and was succeeded a year later by Cochet, who complained that the last French warship at Zanzibar had been there three years before.[8] Apart from the absence of ships, the French consul had further difficulties in that he was paid less than the British consul. It was often said that French influence could not be exerted in Zanzibar to the same

---

[1] Khamis ibn Uthman to Ministry of F.A., 2 May 1847, A.E., Zanz. C.C.1.
[2] Broquant to Ministry of F.A., no. 16, 26 Aug. 1846, and Saiyid Sa'id to Guizot, 13 May 1847, A.E., Zanz. C.C.1.
[3] Belligny to Ministry of F.A., 17 May 1849, A.E., Zanz. C.C.1.
[4] Belligny to Ministry of F.A., no. 4, 26 Nov. 1849, A.E., Zanz. C.C.1.
[5] Guillain to Ministry of F.A., 12 Oct. 1847, M.O., O.I. 14/55; and Zevaco to Ministry of F.A., 5 May 1847, A.E., Zanz. C.C.1.
[6] Belligny to Ministry of F.A., 25 Oct. 1849, A.E., Zanz. C.C.1.
[7] Belligny to Ministry of F.A., no. 7, 9 Jan. 1850, A.E., Zanz. C.C.1; and Ministry of F.A. to Belligny, no. 10, 24 Aug. 1852, A.E., Zanz. C.C.2.
[8] Belligny to Ministry of F.A., 1 May 1855, and Cochet to Ministry of F.A., 29 July 1856, A.E., Zanz. C.C.2.

extent as British because the French consul could not live in so grand a manner.¹

Despite these factors, there remained some feeling in favour of the French at Zanzibar. According to Guillain, Sulaiman ibn Hamad, the governor of Zanzibar, favoured the French because he thought they would support him in his ambitions.² Guillain added that there was a marked preference for the French at Zanzibar, probably due to Arab dislike of drunkenness. Khalid, the Sultan's son who had been likely to succeed him and who had favourable dispositions towards the French, died in 1854, but the French consul also managed to exert great influence on Majid, who succeeded Sa'id.³ When Sa'id died, and Thuwaini in Muscat disputed Majid's succession in Zanzibar, Majid asked for French help.⁴

To the local people of Zanzibar the French provided an alternative to the British, who were regarded as interfering intolerably in the Slave Trade and as exerting a unwanted influence on the Sultan. Several influential people openly declared their preference for the French. It was a time when the presence of Europeans seemed a necessary requirement for economic progress, and so there was a tendency to alignment with one European or other. Moreover, in a society where there was no constitutional means of expressing opposition, dissatisfaction could be indicated by preference for those Europeans who were less influential with the Sultan.

As the 1840s proceeded, Sa'id was drawn further into the British camp. Most French visitors to Zanzibar remarked on his subjection to Hamerton.⁵ When Belligny arrived in 1849, he said Sa'id was totally under the British yoke.⁶ What had made Sa'id fall so completely under British influence when he had struggled for so long to remain free of it? One of the reasons was that he had always held the French out as an

---

¹ Journal of *Le Chasseur*, by E. Bolle, 22 May 1850, showing the British consul was paid twice as much as the French – M.O., Madag. 270/605. The French consul was paid 6,000 francs a year – Ministry of F.A. to Noel, 12 Sept. 1839, A.E., Zanz. C.C.1.
² Guillain to Ministry of F.A., 12 Oct. 1847, M.O., O.I. 14/55.
³ For the high esteem in which Cochet was held, Hamerton to F.O., no. 8, 10 Nov. 1856, F.O. 54/17. Also Cochet to Ministry of F.A., no. 2, 27 Nov. 1856, A.E., Zanz. C.P.1.
⁴ Majid to Cochet, 16 Nov. 1856, A.E., Zanz. C.P.1.
⁵ e.g. Captain of *La Reine Blanche* to Ministry of Marine, no. 37, 25 Sept. 1849, A.N., Marine BB4/665.
⁶ Belligny to Ministry of F.A., 7 May 1849, A.E., Zanz. C.C.1.

alternative and had on several occasions used the threat of an alliance with them to pressurize the British, but once he had signed the 1844 treaty with France and a consul had been sent, he could no longer do this. He was also disappointed in his hope that the French consul would be a rival and a balance to the British – Hamerton and Broquant were firm friends. Then Broquant's death was followed by the absence of a French consul from Zanzibar for over three years, during which time Hamerton's influence reigned supreme. For various reasons Sa'id agreed to co-operate to some extent with British requirements for the cessation of the Slave Trade, and once he had made that decision he opened himself wide to unpopularity among his own people and had to rely on support from those who had encouraged him to make the concessions. In addition, from the end of the 1830s Sa'id was seriously worried by French activities in the Comoro islands, and the possibility that they would extend to his East African possessions. He was too wise not to see that co-operation with a French consul might be a preliminary to acquisition of some of his lands. Sa'id also remained constantly in need of British support to uphold his position in Oman. He knew, from the often discouraging letters he received in answer to requests for help, that it was unlikely that the British would ever assist him on land, but those who threatened him did not know this. On many occasions trouble-makers were warned by the British that any further action would 'be viewed with grave displeasure'. The memory of the defeat of the Qawasim was still alive. Sa'id had to see to it that the British continued to issue such warnings and to send warships to trouble spots. He was in a dangerous situation in Oman in the late 1840s and early 1850s. The chief of Sohar had gathered so much support that there was a possibility that he would aspire to the Imamate, which of course Sa'id did not hold.[1] Moreover, the Wahhabis occupied Buraimi and demanded tribute from Sa'id. He had to pay 5,000 dollars because Thuwaini's request for help from the British had been refused. In fact the British were contemplating aiding him, but were hoping that he would be able to settle his troubles

[1] Bombay to C. of Ds., no. 119, 31 Oct. 1846, P.L.B. 33, and Bombay to Secret Committee, no. 41, 15 Apr. 1846, S.L.B., 1st series 22. Saif ibn Hamud, the son of Hamud ibn Azzan who had been at enmity with Saiyid Sa'id for so long, succeeded to his father's position in Sohar. He managed to capture Buraimi in 1848 which put him in a very strong position. In 1851 there was a truce between Thuwaini and Sohar after Saif had been captured and died in prison at Muscat, but trouble soon broke out again. In 1854 Turki, one of Saiyid Sa'id's sons, was appointed governor of Sohar.

SAIYID SAʿID AND THE WESTERN POWERS, 1839-1856

himself.[1] Then Persia maltreated some of Saʿid's subjects in his ports on the Persian side of the Gulf, and he had to face the likelihood of war.[2] Finally, he never lost hope that the British would assist him to take Bahrain.[3]

It had been easier for Saʿid to avoid British influence when he had no British consul resident with him, but once Hamerton came to live at Zanzibar, circumstances changed. Saʿid could resist his influence to some extent as long as Cogan held out the hope that Hamerton might be removed, but when the Sultan eventually accepted that Hamerton was there to stay, it was difficult to avoid bowing to his influence. In fact, in 1845 Aberdeen had ordered Hamerton's removal after Saʿid's final complaint about him[4] and after the disclosure of Hamerton's indiscreet remarks to the French about British plans for Zanzibar:

'Lord Aberdeen is of the opinion that the conduct of Captain Hamerton is not such as to give him that influence with the Imam of Muscat which it is essential that the British Consular Agent should have.'[5]

The Bombay government, however, was unwilling to find a successor. They did offer the post to Kemball, the Assistant Resident in the Persian Gulf, but he refused it. In fact Bombay was well satisfied with Hamerton, and thought the Sultan had been prejudiced against him by Cogan. While admitting that Hamerton's correspondence left something to be desired, Bombay thought it would be difficult to find anyone as highly qualified for the post as he.[6] Hamerton apparently spoke perfect Arabic.[7] Shortly after the Foreign Office's order to replace Hamerton, Aberdeen was succeeded by Palmerston, and the British consul remained at his post. Hamerton subsequently reported

---

[1] Bombay to C. of Ds., no. 44, 30 Apr. 1845, and no. 90, 26 Aug. 1845; and Supreme Government to Bombay, 6 May 1845, P.L.B. 31.

[2] Bombay to C. of Ds., no. 21, 31 Jan. 1848, P.L.B. 36; and Bombay to Secret Committee, no. 56, 16 June 1847, S.L.B., 1st series 23.

[3] He made another request about this in 1849 – Bombay to C. of Ds., no. 29, 31 Mch. 1849, P.L.B. 39; Bombay to Secret Committee, no. 68, 25 July 1849, and no. 76, 17 Sept. 1849, S.L.B., 1st series 26. The Foreign Office discouraged the Sultan – Saʿid to Palmerston, 18 Mch. 1849, and draft reply from Palmerston, 31 May 1849 – F.O. 54/13.

[4] 'The trouble that I have had is more than I can well bear' – Saʿid to Cogan, 4 Feb. 1846, F.O. 54/10.

[5] F.O. to India Board, 5 Dec. 1845, F.O. 54/9.

[6] Bombay to Secret Committee, no. 93, 26 Aug. 1846, S.L.B., 1st series 22.

[7] De Lagiène to Guizot, 9 Jan. 1844, A.E., Zanz. C.P.1.

an improvement in his relations with the Sultan. In April 1846 he said that for some time Sa'id had evinced towards him 'the most kindly and confidential feeling in every way',[1] and the following year, when Hamerton was seriously ill, he was constantly visited by the Sultan.[2] But Sa'id never came to like Hamerton. 'The British Consul', said the American consul, 'is not a favourite of the Sultan, but he is so much afraid of the injury that he may do him that he is more subservient to him than he would otherwise be.'[3]

It may seem surprising, considering their commercial dealings, that the Americans were not more influential at Zanzibar. One reason was that their consuls were really commercial agents and were not endowed with many diplomatic powers. Sa'id himself regarded them as businessmen, and they gained considerable unpopularity among the commercial people of Zanzibar because of the closeness of their ties with the customs master. Waters, the first American consul, had an arrangement with Jairam, the customs master, which gave the two of them a near monopoly of Zanzibar trade.[4] 'Le pavillon de l'Union', commented a Frenchman, 'se trouve ainsi arboré sur une boutique.'[5] Waters was a pious man, and lamented the fact that the Sultan was not a Christian.[6] He regarded Zanzibar as a land of 'gross darkness',[7] but was

'willing to work hard for a few Years, and be sepperated [sic] from dear friends, if I can acquire a necessary portion of riches'.[8]

The fact that consuls were not paid by the Federal Government but had to support themselves by their commercial transactions meant that the United States could establish consulates in places where there was little diplomatic necessity so to do, when a merchant suggested himself for the post. Apart from the consul at Zanzibar, there were also two successive American consuls at Muscat. The first, Marshall, appointed in 1838, had to leave the following year when his firm collapsed.[9] The

---

[1] Hamerton to Bombay, 24 Apr. 1846, encl. in India Board to F.O., 5 Oct. 1846, F.O. 54/10.
[2] Hamerton to Bombay, no. 2, 4 May 1847, Z.A.
[3] Ward to Abbot, 13 Mch. 1851, Amer.N.A., Zanz. 3.
[4] See Chapter XII, pp. 327-8.
[5] R. Desfossés to Ministry of F.A., 4 Feb. 1845, A.E., Zanz. C.C.1.
[6] Waters' Journal, entry for 23 Aug. 1837, printed in Bennett and Brooks, op. cit., p. 204.
[7] Ibid., entry for 9 Apr. 1837, p. 196.
[8] Ibid., entry for 19 Aug. 1837, p. 203.
[9] Marshall to Forsyth, 15 Feb. 1838 and 10 Dec. 1839, Amer.N.A., Zanz. 1.

second, Frank Powell, said he hoped he would be able to find means of support at Muscat, but he had to leave when he became ill.[1]

Although the Americans were bringing wealth to Zanzibar, the Sultan did not regard them as a powerful people whose interests must be taken into account before he made a diplomatic manœuvre. Unlike the British and French, they possessed no territory in the Indian Ocean, and they did not appear to have a strong navy. Ward, who succeeded Waters as consul, thought the reason the Sultan did not respect the Americans was that he had no idea of the size and power of the American nation. He only saw American merchant vessels, never warships.[2] Sa'id was much struck with the smallness of the American force used in the Mexican War in comparison with the large forces which the English had brought into the field in Europe and were then employing in India.

The State Department itself had little reason to interfere in political matters in Zanzibar and seldom put any pressure on Sa'id. Several times Sa'id wrote to the United States President, but rarely on matters of such importance as those he discussed with Palmerston, Aberdeen, and Guizot.[3] The consuls themselves would have had to be particularly dynamic or meddling men for Sa'id to have regarded the Americans as a power to be consulted. Waters seems to have kept out of Zanzibar politics, although not sufficiently to avoid causing Sa'id to ask for his recall – a request that never reached America because Waters opened the letter prior to forwarding it and tore it up.[4] The attitude of Ward, Waters' successor, did not augur well for happy relations with the Sultan. He regarded Sa'id as 'crafty, deceitful, faithless, and only operated upon by the display of physical powers'.[5]

Although the Europeans were forcing themselves upon the ruler of Muscat, he was himself partially encouraging them to do so. His attitude towards them seems to have been a complex amalgam of political ambition, self-interest, fear, and fascination with occidental technology. He hoped that the British would protect him against his enemies and further his own plans of territorial aggrandizement. He was afraid of both British and French power which, if provoked, might

[1] Powell to Buchanan, 9 Mch. 1847, Amer.N.A., Zanz. 2.
[2] Abbot to Webster, Mch. 1851, Amer.N.A., Zanz. 3, reporting a conversation with Ward.
[3] There are several letters from Sa'id to the President in the Zanzibar Archives.
[4] Edward Brown to Webster, 31 Dec. 1841, Amer.N.A., Zanz. 1.
[5] Abbot to Webster, Mch. 1851, Amer.N.A., Zanz. 3, reporting a conversation with Ward.

undermine his dominions. He was flattered by the interest of European powers and impressed by the extent of their martial success. Britain's prestige stood high after the defeat of Napoleon, and it needed the visit of many French warships to persuade him that France was once again an important nation. He wished to put himself on a par with European states and despatched his own ships round the Cape of Good Hope to Western Europe and the United States.[1]

The purpose of this imitation and enquiry was to westernize his dominions and thereby both develop them and maintain their independence. However, he was playing a dangerous game. By the end of his long life, when he was old and tired, he had almost lapsed into dependence on the British. His attempt to introduce a French presence into Zanzibar to balance that of the British had not been a success. In 1851 Ward, the American consul, said that there was a general impression among the Arabs of Zanzibar that when the Sultan died, the English 'will decide who shall be the new Sultan and that the country will come under the protection of England'.[2] This was not yet to come for a few years, but Sa'id had made it more possible by his dealings with the Europeans and Americans. At the same time, however, these dealings also enabled him to maintain his political position in Oman and extend it on the Swahili Coast. The European support for Saiyid Sa'id was an ever-present threat to those who opposed the Sultan. In addition, the economic development of the Swahili Coast under Saiyid Sa'id can to a large extent be attributed to the coming of the Europeans and Americans and the favourable terms of the trade offered them by Saiyid Sa'id.[3]

[1] See Chapter XII, pp. 367-9.
[2] Ward to Abbot, 13 Mch. 1851, Amer.N.A., Zanz. 3.
[3] See Chapter XII.

CHAPTER VIII

THE SLAVE TRADE ON THE SWAHILI COAST

One of the main reasons for the increasing interest shown by the British in Saiyid Saʻid and his dominions was their desire to suppress the Indian Ocean Slave Trade. The source of supply for this trade was in East Africa. The British campaign to stamp out the traffic and the extent of its success will be described in Chapter IX. First, however, it is necessary to evaluate both the political and economic importance of the Slave Trade on the Swahili Coast. This chapter will attempt to assess how far the Slave Trade was a source of attraction for the Omani Arabs, and whether it influenced their migration from Oman to East Africa. It will also consider the importance of the Slave Trade in the economic structure of the Swahili Coast, whether and for what reasons the relative value of this trade fluctuated during the first half of the nineteenth century, and who derived most profit from it. It will examine the extent to which the Swahili Coast was able to expand both as a commercial centre and an area of primary production and how important the Slave Trade was in supporting this expansion. It will also attempt to discover what regional differences there were in economic development along the Swahili Coast during this period and whether the nature of the Slave Trade had any effect on these local variations. At the same time it will have to consider the extent to which the Slave Trade was an indispensable element in the revenues of the Sultan of Zanzibar.

Demands by the French, newly arrived in the Mascarene islands, caused an expansion of the Slave Trade on the Swahili Coast in the late eighteenth century. Previously there had probably been merely a constant small demand from Arabs, Indians, and Portuguese. In the eighteenth century Frenchmen colonized the islands of Ile de France and Bourbon, where they planted sugar. At first they obtained from the Portuguese the slaves they needed to work their plantations. In the 1770s, however, they were diverted from their usual sources at Mozambique, Ibo and Kerimba by an African rising against the Portuguese.[1] Since it would also be cheaper to buy direct rather than through the Portuguese,[2] the French turned their attention to the port of Kilwa, and made arrangements with its authorities concerning the price of slaves and their regular supply.

On 14 September 1776 Morice, who, like Massieu and Comarmond, was one of the most prominent of the French slave-traders, made a written agreement with the sultan of Kilwa to be furnished with 1,000 Africans a year.[3] Nine years later a further arrangement was made by Saulnier de Mondevit,[4] while in 1785 and again in 1786 the authorities in Oman, who were by then known to have interests on the Swahili Coast, were approached by Rosilly and Kergarion de Loemaria successively in order to discuss terms for the regular purchase of slaves.[5] These activities were bound to arouse the interest of the Omani Arabs.

Between 1782 and 1784 the French took 4,193 slaves from Kilwa.[6] In addition they were buying slaves at Zanzibar; Morice alone took 925 in 1775 and 860 in 1776.[7] It is not known whether the sultan of Kilwa kept his promise to furnish Morice with 1,000 slaves a year, but in 1776 Tostain acquired 416 from that port.[8] Although it was the wish of the governor of Ile de France to introduce 2,000 slaves into his island every year,[9] the death of Morice and the loss of many ships by Comarmond[10] may have meant that the purchase of slaves in the

[1] 'Observations sur le pays et les productions de l'Isle [sic] de Quiloa', by Massieu, 1 Feb. 1778, M.O., O.I. 15/61.

[2] Comarmond's 'Mémoire', 1787, A.N., Colonies C4/85.

[3] The agreement is contained in a note in the Ministry of Marine on the projected French establishment at Kilwa, dated 8 June 1778, M.O., O.I. 15/61.

[4] Extract from the journal of Captain Saulnier de Mondevit, who left Ile de France for this purpose in July 1785, A.N., Colonies C4/80.

[5] De Souillac, governor of Ile de France, to Kergarion, 20 Nov. 1786, A.N., Colonies C4/73.

[6] Report by J. Crassons de Medeuil, 1784/5, printed in Freeman-Grenville, *Select Documents*, pp. 193-4.

[7] Morice to Minister of the Navy, Ile de France, 3 Mch. 1776, A.N., Colonies C4/42.

[8] Description of the voyage of *Le Gracieux* to Kilwa, M.O., O.I. 15/61.

[9] Cossigny, 24 June 1777, in 'Projet d'un établissement', p. 123.

[10] Comarmond to governor of Ile de France, 20 June 1789, A.N., Colonies C4/85.

last quarter of the eighteenth century was irregular. Seton, the British Resident at Muscat in 1802, reported that five to ten slaving vessels from 100 to 200 tons plied annually between Zanzibar and Ile de France.[1]

The sultan of Kilwa, who had ousted the Omanis from his island some years previously, was deriving a large revenue from the export duty of six dollars a head which he charged the French.[2] It may not be without significance that in 1785 the Imam of Oman re-established his authority over Kilwa.[3] This was the same year in which the Frenchman Rosilly, who had previously visited Kilwa, went to Muscat to make commercial arrangements with the Imam.[4] Doubtless the authorities in Oman were informed of the agreements the French had made with Kilwa.

The demand for slaves from Ile de France and Bourbon was maintained well into the nineteenth century, even though in 1810 the British captured both islands and retained the former in the Treaty of Paris at the end of the war. Between 1811 and 1821 about 30,000 Africans were imported into Mauritius (previously Ile de France),[5] and a similar number may have entered Bourbon. If a figure of 50,000 is accepted for the two islands, an average of 5,000 slaves a year was procured from Madagascar, the Portuguese territory, and the Swahili Coast. How many of these actually came from the Swahili Coast is difficult to calculate. In April 1821 Captain Moresby at Zanzibar reported that eight vessels, nominally bound for Bourbon, had lately sailed from Zanzibar with an average of 200 to 400 slaves each.[6] At a rough guess, 2,500 may have come from the Swahili Coast annually. Despite British and French attempts to put an end to the trade, in 1826 a coast patrol found that it still continued, the annual turnover being from 2,000 to 5,000.[7] Due to restrictions (see next chapter) the trade became more devious and the number of slaves going from East Africa to Bourbon and Mauritius probably diminished in the 1830s. None the

---

[1] Seton to Bombay, 9 July 1802, Proc. 27 Aug., B.P.S.P. 381/33.
[2] Rosilly to Minister of Marine, n.d., 1785, A.N., Marine B4/276.
[3] See above, Chapter I, p. 32.
[4] As note 2, and Imam of Oman to Rosilly, 8 Sept. 1785, A.N., Colonies C4/73.
[5] Farquhar to Hastings, 11 May 1821, Proc. 10 Oct., B.P.C. 385/12.
[6] M. K. Jones, 'The Slave Trade at Mauritius 1810-1829' (B.Litt. thesis, University of Oxford, 1936), p. 194.
[7] *Ibid.*, p. 107.

THE SWAHILI COAST

less, the trade continued: Arabs took East African slaves to Bombetok in Madagascar and to Nossi Bé, where they sold them to agents from Mauritius and Bourbon.[1]

In addition to the requirements of Mauritius and Bourbon, there was also a more modest demand for slaves from the Portuguese and Spaniards. Most of the slaves needed by the Portuguese were obtained from the Mozambique region, but Arabs and Indians also carried some from Kilwa and ports to the north to be offered for sale at Mozambique. When W. F. Owen was at Mozambique in 1823, a ship arrived from Kilwa laden with slaves.[2] Portuguese vessels themselves also visited places to the north of Cape Delgado to procure slaves: Owen reported an example of this in 1825.[3] It was difficult to implement the Moresby Treaty[4] at Kilwa and other places on the southern Swahili Coast, so sales of slaves to the Portuguese tended to continue. It is, however, impossible to calculate the number of slaves involved in this trade; they may have fallen after 1830 when the Portuguese themselves put a stop to their subjects trading in slaves.

The number sold to the Spanish is also difficult to estimate. Spaniards took East African slaves round the Cape to South America. The number they took from the Swahili Coast in 1820 was put at 12,000 by Captain Moresby, but this is almost certainly a gross exaggeration.[5] Had they exported such a large number, they would have been noticed far more in documents than is in fact the case. In 1819 Albrand reported that three Spanish ships had traded the previous year at Zanzibar and Kilwa, and one of them had embarked 700 slaves for Havana.[6] Possibly numbers of slaves sold to the Spanish fell after the implementation of the 1820 treaty between Spain and Great Britain concerning the Slave Trade. However, there is subsequent mention of Spanish slavers on the Swahili Coast: sometime between 1832 and 1835 a Spanish vessel visited Zanzibar;[7] in 1837 the American consul recorded that a Spanish slaver

---

[1] Moresby to Bombay, 25 Sept. 1822, Proc. 2 Oct., B.P.C. 385/26; Massieu to Freycinet, 9 Oct. 1822, M.O., Réunion 72/473; and Romain Desfossés to Ministry of Marine, no. 16, 1 Feb. 1845, M.O., Madag. 17/32.

[2] Owen to Bombay, 23 Nov. 1823, Proc. 3 Dec., B.P.C. 385/41.

[3] Owen to Sir Lowry Cole, 4 Aug. 1825, *State Papers*, vol. XIII, p. 329.

[4] For the Moresby Treaty, see next chapter.

[5] Moresby to Bombay, 25 Sept. 1822, Proc. 2 Oct., B.P.C. 385/26.

[6] Albrand's Report, 1819, M.O., Réunion 72/472.

[7] E. Roberts to John Forsyth, 23 Oct. 1835, printed in Bennett and Brooks, *op. cit.*, p. 163.

lay in Zanzibar harbour;[1] and in 1843 a British ship sent to investigate discovered that Spanish schooners still bought slaves in the Kilwa region.[2]

This European demand for slaves, which originated in the 1770s and was maintained until the 1820s when British measures began to take effect, and which even afterwards continued on a lesser scale, must have stimulated economic activity on the Swahili Coast. Not only did the ports involved prosper, but the traditional traders from the north – Arabs and Indians – were forced to organize themselves more efficiently in the face of this new competition. The northward trade in slaves to Arabia and India had existed prior to the arrival of the French, but its volume is difficult to calculate. In 1776 Morice reported that Arabs of Socotra and Muscat came to Zanzibar to fetch millet, slaves, and ivory.[3] He also described Indian vessels arriving in Zanzibar, whence Swahilis went to buy goods which they subsequently exchanged in their own districts for ivory, provisions, and slaves. In March and April, Swahili and Arab traders went to Kilwa to buy slaves.[4]

Whether the volume of this northward trade was affected by the new European demand after the 1770s is difficult to estimate because there are no figures available. What probably happened was that the traditional merchants became more interested in controlling and organizing the supply of slaves. In many cases this would have required settlement on the Swahili Coast. The merchants may also have put pressure on the authorities in Oman to tighten up their control of the Swahili Coast in order to regulate supply and to prevent outsiders from establishing themselves in the region. The traditional merchants would have been given further encouragement to pressurize the authorities by the inevitable rise in prices which accompanied the European demand. In 1785 Saulnier de Mondevit made an arrangement with the sultan of Kilwa that slaves were not to cost more than 25 dollars, but two years later Comarmond complained that prices had doubled in the last five or six years.[5] In 1802 slaves were costing 40 dollars each.[6] As the

[1] Journal of R. P. Waters, entry for 21 Oct. 1837, printed in Bennett and Brooks, *op. cit.*, p. 205.
[2] Lt Christopher to Hamerton, 28 Feb. 1843, encl. in Bombay to Secret Committee, no. 54, 18 July 1843, E.S.L.B. 60.
[3] Morice, 'Projet d'un établissement', pp. 78 and 89.
[4] *Ibid.*, p. 57.
[5] Extract from the Journal of Saulnier de Mondevit, 1785, A.N., Colonies C4/80, and Comarmond's 'Mémoire', 1787, A.N., Colonies C4/85.
[6] Seton to Bombay, 9 July 1802, Proc. 27 Aug., B.P.S.P. 381/33.

THE SWAHILI COAST

European demand diminished, prices fell again – between 1817 and 1819 slaves cost between 15 and 25 dollars[1] – but they had remained high long enough to affect Arab and Indian merchants.

There were other factors which encouraged the Omanis to extend their economic activities on the Swahili Coast, but undoubtedly the European demand for slaves was a most important one. Accompanying this extension came an emphasis of political authority by the rulers of Muscat, who wanted to command the increasing revenues provided by the Swahili Coast. It is significant that the revenues provided by that region rose steadily before the 1820s,[2] and it is not unlikely that the European purchase of slaves played a large part in the increase. Complaints about the extortionate duties the French had to pay are common in their letters. In 1804 Dallons had to pay eleven dollars duty per head at Zanzibar.[3] In 1811, eight dollars duty was paid at Kilwa.[4] If an average of ten dollars duty was paid per head, and 2,500 slaves were exported to Mauritius and Bourbon annually before the 1820s, 25,000 dollars revenue per year could be derived from the Swahili Coast's sale of slaves to those Europeans alone. There were also duties paid by Arabs and Indians, the volume of whose exports is unknown. This 25,000 dollars was a third of the revenue which Saiyid Sa'id obtained from the Swahili Coast in 1818.[5] In 1822 the governor of Mauritius calculated that 40,000 dollars would be fair compensation for Saiyid Sa'id should he prohibit the sale of slaves to Europeans.[6] The Slave Trade therefore provided a large proportion of the revenue Sa'id derived from East Africa. Moreover, in 1802 the revenue from East Africa amounted to a third of the ruler of Muscat's total revenue,[7] and it is very likely that this proportion was maintained or increased. The ruler of Muscat was therefore alive to the potential value of the Swahili Coast, and indeed before the 1820s Saiyid Sa'id had begun to stress his authority there.

---

[1] Sausse to Minister of Marine, 15 Nov. 1817 (15-20 dollars each); Barreaut to Minister of Marine, 15 Oct. 1818 (20-25 dollars each); and Albrand's Report, 1819 (18-22 dollars each) – all from M.O., Réunion 72/472.

[2] See Chapter III, p. 99.

[3] Dallons, 1804, printed in Freeman-Grenville, *Select Documents*, p. 199.

[4] Prior, *op. cit.*, p. 68.

[5] For 80,000 dollars as Sa'id's annual revenue from East Africa, De Tromelin to Minister of Marine, 22 May 1819, M.O., Réunion 72/472.

[6] Farquhar's minute of 7 Feb. 1822, quoted in Moresby to Farquhar, 11 Sept. 1822, Proc. 18 Sept., B.P.C. 385/26.

[7] Seton to Bombay, 9 July 1802, Proc. 27 Aug., B.P.S.P. 381/33, and see Chapter III, p. 100.

THE SLAVE TRADE ON THE SWAHILI COAST

This extension of political authority, already begun when the British started to put pressure on Saiyid Sa'id to forbid the sale of slaves to Europeans, was enforced rather than diminished as a result of that pressure. Sa'id not only had to appear actively in control of the Swahili Coast in order to discourage European intruders, but also had to envisage the consequences of bowing to British demands and to plan alternative sources of revenue.

The restrictions imposed by the British caused a contraction in the European demand for slaves after 1822.[1] The years following this contraction were precisely those in which the plantation economy of Zanzibar and Pemba developed, and there may well have been a connexion between the two occurrences. In the late 1820s and early 1830s vast and ready sources of labour were an urgent requirement for the large clearing operations involved in laying out the plantations.[2] Saiyid Sa'id himself eventually had forty-five of these plantations.[3] Then, when the plantations began to produce cloves, the picking season was highly labour-intensive. In thirty years the clove export rose from almost nothing to 5 million lb. annually.[4] The steady supply of slaves which had formerly gone to European buyers was ready to be diverted to this alternative market in the 1820s, and was an important contributory factor in the establishment and success of the clove plantations of Zanzibar and Pemba. Absorption on the plantations meant that the number of slaves coming to the coast from the interior was maintained at a steady rate. It was not a question of attaining a large stable labour force and then diminishing the purchase of slaves, because the high death rate among agricultural slaves of 22–30 per cent annually meant that the complete force had to be renewed every four years.[5] Local ownership of slaves was not, however, entirely new in the 1830s. In 1811 Smee had observed that many Arabs possessed 800 or 900 slaves each.[6] But as the Omani and Indian settlers proliferated and enriched themselves, more slaves were bought by local people. In

---

[1] See Chapter IX for the restrictions.

[2] Ruschenberger observed such clearing operations – *op. cit.*, I, 73.

[3] Emily Ruete (Salma binti Sa'id), *Memoirs of an Arabian Princess*, trans. Lionel Strachey (London, 1907), p. 109. (First publ. Berlin, 1886.)

[4] Burton, *Zanzibar*, I, 364.

[5] Hamerton to F.O., no. 1, 2 Jan. 1844, F.O. 54/6, and R. F. Burton, *The Lake Regions of Central Africa* (London, 1860), 2 vols, II, 377 (hereafter cited as *Lake Regions*).

[6] Smee's Description of the island of Zanzibar, I.O.L., Marine Records Miscellaneous 586.

THE SWAHILI COAST

the early 1830s some people owned as many as 2,000 slaves.[1] The British consul reported that by 1841 almost every one of the Sultan's subjects owned slaves, the poorer about five, and the wealthier from 400 to 1,500.[2] In 1843 Jairam, the customs master, had 200 slaves, and Saiyid Sa'id 12,000.[3] By the 1840s 7,000-10,000 slaves were being absorbed annually in Zanzibar.[4] A considerable number were also used elsewhere on the Swahili Coast for domestic and agricultural purposes and as porters and defenders of caravans penetrating inland. The Nyika, for example, began to acquire slaves in the 1840s to cultivate their land.[5]

The number of slaves sold on the Swahili Coast was also kept up because the demand from the non-European markets of Arabia and India continued, and more Omani and Indian traders took advantage of the opportunities offered by the Swahili Coast. The British did not attack this branch of the Slave Trade until twenty years after they had insisted that sales to Europeans be prohibited.[6] By the time they were able to impose a treaty designed to suppress the Indian and Arabian trade, it was so firmly established that their opposition was ineffective.

There were various estimates given in the 1840s of the number of slaves East Africa exported to the north. Loarer reckoned that before 1846 7,000-8,000 were sent northwards annually.[7] However, the estimates which the British consul gave before 1846 are higher than this. He claimed that 20,000 slaves were brought to Zanzibar every year, and of these 13,000-15,000 went to the Red Sea, Arabia, the Persian Gulf, and India.[8] According to the customs figures at Zanzibar, 15,000 were imported yearly into that island, but this is not a true figure because many traders, such as the Sultan's family and other members

---

[1] Ruschenberger, *op. cit.*, I, 40.

[2] Hamerton to Bombay, 13 July 1841, encl. in Bombay to Secret Committee, no. 69, 30 Aug. 1841, E.S.L.B. 35; and same to same, no. 2, 2 Jan. 1842, encl. in Bombay to Secret Committee, no. 43, 30 Apr. 1842, E.S.L.B. 44.

[3] Journal of Lt Christopher, 1843, encl. in Bombay to Secret Committee, no. 54, 18 July 1843, E.S.L.B. 60.

[4] Romain Desfossés to Ministry of F.A., no. 7, 5 Feb. 1846, A.E., Zanz. C.C.1.

[5] Guillain's Report, 1849, A.N., Marine BB4/1036.

[6] See Chapter IX.

[7] Loarer's Report, Part I, 1849, M.O., O.I. 5/23.

[8] Hamerton to Bombay, no. 22, 5 Sept. 1844, B.C. 2121. There are many estimates of the volume of the East African coast Slave Trade made at different times by Hamerton, and it is clear that he had great difficulty in obtaining correct information.

of the Al Bu Saʻidi clan, were exempt from the payment of customs dues, and many slaves were also smuggled into the island.[1] In 1846 a French observer estimated that 16,000 slaves went northwards annually.[2] This was the final year before the treaty arranged by the British in 1845 came into operation, and so it is likely that full advantage was taken of what might have been the last season for the export of slaves. Later that year, in two months alone – August and September – 15,000 slaves were taken from Zanzibar to the Persian Gulf and Red Sea.[3] The following year, when the treaty had come into operation, there was a marked decrease in the number of slaves sent northwards, but when no arrests were in fact made by British cruisers the numbers soon crept up again.[4] None the less, whereas before the treaty 210 boats a year had come from the north to Zanzibar, only 170 came in 1848.[5] In 1850 Hamerton reported that great numbers of slaves would be taken from Zanzibar that year,[6] but the presence of H.M.S. *Castor* was some check.[7] In 1851 the slaving ships returned to the Persian Gulf earlier than usual, thereby evading British counter measures.[8] They also carried on the trade under the Persian flag, which could not be apprehended by British vessels.[9] The situation worsened when Saiyid Saʻid and Hamerton left Zanzibar for a while in 1852.[10] In 1856, the year Saʻid died, 15,000 slaves were reported to have been taken from Zanzibar to the Persian Gulf, and 2,500 to the Red Sea.[11] Therefore, despite the British campaign, the numbers of slaves exported from the East African coast to the north had, if anything, increased. East Africa had found a satisfactorily steady market to help replace that lost when the Europeans had ceased to trade in slaves. Doubtless there were fluctuations from year to year, but by the 1840s the northward market was accepting about 15,000 slaves annually.

[1] Hamerton to Bombay, no. 2, 2 Jan. 1842, encl. in Bombay to Secret Committee, no. 43, 30 Apr. 1842, E.S.L.B. 44.
[2] Romain Desfossés to Ministry of F.A., no. 7, 5 Feb. 1846, A.E., Zanz. C.C.1.
[3] Loarer's Report, Part I, 1849, M.O., O.I. 5/23.
[4] *Idem.*
[5] Guillain's Report, 1849, A.N., Marine BB4/1036.
[6] Hamerton to Bombay, no. 5, 15 Feb. 1850, Z.A.
[7] Hamerton to Comm. Wyvill, 8 May 1850, encl. in Bombay to Secret Committee, no. 35, 25 June 1850, E.S.L.B. 102.
[8] Hennell to Bombay, 28 June 1851, B.C. 2442.
[9] Hamerton to Bombay, no. 6, 7 Mch. 1848, Z.A.
[10] Ward to Webster, 14 June 1852, Amer.N.A., Zanz. 3.
[11] Coghlan (Resident at Aden) to Bombay, no. 78, 22 May 1856, encl. in Bombay to Secret Committee, no. 42, 10 June 1856, E.S.L.B. 125.

THE SWAHILI COAST

It is difficult to separate the Indian demand from that of Arabia because in many cases slaves reached India via Muscat. Indian slave-brokers from Bombay would go to Muscat to arrange the purchase of slaves.[1] There was also a flourishing trade from Muscat to Sind and Kutch.[2] A further difficulty encountered when attempting to estimate the number of East African slaves absorbed in India is that some Arab boats would take slaves directly from Zanzibar to India but their destination would be unknown to observers at Zanzibar.[3] The numbers involved cannot have been large because guile had to be resorted to in order to introduce the slaves into British Indian territory. Some boats carried only six or seven slaves, who could be passed off as crew or wives of crew.[4] On arrival in Bombay the women would sometimes be dressed up as men and others would be passed through the guards with bribes.[5] The local agent of the British at Muscat reported that 400-500 slaves from Zanzibar entered India annually.[6]

The number of slaves sold on the Swahili Coast was also kept up by the Portuguese demand which continued to a limited extent after the 1820s. Because it was difficult to implement the treaties on the southern section of the Swahili Coast, sales of slaves to the Portuguese were still taking place in the 1850s. In 1850 a British naval vessel discovered barracoons in the vicinity of Kilwa in which slaves were stored prior to export to the north, or sale to the Portuguese.[7]

After the initial expansion in response to European demand, the total volume of the Swahili Coast Slave Trade – that is, the number of slaves sold both for local use and for export to Europeans, Arabians, and Indians – seems to have been the same at the beginning and end of the period under review. Since Zanzibar became the main slave market, the figures of the yearly import of slaves into that island are a good guide to the total volume of the East African Slave Trade. It was said

---

[1] Bombay to Secret Committee, no. 108, 31 Dec. 1841, S.L.B. 1st series 14.
[2] *Idem.*
[3] Same to same, no. 69, 30 Aug. 1841, S.L.B. 1st series 13.
[4] Hennell to Bombay, 7 Sept. 1841, encl. in Bombay to Secret Committee, no. 97, 30 Nov. 1841, E.S.L.B. 38.
[5] British local agent at Muscat to Hennell, 9 Aug. 1841, encl. in no. 97, as above.
[6] Same to same, 3 Aug. 1841, encl. in no. 97, as above. The local agent obtained this information from the commander of one of Saiyid Sa'id's vessels.
[7] Hamerton to Bombay, no. 8, 20 May 1850, encl. in Bombay to Secret Committee, no. 35, 25 June 1850, E.S.L.B. 102.

THE SLAVE TRADE ON THE SWAHILI COAST

that in 1819 25,000-30,000 slaves were imported into Zanzibar.[1] However, three years later another observer gave a figure of only 8,000, although he did say that there had been a sharp drop recently in imports of slaves.[2] A visitor to Zanzibar in 1833 reported that 6,000-7,000 slaves entered Zanzibar yearly.[3] Cogan's exaggerated figure of 50,000 also dates from the 1830s.[4] Cogan, the negotiator of the 1839 treaty between Sa'id and the British, had an interest in overestimating the figure because he was attempting to persuade Palmerston of the need for a British consul at Zanzibar. Hamerton's figures for the 1840s average at about 15,000 slaves annually imported into Zanzibar.[5] This is corroborated by Ward, the American consul.[6] All these figures are of only limited worth. The slave traders had an interest in concealing the true facts from Europeans, who viewed the Slave Trade with disfavour. Hamerton claimed he obtained his figures from the customs records, but even if this were true (he was unlikely to have been given access to the records to enquire into such a delicate matter), these did not refer to all the slaves imported. In summary, before the 1822 Moresby Treaty possibly as many as 20,000 slaves were sold annually on the Swahili Coast, there was a drop in sales in the 1820s and 1830s due to restrictions imposed on the sale of slaves to Europeans, but in the 1840s once again about 20,000 slaves were sold yearly on the Swahili Coast. Although the Slave Trade was of great commercial importance, the fact that it did not increase in volume contrasted with the rapid development of other forms of economic activity.[7] Hence by the mid 1840s it was possible for Saiyid Sa'id to envisage a reduction in the Slave Trade, even though this traffic had been indispensable to the growth of commercial prosperity on the Swahili Coast.

The importance of the Slave Trade lies less in its overall value than in the fact that it was a catalyst in the economic development of the

---

[1] Albrand's Report, 1819, M.O., Réunion 72/472. A figure of 25,000 for 1819 was also given by Moresby, who did not have access to Albrand's letter, but may have obtained his information from the same source in Zanzibar – Moresby to Bombay, 25 Sept. 1822, Proc. 2 Oct., B.P.C. 385/26.

[2] Moresby to Bombay, idem.

[3] Ruschenberger, op. cit., I, 40. Burton, Zanzibar, I, 351, says that in 1835 6,000-7,000 were imported, and it is likely that he obtained his information from Ruschenberger's book.

[4] Cogan to Palmerston, 6 May 1839, F.O. 54/3.

[5] See above, p. 204.

[6] Ward to Buchanan, Sec. of State, no. 16, 7 Mch. 1847, Amer.N.A., Zanz. 2.

[7] See Chapter XII.

Swahili Coast. It has been demonstrated how the Slave Trade and the establishment of the plantations were linked. In addition, the development of a more efficient method of obtaining slaves was accompanied by the provision of capital, investment in other areas of production, and general economic diversification. The mechanism for the acquisition and sale of slaves became more complex in order to maintain a steady supply. This meant that caravans to the interior had to be organized along more formal lines than in earlier periods. Before the 1830s most of the slaves were brought to the coast by the peoples of the hinterland and interior: there is little evidence to show that coastal people themselves went inland to procure slaves. Morice was of the opinion that 'Moorish' and Arab travellers did not penetrate any distance inland, although he had heard of some journeys to Lake Nyasa and beyond.[1] However, the information gleaned by Lt Hardy, visiting Zanzibar in 1811, indicates that there might have been some penetration from the coast.[2] He was told that traders from the coast went two months and nineteen days inland (about 400 miles at an average of five miles a day) from the Wami River. During the 1830s regular penetration of caravans from the coast developed.[3] This can perhaps be explained by the strain put upon the traditional methods of obtaining slaves which resulted from the constantly high demand for them since the 1770s. In order to investigate how far this is true, a study would have to be made of the whole process of slave acquisition and marketing in the interior – a study which cannot be undertaken here. The traditional methods may, however, have been haphazard, and no longer sufficed to meet the needs of the trade. The old system continued side by side with the new. Coastal caravans gradually pushed further and further inland in search of cheaper slaves and ivory as prices in the interior rose.[4]

The caravan trade was a direct stimulus to the further economic development of the Swahili Coast, and in particular to the expansion of the clove plantations. Capital generated by slave and ivory caravans was often invested in plantations. Poor merchants frequently started out as caravan leaders and, having journeyed three or four times into the interior, gained sufficient capital to buy a property and plant cloves.[5]

[1] Morice, 'Projet d'un établissement', p. 63, and 'Memoir concerning the East Coast of Africa, 15 June 1777 and 26 September 1777', A.N., Colonies C4/42.
[2] Hardy's report on Zanzibar, I.O.L., Marine Records Miscellaneous 586.
[3] See Chapter XII, p. 356.
[4] Burton, *Lake Regions*, II, 61, and J. H. Speke, *What led to the Discovery of the Source of the Nile* (London, 1864), pp. 240-1.
[5] Loarer's Report, Part I, 1849, M.O., O.I. 5/23.

THE SLAVE TRADE ON THE SWAHILI COAST

The profits then made from these plantations would enable the owners to organize, rather than lead, large-scale caravans. However, most of the capital to finance the caravans was provided by Indian merchants. The increasingly attractive economic opportunities of the Swahili Coast encouraged Indians to come to the region.[1] They then provided capital and banking and lending facilities without which the economic development of the Swahili Coast could not have progressed so rapidly. Indians did not personally participate in caravans to the interior, which were conducted by Arabs and Swahilis.[2] They were, however, prominent in the middleman activities of buying and selling on the coast. The slaves brought to the coast by peoples of the interior or the hinterland – the former often passed them on to the latter before final sales in the coastal ports – were purchased mainly by Indian merchants.[3] The slaves would then be stored on the coast prior to shipment to Zanzibar in boats which were chartered from Arabs and Swahilis by Indians or which were owned by the Indians themselves.[4] On reaching Zanzibar, whither vessels from Arabia, India, and the Persian Gulf had come, the slaves would be sold in the slave market. Although, after the 1830s, Arabs, Swahilis, and Indians all participated in the organization of the Slave Trade, it was the Indians who would have been hardest hit financially had the trade diminished.

As already mentioned, one link between the Slave Trade and the economic development of the Swahili Coast was the capital generated by the former which was invested in other economic activities. An attempt should therefore be made to calculate the size of the profits gained from this traffic in human lives. The prices fetched by slaves are an important factor in assessing these. After the Europeans left the market, prices paid for slaves were more moderate. In 1842 slaves cost seven dollars at Kilwa;[5] six years later Guillain discovered that slaves bought there varied in price from 10 to 100 *doti*[6] (a *doti* was a measure of cloth, about ten of which could be bought for a dollar), and Loarer, who accompanied him, observed that slaves cost eight dollars at that

---

[1] See Chapter X, p. 290.
[2] Loarer's Report, Part II, 1849, M.O., O.I. 2/10.
[3] Hamerton to Bombay, no. 2, 2 Jan. 1842, encl. in Bombay to Secret Committee, no. 43, 30 Apr. 1842, E.S.L.B. 44; and Ward to Buchanan, no. 16, 7 Mch. 1847, Amer.N.A., Zanz. 2.
[4] Guillain's Report, 1849, A.N., Marine BB4/1036.
[5] R. P. Waters' notes, 18 Oct. 1842, printed in Bennett and Brooks, *op. cit.*, p. 253.
[6] Guillain's Report, 1849, A.N., Marine BB4/1036.

port.¹ Slaves sold at coastal ports, such as Kilwa, were generally bought by merchants who then took the slaves to the Zanzibar market where they were sold at a profit. Prices were much higher in Zanzibar. In 1842 average prices there were: boys from seven to ten years: 7-15 dollars; boys from ten to twenty years: 15-30 dollars; full-grown men: 17-20 dollars. Females cost more: 'a good stout lass will sell for 35 dollars'.² These prices are corroborated by other sources. Loarer reported that before 1847 a man sold for 15-18 dollars at Zanzibar, and a woman for 50-100.³ The American consul observed in 1842 that slaves sold for 14-25 dollars each at Zanzibar.⁴

What relation did these prices bear to those paid by caravans in the interior? Prices in the interior are difficult to calculate because most of the trade was conducted in barter, and there were of course differences from place to place. 'It is impossible', said Richard Burton, 'to give any idea of the average price of the human commodity, which varies, under the modifications of demand and supply, from two to ten doti or tobes of American domestics.'⁵ None the less Burton mentioned prices at various places in the interior. These were measured in *fundo* of beads (a *fundo* was ten lengths of beads doubled round the throat – or five lengths in some areas – which, according to the type of bead, might cost up to half a dollar in Zanzibar) or *shukkah*, *doti*, and *gorah* of cloth (a *shukkah* measured about six feet, a *doti* was two *shukkah*, and a *gorah* was seven to eleven *doti*).⁶ Generally at remote places, such as Uvira, Ujipa, and Marungu, slaves were cheaper than in the market at Ujiji.⁷ At Karagwe the price of an adult male slave varied from eight to ten *fundo* of white, green, or blue porcelain beads, and a woman in her prime cost two *kitindi* (a coil bracelet of copper, iron, or brass wire, the value of which varied from one to five dollars) and five or six *fundo* of mixed beads.⁸ At Ubena slaves were sold for five or six *fundo* of beads. This may be compared with the price of ivory there: one pound cost one or two *fundo* of yellow and other coloured beads.⁹ At Msene a full-grown girl would cost a *gorah* of *merkani* or *kaniki*¹⁰ (*merkani* was

[1] Loarer's Report, Part II, 1849, M.O., O.I. 2/10.
[2] Kemball, Assistant Resident in the Persian Gulf, to Robertson, 8 July 1842, encl. in Bombay to Secret Committee, no. 106, 30 Sept. 1842, E.S.L.B. 50. Kemball had been making enquiries about the Slave Trade.
[3] Loarer's Report, Part II, 1849, M.O., O.I. 2/10.
[4] Waters' notes, 18 Oct. 1842, printed in Bennett and Brooks, *op. cit.*, p. 253.
[5] Burton, *Lake Regions*, II, 62.
[6] For these measures and values, see Burton, *Lake Regions*, II, Appendix I.
[7] *Ibid.*, II, 121.   [8] *Ibid.*, II, 184.   [9] *Ibid.*, II, 270.   [10] *Ibid.*, II, 79.

unbleached American shirting or sheeting cotton and *kaniki* was indigo-dyed Indian cotton) which cost two to three dollars in Zanzibar.¹ In the interior, therefore, a male cost anything up to the equivalent of three dollars and a woman slightly more. Sometimes a human being could be purchased for less than half a dollar.

It is therefore apparent that large profits could be made by those engaged in the Slave Trade because of the disproportion between prices in the interior and those in Zanzibar. However, profits were not as great as appears from a simple comparison of prices, because of the sometimes extensive cost of caravans and the number of middlemen involved. The largest profits would go to those who commissioned caravans to go into the interior, owned their own coasting vessels on which the slaves would be brought to Zanzibar, and themselves arranged for the sale of those slaves. The leader, porters, and armed guard of the caravan would have to be paid, and there would also be the cost of the cloth, beads, and wire to be used as barter and as tolls. There would also be the customs dues payable on entry to Zanzibar. About 1835 the import duty at Zanzibar varied from half a dollar to four dollars, according to which coastal port the slaves had come from; later on, the duty was two dollars, and by 1857 this had fallen to one dollar.² Taking all these costs into account, and the numerous desertions of slaves that always occurred, a merchant could none the less make 500 per cent profit on slaves brought from the interior.³ The merchant who bought his slaves on the coast, perhaps from one of the African caravans which came down from the interior, would make a smaller, but nevertheless substantial, profit. Paying five to seven dollars for each slave at the littoral port, and two dollars entry at Zanzibar, he would make a profit of 50 per cent or more. Slave dealing was, then, a highly lucrative business.

What part did the buying and selling of slaves play in the economic activities of Indian merchants? When in July 1850 Saiyid Saʻid issued an edict forbidding Indians to trade in slaves, and at the same time a British vessel burnt slave barracoons belonging to Indians at Kilwa and imprisoned their owners,⁴ some Indian merchants suspended their businesses.⁵ Others actually closed their businesses, thereby suffering

---

¹ As note 6, p. 210.
² Burton, *Zanzibar*, I, 465.
³ This is Burton's estimation – *Lake Regions*, II, 62.
⁴ See Chapter IX, p. 243.
⁵ Ward to Clayton, no. 42, 20 July 1850, Amer.N.A., Zanz. 2.

THE SWAHILI COAST

great financial loss, and left the Swahili Coast.¹ In 1850/1 the unsettled situation following Sa'id's edict made trade on the Swahili Coast dull. Indians refused to buy from foreign merchants.² The situation was aggravated by the particular method of trading which had developed at Zanzibar: foreign merchants, particularly Americans, sold their cargoes, mainly to Indians, on six months' credit, but bought local products for cash.³ Presumably it was those who lost confidence, or who derived most of their profits from the Slave Trade, who suffered financial loss in 1850. In fact some Indian businesses and the trade of the Swahili Coast soon revived. In February 1852 an American merchant reported that the market for imports was more healthy and Indians had recommenced trading.⁴ Many Indian businesses were able to continue after Sa'id's edict because they had already invested in other products and were able to fall back on these. They held the buying and selling of almost all the varied products of the Swahili Coast in their hands.⁵ In addition, most of them were representatives of houses in India and could cash drafts on Bombay.⁶ They therefore had ample capital to support them while they invested in other economic activities. After their setback the Indian merchants, who played such a vital part in the economic system of the Swahili Coast, recovered and prospered once again.⁷

Almost inseparable from the part the Slave Trade played in the fluctuating fortunes of Indian businesses was its contribution to the general economy of the Swahili Coast. What part did the Slave Trade play in both the general economy and the fortunes of particular regions? As Kilwa Kisiwani declined, Zanzibar became an increasingly important entrepot,⁸ and superseded Kilwa as the main slave market of the coast. None the less the number of slaves coming from the Kilwa area was not affected; they merely went to Zanzibar for sale instead of being sold

[1] Ward to Abbot, 13 Mch. 1851, Amer.N.A., Zanz. 3; and Hamerton to Bombay, no. 13, 29 Aug. 1851, Z.A.
[2] William McMullan to Michael Shepard, 28 Jan. 1851, and John F. Webb to Michael Shepard, 14 June 1851, printed in Bennett and Brooks, *op. cit.*, pp. 474-5 and 485.
[3] Ward to Abbot, 13 Mch. 1851, Amer.N.A., Zanz. 3.
[4] John F. Webb to Michael Shepard, 22 Feb. 1852, printed in Bennett and Brooks, *op. cit.*, p. 495.
[5] Ward to Buchanan, no. 16, 7 Mch. 1847, Amer.N.A., Zanz. 2.
[6] Burton, *Zanzibar*, I, 329.
[7] *Ibid.*, 327-35.
[8] See Chapter III, pp. 79-80 and 85.

directly at Kilwa. This process had begun by the 1820s. In 1822 Massieu reported that the slave market at Zanzibar was full of slaves from Kilwa, and each day more slaving ships were arriving from there.[1] In 1817 Kilwa provided Zanzibar with half its total import of slaves: of the 25,000 taken there from all the coast, 13,000 were from Kilwa, Tongui, and Lindi.[2] In 1848 8,000-10,000 slaves came from the interior to Kilwa Kivinje and 1,000-1,200 to Lindi, so the number had kept fairly steady.[3] In 1850 Krapf visited Kilwa and reported that 10,000-12,000 slaves were exported each year.[4] When prohibitions were enforced by Saiyid Sa'id in an attempt to co-operate with the British, Kilwa had the advantage of being far from Zanzibar and more able to carry on a direct trade with Arabian boats, which sailed round the east of Zanzibar to evade the Sultan's police.[5]

The other half of the slaves exported from the Swahili Coast came from the area behind Bagamoyo, stretching to Lakes Tanganyika and Victoria Nyanza. The paucity of information in the European sources about slaves exiting at ports opposite Zanzibar during the earlier period when the trade with the French was flourishing does not necessarily mean that they did not do so. In the list of groups composing the cargo of slaves taken by the *Sir Edward Hughes* Indiaman, peoples inhabiting the area opposite Zanzibar are included, such as the Mrima (the general name for the people inhabiting the littoral opposite Zanzibar), Chagga, and Hehe.[6] Among the list Smee compiled from the slave market in Zanzibar in 1811 were Nyamwesi, 'Guru' (Nguru), Doe, Zigua, and Shambala.[7] These were obviously procured from the coastline opposite Zanzibar because Smee places their homelands as 'three days from the coast', 'four days from the coast', etc. At Zanzibar, Lt Hardy, accompanying Smee, acquired much information about this part of the coast, such as a detailed description of peoples inhabiting the hinterland and their trading habits. Slaves are repeatedly named as one of the articles of trade.[8]

However many slaves it had produced before, the African interior opposite Zanzibar was a great slave-supplying area by the 1840s. The

[1] Massieu to Freycinet, 9 Oct. 1822, M.O., Réunion 72/473.
[2] Albrand's Report, 1819, M.O., Réunion 72/472.
[3] Loarer's Report, Part II, 1849, M.O., O.I. 2/10.
[4] Krapf, *op. cit.*, p. 423.
[5] *Ibid.*, p. 424.
[6] Bombay to Smee, 31 Dec. 1810, I.O.L., Marine Records Miscellaneous 586.
[7] Smee's Description of the island of Zanzibar, I.O.L., *ibid.*
[8] Hardy's report on Zanzibar, 1811, *ibid.*

supply of slaves must have been stimulated by the increasing frequency of caravans and by the practice of exchanging muskets for slaves. For example, Zanzibar Arabs would promise Zigua leaders a certain number of muskets in return for slaves, which prompted them to attack neighbouring villages.[1] In the 1850s Kisabengo, a Zigua, who possessed 500 guns, captured almost all the inhabitants of the area between the Usagara and Nguru hills, and sent them to the Zanzibar slave-market.[2] The trade routes of the area from the coast to Lake Tanganyika became well established, and by the mid 1840s traders were passing beyond that lake into the present Uganda region.[3]

The interior behind Mombasa provided far fewer slaves than the areas further south. In 1811 Hardy mentioned that a few slaves were sold by the 'Metane' near Mombasa,[4] but Lt Emery, in charge of the British occupation of Mombasa from 1824 to 1826, did not include slaves in his list of that town's exports.[5] The Arab and Indian merchants who traded with the Kamba did not buy slaves from them.[6] As was the custom, the Arabs and Swahilis at Mombasa possessed slaves, and, as there was no great supply from the interior, Mombasa had to import slaves from elsewhere on the East African coast. By the late 1840s there was an additional demand for slaves in Mombasa because of a system of exchange which had developed. Mombasa was buying slaves from Mongallo, Kilwa, and Zanzibar, which were given to the Nyika in exchange for cattle. These cattle were then passed to the Kamba in exchange for ivory.[7] The rate of exchange with the Nyika was two, three, or four animals for a slave. The system flourished because of the new difficulties of sending slaves to Arabia and because of the Nyika demand for slaves, a demand which had arisen when the Nyika realized the advantages of using slaves in agricultural and herding pursuits and of hiring them as porters for caravans.[8] The Nyika also sold slaves to

---

[1] Krapf, *op. cit.*, p. 121.   [2] Burton, *Lake Regions*, I, 88 and 185.
[3] H. Stuhlmann, *Die Tagebucher von Dr. Emin Pascha*, 5 vols (Hamburg, 1917-27), I, 139 and 154.
[4] Hardy's 'Account of Different Rivers on the Coast from Qualiffe towards Mozambique', I.O.L., Marine Records Miscellaneous 586.
[5] See Chapter III, p. 87.
[6] Emery to W. D. Cooley, 20 Dec. 1833, R.G.S., Emery MS. File.
[7] Guillain, *Documents*, III, 267-8; Guillain's Report, 1849, A.N., Marine BB4/1036.
[8] Guillain's Report, *idem*, and Krapf, *op. cit.*, p. 357. For the suggestion that coastal slave-traders were using Mombasa as an alternative market when their northern trade was affected, Krapf, *op. cit.*, p. 358.

THE SLAVE TRADE ON THE SWAHILI COAST

the Galla. As well as these imported slaves there were still a few which were procured from the interior. By the late 1840s the Swahilis of Mombasa were going to the Chagga area to buy slaves, and on occasion, such as in times of famine, the Nyika sold members of their own group.[1] There must have been some incidental export of slaves because Guillain quotes the dues payable on them.[2]

Slaves were also imported rather than exported at the towns north of Mombasa. On the islands of the Lamu archipelago slaves were used for cultivation and herding purposes, and they were also sold by the inhabitants to the Galla of the opposite mainland.[3] Most of Pate and Lamu's slaves were obtained from Zanzibar.[4]

The expansion of the caravan trade, originally stimulated by the need to maintain a steady supply of slaves, opened up the interior region behind the littoral ports opposite Zanzibar, and also led to the development of those ports. As the central region was opened up, Kilwa and its neighbouring ports in the south were nevertheless able to hold their own in maintaining a steady supply of slaves. They were assisted in this by the ease with which they could evade the Sultan's restrictions. Because Mombasa and the area to the north were less involved in the Slave Trade, its fluctuations had less effect on their economic growth; none the less the particular system of exchange which developed at Mombasa relied heavily on the import of slaves.

Finally, it remains to assess the part the Slave Trade continued to play in the general economy of the Swahili Coast after that economy had diversified during the 1830s. It has already been demonstrated that the Slave Trade continued to be important in the provision of capital for other spheres of economic activity, that merchants were affected by attempts to limit it, and that locally absorbed slaves were a valuable part of the production of cloves in Zanzibar and Pemba. Saiyid Sa'id himself did not invest in slave trading, so he would suffer little personal loss if it were limited. The proportion of the customs revenue provided by the Slave Trade after the 1830s is a subject treated in the next chapter; suffice it to say here that the size of the customs receipts from that traffic and the fact that the customs were in any case farmed out meant that the Zanzibar revenues could withstand a diminution in the sale of slaves. It would be more serious for the economy of the

---

[1] Guillain, *Documents*, III, 268.
[2] *Idem*.
[3] Loarer's Report, Part II, 1849, M.O., O.I. 2/10.
[4] Guillain's Report, 1849, A.N., Marine BB4/1036.

Swahili Coast if the slave and ivory trades were interdependent. When the British imposed their restrictions on slave trading in 1850 the American merchants were afraid that the ivory, which was the most important of East Africa's products, and which they said the slaves brought to the coast, would no longer reach Zanzibar.[1] Although there may have been a temporary recession of trade, the fears of the Americans were not justified, and Zanzibar's ivory export continued to rise.[2] It is true that slaves were used to carry ivory to the coast but this was by no means the sole method of porterage. Inland peoples, particularly the Yao and the Nyamwesi, organized themselves into caravans and carried tusks to the coast.[3] As for the caravans which went inland from the coast, on their return journey it was more common for them to use the porters they had taken inland with them or others they hired in the interior to carry the ivory than for them to load it on to the slaves.[4] Slaves which were already in the possession of the organizers of caravans were also taken inland as porters.[5] Porters were equally needed on the inland journey as on the return to the coast because of the quantities of goods, particularly cloth, which was heavy, which had to be taken for barter purposes. Later in the century, chained gangs of slaves carrying tusks were common, but in this period it was not the regular practice. Although, therefore, a diminution in the Slave Trade would have affected the ivory trade, it would not have ruined it because alternative porterage systems were more common.

In assessing the part the Slave Trade played in the economy of the Swahili Coast, it is important to estimate how great a proportion it was of the total value of the exports from that region. An average of 15,000 slaves were exported annually at a ratio of six men to every five women[6] – that is, about 8,100 men and 6,800 women. Taking average prices as 20 dollars for a man and 35 dollars for a woman, the exports would total 400,000 dollars. This can be compared with the 1859 clove exports, which were valued at 278,330 dollars, and ivory exports, valued at 733,330 dollars.[7] The total value of exports from Zanzibar for 1859

[1] Ward to Abbot, 13 Mch. 1851, Amer.N.A., Zanz. 3.
[2] See Chapter XII, pp. 354-5.
[3] Burton, *Lake Regions*, I, 337, and Loarer's Report, Part II, 1849, M.O., O.I. 2/10.
[4] Burton, *Lake Regions*, I, 337 and 340.
[5] *Ibid.*, I, 337.
[6] Kemball to Robertson, 8 July 1842, encl. in Bombay to Secret Committee, no. 106, 30 Sept. 1842, E.S.L.B. 50.
[7] Burton, *Zanzibar*, II, 413.

was 1,800,410 dollars, excluding the value of slaves.[1] Slaves, therefore, accounted for a fifth of Zanzibar's exports of local produce.

The value of the Slave Trade to the Swahili Coast was diminished by the fact that some of the profit from it drained away to India. Being agents of Indian firms and only temporarily resident on the Swahili Coast, many Indian merchants sent their profits regularly to India. Jairam, the customs master, had thirty millions in a Bombay bank.[2] Specie, mainly brought in by Americans, was the third highest of Zanzibar's exports,[3] and most of it went to India. It would, therefore, be possible for the authorities in Zanzibar to contemplate the limitation of the Slave Trade.

It was the Slave Trade which was originally responsible for generating the increased economic interest of the Omanis in the Swahili Coast. This interest was accompanied by an assertion of political authority. Economic diversification soon followed the better organization which was imposed in order to maintain a steady supply of slaves. Such diversification required a further stressing of political authority, which it seemed possible to achieve only with British support. Consequently the Omani authorities contemplated limiting the Slave Trade in response to British demands so that they could expand further in a territory where their original expansion had been encouraged by that very trade. At the same time, the economic diversification brought about by the Slave Trade facilitated its suppression – but these are the subjects of the next chapter.

[1] *Idem.* Burton does not include the value of slave exports. This figure does not include the value of exports of foreign produce, which had been brought to Zanzibar from Europe, India, the Red Sea, and the Persian Gulf.
[2] Broquant to Ministry of F.A., 14 Feb. 1846, A.E., Zanz. C.C.1. Broquant may mean dollars, or may have converted into francs.
[3] Burton, *Zanzibar*, II, 413.

CHAPTER IX

ATTEMPTS TO SUPPRESS THE SWAHILI COAST SLAVE TRADE AND THEIR EFFECT

The Sultan of Zanzibar wrote to Queen Victoria in 1842:

'It is your desire that the traffic in slaves should cease. And I hear your words and obey your wishes. But be Your Majesty informed that these countries will in consequence be totally and entirely ruined.'[1]

Saiyid Sa'id well knew that his gloomy forecast was far from the truth. He was, however, trying to extort the greatest possible benefits from the British in return for granting their request. The story of British pressure on the Sultan of Zanzibar to suppress the Slave Trade illustrates the capacity of both sides to weigh the balance of mutual advantage and injury and to drive a hard bargain over an issue which involved problems of morality, commercial profit, and political security.

Any opponent of the export of slaves from East Africa had serious problems to face. The co-operation of the sellers and buyers, and in particular of their rulers, would have to be enlisted. British and other European buyers would be the easiest to approach first, since their leaders had generally agreed on the principle of abolition. Other buyers and sellers were a more difficult proposition. Since the ruler of Zanzibar claimed control over the ports of exit of the slaves, the first essential was to obtain his consent to the suppression of the export trade. Even then he might not have the power or inclination to enforce this at the many littoral ports. As for the non-European buyers, these came from so many different places that numerous authorities would have to be approached. It was no use persuading one shaikh to prohibit the Slave Trade if his neighbour continued to indulge in it. He would be jealous of his neighbour growing rich at his expense, and he might

[1] Saiyid Sa'id to Queen Victoria, 11 Feb. 1842, F.O. 54/5.

ATTEMPTS TO SUPPRESS THE SLAVE TRADE

import slaves overland through his neighbour's territory. There was no one authority to whom the British could appeal to put an end to the trade, and whom they could have threatened to supplant unless he co-operated.

Difficulties were enhanced when rulers themselves engaged in, or derived a considerable proportion of their revenue from, the Slave Trade. Even if rulers did assist the British, they would have to have adequate judicial arrangements and naval and police forces to enforce obedience and impose punishment. Since such requirements were generally absent, the whole task of catching and punishing the culprits would tend to fall on the power which had originally initiated the measures.

These problems were so daunting that it was fortunate that the British were not fully aware of them when they began to interfere with the East African Slave Trade. Their attack on the trade was a very gradual affair. It originated when, on 1 January 1808, the Act for the Abolition of the British Slave Trade came into force. Although public indignation had been aroused by the horrors of the Atlantic Slave Trade, this Act applied equally to British subjects in India and the Eastern Seas. It soon became obvious to the British in India and Mauritius that it might be worth while trying to prevent slaves leaving their places of origin, in order to thwart British slave-traders in their attempts to trade. It was Farquhar, the governor of Mauritius, who first tried to do this. The Mauritius slaves came from Portuguese East Africa, Madagascar, the Comoro islands, and the section of the East African coast claimed by the ruler of Muscat. The Portuguese were already being importuned to stop the trade by the British Government, and in 1817 Farquhar arranged with Radama, the ruler of Madagascar, a treaty which forbade the sale of slaves to Europeans.[1]

The subject was first broached with the ruler of Muscat in 1812. Bombay told Sa'id the trade had been prohibited in British India, asking him to proclaim this throughout his dominions so that his subjects would not sell slaves to British subjects.[2] In July 1815, after hearing that a boat carrying slaves from Zanzibar to Muscat had been taken by Persian Gulf pirates, Bombay went even further. Nepean, the governor of Bombay, suggested that Sa'id imitate the principal powers

---

[1] Farquhar sent the treaty to India in Jan. 1821 – Farquhar to Fort William, 21 Jan. 1821, Proc. 10 Oct., B.P.C. 385/12. The success of the treaty waxed and waned with Radama's political fortunes.

[2] Bombay to Sa'id, 4 Mch. 1812, B.P.C. 383/32.

THE SWAHILI COAST

of Europe and abandon the Slave Trade.[1] He added that this would be extremely gratifying to the British Government. It was not the right moment to make such an appeal to Saʻid, for he was enjoying a period of relative peace after the suspension of the Wahhabi invasion. He made no reply to the suggestion.

Farquhar thought approaches to Saʻid should be continued. During his absence from his post as governor of Mauritius between 1817 and 1820, the African Institution in London had begun for the first time to concern itself with the Slave Trade in the Indian Ocean. Although the society had been formed in 1807, there was no mention of the Indian Ocean Slave Trade in its annual reports until 1813. In that year it protested against the decision of the Admiralty Court at the Cape of Good Hope to restore to their owners three slaving ships which had been bound from Madagascar to Mauritius.[2] A protest from the Directors of the Institution to Ministers led the House of Commons to order papers on the subject to be printed. This was the beginning of public concern over the Indian Ocean Slave Trade. Each year thereafter the African Institution reported on the Mauritian Slave Trade and lamented its continuance. Although in fact most of the instances it quoted pertained to Madagascar,[3] Farquhar was convinced that many of the slaves were coming from the East African coast and Zanzibar. He was right.

Farquhar determined to put an end to this situation; he reckoned that, discouraged from buying slaves at Madagascar after the treaty with Radama, the slavers would increase their exertions on the Swahili Coast.[4] His case was reinforced when in 1821 two vessels were captured bringing slaves from Zanzibar.[5] He took it upon himself to initiate negotiations with Saiyid Saʻid, offering him a commercial treaty in return for concessions over the selling of slaves to Europeans.[6] Aware

---

[1] Nepean to Saʻid, 26 July 1815, B.P.C. 383/62.

[2] *7th Report of the Directors of the African Institution*, 1813, p. 6.

[3] For example, in the *9th Report* of 1815, p. 34, it was reported that seven brigs and schooners had foundered off Mozambique and Madagascar in a hurricane, and most of them were slavers.

[4] Farquhar to Hastings, the Governor-General of India, 11 May 1821, Proc. 10 Oct., B.P.C. 385/12. [5] *Idem*.

[6] Farquhar offered to allow the vessels of Saʻid and his subjects into Mauritius, when carrying the produce of Arabia and Persia, on the same footing as British vessels; he also offered to exempt Saʻid's own vessels from the payment of port and quay dues – Farquhar to Saiyid Saʻid, 11 May 1821, Proc. 9 Jan. 1822, B.P.C. 385/17.

that Sa'id had recently co-operated with the British in countering piracy in the Persian Gulf, he likened the Slave Trade by Europeans to piracy. He also sent Captain Moresby in the *Menai* to cruise in Zanzibar waters and to apprehend any British slavers. Moresby seized the *Industry*, with 140 slaves on board, when it was actually in Zanzibar harbour.[1] In considering Farquhar's appeal, Sa'id therefore had to take into account the fact that the British could obviously prevent their ships taking away slaves regardless of his attitude. If he were bound to lose money in any case, he might as well make a virtue of it.

This was not the only factor that influenced Sa'id's decision to forbid the sale of slaves to Europeans. He was also being solicited by the Bombay Council which had been jolted from its inactivity by instructions from the Court of Directors of the East India Company. The Directors themselves were under pressure from the African Institution. The Institution had got hold of a memoir on the Zanzibar slave trade, which it printed in its 15th Report in 1821.[2] This maintained that 10,000 slaves a year were being exported from East Africa to India, Muscat, Bourbon and Mauritius. Alerted by the Institution, the Court of Directors ordered Bombay to renew its 1815 appeal to Saiyid Sa'id.[3] It would be most gratifying, Bombay accordingly told Sa'id, both to the Company Government and to the whole British nation, if he prohibit the slave trade entirely in his dominions, but if he did not find himself able to do this, he should issue orders to all his local authorities to prevent all dealing in slaves carried on by European agents, which was in any case illegal from the point of view of British law.[4] Saiyid Sai'd was further pressurized by the visit of Jukes, who was ordered to stop at Muscat on his way to Persia in order to persuade Sa'id to agree,[5] and by Bruce, the Resident in the Persian Gulf, who had been advised to exert his influence.[6]

[1] Moresby to Farquhar, 7 Aug. 1821, Proc. 9 Jan. 1822, B.P.C. 385/17.
[2] *15th Report of the Directors of the African Institution*, 1821, p. 54. The report quotes and relies heavily on information obtained by Smee in 1811, which was not then published. Possibly it was written by Moresby who did not wish to be named because of his official duties. Moresby could have seen a copy of Smee's report in the Mauritius archives.
[3] Directors of African Institution to C. of Ds., 20 Mch. 1821, *ibid.*, p. 59; and C. of Ds. to Bombay, *ibid.*, p. 63.
[4] Bombay to Saiyid Sa'id, quoted in Bombay to Calcutta, 4 Oct. 1821, Proc. 10 Oct., B.P.C. 385/12.
[5] Instructions to Jukes, 4 Oct. 1821, Proc. 4 Oct., B.P.C. 385/12.
[6] Bombay to C. of Ds., 2 Mch. 1822, P.L.B. 8.

THE SWAHILI COAST

Saiyid Sa'id had to review his political and economic position before he decided whether it was worth while agreeing to the British proposals. It has already been shown that at this time a significant proportion of his revenue derived from the sale of slaves to Europeans.[1] On the other hand, he had to take account of the fact that, in the eyes of the Persian Gulf chiefs, he was firmly in the British camp. He had just participated in the expeditions of 1819 against the Qawasim and 1820 against the Bani Bu Ali. Such activities would not have contributed to his popularity in the Gulf, and if he forfeited British goodwill now he would stand alone. Sa'id was also faced by the strength and power of the British in the Persian Gulf; she had just placed a military force on the island of Qishm.

Sa'id would also have to consider how far a concession would affect his political position in East Africa. It was to his advantage that many of the slave dealers were Indians who were uninterested in political dissent because they were not permanent residents on the Swahili Coast. The attitude of the Swahilis was a more formidable obstacle. Yet the northern section of the Swahili Coast, which was that with which Sa'id was having most trouble at this time, was not the region from which slaves were exported. So far as the Slave Trade was concerned, the most likely centres of political opposition would be Kilwa Kisiwani and Zanzibar. Sa'id had recently removed the troublesome Abdullah ibn Jum'ah from his position as governor of Zanzibar, replacing him with an altogether more co-operative man.[2] This left Kilwa as the most likely seat of resistance, especially since recently it had offered to help the French take Zanzibar.[3]

Despite these dangers, Saiyid Sa'id decided to go ahead with his concessions, being prepared to blame the British for them should they provoke unrest. His discussions with Moresby over sanctions indicate that he intended to do this.[4] Moresby's first proposal was that Sa'id should hand over culprits to the British. Sa'id rejected this, probably because of the obligation it would place upon him, and the unpopularity he might face if he implemented it. It is evident throughout the negotiations for the subsequent treaty that Sa'id was unwilling to agree to anything which put him under a heavy obligation to see that the treaty was observed.

[1] See Chapter VIII, p. 202.
[2] See Chapter V, p. 131, and governor of Zanzibar to Saiyid Sa'id, n.d., but 1822, Proc. 26 June 1822, B.P.C. 385/24.   [3] See Chapter VI, p. 135.
[4] Moresby to Farquhar, 11 Sept. 1822, Proc. 18 Sept., B.P.C. 385/26.

Having decided to submit to the combined pressure from Farquhar and Bombay, Sa'id sent a directive to his governor in Zanzibar to prohibit the sale of slaves to 'Christians'.[1] The directive was confirmed by the treaty negotiated by Moresby who went to Muscat for this purpose at the end of August 1822. Moresby was hampered by the absence of a competent interpreter at Muscat.[2] Nevertheless, he was able to persuade Sa'id to sign a 'requisitions and answers' version of the original proposals. It was not until this Arabic version was translated into English at Bombay that the British could discover whether the Arabic treaty corresponded with the original British proposals.[3] There were some significant differences, but, since the Arabic was the only version to which Sa'id could be beholden, it was that which the British should have accepted. Indeed, in the official publication of treaties arranged with local powers compiled by Aitchison at the end of the nineteenth century, it is the translation of the Arabic version which is included.[4] In 1822, however, Bombay seemed to consider that Moresby's own version was the correct one, and in the *Selections from the Bombay Records*, printed in 1856, it is that which is included.[5]

Article 1 forbade all sales of slaves to 'Christians of every description'. Article 2 concerned evasion and punishment. In Moresby's version Sa'id's officials were to send culprits to Sa'id for punishment, but in the Arabic version officers were to inflict the punishment themselves. This could have been a deliberate attempt by Sa'id to diminish his own obligations. It was also provided that a British agent be resident in Sa'id's dominions to 'have intelligence of' sales of slaves to Christians, but there was no mention that culprits should be handed to this agent, although this was Moresby's original intention.[6] The treaty also stipulated that Omani Arab ships were liable to seizure by British cruisers if found with slaves east of a line passing sixty miles east of Socotra, on to Diu Head, and would be treated (but only in the English version) 'in the same manner as if they were under the English flag'.

Such confusion and differences of wording did not augur well for

[1] Saiyid Sa'id to Bombay, 13 Dec. 1821, Proc. 9 Jan. 1822, B.P.C. 385/17, reporting the measures he had taken; and governor of Zanzibar to Saiyid Sa'id, n.d., but 1822, Proc. 26 June 1822, B.P.C. 385/24, saying the order had been executed.
[2] Moresby to Farquhar, 11 Sept. 1822, Proc. 18 Sept., B.P.C. 385/26.
[3] Translation of Arabic version in Proc. 25 Sept. 1822, B.P.C. 385/26.
[4] Aitchison, *op. cit.*, XI, 289.
[5] *Bombay Selections XXIV*, pp. 654-7.
[6] Moresby to Farquhar, 11 Sept. 1822, Proc. 18 Sept., B.P.C. 385/26.

THE SWAHILI COAST

the success of the treaty. There was little diminution in the sale of slaves to Mauritius and Bourbon.[1] The French Government could not enforce its own prohibition against its subjects trading in slaves, because the Council at Bourbon was so obstructive.[2]

However, the sale of slaves to Europeans was no longer carried out openly, and possibly not at all at Zanzibar. Massieu, captain of the French corvette *L'Espérance*, reported during a visit to Zanzibar in 1822 that slaves were no longer sold to European ships and the price of a good slave had fallen. As a result, the English were detested at Zanzibar, particularly by the traders, who thought they would be ruined.[3] Commodore Nourse, at Zanzibar in December of the same year, said that just before his arrival a vessel under French colours, which had come to purchase slaves, was refused a sale.[4] Moresby himself said the sale of slaves to foreigners on the Swahili Coast had virtually ceased,[5] and so sales must have been well concealed from him.

From these small beginnings developed a general attack on the Indian Ocean Slave Trade. To stop Mauritians getting slaves from East Africa, Saiyid Sa'id had been persuaded to forbid the sale of slaves to 'Christians'. There was no mention in the treaty of the prevention of sale to British subjects who were not Christians – such as British Indians. This omission was due to the preparation of the treaty by the governor of Mauritius. The trade in slaves to India, and particularly into the British states, was a problem which caused much concern among Indian administrators. It became obvious that it would be stopped only if the entire Slave Trade of the Indian Ocean were suppressed; otherwise the slaves would still slip in. It was Saiyid Sa'id again who would have to be approached about this – not only because he had co-operated in 1821, but also because the slaves were obtained from his East African territories, and were mainly carried in his subjects' vessels.

There was, however, no coherent policy of pressure on Saiyid Sa'id.

---

[1] 'Mémoire sur l'abolition de l'esclavage dans les colonies françaises et principalement à Bourbon', by C. V. Barbaroux, 13 Apr. 1839', M.O., Généralités 174/1402.

[2] See Chapter VIII, p. 199.

[3] Massieu to Fréycinet, 9 Oct. 1822, M.O., Réunion 72/473. It is interesting that it was the English who were 'hated', not Sa'id. His attempt to appear to have been forced into acceding to the treaty was working.

[4] Farquhar to R. W. Horton, M.P., 22 Jan. 1823, quoting Nourse to Farquhar, 8 Dec. 1822, *State Papers*, vol. XI (1824), p. 630.

[5] Moresby to Bombay, 25 Sept. 1822, Proc. 2 Oct., B.P.C. 385/26.

ATTEMPTS TO SUPPRESS THE SLAVE TRADE

Indeed, the British were not prepared to press their demands too hard and thereby risk losing the co-operation of the ruler of Muscat and Zanzibar. The Owen incident of 1824-6 well illustrates this constant reference to mutual advantage. Captain Owen, whose orders were solely concerned with execution of a nautical reconnaissance of the East African coast, decided at the same time to carry out a private campaign against the Slave Trade in that region. This included illegally accepting the sovereignty of Mombasa for the British and establishing a colony of freed slaves there.[1] However, when the news of Owen's activities reached London and Bombay, accompanied by fierce protests from Saiyid Sa'id against the British action, the British were not prepared to jeopardize their relationship with the ruler of Muscat.

Bombay was reluctant to abandon its ally:

'The present Imaum of Muscat has, ever since his accession, been very closely connected with the British Government in India. He has co-operated in all measures which have been adopted for the suppression of Piracy, on the coasts of Arabia, and Persia, and has more than once foregone, at our request, very favourable opportunities of aggrandizing himself, which would have been inconsistent with our policy, as disturbing the peace of the Persian Gulph. He has also on many occasions/especially on that of his agreement with Captain Moresby/ evinced his readiness to co-operate, although with considerable loss of revenue to himself, in the extinction of the trade in slaves carried on with the European colonies.

'The compliances on the Imaum's part have been repaid by assurances of friendship on ours, although accompanied with frequent explanations, that it was impossible for us to afford him any assistance, in his wars with different powers in his neighbourhood, from a fixed practice of our Government, to forbear all interference in the disputes of the Princes of those countries.'[2]

Elphinstone, the governor of Bombay, added that Saiyid Sa'id had great reason to complain because the British not only refused to help him against his enemies, but actually helped his enemies against him.[3] The British thought their alliance with Sa'id – which they felt to be important not least because he was their chosen collaborator on the

[1] See Chapter VI, pp. 139-42; and Emery's Journal, *passim*, Adm. 52/3940.
[2] Bombay to Commodore Christian, 8 Sept. 1826, Proc. 13 Sept., B.P.C. 386/11.
[3] Minute by Elphinstone, 14 Jan. 1826, Proc. 15 Feb., B.P.C. 386/4.

Slave Trade issue – would be severely shaken, if not destroyed, should they keep Mombasa. London gave the order to withdraw the British Establishment.¹

Since they had rejected Owen's method of campaign against the Slave Trade, Bombay was obliged to press Saiyid Saʻid for further concessions, particularly after it was given evidence that the Moresby Treaty was being flouted.² Elphinstone considered the likelihood of Saʻid's abolishing the Slave Trade entirely if he were given adequate compensation.³ The question of compensation had first been raised four years earlier when Farquhar hinted to Saʻid that he might be given 40,000 dollars if he abolish the Slave Trade entirely. Saʻid had said that if it were 140,000 he might have considered it.⁴ Then in 1825 the Resident in the Persian Gulf had suggested the entire abolition for some compensation.⁵ Now Elphinstone raised the question again, but left it to Saʻid to suggest adequate terms.

The terms Saiyid Saʻid put forward were severe. His anger had been aroused by a threat from Owen to his governor at Zanzibar that unless Saiyid Saʻid abolished the Slave Trade at all his ports on the East African coast he should be deprived of all his possessions there. Owen added, however, that if Saiyid Saʻid consented, the possessions of the Portuguese should be taken from them and given to him.⁶ Saʻid took Bombay up on Owen's unauthorized promise. He said he would suppress the Slave Trade entirely on one of three conditions – that he be given Mozambique, or the British promise to defend him by land and sea against his enemies, or a money provision be given him so that he might reside in Zanzibar and give up his native country. He claimed that it would be impossible to stay in his own country after he had abolished the trade in slaves because all Muslims would be his enemies.⁷ This last provision indicates that Saiyid Saʻid did not intend to comply with the British desire – he could hardly regard the Slave Trade as effectively abolished if he immediately left the country in the hands of the anti-abolitionists. He was in any case, regardless of the Slave Trade,

¹ See Chapter VI, p. 142.
² Owen to Sir Lowry Cole, 4 Aug. 1825, *State Papers*, vol. XIII (1825), p. 328; and Owen to Bombay, 23 Nov. 1823, Proc. 3 Dec., B.P.C. 385/41.
³ Minute by Elphinstone, 14 Jan. 1826, Proc. 15 Feb., B.P.C. 386/4.
⁴ Moresby to Farquhar, 11 Sept. 1822, Proc. 18 Sept., B.P.C. 385/26.
⁵ Bombay to C. of Ds., 24 June 1825, P.L.B. 9.
⁶ Governor of Zanzibar to Saiyid Saʻid, n.d., encl. in Resident, Persian Gulf, to Bombay, 14 May 1825, Proc. 8 June, B.P.C. 385/60.
⁷ Saiyid Saʻid to his agent in Bombay, n.d., Proc. 15 Feb. 1826, B.P.C. 386/4.

considering moving to Zanzibar, but he had no intention of abandoning Oman, for he was at this very time planning to attack Bahrain. Sa'id's reluctance to do anything further about the Slave Trade was also demonstrated by his alternative suggestions. He must have known that only the utmost strength of purpose, which the British had not previously exhibited in their campaign against the Slave Trade, would prompt them to attack the Portuguese in Mozambique and hand the area to him. The chances of acceptance of his Mozambique proposal were so slim as to be almost non-existent; none the less, Sa'id did not yet know that the British had decided to withdraw from Mombasa, and if they were prepared to take that place in order to counter the Slave Trade, they might consider operations in the Mozambique region. It would be wise to have a stake in such activities. It is more likely, however, that Sa'id was deliberately bargaining with impossible suggestions so that the British would withdraw their request, because, in the very same month that Sa'id made these suggestions, he was arranging a commercial treaty with Mozambique, and trying to settle a border dispute with that region.[1]

That Saiyid Sa'id refused to consider the British request of 1826 was due to a number of factors. In 1826 the memory of the British expeditions against the pirates was less immediate, and that nation had also disgraced itself by taking Mombasa; the French had by now arisen as possible alternative champions. Also important was the difference in approach and content of the British demands of 1821 and 1826. On the former occasion Sa'id had actually been presented with a treaty to sign; in 1826 he was merely having his views sounded out. The first demand was also much milder in content than the second. The total abolition of the sale of slaves would have seriously affected Sa'id's East African revenues, and as yet alternative economic activities on the Swahili Coast were unestablished. There were political considerations too: the previous year the influential religious and territorial chiefs of Oman had gathered and censured their ruler,[2] and in East Africa a town near Kilwa had abandoned its connexions with the ruler of Zanzibar and was making independent profits from the sale of slaves to Europeans.[3]

[1] Gray, *History of Zanzibar*, p. 176.
[2] Saiyid Sa'id to his agent in Bombay, n.d., Proc. 15 Feb. 1826, B.P.C. 386/4.
[3] The name of the town is difficult to decipher, but may be Ngao (Mongallo?) – Memo. from Persian Secretary at Bombay, and Saiyid Sa'id to Ahmad ibn Saif, his governor in Zanzibar, 24 Jan. 1827, Proc. 28 Feb., B.P.C. 386/19.

THE SWAHILI COAST

Bombay abandoned its suggestions of 1826, but continued to be concerned about the importation of slaves into the British Indian States and Protected States. Willoughby, a member of the Bombay Council, worked hard to end the trade, particularly that with the Protected States. Saiyid Sa'id figured largely in the discussions Willoughby provoked because it was discovered that the slaves were chiefly supplied from his territories.[1] Willoughby was in favour of another approach being made to Saiyid Sa'id, but Calcutta would not allow this. Calcutta preferred to leave the matter to the Law Commission appointed in 1835, and to await its report.[2]

The attention of Parliament and the British public was also being drawn to the Indian Ocean Slave Trade. The Anti-Slavery Society, founded in 1823, became concerned about the trade, details of which it published in the *Anti-Slavery Reporter*. In 1826 this monthly magazine carried an article on the Slave Trade at Mauritius which accused Farquhar of tolerating the importation of slaves into Mauritius from Madagascar and East Africa. At the same time T. F. Buxton exposed the case in the House of Commons, which set up a Commission of Enquiry.[3] Events such as these made Parliament and the public aware of the East African Slave Trade.

Palmerston's attention was aroused by a new plea from W. F. Owen that the British should assume control of Mombasa to put down the Slave Trade.[4] Opportunists learnt what an effective tool the Slave Trade could be. Robert Cogan, who was trying to establish a commercial house at Zanzibar, used the Slave Trade question as a bait when in 1838 he wanted the British to have a consul at Zanzibar and arrange a commercial treaty with the Sultan.[5] He reminded the India Board that the Sultan had helped Britain a great deal over the Slave Trade question: 'I am further of the opinion much may be done through His Highness' influence by stopping the export of slaves from his dominions in Africa into Arabia, Persia, and the independent native states of India,

---

[1] 'Memo. on slavery in Kutch and Kattywar', by Willoughby, 1 Dec. 1835, Proc. 23 Dec., B.P.C. 388/8.

[2] Bombay to C. of Ds., 29 Mch. 1837, P.L.B. 19, and D. R. Banaji, *Slavery in British India* (Bombay, 1935), Part I, pp. 178, 189.

[3] *Hansard*, 1826, New Series XV, pp. 1015-37, and 'Report of the Commissioners of Enquiry on the Slave Trade at Mauritius', *Parliamentary Papers*, 1829, XXV, 49-93.

[4] Owen to Palmerston, 8 Sept. 1834, F.O. 54/1, and see Chapter VI, p. 158.

[5] Cogan to Carnac, 5 Jan. 1838, encl. in Carnac to India Board, 3 Feb. 1838, F.O. 54/2.

as well as to the Eastern Archipelago.'[1] He gave warning, however, that Saiyid Sa'id would require much encouragement and support from the British Government if he were to agree. The original draft of the 1839 treaty made provision for measures against the Slave Trade, but these propositions were soon refined out of it under the influence of Cogan and the Secret Committee of the Court of Directors.[2] The Committee said that all the Sultan could safely do about the Slave Trade was 'to discountenance with a view to its general suppression the transport of slaves between his dominions and other countries'.[3] Having used the Slave Trade to initiate the preparation of a treaty, Cogan did not want the proposals to be so extreme as to be bound to be rejected by the Sultan. He said the Sultan would not agree to the proposed articles 16 and 17,

'particularly when I keep in view the number of Mahometan chieftains and petty states deeply interested in the continuance of slavery, and some of them powerful as regards the Sultan's government and who from time immemorial have been supplied with slaves from His Highness' African possessions'.[4]

The articles would lead, he continued, to the destruction of the Sultan's authority. He suggested instead the gradual abolition of the Slave Trade by Saiyid Sa'id, but even this should only be effected by verbal agreements.

The mention of the 'destruction of the Sultan's authority' convinced the East India Company, which had so long supported Sa'id's position. The Secret Committee actually directed the Governor-General not to insist on the abolition of the Arab Slave Trade.[5] At this stage diplomatic interests were also more important to the Foreign Office than the abolition of the Indian Ocean Slave Trade. The offending articles were toned down. It seems that Palmerston was not at this time contemplating a campaign against the Arab Slave Trade; indeed, he thought the

[1] Cogan to Hobhouse, 22 Feb. 1838, encl. in India Board to Palmerston, 7 Mch. 1838, F.O. 54/2.
[2] F.O. to India Board, 28 Aug. 1838, and other correspondence in F.O. 54/2.
[3] Secret Committee to India Board, 13 Sept. 1838, encl. in India Board to F.O., 17 Sept. 1838, F.O. 54/2.
[4] Cogan to India Board, 5 Sept. 1838, encl. in India Board to F.O., 17 Sept. 1838, F.O. 54/2.
[5] Secret Committee to Governor-General, 28 Sept. 1838, F.O. 54/2.

only point at issue was the sale of slaves to Europeans.[1] He was unaware of the problems of the Indian Government.

The Indian Government, however, interpreted Cogan's mission to negotiate the treaty with the Sultan differently from the London authorities. Lord Auckland, the Governor-General, wanted to negotiate 'an important arrangement for the entire suppression of the Slave Trade in ... the Sultan of Muscat's dominions'.[2] As for Bombay, the Presidency thought 'the main object of Captain Cogan's mission was a furtherance of the humane efforts of Her Majesty's Government for the preventing of a traffic in slaves'.[3] On Auckland's orders, they gave Cogan a summary of their proceedings for the suppression of the Slave Trade.[4]

Nevertheless Cogan preferred to follow the advice of London and not jeopardize his treaty. He emerged from his discussions with the Sultan about the Slave Trade with a mere renewal of the 1822 Treaty and a removal of the anomaly to which Bombay had objected – that only ships of the British Navy and not those of the Company Marine were allowed to seize slavers.[5] He had, however, raised the question of further concessions. As usual Saʻid tried to bargain, proposing that, in return for Britain giving him Bahrain, he prevent the exportation of slaves from his dominions to any ports or places south-west of Burma, and to the coasts of Persia, Makran, Sind, and Kutch.[6] It was Cogan who had planted in him the idea that he might be compensated with Bahrain.[7]

As far as the Indian Government was concerned, Cogan's mission had been a failure. It therefore went ahead with its own measures to suppress the Indian Ocean Slave Trade. Keir's treaty of 1820 with the shaikhs of the Persian Gulf contained an article which read: 'The carrying off of slaves (men, women, or children) from the coasts of Africa or elsewhere and the transporting of them in vessels is plunder and piracy, and the friendly Arabs should do nothing of this nature.'[8] This article had not been proposed by Bombay; in fact, Keir had failed to wait for their instructions before he arranged the treaty and had

[1] Palmerston to Glenelg, 24 Sept. 1838, F.O. 54/2.
[2] Cogan to Palmerston, Bombay, 19 Jan. 1839, F.O. 54/3.
[3] Bombay to Secret Committee, no. 14, 20 Feb., S.L.B. 2nd series 6.
[4] *Idem.*
[5] The treaty is printed in *Bombay Selections XXIV*, p. 255. Also Cogan to Palmerston, 31 July 1839, F.O. 54/3.
[6] Cogan to Palmerston, 31 July 1839, F.O. 54/3.
[7] *Idem.*
[8] The treaty is printed in *Bombay Selections XXIV*, p. 78.

allowed his translator, Captain T. Perronet Thompson, a more or less free rein. Thompson, a vigorous supporter of the abolition of the Slave Trade (he had donated £100 to the African Institution[1]), inserted the article, saying 'it is very likely this article will pass in the crowd'.[2] The shaikhs may have agreed to it because they misunderstood its meaning, thinking it referred to stealing people rather than buying them in the normal manner. Bombay had decided to accept Keir's treaty as it was in order not to upset their delicate relationship with the shaikhs. The article concerning slaves was a dead letter from the beginning: it was put into operation only once – in 1824.[3] It came under discussion again in 1838 when Hennell, the Resident in the Persian Gulf, induced four Gulf shaikhs to forbid the sale of Somalis, who were technically 'hurr' or 'free' in Islamic law.[4] Shortly afterwards the shaikhs were persuaded to accede to another request: that British vessels should have the right of search and seizure (if found carrying slaves) of vessels belonging to the subjects of these rulers, if the vessels were beyond a line drawn from Cape Delgado passing two degrees east of Socotra, to Pasni, on the Makran coast.[5] Saiyid Sa'id also became party to that agreement in December 1839. The engagement was designed, as was a similar article in the Moresby Treaty, to prevent the sale of slaves to Mauritius and India. By moving the line beyond which slaves could not be carried, it remedied a defect in the Moresby Treaty which had not prevented slaves from being taken to Kutch and Kathiawar, whence they often found their way to British India.[6]

Saiyid Sa'id would not abolish the Slave Trade entirely when this was suggested in 1826 and 1839, but he did agree to do so in 1845. What happened to induce this change of attitude? In the first place, he was now accompanied by a British consul who continuously agitated the question. Although Coupland said of the appointment of the consul, 'on the side of the British Government it was almost wholly to maintain its efforts for the suppression of the Slave Trade',[7] this was not in fact the case. As has already been shown, Palmerston was willing to tone down the articles about the Slave Trade in the 1839 treaty, and

[1] List of donations in the *6th Report of the Directors of the African Institution*, 1812.
[2] Thompson to John Smith, M.P., quoted in Moyse-Bartlett, *op. cit.*, p. 111.
[3] Bombay to C. of Ds., 14 Jan. 1824, P.L.B. 9.
[4] Aitchison, *op. cit.*, XI, 249.
[5] *Ibid.*, pp. 249-50.
[6] Bombay to C. of Ds., 23 May 1840, P.L.B. 23.
[7] Sir R. Coupland, *The British Anti-Slavery Movement* (London, 1933), p. 203.

any concern with the Slave Trade is conspicuously absent in his discussions about the appointment of a consul.[1] But Bombay soon saw what a useful role the consul could play in their attempts to suppress the importation of slaves into India. They asked Hamerton, who was appointed consul, to investigate a report that Saiyid Saʻid's vessels were in the habit of bringing slaves from Africa for sale at Bombay and of taking back Hindu females as slaves to Zanzibar.[2] Hamerton discovered that this was practised, but not on a large scale.[3]

At first Hamerton's view was that Saiyid Saʻid himself could not be relied on to do anything further about the Slave Trade. He would have to be actively supported if any proposal were to succeed:

'No negotiation nor remonstrance of any kind, nor on the part of anyone, will succeed with His Highness for the suppression of the Slave Trade in his dominions unless backed by force; nor need the force be very considerable.'[4]

It so happened that soon afterwards two naval vessels, H.M.S. *Lily* and H.M.S. *Grecian*, paid separate visits to Zanzibar.[5] The latter was ordered to investigate the Slave Trade in Saiyid Saʻid's dominions.[6] Such visits demonstrated to the Sultan not only Great Britain's power but also its concern about the Slave Trade. The presence of a consul and regular visits from naval ships meant that it was more difficult for Saʻid to evade putting into practice the agreements he had made. These evasions may not have been deliberate, for even had Saʻid wanted to enforce the treaties, he did not have the strength to do so. Recently a Spanish slaver at Kilwa had taken all hands from two of his ships and enslaved them.[7]

---

[1] For the reasons for the appointment of a consul, see Chapter VI, pp. 157-61 and Chapter VII, pp. 169-71.

[2] Bombay to Hamerton, 26 Feb. 1841, Z.A.

[3] Hamerton to Bombay, 1 July 1841, encl. in Bombay to Secret Committee, no. 69, 30 Aug. 1841, E.S.L.B. 35.

[4] Hamerton to Bombay, 13 July 1841, encl. in Bombay to Secret Committee, no. 69, 30 Aug. 1841, E.S.L.B. 35.

[5] Hamerton to Bombay, 20 Aug. 1841, encl. in India Board to Aberdeen, 12 Jan. 1842, F.O. 54/4.

[6] It was also to protect British commerce – Capt. Smyth to Hamerton, 3 Dec. 1841, encl. in Bombay to Secret Committee, no. 41, 30 Apr. 1842, E.S.L.B. 44.

[7] Hamerton to Bombay, 13 July 1841, encl. in Bombay to Secret Committee, no. 69, 30 Aug. 1841, E.S.L.B. 35.

ATTEMPTS TO SUPPRESS THE SLAVE TRADE

The *Grecian* brought a letter which was to encourage Hamerton to increase his pressure on the Sultan about the Slave Trade:[1] it was from Lord Leveson-Gower, under-secretary at the Foreign Office. This letter was a landmark in the history of the campaign against the Slave Trade in the Indian Ocean. It expressed a change in the attitude of the Foreign Office. This may have been because they had read two reports, one of which was a memoir from Bombay on British efforts to suppress the trade,[2] and the other a study by Dr Mackenzie of the Slave Trade on the East African coast. Mackenzie's report had been forwarded by Bombay to London in February 1841, and the East India Company passed it on to Palmerston.[3] Whereas, during the preparation of the 1839 treaty, there had been no insistence on the insertion of articles concerning the Slave Trade, now 'it would be desirable that the Imam and the Arabian chiefs should be made to understand that the British Government is determined at all events to put this Slave Trade down, and is conscious that it has the means of doing so'.[4] The Sultan and the Arab chiefs should be asked 'to forbid all slave trading by sea and to permit British ships of war to search, seize and confiscate all native vessels found with slaves on board wherever navigating'. This was extreme, and was doubtless due to the Foreign Office's recognition of how ignorant they had previously been of the true extent of the Indian Ocean Slave Trade. Cogan had told them that 50,000 slaves were annually exported from East Africa,[5] but he had not given any details of the trade. Now Bombay had provided these.

Hamerton laid Leveson-Gower's letter before Saiyid Sa'id, who asked whether it was from the Company or 'the Government of the Crown'.[6] He was always more awed by the latter. Sa'id was most displeased by the contents of the letter.[7] What were the chances of his agreeing to its

[1] Hamerton to Bombay, 27 Dec. 1841, encl. in Bombay to Secret Committee, no. 41, 30 Apr. 1842, E.S.L.B. 44.
[2] Bombay to C. of Ds., no. 15, 20 May 1840, recd. 27 July 1840, F.O. 54/5.
[3] Bombay to Secret Committee, 28 Feb. 1841, no. 16, S.L.B., 1st series 13, enclosing Mackenzie's report. A copy of the report was sent to Palmerston – note by Secret Committee on the back of the letter.
[4] Leveson-Gower (Granville) to Board of Control, 8 June 1841, Proc. 17 Nov., B.P.C. 390/2.
[5] Cogan to Palmerston, 6 May 1839, F.O. 54/4.
[6] Hamerton to Secret Committee, 9 Feb. 1842, encl. in Bombay to Secret Committee, no. 58, 23 May 1842, E.S.L.B. 45.
[7] *Idem.*

demands? Hamerton had continually nagged Saʻid about the Slave Trade:

'I have in various ways and on many occasions, whenever the least opportunity offered for my so doing, always tried to impress upon the Imam and also upon his sons the great interest the people of England felt for the suppression of slavery.'[1]

Hamerton had refused to allow Saʻid to sell slaves under the free-labour system to Mauritius – an action which had almost succeeded in estranging the Sultan from his friendship with the British.[2] The British consul had aroused resentment against both himself and the British nation by also interfering in other matters.[3] 'Certainly', said the Sultan, '... I did not experience the same kindness from the British Government of late years as formerly ... I had done.'[4]

On the other hand, Saʻid had to consider his international situation. This was the period when he was concerned about the intentions of the French.[5] He had written to the governor of Bourbon to protest about French activities.[6] He must have felt that, by doing this, he had antagonized the French. His international situation therefore compelled him to consider Leveson-Gower's letter seriously. Financial matters must also have played a part in Saʻid's calculations. He himself claimed that he would lose 35,000-40,000 dollars,[7] but this was a deliberately high estimate in the hope that he would receive generous compensation. At this stage he farmed out the collection of customs dues at his various ports. If 15,000 slaves a year paid dues of two dollars each (and some only paid one dollar),[8] the total loss to all his customs farmers would be 30,000 dollars. The customs farmer at Zanzibar, who paid a rental of 150,000 dollars, made great profits from his office.[9] What he would lose was not a large proportion of his receipts. Even if Saʻid did reduce

[1] Hamerton to Bombay, no. 4, 3 Jan. 1842, Z.A.
[2] Same to same, no. 30, 4 Oct. 1841, Z.A., and Hamerton to governor of Mauritius, 17 Aug. 1841, F.O. 54/4.
[3] See Chapter VII, p. 178.
[4] Hamerton to Bombay, 27 Dec. 1841, encl. in Bombay to Secret Committee, no. 41, 30 Apr. 1842, E.S.L.B. 44.
[5] See Chapter VII, p. 168.
[6] Saiyid Saʻid to governor of Bourbon, 3 Nov. 1840, F.O. 54/4.
[7] Hamerton to Aberdeen, no. 7, 4 Oct. 1845, encl. in Bombay to Secret Committee, no. 38, 14 Apr. 1846, E.S.L.B. 80.
[8] For the duties on slaves, Guillain's Report, 1849, A.N., Marine BB4/1036.
[9] Hamerton to Bombay, no. 2, 2 Jan. 1842, encl. in Bombay to Secret Committee, no. 43, 30 Apr. 1842, E.S.L.D. 44.

the rentals, he need not have lowered them to the full amount of the customs farmers' loss. At the most Sa'id would probably stand to lose 15,000-20,000 dollars annually. His total revenue was about 400,000 dollars a year,[1] so the receipts from the Slave Trade were not a large proportion. Sa'id must also have been aware that the Zanzibar merchants and the Zanzibar economy could afford a diminution in the sale of slaves.[2] The economy was stronger and more diversified than in 1826, when Sa'id had refused to consider putting an end to the trade in slaves.

The offer of £2,000 as compensation may have influenced Sa'id's decision. He claimed that this was not enough and the sum may have been increased. Loarer said that Sa'id, by abolishing the Slave Trade, had sold the interest of his people for a silver teaset 'et une pousson de 40,000 piastres'.[3] The latter may have been a reference to compensation. In 1846 Romain Desfossés mentioned that an indemnity of 40,000 dollars had been promised to Sa'id.[4] However, there is little evidence that compensation as such was paid. When Sa'id sent his ship *Caroline* to England in 1845, she needed repairs, the cost of which amounted to £3,484. The bill was paid by the British Government, because, said the Foreign Office, Great Britain had promised to pay £2,000 in compensation for Sa'id's measures against the Slave Trade, but nothing had yet been paid.[5]

There were, therefore, a number of factors influencing Sa'id in his decision, the most compelling of which was probably the obvious strength of the British and Sa'id's political reliance upon them. 'I well know', he said, 'the English have the power to stop the carrying of slaves by sea.'[6] His comment on Leveson-Gower's letter was ' . . . it is the same as the orders of Azrael, the Angel of Death: nothing but to

[1] Cogan's Report on the Sultan and Zanzibar, 5 Dec. 1839, F.O. 54/3.
[2] See Chapter VIII, p. 216-17.
[3] Loarer's Report, Part I, 1849, M.O., O.I. 5/23. The reference to a silver teaset concerned one the British had recently sent Sa'id as a present. When it arrived in Zanzibar Hamerton, wanting to impress the Sultan with the splendour of the present, took the labelled box unopened into his presence. With much ceremony the lid was raised, only to reveal a tombstone. Sa'id took the mistake in labelling in good humour. He did eventually get his teaset – Hamerton to F.O., no. 6, 26 Mch. 1845, F.O. 54/7.
[4] Romain Desfossés to Ministry of F.A., no. 7, 5 Feb. 1846, A.E., Zanz. C.C.1.
[5] Admiralty to F.O., 12 Sept. 1845, and note by F.O. in the margin, F.O. 54/8.
[6] Hamerton to Bombay, no. 2, 2 Jan. 1842, encl. in Bombay to Secret Committee, no. 43, 30 Apr. 1842, E.S.L.B. 44.

obey'.¹ But he was not going to submit unless absolutely necessary or unless he could obtain favourable compensation. He determined to send an envoy to London to plead with the Queen and the Foreign Office.² The envoy was directed to say that the £2,000 offered as compensation was not enough, and that the ivory trade would be affected because the slaves brought down ivory, but that the Sultan might consider the matter on two conditions – that Britain give him Bahrain and defend him against France:

'Let the whole injury which may happen to us from the French be upon the English Government. And if this be disagreeable to you, and you abandon us, then we will repair our condition with the French in the best way we can.'³

But the international situation had changed. Palmerston, who had been sympathetic towards Sa'id, was no longer in office. Aberdeen, who had replaced him, had arranged a rapprochement with Guizot and the Anglo-French tension in the Middle East had slackened. Now it was far less important to retain the co-operation of the ruler of Muscat and to block French activities in the Indian Ocean. There was no question of giving Muscat Bahrain. The envoy, Ali ibn Nasir, was sent home to Zanzibar with no concessions to offer his sovereign.⁴

Saiyid Sa'id had not expected this. Although he had, on the suggestion of Bombay and Calcutta, been persuaded to issue a proclamation forbidding the Qawasim, who came down from the north to buy slaves, from visiting his African possessions,⁵ he suspended the order until Ali ibn Nasir should return.⁶ When the envoy came back empty-handed, the Sultan's hopes were not altogether dashed. He wrote again to Aberdeen saying Ali ibn Nasir had not brought him any reply concerning British feeling about French activities on the East African

---

¹ Hamerton to Secret Committee, 9 Feb. 1842, encl. in Bombay to Secret Committee, no. 58, 23 May 1842, E.S.L.B. 45.
² *Idem*, and Hamerton to F.O., 10 Feb. 1842, F.O. 54/4. Ali ibn Nasir was sent, with an interpreter, Muhammad ibn Khamis, on board the Sultan's ship, the *Sultana*.
³ Sa'id's Instructions to Ali ibn Nasir, Feb. 1842, F.O. 54/4.
⁴ Hamerton to Bombay, no. 10, 3 Mch. 1842, encl. in Bombay to Secret Committee, no. 58, 23 May 1842, E.S.L.B. 45.
⁵ Hamerton to Bombay, no. 24, 24 May 1842, encl. in Bombay to Secret Committee, no. 68, 17 June 1842, S.L.B., 1st series 16.
⁶ Sa'id's letter enclosed in Hamerton to F.O., 14 Feb. 1843, F.O. 54/5.

coast.¹ Aberdeen returned a discouraging answer, which indicated that Sa'id should not rely on British support.² Simultaneously Hamerton managed to block the attempts of Kerdudal, sent by the governor of Bourbon, to make a treaty with Sa'id concerning the acquisition of free labourers.³ Possibly Sa'id's view was that his co-operation, albeit reluctant, over this matter justified his making a further appeal to Aberdeen. He asked Cogan, who had been running a sugar plantation at Zanzibar and was now returning to England, to take letters to the Foreign Secretary, and to tell him that the Sultan was willing to exchange a concession over the Slave Trade for the grant of Bahrain and the removal of Hamerton.⁴ There was a proviso in the letters: the transit of slaves on the East African coast between Lamu and Kilwa should not be affected by any agreement, and the Sultan would not be answerable for any breach of an agreement. The former proviso was designed to leave the coastal trade in slaves unaffected; in fact Sa'id had always considered that this coastal trade, which of course included the transport of slaves to the Zanzibar market, should not be touched by any agreement.⁵ The latter stipulation was typical of the attitude Sa'id had held ever since he had begun to make concessions about the Slave Trade. It would lighten the blow to his popularity if he released himself from any obligation to enforce a treaty.

The question of the enforcement of the Moresby Treaty had arisen in 1844. Bombay, using Moresby's original version, thought that Sa'id was under an obligation to assist in the seizure of British subjects engaged in the Slave Trade within his territories. This stipulation occurred neither in Moresby's revised version nor in the Arabic version. Apparently unaware of its absence in Moresby's revised version, Bombay ordered Hamerton to get the Arabic version altered. Sa'id refused to change the Arabic version, but did give the consul a verbal promise that he would assist in the apprehension of British culprits.⁶ By insisting on the proviso in his letter to Aberdeen, Sa'id put himself in a position in which he could answer critics of the measure with the argument that it had been forced upon him by the British and he did not intend to insist on its implementation. Sa'id had already been blaming

[1] F.O. to Hamerton, 11 July 1843, F.O. 54/5.
[2] See Chapter VII, p. 181. [3] See Chapter VII, p. 180.
[4] Saiyid Sa'id to Cogan, 11 Apr. 1844, and Saiyid Sa'id to Aberdeen, 8 Apr. 1844, F.O. 54/6.
[5] Cogan to Palmerston, 7 June 1839, F.O. 54/5.
[6] Bombay to C. of Ds., no. 100, 31 Dec. 1844, P.L.B. 30; and Hamerton to Bombay, 1 Sept. 1845, B.C. 2157, Dr. 786.

the British for the Slave Trade concessions he had made. Much of the disapproval had fallen on Hamerton.[1] Hamerton informed Bombay that the Sultan had told him 'that the people troubled him much about my coming here, and that they constantly asked him if I was come here to emancipate the slaves and stop the trade'.[2]

On receipt of Sa'id's letter, Aberdeen decided to refuse both to remove Hamerton and to give the Sultan Bahrain.[3] Not to have met Sa'id's suggestion about the Slave Trade between Lamu and Kilwa would have been to attack the system of slavery itself in Zanzibar, which would have jeopardized the whole of the proposed treaty. The Foreign Office was unaware of the very strong position the British held in relation to Saiyid Sa'id. At this time he faced great danger from Faisal ibn Turki in Oman.[4] Indeed, it may have been Sa'id's hope that the British would come to his aid which prompted him to send letters to England with Cogan promising concessions about the Slave Trade. His son had been refused help by Bombay, but Sa'id did not easily give up. Sa'id's judgment was accurate: when the Foreign Office and India Board heard of his situation in Oman, they suggested aiding him in return for wringing from him fullest concessions about the Slave Trade.[5] The Foreign Office wished to express 'the interest felt by H.M.'s Government for the Imam of Muscat and the security of his dominions'.[6] Two warships were sent to help the Sultan, which pleased him greatly.[7] It was not only for bargaining purposes that this assistance was given to Sa'id: by now the British had had such detailed and lengthy negotiations with him about the Slave Trade that, were his power destroyed, the agreements which had been exacted with such difficulty might be nullified. As the British demanded more concessions, so they had to ensure that the authority which granted those concessions did not collapse.

Shortly afterwards a Treaty concerning the Slave Trade was signed by Great Britain and Sa'id. It was to come into force on 1 January 1847.

---

[1] Hamerton to Bombay, no. 2, 2 Jan. 1842, encl. in Bombay to Secret Committee, no. 43, 30 Apr. 1842, E.S.L.B. 44.
[2] Hamerton to Bombay, 13 July 1841, F.O. 54/4.
[3] Aberdeen to Saiyid Sa'id, 21 Dec. 1844, F.O. 54/6.
[4] See Chapter VII, pp. 182 and 184.
[5] Draft of instructions to the Government of Bombay, encl. in India Board to F.O., 8 Sept. 1845, F.O. 54/9.
[6] F.O. to India Board, 7 Oct. 1845, F.O. 54/9.
[7] Hamerton to Bombay, no. 9, 3 Mch. 1846, encl. in Bombay to Secret Committee, no. 46, 3 June 1848, E.S.L.B. 98.

ATTEMPTS TO SUPPRESS THE SLAVE TRADE

Saʻid was to prohibit the export of slaves from his African dominions, and the import of slaves from any part of Africa into his possessions in Asia, and was to use his influence with chiefs in Arabia, the Red Sea, and the Persian Gulf to prevent the introduction of slaves from Africa into their countries.[1] This treaty, the culmination of five years of persuasion and bargaining, strengthened the alliance between Saiyid Saʻid and Great Britain. The constant need to see that the treaty was observed meant that Hamerton became more influential at Zanzibar.[2]

The treaty had some effect the first year after it came into operation, but the numbers of slaves exported soon crept up again.[3] Before the treaty was signed, Saʻid had cleverly forbidden the public sale of slaves. This was not designed to have any effect on the slave traffic, but its purpose was to move slave dealing from its traditional place in the slave market to places outside the town, where Europeans could not observe it.[4] A similar arrangement was made at Muscat.[5] The treaty failed to have much effect because Saiyid Saʻid was unable to enforce its conditions, even had he wished to do so. His officers showed great indifference to the treaty:

'It is notorious that the Imam's officers pay but little attention to any orders he ever issues, which they consider at variance with their own interests or inclinations.'[6]

Hamerton said that to hope that

'the Imam will ever suppress the Slave Trade is out of the question. He most positively does not possess the means to do it, and his authority on the coast is merely nominal.'[7]

In Muscat, so far removed from Saʻid's eye, there was no co-operation.[8] He does seem to have made occasional attempts to enforce, or at least make known, the provisions of the treaty. In December 1846 he told

[1] Aitchison, *op. cit.*, XI, 300.
[2] Loarer's Report, Part I, 1849, M.O., O.I. 5/23.
[3] See Chapter VIII, p. 205.
[4] Hamerton to Bombay, 19 Mch. 1844, Z.A.
[5] An order was issued that slaves were only to be sold privately in the brokers' houses – British local agent at Muscat to Bombay, 8 May 1843, B.C. 2014, Dr. 666.
[6] Hamerton to Bombay, no. 6, 7 Mch. 1848, Z.A.
[7] Hamerton to Bombay, no. 10, 5 Sept. 1850, Z.A.
[8] Hennell to Bombay, 7 Aug. 1848, encl. in Bombay to Secret Committee, no. 17, 2 Feb. 1849, E.S.L.B. 98, and Bombay to Secret Committee, no. 84, 31 Oct. 1849, S.L.B., 1st series 26.

every slave-broker in Zanzibar not to sell slaves on any account to northern Arabs, on pain of death.[1] He also wrote to Sultan ibn Saqr, and other Persian Gulf shaikhs, that their subjects would suffer the disapprobation of the British Government if they embarked slaves in East Africa. He was careful to imply that this was a measure not of his doing. He said he had been asked by the Queen to issue the order, and had agreed 'as it is impossible that I in particular, without reference to others, can refuse what is requested, considering that I am overwhelmed with their favour'.[2] In 1850 Hamerton reported that the Sultan did more than ever before to see the treaty was obeyed. He had slave-brokers flogged for selling slaves to northern Arabs and sent guards of Baluchis (though every one of them a slave-dealer) to prevent slaves being embarked.[3] The following year the slave market was closed until the northern Arabs had left.[4]

Despite these measures, the trade continued. The northern Arabs violated the convention, carrying on the trade under the Persian flag, and also stealing slaves.[5] Sa'id had no force with which to control them. Hamerton grew disillusioned, and wrote:

'After the most mature consideration ... knowing the feeling of the people as well as I do, I believe that the interposition of the Almighty alone will ever make the Mohameddans or the Portuguese relinquish the traffic.'[6]

Hamerton said the Sultan could do nothing when everyone, including his own children, was against him; he was right to put the burden of enforcement of the treaty wholly upon the British Government.[7] Hamerton suggested fast sailing vessels should be employed at the entrance of the Red Sea, along the eastern coast of Arabia, and all along the entrance to the Persian Gulf.[8]

[1] Hamerton to Bombay, no. 15, 29 Apr. 1847, Z.A. Nor were northern Arabs that year permitted to hire houses in town for their stay in Zanzibar – Hamerton to Bombay, no. 6, 3 Apr. 1847, Z.A.

[2] Saiyid Sa'id to Sultan ibn Saqr, 11 Apr. 1846, Z.A. Also Hennell to Bombay, 17 Aug. 1846, encl. in Bombay to Secret Committee, no. 122, 15 Oct. 1846, E.S.L.B. 83.

[3] Hamerton to Bombay, no. 5, 15 Feb. 1850, Z.A.

[4] Hamerton to Bombay, no. 3, 9 Apr. 1851, Z.A.

[5] Hamerton to Bombay, no. 6, 7 Mch. 1848, and no. 15, 10 May 1848, Z.A. Also Hamerton to F.O., no. 16, 23 Dec. 1846, Z.A.

[6] Hamerton to Bombay, no. 13, 25 Oct. 1849, encl. in Bombay to Secret Committee, no. 35, 25 June 1850, E.S.L.B. 102.

[7] Hamerton to Bombay, no. 5, 15 Feb. 1850, Z.A.   [8] As note 6.

However, British attempts to enforce the treaty were almost as ineffectual as the Sultan's. After a seizure had been made in 1847 it was discovered that the treaty was defective in not providing for a tribunal for adjudicating in seizures, as in the Slave Trade treaties with European powers. There was no legislative enactment to give British courts municipal court jurisdiction.[1] The captives therefore had to be freed, and Bombay tried to cover up the difficulty by issuing a statement that, as this was the first seizure, the captives had been magnanimously set free.[2] A supplement to the treaty and an Act of Parliament had to be arranged to remedy the defect.[3] As well as this, the force appointed to suppress the trade during the season of traffic was completely inadequate to perform its duties effectively.[4] Bombay tried to shift the responsibility of policing the East African shores on to the Cape of Good Hope.[5] Arrangements also had to be made with the Porte,[6] the chiefs of the Persian Gulf, and Persia, to co-operate; otherwise slaves were imported through their lands, or slave ships flew their flags.[7] Bombay succeeded in persuading the Persian Gulf shaikhs to prohibit, after 10 December 1847, the import of slaves from the African coast or elsewhere, and to give the authority of search to Company cruisers.[8] Persia also made concessions: the importation of slaves by sea on board Persian vessels was made illegal.[9]

By 1856 there had been no diminution in the number of slaves exported from East Africa.[10] The 1845 treaty must therefore have been less of a blow to Sa'id's political system than it might have been had it been rigidly enforced. Sa'id blamed the British and survived. He doubtless made it clear to his people, as he did to Hamerton, that it was the

[1] Report by Advocate General, 20 Oct. 1847, B.C. 2235, Dr. 294.
[2] Bombay to Secret Committee, no. 107, 31 Dec. 1847, S.L.B., 1st series 23; and Minute by governor, 5 Nov. 1847, B.C. 2235, Dr. 294.
[3] Act of Parliament of 5 Sept. 1848; Chap. 128 of 11 and 12 Vict., 1 Aug. 1849, and Chap. 84 of 12 and 13 Vict.
[4] Hennell to Bombay, no. 58, 23 Sept. 1847, B.C. 2235, Dr. 294.
[5] Commodore Sir R. Oliver to governor of Bombay, 28 Oct. 1847, B.C. 2235, Dr. 294.
[6] Bombay to Secret Committee, no. 84, 31 Oct. 1849, S.L.B., 1st series 26.
[7] Minute by Willoughby, 30 June 1847, encl. in Bombay to Secret Committee, no. 65, 19 July 1847, E.S.L.B. 88.
[8] Bombay to Hennell, 11 July 1847, encl. in Bombay to Secret Committee, no. 65, 19 July 1847, E.S.L.B. 88.
[9] Minute by the governor, 12 Sept. 1848, encl. in Bombay to Secret Committee, no. 17, 2 Feb. 1849, E.S.L.B. 98.
[10] See above, Chapter VIII, p. 205.

last concession which could possibly be forced from him. 'His Highness', said Hamerton, 'evinces the greatest possible reluctance to converse or to hear anything relative to the last slave treaty; he always appears hurt and distressed'.[1] The northern Arabs, some of whom had suffered so severely from British bombardment in 1809 and 1819, could well understand the necessity of bowing to British demands.

The 1845 treaty did not touch one problem at Zanzibar which had been discussed for some time – that of the possession of slaves by British subjects at Zanzibar. Norsworthy, a British merchant at Zanzibar, had asked in 1841 whether the Indian banians were British subjects, pointing out that, if they were, this could be an important factor in the suppression of the Slave Trade, since they were the most active participants in it.[2] Jairam, the customs master, had 200 slaves.[3] Worried, he approached the Sultan, encouraging him to get all the banians in Zanzibar to sign a paper saying that they were subjects of Zanzibar, and not of Great Britain.[4] All but three, however, refused to sign, putting their wives and children resident in British India before their interests in Zanzibar. Bombay discussed the matter in 1843, asking the Advocate General for his opinion about what could be done.[5] He said British subjects could only be made answerable to British law if the countries in which they resided had arrangements with Great Britain to that effect.[6]

Meanwhile, Hamerton was taking more practical steps to put a stop to the possession of slaves by British subjects. He persuaded the Sultan to issue a proclamation on 7 December 1843, saying he would punish with great severity any of his subjects 'who would henceforth sell to, or buy, slaves from a British subject'.[7] This caused great excitement in Zanzibar, and delight to the Arabs who thought the banians would be driven from the trade, leaving the field free for them.[8] Hamerton could

[1] Hamerton to Bombay, no. 8, 10 Mch. 1848, Z.A.
[2] Norsworthy to Chamber of Commerce, Bombay, n.d. (c. Sept. 1841), F.O. 54/4.
[3] Journal of Lt Christopher, 1843, encl. in Bombay to Secret Committee, no. 54, 18 July 1843, E.S.L.B. 60.
[4] Hamerton to Bombay, 28 Sept. 1841, F.O. 54/4; and Hamerton to Secret Committee, 9 Feb. 1842, encl. in Bombay to Secret Committee, no. 58, 23 May 1842, E.S.L.B. 46.
[5] Minute by governor, n.d. (c. 25 Feb. 1843), B.C. 2014, Dr. 666.
[6] Advocate General to Calcutta, 16 May 1843, B.C. 2238, Dr. 253.
[7] Hamerton to Bombay, no. 33, 9 Dec. 1843, B.C. 2034, Dr. 253.
[8] Idem.

ATTEMPTS TO SUPPRESS THE SLAVE TRADE

do little about enforcing the proclamation, and he did not try very hard. The French suggested this was because he might lose his subjects if he pressed the point.[1] He could then have been withdrawn from his position. The American consul, Ward, condemned Hamerton's equivocal attitude as a result of which the banians claimed to be either Arab or English subjects as suited their purpose. Ward reported that, when he broached the question with Hamerton, the British consul said the matter was best left alone 'for these people would not understand anything about it'.[2] Furthermore, said Ward, the Sultan claimed that banians who possessed slaves were his subjects, and those who did not were British subjects.[3]

It was easier to prevent banians dealing in slaves than possessing them. When H.M.S. *Castor* visited Zanzibar in 1850, Hamerton ordered its captain to investigate the Slave Trade at Kilwa. The captain discovered that some banians had large barracoons near Kilwa in which they stored slaves. He proceeded to destroy these and imprison some of the owners.[4] This was a severe blow to slave-dealing by Indians.[5] They were also vulnerable as a result of the system whereby the Arabs allowed Indians to work their plantations and take the profits in return for a financial loan.[6] The Indians depended on slave labour to work the plantations. When this aspect of the Indians' plight was revealed, the Advocate General in India thought that they should be able to claim compensation in a similar way to the West Indian merchants and plantation owners, but his suggestion was not followed up.[7]

By the time Saiyid Sa'id died in 1856, the British had achieved extensive written agreements for the suppression of the Indian Ocean Slave Trade, but these were of little practical use. To make them effective required a much larger policing force. That was the problem that had to be faced in the 1860s and 1870s. The campaign to get the written agreements, without which policing operations were not possible, had begun with the need to make the 1807 Act of Parliament

---

[1] Loarer's Report, Part I, 1849, M.O., O.I. 5/23.
[2] Ward to Buchanan, no. 16, 7 Mch. 1847, Amer.N.A., Zanz. 2.
[3] Ward to Buchanan, no. 17, 13 Mch. 1847, Amer.N.A., Zanz. 2.
[4] Hamerton to Bombay, no. 8, 20 May 1850, encl. in Bombay to Secret Committee, no. 35, 25 June 1850, E.S.L.B. 102, and see also Chapter VIII, p. 211.
[5] See Chapter VIII, pp. 211-12.
[6] Hamerton to Bombay, no. 33, 9 Dec. 1843, Z.A.
[7] Advocate General to Bombay Council, n.d. (*c.* June 1844), B.C. 2066, Dr. 873.

THE SWAHILI COAST

effective within British possessions in the Indian Ocean. The difficulties of doing this successfully when other powers were openly trading in slaves, and the promptings of various enthusiasts such as Owen, Willoughby, and Thompson, soon extended the campaign into one against the whole Indian Ocean Slave Trade. It was not long before slave trading came to be regarded as morally wrong. The obvious ruler to approach for any concessions was Saiyid Sa'id. Not only did he have a long history of co-operation with the British, but it was also from his territories that the slaves were coming. At one point the British did have in mind the possibility of finding alternative collaborators, but this was not a very serious suggestion. A questionnaire was sent to Hamerton of which Question 11 was:

'Is there in the state in which you reside a party favourable to the abolition of slavery, and what is the extent and influence of such a party? And is such a party on the increase or otherwise?'

However, the first few words of the questionnaire indicate that it was a general one sent round to several consuls. Hamerton replied that there was no such party.[1]

British dealings with Saiyid Sa'id about the Slave Trade were important in their establishment of influence over him. The British and the Sultan became mutually dependent. The Sultan's connexion with the British had originated in the Napoleonic Wars and had been reinforced by the two joint actions against the pirates in 1809 and 1819. Thereafter on several occasions the British came to Sa'id's aid when his position was threatened, and his concessions over the Slave Trade were designed to encourage the British to continue this policy. The fact that British requests for concessions were haphazard, with long intervals between them, made it easier for Sa'id to accede to them. The British campaign was not single-minded or planned. As one loophole or another was discovered, relevant arrangements were made. The British were fortunate in that they did not ask Sa'id to abolish the export of slaves entirely until he had established a fairly prosperous and varied economy at Zanzibar. The varied economy allowed Sa'id to prohibit the export of slaves without ruining himself or his country. The Sultan's concessions about the Slave Trade may even have helped his Arabian possessions to grow apart from his East African ones, although there were several other factors involved in this. When Loarer

---

[1] Hamerton to F.O., 2 Jan. 1844, F.O. 54/6.

said that Saʻid had sold the interest of his people for a silver teaset and 40,000 dollars, he missed the most important point: Saʻid had also gained a powerful protector whose solicitude allowed him to reign for fifty-two years and to create a prosperous empire. Under the protection of a larger empire, Saʻid created his smaller one.

CHAPTER X

ZANZIBAR: THE CONSOLIDATION OF OMANI AUTHORITY

In the second and third decades of the nineteenth century, Saiyid Sa'id made persistent attempts to extend his authority over ports on the Swahili Coast. Although he suffered many setbacks he was in the main successful. Zanzibar was chosen by Sa'id as the headquarters from which to exercise his power along the coast. It has already been demonstrated that in the eighteenth and early nineteenth centuries Zanzibar had become the most secure seat of Omani authority on the Swahili Coast and that its economic and commercial development was outstripping that of rival ports. By 1856 Zanzibar had become the administrative and commercial capital of the Omanis on the Swahili Coast. Saiyid Sa'id himself had taken up permanent residence there; it was the largest town on the Swahili Coast; American, French, and British consulates had been established there; most exports and imports for the coast passed through it; and the fertile region of the island had been extensively planted with cloves. What had caused these developments?

Because of the personal nature of political authority on the Swahili Coast, first it is necessary to establish when and why the ruler of Muscat came to live permanently in Zanzibar. If information given to the French consul at Zanzibar in the 1840s is correct, Sa'id first visited the Swahili Coast in 1802.[1] Although he was then only about eleven years old, he may have been attracted by the prospects of the region. Despite his interest and active interference in the area after 1817, Saiyid Sa'id did not go to the Swahili Coast again until 1828.[2] His visit was

[1] Broquant to Ministry of F.A., no. 3, 14 Feb. 1845, A.E., Zanz. C.C.1.
[2] Correspondence between Sa'id and the Bombay Council from 1807 to 1828 shows that Sa'id did not leave the Persian Gulf except for a pilgrimage

ZANZIBAR: THE CONSOLIDATION OF OMANI AUTHORITY

only brief, but Sa'id left Muscat for Zanzibar again in December 1829,[1] and this time he stayed six months.[2] Thereafter he was in Zanzibar from December 1831 to September 1832, December 1833 to some time in 1835, early 1837 until September 1839, December 1840 to April 1851, and December 1852 to April 1854.[3] Sa'id spent the periods in between in Muscat. He died at sea on his way back to Zanzibar on 19 September 1856.[4] It appears, therefore, that in about 1840 the ruler of Muscat decided to reside more or less permanently in Zanzibar.

Many factors provoked Sa'id's decision. It has already been shown how his interest in the Swahili Coast was originally aroused by the commercial opportunities of East Africa, by the interference of the Europeans, and by the possibility that his authority in Oman might be challenged directly or indirectly from East Africa. Two particular points caused him grave disquiet in the 1820s: the Moresby Treaty of 1822 concerning the Slave Trade, and the British Establishment at Mombasa from 1824 to 1826. Both incidents encouraged him to strengthen his hold on the Swahili Coast. In 1827 he was corresponding with his governor in Zanzibar about the wisdom of despatching a force to quell rebellious elements near Kilwa and at the same time he was trying to negotiate a settlement with Mombasa.[5] These difficulties on the Swahili Coast probably prompted him to pay a personal visit to the region in 1828. That he was contemplating more than a brief and isolated visit is evident from the orders he sent ahead that a palace be built for him at Mtoni, on Zanzibar.[6] His stay seems to have encouraged Sa'id to emphasize his authority further on the Swahili Coast and to

to Mecca in 1825 – B.P.C., *passim*. For the 1828 visit to Zanzibar, Edmund Roberts to Saiyid Sa'id, 27 Jan. 1828, Z.A., and Guillain, *Documents*, I, 589.

[1] British broker at Muscat to Bombay, 8 Jan. 1830, Proc. 10 Feb., B.P.C. 386/61.   [2] Bombay to C. of Ds., no. 37, 16 Nov. 1831, P.L.B. 14.

[3] Saiyid Sa'id to Bombay, 25 Dec. 1831, Proc. 25 Jan. 1832, B.P.C. 387/20; Bombay to C. of Ds., no. 31, 14 Aug. 1833, P.L.B. 16; Hart's Report, Proc. 21 May 1834, B.P.C. 387/58; Bombay to C. of Ds., no. 31, 30 June 1837, P.L.B. 20; Journal of R. P. Waters, entry for 20 Mch. 1837, printed in Bennett and Brooks, *op. cit.*, p. 195; Saiyid Sa'id to Bombay, 7 Oct. 1839, encl. in Bombay to Secret Committee, no. 127, 28 Nov. 1839, E.S.L.B. 30; Bombay to Secret Committee, no. 108, 30 Dec. 1840, S.L.B., 1st series 12; Hamerton to Bombay, no. 6, 14 May 1851, no. 31, 4 Sept. 1852, and no. 16, 18 Apr. 1854, Z.A.

[4] Cochet to Ministry of F.A., no. 1, 26 Oct. 1856, A.E., Zanz. C.P.1.

[5] Saiyid Sa'id to Ahmad ibn Saif, his governor in Zanzibar, 24 Jan. 1827, Proc. 28 Feb. 1827, B.P.C. 386/19; and Saiyid Sa'id to the Mazrui shaikhs of Mombasa, Jan. 1827, Proc. 14 Feb., B.P.C. 386/18. See also Chapter XI, p. 305.

[6] For the orders, Guillain, *Documents*, I, 589.

develop the economic and commercial potential of the region. It was a happy coincidence that an American merchant called at Zanzibar at the same time, and discussed the possibility of making commercial arrangements.[1] Saʿid also observed how well cloves planted some years earlier were growing on Zanzibar, and he confiscated some plantations for his own use.[2] Saʿid had considered Zanzibar one of his most important possessions as early as 1822;[3] now he concentrated on developing it. In December 1829 he took most of his property and household furniture to Zanzibar.[4] Troubles in Oman drew him back to the Persian Gulf several times in the 1830s, but he estimated, correctly, that the British would buttress his position in Oman were it seriously undermined. He therefore devoted most of his energies to the Swahili Coast. Not only was the region undergoing rapid commercial development in the 1830s, but also various of its ports remained reluctant to accept the ruler of Zanzibar's authority and had to be perpetually watched and coerced. With his presence required in both the Persian Gulf and East Africa, the 1830s were a decade of tension and anxiety for Saiyid Saʿid.

The events of the early 1840s confirmed Saʿid in his inclination to spend most of his time on the Swahili Coast. By then the region was responding well to economic development, and the revenues it furnished had overtaken those provided by Saʿid's possessions in the Persian Gulf. His private commercial ventures also had more scope in East Africa. Saʿid was a merchant-prince. His authority partly stemmed from the fact that he could command resources necessary to maintain a fleet, to hire mercenaries, and to offer chieftains financial incentives to support him and provide him with troops. Many of these resources had to come from his own commercial and agricultural activities. As early as 1833 Saʿid himself explained his presence in Zanzibar thus: '... my revenues ... in Oman are very small and my expenses very great'.[5] The following year Captain Hart was told that the East African revenues exceeded those from Oman.[6] Hart also concluded that Saʿid's ability to maintain a fleet and establishment was due not only to his formal revenues but also to his own trading ventures. During the 1840s Saʿid's

[1] See Chapter XII, p. 326.
[2] Guillain, *Documents*, II, 49, and see below, p. 268.
[3] Duplessis-Parseau to Freycinet, n.d. (but end 1821), A.N., Marine BB4/435.
[4] British broker at Muscat to Persian Gulf Resident, 21 Dec. 1829, Proc. 3 Mch. 1830, B.P.C. 386/61.
[5] Saiyid Saʿid to his agent in Bombay, n.d., received 5 Mch. 1833, Proc. 20 Mch, B.P.C. 387/43.
[6] Hart's Report, Proc. 21 May 1834, B.P.C. 387/58.

ZANZIBAR: THE CONSOLIDATION OF OMANI AUTHORITY

revenues from the Swahili Coast continued to surpass those from Oman.[1] Zanzibar was therefore the more preferable place to reside, even without taking into account its climatic and topographical superiority to Muscat. According to Hart, in 1834 it was supposed at Zanzibar that Sa'id would at some later date make that island his permanent residence in preference to Muscat, and in 1842 Hamerton said that it was the Sultan's intention always to live at Zanzibar because it had become the most important part of his territories in every way.[2]

The French explanation for this change was that Saiyid Sa'id left Muscat to escape British domination.[3] Had this really been a factor in Sa'id's decision, his hopes were illusory, since his removal to Zanzibar in 1840 was rapidly followed by the appointment of a British consul. In 1833 Sa'id himself had given a curious reason for his presence in Zanzibar: '... it is now five years since all the chief men have died out of Oman and none but the low and mean remain, and I am ashamed to live near such despicable people'.[4] This may well indicate a dissatisfaction with his political situation in Oman and a consequent desire to establish a firm position elsewhere. Moreover, at the beginning of the 1840s he felt his position on the Swahili Coast was threatened by the French. Indeed, it was to investigate French activities that he went to East Africa in 1840, a visit which began his uninterrupted residence there for eleven years. In the mid 1840s he may well have felt that the troubled state of affairs in the Lamu archipelago required his constant presence on the Swahili Coast. None the less Sa'id never envisaged abandoning his position in Oman: his visits to that country in the early 1850s in order to settle uprisings, demonstrate this point. He did, however, understand the difficulties faced by the ruler who attempted to manage both Oman and the Swahili Coast. Although the distance between Oman and East Africa was lessened by the monsoon winds, personal government still depended largely upon personal presence. By 1844 Sa'id had decided that, when he died, the two parts of his dominions would be divided between two of his sons. He informed the British

[1] See Chapter XII, p. 373.
[2] Hart's Report, Proc. 21 May 1834, B.P.C. 387/58; and Hamerton to Bombay, 29 May 1842, encl. in Bombay to Secret Committee, no. 82, 18 July 1842, E.S.L.B. 48.
[3] Noel to Ministry of F.A., 12 Feb. 1841, A.E., Zanz. C.C.1; Kerdudal to Bazoche, 24 May 1843, M.O., O.I. 15/63; and De Lagiène to Guizot, 9 June 1844, A.E., Zanz. C.P.1.
[4] Saiyid Sa'id to his agent in Bombay, n.d., received 5 Mch. 1833, Proc. 20 Mch., B.P.C. 387/43.

Foreign Office that Khalid would succeed him in Zanzibar and Thuwaini in Oman, although he supplied no details about the financial and administrative separation this would entail.[1] However, when Khalid died in 1854,[2] Sa'id made no further provision for the separation of his dominions. Whether or not he had changed his mind is unclear. His omission to state his views was to lead to a dangerous dispute upon his death in 1856 when his son Majid assumed authority in Zanzibar while Thuwaini, in Muscat, claimed the whole of his father's dominions.

By 1856 the Swahili Coast had developed to such an extent that its economy was able to support an independent administration. This administration, centred at Zanzibar, owed its viability to a number of factors. Although these were mainly of a social and economic character, it would be unwise to overlook the importance of Saiyid Sa'id's personality in confirming Omani power at Zanzibar. Sa'id had the advantage that he was a physically imposing man. Almost all the Westerners who wrote about him were impressed by his presence. For example, Maurizi, Wellsted, Ruschenberger, Hart, Waters, Loarer, Guillain, and Putnam all commented on this attribute.[3] Sa'id was tall, strong, and good-looking, retaining his physical prowess well into his fifties.[4] Most of the descriptions of Sa'id's personality which are available were written by Europeans and Americans and therefore may be distorted because he tended to be cold, though courteous, in his relationships with people from the West.[5] Many of these accounts comment on Sa'id's shrewdness and intelligence. Maurizi remarked on his sound understanding, De Lagiène on his measured and circumspect replies to questions, and Hart on his sharpness of eye, clarity and intelligence.[6] In 1854 Hamerton, despite his reservations about the Sultan, described him as 'a very extraordinary old gentleman, certainly the most clear-sighted

[1] Saiyid Sa'id to Aberdeen, 23 July 1844, F.O. 54/6. See also below, p. 276.
[2] Hamerton to Bombay, no. 29, 15 Nov. 1854, Z.A.
[3] Vincenzo Maurizi, *History of Seyd Said, Sultan of Muscat* (London, 1819), p. 17; J. R. Wellsted, *Travels in Arabia* (London, 1838), 2 vols, I, 6; Ruschenberger, *op. cit.*, I, 109; Hart's Report, Proc. 21 May 1834, B.P.C. 387/58; Journal of R. P. Waters, entry for 20 Mch. 1837, printed in Bennett and Brooks, *op. cit.*, p. 195; Loarer's Report, Part I, 1849, M.O., O.I. 5/23; Guillain, *Documents*, II, 220; and Journal of H. B. Putnam, 1849, printed in Bennett and Brooks, *op. cit.*, p. 428.
[4] Loarer's Report, as above.
[5] Kerdudal to Bazoche, 24 May 1843, M.O., O.I. 15/63; Guillain, *Documents*, II, 220.
[6] Maurizi and Hart as note 3; De Lagiène to Guizot, 9 June 1844, A.E., Zanz. C.P.1.

ZANZIBAR: THE CONSOLIDATION OF OMANI AUTHORITY

Asiatic I have ever met'.[1] The sole dissentient pen is that of Loarer, who found Sa'id very ignorant, obstinate, distrustful, and obtuse.[2]

That Sa'id was astute is obvious from his anxiety to learn and his interest in the societies, politics, geography, culture, and technical progress of other countries – a curiosity which was not always due to his own political stratagems. When Sa'id was in his teens Maurizi commented on his desire to learn from Europeans;[3] later in his life he delighted to receive foreign journals, particularly those in which he was mentioned.[4] Albrand told of the Arabs of Zanzibar forming an exalted opinion of French civilization when they were shown a book printed in Paris containing some letters written by the Imam of Oman.[5] Many Europeans and Americans remarked on Sa'id's interest in the politics and military and naval history of the West. His personal hero was Napoleon, from whom his father had received a letter in 1799.[6] In 1834 he asked an American about the state of the political parties in France, observing that the French would never have another leader like Napoleon.[7] Sa'id sent envoys and ships to America, England, and France – not solely, one suspects, to negotiate and trade, but also to observe.[8] The first envoy to England, Ali ibn Nasir, visited the industrial towns of Manchester and Birmingham.[9] Sa'id was fascinated by technology and made several attempts to introduce machinery to Zanzibar. According to Richard Burton, he gave the *Liverpool* to King William in the hope that he would be presented with a steam-ship in return, but this may have been one of the explorer's flights of fancy because such an intention was never hinted at when the gift was made.[10] Sa'id also tried to set up a steam-driven sugar-mill and institute the

[1] Hamerton to F.O., 26 June 1854, F.O. 54/16.
[2] Loarer's Report, Part I, 1849, M.O., O.I. 5/23.
[3] Maurizi, *op. cit.*, p. 17.
[4] Kerdudal to Bazoche, 24 May 1843, M.O., O.I. 15/63, and De Lagiène to Guizot, 9 June 1844, A.E., Zanz. C.P.1.
[5] Albrand's Report, 1819, M.O., Réunion 72/472. The book must have been Silvestre de Sacy, *Chrestomathie Arabe*, 3 vols (Paris, 1806), in which are printed and translated some letters of Sa'id ibn Ahmad and Khalfan ibn Muhammad to Rousseau at Basra – vol. III, pp. 267-86 and 332.
[6] Noel to Ministry of F.A., 12 Feb. 1841, A.E., Zanz. C.C.1. The letter from Napoleon is printed in Miles, *Persian Gulf*, p. 290.
[7] Ruschenberger, *op. cit.*, I, 110.
[8] See Chapter VII, pp. 175, 178, 181. The envoy to France, Hajji Dervish, was sent in 1849 – Belligny to Ministry of F.A., 7 May 1849, A.E., Zanz. C.C.1.
[9] F.O. to Board of Trade, 8 Sept. 1838, F.O. 54/2.
[10] Burton, *Zanzibar*, I, 269, and see above, Chapter VI, pp. 156, 157 and 159.

production of indigo dye at Zanzibar.[1] But machinery requires engineers and Saʻid's inability to obtain them, or rather to keep them alive in malaria-ridden Zanzibar, meant that his technological ventures were doomed.[2] In Réunion (Bourbon before 1849) Zanzibar was known as the tomb of Europeans.[3] During the hot season of 1846 seven of the fifteen Europeans living at Zanzibar died.[4] Saʻid's fascination with machinery was manifested on a lesser scale by his passion for clocks, musical boxes, and small mechanical objects of all sorts.[5] He also sent a Parsee to France to study watchmaking.[6]

Saiyid Saʻid's eagerness to learn from the West was further demonstrated by his acceptance of Western missionaries, consuls, merchants, explorers and residents.[7] These were never present in large numbers: Zanzibar seldom had more than twenty European residents at any one time.[8] The importance of the missionaries did not lie in their religious teachings, which actually made little impact on the local population. Krapf, the leader of the Mombasa mission, implicitly admitted this failure when he described himself as 'scattering the seed, not disheartened though so little had fallen upon good ground'.[9] After ten years, he only had one convert.[10] The importance of the missionaries in this period lay rather in the information which they transmitted home, information which stimulated further commercial and political interest in East Africa. One manifestation of this interest was the spread of European exploration. These increased Western activities stimulated the Swahilis' and Omanis' curiosity about the West and made them familiar with the world outside the Indian Ocean.

The influence of the Western consuls and merchants was more precise and conspicuous than that of the missionaries and explorers.

[1] Hart's Report, Proc. 21 May 1834, B.P.C. 387/58; Hamerton to Aberdeen, 2 Jan. 1844, F.O. 54/6; Belligny to Ministry of F.A., 7 May 1849, A.E., Zanz. C.C.1; and Commander of Réunion and Madagascar to Ministry of Marine, 10 Sept. 1850, M.O., O.I. 15/65.

[2] As note 1, and Hamerton to Bombay, no. 27, 14 Oct. 1844, Z.A.

[3] Commander of Réunion and Madagascar to Ministry of Marine, as note 1.

[4] Wyvill to Adm., 14 Jan. 1846, encl. in Adm. to F.O., 24 Mch. 1846, F.O. 54/10.

[5] Loarer's Report, Part I, 1849, M.O., O.I. 5/23.

[6] British consul at Marseilles to Hamerton, 10 June 1856, Z.A.

[7] In this book the activities of the explorers and missionaries will not be treated in detail. For the former, see Bridges, *op. cit.*, and for the latter see Roland Oliver, *The Missionary Factor in East Africa* (London, 1952).

[8] e.g. Hamerton to F.O., no. 1, 2 Jan. 1844, F.O. 54/6.

[9] Krapf, *op. cit.*, p. 208.   [10] *Ibid.*, p. 211.

ZANZIBAR: THE CONSOLIDATION OF OMANI AUTHORITY

Under some obligation to make the Slave Trade treaties work, and at the same time to restrain European political ambitions, Saiyid Saʻid was compelled to bring some order into his government. For example, he decreed that his ships should register and carry passes: this order was given on the Bombay Council's instigation, to assist the apprehension of slaving vessels.[1] The notion of having 'subjects' was also introduced to Saʻid's mind when the American consul criticized his laxity in not enforcing his orders on the Indians, who claimed to be under the jurisdiction either of the Sultan or the British according to the circumstance.[2] The treaties arranged with the West introduced political and legal definitions; disputes arising from them forced Saʻid to consider such matters as territorial boundaries, citizenship, and regular penalties for crime. The French insisted that he seek out and punish the murderer of their explorer, Maizan.[3] This he should have done according to his treaty with the French, although it was not yet ratified when the murder took place. Many disputes which made Saʻid aware of Western legal systems and laws arose from the fact that his treaties with the British, French, and Americans omitted to define any procedure to be followed when one of Saʻid's subjects was the complainant against a foreigner, although the British and French treaties did stipulate that, when one of Saʻid's subjects was plaintiff against one of their nationals, the case was to be tried by Saʻid's authorities in the presence of the relevant foreign consul.[4] Saiyid Saʻid was provoked into writing to the United States President when one of his 'headmen' was murdered by an American sailor and the consul did not punish the offender. According to his own law, Saʻid wanted blood money to be paid, but according to American law the consul found there was insufficient evidence to convict the man.[5] When another of his subjects was murdered, this time by a

[1] Bombay to Hamerton, 25 Sept. 1841, and Hamerton to Bombay, no. 23, 28 Aug. 1846, Z.A. In fact it was stipulated in Article VI of the Moresby Treaty of 1822 that Saʻid's vessels should carry passes, but this was not implemented.

[2] See above, Chapter IX, p. 243, and Saiyid Saʻid to Aberdeen, 28 Sept. 1845, F.O. 54/7, asking whether children of natives of India born in his dominions were his subjects or British.

[3] See above, Chapter VII, p. 189, note 3, and below, Chapter XI, p. 317.

[4] Article V of the 1839 Treaty with Great Britain and Article VI of the 1846 Treaty with France – printed in *Bombay Selections XXIV*, pp. 252 and 267. Article IX of the 1833 Treaty with America only attended to the question of disputes between American citizens – *ibid.*, p. 263.

[5] Saiyid Saʻid to President James Polk, 9 Aug. 1846; Ward to Saiyid Saʻid, n.d.; and Ward to Buchanan, no. 11, 14 Sept. 1846, Amer.N.A., Zanz. 2. Also much correspondence in the Zanzibar archives.

British seaman, Saʻid must have been surprised to observe the British consul sending the accused and the witnesses to Mauritius for trial.[1]

Saiyid Saʻid's connexions with the Europeans also compelled him to specify the limits of his territories; by the inclusion of these limits in treaties, the extent of his dominions became defined in international law. Furthermore, the Sultan's correspondence with the British Foreign Office, and his protests to Guizot about French activities in Nossi Bé and the Comoro islands, induced him to examine and define the legitimacy of his claims to those places.[2]

Although incited by his relations with the West to bring more order and definition to his government, at the same time the ruler of Zanzibar struggled to avoid the danger faced by all peoples seeking to profit from Western knowledge: that of becoming politically subordinated to the Great Powers. His attempt to escape this led not only to the political manœuvrings described elsewhere in this book, but also to a more simple desire to remove from his presence any representative of a foreign power whom he felt to be interfering unduly in his government. He repeatedly complained about Hamerton to the Foreign Office, but failed to get the British consul withdrawn.[3] The British domination of Saʻid was due as much as anything to Hamerton's ability to survive the malarial climate of Zanzibar; he lived close to Saʻid longer than any other European.[4] Saʻid's attempts to remove Waters were frustrated when the American consul opened the Sultan's letter to the President and tore it up.[5] It was probably to bait Waters' successor, Ward, into resigning that Saʻid refused to fire a salute on 4 July 1850. Ward fell into the trap and thus the Sultan succeeded at least once in removing a meddling consul.[6]

Saiyid Saʻid's determination to profit from Western knowledge was an aspect of his character which, by bringing benefits to his people, helped him to win their confidence. At the same time he possessed other traits likely to diminish people's respect for him as a leader. More than one description of him records that he was parsimonious and greedy, and Loarer claimed that he always allied economy with

[1] Hamerton to governor of Mauritius, no. 48, 31 Aug. 1842, Z.A.
[2] See Chapter VII, pp. 167-8, 171-3, 183, and 189, and Chapter XI, p. 296.
[3] See Chapter VII, p. 178.
[4] Hamerton survived Saʻid by only a few months, dying in July 1857 – Majid ibn Saʻid to Clarendon, 25 July 1857, F.O. 54/17.
[5] W. B. Smith to Webster, 23 Nov. 1841, Amer.N.A., Zanz. 1.
[6] Charles Ward to Clayton, no. 41, 13 July 1850, Amer.N.A., Zanz. 2.

generosity.¹ It is true that his gifts to Europeans were lavish, but these can be discounted because they were made for political reasons.² He was said to have an angry impatience in his blood;³ on one occasion he struck a soldier when he thought a French captain was out of sight,⁴ and on another he seized a man's beard and cut it off when he was displeased with him.⁵ Unfortunately there is only one intimate description of Sa'id: that of Salma, his daughter by a Circassian secondary wife. Salma ran away from Zanzibar with Ruete, a German trader, and spent the rest of her life in Germany, where she became acquainted with Bismarck. She wrote a book giving an intimate account of Sa'id's family and the harem at Zanzibar.⁶ She remembered her father as benevolent, very kind to all his children, and giving all of them his attention despite their numbers.

Whatever the importance of Saiyid Sa'id's personal qualities as a leader, he needed more formal instruments of authority to assert the position of the Omanis on the Swahili Coast. First among these were a force of armed mercenaries and the Sultan's fleet. Sa'id maintained small garrisons of mercenary soldiers, mainly Baluchis, at most of the ports of the Swahili Coast. Sai'd had copied the system of using Baluchis from his father, who preferred using these mercenaries to relying on Omani tribesmen.⁷ When Sa'id required extra Baluchis, he would send a vessel to recruit at Gwadur and Mukalla.⁸ At Zanzibar the number of Baluchis varied: in 1819 there were 50-60, in 1843 there appeared to be only 30, and in 1848 and 1856 there were 80.⁹ They were,

¹ Loarer's Report, Part I, 1849, M.O., O.I. 5/23; and Cogan's Report on the Sultan and Zanzibar, 5 Dec. 1839, F.O. 54/3.

² There is much correspondence in F.O. 54 about Sa'id's regular gifts, particularly of horses, to Queen Victoria. For his gifts to the American President, Martin van Buren, see *Select Documents of the Senate of the U.S.A.*, 1839-40, vol. VII, no. 488. For his gifts of horses to the French President in 1849, Préfet des Bouches de Rhône to Ministry of Interior, 15 May 1849, A.E., Zanz. C.C.1.

³ De Lagiène to Guizot, 9 June 1844, A.E., Zanz. C.P.1.

⁴ Kerdudal to Bazoche, 24 May 1843, M.O., O.I. 15/63.

⁵ Ward to Abbot, 12 May 1851, Amer.N.A., Zanz. 3.

⁶ Emily Ruete (Salma binti Sa'id), *op. cit.*, *passim*. See also Rudolph Said Ruete (her son), *Said bin Sultan* (London, 1929), and note on Salma by Sir John Gray in *T.N.R.*, no. 37 (July 1954), pp. 49-70.

⁷ Burton, *Zanzibar*, II, 162, and *Lake Regions*, I, 14. See also Maurizi, *op. cit.*, p. 6.

⁸ Burton, *Zanzibar*, I, 266. There were also men from Hindustan, the Hadramaut, and Afghanistan – *ibid.*, II, 162; and Guillain, *Documents*, II, 238.

⁹ Sausse to Milius, 29 May 1819, M.O., Réunion 72/472; Journal of Lt Christopher, 1843, encl. in Bombay to Secret Committee, no. 54, 18 July 1843, E.S.L.B. 60; Guillain, *Documents*, II, 238; and Burton, *Zanzibar*, I, 266.

THE SWAHILI COAST

however, reinforced by a number of armed slaves.[1] Some of the mercenaries, clad in second-hand sepoy uniforms, formed a guard of honour for Saiyid Sa'id.[2] They were all commanded by a Jamadar, who seems to have made a profit from his position as their paymaster, although they were only paid two to three dollars a month.[3] The Baluchis were billeted in Zanzibar fort, which doubled as the jail; it was an unimpressive building which Western observers thought would not stand up to a broadside.[4] The Baluchis were armed with daggers, sticks, and matchlocks, the ammunition for which was kept by the Jamadar.[5] They were sometimes used as soldiers – for example, in the attacks on Pate – but their main duty seems to have been to act as a sort of police force in Zanzibar. If an arrest had to be made, the Baluchis would do it.[6] They were not, however, always entirely effective in their role as police: according to Burton, sometimes when Arabs were ordered to be arrested at Zanzibar they collected their friends, armed their slaves, and fortified their houses.[7]

Sa'id's entire force stationed in Zanzibar and other ports of the Swahili Coast only amounted to 400 regular troops.[8] However, he did not have to rely entirely upon this small force to assert his authority; he could also, when necessary, arrange for casual soldiers to be conscripted. Most of these he obtained from Oman, but on occasion he also raised men locally in Zanzibar, and procured soldiers from the Hadramaut, Comoro islands, and Madagascar. In 1819 Albrand reported that, on the death of the previous governor of Zanzibar, a vessel had been sent to Muscat to get reinforcements to assure the authority of the new governor.[9] About the same period men from Hadramaut were brought in to put down a slave revolt in Zanzibar.[10] In 1843 or 1844 Sa'id obtained 400 soldiers from the queen of Mohelli to assist in his attack

---

[1] Hart's Report, Proc. 21 May 1834, B.P.C. 387/58; and Burton, *Zanzibar*, I, 266.

[2] Burton, *Zanzibar*, I, 265; and Journal of R. P. Waters, entry for 26 Apr. 1837, printed in Bennett and Brooks, *op. cit.*, p. 197.

[3] Burton, *Zanzibar*, I, 266 and II, 164-5; and Guillain, *Documents*, II, 238.

[4] Albrand's Report, 1819, M.O., Réunion 72/472; Massieu to Freycinet, 9 Oct. 1822, M.O., Réunion 72/473; Guillain, *Documents*, II, 134; and Burton, *Zanzibar*, I, 88.

[5] Burton, *ibid.*, II, 163, and I, 107-8. In the latter reference, however, it is said that cartridges and powder were carried.

[6] Hart's Report, Proc. 21 May 1834, B.P.C. 387/58; and Guillain, *Documents*, II, 237.

[7] Burton, *Zanzibar*, I, 262.   [8] Guillain, *Documents*, II, 238.

[9] Albrand's Report, 1819, M.O., Réunion 72/472.

[10] Massieu to Freycinet, 9 Oct. 1822, M.O., Réunion 72/473.

ZANZIBAR: THE CONSOLIDATION OF OMANI AUTHORITY

on Pate.[1] During his war against Mombasa he tried to get 2,000 men from the queen of Madagascar,[2] but it is unlikely that he succeeded. Sa'id's main source of supply for soldiers was Oman. A good description of how he raised troops there was given by Buckingham who visited Muscat in the mid 1820s. When he required troops, Sa'id would address letters to the shaikhs, heads of families, and men of greatest influence and power, calling upon them to prove their allegiance by raising a body of men – he would specify the number required. Each man brought his own weapons but ammunition was provided. The heads of the districts were responsible for maintaining the subsistence of their men. These heads would be paid for this either in money or by being exempted from tithes and duties. Apart from the spoils of war which were divided among all participants, there was a stipulated daily pay for each man according to his rank, and also ample rewards were made to everyone at the close of the war.[3] This was probably an idealized version of the remuneration offered, but Sa'id's ability to raise troops, and the number which would be provided, largely depended on his financial resources.

Numbers given by Europeans, although they should be treated with caution, do give some guide to the strength of Sa'id's land forces. Maurizi, the Italian commander of Sa'id's forces in Oman, said that in 1809 the ruler of Muscat had 2,000 foreign mercenaries and could, if required, increase his army to 15,000 or 20,000 infantry and 1,000 cavalry.[4] When Sa'id was at war in the 1820s, Buckingham reported that he had 20,000 men on foot and 100 regular gunners.[5] In 1839 Cogan claimed that Sa'id would be able to assemble 50,000 men if required.[6] His regular force in Oman, however, numbered only 300 or 400 in 1840.[7] For his East African battles Sa'id obtained far fewer troops than the estimates given above. This was partly due to the difficulty of transporting them from Oman, but he also had some trouble in raising them: in 1844 Hamerton said that far fewer troops

[1] Romain Desfossés to Ministry of F.A., no. 69, 11 Feb. 1846, M.O., Madag. 17/32.
[2] Hart's Report, Proc. 21 May 1834, B.P.C. 387/58.
[3] Buckingham, *op. cit.*, p. 92.
[4] Maurizi, *op. cit.*, p. 30. For Maurizi as commander (probably self-styled) of Sa'id's forces, see the preface to his book.
[5] Buckingham, *op. cit.*, pp. 91–2.
[6] Cogan's Report on the Sultan and Zanzibar, 5 Dec. 1839, F.O. 54/3.
[7] Bombay to Secret Committee, no. 10, 28 Feb. 1840, S.L.B., 1st series 11.

THE SWAHILI COAST

had come from Oman to fight against Pate than Sa'id had expected.[1] When Hart visited Sa'id at Zanzibar in 1834, the Sultan had with him 200 or 300 soldiers from Muscat.[2] It was estimated that about 1,000 men came from Oman for the 1843 attack on Pate,[3] and 1,000–1,500 for that of 1844.[4] To investigate from which groups in Oman these men came is beyond the scope of this book, but a list of tribes from which those who gathered in 1844 to fight Pate came, compiled by the British local agent at Muscat, is interesting: Bani Bu Hasan, Bani Jabir, Bani Ruwaihah, Hajriyin, and Hasham.[5] There also was the shaikh of Dubai with some of his people.[6]

Sa'id's ability to levy even limited numbers of troops in Oman was of decisive importance in the extension of his authority on the Swahili Coast. This was underlined by the difficulties he experienced in raising soldiers from among the people of the Swahili Coast themselves. There is very little evidence to show that he ever made such local levies, and indeed the absence of the same tribal system as existed in Oman would have meant that it was impossible to recruit men in the same way. It is true, however, that the governor of Zanzibar succeeded in gathering men from both that island and the Lamu archipelago to repel the Sakalava from the Mafia region shortly before 1820,[7] but there appears to have been no repetition of such an achievement. In any case that example is not apt because on that occasion the Swahilis were fighting to regain something they themselves had lost, whereas Saiyid Sa'id's wars were fought against sections of the Swahili people, and to inspire other Swahilis to participate in them was difficult. Sa'id also experienced troubles in persuading the Zanzibar Arabs to join his troops: in 1844 they at first refused to accompany the expedition to Pate, and then later only a few of them yielded and joined Sa'id's force.[8] Loarer, however, gives a list of prominent East African Arabs who took part.[9] He also

[1] Hamerton to Bombay, no. 21, 14 Apr. 1845, Z.A.
[2] Hart's Report, Proc. 21 May 1834, B.P.C. 387/58.
[3] Romain Desfossés to Ministry of Marine, 23 Nov. 1844, M.O., Madag. 17/32.
[4] Broquant to Ministry of F.A., no. 3, 14 Feb. 1845, A.E., Zanz. C.C.1 (1,500); British local agent at Muscat to Bombay, 21 Dec. 1844, encl. in Bombay to C. of Ds., no. 24, 27 Feb. 1845, B.C. 2121, Dr. 29 (1,000); Loarer's Report, Part II, 1849, M.O., O.I. 2/10 (1,000–1,200 and 300 Baluchis).
[5] British local agent at Muscat to Bombay, *idem*.
[6] *Idem*, and Hamerton to Bombay, no. 21, 14 Apr. 1845, Z.A.
[7] See Chapter V, p. 130. The Sakalava had joined the Betsimisaraka in their raids.
[8] Hamerton to Bombay, no. 29, 22 Nov. 1844, and no. 21, 14 Apr. 1845, Z.A.
[9] Loarer's Report, Part II, 1849, M.O., O.I. 2/10.

ZANZIBAR: THE CONSOLIDATION OF OMANI AUTHORITY

adds that there were 6,000-7,000 volunteers from the Swahili Coast, but his report cannot be trusted because he got his information four years after the event, whereas Hamerton and Broquant, who also described the incident, were there at the time.

Saiyid Sa'id's armed strength was bolstered by his ability to employ slaves as soldiers. Hamerton, watching the embarkation of troops on vessels of all sorts for the 1843 expedition, said there were almost 16,000 slaves among the men.[1] The following year far fewer appear to have been taken, probably because the decisive defeat of 1843 had demonstrated their inefficacy.

However great an advantage the Omani levies may have given Saiyid Sa'id in his East African expeditions, it should not be thought that they afforded him an overwhelming military superiority. Indeed, the quality of these levies left much to be desired and they were deficient in both organization and armaments. Although in 1844 Sa'id outwardly proclaimed a victory over Pate, privately he confided to Hamerton that he had suffered a heavy defeat and that the Omani troops had behaved in an infamous manner, being concerned only to acquire plunder.[2] It is known that in both 1843 and 1844 Sa'id took artillery to Pate, because it was captured from him on the two occasions.[3] He seems to have had a large number of cannons in his possession: in 1848 Guillain observed fifty at Zanzibar, in addition to the twenty-one forming the battery of the fort.[4] Hamerton, however, claimed that the cannon were deficient,[5] and this is not surprising considering Sa'id's lack of gunners. The Arabs themselves seem to have had little knowledge of artillery. Early in the century it had been the practice of the rulers of Muscat to hire Europeans – particularly Frenchmen – to act as gunners,[6] but later this was no longer done. In the 1843 attack on Pate there was only one gunner, a Turk from the army of Muhammad

[1] Hamerton to Bombay, no. 32, 29 Nov. 1843, Z.A. Loarer, as above, gave a similar number: 15,000.

[2] Hamerton to Bombay, no. 21, 14 Apr. 1845, Z.A.

[3] *Idem.* For other accounts of the rout of the Omani troops, Kerdudal to Bazoche, 3 May 1844, M.O., O.I. 15/59; Broquant to Ministry of F.A., no. 3, 14 Feb. 1845, A.E., Zanz. C.C.1; Hamerton to Bombay, no. 11, 20 Mch. 1844, Z.A.; and Loarer's Report, Part II, 1849, M.O., O.I. 2/10.

[4] Guillain, *Documents,* II, 134.

[5] Hamerton to Bombay, no. 21, as above.

[6] Lt T. Dobinson to Bombay, 11 May 1799 and Saif ibn Muhammad to Mehdi Ali Khan, n.d., Proc. 17 May 1799; Sultan to Bombay, 8 Apr. 1799, Proc. 31 May – all from B.P.S.P. 381/3; and Malcolm to Bombay, 4 Feb. 1800, Proc. 5 Mch., B.P.S.P. 381/10.

THE SWAHILI COAST

Ali of Egypt, and he was killed.[1] In the expedition of the following year there were only three artillerymen, all Turks.[2] As for the equipment of the foot-soldiers, this cannot have been of high quality if it was true, as Buckingham claimed, that every irregular soldier had to provide his own arms. From the descriptions of Loarer and Guillain, it would appear that a large number of Saiyid Sa'id's troops had guns, which they threw down as they retreated in the 1844 battle against Pate.[3] Firearms – mostly British tower muskets – were imported regularly into Zanzibar from America, but these were mainly for the caravan trade.[4] Before the 1844 expedition Sa'id ordered munitions from Bombay[5] which he may have distributed among his troops. In the same year the Sultan told Cogan to buy guns for him in England.[6] As for ammunition, before the 1843 battle each man was given five cartridges.[7] However many firearms Sa'id's soldiers had, the people of Pate also had a large number. In 1833 Sa'id had restricted the sale of muskets, powder, and ball on the Swahili Coast to the government of Zanzibar because he did not want dissident elements to arm themselves.[8] But in 1838, when he felt safer after his defeat of Mombasa, he lifted this restriction.[9] If Loarer is correct, before the second attack on Pate the rebel leader had bought 1,000 muskets and a barrel of powder from an American merchant house at Zanzibar.[10] When Guillain was at Zanzibar in September 1846, an English vessel left for Pate with arms, with the knowledge of the Sultan.[11]

Since the Swahili Coast was above all a maritime region, it was essential for Saiyid Sa'id to possess some form of naval power. The fact that he had a fleet was an important asset in extending his authority over the area. Their ships had always been a buttress of the powers of the rulers of Muscat. Saiyid Sa'id's original successes on the Swahili Coast – at Lamu, Pate, and Pemba – had been attained by his despatch

---

[1] Hamerton to Bombay, no. 11, and Kerdudal to Bazoche, as note 3, p. 259.
[2] Hamerton to Bombay, no. 21, as above. Loarer (as above) claimed there were twelve to fifteen Turkish gunners, of whom three survived.
[3] Loarer, as above, and Guillain, *Documents*, III, 101-2.
[4] Lists of cargoes of American vessels in Amer.N.A. Zanz. 1-3.
[5] Loarer, as above.
[6] Saiyid Sa'id to Cogan, 1 May 1844, F.O. 54/6.
[7] Burton, *Zanzibar*, I, 298.
[8] Article II of the treaty with America – *Bombay Selections XXIV*, p. 262.
[9] Waters to Forsyth, no. 8, 24 May 1838, Amer.N.A., Zanz. 1.
[10] Loarer, as above.
[11] Guillain to Ministry of Marine, 24 Oct. 1847, M.O., O.I. 2/10.

of soldiers from Oman in the ships he had at his disposal. Mombasa, too, had to be attacked from the sea. In 1828 Sa'id threatened that port with the *Liverpool* (74 guns), *Shah Alam* (50 guns), two corvettes, and six or seven baghlas with four to six guns each.[1] His vessels were also used to blockade the Swahili Coast ports: Mombasa was blockaded several times after 1828,[2] and Siu suffered the same treatment in 1845.[3] Sa'id's possession of armed vessels enabled him to bombard ports which were open to the sea. This was of particular danger to Mombasa, with its fort on the island shore, and to the Banadir ports, which faced the open sea. In addition, Sa'id was capable of transporting large numbers of troops to trouble spots. In November 1842 and also the following year the *England*, *Prince of Wales*, and several baghlas took troops to Pate.[4]

It is true that Sa'id's lack of success in battle on many occasions somewhat diminishes the importance of his fleet; none the less, despite the fact that repeated attacks had to be made, Mombasa and Pate eventually submitted to the Sultan. Other Swahili Coast ports were probably deterred from taking an independent line by the knowledge that Sa'id could attack them. Guillain was right when he said that, because the coastal towns did not have a marine force and Saiyid Sa'id did, there was no real independence possible for the former.[5]

An attempt should be made to estimate Sa'id's naval strength. He made his vessels serve a dual purpose – that of war and commerce. In the mid 1830s his fleet consisted of the *Liverpool* (74 guns, built 1826), the *Shah Alam* (50 guns, built 1820), the *Piedmontese* (36 guns, built 1829), the *Mustafa* (26 guns), the *Rahmani* (24 guns, built 1833), the *Sultana* (10 guns, built 1833), the *Taji* (6 guns, built 1829), the *Caroline* (40 guns, built 1814), the *Prince of Wales* (36 guns), the *Hamayun Shah* (36 guns), the *Falak* (18 guns), the *Sulaiman Shah* (18 guns), the *Curlew* (12 guns), the *Psyche* (12 guns), the *Vestal* (6 guns), and the *Elphinstone* (6 guns). There were also ninety small

[1] Guillain, *Documents*, I, 585.
[2] See Chapter XI, pp. 305-8, and also E. Roberts to masters of American vessels in the dominions of the ruler of Muscat, 10 Oct. 1835, printed in Bennett and Brooks, *op. cit.*, pp. 162-3.
[3] Hamerton to Bombay, no. 21, 14 Apr. 1845, Z.A.
[4] Notes by R. P. Waters, 28 Nov. 1842, printed in Bennett and Brooks, *op. cit.*, pp. 254-5; and Hamerton to Bombay, no. 32, 29 Nov. 1842, Z.A.
[5] Guillain to Ministry of Marine, 24 Oct. 1847, M.O., O.I. 2/10.

vessels with anything from four to eighteen guns.[1] The number of guns on the large vessels varied from time to time. By 1848 the *Liverpool* had been given to the British, the *Prince of Wales, Mustafa, Elphinstone,* and *Vestal* had been abandoned or sold because they were old, and the *Sulaiman Shah* and *Hamayun Shah* had been wrecked.[2] These had been replaced by the *Victoria* (40 guns, built 1843), *Faẓa Alam* (24 guns), *Artemise* (18 guns, built 1848), *England* (18 guns, built before 1842), *Antelope* (6 guns), *Gazelle* (10 guns), *Nasiri* (10 guns), *Meuntès* (*Mumtaẓ?*) (24 guns), and *Shatt al-Furat* (without guns).[3] When Sa'id died in 1856 his vessels and their armaments were the *Shah Alam* (50 guns), the *Caroline* (40 guns), the *Piedmontese* (36 guns), the *Victoria* (40 guns), the *Rahmani* (24 guns), the *Artemise* (10 guns), the *Salihi* (300 tons), and the *Taji*. There were also twenty smaller vessels with from two to six guns.[4] Sa'id's naval strength was therefore at its greatest in the 1830s, but he continued to maintain an adequate fleet up to his death.

A list of the number and fire-power of Sa'id's vessels is of little use without an examination of their condition. Most Europeans made disparaging remarks about Sa'id's ships. Observing them stripped down to their lower masts at Zanzibar, they concluded that they were ill-equipped.[5] However, it was the practice to take every removable part from the ships when they were to spend some time in port. In the humid climate of Zanzibar spars and sails soon rotted, and guns rusted. But certainly Sa'id had great difficulty in maintaining his ships in good condition. They were built at Omani ports, in Bombay, or brought from Europe or America;[6] only one, the *Nasiri*, was built at Zanzibar, and

---

[1] List compiled from many letters to the Bombay Presidency in the I.O.L., and also from E. Roberts to Louis McLane, 14 May 1834, printed in Bennett and Brooks, *op. cit.*, pp. 158-9; and Hart's Report, Proc. 21 May 1834, B.P.C. 387/58.

[2] Guillain, *Documents*, II, 242.

[3] Information from Guillain, *Documents*, II, 242; Hamerton to Bombay, no. 32, 29 Nov. 1843, and no. 14, 11 May 1844, Z.A.; Notes of R. P. Waters, 28 Nov. 1842, and Journal of Ephraim A. Emmerton, entry for 18 Oct. 1848 – both printed in Bennett and Brooks, *op. cit.*, pp. 158 and 415.

[4] Burton, *Zanzibar*, I, 267-8.

[5] *Ibid.*, pp. 77-8; Guillain, *Documents*, II, 242; Loarer's Report, Part I, 1849, M.O., O.I. 5/23; and Hamerton to Bombay, 9 June 1840, encl. in Bombay to Secret Committee, no. 37, 22 June 1840, E.S.L.B. 23.

[6] For where built, Guillain, *idem*; Burton, *Zanzibar*, I, 267-8; Hart's Report, Proc. 21 May 1834, B.P.C. 387/58; E. Roberts to L. McLane, as above, and miscellaneous letters in B.P.C.

ZANZIBAR: THE CONSOLIDATION OF OMANI AUTHORITY

its construction was attended with such difficulties and expense, most of the materials and craftsmen having to be brought from India, that the experiment was not repeated.[1] There were no repair facilities at Zanzibar;[2] consequently Sa'id's ships, which he preferred to have with him when he began to live permanently on the Swahili Coast, deteriorated there. He did, however, send them to Bombay for repair.[3] In 1840 Hamerton said that of late years Sa'id had spent hardly any money on keeping up or repairing his ships,[4] but two years later we find him sending the *Rahmani* and *Curlew* to Bombay for repair.[5] In 1849 the French consul's voyage from Aden to Zanzibar was interrupted when the *Taji* had to put in to Muscat for repair because it was in such a leaky state.[6] In 1852 repairs to the *Artemise* at Bombay cost Sa'id 22,000 Co. rupees.[7] Sa'id also replaced his vessels when they were past repair:[8] according to Loarer it was one of his passions to get a new ship built every year.[9] All this must have occasioned him considerable expense – for example, the *Victoria* alone cost 207,000 rupees.[10]

Sa'id experienced difficulties with the equipment and manning of his vessels. He regularly bought guns for them,[11] but often the crews left much to be desired. He appeared to have less trouble obtaining crews earlier in his life, when he resided mostly at Muscat. In 1834 Ruschenberger found his ships in effective discipline, and Roberts said he had an abundance of sailors.[12] By 1843, however, the fleet at Zanzibar seemed to be without officers and men.[13] When he was at Zanzibar it was not Sa'id's practice to keep regular crews on his ships –

[1] Loarer's Report, Part I, 1849, M.O., O.I. 5/23.
[2] Burton, *Zanzibar*, I, 269; and Mansfield to Mancy, 31 Jan. 1856, Amer.N.A., Zanz. 3.
[3] Burton, *ibid.*, 268; and Romain Desfossés to Ministry of F.A., no. 4, 4 Feb. 1845, A.E., Zanz. C.C.1.
[4] Hamerton to Bombay, 9 June 1840, encl. in Bombay to Secret Committee, no. 37, 22 June 1840, E.S.L.B. 23.
[5] Hamerton to Bombay, no. 46, 20 Aug. 1842, Z.A.
[6] Belligny to Ministry of F.A., 1 Sept. 1849, A.E., Zanz. C.C.1.
[7] Hamerton to Bombay, no. 39, 24 Nov. 1852, Z.A.; and Burton, *Zanzibar*, I, 268. A rupee was worth slightly less than half a dollar.
[8] For this policy, Hamerton to Bombay, as note 4.
[9] Loarer's Report, Part I, 1849, M.O., O.I. 5/23.
[10] Hamerton to Bombay, no. 14, 11 May 1844, Z.A.
[11] e.g. Bombay to C. of Ds., 7 Jan. 1819, P.L.B. 6.
[12] Ruschenberger, *op. cit.*, I, 140; and E. Roberts to L. McLane, 14 May 1834, printed in Bennett and Brooks, *op. cit.*, p. 157.
[13] Journal of Lt Christopher, 1843, encl. in Bombay to Secret Committee, no. 54, 18 July 1843, E.S.L.B. 60.

perhaps it was too expensive. He recruited men when necessary.[1] That he often had difficulty obtaining trained sailors detracted from the efficiency of his fleet. There were, however, a few well-trained sailors among his subjects, who had been educated at Bombay and Calcutta and were skilled in practising lunar observations and using chronometers.[2] In particular, there was Hasan ibn Ibrahim, who had studied mathematics, navigation, and English at Bombay and Calcutta.[3] In 1865 the captain of the fleet was Muhammad ibn Khamis, who had studied navigation and modern languages in London.[4] For the long voyages round the Cape of Good Hope to the West, Sa'id employed European and American captains.[5]

Despite the often unsatisfactory condition of his vessels, they were regularly used by Saiyid Sa'id for naval and commercial operations. That they were able to complete the long voyages to France, England, and America indicates that their condition was not as bad as Western critics made out. Although, on these journeys, the captains were European or American, the crews were composed of Arabs, Swahilis, and slaves.[6] Of the 100 sailors who took the *Sultana* to London in 1842, only fourteen survived. The others were inadequately clothed and could not endure the cold.[7] One of them was left in hospital in London, where he stayed two years.[8]

Saiyid Sa'id's fleet assisted him to establish his authority over the Swahili Coast ports, brought him respect from other Arabs, and inflated his political importance in the eyes of Europeans and Americans. While the naval officers might find faults, the rulers of France, the United States of America, and Great Britain would have been most impressed by the appearance of a vessel of an Arab ruler in their ports. Perhaps he was of some moment.

However ambitious Sa'id's maritime activities may have been, the basis of his power after the 1830s centred on the island of Zanzibar itself. Without the security which this commercially prosperous and

---

[1] Guillain, *Documents*, II, 233, 245 and 246; and Burton, *Zanzibar*, I, 78.
[2] As note 12, p. 263.   [3] Ruschenberger, *op. cit.*, I, 28.
[4] Burton, *Zanzibar*, I, 268.
[5] Guillain, *Documents*, II, 245. Examples: Contract between Saiyid Sa'id and J. D. Walker, 1849, Z.A.; and Belligny to Ministry of F.A., no. 8, 31 Jan. 1850, A.E., Zanz. C.C.1, concerning the employment of a French captain.
[6] When the *Caroline* was in London in 1846 it was thought that some of the crew were slaves, and a court case was brought – Newman Hunt to F.O., 31 Jan. 1848, and newspaper report of the case in F.O. 54/10.
[7] Guillain, *Documents*, II, 249.   [8] Krapf, *op. cit.*, p. 415.

ZANZIBAR: THE CONSOLIDATION OF OMANI AUTHORITY

politically stable society gave him, Sa'id would have been unable to exercise authority on the Swahili Coast. An attempt should therefore be made to describe the nature of this society and to analyse the causes of its comparative tranquillity.

As was shown in Chapter I, the population of Zanzibar was made up of a number of different groups. At the apex of the social pyramid there stood the Arabs. To a certain extent one can discern two groups among these: the descendants of those Arabs – mostly from Oman – who had come to East Africa during the eighteenth century; and those who came to Zanzibar after Saiyid Sa'id began to show an interest in the island. In 1804 there were about 300 Arabs in Zanzibar,[1] who formed a wealthy and socially dominant clique of merchants and landowners.[2] In 1819 Albrand estimated there were about 1,000 Arabs in Zanzibar 'capable of carrying arms', distinguishable from the rest of the population by the olive colour of their skin.[3] Three years later Massieu put the number of Arabs at 2,000, and by 1848 Guillain guessed there were 3,000.[4] Accurate figures were difficult to obtain, not only because it was often impossible to distinguish Arabs from Swahilis, but also because observers would not have noticed Arab women, who were very restricted in their social activities. The difficulties are illustrated by the discrepancy between Guillain's figure and those given by Hamerton, himself actually resident in Zanzibar. In 1842 Hamerton said there were not 500 Arabs in Zanzibar, and two years later he said there were 800.[5] By the time Saiyid Sa'id died in 1856 there were probably about 5,000 Arabs on the island.[6] There was also a mobile population, mostly composed of Hadramaut Arabs, numbering from 200 to 400.[7] The number of Arabs in Zanzibar seems small, and it is clear that only limited numbers of Omanis followed Saiyid Sa'id's example and settled there. Even in 1924, when a census was taken, there were still only 16,000 Arabs in Zanzibar.[8]

The number of Arabs is, however, of restricted interest without estimates of the total population of Zanzibar island and that of Zanzibar

[1] See Chapter I, p. 27.   [2] See Chapter III, p. 83.
[3] Albrand's Report, 1819, M.O., Réunion 72/472.
[4] Massieu to Freycinet, 9 Oct. 1822, M.O., Réunion 72/473; and Guillain, *Documents*, II, 78.
[5] Hamerton to Bombay, no. 2, 2 Jan. 1842, encl. in Bombay to Secret Committee, no. 43, 30 Apr. 1842, E.S.L.B. 44; and Hamerton to Aberdeen, 2 Jan. 1844, F.O. 54/6.
[6] Burton, *Zanzibar*, I, 368.
[7] *Ibid.*, p. 378; and Guillain, *Documents*, II, 79.   [8] Ingrams, *op. cit.*, p. 28.

town itself. Figures given by European observers are merely a guide and should be treated with caution. Estimates given for the population of Zanzibar island at various times during the period under review are: 200,000 (1811), 50,000 (1822), 150,000 (1834), 100,000 (1844), 450,000 (1844), 150,000 (1847), and 150,000 (1851).[1] The census of 1924 recorded 186,000 people on the island.[2] Estimates for the population of the town are: 5,000-6,000 (1819); 10,000-12,000 (1834); 20,000-25,000 (1848); 60,000-80,000 (1851).[3]

After Saiyid Sa'id came to Zanzibar there was some ill-feeling between older-established Arabs and newly arrived Arabs. Prominent among the older-established Arabs was the Al Harthi clan. Some people named Al Harthi appear to have come to East Africa from Central Arabia before the Portuguese period,[4] but the Al Harthi were also an important Omani clan and probably came to Zanzibar in considerable numbers during the course of the eighteenth century. In 1804 Dallons said that the Al Harthi often supported the governor of Zanzibar in his violent actions, and in 1819 Albrand described them as a powerful faction on the island.[5] Saiyid Sa'id appointed an Al Harthi, Abdullah ibn Jum'ah, as governor of Zanzibar sometime before 1819, possibly in an attempt to gain the allegiance of this powerful clan. The attempt was a failure and Abdullah was dismissed from his post.[6] Thereafter he indulged in intrigues against Sa'id's government,[7] and probably inspired others of his clan to become disaffected. It may have been an Al Harthi who was causing trouble near Kilwa in the mid 1820s: the documents, which are difficult to decipher, name a man as 'Hautee', or possibly

[1] Smee's Report on Zanzibar, 1811, I.O.L., Marine Records Miscellaneous 586; Massieu to Freycinet, 9 Oct. 1822, M.O., Réunion 72/473; Ruschenberger, *op. cit.*, I, 64 (1834); Krapf, *op. cit.*, p. 124 (100,000 – 1844); Hamerton to Aberdeen, 2 Jan. 1844, F.O. 54/6 (450,000); 'A Visit to Zanzibar', 1847 by H. B. Putnam, printed in Bennett and Brooks, *op. cit.*, p. 400; and Ward to Abbot, 13 Mch. 1851, Amer.N.A., Zanz. 3. [2] Ingrams, *op. cit.*, p. 28.

[3] Sausse to Milius, 29 May 1819, M.O., Réunion 72/472; Ruschenberger, *op. cit.*, I, 64 (1834); Guillain, *Documents*, II, 80 (1848); and Ward to Abbot, 13 Mch. 1851, Amer.N.A., Zanz 3.

[4] See H. C. Baxter, 'Pangani – the trade centre of Ancient History', *T.N.R.*, no. 17 (June 1944), p. 19, for the Al Harthi possibly arriving in Pangani as early as A.D. 909. See Gray, *History of Zanzibar*, p. 22, for Al Harthi activities on the Banadir coast in the tenth century.

[5] Dallons' Report, 1804, printed in Freeman-Grenville, *Select Documents*, p. 199; and Albrand's Report, 1819, M.O., Réunion 72/472.

[6] See Chapter V, p. 131, and Albrand's Report, as above.

[7] *Ibid.*

'Haritee', at the centre of this discord.[1] The Al Harthi clan remained a potential focus for opposition to Saiyid Saʻid. That it was necessary for him to be careful not to antagonize the group is demonstrated by their threat to make trouble in 1854 on the death of Khalid, Saʻid's son left in charge of Zanzibar;[2] and by their support of Barghash in his rebellion against his brother, Sultan Majid, in 1859.[3] In 1856 Burton put the number of Al Harthi in Zanzibar at 300.[4] A few years later the Al Harthi were described as the oldest Arab settlers on Zanzibar, and as wanting to gain the sovereignty of the island.[5] They were 800 strong and their leader, Abdullah ibn Salim, had 1,500 armed slaves. According to one source, Saiyid Saʻid used to take Abdullah ibn Salim with him as a hostage whenever he went to Oman.[6]

It is not clear whether the dissident Al Harthi group was swelled by additional Al Harthi who joined it from Oman during the time of Saiyid Saʻid.[7] The Al Harthi in Oman did not always co-operate as a united group,[8] and the same situation seems to have existed in Zanzibar. For example, a prominent Al Harthi who loyally supported Saʻid in Zanzibar was Ali ibn Nasir, who twice went to England as envoy and who was killed in one of the battles against Siu.[9]

A second group of old-established Arabs, who in fact were at enmity with the Al Harthi when Albrand visited Zanzibar in 1819, were those who deferred to a rich merchant, Salih ibn Haramili al-Abri.[10] Salih,

[1] Saiyid Saʻid to Ahmad ibn Saif, his governor in Zanzibar, 24 Jan. 1827, and Saiyid Saʻid to Stannus, Dec. 1826, Proc. 28 Feb. 1827, B.P.C. 386/19. Saʻid said the man originated from Zanzibar.
[2] Hamerton to Bombay, no. 29, 15 Nov. 1854, Z.A.
[3] E. D. Ropes to Lewis Cass, 20 Oct. 1859, Amer.N.A., Zanz. 4; and Rigby to Grey, 20 Oct. 1859, F.O. 54/17. Rigby said several hundred Al Harthi supported the rebellion.
[4] Burton, *Zanzibar*, I, 373.
[5] *Proceedings of the Commission of Disputes between the Rulers of Muscat and Zanzibar* (Bombay, 1861), p. 97.
[6] *Ibid*. This was probably the same Abdullah ibn Salim listed by Loarer in 1849 as one of Zanzibar's richest merchants: Loarer's Report, Part I, 1849, M.O., O.I. 5/23.
[7] Miles, gathering information in the 1870s, said large numbers of Al Harthi had gone to Zanzibar from Oman – *Persian Gulf*, p. 290.
[8] Information kindly supplied by Dr J. C. Wilkinson.
[9] For his death, Hamerton to Bombay, no. 21, 14 Apr. 1845, Z.A. For his membership of the Al Harthi family, Muhammad ibn Abdullah al-Salimi, *Nuhdat al-Ayan* (Cairo, n.d., c. 1961) – reference supplied by Dr J. C. Wilkinson.
[10] Albrand's Report, 1819, M.O., O.I. 72/472, where the man is merely named Salih. For the full name, Gray, *History of Zanzibar*, p. 129, using local tradition.

himself actually born in Muscat, had enriched himself by trading with the French of Bourbon and Mauritius, where he had observed cloves growing, and had acquired estates upon Zanzibar where he experimented with clove cultivation. About fifty years old in 1819, he spoke French and was liable to call upon that nation for help should his prosperity or power be threatened by the arrival of new Arabs from Oman.[1] When he first went to Zanzibar in 1828, Saiyid Sa'id observed the power and riches of Salih and as a consequence confiscated his plantations, using as a pretext the plea that Salih was continuing to sell slaves to the French.[2] This action appears to have effectively removed a potential source of opposition to the establishment of Sa'id's administration in Zanzibar because nothing more is heard of Salih – Burton implied that he died a beggar.[3]

That the old-established Arabs resented the newer arrivals and remained a possible disruptive force is evident from some details given by the French consul in 1845. Although the French were generally prone to exaggerate the instability of Saiyid Sa'id's position because they had vague ambitions to take over his territories, their descriptions of disaffected sections of the Sultan's people are useful. Broquant said there were two parties in Zanzibar town composed of Arabs who had enriched themselves by various misdealings before Sa'id imposed a regular administration and whose activities had been curbed by the presence of Sa'id and the imposition of regular customs dues. They were awaiting, said Broquant, a propitious moment to return to their former way of life.[4]

It is difficult to establish which groups from Oman came to Zanzibar in the eighteenth and early nineteenth century, and which came during Saiyid Sa'id's time. Burton named the groups of Arabs in Zanzibar in 1856, dividing them into Hinawi and Ghafiri sections. As Hinawi he listed the Al bu Sa'id, Harisi (Harthi), Benu Lamk, Benu Yas, Benu Menasir (Manāsīr), Benu Ali, Benu Baktashi (Battāsh), Benu Uhaybi (Al Wahība or Bani Wahīb?), Benu al Hijri (Al Hajriyīn), Benu Kalban, (Bani Kilbān), Benu el Abri (Al Abriyīn), Benu bu Hasan, Benu Dafri or Dafil (?), Ammari (?), Adwani (Adāwini), Kuruni (Qurūn), Khuzuri (Khazair), Salahameh (Sālahima), and Nayyayareh (Nayāyira).

[1] Albrand, *idem.*
[2] Guillain, *Documents*, II, 50.
[3] Burton, *Zanzibar*, I, 361-2 (if Burton is referring to the same person). Hart, Ruschenberger, and Hamerton never mention Salih.
[4] Broquant to Ministry of F.A., no. 3, 14 Feb. 1845, A.E., Zanz. C.C.1.

ZANZIBAR: THE CONSOLIDATION OF OMANI AUTHORITY

As Ghafiri Burton listed the Masakirah or Maskari (Al Masākira), Jenabah (Janaba), Bimani (?), Benu Katūb (Bani Qitab), Benu bu Ali, and the Benu Riyām.[1] The only numbers given by Burton are 300 for the Al Harthi and '2,000 sabres' for the Al Masakira. Some of these groups were regular traders from Oman and lived only periodically in Zanzibar.[2]

Their economic pursuits did not distinguish old-established from newly arrived Arabs. The French consul said that Arabs who dealt with commercial matters and the coastal trade lived in the old part of Zanzibar to the south of the fort, whereas those who concerned themselves with agriculture, plantation, and building inhabited the new part of Zanzibar town to the north of the fort. By adding that the older-established Arabs lived in the old part, the consul implied that there was a division of function between old and new Arabs.[3] However, the evidence does not bear this out. Arabs were land-owners before Sa'id came to Zanzibar, and it appears to have been a matter of choice whether Omanis invested more in commerce or land when they came to settle.[4] Indeed, many of the wealthier Omanis invested in both: prominent among these were the Sultan himself, his son Khalid, and the governor Sulaiman ibn Hamad.[5]

To understand the nature of Zanzibar society and the strains to which it was subjected it is necessary to study the political position of the Arabs there in some detail. Both old and new Arabs composed the politically dominant class in Zanzibar, and their position was reinforced when Saiyid Sa'id began to live in East Africa. The functionaries and dignitaries of Zanzibar came to be drawn almost exclusively from the Arabs; very few people with an influential role could be classed as Swahili.

The supreme dignitary was Saiyid Sa'id himself. We have already studied the instruments of his authority; now it is necessary to analyse

---

[1] Burton, *Zanzibar*, I, 373-4. Ingrams, *op. cit.*, p. 194, gives a longer list of groups who were at Zanzibar at the beginning of the twentieth century, but some of these may have come after the time of Saiyid Sa'id. I am grateful to Dr J. C. Wilkinson for helping me identify the groups named by Burton.

[2] Burton, *idem*. See also below, p. 293.

[3] Broquant to Ministry of F.A., no. 3, 14 Feb. 1845, A.E., Zanz. C.C.1.

[4] See Chapter I, pp. 29-30.

[5] Guillain, *Documents*, II, 24; Guillain's Report, 1849, A.N., Marine BB4/1036; and Loarer's Report, Part I, 1849, M.O., O.I. 5/23. Loarer gives a list of leading land-owners and merchants which indicates that wealthy men participated in both activities.

the nature of that authority and what sort of obedience it was able to command. The most important characteristic of the Sultan's rule was that it was nebulous and ill-defined. It is true that it was a personal system of government, but in only a very restricted sense can such words as 'authoritarian' and 'autocratic' be used to describe it. In order to survive Saiyid Sa'id was forced to work to maintain the support of the majority of the Arabs, or at least to strike a balance between rival Arab factions. He therefore had to be a master of compromise, procrastination, and conciliation. It has already become evident that he achieved such mastery in his dealings with Europeans. We shall see that he developed the same skill with his own countrymen and his East African subjects. The need to use such a technique was caused by the transference of certain features of Arab political and social organization from Oman to the Swahili Coast. In Oman, leaders depended for their success largely on the manipulation of the clan system. This was one of the features of Omani society which the Arabs had taken to their new home in Zanzibar. In the 1890s all the Arabs in Zanzibar were divided into clans, and this was doubtless also the case beforehand.[1] According to Richard Burton, whenever a new measure was proposed, the chiefs of the clans assembled and addressed the Sultan, treating him more like an equal than a superior.[2] Saiyid Sa'id's consultation of notables was one of the ways in which he was able to maintain his position. Indeed, it appeared to outsiders that he exercised little direct authority. Guillain commented on his equality among the Arabs and his accessibility to all who wished to consult him; Hamerton described Sa'id's government as 'positively of a purely patriarchal nature', without any administrative establishments; and Cogan considered it as a 'too mild if not nerveless system of government'.[3]

Since political decisions were evidently made after consultations with clan notables, it will perhaps be rewarding to examine a number of the more influential citizens about whom information is available. No exhaustive study of this subject can be made because of the lack of documentary evidence. Those individuals described below are characterized by a knowledge of foreign languages, which brought them to the notice of Western visitors. However, importance in a clan may not necessarily have been associated with linguistic ability. In fact, many of Sa'id's translators and envoys were not even of Omani origin, having

---

[1] Baumann, *op. cit.*, p. 24.   [2] Burton, *Zanzibar*, I 261.
[3] Guillain, *Documents*, II, 222; Hamerton to Bombay, no. 10, 24 Mch. 1855, Z.A.; and Cogan's Report on the Sultan and Zanzibar, 5 Dec. 1839, F.O. 54/3.

ZANZIBAR: THE CONSOLIDATION OF OMANI AUTHORITY

risen to prominence as a result of the expansion of relations with Europeans which necessitated the use of men with a good knowledge of languages.

For example, Khamis ibn Uthman, who was prominent in the discussions which preceded the establishment of a French consul, originated from Lamu.[1] Although Khamis' fortunes fluctuated, in the opinion of Guillain, 'si Khamis vient à mourir, cet évenement fera une revolution dans les relations extérieures de Zanzibar'.[2] Khamis'son, Muhammad, was similarly influential. He was educated in England and rose to the command of Saiyid Sa'id's fleet.[3] Another influential non-Omani was Ahmad ibn Nahman, who came from Basra and began his life as a cabin boy.[4] His ability and command of languages led him to be sent as an envoy to America in 1839, to Bourbon in 1843, and to Oman to raise soldiers in 1850.[5] There was, however, one envoy of Omani origin – Ali ibn Nasir Al Harthi, who visited England.[6]

Although these interpreters and envoys played a significant role in Zanzibar's foreign policy, they did not hold official positions on the island. It remains, therefore, to consider the clan loyalties of those men to whom Saiyid Sa'id entrusted official authority. The only official post which existed was that of governor of Zanzibar. When Saiyid Sa'id came to power he retained as governor his father's appointee, Yaqut, a former Abyssinian slave.[7] This type of appointment must have been successful because Yaqut was followed by another Abyssinian slave, Ambar.[8] When Ambar died Sa'id entrusted the post to a local man Abdullah ibn Jum'ah Al Harthi, who proved unsatisfactory and was

[1] Noel to Ministry of F.A., 12 Feb. 1841, A.E., Zanz. C.C.1. See also Chapter VI, p. 157.
[2] Guillain, *Documents*, II, 131.
[3] Ruschenberger, *op. cit.*, I, 45; Loarer's Report, Part I, 1849, M.O., O.I. 5/23; and Burton, *Zanzibar*, II, 286.
[4] Burton, *Zanzibar*, I, 263. His full name was Ahmad ibn Nahman ibn Muhsin ibn Abdullah al-Ka'abi al-Bahrani – extracts from Ahmad ibn Nahman's account book, printed in *T.N.R.*, no. 31 (July 1951), pp. 25-31.
[5] For the journey to America, the account book, as above; for that to Bourbon, Bazoche to Ministry of Marine, no 384, 4 Aug. 1843, M.O., O.I. 15/63; and for that to Oman, Heskiel ibn Yusuf to Bombay, 7 and 27 May 1850, encl. in Bombay to Secret Committee, no 35, 3 Oct. 1850, E.S.L.B. 103.
[6] See Chapter VII, p. 176.
[7] Dallons, 1804, printed in Freeman-Grenville, *Select Documents*, p. 199; and Smee's log, entry for 24 Feb. 1811, I.O.L., Marine Records Miscellaneous 586.
[8] Gray, *History of Zanzibar*, p. 126.

removed by 1819.¹ He was succeeded by Sa'id ibn Muhammad al-Akhbari, in his turn to be followed by Ahmad ibn Saif ibn Muhammad and Nasir ibn Hamad. The last two of these belonged to Saiyid Sa'id's own clan, the Al Bu Sa'idi, Ahmad being the Sultan's maternal uncle and Nasir being far more distantly related. Nasir and Saiyid Sa'id had had a common ancestor five generations previously.²

Sa'id continued the policy he had adopted in 1824 of appointing members of his own clan as governors of Zanzibar when Nasir was succeeded by his brother, Sulaiman ibn Hamad. This appointment was made when the Sultan, having visited Zanzibar in the late 1820s, was obliged to return to Oman and leave his young son as regent in East Africa. Sulaiman was ordered to oversee the actions of the youth.³ Even when Saiyid Sa'id began to reside permanently in Zanzibar, Sulaiman retained his position and continued to be influential. The Sultan held an audience with him daily and paid great attention to his advice. On many occasions judicial and other matters were referred to Sulaiman for decision.⁴ Sulaiman was the greatest land-owner in

[1] See Chapter V, p. 131.

[2] If the 'Saidi' of Albrand (Report, 1819, M.O., Réunion 72/472) and the 'Saydi' of Massieu (to Freycinet, 9 Oct. 1822, M.O., Réunion 72/473) refer to Sa'id ibn Muhammad, he was governor as early as 1819 or 1822. He was definitely governor in Feb. 1824 and late in 1824: for 'Seid Larkbree', Owen, I, 359; for 'Sueed bin Mahomed', Saiyid Sa'id to Bombay, 29 Oct. 1824, Proc. 1 Dec., B.P.C. 385/53; for 'Sueed bin Mohammed il-Akburee', Saiyid Sa'id to King of England, n.d., Proc. 19 Jan. 1825, B.P.C. 385/55; and for 'Saïd-ben-Mohhamed el-Akhabiri' as governor of Zanzibar in 1824, Guillain, *Documents*, I, 580. By 1825 Ahmad ibn Saif had succeeded to the post: for 'Hammer ben Safe', Emery's Journal, entry for 12 Mch. 1825; and for 'Syed Ahmed been Seife', Nasir ibn Sulaiman ibn Qasim to Saiyid Sa'id, 12 May 1825, Proc. 8 June, B.P.C. 385/60. Ahmad was still governor in 1827 – Saiyid Sa'id to Ahmed bin Seif bin Mohamed, *wali* of Zanzibar, 24 Jan. 1827, Proc. 28 Feb., B.P.C. 386/19. For Ahmad as the Sultan's maternal uncle, Burton, *Lake Regions*, I, 125. The Sultan's mother was Ghani binti Saif Al Bu Sa'idi – Ibn Ruzayq, *op. cit.*, p. 229, and Pullicino, *Aulad el Imam*, notes to table I. For Nasir ibn Hamad as governor in 1828, Farsy, *Said bin Sultan* (Zanzibar, n.d.), p. 33, and Gray, *History of Zanzibar*, p. 127. The common ancestor of Nasir and the Sultan was Khalaf: Nasir ibn Hamad ibn Sa'id ibn Muhammad ibn Abdullah ibn *Khalaf*, and Sa'id ibn Sultan ibn Ahmad ibn Sa'id ibn Muhammad ibn *Khalaf* – *Aulad el Imam*, table I, and Guillain, *Documents*, II, 24 (the latter gives Nasir's father as 'Ahmad' rather than 'Hamad').

[3] Hamerton to F.O., no. 9, 24 Oct. 1845, F.O. 54/7, and Burton, *Zanzibar*, I, 261.

[4] Kerdudal to Bazoche, 24 May 1843, M.O., O.I. 15/63, and Loarer's Report, Part I, 1849, M.O., O.I. 5/23.

ZANZIBAR: THE CONSOLIDATION OF OMANI AUTHORITY

Zanzibar after the Sultan and was also an important trader.[1] He was most useful to Saiyid Saʻid because of his popularity among the African chiefs of the mainland.[2] Guillain thought him liberal and tolerant and Hamerton held a similar opinion, describing him as 'not a clever man, but a kind, good sort of man'.[3] Sulaiman survived his ruler by seventeen years.[4]

Although it is true that the last three governors of Zanzibar appointed by Saiyid Saʻid belonged to the Al Bu Saʻidi clan, the Sultan's administration was not dominated by members of his own clan. Rather he relied for guidance upon men with linguistic ability, notables from other clans, and religious leaders. Nevertheless it was of utmost importance to him that he should keep the loyalty of his immediate family. Too often in the past Omani leaders had fallen when their close kinsmen took up arms against them. On the whole Saiyid Saʻid kept his family united, although his quarrels with his eldest son, Hilal, led him into difficulties on more than one occasion. Saʻid had about thirty-six children, eighteen of whom were sons and eighteen daughters.[5] None of these were children of his three primary wives, being rather the offspring of his secondary wives, of whom there were sixty-nine at the time of his death.[6] Nevertheless, under Islamic law they were his legitimate heirs. Three sons – Hilal, born about 1815, Khalid, born about 1819, and Thuwaini, born about 1821 – were older than the other children and therefore more prominent in politics.[7]

It was the eldest son, Hilal, who posed the greatest danger to the Sultan. Hilal had been left in charge of Oman when Saiyid Saʻid first went to East Africa, but by 1837 he had been replaced as regent by his brother Thuwaini.[8] He then became governor of Barqa but was also

[1] Loarer, *idem*, and Part II, 1849, M.O., O.I. 2/10 for Sulaiman's plantations in Pemba; Guillain's Report, 1849, A.N., Marine BB4/1036; and Guillain, *Documents*, II, 24.

[2] Hamerton to Bombay, no. 10, 24 Mch. 1855, Z.A.

[3] Hamerton, *idem*, and Guillain, *Documents*, II, 24.

[4] Gray, *History of Zanzibar*, p. 128.

[5] Emily Ruete, *op. cit.*, p. 10. Pullicino, *Aulad el Imam* lists 26 children, although in the notes to table V it is said that Saʻid left 32 children surviving him, of whom 16 were sons. In 1845 Broquant said the Sultan had 26 children – Broquant to Ministry of F.A., no. 3, 14 Feb. 1845, A.E., Zanz. C.C.1.

[6] Emily Ruete, *op. cit.*, p. 10.

[7] Guillain, *Documents*, II, 224, 228, and 229, and Hamerton to Bombay, no. 10, 24 Mch. 1855, Z.A.

[8] J. B. Kelly, *Britain and the Persian Gulf, 1795–1880* (Oxford, 1968), pp. 226, 243, 324, 354, and 360 (hereafter cited as *Persian Gulf*).

removed from this position and transferred his seat of residence to Zanzibar. Various explanations of the disagreement between Hilal and his father have been put forward. In 1879 the British Resident at Muscat, investigating the matter, said that Hilal's immense popularity in Oman caused Saiyid Sa'id to be apprehensive about leaving him there in any position of authority. According to this source, Saiyid Sa'id actually ordered Hilal to go to Zanzibar in 1841 so that he could keep an eye on him.[1] The relationship between father and son then seems to have deteriorated further. One rumour had it that Hilal had violated his father's harem, but the British consul thought this was unlikely, adding that, even were it true, it would not have caused the estrangement because Sa'id had done the same to his own father's harem.[2] Sa'id himself told the British consul that the offences of his son were such that he could not mention them; they were contrary to the laws of god and man.[3] The Sultan's estrangement from his eldest son was explained in another source as being due to the influence of the mother of Sa'id's second son, Khalid. She had ambitions for Khalid which entailed removing Hilal from his father's favour. Hilal's own mother, an Abyssinian, had died giving birth to him, whereas Khalid's mother, a Malabari named Shurshit, was a woman of great energy and intelligence who wielded considerable political influence.[4] Another contribution to the story came from Hilal's sister, Salma, who said Hilal was a drunkard and under the bad influence of the French consul. He was also supplied with money by his sister Khaduj, whom he frequently visited in the harem.[5] This may indeed have been the origin of the rumours suggesting that Hilal had violated the harem.

Whatever the truth, the estrangement of father and son gave rise to incidents of political and diplomatic importance. Hilal went to England

[1] *Report on the Administration of the Persian Gulf Political Residency and Muscat Political Agency, 1879* (Calcutta, 1880), p. 34.

[2] Loarer's Report, Part I, 1849, M.O., O.I. 5/23; Hamerton to Bombay, no. 12, 10 Sept. 1850, Z.A.; and Guillain, *Documents*, II, 121 and 226.

[3] Hamerton to Bombay, *idem*.

[4] Broquant to Ministry of F.A., no. 3, 14 Feb. 1845 and R. Desfossés to Ministry of F.A., no. 7, 5 Feb. 1846, A.E., Zanz. C.C.1; Emily Ruete, *op. cit.*, p. 41; Guillain, *Documents*, II, 228; Pullicino, *Aulad el Imam*, table VII; and Loarer's Report, as above.

[5] Emily Ruete, *Mémoires d'une Princesse Arabe* (Paris, 1905), p. 138. This translation of the memoirs is fuller than the English version already cited. Except where indicated, the page numbers will refer to the English version.

in an attempt to procure a reversal of his disinheritance.¹ The British Government obtained a favourable impression of him and exhorted Sa'id to heal the rift. This prompted Sa'id to reply, 'you say he is my eldest son, yet amongst the Arabs being the eldest son is of no consequence, but the ornament and dignity of a man is from his conduct'.² The popularity of Hilal in Zanzibar made the breach more serious as it meant that the prince could become a focus for discontented elements. Apparently he was a personable, charming, and generous young man.³ Saiyid Sa'id was conscious of the danger, at first allowing Hilal to reside only where he himself was living, and later unsuccessfully attempting to lure him to Mecca – where he hoped the Sharif would imprison him.⁴ Eventually Sa'id exiled Hilal, an unwise move because Hilal went to Lamu in 1850 and replaced its garrison with his own supporters. However, Hilal's assertion of independence came to nothing.⁵ His death shortly afterwards in June 1851 solved the problem for the Sultan.⁶

Saiyid Sa'id was fortunate in that his second son, Khalid, was prepared to bide his time throughout his father's long reign and never set himself up as a rival. He was of course secure in the knowledge that his father wished him to succeed to the sultanate. Khalid's ability to assume the rule of Zanzibar during his father's absences, and his willingness to relinquish the position when the Sultan returned, was an important factor in Sa'id's retention of control over the island. It was, however, fortunate that Khalid's death in 1854 precluded his succession to the sultanate because, unlike his father and elder brother, he was not popular in Zanzibar.⁷ His love of gain led him to be called 'the banian'.⁸

¹ Hilal to F.O., 20 Nov. 1845, F.O. 54/7, and Hamerton to Bombay, no. 8, 3 Mch. 1846, Z.A.
² Saiyid Sa'id to F.O., 9 Feb. 1846, F.O. 54/10.
³ For Hilal's popularity, Hamerton to F.O., no. 3, 31 July 1844, F.O. 54/6; Loarer's Report, Part I, 1849, M.O., O.I. 5/23; Kerdudal to Bazoche, 24 May 1843, M.O., O.I. 15/63; R. Desfossés to Ministry of F.A., no. 7, 5 Feb. 1846, A.E., Zanz. C.C.1; and Guillain, *Documents*, II, 227.
⁴ Hamerton to F.O., no. 3, as above, and Hamerton to Bombay, no. 21, 5 Nov. 1849, Z.A.
⁵ Heskiel ibn Yusuf to Bombay, 7 May 1850, encl. in Bombay to Secret Committee, no. 51, 3 Oct. 1850, E.S.L.B. 103, and Guillain, *Documents*, III, 450.
⁶ Hamerton to Bombay, no. 9, 23 July 1851, Z.A.
⁷ For his death, Hamerton to F.O., 26 June 1854, F.O. 54/16. For his unpopularity, Emily Ruete, *op. cit.*, p. 96.
⁸ Guillain, *Documents*, II, 228.

THE SWAHILI COAST

He lacked generosity and had a tendency to be cruel and grasping.[1] The governor of Bourbon thought him 'avide, cruel, et d'une intelligence bornée'.[2] Khalid's appearance also made it difficult for him to present a good public image; he was incapacitated by elephantiasis and hydrocele which made him physically unattractive.[3]

Sa'id's third son, Thuwaini, whose mother was a Georgian, also assisted his father to retain his position.[4] After Hilal fell into disfavour it was Thuwaini whom Sa'id always left in charge of Oman when he went to Zanzibar. Thuwaini remained consistently loyal, never taking advantage of his powerful position to set himself up as a rival to his father. Like Khalid, he expected to succeed Sa'id. He was confident that he would succeed in Oman and hopeful that he would also acquire the East African possessions. Quite what Sa'id intended to do about his diverse possessions on his death is unclear. It appears that he envisaged a division between Oman and East Africa; certainly this was the impression he gave the British Foreign Office in 1844 when he informed them that Khalid would succeed him in Zanzibar and Thuwaini in Oman.[5] Khalid's death in 1854 destroyed the plan. The Sultan was in Oman at the time and had to appoint a new regent in Zanzibar. His eldest son actually present in Zanzibar was Majid, who was accordingly appointed regent.[6] If Sa'id gave any instructions about who was to succeed him in Zanzibar after his own death, they are not known to us. Although Majid, nineteen years old in 1854 and the son of an Abyssinian, was amiable and popular in Zanzibar, he was not entirely suitable as a successor to the sultanate because he was subject to fits which sometimes struck him unconscious for several hours at a time.[7] However, it was he who assumed power in Zanzibar when Sa'id died in 1856.

Saiyid Sa'id therefore relied heavily on the loyalty of his own sons

---

[1] Hamerton to F.O., no. 3, 31 July 1844, F.O. 54/6; Broquant to Ministry of F.A., no. 3, 14 Feb. 1845, A.E., Zanz. C.C.1; and Loarer's Report, Part I, 1849, M.O., O.I. 5/23.

[2] R. Desfossés to Ministry of F.A., no. 7, 5 Feb. 1846, A.E., Zanz. C.C.1.

[3] Loarer's Report, Part I, as above; and Guillain, *Documents*, II, 228.

[4] For his mother, Guillain, *Documents*, II, 229.

[5] Saiyid Sa'id to Aberdeen, 23 July 1844, F.O. 54/6, and see above, pp. 280-1.

[6] Kemball to Thompson, 15 Mch. 1855, encl. in Kemball to Bombay, no. 25, 19 Mch. 1855, B.C. 2625; and Emily Ruete, *op. cit.*, p. 105.

[7] For his age, Hamerton to F.O., 26 June 1854, F.O. 54/16. For his mother, Emily Ruete, *op. cit.*, p. 16 (but Speke, *op. cit.*, p. 160, says his mother was Circassian). For his popularity and his fits, Emily Ruete, *op. cit.*, pp. 16 and 47.

for the maintenance of his position in Zanzibar and Oman. Apart from his treatment of Hilal, he had amicable relations with all his sons, placing the older ones in positions of authority. Muhammad (twenty-eight in 1854) was governor of Samayil, and in 1854 Turki was appointed governor of Sohar at the age of twenty-two.[1] The only other son old enough to make a mark was Barghash, who was seventeen years of age in 1854 and was attending his father in Muscat when Khalid died.[2]

The support of members of his own family was important to Sa'id but he did not rely upon it exclusively for the maintenance of his position. It has been shown how, although the last three governors of Zanzibar were Al Bu Sa'idi, most of Sa'id's advisers were either notables from other clans or educated men. It remains to consider yet another group with which the Sultan worked – the religious leaders. Since the law was mostly Koranic, this of course included the men responsible for settling legal matters. Unlike his eighteenth-century predecessors in Oman, Sa'id was not actually head of the religious establishment because he never became Imam. In his letters he described himself merely as 'Sultan of Muscat and countries in Africa'.[3] He had no aspirations to the post of Imam, since he wisely considered that it would be a liability rather than an asset. Neither did he appear perturbed when in 1846 five hundred notables of Oman met and elected an Imam.[4] The fact that Sa'id did not insist upon being recognized as a supreme religious authority made him more acceptable to his people. At the beginning of his period of residence in Zanzibar his name was not even invoked in the Friday prayers when the favours of heaven were invited to fall upon the ruler.[5] However, Saiyid Sa'id did manage to change this after a while by making a gift to the head priest, but even then the name of the *mwenyi mkuu* was cited before his own.[6]

Matters of religion and litigation were controlled by *qadhis* and *ulama*.[7] There were two main *qadhis*, one of the Sunni and one of the Ibadhi school.[8] The *qadhis* settled disputes according to their own

[1] Hamerton to F.O., as above; Hamerton to Bombay, no. 16, 18 Apr. 1854, Z.A.; and Pullicino, *Aulad el Imam*, table VII.
[2] Emily Ruete, *op. cit.*, p. 104.
[3] e.g. Saiyid Sa'id to Hamerton, 13 Mch. 1847, Z.A.
[4] Hamerton to Bombay, no. 26, 9 Sept. 1846, Z.A., and Kelly, *Persian Gulf*, p. 391.
[5] Guillain, *Documents*, II, 105.
[6] *Idem*, and Loarer's Report, Part II, 1849, M.O., O.I. 2/10.
[7] Burton, *Zanzibar*, I, 263.   [8] *Idem*, and Guillain, *Documents*, II, 95.

schools of law and customs and imposed punishments such as whipping, fines, fetters, imprisonment, and confiscation. Mutilation was very rare.[1] Before Saiyid Saʻid settled permanently in Zanzibar, a sort of court was held daily at the fort gates, at which Khalid, the governor Sulaiman ibn Hamad, and three *qadhis* proclaimed judgment.[2] This practice was discontinued when Saʻid came to Zanzibar, but his subjects could always appeal to him against decisions of the *qadhis*. In 1845 Saʻid issued a proclamation which implied a right of appeal:

'With reference to *qadhis*, if one errs in his decision according to his school of law, the matter should be referred to those possessing better knowledge. Each school is to follow its own doctrines – this has been the practice since old times.'[3]

In practice the most serious disputes, particularly those which in European law would be classed as 'criminal' rather than 'civil', were taken straight to the Sultan for decision.[4] He also settled legal matters of the non-Muslim residents who did not come under consular jurisdiction. For example, when a Hindu merchant went bankrupt in 1847, the Sultan appointed receivers and gave an order for the sale of the debtor's three clove plantations, 175 slaves, real estate, and personal property.[5] Only the Sultan could impose penalty of death, and he exhibited great reluctance ever to do so. There was a case in 1847 of a murderer being dragged through the city and then thrown into the sea to die.[6] According to the British consul, however, Said would go to great lengths to avoid having to order a man to be put to death; he would even raise the substitute blood money of 800 dollars himself if this proved necessary.[7]

Saiyid Saʻid's attitude towards his judicial function was consistent with the general character of his administration. His system of govern-

---

[1] Ward to Buchanan, no. 11, 14 Sept. 1846, Amer. N.A., Zanz. 2; Guillain, *Documents*, II, 237; Burton, *Zanzibar*, I, 258 and 263; and *Rigby's Report*, 1860.

[2] Ruschenberger, *op. cit.*, I, 56.

[3] Proclamation by Saiyid Saʻid, Mch. 1845, Z.A.

[4] Ward to Buchanan, no. 11, 14 Sept. 1846, Amer.N.A., Zanz. 2; Loarer's Report, Part I, 1849, M.O., O.I. 5/23; Hamerton to Bombay, no. 10, 24 Mch. 1855, Z.A.; *Rigby's Report*, 1860; and Guillain, *Documents*, II, 237.

[5] Ward to Buchanan, no. 16, 7 Mch. 1847, Amer.N.A., Zanz. 2.

[6] H. B. Putnam, 'A Visit to Zanzibar, 1847', printed in Bennett and Brooks, *op. cit.*, pp. 402-3.

[7] Hamerton to Bombay, no. 49, 3 Sept. 1842, Z.A.; Ward to Buchanan, no. 11, 14 Sept. 1846, Amer.N.A., Zanz. 2; and *Rigby's Report*, 1860.

ZANZIBAR: THE CONSOLIDATION OF OMANI AUTHORITY

ment was casual rather than systematic, for it lacked a clearly defined set of institutions. The amorphous nature of Sa'id's rule was one reason for its success. At the same time Sa'id was fortunate in that conditions among the Arabs in Zanzibar during his reign were favourable to the kind of regime which he represented. The Arabs, as the politically dominant group, were disposed to be co-operative because they enjoyed a position of social and economic superiority. Benefiting from a higher standard of living than they would have had in Oman, their power and wealth was out of all proportion to their numbers. It is true that on many occasions they were subject to irritants, particularly in matters concerning the Slave Trade – at one time Hamerton said the Sultan was 'in a sea of difficulties with his people' – but in general they had few grievances.[1] For example, they were not required to pay any formal taxes. Most of them derived considerable personal power from their ownership of landed estates and slaves. Some Arabs, of whom Salim ibn Abdullah is an example, owned as many as 2,000 slaves, many of whom were armed with muskets.[2] This was a potential danger to the Sultan – indeed, Salim ibn Abdullah waged a petty war with Saiyid Sa'id's men – but in general it provided the Arabs with a power which they did not find occasion to use.[3]

Saiyid Sa'id's position depended on the support of the dominant Arab group. Yet he would have faced grave dangers if there had been massive opposition to his rule from the Swahili inhabitants of Zanzibar. Such a threat was, however, made less likely by the extent of cultural assimilation between the Arabs and the upper-class Swahilis. The rapidity of this assimilation owed a great deal to the widespread Arab habit of taking secondary wives. Most of these women were slaves brought from the African mainland: Abyssinians were particularly popular.[4] They learnt to speak Swahili rather than Arabic and their children were often dark in colour. Athough in 1819 Albrand said the Arabs could be recognized by the olive colour of their skin, by 1834 Ruschenberger found the colour of the Arabs almost as deep as that of the Africans, and by 1848 Guillain said it was often difficult to distinguish Arabs from Swahilis by appearance.[5] The operation of the harem

---

[1] Hamerton to Bombay, 14 July 1841, Z.A.
[2] Same to same, 13 July 1841, Z.A.; Ruschenberger, *op. cit.*, I, 40; and Burton, *Zanzibar*, I, 262.
[3] Burton, *idem*.   [4] Emily Ruete, *op. cit., passim*.
[5] Albrand's Report, 1819, M.O., Réunion 72/472; Ruschenberger, *op. cit.*, I, 47; and Guillain, *Documents*, II, 78.

system meant that the children were under the influence of their mothers rather than their fathers during their formative years. By the late 1840s few Arabs in Zanzibar spoke Arabic, the Swahili language being almost exclusively used.[1] Saiyid Sa'id himself had only one Arab wife – Adza (Izzha?) binti Saif, the daughter of the Musa binti Ahmad who had helped him come to power in Oman.[2] His two other primary wives, both Persians, and his many Circassian and African secondary wives would not have introduced any Arab influences into his household.[3] How far Zanzibar Arab households had diverged from their Omani counterparts was demonstrated when some members of the Sultan's family visited Oman in 1854. The light-skinned Omani branch of the family disapproved of their 'African' relatives who were unable to speak Arabic.[4] Even Sa'id's educated daughter, Salma, spoke only Swahili. Sa'id's household, typical of those maintained by Zanzibar Arabs, illustrated the rapid assimilation which had taken place.

The growing similarity between the Arabs and the upper-class Swahilis assisted the acceptance of the former by the latter, but there was no complete fusion, and many strains still remained. Comments from European observers describe the resentment which the Swahilis felt towards the Arabs: in 1775 it was said that for a long time Arabs and Swahilis had experienced feelings of jealousy and rivalry, and in 1821, 1822 and 1848 the Swahilis were said to hate the Arabs.[5] It must be borne in mind, however, that all these comments were made by Frenchmen, who had a direct interest in exploiting the strains within Zanzibar society. Swahili antagonism did not lead to the expulsion of the Arabs or the overthrow of Sa'id's regime. This was partly because

[1] Guillain, *Documents*, II, 94.
[2] *Ibid.*, pp. 157 and 224; Broquant to Ministry of F.A., no. 3, 14 Feb. 1845, A.E., Zanz. C.C.1; and Ibn Ruzayq, *op. cit.*, p. 261. But Pullicino, *Aulad el Imam*, table IV, makes Adza the daughter of Saif, the son of the first Al Bu Sa'idi Imam. If this were the case she would be the sister of Musa and the aunt of Saiyid Sa'id. Burton, in *Zanzibar*, I, 309, calls her Adza binti Musa and says she was a grand-daughter of the Imam Ahmad. However, in Saiyid Sa'id's will, dated 17 Feb. 1850, Z.A., Adza is described as the daughter of Saif ibn Ali.
[3] For the three primary wives, Guillain, *Documents*, II, 224 and III, 95 and 197; Burton, *Zanzibar*, I, 300 and 302; and Emily Ruete, *op. cit.*, pp. 10 and 51.
[4] Emily Ruete, *op. cit.*, pp. 93-4.
[5] Morice's Memoir concerning the East Coast of Africa, 15 June and 26 Sept. 1777, A.N., Colonies C4/42, 'Projet de livrer l'île de Zanzibar au français', n.d., 1821, Réunion 72/472; Vandries to Philibert, Feb. 1822, M.O., O.I. 17/89; and Loarer's Report, Part II, 1849, M.O., O.I. 2/10.

ZANZIBAR: THE CONSOLIDATION OF OMANI AUTHORITY

of the degree of social fusion between the Arabs and the old Swahili elite, which in 1856 consisted of about a hundred families.[1] But although the Swahilis dressed the same, looked the same, and followed the same economic pursuits as the Arabs, they were not really on an equal footing with the newcomers because they had had much of their political power eroded.[2] It is true that individual Swahilis such as Khamis ibn Uthman and Muhyi al-Din had important roles, but in general the Swahili elite was not in an influential position. Although the Swahilis had their own leader, called the *mwenyi mkuu*, his political power was limited and operated only within his own community.[3] Sir Bartle Frere, writing in 1873, said Saiyid Sa'id made an agreement with the *mwenyi mkuu* according to which the latter received a pension but retained only limited sovereignty.[4] This appears to have been a confirmation of a previous engagement by which the people of Zanzibar had yielded sovereignty to the Omanis on condition that their leader and his descendants should be paid a large annuity – one source gives a figure of 8,000 dollars and another puts it as high as 15,000 dollars.[5] This arrangement does not seem to have been strictly adhered to: in 1848, for example, the *mwenyi mkuu* was allowed to keep 2,000 dollars from the taxes he collected for the Sultan, and in addition received a direct payment of 2,000 dollars from Saiyid Sa'id.[6]

The *mwenyi mkuu* was concerned with the settlement of disputes among his own people and the collection of taxes for the Sultan. He was therefore important to Saiyid Sa'id as an intermediary between the Swahilis and Arabs and as an instrument for the raising of revenue. At the beginning of Saiyid Sa'id's reign, taxation appears to have been irregular: in 1811, for example, Smee reported that there was no consistent land tax but that the Sultan sometimes resorted to imposing one. Upon receiving an order to send 25,000 dollars to Oman in 1811, the governor of Zanzibar had ordered the chiefs in each district on pain of imprisonment to collect specified amounts of money.[7] Later it seems that regular taxation was imposed on the Swahilis, at first at a rate of

[1] Burton, *Zanzibar*, I, 411.
[2] *Ibid.*, pp. 411 and 433; and Guillain, *Documents*, II, 74 and 78.
[3] For a discussion of the *mwenyi mkuu*, see Chapter I, pp. 27-8.
[4] Gray, *History of Zanzibar*, p. 160.
[5] *Idem*, quoting E. Roberts to L. Woodbury, Dec. 1828; and Owen, *op. cit.*, I, 361.
[6] Guillain, *Documents*, II, 77. See also Burton, *Zanzibar*, I, 411.
[7] Smee's Description of the island of Zanzibar, 1811, I.O.L., Marine Records Miscellaneous, 586.

two dollars per family head, and later at a lesser rate.¹ The *mwenyi mkuu* was also responsible for organizing the *corvée* and it may have been in return for a reduction of this that regular taxation was imposed. The *corvée* still existed in 1848, although it was less burdensome than it had been before.² The Swahilis had to work on the plantations for a month, receiving food but no pay. The important role of the *mwenyi mkuu* in collecting taxes and organizing the *corvée* may partly explain his continued existence under the Omani regime. The Sultan would also have had to work through him to raise Swahili troops. In 1860 Rigby said the *mwenyi mkuu* was influential in time of war because it depended on him whether or not the Swahilis answered a call to arms.³ However, the Sultan does not appear to have used Swahili troops to any great extent. The British consul, watching the embarkation of troops for the war against Pate, did not describe any large Swahili contingent, commenting rather on the use of great numbers of slaves.⁴

Athough the *mwenyi mkuu* was important to Saiyid Sa'id as an intermediary and an executor of administrative demands, he had no real power in other matters. His sole means of putting pressure on the Sultan was by withholding payment of the taxes – as he appears to have done in 1833.⁵ It was probably because he felt his position so circumscribed in Zanzibar town that he went to live inland at Dunga at some time after 1828.⁶ Guillain described the *mwenyi mkuu* as a ruler only in name and Burton said he was admitted to no equality with the Sultan.⁷ Indeed on one occasion Saiyid Sa'id appears to have put him in prison.⁸ Although he was impotent to influence the external affairs of Zanzibar, the *mwenyi mkuu* was highly respected among his own people.⁹ He was the ultimate authority to whom the village Swahilis could

¹ Ruschenberger, *op. cit.*, I, 64; Hamerton to Mauritius, 15 Feb. 1845, Z.A.; Guillain, *Documents*, II, 77; and Burton, *Zanzibar*, I, 414. From *Rigby's Report* it appears that a lesser amount was being paid in 1860, but this may have been the result of tax avoidance.

² Ruschenberger, Hamerton, Guillain, and Rigby as above. Also Ward to Buchanan, no. 16, 7 Mch. 1847, Amer.N.A., Zanz. 2; and Loarer's Report, Part I, 1849, M.O., O.I. 5/23.

³ *Rigby's Report*, 1860.   ⁴ See above, p. 259.

⁵ Letter of Saiyid Sa'id to the *mwenyi mkuu*, 1833, quoted in Gray, *History of Zanzibar*, p. 161.

⁶ Gray, *ibid.*, p. 160; and *Rigby's Report*, 1860. There is a picture of the Dunga palace in Pearce, *op. cit.*, p. 171.

⁷ Guillain, *Documents*, II, 77; and Burton, *Zanzibar*, I, 411.

⁸ Pearce, *op. cit.*, p. 172; and Ingrams, *op. cit.*, p. 151.

⁹ Pearce, *op. cit.*, p. 172.

ZANZIBAR: THE CONSOLIDATION OF OMANI AUTHORITY

appeal, for he headed the local organization of village headmen.[1] The Arabs did not interfere with this local administration – indeed, to have done so would have meant that they would have had to construct one of their own. The Swahilis were left alone to follow their Shafi'i beliefs and worship in their own mosques.[2] They could appeal to their own chief *qadhi*, Muhyi al-Din, to settle legal disputes.[3]

The fact that the Swahilis were allowed to have their own leaders helped to prevent them from becoming disaffected. A further explanation for the absence of disaffection lies in the division between groups of Swahilis. Firstly, there were the upper-class or 'Shirazi' families who had been the political elite in Zanzibar before 1698. Many of these left Zanzibar for Mafia after the coming of the Omanis.[4] Those who were left lost their political status and as a result probably held, as Loarer remarked in 1849, 'a vague desire for independence'.[5] However, there were too few of them to take practical steps to gratify this desire without outside assistance. Secondly, there were the less prosperous town Swahilis: the middlemen, masons, boat-builders, carpenters, and seamen. This was a motley group whose members originated from all parts of the Swahili Coast. Their lack of organization, together with their participation in the economic system dominated by the Omanis and Indians, prevented them from becoming an effective opposition. Thirdly, there were the village Swahilis – the agriculturalists and fishermen. It was this last group which had the strongest motive to resent the coming of the Omanis. It has been shown in Chapter I that initially their lives may not have been greatly affected by the establishment of the Arab regime. However, as the nineteenth century progressed, they had more compelling grounds for resentment.

Their major grievance was the takeover of the best land on Zanzibar island for Arab clove plantations. It is difficult to establish the exact scale and timing of this takeover. European sources do not provide much evidence about this subject because in the first half of the nineteenth century most Western visitors to Zanzibar failed to penetrate far

[1] Guillain, *Documents*, II, 76; and *Rigby's Report*, 1860. See also Chapter I, p. 31.
[2] Krapf, *op. cit.*, p. 125; Guillain, *Documents*, II, 95 and 105; and Burton, *Zanzibar*, I, 84.
[3] Loarer's Report, Part I, 1849, M.O., O.I. 5/23; Hamerton to Bombay, no. 10, 24 Mch. 1855, Z.A.; *Rigby's Report*, 1860; Guillain, *Documents*, II, 237; and Burton, *Zanzibar*, I, 263 and II, 193.
[4] See Chapter I, p. 27.
[5] Loarer's Report, Part II, 1849, M.O., O.I. 2/10.

into the island, preferring rather to remain in the town or to take short rides to nearby Arab plantations.[1] The Arabs already possessed some landed estates in 1811,[2] but it was the spread of clove planting in the next two decades that brought about the real Arab expansion. By the late 1820s Kichwele plantation, which was some distance to the north of Zanzibar town, had been established.[3] In the late 1840s Guillain reported that clove cultivation was still extending every year.[4] By the end of Saʻid's reign the plantations reached as far north as Bumbwini and Mangapwani, fifteen miles from Zanzibar town, and as far west as Kizimbani and Selem.[5] The scale of Arab land colonization is evident from a comparison of the clove exports for 1839 and 1856. At the former date Zanzibar produced 315,000 lb. of cloves and at the latter 5,000,000 lb.[6] Each tree produced a maximum of 6 lb. of cloves a year, although in some years thirty trees would only yield 35 lb.[7] If an annual average of 3 lb. a tree is taken, and each tree needed an area of 400 square feet (trees were set 20 feet apart), about 15,300 acres of land must have been planted to obtain 5 million lb. of cloves.[8]

By the end of Saiyid Saʻid's reign, then, a good part of the fertile area to the north and east of Zanzibar town had been taken over for clove plantations. Originally indigenous agriculturalists would have occupied some of this land.[9] It is true that some contemporary observers commented on the absence of cultivation in Zanzibar, but this is not necessarily significant.[10] These observers did not go any distance from Zanzibar town, and in any case the local cultivators engaged in

[1] For example, Ruschenberger, *op. cit.*, I, 70; Waters' Journal, entry for 2 Aug. 1837, printed in Bennett and Brooks, *op. cit.*, p. 200; Guillain, *Documents*, II, 47; and Burton, *Zanzibar*, I, 358.

[2] See Chapter I, pp. 29-30.   [3] Guillain, *Documents*, II, 50.

[4] Guillain's Report, 1849, A.N., Marine BB4/1036.

[5] As note 3, and Waters' Journal, entry for 21 Dec. 1839, printed in Bennett and Brooks, *op. cit.*, p. 213. See also Middleton, *op. cit.*, p. 12.

[6] Guillain, 'Côte de Zanguébar et Mascate, 1841', in *Revue Coloniale* (Paris, 1843), pp. 520-62 (here p. 538); and Burton, *Zanzibar*, I, 364.

[7] Burton, *ibid.*, p. 363. Pearce, *op. cit.*, p. 301, for an average of 5 lb. a year.

[8] For the distance trees were set apart – Burton, *Zanzibar*, I, 362, for 20 ft; Journal of Lt Christopher, 1843, encl. in Bombay to Secret Committee, no. 54, 18 July 1843, E.S.L.B. 60, for 14 ft; and Pearce, *op. cit.*, p. 299, for 30 ft.

[9] Such is the opinion of Baumann, *op. cit.*, p. 19, Pearce, *op. cit.*, p. 249, and Gray, *History of Zanzibar*, p. 157. For an opposite view, J. Middleton, *Land Tenure in Zanzibar* (HMSO, 1961), p. 12.

[10] e.g. Albrand's Report, 1819, M.O., Réunion 72/472; and Massieu to Freycinet 9 Oct. 1822, M.O., Réunion 72/473.

ZANZIBAR: THE CONSOLIDATION OF OMANI AUTHORITY

primarily subsistence agriculture and tilled small plots of land, which would have been less easy to observe than large estates. Even after extensive planting of cloves Europeans were liable to comment on the apparent absence of cultivation.[1] That the local agriculturalists had previously cultivated the fertile area on the west side of the island is indicated by the fact that by 1856 they still held land on the very edge of that area. The *mwenyi mkuu* had built a large house at Dunga on the outskirts of the fertile region, around which the land was tilled. After the death of the last *mwenyi mkuu*, in 1873, the house and surrounding land was taken over by the Sultan – which may be taken as an example of the sort of development which had taken place elsewhere during the period of the Arab expansion.[2] As we have seen in Chapter I, as a result of the Arab expansion many of the indigenous inhabitants went to live in the eastern and southern parts of the island.

Some clues to the extent to which Swahili agriculturalists may have suffered when the Arabs encroached on the fertile region of Zanzibar may be obtained from a study of the Arab method of acquiring land. Saiyid Sa'id himself considered that in some sense all Zanzibar belonged to him. For example, in 1834 he granted the French some land on the north-west side of the island, retaining a reversionary right should that land become unoccupied.[3] Another example of this type of grant was Sa'id's gift of Latham's Island, near Zanzibar, to Robert Cogan. The agreement specified that the produce of the island (guano deposit) and not the island itself were granted to Cogan 'as long as he wishes to keep it or use it'.[4] Other Arabs, however, probably acquired their land by a variety of methods, following a mixture of Zanzibar and Arab land law and practice.

According to local practice, there were three types of land: *wanda* land which was bushland; *kiambo* land which was a family building site; and *msitu* land which was village scrubland. *Kiambo* ownership was shared by those patrilineally descended from the man with the first right of occupancy. If a shareholder vacated his plot kinsmen or strangers could get permission to plant crops on it, but this did not destroy the owner's priority, and he could return. The *wanda* land belonged to the village and its rights were controlled by the guardian

---

[1] e.g. Guillain, *Documents*, II, 72, and *Rigby's Report*, 1860.
[2] Baumann, *op. cit.*, p. 42.
[3] Guillain to Ministry of Marine, 21 Oct. 1840, and Guillain to governor of Bourbon, 9 Jan. 1841, M.O., O.I. 10/45.
[4] Saiyid Sa'id to whom it may concern, n.d. (? Feb. 1846), Z.A.

of the soil, the *mviale*. It could not be cultivated without his permission. He could give this permission to members of the locality, who had the first right of occupancy, or even to strangers if they paid a fee. However, when the land was abandoned it reverted to the village.[1] It probably happened, then, that some of the land the Arabs occupied was classed as *wanda* land and they acquired permission from local *mviale* to cultivate it. This is borne out by Albrand's report in 1819 that land was obtainable by giving half a dollar to the local headman and paying him an annual rent of 200 to 300 lb. of rice.[2] Later, however, as clove cultivation proved unexpectedly profitable, the payment of rent probably lapsed, as did the understanding that *wanda* land was ultimately the property of the village. The Arabs may even have applied their own land law according to which it was possible to gain title to vacant land by right of occupation. Another legal argument that might have been used was the rule that property of a usurped object can be acquired if that object's main uses are changed. Usurpation is not really recognized in Islamic law, but its effects are, because claims to ownership of land against the possessor cannot be entertained after a number of years has passed. There may, therefore, have been a confusion between rights to usufruct, which the Swahilis thought they were conferring, and rights to ownership, which the Arabs thought they were receiving.

Unfortunately there is little evidence available to study what happened in practice, and the examples that occur refer to the transfer or lease of land from one alien to another. In 1844 the American consul, Waters, reported that the governor, Sulaiman ibn Hamad, was going to lease him a plantation for fifty years.[3] When Hamerton described the mortgage system he omitted to say to whom the original money was paid and what type of tenure payment gave the buyer.[4] In 1860 Rigby reported that land was available for purchase, but he did not say from whom.[5] A large area of the land may have been taken by Saiyid Sa'id himself without payment to anyone. This is the impression given by Guillain when he said that the Sultan used to ask his neighbours if he could take over their lands, a request which they dare not refuse.[6]

[1] For Zanzibar land law see Pakenham, *op. cit.*; Prins, *Swahili-speaking Peoples*, pp. 61-4; and Middleton, *op. cit.*

[2] Albrand's Report, 1819, M.O., Réunion 72/472.

[3] R. P. Waters' notes, 3 Apr. 1844, printed in Bennett and Brooks, *op. cit.*, p. 256.

[4] Hamerton to Bombay, no. 33, 9 Dec. 1843, Z.A.

[5] *Rigby's Report*, 1860.   [6] Guillain, *Documents*, II, 51.

Since Saiyid Saʻid owned a large part of the plantation area and produced one-third of Zanzibar's cloves, many Swahilis may have been dispossessed in this fashion.¹ The Sultan may also have taken other land and granted it to his Arab subjects in the same way as he made grants to Europeans.²

The deepest grievances of the Swahilis against the Arabs would have been connected with the extension of Arab plantations. A further cause of discontent was the raids which Arab slaving vessels from the north carried out on the east side of Zanzibar island.³ The Arab colonists, however, did not enslave the Swahilis.⁴ Despite having cause for resentment against the Arabs, the Swahilis did not seriously threaten Saiyid Saʻid's regime. They merely withdrew to the west and south of the island where, for the time being, the Arabs left them to administer their own affairs without interference.

Far greater in number than either Arabs or Swahilis were the slaves of Zanzibar. It is therefore important to study this group's position within the island's social and political structure and to estimate how important it was for the Arabs to keep control over the slave population. Various estimates were given of the number of slaves in Zanzibar: in 1811 it was said that they formed three-quarters of Zanzibar's total population of 200,000; the figure for 1819 was 15,000 slaves; in 1834 they were estimated as two-thirds of Zanzibar's population of 150,000, and in 1844 as four-fifths of a population of 450,000; in 1847 a figure of 60,000 slaves was given; in 1856 it was said that two-thirds to three-quarters of Zanzibar's population was in slavery; and in 1860 Rigby said that slaves formed the great bulk of the population of Zanzibar.⁵ Bearing in mind that most Arab proprietors and Indian merchants owned slaves, and that Saiyid Saʻid had about 10,000,

---

¹ Ward to Abbot, 13 Mch. 1851, Amer.N.A., Zanz. 3. Loarer's Report, Part I, 1849, M.O., O.I. 5/23, said two-thirds of the plantations belonged to Saʻid in 1840 and one-third in 1845. See Emily Ruete, *op. cit.*, p. 109, for Saʻid having forty-five plantations.

² This is the view of Middleton, *op. cit.*, p. 12.

³ *Rigby's Report*, 1860, and Baumann, *op. cit.*, p. 20.

⁴ Hamerton to Mauritius, 15 Feb. 1845, Z.A.

⁵ Smee's Description of the island of Zanzibar, 1811, I.O.L., Marine Records Miscellaneous 586; Albrand's Report, 1819, M.O., Réunion 72/472; Ruschenberger, *op. cit.*, I, 64; Hamerton's answers to a questionnaire, encl. in Hamerton to F.O., no. 1, 2 Jan. 1844, Z.A.; H. B. Putnam, 'A Visit to Zanzibar, 1847', printed in Bennett and Brooks, *op. cit.*, p. 400; Burton, *Zanzibar*, I, 463; and *Rigby's Report*, 1860.

THE SWAHILI COAST

a tentative estimate can be made of 60,000 slaves on Zanzibar in the 1850s.[1]

The slaves' position in the society of Zanzibar differed according to what job they were given and also according to whether they were locally born of slave parents or brought from Africa as children or adults.[2] Locally born slaves were used for work in the household whereas imported slaves, other than women who became secondary wives, were usually put to work on the plantations. The imported boys, however, like the locally born boys, were given an Islamic education and taught a trade so that they could remit part of their earnings to their owners or so that when they died they might leave their owners the property they had acquired.[3] For example, Saiyid Sa'id inherited property from his rich slave, Tengweni, and 500,000 dollars from Yaqut, the Abyssinian slave governor of Zanzibar.[4] Slaves became blacksmiths and carpenters and also worked on vessels as stewards, superintendents, and supercargoes.[5] Many of them attained positions of considerable importance, conducting trade, organizing caravans, commanding garrisons, and even becoming governors.[6] The governors of Zanzibar, Yaqut and Ambar, were both slaves, and in 1834 the Baluchi soldiers at Zanzibar were commanded by an Abyssinian slave.[7] Some slaves became so distinguished that they were able to buy slaves themselves.[8]

Slaves were also used as porters for caravans and as an irregular armed force.[9] Those who were put to work on the plantations were given small plots of land on which they lived and from which they had to obtain their subsistence.[10] Consequently when a plantation changed

---

[1] For Saiyid Sa'id's slaves, Journal of Lt Christopher, 1843, encl. in Bombay to Secret Committee, no. 54, 18 July 1843, E.S.L.B. 60.

[2] Burton, *Zanzibar*, I, 463 and *Lake Regions*, II, 369, distinguishes between the *muwallid* or domestic born in captivity, and the slave imported from Africa.

[3] Burton, *Zanzibar*, I, 467; and *Rigby's Report*, 1860.

[4] Albrand's Report, 1819, M.O., Réunion 72/472; and Guillain, *Documents*, II, 50.

[5] Hamerton to Bombay, no. 2, 2 Jan. 1842, encl. in Bombay to Secret Committee, no. 43, 30 Apr. 1842, E.S.L.B. 44; and Burton, *Zanzibar*, I, 467-8.

[6] Krapf, *op. cit.*, p. 128; Guillain, *Documents*, II, 81; and Burton, *Lake Regions*, II, 370.

[7] For Yaqut and Ambar, see above, p. 271. For 1834, Ruschenberger, *op. cit.*, I, 69.

[8] *Rigby's Report*, 1860.

[9] Burton, *Lake Regions*, I, 337. See also above, p. 259.

[10] Burton, *Zanzibar*, I, 149; Loarer's Report, Part I, 1849, M.O., O.I. 5/23; and Hamerton to Bombay, 13 July 1841, Z.A.

ZANZIBAR: THE CONSOLIDATION OF OMANI AUTHORITY

hands its slaves usually went with it.[1] They worked three days a week for their owners and four for themselves, selling their produce in the market.[2]

Superficially it might appear that the large numbers of slaves and the fact that some of them attained influential positions would have posed a threat to the Arab regime. In 1822 a Frenchman observed that the disproportion between Arabs and slaves would be fatal to the former.[3] The danger would have been great had the slaves acquired firearms. It is true that some slaves were armed by their owners, but this was the exception rather than the rule.[4] Gangs of plantation slaves would often have feuds with other gangs, but their lack of firearms prevented them from becoming dangerous to the Arabs. However, on two occasions groups of slaves did organize themselves sufficiently to threaten the Arabs in a serious way. Some time before 1822 a slave revolt was put down by the Zanzibar governor who assembled all the Arabs to fire the bush and flush the rebels out, and on the second occasion (between 1825 and 1828) mercenaries from the Hadramaut were brought in to wage war against a group of Zigua slaves who had retired into the bush. On this latter occasion the slaves were given as prizes to their captors.[5]

In general, however, the slaves did not act together as a group, and their interests were more personal than political: to obtain manumission, to escape, or to better themselves and become absorbed in society. Manumission was often granted by a master at the point of his death: for example, in his will Saiyid Sa'id declared free after his death all his male and female slaves, excepting those on his plantations.[6] Many slaves, reluctant to await such a turn of fortune, took matters into their own hands and escaped. If lucky they were able to reach a runaway slave settlement such as that at the Shimba hills.[7] Domestic slaves could

[1] Hamerton to Bombay, *idem.*

[2] H. B. Putnam, 'A Visit to Zanzibar, 1849', printed in Bennett and Brooks, *op. cit.*, p. 427. However, three sources say the slaves worked five days a week for their masters and two for themselves – Ruschenberger, *op. cit.*, I, 41; Journal of Lt Christopher, 1843, encl. in Bombay to Secret Committee, no. 54, 18 July 1843, E.S.L.B. 60; and *Rigby's Report*, 1860.

[3] Massieu to Freycinet, 9 Oct. 1822, M.O., Réunion 72/473.

[4] Speke, *op. cit.*, p. 194; and Burton, *Zanzibar*, I, 466 and *Lake Regions*, II, 371.

[5] For the plantation gangs, Burton, *Zanzibar*, *idem.* For the first revolt, Massieu, as note 3. For the second revolt, Burton, *Lake Regions*, I, 125.

[6] Saiyid Sa'id's will, 17 Feb. 1850, Z.A.

[7] Burton, *Zanzibar*, II, 105 and *Lake Regions*, II, 374.

often leave one house and find employment in another. The less fortunate, however, were driven to become petty criminals and suffered great degradation if they were caught.[1] Recaptured slaves had iron collars fastened to a heavy chain put around their necks, and were left exposed all day in the public thoroughfare. They remained chained in this way until they were claimed by their owners.[2]

Less numerous than the slaves, but with an economic importance out of all proportion to their numbers, were the Indian residents of Zanzibar. It is therefore important to investigate the response of this section of the island's society to Arab rule. Considerable numbers of Indians came to Zanzibar in Saiyid Sa'id's reign. From just over 200 in 1819 their numbers rose to 350 in the mid 1830s, about 700 in the mid 1840s, and between 5,000 and 6,000 in 1859.[3] Many of these Indians were Hindus from Kutch, Surat, and Bombay, and they included a large proportion of Batias. From the 1830s Muslim Indians, particularly Khojas and Bhoras, began to settle in Zanzibar town. The Indians were mainly merchants, money-lenders, and bankers; the less wealthy among them became shopkeepers and experts at handicrafts.[4]

At first the relationship between the Arabs and Indians was strained. The Arabs resented the presence of Indian merchants in Zanzibar and attempted to restrict their commercial activities by only allowing them to stay on the Swahili Coast for the period of one monsoon.[5] None the less the Indians established themselves in the Zanzibar business world. Their position improved when a British consul was appointed to Zanzibar. Indeed, it had been British and British Indian merchants who had helped initiate the move to establish British representation there.[6]

[1] Loarer's Report, Part I, 1849, M.O., O.I. 5/23; and Burton, *Lake Regions*, II. 370. [2] *Rigby's Report*, 1860.

[3] Albrand's Report, 1819, M.O., Réunion 72/472 (214); Ruschenberger, *op. cit.*, I, 42, 1834 (350); Cogan's Report on the Sultan and Zanzibar, 5 Dec. 1839, F.O 54/3 (900); Krapf, *op. cit.*, p. 122 (700); Hamerton to Bombay, 13 July 1841, F.O. 54/4 (700); Hamerton to Aberdeen, 2 Jan. 1844, F.O. 54/6 (800); Hamerton's Memo. on British Indian subjects at Zanzibar, 29 Jan. 1846, F.O. 54/9 (1,000); and *Rigby's Report*, 1860 (5,000-6,000).

[4] Hamerton to Bombay, 9 Feb. 1842, encl. in Bombay to Secret Committee, no. 58, 23 May 1842, E.S.L.B. 45; Hamerton's Memo., 1846, as above; Guillain, *Documents*, II, 80; Loarer's Report, Part I, 1849, M.O., O.I. 5/23; Burton, *Zanzibar*, I, 327 and 336; and *Rigby's Report*, 1860.

[5] Hamerton to Bombay, no. 26, 6 Sept. 1841, Z.A.; and Loarer's Report, Part I, as above. See also Chapter III, pp. 78-9.

[6] Norsworthy to Secretary of the Bombay Chamber of Commerce, n.d., 1841, F.O. 54/4. See also Chapter VI, pp. 158-9.

ZANZIBAR: THE CONSOLIDATION OF OMANI AUTHORITY

The subsequent exertions of the British consul to improve the lot of the Zanzibar Indians encouraged more of them to come to the town and exploit its economic opportunities.[1] Afraid of this increased commercial competition, the Arab merchants were delighted when in 1843 restrictions were imposed on Indians dealing in slaves.[2] They hoped that all commerce would fall into their hands. The measures were, however, ineffectual and the numbers of Indians in Zanzibar continued to increase. Apprehensive though they were, the Arabs allowed the Indians to remain because they were dependent on them for capital, with which they financed expeditions to the African interior or bought land for plantations.[3] Saiyid Sa'id himself was alive to the importance of Indian capital and banking to the Zanzibar economy. He encouraged Parsees to come to Zanzibar[4] and did not hesitate to borrow large sums for his own projects and expenses. In 1851, for example, he borrowed 50,000 dollars to pay his war expenses in Oman.[5]

One might have expected that the Indians' expanding wealth and numbers would have been accompanied by an increase in their political influence. There were, however, certain factors working against this. Although most of the Indians in Zanzibar were actually the subjects of British Indian States or Protected States, the blurred definitions of nationality then existent enabled them to claim that they were either British or Zanzibari according to their immediate commercial purposes.[6] They ceased to be able to do this when the British, concerned to suppress the Slave Trade, began to make sure that their own subjects neither dealt in nor held possession of slaves. For the first time the Indians were forced to define their position. In 1841 the Zanzibar customs master, himself an Indian, suggested that his fellow-countrymen sign a paper declaring themselves to be the subjects of the Sultan of Zanzibar. In his opinion this would give them the right to continue dealing in slaves. His suggestion was not followed, all but three Indians refusing to sign the paper.[7] They obviously felt that such an action would threaten their interests in India and break the links which they retained with their mother country. Not regarding East Africa as their permanent home,

[1] Hamerton to Bombay, 6 Sept. and 5 Dec. 1841, Z.A.; 28 Sept. 1841, F.O. 54/4; and no. 8, 3 Feb. 1842 and 9 Feb. 1842, encl. in Bombay to Secret Committees, nos. 57 and 58, 23 May 1842, E.S.L.B. 45.
[2] Hamerton to Bombay, no. 33, 9 Dec. 1843, B.C. 2034.
[3] See Chapter XII, p. 358.   [4] Burton, *Zanzibar*, I, 336.
[5] Charles Ward to Andrew Ward, 13 Jan. 1851, printed in Bennett and Brooks, *op. cit.*, p. 472.
[6] See Chapter XII, p. 348.   [7] See Chapter IX, p. 242.

most of them left their families in India and planned to return home after a few years.¹ They also had commercial interests in India and remitted thither most of the profits they made.² To have renounced their British nationality would have meant that they would be prohibited from holding real estate in Bombay.³ At the same time they wished to continue dealing in slaves in East Africa. As a result they were in an ambiguous position and their need to keep quiet prevented them from involving themselves in political matters at Zanzibar.

As a group the Indians were lacking in political influence. However, certain individuals among them had great power. These were mainly rich merchants, such as the brothers Jairam and Abji Sewji, Rensha Ramji, and Topan Tajir, who had close relations with foreign firms and therefore considerable influence over the relationships between foreigners and Zanzibar.⁴ In a particularly prominent position was Jairam Sewji, the customs master. It was Omani practice to farm out the customs collections. The posts usually went to Indians because Arab rulers preferred politically impartial men in such influential offices and because Indians had the capital necessary to make high bids and regular payments thereafter.⁵ In 1834, Jairam Sewji of Kutch bought the customs collection at Zanzibar. He kept it until 1853 when he was succeeded by Ladha Damji.⁶ Jairam's office gave him the opportunity to direct the sale of cargoes at great profit to himself and to exclude undesirable competitors.⁷ To help him in this purpose he possessed 150 to 200 slaves armed with matchlocks.⁸ In many spheres Jairam

---

[1] Guillain's Report, 1849, A.N., Marine BB4/1036; Hamerton to F.O., no. 6, 26 July 1849, F.O. 54/13; Loarer's Report, Part I, 1849, M.O., O.I. 5/23; and Burton, *Zanzibar*, I, 329.

[2] See Chapter VIII, p. 217.

[3] Ward to Abbot, 13 Mch. 1851, Amer.N.A., Zanz. 3.

[4] Guillain's Report, 1849, A.N., Marine BB4/1036; Hamerton to Wyvill, 13 Mch. 1851 and Hamerton to Bombay, no. 5, 15 Feb. 1853, Z.A.; B. F. Fabens to M. Shepard, 4 Jan. 1845, printed in Bennett and Brooks, *op. cit.*, p. 340; Journal of the Brig *Richmond*, 9 June 1845, *ibid.*, p. 267; McMullan to Shepard, 28 Jan. 1851, *ibid.*, p. 475; and R. P. Waters' notes, 3 Sept. 1844, *ibid.*, p. 257.

[5] e.g. in 1845 the family of Gopal farmed the Muscat customs – British local agent at Muscat to Resident, Persian Gulf, 17 Oct. 1845, B.C. 2174.

[6] Waters to Forsyth, 6 May 1837, printed in Bennett and Brooks, *op. cit.*, p. 216; Hamerton to Bombay, no. 23, 24 Sept. 1853, Z.A.; and Burton, *Zanzibar*, I, 271.

[7] See Chapter XII, p. 327.

[8] Journal of Lt Christopher, 1843, encl. in Bombay to Secret Committee, no. 54, 18 July 1843, E.S.L.B. 60.

ZANZIBAR: THE CONSOLIDATION OF OMANI AUTHORITY

exercised more authority than the Sultan himself.[1] Sa'id recognized and accepted this. On one occasion when the customs came up for sale the Sultan accepted Jairam's bid even though he received a higher offer from someone else.[2]

A few more groups contained in the motley society of Zanzibar remain to be considered. There were the mainland Africans and people from Madagascar and the Comoro islands who came to settle in Zanzibar when it began to develop economically. The former, particularly Zigua, Segeju, and Digo, earned a living by fishing or hiring themselves out as plantation labour, often acquiring a small patch of ground from the estate owner.[3] Madagascans and Comoro islanders, numbering about 2,000 in 1856, lived in the easternmost part of the town and occupied themselves as artisans, labourers, and sailors.[4] The dockers and harbour workers were mostly Arabs from the Hadramaut.[5]

These settlers caused no serious trouble to Saiyid Sa'id's regime. A far more disruptive element was the seasonal population which came down from Arabia on the north-east monsoon from mid-November onwards and did not leave Zanzibar until the south-west monsoon set in during April. The Omanis themselves had belonged to this group before they settled on Zanzibar, but once they became permanent residents they disliked the antisocial activities of the several thousand non-settled maritime Arabs. Those from the Trucial Coast recognized no allegiance to Saiyid Sa'id; rather they had a tradition of rivalry with him, and they extended their piratical activities from the Persian Gulf into East African waters. They would often steal slaves in Zanzibar town and elsewhere on the island.[6]

Saiyid Sa'id's loose authority was not of the type which could easily limit the activities of the 'northern Arabs', as they came to be known. The force he maintained in Zanzibar could not deal with them, particularly when it came to imposing restrictions on the Slave Trade. Occasionally he was able to exercise some authority – for example,

[1] *Idem*, and Hamerton to Bombay, 1 July 1841, encl. in Bombay to Secret Committee, no. 69, 30 Aug. 1841, E.S.L.B. 35.
[2] W. C. Waters to R. P. Waters, 1 Oct. 1841, printed in Bennett and Brooks, *op. cit.*, p. 232.
[3] Burton, *Zanzibar*, I, 344-5.
[4] *Ibid.*, pp. 339-42, and *Rigby's Report*, 1860.
[5] Burton, *Zanzibar*, I, 378; *Rigby's Report*, 1860; and Guillain, *Documents*, II, 79.
[6] Hamerton to F.O., no. 16, 23 Dec. 1846, and Hamerton to Bombay, no. 15, 29 Apr. 1847, Z.A.; and *Rigby's Report*, 1860.

when he imprisoned a man from Ras al-Khaima for piracy and slave stealing.[1] However, although he issued orders that no slaves were to be sold to the northern Arabs, closed the slave market until the monsoon had turned, posted Baluchis to stop slaves being embarked, and confined the seasonal visitors to their vessels, the numbers of slaves exported from Zanzibar to the north did not diminish.[2] Their ability to evade the Sultan of Zanzibar's restrictions made it unnecessary for the northern Arabs to attack Saiyid Sa'id's position. Moreover, their interests were commercial rather than political. Being seasonal visitors and coming from a number of different areas – the coast of Oman, the Trucial Coast, Hadramaut, and the Red Sea – they were incapable of organizing any sustained opposition.

From this survey it has become evident that the only group in Zanzibar which could have removed the Sultan was that of the Omanis themselves. However, although this group was sometimes split by clan divisions, it enjoyed a power and prosperity which left it indisposed to protest. The Omani regime owed its stamina largely to its loose organization and lack of visible administrative structures. Although the Swahilis lost their political and economic superiority, for the time being they were permitted to run their own affairs. The village Swahilis who were dispossessed of their land were as yet incapable of physical resistance to the Arabs. Although the Sultan's fleet and soldiers were far from effective in practice, they remained as a threat to the local population. The comparatively recent consolidation of Arab rule in Zanzibar meant that there had been insufficient time for local grievances to develop and find political expression. In any case, Omani rule was not yet being exercised rigorously enough to provoke organized opposition among the disparate elements which were subjected to it.

[1] Hamerton to Resident, Persian Gulf, no. 13, 27 June 1853, and no. 3, 10 Jan. 1854, Z.A.
[2] Hamerton to Bombay, no. 6, 3 Apr. 1847, Z.A. See also Chapter IX, pp. 240-1.

CHAPTER XI

THE SWAHILI COAST

THE CONSOLIDATION OF OMANI AUTHORITY
AND LOCAL REACTIONS TO IT

From their capital in Zanzibar the Omani Arabs extended their rule over a section of the East African coast between Mogadishu in the north and Cape Delgado in the south. The nature of this rule varied from settlement to settlement along the littoral: in some places Omani governors and garrisons were established, and in others there was merely a tacit acceptance of Omani authority. This is why there were so many conflicting opinions about both the nature and extent of Omani rule in East Africa. The Sultan of Zanzibar's own opinion on the matter cannot be given too much credence because he had many reasons to distort the true state of affairs, sometimes in order to minimize his own influence and sometimes in order to exaggerate it. In 1847 he claimed his territory extended from Mogadishu to Tongui and included the two islands of Mohelli and Grand Comore.[1] Europeans who investigated the question were not told the truth because the Arabs wanted to prevent them visiting the littoral and penetrating to the African interior. The Omanis consequently stressed the extent of their rule and exaggerated the hostility of the Africans of the hinterland to any penetration.[2] Even the direct observations of Europeans were sometimes mistaken because of their own ulterior motives or because they were confronted with a type of rule which they had little experience of and did not understand. Thus in 1819 Albrand exaggerated the independence of Kilwa because he wanted the French to obtain it; likewise in the 1840s Guillain found the inhabitants of the Banadir coast conveniently anxious to free themselves

---

[1] Saiyid Sa'id to Guizot, 18 Aug. 1847, M.O., Madag. 270/605.
[2] Albrand's Report, 1819, M.O., Réunion 72/472; and Burton, *Lake Regions*, I, 16 and 31.

from Saiyid Sa'id's rule.[1] The missionary Krapf, stung by obstructions Africans put in his way, claimed that Sa'id's authority was non-existent in most places.[2] Hamerton, too, found it difficult to understand Sa'id's almost indefinable authority, and concluded that it hardly existed; at the same time he refused openly to admit this because he did not want the French to step in with territorial claims.[3]

The extension of Omani authority over some places on the Swahili littoral in the early years of Saiyid Sa'id's reign has already been described. The timing of later expansion was affected by external pressure from Europeans as much as by local factors. Omani expansion was directly stimulated by aggressive territorial moves on the part of European powers and the rising competitive hysteria of the French and British, and indirectly encouraged by the wish of these powers to have the Omanis rather than their rivals rule the Swahili Coast. Moreover, the Omanis found it commercially expedient to control the Swahili ports. They were mainly concerned, particularly in the period before cloves became well established in Zanzibar, with channelling three staples produced in East Africa – ivory, gum copal, and slaves – through the island of Zanzibar. Because vast tracts of land had to be combed for ivory and slaves they emerged from Africa at a great number of exit points, all of which it was desirable to control. By the end of his reign Saiyid Sa'id had established some sort of control over exit points along 600 miles of coastline.

A satisfactory investigation into the nature of Omani rule and the local reaction to it can only be conducted by studying separately all the different places which were affected. The northernmost point on the East African littoral in which Sa'id had some sort of authority was Mogadishu on the Banadir coast. His writ did not extend north of Mogadishu or into the Red Sea, although he had vague ambitions in that region. In fact, in 1842 Sa'id asked the British Foreign Secretary if he had any objection to his extending his authority from Ras Hafun to Berbera, and the following year he several times mentioned to Lt Christopher that he wanted to control Berbera.[4] The Sultan had

[1] Albrand, as above; and Guillain to Ministry of Marine, 24 Oct. 1847, M.O., O.I. 2/10.   [2] Krapf to Kuhlmann, 3 Oct. 1854, A.E., Zanz. C.P.1.
[3] Hamerton's Report on the Proceedings of the French, 1842, F.O. 54/4; and Hamerton to Bombay, no. 10, 5 Sept. 1850, Z.A. For Hamerton's refusal to admit this, Krapf to Kuhlmann, as above.
[4] Saiyid Sa'id to Aberdeen, 19 June 1842, F.O. 54/4; and Journal of Lt Christopher, 1843, encl. in Bombay to Secret Committee, no. 54, 18 July 1843, E.S.L.B. 60.

THE SWAHILI COAST AND OMANI AUTHORITY

probably heard of British activities in the Berbera region and hoped that he might participate in the spoils. Nothing came of these manœuvres and he had to be content with Mogadishu as his northern outpost on the East African littoral.

Saiyid Sa'id's first contact with the Banadir coast had been in 1822 when Hamad ibn Ahmad, the commander of the fleet he had despatched to effect the subjection of Pate, put in to water at Brava.[1] Hamad appears to have indulged in more than provisioning activities because the following year Captain Owen reported that Brava and Marka had recently been 'subjected' by Saiyid Sa'id.[2] Mogadishu was not included in this initial move, but late in 1823 it, too, suffered at Omani hands. That year Sa'id sent another expedition to Pate and on the way the commander, Abdullah ibn Sulaiyim, anchored at Mogadishu and seized some men whom he later ransomed at Zanzibar for 2,000 dollars.[3] This may have been a private commercial enterprise on the part of Abdullah, but it had important political repercussions. It prompted Captain Owen, whose activities at Mombasa have already been described, to intervene with the governor of Zanzibar to free the men and later to visit the Banadir coast himself. Owen took with him Rashid ibn Ahmad al-Mazrui of Mombasa who endeavoured to canvass the support of the inhabitants of the Banadir for Mombasa's cause. He had no success at Mogadishu but Brava raised the British flag in return for agreeing to renounce the trade in slaves.[4] Saiyid Sa'id was given a somewhat exaggerated description of these events by his governor in Pemba, Nasir ibn Sulaiman.[5] It added weight to his protests to the British Government and confirmed him in his suspicion that to subdue Mombasa successfully he must also extend his control over that town's possible allies.

Saiyid Sa'id did not take immediate action because the British withdrew from East Africa. In 1828, however, he despatched an expedition against Mombasa and ordered its commander, Hamad ibn Ahmad, to put in at Mogadishu on his return voyage to Oman and bombard the town. One story has it that Abdullah ibn Sulaiyim was killed in the ensuing fight and the people of Mogadishu were so apprehensive of Sa'id's reaction to this event that they sent their submission to Oman.[6]

[1] Guillain, *Documents*, I, 572-3.   [2] Owen, *op. cit.*, I, 355.
[3] *Ibid.*, p. 359; and Guillain, *Documents*, I, 582.
[4] Boteler, *op. cit.*, II, 232.
[5] Nasir ibn Sulaiman to Saiyid Sa'id, 12 May 1825, Proc. 8 June, B.P.C. 385/60.   [6] Guillain, *Documents*, I, 590.

There is a similar story about Marka at about the same date: that the killing near Marka of a soldier of the Bani Bu Hasan people of Oman caused the people of Marka to declare themselves the subjects of Saiyid Saʻid in order to escape his reprisals.[1]

The Banadir coast was not central to Saiyid Saʻid's ambitions. In the early 1830s he was able virtually to ignore the region because it was not actively hostile to him. In those years his energies were consumed by the struggle with Mombasa and the expansion of the economy of Zanzibar. It was not until Mombasa was finally overcome in 1837 that Saiyid Saʻid again turned his attention to the Banadir coast. In that year he sent his first official to Brava, probably as a collector of customs dues.[2] His interest in the Banadir had quickened because American vessels had started to go there to trade and by his 1833 treaty with the United States he could receive 5 per cent import duties on American goods at his ports.[3] But the true stimulus for his interest in the region came in 1840 when Commander Guillain, while trying to establish a French consul in Zanzibar, made enquiries about the situation at Mogadishu and Brava. He then proceeded to Muscat, where he continued his investigations.[4] It was doubtless concern about this French interest that prompted Saʻid to put in at Marka on his return from Oman to Zanzibar late in 1840 or early in 1841.[5] In an attempt to forestall future French moves, on his arrival in Zanzibar he sent flags to all the different ports on the coast to which he laid claim.[6]

Mounting European pressures forced Saiyid Saʻid to strengthen his tenuous hold on the Banadir. In 1841 both the British and Americans complained that the Sultan's official at Brava was charging them duties higher than those stipulated in their respective treaties.[7] Saʻid sent orders that this was to be stopped and despatched an envoy, Muhammad

---

[1] Guillain, *Documents*, III, 120.   [2] *Ibid.*, pp. 171-2.
[3] For American trade with the Banadir, Waters' Journal, entry for 19 Nov. 1837, printed in Bennett and Brooks, *op. cit.*, p. 206.
[4] De Hell to Guillain, 18 May 1840, M.O., O.I. 10/45; and Hennell to Bombay, 5 Aug. 1840, encl. in Bombay to Secret Committee, no. 56, 22 Aug. 1840, E.S.L.B. 23.
[5] For this visit to Marka, Guillain, *Documents*, III, 145. Saʻid left Muscat for Zanzibar on 10 Nov. 1840 – Bombay to Secret Committee, no. 108, 30 Dec. 1840, S.L.B., 1st series 12.
[6] Hamerton's Report on the Proceedings of the French, 1842, F.O. 54/4.
[7] *Idem*, and R. P. Waters to John Shirley, 19 June 1841, printed in Bennett and Brooks, *op. cit.*, p. 231.

ibn Nasir, to the Banadir to obtain information about its commercial movement and to regulate the customs dues.[1] The resultant report must have been favourable because the following year Sa'id sent Ali ibn Muhammad to be both governor and customs master of Mogadishu. The local rulers' support for this arrangement was sought by promising them that they would suffer no financial loss. Saiyid Sa'id engaged to pay them what they would formerly have received from customs dues. Whether this arrangement worked is unknown; certainly Sa'id's officials had little means to enforce their authority because they were accompanied by only one or two soldiers.[2]

Saiyid Sa'id's activities on the Banadir coast stopped short at the imposition of customs officials at Marka, Brava, and Mogadishu. The local shaikhs and sultans continued to exist as before.[3] Although these rulers would sometimes turn to the Sultan for assistance in their internal disputes, he had no practical authority over them. In 1846 Hamerton said that it was only by making occasional presents to the shaikhs of Brava that Saiyid Sa'id possessed any influence there. Occasionally those shaikhs visited Zanzibar to consult the Sultan, and they would also appeal to him if a dispute arose concerning Europeans, with whom Sa'id had a far closer relationship than themselves.[4] In 1842, for example, Shaikh Uwais of Brava complained to Saiyid Sa'id about the activities of Norsworthy, a British merchant.[5] In reality the leaders of the hinterland Somalis had greater influence in the Banadir towns than did Sa'id: particularly important in this respect were Yusuf and his successor, his brother Ibrahim.[6] Like the Swahili towns, the ports of the Banadir coast relied for their prosperity on their role as entrepot between maritime trade and the commerce of the interior. Their caravans had to pass through Yusuf's lands to reach their inland destinations. The rulers of the hinterland were therefore able to acquire considerable influence over the coast towns and to impose passage dues.[7] This may, indeed, have been one of the reasons why Saiyid Sa'id did not put more soldiers into the Banadir towns: unable to compete with Yusuf, the

[1] Waters, *idem*, and Guillain, *Documents*, II, 529.
[2] Guillain, *Documents*, II, 529, and III, 120 and 147.
[3] *Ibid.*, II, 527, and III, 170; and Journal of Lt Christopher, 1843, encl. in Bombay to Secret Committee, no. 54, 18 July 1843, E.S.L.B. 60.
[4] Hamerton to Bombay, no. 7, 3 Mch. 1846, Z.A.
[5] Hamerton to Bombay, no. 50, 30 Sept. 1842, Z.A.
[6] Guillain, *Documents*, III, 187 and 445.
[7] Isaacs, *op. cit.*, II, 314; and Guillain to Ministry of Marine, 24 Oct. 1847, M.O., O.I. 2/10.

Sultan of Zanzibar co-operated with him by sending him arms and powder.[1]

Saiyid Sa'id was content to let the Banadir towns remain on the periphery of his ambitions provided he could derive a small profit from them and feel confident that they would not be taken over by Western powers. Although in 1848 his official at Brava, Stambuli ibn Kombo, possessed the grand title of governor of the Banadir,[2] Saiyid Sa'id made little attempt to impose his authority in the region. He actually admitted the insubstantial character of his influence there when he was called upon to stipulate the limits of his East African domain in a written treaty with the British. In that instance he named Lamu and nearby Kiwaiyu island as his northern outposts.[3] However, he made grander claims when it suited his purpose. In order to curtail French ambitions he informed Paris in 1847 that his authority extended as far north as Mogadishu.[4]

The Lamu archipelago was far more central to Sa'id's ambitions than the Banadir coast. It was not long before difficulties arose for the governors whom he had placed there in the early 1820s. Hostility to the Omanis was fomented by Fumoluti ibn Shaikh, a discontented local notable who laid claim to the rulership of Pate, a post which still existed side by side with the Omani governorship. Having failed, despite assistance from the Mazruis, in a bid he made in 1822 to establish himself as the ruler of Pate, Fumoluti had set himself up as ruler of Ozi, on the mainland.[5] Two years later Fumoluti observed with great interest that the British had taken Mombasa under their protection. He hoped that the newcomers would also come to his assistance and support his claims in Pate. When, therefore, Saif ibn Ahmad, Saiyid Sa'id's major governor in the Lamu archipelago, sent an expedition against Ozi, Fumoluti's henchmen raised the British flag over their settlement.[6] This action caused the attacking force to withdraw. The flag had in fact been raised without British authorization, but its dramatic deterrent effect must have strengthened Fumoluti's desire to obtain British support. He extracted a promise from Captain Owen at Mombasa that the British would protect Ozi.[7] Owen sent midshipman

[1] Guillain, *idem*.
[2] Guillain, *Documents*, III, 145-7 and 172.
[3] Aitchison, *op. cit.*, XI, 300.
[4] Saiyid Sa'id to Guizot, 18 Aug. 1847, Madag. 270/605.
[5] See Chapter V, p. 124.
[6] Emery's Journal, entry for 30 Oct. 1824.   [7] *Ibid.*, 17 Nov. 1824.

THE SWAHILI COAST AND OMANI AUTHORITY

Philips to Fumoluti's stronghold to make the necessary arrangements, and this put an effective stop to any direct action against Fumoluti by the Omani governor of Lamu.¹ However, Saif ibn Ahmad managed to enrage the ruler of Ozi in other ways. He imprisoned Fumoluti's brother and murdered his uncle, actions which caused the ruler of Ozi to march to Siu on Pate island, where he acquired the support of the local shaikh, Bwana Mataka ibn Mubarak. It is unlikely that Saiyid Sa'id had any soldiers in Siu, relying rather on his garrison in Pate town to control the whole island. Fumoluti and his new allies then attacked Pate town itself, but they were not altogether successful and withdrew to Siu. This aroused a quick response from Saif ibn Ahmad in Lamu. He despatched a force to Siu, but it failed to take the town.² There was no resolution to the uneasy situation for several years. When Saiyid Sa'id first visited Zanzibar in 1828 he attempted to settle the affair by ordering a fort to be built at Siu.³ It is unlikely, however, that Bwana Mataka allowed this to be done. Fumoluti died shortly afterwards, but Mataka continued his policy of non-co-operation.

The rebels against Omani authority in the Lamu archipelago were closely associated with those pursuing the same purpose in Mombasa.⁴ However, the collapse of the Mazruis in 1837 was not accompanied by a corresponding weakening of resistance in Pate. In fact Saiyid Sa'id's problems there had been aggravated by the hostility towards him of the new ruler of Pate town, Fumobakari ibn Shaikh. Formerly, whereas the rulers of Siu and Ozi had maintained an independent stand, the ruler of Pate town itself had co-operated with the governor and soldiers sent by Saiyid Sa'id. In about 1839, however, Fumobakari expelled the Omanis from his town.⁵ By 1840, then, Saiyid Sa'id no longer had any hold on Pate island. He did still retain a governor and garrison in Lamu, where his influence had always been stronger. Lamu had developed into a settled commercial community which paid customs dues to Zanzibar.⁶

The early 1840s saw a new bid by the Sultan of Zanzibar to subdue the towns on Pate island. As long as they were hostile to him they

¹ *Ibid.*, 24 Jan. 1825.
² For these events, *ibid.*, 12 Mch. and 27 June 1825, and *Pate Chronicle*, p. 88.
³ Saiyid Sa'id to Shaikhs Ishaq ibn Bwana Miya, Abubakr ibn Muhammad ibn Shaikh, and Yusuf ibn Shaikh, 17 Jan. 1828, Z.A.
⁴ Mazrui MS., p. 69; and Guillain, *Documents*, I, 599.
⁵ Guillain, *Documents*, I, 601 and III, 97, and *Pate Chronicle*, p. 89.
⁶ Isaacs, *op. cit.*, II, 323.

remained a focus for elements which were discontented with Saiyid Sa'id's position on the Swahili Coast. The Pate towns were not easy to occupy. From a military point of view they were excessively difficult to attack and from a political standpoint they were so fragmented that it was unusual for any outsider to retain a core of support for long. Economic factors further complicated the task of any foreigner who aspired to rule there. Unlike Yusuf of the Banadir hinterland and Kimwere of the Pangani region, who were able to impose passage dues which could coexist with the customs duties charged by the Sultan of Zanzibar, the rulers of the Pate towns had to rely on customs dues for their revenue.

Saiyid Sa'id sent two major expeditions against Bwana Mataka in Siu – in December/January 1833/4 and December/January 1844/5. He may also have despatched a smaller expedition before this.[1] The first of these major campaigns was led by Khalid, Saiyid Sa'id's son, and consisted of about 250 Arabs and Baluchis from Zanzibar, several thousand slaves (Hamerton said 16,000), and probably about 1,000 Arabs from Oman.[2] The expedition returned to Zanzibar on 5 February 1844, having suffered complete defeat. All the Sultan's guns had been captured and the one trained artilleryman had been killed.[3] Saiyid Sa'id determined to avenge the defeat and go in person to attack Siu. In December he took a force to Lamu where he was joined by Hamad ibn Ahmad at the head of 2,000 troops which had been raised in Oman.[4] The force disembarked on Pate island and marched towards Siu, leaving its artillery behind on the shore. The guns were then captured by Mataka's men, a disaster which, together with the death of the general, Hamad ibn Ahmad, caused Sa'id's troops to flee back towards the sea and the safety of their ships. They were pursued by Mataka's men, who slaughtered the swimming soldiers with gunfire. Saiyid Sa'id, who had

---

[1] For a possible earlier expedition, see Loarer's Report, Part II, 1849, M.O., O.I. 2/10.

[2] R. P. Waters' notes, 28 Nov. 1842 (this is misdated – the year should be 1843), printed in Bennett and Brooks, op. cit., pp. 254-5 (Waters said 2,000 soldiers left Zanzibar for Lamu); and Hamerton to Bombay, no. 32, 29 Nov. 1843, Z.A. (Hamerton said Sa'id expected 3,000 Arabs to come from Oman).

[3] Hamerton to Bombay, no. 11, 20 Mch. 1844, Z.A.; and Kerdudal to Bazoche, 3 May 1844, M.O., O.I. 15/59.

[4] Hennell to Bombay, no. 148, 13 Dec. 1844, and Heskiel ibn Yusuf to Bombay, 21 Dec. 1844, B.C. 2121, Dr. 29. Hamad ibn Ahmad may also have commanded the Omani troops on the first expedition – Ibn Ruzayq, op. cit., p. 355, and Bombay Selections XXIV, p. 215.

himself remained at Lamu, was highly displeased with his troops' retreat, blaming it on the cowardice of the Omani levies.[1]

The Sultan of Zanzibar could not run the risk of suffering a third defeat; in any case it is unlikely that he would have been able to raise any more troops in Oman. The geographical position of Siu made it extremely difficult for a military operation against it to succeed. A force had to come by sea and then march a long way through swampy ground, where it was open to ambush, before reaching the town. It was, therefore, unable to transport or position its guns effectively. In the face of such obstacles, Sa'id therefore reverted to diplomacy in order to regain a hold on Pate. He sent Muhyi al-Din, the Swahili *qadhi* of Zanzibar, to negotiate with Bwana Mataka. The Siu leader may have been willing to come to an arrangement because the Sultan still commanded the sea and had imposed a blockade on Pate island. Some sort of peace was negotiated and the captured guns were returned to Sa'id. The Sultan then sent a governor and five soldiers to Pate.[2] However, even though Mataka died in November/December 1848, some of the inhabitants of Pate island, notably Muhammad ibn Shaikh, Fumobakari, and Ali ibn Nasir, continued to be hostile to the rule of Zanzibar.[3]

In view of this state of affairs, the defection to Lamu in 1849 of Saiyid Sa'id's estranged son, Hilal, was a serious danger to the Sultan. In a bid to set up his own domain, Hilal killed Ali ibn Saif, the Omani governor of Lamu.[4] Until then, in spite of the troubles of Pate, Saiyid Sa'id had maintained his hold on Lamu, but now the whole archipelago

---

[1] For contemporary accounts of the battle, which took place in mid-January 1845, Hamerton to Bombay, no. 21, 14 Apr. 1845, Z.A.; and Broquant to Ministry of F.A. no. 3, 14 Feb. 1845, A.E., Zanz. C.C.1. For later and probably less accurate accounts (although in some respects more detailed), Loarer's Report, Part II, 1849, M.O., O.I. 2/10; Guillain, *Documents*, III, 101-2; Burton, *Zanzibar*, I, 298-9 (but Burton seems to confuse the two expeditions); and *Pate Chronicle*, pp. 92-4.

[2] Saiyid Sa'id to Waters, 1 Jan. 1847, printed in Bennett and Brooks, *op. cit.*, p. 372; R. Desfossés to Ministry of F.A., no. 69, 11 Feb. 1846, M.O., Madag. 17/32; Guillain to Ministry of Marine, 24 Oct. 1847, M.O., O.I. 2/10; Guillain, *Documents*, III, 103; Burton, *Zanzibar*, I, 299-300; and Heskiel ibn Yusuf to Bombay, 5 Mch. 1847, B.C. 2203, Dr. 700 (Heskiel said there was some disagreement among Mataka's men which allowed Sa'id to make terms).

[3] Loarer's Report, Part II, 1849, M.O., O.I. 2/10; and Guillain, *Documents*, III, 444.

[4] Heskiel ibn Yusuf to Bombay, 7 May 1850, encl. in Bombay to Secret Committee, no. 51, 3 Oct. 1850, E.S.L.B. 103; and Ward to Abbot, 12 May 1851, Amer.N.A., Zanz. 3.

had slipped from his grasp. He immediately sent to Oman for soldiers to fight Hilal, but none were forthcoming.[1] Hilal kept Lamu for two years, until he died in 1851.[2] Saiyid Saʻid then regained the island, but in 1856 its inhabitants were still causing trouble.[3] Siu, too, was more subdued after the Sultan of Zanzibar seized and imprisoned Muhammad, Mataka's son, who had succeeded to the rulership.[4]

Saiyid Saʻid's skirmishes in the Lamu archipelago illustrated the weaknesses of the type of rule he imposed on the Swahili Coast. It is true that in many places his authority derived its strength from its casual nature which made it more easily acceptable, but in others, where the traditional rulers had greater motives for and means of resistance, Saʻid's governors and garrisons were liable to be ejected. Pate island was a particularly difficult place to hold because it regularly suffered struggles over the succession. In such a situation the presence of a foreigner attempting to impose some authority, however slight, provided an excellent motive for opposition to the existing local ruler who might be collaborating with the newcomers in a bid to survive. Pate town also contained three major settlements, and no sooner would resistance be overcome in one of these than it arose in another. That opposition to foreign rule could be a rallying cry is evident from the emergence of Mataka as ruler of Siu. A man of apparently ordinary birth, his success was due to his own ambition, energy, and ability to embrace a topical cause.[5]

The Sultan of Zanzibar could not have omitted Pate from his East African designs. Originally the focus of rivalry between the Mazruis and Omanis, the Lamu archipelago had become too central to Saʻid's ambitions to be abandoned when that rivalry shifted to Mombasa itself. Until the Mazruis were subdued there was always the possibility that they might derive support from factions in the Lamu archipelago, and by the time they had been overcome Saʻid's involvement in the

---

[1] Heskiel ibn Yusuf to Bombay, 27 May 1850, encl. in Bombay to Secret Committee, no. 51, as above; and Hamerton to Bombay, no. 21, 5 Nov. 1849, Z.A.

[2] Political agent, Aden, to Bombay, 24 June 1851, Z.A.

[3] Guillain, *Documents*, III, 454, for Saʻid reimposing his authority when he put in to Lamu in Dec. 1852/Jan. 1853 on his return from Muscat to Zanzibar. For trouble in 1856, Cochet to Ministry of F.A., 30 Oct. 1856, A.E., Zanz. C.C.2.

[4] Hardinge, *op. cit.*, p. 14.

[5] Guillain to Ministry of Marine, 24 Oct. 1847, M.O., O.I. 2/10. But for the view that Mataka was of shaikhly family, Hardinge, *op. cit.*, p. 14, and A. Werner and W. Hichens (eds), *The Advice of Mwana Kupona upon the Wifely Duty* (Medstead, 1934), p. 16.

THE SWAHILI COAST AND OMANI AUTHORITY

development of the Swahili Coast had deepened to such a degree that it was impossible for him to contemplate the loss of Pate and Lamu.

Saiyid Sa'id's attitude towards the Swahili Coast was initially conditioned by his struggle with Mombasa, and it was as a result of this struggle that he developed an inclination to extend his authority over the whole region. It is most likely that he first came to East Africa in 1828 in order personally to review the state of hostilities with Mombasa. The British protectorate over that town had shocked him into a realization of the hazards of allowing the Omani hold on various Swahili settlements to continue in its former casual manner.

It took Sa'id eleven years to expel the Mazruis after the British left Mombasa. At first he was undecided about whether a complete expulsion was necessary, or whether he should construct some method of government which would allow them to retain at least some measure of their authority. Initially he attempted to compromise with the Mazruis; it may be, however, that such efforts were designed to conceal a wider plan for a complete takeover. Sa'id wrote to the Mazrui shaikhs proposing four conditions, one of which they must accept. The Mazruis could surrender the fort and go and live in Mombasa town; in this case they could keep the town's revenues. Alternatively they could go and live anywhere they wished and receive a pension of 10,000 dollars a year. Lastly, they could govern either Lamu or Pemba instead of Mombasa.[1] The Mazruis replied that they would recognize the authority of Sa'id but would not give up the fort.[2] Dissatisfied with this answer, in 1828 Saiyid Sa'id took to Mombasa 1,200 men on four large and six small vessels.[3] Confronted by such a force, the governor Salim had to capitulate. In any case he could not have held out because there had been a split in the Mazrui ranks and Sa'id had won over – by bribes, it is said – two prominent Mazruis to his side.[4]

Salim ibn Ahmad had succeeded the aged Sulaiman ibn Ali as governor in 1826 when a group of younger Mazruis felt the need for stronger leadership.[5] It is most likely that they were dissatisfied with Sulaiman's reluctance to press the British to keep to the original terms of their agreement to regain Pemba for Mombasa, and were generally

[1] Saiyid Sa'id to Shaikhs Mubarak, Salim, and Khamis al-Mazrui, n.d., encl. in Saiyid Sa'id to Bombay, n.d., Proc. 14 Feb. 1827, B.P.C. 386/18.
[2] Guillain, *Documents*, I, 584.
[3] *Ibid.*, p. 585; Burton, *Zanzibar*, I, 293; and E. Roberts to Saiyid Sa'id, 27 Jan. 1828, Z.A.
[4] Guillain, *Documents*, I, 586; and Mazrui MS., p. 57.
[5] See Chapter II, pp. 50-1.

discontented with the British presence. However, Salim's forthright leadership aroused hostility among certain Mazruis, and it was these who saw their chance in collaboration with the Omani leader.

Salim arranged a convention with the Omanis by which the fort was to be garrisoned by Saiyid Sa'id with fifty soldiers of a tribe tolerable to the Mazruis, but at the same time its buildings could continue to be inhabited by the Mazrui governor and his family. The Mazruis would recognize the rights of Saiyid Sa'id to the sovereignty of Mombasa, but Salim could retain the governorship for himself and his descendants, with no other obligation than to divide with the Omanis the customs dues, the collector of which was to be nominated by the Mazruis.[1]

Perhaps not surprisingly, the arrangement did not work. Saiyid Sa'id may have always intended to abrogate it, or he may have been influenced to do so by Nasir ibn Sulaiman, his governor in Pemba. Nasir informed Sa'id that the Mazruis were planning rebellion and then, either on his own initiative, or in response to orders from the Sultan, he went to Mombasa and occupied the fort.[2] It appears that the Mazruis had previously left their stronghold and gone to live in the town. One story has it that they had withdrawn because they found it impossible to inhabit the fort alongside the Omani garrison,[3] and another claims that 350 soldiers had been introduced instead of the 50 Sa'id had promised originally and these had forced out the Mazruis.[4] In any case they did not take kindly to their removal and prepared a siege of the fort. After about eight months Nasir and the Omani soldiers surrendered, having been reduced to such extremity that they were forced to eat the leather of their shields, and rats, the price of which had risen to a dollar each.[5]

The expulsion of his garrison must have appeared to Saiyid Sa'id as a threat to his entire position on the Swahili Coast. Immediately the monsoon was favourable, in December 1829 he accompanied another expedition from Oman.[6] Despite having a large number of men (esti-

---

[1] Guillain, *Documents*, I, 587-8; and Mazrui MS., p. 58. Guillain, however, must be mistaken in saying the Mazruis would accept men of the Hinawi faction.

[2] Guillain, *ibid.*, pp. 591-2; and Mazrui MS., p. 59. For Nasir ibn Sulaiman, see Chapter V, p. 127.

[3] Mazrui MS., p. 58.   [4] Guillain, *Documents*, I, 588.

[5] *Ibid.*, pp. 592-3, and Mazrui MS., pp. 60-1. Also poem by an eye-witness, Muhyi al-Din ibn Shaikh al-Qahtani, included in the Mazrui MS., p. 62. An American ship visited Mombasa during the siege – log of *Virginia*, entry for 3 Sept. 1828, printed in Bennett and Brooks, *op. cit.*, p. 152.

[6] Broker at Muscat to Bombay, 8 Jan. 1830, Proc. 16 Feb., B.P.C. 386/61.

THE SWAHILI COAST AND OMANI AUTHORITY

mates vary from 1,400 to 2,000) the Omanis failed to take Mombasa.[1] Their mistake was to attempt to attack the town by land without ascertaining the feeling of the inhabitants of the place where they landed – Kilindini village, on the opposite side of Mombasa island from Mombasa town. It has been shown that an assailant's problem in attacking Mombasa was the dominance of the harbour entrance by the guns of the fort. Mere bombardment of the fort from the sea was unlikely to succeed, and even if it did silence the citadel's guns, there still remained the task of getting enough men ashore in small boats to scale the towering walls. Even then, the defenders could retreat and rally behind the walls of the town, which lay beside the fort. About 5 feet thick, with raised towers, the town wall was built on the ruins of the old Portuguese wall shortly before 1824 and was strengthened a few years later by the governor Salim.[2] It was, therefore, a sound idea to land soldiers elsewhere on the island and march to attack the town and fort from the landward side. However, in 1829 the Omanis failed to choose a good landing place, with the result that 900 of them were killed by the inhabitants of Kilindini village.[3] The Omanis withdrew and Saiyid Sa'id imposed a blockade on Mombasa. Even this method of procedure, however, caused only limited inconvenience to the Mombasans because the blockade had to be lifted every time the monsoon changed.[4]

The Sultan of Zanzibar attempted another direct attack on Mombasa in 1833. This time his troops placed their guns on the mainland opposite Mombasa town and bombarded the fort from there. As usual, however, it was difficult to follow up the attack, and the Omanis eventually withdrew.[5] It was now becoming doubtful whether Sa'id would ever take Mombasa if its inhabitants' determination to resist remained firm. But cracks soon appeared in Mombasa's united front. The town had been held together by the leadership of the governor, Salim ibn Ahmad. When Salim died in March 1835 there was a dispute over the succession, the repercussions of which revealed how important it was for the Mazruis, of whom there were now about 1,500,[6] to remain united among themselves and to keep the support of the Swahili people of Mombasa.

[1] Guillain, *Documents*, I, 594 for 1,400; and Mazrui MS., p. 66, for 2,000.
[2] Boteler, *op. cit.*, II, 20; Guillain, *Documents*, III, 236; and Mazrui MS., p. 69.
[3] Mazrui MS., pp. 57-68; and Guillain, *Documents*, I, 594-5.
[4] For the raising of the blockade for this reason in 1832 and 1833, Guillain, *Documents*, I, 597 and 599.
[5] *Ibid.*, p. 598.   [6] *Ibid.*, III, 236.

THE SWAHILI COAST

Instances of the dangers of Mazrui disunity had occurred before – for example, in 1828 – but Salim had managed to retain his position. One branch of the Mazruis, led by Rashid ibn Salim ibn Abdullah, had set themselves up in Takaungu after a disagreement with Salim.¹ Salim had also succeeded in retaining Swahili support, although there had been difficulties in this respect – for example, during the siege of the fort in 1828 some Swahilis had fired maize cobs attached to arrows into the garrison at night.² However, Salim's treatment of the Swahilis encouraged them to accept his authority. According to the Mazrui MS.,

'he never initiated any course of action without consulting the distinguished men and leaders of the country. The people therefore had a great affection for him and the leaders of the Twelve Tribes began to consider that they shared in his government, especially the leaders of the Three Tribes, whom he treated as brothers'.³

Now, however, the Mazrui quarrels over the succession, which coincided with the advent of a plague in Mombasa, induced a feeling of disillusionment among the Swahilis. The shaikh of the Kilindini and other Swahili leaders therefore went to Muscat to request Saiyid Sa'id's assistance.⁴ Sa'id seized this instance of disunity as an opportunity to send vessels to Mombasa. This time his troops met with no resistance when they landed at Kilindini village, and it became obvious to Rashid ibn Salim, who had by then been proclaimed as his father's successor, that he would have to come to terms with the Omanis or be ejected. The convention he signed was similar to that of 1828 except that the Mazruis were not allowed to reside in the fort.⁵ From Sa'id's point of view this was only a temporary measure; he had suffered so much humiliation at the hands of the Mazruis that he could not afford to give them the chance to make any more mischief. He tried to induce Rashid to live in Zanzibar, but when this failed he seized the former governor, together with thirty other leading Mazruis, and took them to the Persian Gulf where they perished in prison.⁶ Thus ended over a century of Mazrui rule over Mombasa.

---

¹ Mazrui MS. p. 71.   ² *Ibid.*, p. 60.   ³ *Ibid.*, pp. 71-2.
⁴ Omari bin Stamboul, *op. cit.*, p. 35; and Guillain, *Documents*, I, 602. For the plague, *ibid.*, III, 236.
⁵ Guillain, *Documents*, I, 602-5. Gray, *The British in Mombasa, 1824-1826*, p. 189, is probably mistaken when he names Salim's successor as Rashid ibn Salim ibn Abdullah rather than Rashid ibn Salim ibn Ahmad.
⁶ Guillain, *Documents*, I, 607-8; Burton, *Zanzibar*, I, 298; and Mazrui MS., p. 72.

When the Mazruis were expelled, Saiyid Sa'id installed a governor, garrison, and customs master in Mombasa. The garrison was larger than that which he maintained in Zanzibar: in 1847 it consisted of 400 men and in 1847 about 215, most of whom were Baluchis.[1] The garrison commander, Tangui ibn Chenbe, was a forty-year-old Baluchi from Makran who was unable to read or write but was renowned for his *akl* or intellect.[2] Partly because of his extensive commercial dealings, he appears to have had almost more power in Mombasa's affairs than the Omani governors of the town. The first of these was Ali ibn Mansur, who was succeeded by Ali ibn Nasir. The latter twice went to England as the Sultan's envoy but had his career cut short by his death in the second campaign against Pate.[3] The succeeding governors of Mombasa became preoccupied with their commercial operations, behaving as prominent merchants rather than administrators. Because they received no payment for their office, governors used their position to enrich themselves.[4] Apart from the governor and the garrison commander, Mombasa also had a customs master who, according to usual practice, was an Indian.[5]

Despite Mombasa's lengthy resistance, Saiyid Sa'id did not alter his habit of leaving in the hands of the local inhabitants the administration of their own affairs. This habit arose partly from necessity – the Sultan did not have the personnel capable of undertaking such tasks – and partly from design – it was a means of inviting co-operation. Consequently, on 21 December 1836 an agreement was made with the leaders of the Twelve Tribes to the effect that 'whenever a difference arises amongst members of his [the Swahili leader's] community, such a difference shall be dealt with between themselves. ... It is upon them to bring pressure to their own folk and the *liwali* [governor] will not enforce judgment on internal matters', and 'in all internal and domestic affairs the *liwali* shall keep to their advice'.[6] At the same time the Sultan

[1] Krapf, *op. cit.*, p. 119; and Guillain, *Documents*, II, 238 and III, 254.
[2] Krapf, *op. cit.*, p. 298; Guillain, *Documents*, III, 199, 223 and 262; and Burton, *Zanzibar*, II, 79.
[3] Hamerton to F.O., no. 21, 14 Apr. 1845, F.O. 54/9; and Guillain, *Documents*, III, 261-2.   [4] Guillain, *Documents*, III, 204.
[5] *Ibid.*, p. 262; and Burton, *Zanzibar*, II, 79.
[6] Deed of 21 Dec. 1836, signed by Sulaiman ibn Muhammad (Hamad), governor of Zanzibar. Shaikh M. Qasim Mazrui has a copy of the deed, and it was also displayed in the case of Abdullah ibn Shaikh ibn Yunis on behalf of the Three Tribes and W. N. Macmillan *v.* the Wakf Commissioners and the Land Officer, Civil Appeal no. 12 of 1913 in the High Court of British East Africa.

of Zanzibar kept some control over the political life of the Swahilis by participating in the choice of their shaikhs. The shaikhs, one of whom would represent the Three Tribes and one the Nine, would be selected by their own people, but their appointment had to be confirmed by Saʻid.[1] In 1836 Shaikh Mshirazi was approved as leader of the Three Tribes – 'we have agreed between ourselves and Shaikh Mshirazi that he is the recognized leader of his community'[2] – and in 1838/9 Muhammad ibn Shahali's appointment as leader of the Changamwe was confirmed by Saʻid.[3] Other controls established by the Sultan of Zanzibar were the holding of regular meetings for which the shaikhs came to Zanzibar, and the payment to the Swahili leaders of an annual sum in recompense for forfeiting the right to receive customs dues.[4] In 1839 it was agreed that 'Shaikh Mshirazi has 150 dollars for himself and 250 for his relatives the Three Tribes. This amount has been granted to him ... for the surrender of the right of imposing customs'.[5] Such an arrangement gave Saiyid Saʻid considerable influence because he could withhold payment. Indeed, Guillain reported that by 1847 the shaikhs were receiving only 100 dollars a year because of various misdemeanours committed by the people of Mombasa.[6] The Sultan of Zanzibar also had some influence in the appointment of the two chief *qadhis*, one for the Three and one for the Nine Tribes.[7]

There is no record of the reaction of the Mombasa Swahilis to the imposition by the ruler of Zanzibar of a governor, garrison, and customs dues. Since Saiyid Saʻid allowed them to retain some say in their own affairs their position cannot have seemed greatly different from that which they had held under Mazrui overlordship. There is evidence, however, that there were certain side-effects of Saʻid's rule which displeased the Mombasa Swahilis. In the wake of the Omanis came Indian traders whose activities, in Guillain's opinion, were more harmful than the Mazrui taxes had been. They took much of the export trade out of Swahili hands.[8] The Indians were not entirely new to Mombasa – in 1824 Boteler recorded the presence of Indian merchants and moneylenders – but they increased in number.[9] In 1844 there were

[1] Guillain, *Documents*, III, 260. [2] Deed of 21 Dec. 1836, as above.
[3] Saiyid Saʻid to whom it may concern, 1254 (1838/9), Z.A.
[4] Guillain, *Documents*, III, 260-1; and Burton, *Zanzibar*, II, 76.
[5] Deed dated 9 May 1839 signed by Saiyid Saʻid, in the possession of Shaikh M. Qasim Mazrui of Mombasa.
[6] Guillain, *Documents*, III, 261. [7] *Idem*; and Burton, *Zanzibar*, II, 76.
[8] Krapf, *op. cit.*, p. 118; and Guillain, *Documents*, III, 262.
[9] Boteler, *op. cit.*, II, 106.

thirty or forty, in 1847 about fifty, and ten years later about eighty, fifty of whom were Batias and twenty-five to thirty Muslims.[1] The Swahilis did not, however, suffer financial disaster because they kept hold of the trade with the interior.[2]

The inhabitants of Mombasa who classed themselves as Arabs – the remaining Mazruis and recent immigrants – fared worse than the Swahilis after Sa'id's capture of the town. Having lost their position as the political elite, many left Mombasa, but about 230 Arabs (forty families) remained.[3] In 1857 there were 350 Arabs in Mombasa. They were allowed to have their own representative shaikh and *qadhi*.[4]

As for the peoples of the hinterland, they were little affected by Mombasa's change of masters. The Mazruis had lived in reasonable peace with the Nyika and there had been regular contact between the inhabitants of town and country. These contacts continued under Omani rule, but the Nyika owed no allegiance to the governor of Mombasa. They levied arbitrary passage dues which the governor was powerless to prevent. When the Duruma demanded of Krapf payment of sixteen dollars to pass through each village, his complaints to the governor of Mombasa evoked no response.[5] The Nyika would not attend audience with the governor without first receiving a present of cloth worth two dollars.[6] It would have been unlikely that the Nyika, who had previously been ready to fight for the Mazrui governors of Mombasa, would answer a similar call to arms from the Omanis. Even the Twelve Tribes exacted a promise from the Sultan that they would not be conscripted.[7] Despite their aloofness, the Nyika posed no danger to Sa'id's authorities because they were reliant on Mombasa's commerce for their prosperity and because they did not possess fire-arms. In 1857 there appears to have been a prohibition on the importation of powder to Mombasa, a measure which may have been designed to prevent the hinterland peoples acquiring fire-power.[8] Nyika weakness in this respect was demonstrated in 1857 when the Masai raided

[1] Krapf, *op. cit.*, p. 118; Guillain, *Documents*, III, 238; and Burton, *Zanzibar*, II, 75.
[2] Burton, *Zanzibar*, II, 24.   [3] Guillain, *Documents*, III, 237 and 263.
[4] *Ibid.*, p. 260; and Burton, *Zanzibar*, II, 76.
[5] Krapf to Kuhlmann, 3 Oct. 1854, A.E., Zanz. C.P.1.
[6] Guillain, *Documents*, III, 245.
[7] Article 12 of Deed of 21 Dec. 1836, as above. However, the translation of this article in Shaikh M. Qasim Mazrui's copy of this deed reads: 'No ill-action should be done on them by our representative.'
[8] Burton, *Zanzibar*, II, 53.

THE SWAHILI COAST

most of their cattle and the Mombasa garrison commander seized advantage of their plight to capture the remainder of their livestock.[1]

After 1837 there was never any serious threat to Sa'id's rule from the inhabitants of Mombasa. The Mazruis did, however, raise a small revolt in 1839 from their new base at Gazi. After they were defeated at Mombasa some Mazruis went north to Takaungu and some south to Gazi. Those at Takaungu lacked the resources to raise effective opposition – they had only three small vessels in which they sent the grain they produced to Mukalla – and they may even have paid customs dues to the Sultan of Zanzibar.[2] Those at Gazi, however, were in a stronger position. They were led by a spirited woman, Khasa binti Ahmad, the former governor Salim ibn Ahmad's sister, who gained the allegiance of 500 slaves. In 1839 they swept down on Tanga and were only repulsed when soldiers were sent from Zanzibar.[3] This was the last time the Mazruis made a bid for power in Saiyid Sa'id's reign; when Burton visited Gazi in 1857 the Mazruis had settled down to an agricultural existence.[4]

There was never any chance of the Mazruis regaining the position which they had formerly held in Pemba. Nasir ibn Sulaiman, Sa'id's first governor there, was killed by the Mazruis after his surrender in Mombasa fort,[5] but he must have been replaced by somebody equally loyal to the Sultan because there is no record of any trouble from Pemba in Sa'id's reign. In 1841 the Omani governor was one Nasir ibn Khalaf, who was later succeeded by his son, Muhammad.[6] There was also an Indian customs master and a garrison of twenty men. Pemba developed into a commercial community with several Indian residents, and also proved as fertile as Zanzibar for the cultivation of cloves.[7] Following his usual practice, Saiyid Sa'id retained the traditional political system, with its *diwani*.[8]

Once the Omanis had become deeply involved in the struggle to obtain the Lamu archipelago and Mombasa their expansion in other

---

[1] Burton, *Zanzibar*, II, 71.

[2] Krapf, *op. cit.*, pp. 114-16; and Guillain, *Documents*, III, 265.

[3] Local agent at Muscat to Bombay, 12 Mch. 1839, encl. in Bombay to Secret Committee, no. 87, 16 July 1839, E.S.L.B. 14; Guillain, *Documents*, III, 264; and Omari bin Stamboul, *op. cit.*, p. 35.

[4] Burton, *Zanzibar*, II, 105-6.

[5] Mazrui MS., p. 59. For a different version, Guillain, *Documents*, I, 594.

[6] Hamerton to Bombay, 15 May 1841, Z.A.; Loarer's Report, Part II, 1849, M.O., O.I. 2/10; and Burton, *Zanzibar*, II, 11-12.

[7] Burton, *idem*.   [8] Ingrams, *op. cit.*, pp. 158-9.

THE SWAHILI COAST AND OMANI AUTHORITY

places began to accelerate. The ports on the mainland littoral opposite Zanzibar, known as the Mrima, were points of exit for most of the ivory and slaves which passed through Zanzibar. They were therefore potential sources of customs revenue as well as desirable places to hold in order to control the trade. Since the northernmost settlements of the Mrima – from Pangani northwards – owed some allegiance to Mombasa,[1] Saiyid Sa'id had to ensure that they gave that town no assistance during his campaign against it. By 1824 Sa'id's forces had already harassed Wasin and Tanga. The inhabitants of Wasin had been driven off their island and robbed of their vessels, property and slaves, and Tanga's population had fallen to 300, to the serious detriment of its ivory trade.[2] The traditional history of Wasin describes the advent of the Omanis thus: when the *diwani* of Wasin, who feared that Saiyid Sa'id would treat his town in the same way as he had Pate, heard the Omani ships were near, he fled to the mainland with his people. Sa'id's force then called at Wasin, found it deserted, and sacked the town. Afterwards the people returned to their settlement.[3] Saiyid Sa'id did not follow up his action by appointing governors to Wasin and Tanga, probably because at the time he was too involved elsewhere, and he considered them of minor importance. They retained their traditional methods of government and continued their connexion with Mombasa.[4] When Mombasa was finally overcome, Saiyid Sa'id found it unnecessary to place officials in these towns, but in 1839 he had to do so at Tanga. That year the Mazruis of Gazi attacked Tanga, whereupon Sa'id despatched thither Sulaiman ibn Hamad and Muhyi al-Din, together with some soldiers. Fifteen soldiers were then left in Tanga and a fort was constructed.[5] In 1856 the garrison was still present at Tanga.[6]

About 1839 there was a general expansion of Saiyid Sa'id's activities on this section of the coastline. This was a direct result of Zanzibar's developing commercial interests and the Sultan's determination to control trade in the Mrima region. The arrival of American and European merchants meant that customs duties had to be regulated by treaty. It occurred to Sa'id that merchants might go directly to ports on the African coast where there were no customs officials, and thus

---

[1] See Chapter II, p. 59.
[2] Boteler, *op. cit.*, II, 178 and 181.
[3] Hollis, *op. cit.*, p. 290.
[4] Emery's Journal, entry for 2 Apr. 1825.
[5] Local agent at Muscat to Bombay, 12 Mch. 1839, encl. in Bombay to Secret Committee, no. 87, 16 July 1839, E.S.L.B. 14; Omari bin Stamboul, *op. cit.*, p. 35; and Guillain, *Documents*, III, 264.
[6] Burton, *Zanzibar*, II, 116.

THE SWAHILI COAST

evade paying the duties stipulated in the treaties. He tried to prevent this by prohibiting Europeans from visiting the Mrima region, but he still had another problem to face – that of the Indian merchants, who would now sail under the British flag in order to pay only the 5 per cent import duty applicable to British merchants.[1] Saiyid Saʻid therefore had to place customs officials, many of whom were supported by a few soldiers, at all the major Mrima ports.

There were a number of reasons why Saʻid's officials were acceptable to the inhabitants of the Mrima settlements. In the first place, the Sultan allowed the local systems of government to continue, although he did insist on exercising a personal right to approve the *diwani* who were chosen as rulers.[2] It is not clear what happened to the *diwani's* former methods of raising revenue when Saʻid took over the collection of customs dues, but it is likely that local rulers retained some proportion of the dues for themselves.[3] Furthermore, Saʻid's authority was acceptable because it provided some protection, even if only theoretical, against the hinterland peoples who remained a continuous threat to the littoral villages. Behind Pangani and the settlements immediately to its north dwelt the Digo, Segeju, and Shambala peoples. The hinterland a little to the south was inhabited by the Zigua. These groups had feuds among each other which affected the coastal villages because they could influence the safe penetration of caravans and could force the villages to take sides. The Shambala, headed by the chief Kimwere, had feuds with the Digo and Zigua, but were on friendly terms with the Segeju, who were also hostile to the Zigua.[4] In 1857 Burton observed that of late years the people of Tanga had been having trouble with the Digo and had turned to both Kimwere and the Zigua for protection.[5] But in those years Kimwere himself was in difficulties with his neighbours and had to seek assistance from Saiyid Saʻid.

The relationship the Sultan of Zanzibar had with the powerful chief of the Shambala was similar to that which he enjoyed with Yusuf of the Banadir hinterland. Uninterested in territorial expansion as such, Saʻid was content that the hinterland of Pangani should be ruled by a chief not hostile to his interests. He was satisfied that the littoral villages owed some allegiance to Kimwere as long as they also recognized his

---

[1] For Saʻid's concern about this matter, Guillain, 'Côte de Zanguébar et Mascate, 1841', in *Revue Coloniale* (Paris, 1843), p. 543.
[2] Krapf, *op. cit.*, p. 416; and Burton, *Zanzibar*, II, 109, 121, 124, 136 and 148.
[3] For evidence that they did so, Velten, *Desturi*, pp. 230-1.
[4] Burton, *Zanzibar*, II, 119 and 149.   [5] *Ibid.*, p. 119.

own authority. Kimwere had influence in the appointment of *diwani* (in fact both Krapf and Burton claim that Kimwere actually appointed the *diwani* of Pangani),[1] and he also required them to give him presents of cloth every two or three years.[2] This arrangement was acceptable to the Sultan of Zanzibar who had to keep on good terms with the Shambala because the great inland caravan route from Pangani passed through their territory. It was probably to protect this route against Zigua raids that,[3] towards the end of his reign, Sa'id established two garrisons a short distance inland behind Pangani – at Chogwe and Tongwe, seven and nine miles respectively from the coast. The garrisons were, however, small – there was a commander and twenty soldiers at Chogwe but only two Baluchis at Tongwe.[4] There are two other explanations for Sa'id's establishment of these garrisons. Burton, who actually visited the two forts in 1858, said they were the result of a response by an angry Sa'id to Krapf's claims that the Sultan had 'not one inch of ground between the island of Wasin and the River Pangani'.[5] They may, however, have been built after a disagreement between Sa'id and Kimwere.[6]

The garrisons at Chogwe and Tongwe were the farthest inland that Saiyid Sa'id ever placed soldiers. South of Pangani he confined his authority to the coastal villages. The settlements on the littoral between Pangani and Mafia, which had formerly owed no allegiance to either Mombasa in the north or Kilwa in the south, were especially vulnerable to the whims of hinterland peoples, and may therefore have welcomed any approach by the Sultan of Zanzibar. Since these villages – the most prominent of which were Buyuni, Sadani, Bagamoyo, Kaole, and Mbwemaji – were directly opposite Zanzibar and were the exit points for caravans from the rich Unyamwesi region, they must have come early to the attention of the Zanzibar authorities. It is most likely that Zanzibar agreed to defend them with a governor and a few soldiers in return for receiving the right to collect customs duties. In fact, in 1841 Hamerton reported that many chiefs on the coast had become subject to Sa'id's authority on the condition that he would protect them, and a few years later a Frenchman confirmed this view when he said that

[1] *Ibid.*, p. 148; and Krapf, *op. cit.*, p. 416.   [2] Krapf, *op. cit.*, p. 375.
[3] Erhardt to Venn, 9 Apr. 1853, F.O. 54/15. For Zigua raids, see also Burton, *Zanzibar*, II, 149.
[4] Burton, *Zanzibar*, II, 159 and 172; and Speke, *op. cit.*, p. 174.
[5] Burton, *Zanzibar*, II, 159.
[6] For the disagreement, Erhardt to Venn, 9 Apr. 1853, F.O. 54/15.

the coastal chiefs had to seek a more powerful protector in order to survive among their turbulent neighbours.[1] A traditional history of Bagamoyo claims that the *jumbe* of that village asked for Sa'id's assistance because the Doe were making exorbitant demands on them.[2] It is not easy to date the placing of governors, garrisons, and customs officials at Bagamoyo, Kaole, Buyuni, Mbwemaji, and Sadani, but it is most probable that this was done before 1840.[3]

In actual fact the protection Sa'id could give the littoral villages was limited. Behind them dwelt the Zigua, Doe and Zaramo,[4] who posed not so much a physical danger to the coastal villages as a commercial threat; they could charge exorbitant passage dues to caravans travelling to and from the coast and thereby disrupt trade. The Zigua were the most formidable as they early acquired firearms. There were also occasional skirmishes between the hinterland peoples and the littoral villages: for example, a host of Zaramo attacked Kaole in 1844 and young men sometimes undertook plundering expeditions to Bagamoyo and Mbwemaji. Caravans, too, were subject to attack if inadequately armed: in 1856, for example, Salim ibn Nasir Al Bu Sa'idi was murdered on a caravan in the Usagara mountains.[5]

Saiyid Sa'id could do very little about such disturbances. He wanted as far as possible to avoid involvements with the African peoples because he had neither the means nor the inclination to expand territorially into Africa. He could neither control the hinterland peoples nor assume responsibility for keeping peace between them without employing large armies of men, which he did not possess. He did, however, offer a limited protection to the coastal settlements. In 1844 his men defended Kaole when it was attacked by the Zaramo,[6] and in 1847 he very reluctantly took action to avenge the murder by a Zaramo

---

[1] Hamerton to Bombay, 13 July 1851, Z.A.; and Passot, commander of Mayotte, to Ministry of Marine, 22 Oct. 1846, M.O., Madag. 270/605.

[2] The History of Bagamoyo, printed in Velten, *Prosa und Poesie*, pp. 300-5, and in Freeman-Grenville, *Select Documents*, pp. 238-40.

[3] For the governor at Buyuni, Krapf, *op. cit.*, p. 418; for the governor at Sadani, Burton, *Zanzibar*, II, 272; for the garrisons at Kaole and Bagamoyo, Burton, *Lake Regions*, I, 13, 20, and 89.

[4] Krapf, *op. cit.*, pp. 392 and 418; Burton, *Zanzibar*, II, 267-8, and *Lake Regions*, I, 43-4, 107, 123, and 125. For the present position and details of the history of these peoples, see T. O. Beidelman, *The Matrilineal Peoples of Eastern Tanzania* (London, 1967).

[5] For all the above information, Burton, *Lake Regions*, I, 44, 112-13, 125, and 233.

[6] *Ibid.*, pp. 43-4.

chief of the French explorer Maizan. It is unlikely that he would have done anything in the latter case had he not been strongly pressed to take action by the French and been loath to admit to Europeans that he had no authority over hinterland peoples.[1] As it was, the action he took could not have antagonized the Zaramo. Although he claimed that he had despatched 400 men, captured the principal minister of the offending chieftain, and burned his village, in fact all he really did was to seize a Zaramo villager and hand him over to the French for punishment.[2]

Despite the restricted protection offered by the Sultan of Zanzibar, the littoral villages were content to accept his governors and customs officials provided their own arrangements were not too stringently interfered with. Following his usual practice, Saiyid Sa'id allowed the local systems of government to continue.[3]

This was not the case, however, with Kilwa Kisiwani, further to the south. The rulers of Kilwa, like those of Mombasa, had been rather more powerful than the numerous petty *diwani* and *jumbe* of the Mrima settlements, and they were consequently more dangerous to the Sultan. For a while he retained the sultanate of Kilwa, but he gradually eroded its powers. This task was made easier by the economic decline of Kilwa Kisiwani. In 1819 it was already being described as 'a miserable village', and by 1842 the 2,000–3,000 inhabitants had shrunk to a mere few hundred.[4] By the original agreement made with Zanzibar, the sultan of Kilwa retained one-fifth of the customs dues provided by the town's declining commerce,[5] but later even this prerogative was removed. According to one story, Sa'id curtailed the privilege by sending the governor of Zanzibar to Kilwa to lure the three brothers of the ruling family on to his ship and sail away with them to Muscat. He then offered to release them in return for being given the whole of Kilwa's revenues. He did, however, offer a small palliative by allowing the sultan of Kilwa quarter of a dollar for each slave exported from Kilwa to Muslim states.

[1] At first Sa'id told the governor of Bourbon that the Zaramo chief was one of his subjects, but later he admitted that this was not so – R. Desfossés to Ministry of F.A., no. 8, 27 Feb. 1846, M.O., Madag. 17/32; and Guillain to Saiyid Sa'id, 5 Oct. 1846, M.O., O.I. 2/10.

[2] Saiyid Sa'id to R. Desfossés, 31 Dec. 1846, and Guillain to Ministry of Marine, 24 Oct. 1847, M.O., O.I. 2/10.

[3] Burton, *Lake Regions*, I, 16-17.

[4] Albrand's Report, 1819, M.O., Réunion 72/472; and Kerdudal, 'Quiloa ou Keloua', *Revue Coloniale* (Paris, Feb. 1844), pp. 215-17. For 2,000–3,000 inhabitants, Prior, *op. cit.*, p. 69.

[5] See Chapter I, p. 33.

THE SWAHILI COAST

The offer was accepted and the three brothers returned home.[1] No date is given for this event, but it is likely that it occurred after 1822 because the use of the words 'Muslim states' in the conditions for release indicates that the Moresby treaty had already been arranged.

The sultanate of Kilwa seems to have been still in existence in the late 1840s when Loarer visited the region, because he did not remark on its disappearance. In fact, the 'king of the Mrima' mentioned a few years previously by both Norsworthy and Kerdudal may well have been the sultan of Kilwa.[2] Kerdudal named this person as Sultan Assagni [Hasan] and said that, although the Sultan of Zanzibar was suzerain over the region, Hasan was independent of his governors and retained in his own hands the 'rights of jurisdiction and justice'. In 1843 another visitor, Passot, also reported the existence of a sultan of Kilwa, commenting on the ill-feeling between him and the Sultan of Zanzibar.[3] Sometime after Loarer's visit Saiyid Sa'id seized and deported to Muscat the last sultan of Kilwa, Muhammad, and the ruling clan was scattered abroad.[4] There is an unfortunate absence of information about this event, and one can only speculate that it was the result of Saiyid Sa'id's expanding authority and the rising importance of nearby Kilwa Kivinje. By 1859 Kilwa Kisiwani had declined into a small fishing village.[5]

During the first half of the nineteenth century Kilwa Kivinje, seventeen miles to the north of Kilwa Kisiwani, became the most important port between Zanzibar and Mozambique. According to Burton, Kilwa Kivinje was built by the inhabitants of Kilwa Kisiwani when fleeing from Saiyid Sa'id, but, if this were the case, they must have occupied an already existing village because Morice mentioned Kivinje in the 1770s.[6] A local tradition maintains that Kivinje was founded by three families who came from the Lake Nyasa region towards the end of the eighteenth century.[7] Whatever its origins, Kivinje was important enough by 1819 to have had an Omani governor appointed.[8] By the 1840s Kivinje was the destination for all the great caravans from the Lake Nyasa region, and its commercial movement was immense in

[1] Loarer's Report, Part II, 1849, M.O., O.I. 2/10.
[2] Kerdudal, 'Quiloa ou Keloua', as above, and Norsworthy to Bombay Chamber of Commerce, n.d., 1841, F.O. 54/4.
[3] Passot to governor of Bourbon, 6 Sept. 1843, M.O., O.I. 15/59.
[4] Burton, *Zanzibar*, II, 366. [5] *Ibid.*, p. 367.
[6] *Ibid.*, p. 341, and Morice, 'Projet d'un établissement', p. 62.
[7] 'Some notes on Kilwa compiled from various sources', *T.N.R.*, no. 2 (Oct. 1836), p. 94.
[8] Albrand's Report, 1819, M.O., Réunion 72/472.

comparison with that of other ports in the area. It had thirty stone houses, an unusually large number for a Swahili settlement of that time, and its customs house was the finest on the East African coast.[1] Its population had also reached large proportions: in 1844 Krapf estimated it as 12,000-15,000, and in 1848 Loarer reckoned it was 50,000.[2]

Because Kivinje lacked a tradition of local rulership, it might have seemed easier for the Sultan of Zanzibar to maintain uninterrupted authority there and derive great commercial benefit. This was not, however, the case. Although Sa'id did keep a governor and garrison at Kivinje, the person he chose as governor caused him difficulties in the early 1840s. This was partly the result of Sa'id's attempts to compromise with European powers over the sale of slaves and the reluctance of the Kilwa officials, who made great profits from the slave trade, to comply with their ruler's orders. In 1841 Saiyid Sa'id arrested the governor and customs master of Kilwa Kivinje because they were putting commercial obstructions in his way.[3] Thereafter the position seems to have improved because when *La Grenouille* visited Kivinje in 1848 the governor obeyed Sa'id's restrictions on European trading with the Mrima and refused to allow it to make purchases.[4] Shortly afterwards Loarer, who was making commercial enquiries in the region, was treated in an unfriendly manner.[5]

Kivinje's example showed that the Sultan of Zanzibar faced dangers not only from discontented Swahili rulers but also from his own officials. In this instance he was able to regain control. His influence in this southern region was not, however, firmly established. In Mafia, for example, his authority was slight. There the 'notable' Swahili families retained their position as the commercial elite and also exercised more authority than Saiyid Sa'id's governor. In the late 1840s the al-Shatri family provided the local ruler, who was Sa'id Bakr ibn Abdullah al-Shatri.[6]

[1] Loarer's Report, Part II, 1849, M.O., O.I. 2/10; and Burton, *Zanzibar*, II, 342.
[2] Krapf, *op. cit.*, p. 243, and Loarer, as above.
[3] Hamerton's Report on the Proceedings of the French, 1842, F.O. 54/4; and Hamerton to Bombay, no. 2, 2 Jan. 1842, encl. in Bombay to Secret Committee, no. 43, 30 Apr. 1842, E.S.L.B. 44.
[4] Journal of *La Grenouille* (Capt. Bisson), entry for 6 Sept. 1849, A.E., Zanz. C.C.1.
[5] Loarer's Report, Part II, 1849, M.O., O.I. 2/10.
[6] *Idem.* For the Omani governor, Amr Umar Sa'adi, 'The History and Traditions of Mafia', *T.N.R.*, no. 12 (Dec. 1941), pp. 23-7.

THE SWAHILI COAST

South of Kilwa Kivinje lay the three settlements of Kisuere, Lindi, and Tongui. Kisuere had no governor or customs master appointed by Zanzibar[1] and consequently gained in importance as the restrictions on the sale of slaves to Europeans were more firmly enforced. In 1827 an American ship reported that the French were trading there for slaves, and in the 1840s Krapf saw there two slave vessels bound for Mozambique.[2] Europeans made similar use of Lindi to load slaves clandestinely, but there Saiyid Sa'id did maintain a governor and garrison, which had been imposed some time before 1824.[3] None the less one of the rulers of Lindi, Ibrahim ibn Isa (whether he was a local Swahili ruler or a governor appointed by Saiyid Sa'id is unclear) took a very independent line and terrorized the neighbouring coast, committing acts of piracy on passing vessels. Ibrahim died in 1833/4 and was succeeded by his brother Muhammad. By the late 1840s the situation was calm once again and two Indians appointed by Jairam, the customs master at Zanzibar, were levying customs dues at Lindi.[4] It was also at some settlement in this region that Saiyid Sa'id suffered trouble from a rebel leader in 1826.[5]

Tongui was the southernmost point on the Swahili Coast over which Saiyid Sa'id claimed authority. He did not appoint any officials there until the 1840s because there was a long-standing dispute with the Portuguese about whether it came under his or their jurisdiction. The matter was settled in Sa'id's favour in 1843 when the governor of Mozambique visited Zanzibar.[6]

It would have been difficult for the Omanis to expand any further south than Tongui because the Portuguese had been in possession of the Mozambique region for centuries. Sa'id did, however, try to claim some southern islands, particularly Mohelli and Grand Comore, with which Zanzibar had commercial links.[7] He also had dreams of some

---

[1] Loarer's Report, Part II, 1849, M.O., O.I. 2/10.

[2] Log of the brig *Ann* of Salem, entry for 17 Nov. 1827, printed in Bennett and Brooks, *op. cit.*, p. 148; and Krapf, *op. cit.*, p. 430.

[3] Boteler, *op. cit.*, II, 48. See also E. Roberts to L. McLane, 14 May 1834, printed in Bennett and Brooks, *op. cit.*, p. 157. For the slaves, log of *Ann*, as above.

[4] Loarer's Report, Part II, 1849, M.O., O.I. 2/10.

[5] See Chapter X, pp. 266-7.

[6] Hamerton to Bombay, 24 Aug. 1843, Z.A. Gray, *History of Zanzibar*, pp. 175-9, describes Saiyid Sa'id's relations with the Portuguese.

[7] For the commerce, Massieu to Freycinet, 9 Oct. 1822, M.O., Réunion 72/473.

sort of alliance with Madagascar, where a few Omani traders had settled.¹ His attention may well have been drawn to Madagascar when the ruler Radama expelled Arab merchants from Bombetok in the 1820s.² Soon afterwards Radama was succeeded by Queen Ranavalano, with whom Saiyid Sa'id tried to make a marriage alliance. His offer was refused by the queen³ but, undaunted, he then tried to obtain the co-operation of her enemies, the Sakalava. When the French became interested in their territory, the Sakalava were glad to accept Sa'id's offer of protection, and treaties were arranged to this effect.⁴ Sa'id's initial intention was to place a garrison in the region, but he had so many commitments nearer home that he had to be content with keeping agents in the Comoro islands and making representations to the French that they should avoid the area. He also tried to involve the British in supporting his slender claims. Although the British were anxious to prevent French expansion in the region, after making an investigation they thought Sa'id's claims too flimsy to uphold and refused to help him.⁵ The French also ignored Sa'id's complaints.⁶ He made one last unsuccessful attempt to establish himself in the region in 1850, when he offered to marry the queen of Mohelli.⁷

By 1856 the Sultan of Zanzibar could claim some sort of authority over most of the towns and villages of the East African coast between Lamu in the north and Tongui in the south. This represented a considerable extension of Omani rule since the time of his accession. The conditions which allowed this extension had indeed existed at the beginning of Saiyid Sa'id's reign. The Omanis had already been present on the Swahili Coast for a century. Commercial links had been developed and Omani influence was making itself felt at several places along the coast. The local systems of government also provided favourable conditions for Omani expansion. The agitated political state

[1] *Idem.*
[2] Instructions to Vailhen from governor of Bourbon, 1834, M.O., Réunion 86/569.
[3] Hart's Report, Proc. 21 May 1834, B.P.C. 387/58.
[4] See Chapter VII, pp. 167-8.   [5] See Chapter VII, p. 173.
[6] Noel to Ministry of F.A., 15 July 1842, A.E., Zanz. C.C.1; Governor of Bourbon to commander of *Crocodile*, 17 Oct. 1846, Passot to Ministry of Marine, 22 Oct. 1846, and Belligny to Ministry of F.A., 27 Mch. 1850, M.O., Madag. 270/605; R. Desfossés to Ministry of F.A., no. 8, 27 Feb. 1846, M.O., Madag. 17/32; and R. Desfossés to Ministry of Marine, 3 Feb. 1847, A.N., Marine BB4/651.
[7] E. Bolle's Report on the voyage of *Le Chasseur*, 22 May 1850, M.O., Madag. 270/605.

of several settlements afforded fertile ground for interference by outsiders.

However, if the Omanis were to consolidate and extend their position on the Swahili Coast they required a stimulus. This was provided by the Mazrui interference in the Lamu archipelago which threatened to disturb the *status quo*. The entry of the British in support of the Mazruis made the situation infinitely more serious for Sa'id. He envisaged losing his entire position on the Swahili Coast. As soon as events in Oman and the Persian Gulf allowed him a respite he went personally to East Africa in order to assert his interests. Thereafter, he entered upon an involvement in the political squabbles of the Swahili Coast, an involvement from which he would have been reluctant to withdraw. There was seldom a period when he could relax his vigilance. At first he embarked on a campaign against the Mazruis, and then found it necessary to subdue Pate. Meanwhile pockets of resistance arose in places like Tanga and Kilwa Kivinje. His was not a sudden decision to overcome all the Swahili Coast; rather he was drawn into a web of interrelated political adventures. This political involvement was reinforced by the successful economic development of Zanzibar, a development which was itself encouraged by European and American interests. The Europeans posed a political threat, but they also offered a commercial market. Saiyid Sa'id devoted himself to striking a balance on the Swahili Coast between welcome foreign trade and undesirable foreign competition. That he succeeded in this was largely due to the fact that the Europeans had not yet started to expand politically in this area. At the same time the startling success of clove-planting and the development of Zanzibar and Pemba as plantation islands made it increasingly improbable that Saiyid Sa'id would return to Oman.

The system which the Omanis established on the Swahili Coast during the first half of the nineteenth century would have collapsed had they not achieved the co-operation of sections of the local populace, a co-operation which was won partly by leaving the details of local administration in the hands of traditional leaders. The system did not allow local leaders who were openly hostile or obstructive to remain in office but it did give an opportunity for Swahili notables who were prepared to arrange some compromise to continue their former way of life. The petty *diwani* and *jumbe* of the Mrima region were therefore more likely to remain in office than the ambitious and powerful leaders of the larger towns. They were also the ones who would derive most benefit from the protection of an alien overlord. Provided Zanzibar

THE SWAHILI COAST AND OMANI AUTHORITY

did not interfere too stringently with their own arrangements they might even have sought and certainly have welcomed a governor, garrison, and customs master. This capacity to exercise control while at the same time avoiding responsibility for internal details was essential to the success of Sa'id's regime on the Swahili Coast. The biggest disadvantage as far as the Swahilis were concerned was that the newcomers might usurp their livelihood. Although this did happen in certain cases – particularly in Zanzibar – in general the Swahilis participated in and benefited from the economic expansion. Perhaps this was the major reason why, despite political turbulence on a local level, the Omanis' rule on the Swahili Coast avoided provoking large-scale Swahili resistance.

CHAPTER XII

THE ECONOMIC DEVELOPMENT OF THE SWAHILI COAST

The economy of the Swahili Coast expanded steadily between 1820 and 1856. To some extent this was a continuation of a process which had already begun, but there were also momentous developments which accelerated the process and caused it to assume new characteristics.

It was shown in Chapter III that conditions for further economic expansion were favourable in 1820. Omani Arabs maintained a regular intercourse with East African ports, and Indian merchants lived there seasonally in considerable numbers, providing necessary financial services as well as a lively market. The centralization of trade at Zanzibar enabled the Omanis better to control the commercial movement of the Swahili Coast and to embark upon the task of transforming Zanzibar into a centre of production. They had recently planted cloves which were thriving in the coastal climate.

After 1820 the commercial movement of the Swahili Coast was stimulated by new factors. In the first place, the British began to protest about the East African Slave Trade. Saiyid Sa'id was prepared to go a certain distance towards meeting their demands that it be suppressed, particularly since he thought that some limited acquiescence would have little effect upon his own prosperity and that of his people. But he and other Omanis none the less took the safe course of diversifying their economic activities in case they should be hard hit by the restrictions. It was at this time – in the late 1820s and the 1830s – that they acquired land on Zanzibar island and planted cloves. Certainly Saiyid Sa'id himself obtained large estates, although one cannot be sure that this was entirely due to the apprehension he felt when he introduced measures to curtail the sale of slaves to Europeans.

THE ECONOMIC DEVELOPMENT OF THE COAST

Although the personal role of Saiyid Sa'id in the economic development of the Swahili Coast should not be overstressed, it does appear that at the outset he encouraged those activities which were to prove the most successful commercial ventures. The arrangement in 1822 of the Moresby Treaty to limit the Slave Trade coincided with the reluctance of the Mombasans to accept Sa'id's authority and their subsequent support by the British. These political considerations caused Saiyid Sa'id to affirm his authority on the Swahili Coast and to pay it a personal visit in 1828. At this juncture he decided to tighten his economic ties with the region, an intention which was encouraged by his observation that cloves planted in Zanzibar some years beforehand were thriving. By 1834 Saiyid Sa'id was influencing the development of Zanzibar as a plantation island by order as well as example. Not only had he planted a large area of his own land with cloves, but he had also issued instructions that estates would be confiscated unless their owners planted three clove trees for every coconut tree.[1]

Just as Western interests prompted Sa'id to strengthen his hold on East Africa, so also they helped to provide the market for the produce which resulted from that extended authority. The French had been trading for some time with the Swahili Coast, but now other Western merchants appeared – the British and Americans. The advent of the British was due in part to their political manœuvrings and the consequent increase in their knowledge of the region. Early in the 1830s a British firm, Newman Hunt and Christopher, started to trade with East Africa. They may have been encouraged in this enterprise by the favourable reports of Emery and Owen about the area's economic potential because in the *Journal of the Royal Geographical Society* printed in 1833 there appeared an account of Mombasa by Lt Emery,[2] and in the same year Newman Hunt sent the brig *Sandwich* on an experimental voyage to the East African coast under the direction of R. B. Norsworthy.[3] Newman Hunt may also have been influenced by the reports of Nathaniel Isaacs, who had visited East Africa in 1831/2 in the brig *Mary* and who believed that 'Eastern Africa offers a scene for commercial enterprise which ought not to be neglected by so extensive a commercial and manufacturing nation as Great Britain'.[4]

[1] Hart's Report, Proc. 21 May 1834, B.P.C. 387/58; and Pearce, *op. cit.*, p. 122. For the development of the clove plantations, see Chapter X, pp. 283-4.
[2] Emery, 'A Short Account of Mombas', *J.R.G.S.*, vol. III (1833), pp. 280-3.
[3] Petition from Newman Hunt, Proc. 20 Dec. 1837, B.P.C. 388/50.
[4] Isaacs, *op. cit.*, II, 326.

Isaacs' descriptions were not published until 1836, but Newman Hunt may have heard about his voyage privately, a conjecture which is supported by his despatch of his first vessel to Lamu, about which Isaacs had given a particularly favourable account.

It seems to have been a mere coincidence that American traders came to the East African coast at the same time as Saiyid Sa'id began to show a wider interest in the region. But it was a happy coincidence because the Americans provided the market which stimulated East Africa to develop its commerce. The Americans first came to the Swahili Coast in 1818 when Captain Forbes of the *Titus* made commercial enquiries at Zanzibar. Three years later his brother sold a cargo there.[1] Gradually American ships began to trade with Zanzibar, but they were hindered by the restrictions and impositions on foreign merchants issued by its governor.[2] They might have abandoned their enterprise had not one trader – Edmund Roberts – taken advantage of Sa'id's visit to East Africa in 1828 to negotiate more favourable terms for the Americans.[3] In contrast with his East African officials, whose policy was to exact the highest possible tariffs from foreign merchants, Saiyid Sa'id foresaw the opportunities of an expanded market which should result from better terms of trade. He agreed to proposals for a treaty, which was signed in 1833.[4] The treaty's most important stipulation was that Americans would pay only 5 per cent duty on the articles they took to the Swahili Coast and no duty at all on those they bought there. Now the way lay open for the expansion of American trade with East Africa.

Between 1830 and 1837 thirty-three visits to Zanzibar were made by American merchant vessels.[5] At first their main purchases were of gum copal and ivory, which they exchanged for specie and guns. Later, in about 1837, they bought the cloves which had begun to come on to the Zanzibar market in exportable quantities. They soon found they were taking from Zanzibar rather more than they brought and had to pay for the excess in specie. Consequently they tried out American cottons on the Zanzibar market – an experiment which was to have profound effects.[6]

[1] Broquant to Ministry of F.A., no. 4, 12 Mch. 1845, A.E., Zanz. C.C.1.
[2] See Chapter III, pp. 80-1.
[3] E. Roberts to Saiyid Sa'id, 27 Jan. 1828, Z.A.
[4] For the events leading to the treaty, see Chapter VI, pp. 149-51.
[5] List compiled by N. Bennett in 'Americans in Zanzibar, 1825-1845', *T.N.R.*, no. 56 (Mch. 1961), pp. 93-108 (here pp. 107-8).
[6] For their articles of trade, Journal of R. P. Waters, entries for 2, 3, and 19 Aug. 1837, printed in Bennett and Brooks, *op. cit.*, pp. 201-3; and Guillain, 'Côte

THE ECONOMIC DEVELOPMENT OF THE COAST

The interests of the Americans in Zanzibar were furthered in 1837 when R. P. Waters was appointed American consul. Himself a merchant, he devoted himself to expanding American trade with Zanzibar.[1] Waters worked in partnership with Jairam, the customs master, buying and selling cargoes only through his agency: indeed, by December 1839 Waters was doing nine-tenths of his business through Jairam.[2] Captains of incoming vessels would give Waters details of their cargoes and this information the consul would pass on to Jairam, who would then call the merchants together at Waters' house, show them samples, and fix a price. The goods ordered would then be delivered to Jairam who would pay for them and distribute them to their purchasers.[3] This system could work as long as there was only restricted competition between American or European firms and prices could be maintained at a reasonable level. Soon, however, the number of American firms trading to Zanzibar began to expand and Jairam saw that he would make greater profits if he had dealings with more merchants. He therefore ceased to work so closely with Waters.

Initially the American merchants thought that the British traders at Zanzibar would be serious rivals. Newman Hunt and Christopher started business in an adventurous manner, working through the agency of Khamis ibn Uthman, who had accompanied Owen on his East African voyage in the early 1820s. They also maintained a British agent, R. B. Norsworthy, in Zanzibar. They developed the practice of using small vessels to bring goods from the mainland littoral to Zanzibar: for example, two or three small schooners were kept in the Lamu area to procure hides. Apprehensive of competition, an American merchant said disconsolately that Hunt's vessels 'swarmed the coast'.[4] Although the method employed by the British firm was presumably designed to by-pass local middlemen, it turned out to be too expensive. Soon the firm ran into financial difficulties and Hunt went out to

de Zanguébar et Mascate, 1841', *Revue Coloniale* (Paris, 1843), p. 527. The latter will hereafter be cited as *Côte de Zanguébar*.

[1] For the consul's early connexion with the firm of Shepard and Bertram, Journal of R. P. Waters, entry for 9 June 1837, printed in Bennett and Brooks, *op. cit.*, p. 198.

[2] R. P. Waters to W. C. Waters, 17 Dec. 1839, printed in Bennett and Brooks, *op. cit.*, p. 223.

[3] R. P. Waters to P. S. Parker, 1 Jan. 1840, *ibid.*, pp. 224-5.

[4] J. G. Waters to G. West, 30 May 1838, *ibid.*, p. 221. For a description of the British methods, Guillain *Côte de Zanguébar*, pp. 529-34.

Zanzibar to investigate.[1] Dissatisfied with Norsworthy's management of his business, he replaced him with Thorn.[2] There was, however, little improvement. A major difficulty was the commercial manipulations of Jairam and Waters, which forced most foreign vessels to purchase and sell goods through their agency. Since all articles had to pass through the hands of the customs master, he had first option of purchase, or could give preference to any buyer he wished. A further problem was that Jairam would inform potential purchasers of the valuation of the goods which he had made when levying customs dues. Any purchaser who possessed such information could therefore refuse to pay the higher prices demanded by the seller.[3] Norsworthy, who carried on his own business at Zanzibar after his dismissal by Hunt, complained bitterly to Bombay about this state of affairs.[4] It was partly as a result of his protests that British officials became really aware of the commercial opportunities offered by the Swahili Coast and established a consulate at Zanzibar.[5]

By the end of the 1830s, then, one of the essential conditions for economic development had occurred on the Swahili Coast – the market had been expanded by the entry of foreign buyers. The economic expansion of the region continued throughout the remainder of Saiyid Sa'id's reign. It is necessary to investigate how far European and American trade continued to stimulate the economy of the Swahili Coast after its initial impact; what proportion of the total value of the region's trade the Western enterprises represented; and whether or to what extent Western merchants usurped the position of Indian and Arab traders.

The Americans continued to be the most prominent Western merchants in Zanzibar. Their success was partly due to the rivalry which existed between the different American houses. The two largest

[1] Journal of R. P. Waters, 7 Aug. 1837, printed in Bennett and Brooks, *op. cit.*, p. 202.
[2] For Norsworthy's general misconduct, Cogan to India Board, 9 June 1838, F.O. 54/2. For Thorn, J. G. Waters to G. West, 30 May 1838, printed in Bennett and Brooks, *op. cit.*, p. 221.
[3] Hamerton to Bombay, no. 8, 3 Feb. 1842, encl. in Bombay to Secret Committee, no. 57, 23 May 1842, E.S.L.B. 45; and Loarer's Report, Part I, 1849, M.O., O.I. 5/23.
[4] Norsworthy to Secretary of Bombay Chamber of Commerce, n.d., 1841, F.O. 54/4. For Norsworthy's business, Hamerton to Norsworthy, 19 Sept. 1843, Z.A.
[5] See Chapters VI and VII.

THE ECONOMIC DEVELOPMENT OF THE COAST

of these were the firms of Pingree and West, and Shepard and Bertram. Waters, the American consul, did some business to start with for Shepard, but he later became the agent for Pingree and West. When he retired from the consulate, the Shepard concern was quick to offer the new consul the job of being their agent, even though they already had a satisfactory representative in Zanzibar.[1] This incident illustrates the severe competition between the two firms in Zanzibar, each of which hurried to get its cargoes back to Salem before the ships of their rivals returned.[2] Pingree and West put another vessel into the trade in an attempt to hinder Shepard's operations.[3] In order to pre-empt the rival firm, Ward, the American consul who had succeeded Waters and who acted as agent for Shepard, would go to the customs master's house every night and copy from his books the names of the people to whom the ivory arriving in Zanzibar belonged. The following morning, armed with the list, he and his brother would approach the sellers. 'Thus', said Ward, 'we had great advantage over our opponents.'[4] When a third American firm tried to enter the Zanzibar trade, Pingree asked the consul to do all he could to prevent it buying successfully in Zanzibar and to inflict hindrances 'sufficient to disgust and sicken them of Zanzibar and its trade'.[5] Nevertheless, in the 1850s a third firm did establish an agent in Zanzibar – Rufus Greene and Co. of Providence, Rhode Island.[6]

The American commercial success in Zanzibar which enticed a third firm into the trade was due to a number of factors. American ships would call at Zanzibar, leave part of their cargo there and place their orders, and then go north to the Red Sea, Muscat and Bombay. Finally, they would put in at Zanzibar on their return to America to pick up the cargo they had ordered.[7] In this way they took full advantage of the monsoon and did not have to wait idly at Zanzibar until it changed. Moreover, their agents could unhurriedly procure the best terms of purchase.

[1] Shepard to Fabens, 4 Oct. 1845, printed in Bennett and Brooks, *op. cit.*, p. 344.
[2] Pingree and West to R. P. Waters, 30 Dec. 1841, *ibid.*, p. 235.
[3] J. G. Waters to R. P. Waters, 9 June 1844, *ibid.*, p. 250.
[4] Charles Ward to Shepard, 3 Jan. 1850, *ibid.*, p. 452.
[5] R. P. Waters to W. C. Waters, 13 Nov. 1844, *ibid.*, p. 251.
[6] Shepard to J. F. Webb, 3 July 1851, *ibid.*, p. 486; and Rufus Greene to F. Seward, 4 May 1863, Amer.N.A., Zanz. 4.
[7] General remarks in the returns of American vessels at Zanzibar, Jan.-July 1838, encl. in Waters to Forsyth, 1 Nov. 1838, Amer.N.A., Zanz. 1.

THE SWAHILI COAST

In the second place, the Americans succeeded because they brought to Zanzibar an article highly prized in the African interior – cloth. Before the Americans arrived, all the cloth used for barter had been brought to Zanzibar from India. According to one source, by 1841 800-1,000 bales, each consisting of twenty-five pieces thirty yards long (worth $3¼ to $4 a piece) of American cotton were entering Zanzibar in comparison with 250-300 bales of English cotton, each bale containing thirty pieces of a length of forty yards (worth $5 to $7 a piece), and 500 pieces of printed Indian cottons (each twenty-eight yards long and worth $2½).[1] A different source calculated that in 1841 the Americans brought to Zanzibar $70,000 worth of unbleached cotton, $5,000 of bleached cotton, and $3,000 of other dyes.[2] In the year between August 1846 and July 1847 the amount of cotton the Americans brought into Zanzibar had risen to 55,000 unbleached pieces (now $3 each) worth $165,000, 6,000 bleached pieces (now $3½ each) worth $19,500, and 1,500 dyed pieces worth $5,250. In 1848, 4,250 bales of various types of pieces, altogether worth $239,655, were taken to Zanzibar by American vessels.[3] By 1856, sales of American cotton in Zanzibar had risen to $529,788, and three years later 6,950 bales worth $421,850 were sold.[4]

The Americans also brought to Zanzibar guns and powder, household goods such as crockery, glassware, chairs and soap, foods like white sugar and biscuits, articles of value in the African interior like beads and brass wire, and miscellaneous items of hardware. Also included in their cargoes were spirits, turpentine, iron hoops, cordage, and paints.[5] In 1841 the relative importance of the major American sales was thus: cottons ($78,000), naval stores ($5,000), powder and guns ($3,000), furniture, pottery and glassware ($2,000), and biscuits and other foods ($2,000).[6] Over the years there were various changes in both the volume of the sales and the relative importance of the

[1] Guillain, *Côte de Zanguébar*, pp. 540-1.
[2] Loarer's Report, Part I, 1849, M.O., O.I. 5/23.
[3] *Idem*.
[4] Cochet to Ministry of F.A., no. 6, 15 Jan. 1857, A.N., Aff.Etr. B3/438; and Rigby to F.O., no. 3, 1 May 1860, F.O. 54/17.
[5] Lists of cargoes in returns of trade by American consuls, Amer.N.A., Zanz. 1, 2, and 3; Guillain, *Côte de Zanguébar*, *passim*; Kerdudal to Bazoche, 3 May 1844, M.O., O.I. 15/59; and Loarer's Report, Part I, 1849, M.O., O.I. 5/23.
[6] Loarer, *idem*.

THE ECONOMIC DEVELOPMENT OF THE COAST

different articles which were sold. In the year between August 1846 and July 1847 the following picture emerges: cottons ($189,750), foodstuffs ($4,500), 1,000 guns at $3½ each ($3,500), and naval stores ($2,500). In 1848 there was a further change. That year the Americans sold cottons worth $239,655; ironware, clocks, furniture and glassware worth $6,000; foodstuffs worth $5,000; 1,000 barrels of powder at $3 each ($3,000); 600 guns at $3½ each ($2,100); naval stores worth $1,500; and other articles to a value of $2,500.[1] In 1856 their sales of cottons had risen to $529,788, and they also brought gunpowder ($12,926), guns ($10,000), soap ($2,614), copper wire ($1,650), flour ($1,350), sugar ($1,037), and sundries worth $5,535.[2] Three years later they provided Zanzibar with 6,950 bales of cotton ($421,850), 11,000 barrels (each of 25 lb.) of gunpowder ($38,150), 8,000 muskets ($30,000), 200 barrels of flour ($24,000), 1,900 barrels of brass wire ($1,900), 500 boxes (each of 224 lb.) of tobacco ($3,750), 900 clocks ($3,600), 3,000 chairs ($2,475), 2,000 boxes of soap ($1,625), 800 boxes of biscuits ($1,600), and 1,000 deal planks ($750).[3]

Another factor which contributed to the American commercial success, at least at the outset, was their unscrupulous exploitation of the Arabs' ignorance of the true value of certain coins. The Americans introduced large amounts of coin to pay for their purchases; for example in the year between August 1846 and July 1847 they paid 100,000 piastres.[4] Far from suffering from parting with such large amounts of coin, the Americans were able to make a profit by deliberately failing to reveal a confusion among Zanzibar traders between the type of pesetas consisting of four reals and the type composed of five reals. Both sorts of pesetas were lesser denominations of the Spanish piastre, a coin of equivalent value to the Maria Theresa dollar, and also used as currency in the Indian Ocean. It was not until 1847 that the Zanzibaris noticed their error, and the following year the Americans introduced no specie into Zanzibar.[5]

Several sources provide figures which are a guide to the rate of increase and the total volume of American sales in Zanzibar. According

[1] *Idem.*
[2] Cochet to Ministry of F.A., no. 6, 15 Jan. 1857, A.N., Aff.Etr. B3/438.
[3] Rigby to F.O., no. 3, 1 May 1860, F.O. 54/17.
[4] Loarer's Report, Part I, 1849, M.O., O.I. 5/23.
[5] *Idem.*

to the returns of shipping compiled by the American consul, the value of the annual sales was as follows:

1838— $96,923	1844—incomplete	1850—$275,242
1839—$113,141	1845—$240,396	1851—unavailable
1840—$101,922	1846—$186,675	1852—$471,200
1841—$218,712	1847—incomplete	1853—$375,675
1842—$196,982	1848—$214,757	1854—$494,806[1]
1843—$179,372	1849—$380,000	

It must be borne in mind that these figures may not be altogether accurate because they were compiled by the consul from information given him by the vessels and rivalry between the different firms may well have led them to falsify their figures. Non-American sources also give occasional estimates for American sales in Zanzibar. According to Guillain in 1841, the Americans brought money and goods to the value of $130,000-$135,000 a year.[2] Writing a few years later, Loarer valued the American sales in 1841 at $90,000.[3] In 1844 Kerdudal put the figure at $200,000.[4] Between August 1846 and July 1847 the Americans introduced $208,250 of goods and $100,000 of specie, whereas in 1848 their sales reached $259,755.[5] The following year Guillain said that American sales approximated to $300,000-$350,000 a year.[6] At the end of Saiyid Sa'id's reign, in 1856, the volume had almost doubled, reaching $563,972, and three years later it was at a similar level – $534,100.[7]

Various conclusions can be drawn from these facts and figures. However inaccurate the figures, it is clear that there was a considerable expansion of the Americans' trade with the Swahili Coast; the total value of their sales rose from just under $100,000 in 1838 to just over $550,000 in 1856. The major increase was in the sales of cottons, of which the unbleached type was more popular than the bleached because it was stronger and the buyers preferred to do their own bleaching.[8]

---

[1] Consular returns of shipping, Amer.N.A., Zanz. 1, 2, and 3.
[2] Guillain, *Côte de Zanguébar*, p. 528.
[3] Loarer's Report, Part I, 1849, M.O., O.I. 5/23.
[4] Kerdudal to Bazoche, 3 May 1844, M.O., O.I. 15/59.
[5] Loarer's Report, as above.
[6] Guillain's Report, 1849, A.N., Marine BB4/1036.
[7] Cochet to Ministry of F.A., no. 6, 15 Jan. 1857, A.N., Aff.Etr. B3/438; and Rigby to F.O., no. 3, 1 May 1860, F.O. 54/17.
[8] Guillain's Report, 1849, A.N., Marine BB4/1036.

THE ECONOMIC DEVELOPMENT OF THE COAST

British merchants tried to compete with the Americans in sales of cloth but they achieved little success because their product was inferior, weighing less per piece.[1] The Americans also had great success with their sales of naval stores and were the almost exclusive providers of such articles. Initially they also sold large numbers of guns, but soon this branch of trade was usurped by British merchants. Later, as the British left the Zanzibar trade, American sales of arms rose again. Another trend was the decline in the introduction of specie by the Americans.

The value of American purchases in Zanzibar matched that of their sales. The following table of their major purchases illustrates the diversity and the increase in the volume of their trade.[2]

	1841 lb.	1848 lb.	1856	1859 lb.
ivory	66,000-78,500 (30-35 tons)	121,000 worth $196,000	$175,926	227,500 worth $325,000
copal	463,000-493,000 (210-220 tons)	unknown	$358,704	595,000 worth $93,500
cloves	110,220-112,000 (50 tons)	210,000	$5,833 (a mistake?)	840,000 worth $48,000
coconut oil	330,660-336,000 (150 tons)	unknown	unknown	unknown
hides	unknown	unknown	$5,000	40,000 worth $50,000
tortoise-shell	unknown	unknown	$4,211	unknown
red pepper	unknown	unknown	unknown	70,000 worth $2,600

The Americans also acquired at Zanzibar, in lesser amounts, coir, tallow, beeswax, aloes, shells, tobacco, camphor, senna, drugs, dyes,

[1] Loarer's Report, Part I, 1849, M.O., O.I. 5/23.
[2] For 1841, Guillain, *Côte de Zanguébar*; for 1848, Loarer, as above; for 1856, Cochet to Ministry of F.A., no. 6, as above; and for 1859, Rigby to F.O., as above. Guillain gave the 1841 figures in tons, without specifying what type of ton he was using. The translation into pounds is therefore only approximate. Where the word 'unknown' occurs, the source gave no figure.

mother-of-pearl, arrowroot, asafoetida, and sesame.[1] The total volume of their purchases of local produce rose through the following stages:

1838— $52,667	1845—$179,742	1851—unavailable
1839—$164,026	1846—$294,810	1852—$415,500
1840— $27,209	1847—incomplete	1853—$264,100
1841—$209,056	1848—$246,270	1854—$501,722
1842—$169,899	1849—$305,648	1856—$565,925
1843—$234,020	1850—$444,669	1859—$534,100[2]
1844—incomplete		

From these figures it is clear that the expansion was fairly steady and that the value of American sales and purchases was well balanced. Over the whole period their purchases exceeded their sales by only $36,000 out of a total of $3,500,000, although there were exceptional years of imbalance such as 1840 and 1853. The 1853 drop in purchases may have been due to trouble on the mainland in the previous year which caused copal and ivory to enter Zanzibar in only very small quantities.[3] The situation was aggravated by the increase in the number of Western firms in Zanzibar which raised prices beyond the Americans' reach.[4]

The success of the Americans in the trade of the Swahili Coast owed much to their capture of the cloth market, their initial duplicity over the introduction of specie, their full use of the Indian Ocean winds to spend only the minimum time necessary at Zanzibar, and their willingness to take only small profits on their sales in Zanzibar and make up the loss on their sales in America. At Zanzibar they seldom made more than 7 or 8 per cent profit on their transactions, whereas in America they sold their cargoes at 25 per cent profit.[5] Once they had established themselves in the Swahili Coast trade they became popular merchants because of the regularity of their arrival and steadiness of their purchases. For this reason the Indian middlemen preferred them to traders of other nationalities.[6]

---

[1] Lists of cargoes from consular returns of American vessels at Zanzibar, Amer.N.A., Zanz. 1, 2, and 3; Guillain, *Côte de Zanguébar*, p. 528; and Loarer's Report, Part I, 1849, M.O., O.I. 5/23.

[2] For figures up to 1854, consular returns of shipping, Amer.N.A., Zanz. 1, 2, and 3. For 1856, Cochet to Ministry of F.A., no. 6, 15 Jan. 1857, A.N., Aff.Etr. B3/438. For 1859, Rigby to F.O., no. 3, 1 May 1860, F.O. 54/17.

[3] J. F. Webb to Shepard, 27 Jan. 1852, printed in Bennett and Brooks, *op. cit.*, p. 493.

[4] Same to same, 22 Feb. 1852, *ibid.*, p. 494.

[5] Loarer's Report, Part I, 1849, M.O., O.I. 5/23. [6] *Idem.*

THE ECONOMIC DEVELOPMENT OF THE COAST

While American trade at Zanzibar expanded, that of the British decreased. Even the British treaty of 1839 did not assist matters. It was similar to the American treaty, imposing a 5 per cent duty on imports only. By that date, however, the firm of Newman Hunt and Christopher was in such difficulties that it did not revive. Hunt ceased his operations in the early 1840s. Despite the failure of the British firm, Cogan, who had negotiated the treaty, decided to try his fortune in Zanzibar, backed by Henderson of Bombay.[1] He became a favourite of Saiyid Sa'id, who granted him Latham's Island, rich in guano, to the south of Zanzibar.[2] But Cogan was unable to exploit his island because the British consul forbade him to use slave labour.[3] Cogan also tried his hand at sugar manufacture, making an agreement with Saiyid Sa'id, who would provide the canes and slaves, while Cogan would provide the supervision and the mill. Cogan and the Sultan were each to get a half of the sugar produced.[4] However, Cogan did not prosper at Zanzibar – two of his ships were wrecked, possibly deliberately.[5] Eventually he quit Zanzibar for Aden, leaving his affairs in the charge of Francis Peters.[6] When Peters died in 1848 the business was wound up.[7] Cogan suffered from the same disadvantage as had Hunt: he had difficulty in paying for his purchases because Great Britain did not provide the coarse cottons able to challenge the American article. Cogan had tried to solve the problem by setting up small industry in Zanzibar, but this had also failed, partly because there was no legitimate labour force available while slavery existed.

The only other British enterprises in East Africa in Saiyid Sa'id's reign were those of Norsworthy, who has already been mentioned, of Parker, an agent sent out by the Liverpool firm of Cram, and of Wilson and Pollock, two independent merchants whose achievements were minimal.[8] Cram sent three vessels to Zanzibar, but Parker

[1] W. Henderson and Co. to Aberdeen, 27 May 1846, Z.A.; and British agent, Muscat, to Bombay, 4 Apr. 1841, encl. in Bombay to Secret Committee, no. 29, 26 Apr. 1841, E.S.L.B. 31.
[2] Deed signed by Saiyid Sa'id, archives no. 26/283, Z.A.
[3] Hamerton to F.O., no. 5, 24 Mch. 1845, F.O. 54/7.
[4] Same to same, 2 Jan. 1844, F.O. 54/6.
[5] Bombay to C. of Ds., no. 11, 25 Feb. 1843, P.L.B. 27; and same to same, no. 33, 12 Mch. 1847, P.L.B. 34.
[6] Haines to Bombay, 5 Jan. 1847, B.C. 2203, Dr. 700; and Hamerton to F.O., no. 3, 25 Mch. 1847, F.O. 54/11.
[7] Ephraim Emmerton's Journal, entry for 1 Oct. 1848, printed in Bennett and Brooks, *op. cit.*, p. 412. For Peters' death, Ward to B. F. Fabens, 3 Jan. 1843, *ibid.*, p. 390.   [8] Loarer's Report, Part I, 1849, M.O., O.I. 5/23.

mismanaged his business. He wanted to exploit some antimony mines near Mombasa and proposed to the Sultan that they share the working of them on equal terms of profit and loss. When Saiyid Sa'id showed no interest in the idea, Parker abandoned the East African trade.[1]

Before the British left East African commerce they tried to sell the articles most required at Zanzibar, and offered glassware, earthenware, hardware, utensils, syrups, cloths, silks, woollens, copper, brass and iron wire, wines and spirits, beads, guns and powder.[2] Until 1848 they sold annually about 1,000 guns and 2,000 barrels of powder, which formed a large proportion of Zanzibar's import of arms.[3] The inhabitants of the Swahili Coast preferred British guns and powder to those of any other country.[4] Muskets sold in Zanzibar at $3½ each, although the price fell to $3 when the *Caroline* brought a great number from London.[5] The British were also successful in their sales of Venetian beads, which formerly had reached Zanzibar from Italy by way of Egypt and the Red Sea. Less impressive were their attempts to sell cloth. Although it is true that for a while Newman Hunt and Christopher copied in London materials which Zanzibar obtained from Muscat, and those found a ready sale, the Americans and Indians continued to dominate the cloth trade.[6]

The most flourishing year for British commerce in Zanzibar was 1846/7. Sales for that year[7] are shown in table on p. 337.

At first the British also experimented in an enterprising manner with the articles they purchased at Zanzibar. They obtained coconut oil for $64 a ton in Zanzibar and sold it for $220 in London.[8] On one occasion Peters bought a consignment of 18,000-20,000 *frasela*, and Saiyid Sa'id himself sent 5,000-6,000 *frasela* of coconut oil to the London market.[9] Tortoise-shell was also regularly despatched to London: Peters, for example, purchased 1,000-1,200 lb. annually.[10] The British also bought the staple articles provided by the Swahili Coast – copal, ivory and cloves. In 1839 they took from Zanzibar 14,000-15,000 *frasela* of copal, 7,000 *frasela* of coconut oil, and 1,200 *frasela* of ivory.[11] In 1838 the

[1] Hamerton to F.O., no. 10, 15 Dec. 1848, F.O. 54/12; Hamerton to E. Parker, 12 Apr. 1847, Z.A.; and Krapf, *op. cit.*, pp. 166-7.
[2] Guillain, *Côte de Zanguébar*, p. 534, and Loarer's Report, Part I, 1849, M.O., O.I. 5/23.
[3] Loarer, *idem*.   [4] Guillain's Report, 1849, A.N., Marine BB4/1036.
[5] Loarer, as above.   [6] *Idem*.   [7] *Idem*.
[8] Guillain, *Côte de Zanguébar*, p. 538.
[9] Loarer, as above.
[10] *Idem*.   [11] Guillain, *Côte de Zanguébar*, p. 534.

British sales at Zanzibar, 1846/7

		$
1,000 guns at $3½		3,500
1,500 barrels of powder at $3½		4,250
cotton	white	18,500
	printed	20,500
	dyed	8,200
silk, silk and cotton, silk and wool, and gold-threaded silk		12,500
wool	light	8,250
	merino	6,000
	printed	3,000
beads		55,000
drinking glasses, crystal, and pottery		6,500
ironmongery		6,000
iron wire		7,800
brass and copper wire		35,000
foods, wines, spirits		4,500
sundries		15,000
		214,000

British received (including what Saiyid Sa'id sent on the *Caroline*) 1,000 *frasela* of ivory at $25, 1,500 at $30, and 1,200 at $34, a consignment which was altogether worth $110,800.[1] The British also purchased, in lesser amounts, hides, sesame, wax, drugs, and rhino-horn.[2]

After 1848, however, the British trade with Zanzibar virtually came to an end, and there is no record of British merchant vessels visiting that port until 1855, when two ships, with an aggregate tonnage of 409, went there for commercial purposes.[3] The following year two British ships again traded at Zanzibar, a number which rose to three in 1857.[4] The failure of British commercial enterprise in Zanzibar, in contrast to British political influence, is difficult to account for. Perhaps the most important factor in the failure was the presence of Indian merchants who introduced British goods to the Swahili Coast via India. Financially well-backed and able to accept smaller profits than could British firms, the Indians narrowed the market for goods coming directly from England. For example, much of the cloth which the Indians sold in Zanzibar originated from England. British merchants were unable to

[1] Loarer's Report, Part I, 1849, M.O., O.I. 5/23.
[2] *Idem*, and Guillain, *Côte de Zanguébar*, p. 534.
[3] Rigby to F.O., no. 3, 1 May 1860, F.O. 54/17.
[4] *Idem*. Rigby gives the 1856 tonnage as 1,167, and the 1857 as 770. Cochet gives the 1856 tonnage (2 vessels) as 737 – Cochet to Ministry of F.A., no. 6, 15 Jan. 1857, A.N., Aff.Etr. B3/438.

find suitable alternative articles to offer for sale. They had, it is true, some success with their firearms, but their market for that article was also usurped, this time by the Americans. Although the firearms which the Americans introduced were British in manufacture, the willingness of the traders of that nation to accept small profits in Zanzibar enabled them to sell the guns at the same price as those brought directly from England. Another factor which may be relevant in the failure of British trade was the lack of stimulus for firms who might be willing to trade with Africa. This was partly the result of the commercial disinterest of the British consul, Atkins Hamerton, who unlike his fellow officers of other nations, composed no detailed reports of the economic life of the region in which he resided for so long. He drew up only one table of British trade returns – for the year 1847, according to which the British sold to Zanzibar goods worth £11,160 and made purchases to the value of £12,091.[1]

A late foreign participant in the trade of the Swahili Coast was metropolitan France. For many years the French colonies had traded with Zanzibar, and commercial treaties between Zanzibar and Bourbon had been arranged in 1822 and 1827.[2] The prosperous Bourbon house of Rontaunay sent occasional vessels to Zanzibar in the 1820s,[3] and in 1835 Vailhen was sent from Bourbon to make a commercial arrangement with Zanzibar, a mission he did not complete.[4] There was then a gap until the next merchant vessel came in 1840.[5] Around that date ships from metropolitan France were stimulated to visit East Africa by the recent commercial reports of Guillain, which were printed in the *Revue Coloniale*.[6] A Bordeaux vessel, the *Mexicaine*, had traded at Zanzibar in 1835, but now two ships from the same port came to sample the market.[7] These initial enterprises cannot have been outstandingly

---

[1] Hamerton to F.O., no. 4, 14 Feb. 1848, F.O. 54/12. £1 equalled $4½-4¾.

[2] Governor of Bourbon to Ministry of Marine, 22 Sept. 1827, A.E., Zanz. C.C.1; and Hamerton to Aberdeen, 31 Aug. 1843, F.O. 54/5.

[3] Gaultier de Rontaunay to Sainte-Hilaire, 26 Jan. 1829, M.O., Réunion 80/529.

[4] See Chapter VI, pp. 153-4.

[5] E. G. Kimball to G. West, 7 June 1840, printed in Bennett and Brooks, *op. cit.*, p. 226. This could not have been the warship *Dordogne* because that did not arrive in Zanzibar until 19 June – Noel to Ministry of F.A., 12 Feb. 1841, A.E., Zanz. C.C.1.

[6] *Revue Coloniale* (Paris, 1843), pp. 520-62.

[7] Broquant to Ministry of F.A., no. 4, 12 Mch. 1845, A.E., Zanz. C.C.1. The two ships were *L'Ankobar* and *L'Africaine*.

THE ECONOMIC DEVELOPMENT OF THE COAST

successful because it was several years before a regular trade between France and Zanzibar developed. A Bordeaux vessel visited Zanzibar in 1844, returning again in the following year.[1]

The arrangement in 1844 of a commercial treaty[2] almost identical to that of the British did not seem to encourage merchants, but the detailed exploration of the commercial possibilities of East Africa by the Guillain expedition of 1846-9 had a more favourable effect. It was a well-organized project backed by different French ministries. The Ministry of Marine and Colonies contacted the Ministry of Agriculture and Commerce which asked the Chambers of Commerce and the manufacturers of Paris, Marseilles, Rouen, St Etienne, Sedan, Roubaix, Lodèves, and Elbeuf to provide samples of their products to be taken to East Africa.[3] The Nantes Chamber of Commerce was ordered to choose a representative to make commercial enquiries on the voyage and they appointed Loarer, who had already been to East Africa.[4] This formal government enquiry, of a kind conducted by no other country, had important commercial effects. Whereas in both 1848 and 1849 only one French vessel visited Zanzibar,[5] in 1850 and 1851, inspired by the reports from the French expedition, two rival houses from Marseilles – Vidal Bros and Rabaud Bros – sent several ships to Zanzibar.[6] By December 1851 Vidal Bros had established a factory in Zanzibar.[7] Being one of the largest commercial houses in Marseilles, they had a large amount of capital, which enabled them to buy at higher prices than the Americans and Germans.[8] In order to procure hides, both the French houses established agents on Lamu, which gave them purchasing

---

[1] B. F. Fabens to Shepard, 27 Sept. 1844 and 22 Dec. 1845, printed in Bennett and Brooks, *op. cit.*, pp. 251 and 348.

[2] See Chapter VII, pp. 184-5.

[3] Ministry of Agriculture and Commerce to Ministry of Marine, 4 Mch. 1846, M.O., O.I. 2/10.

[4] Same to same, 14 Nov. 1845, M.O., O.I. 2/10.

[5] Ephraim Emmerton's Journal, entry for 1 Oct. 1848, printed in Bennett and Brooks, *op. cit.*, p. 412 (for *La Grenouille* in 1848); and 'Navigation de Zanzibar, 4e trimestre, 1849', A.E., Zanz. C.C.1.

[6] Belligny to Ministry of F.A., 5 May and 7 Oct. 1850, A.E., Zanz. C.C.1. The returns of French vessels at Zanzibar in 1851 (in A.E., Zanz. C.C.2) show that 14 French ships were in Zanzibar that year, but, as no names are given, several vessels may have put into the port more than once. The 1852 returns also show 14 vessels.

[7] Belligny to Ministry of F.A., no. 28, 27 Feb. 1852, A.E., Zanz. C.C.2.

[8] F. Ward to C. Ward, 18 Dec. 1851, and Webb to Shepard, 22 Feb. 1852, printed in Bennett and Brooks, *op. cit.*, pp. 492 and 495.

superiority over the Americans, who had no agent there.¹ The activities of the two French firms must have been successful because at the end of 1854 they were joined in the East African trade by another powerful Marseilles firm – Régis Bros.² This house had already despatched an unsuccessful vessel to Zanzibar in 1848 and the same ship again in 1850,³ but it now embarked upon a more active participation in the trade.

The French faced many early difficulties in their commercial exchanges with Zanzibar. They did not produce the required type of cloth, and their firearms, of a different design from and a higher price than those supplied by the British, were not popular.⁴ Consequently they would have preferred to pay for some of the goods they purchased with specie, and in particular with the five-franc pieces used in Bourbon. These coins were not, however, popular in Zanzibar, having only a poor exchange rate of 108 to 100 dollars. The French tried to get Saiyid Sa'id to proclaim officially a more favourable exchange rate, but he could not affect the dealings of the money-changers with any legislation.⁵ A further difficulty encountered by French merchants was the high duties to which East African goods were subject in French ports.⁶

None the less there was a startling growth of French trade with the Swahili Coast in the 1850s. In 1855 thirteen French vessels (5,523 tons altogether) entered Zanzibar; in 1856 either twenty-two (10,079 tons in all) or twenty-three (9,584 tons in all) French ships, of which two were from French colonies, traded at the port.⁷ They concentrated on bringing to Zanzibar household goods and luxuries, as well as food, drink, and some firearms. In 1856 the articles they sold in Zanzibar, in order of importance, were guns (3,000), cloth, spirits, wine, beads, mirrors, clocks, olive oil, flour, liqueurs, porcelain, pottery, refined

¹ Burton, *Zanzibar*, I, 319.
² Ernst Hieke, *Zur Geschichte des Deutschen Handels mit Ostafrika* (Hamburg, 1939), p. 140.
³ Belligny to Ministry of F.A., no. 7, 9 Jan. 1850, A.E., Zanz. C.C.1; and Cochet to Ministry of F.A., 19 Jan. 1857, A.E., Zanz. C.C.2.
⁴ Loarer's Report, Part I, 1849, M.O., O.I. 5/23.
⁵ C. Ward to M. Shepard, 20 Jan. 1851, printed in Bennett and Brooks, *op. cit.*, p. 473. For the struggle to get a better exchange rate, R. Desfossés to Ministry of F.A., no. 8, 27 Feb. 1846, M.O., Madag. 17/32; Broquant to Ministry of F.A., no. 15, 14 Feb. 1846, A.E., Zanz. C.C.1; Ministry of F.A. to Belligny, no. 1, 26 Apr. 1849, *ibid.*; and Saiyid Sa'id to Belligny, 28 Dec. 1849, A.E., Zanz. C.P.1. ⁶ Loarer's Report, Part I, 1849, M.O., O.I. 5/23.
⁷ Rigby to F.O., no. 3, 1 May 1860, F.O. 54/17. For the alternative number, Cochet to Ministry of F.A., no. 6, 15 Jan. 1857, A.N., Aff.Etr. B3/438.

THE ECONOMIC DEVELOPMENT OF THE COAST

sugar, paper and perfume.[1] The following list gives a detailed picture of their sales three years later:[2]

	$
Venetian glass beads	41,000
7,000 muskets	21,000
2,000 fowling pieces	14,000
spirits	4,250
3,150 dozen cotton handkerchiefs	3,937
glassware	3,950
macaroni and vermicelli	2,200
10 bales of broadcloth	1,800
mirrors	1,000
10,080 lb. refined sugar	900
sherbet	480
157 pieces of chintz	414
olive oil	400
40 pigs of lead	240
chinaware	200
300 iron cooking utensils	200
wax candles	200
200 deal planks	150
60 boxes of soap	90
14 boxes of preserves	50
sundries	20,000

In 1856 the total value of the sales of French goods in Zanzibar was $45,468, and three years later $116,451. In addition, in those two years the French introduced $37,037 and $400,000 in specie.

This large import of coin into Zanzibar was caused by the discrepancy in the value of French sales and purchases. The following table lists French purchases in the years 1856 and 1859:[3]

	1856	1859
sesame	$225,850	5,600,000 lb. worth $67,500
copra	113,519	2,450,000 lb. worth $60,000
cloves	47,983	1,050,000 lb. worth $60,000
cowries	38,770	—
hides	21,190	25,000 worth $30,000
copal	12,405	—
ivory	9,321	—
coconut oil	7,369	—
beeswax	1,368	—
tortoise-shell	968	—
tallow	747	—
sundries	23,978	worth $30,000

[1] Cochet to Ministry of F.A., *idem.*
[2] Rigby to F.O., no. 3, 1 May 1860, F.O. 54/17.
[3] Rigby and Cochet, as above.

In 1856, therefore, the total value of French purchases was $503,469, whereas in 1859 it was $247,500. If these figures are correct, the initial boom had not continued. This state of affairs was confirmed by Richard Burton who reported in 1857 that the French merchants were in difficulties. Vidal, he said, had been named for a loss of $400,000, which it would be impossible to recoup.[1] A most interesting feature of the French purchases in Zanzibar is the size of their requirement of sesame, which was far larger than that of any other country. They also bought less ivory and copal than traders of other nations, and were the only Westerners to take a large amount of copra. This concentration on two articles which were not required by rival foreign buyers helped the French establish themselves in the trading community of the Swahili Coast. It must also have contributed to their success in raising the amount of their purchases at Zanzibar to a level similar to that of the Americans in the short space of a few years.

Other late-comers to the East African market were Germans; like the metropolitan French, they entered the trade when contacts with Europeans were already well established. They came in search of one particular article – the cowry shell. Cowries were used as currency in West Africa, which obtained large numbers of its shells from the Maldive and Laccadive islands in the Indian Ocean. In 1844 the Hamburg house of Hertz, which was engaged in the cowry trade to West Africa, decided to seek the shells farther afield and sent a vessel to Zanzibar to investigate whether it could provide them in a suitable quantity.[2] The East African cowries were found to be bigger than those of the Maldives and Laccadives, but a trial indicated that they were acceptable in West Africa. Thus there began a regular trade by German vessels from East to West Africa. Also in 1844 another Hamburg firm, Wilhelm O'Swald, which had been somewhat unsuccessfully trading with China, made enquiries about East Africa's commercial possibilities.[4] The results of their investigations were so favourable that another vessel was sent in 1847. It soon became apparent, however, that an agent would have to be appointed if the firm were to compete successfully with other Western traders in Zanzibar.

In June 1849 O'Swald opened a factory at Zanzibar and appointed Schmeisser as his agent.[3] The firm joined Hertz in taking cowries to West Africa, and their operations caused a boom in the East African cowry trade at the end of the 1840s. The Germans tried to conceal the

[1] Burton, *Zanzibar*, I, 320.   [2] Hieke, *op. cit.*, p. 68.
[3] *Ibid.*, p. 101.   [4] *Ibid.*, pp. 108, 109.

THE ECONOMIC DEVELOPMENT OF THE COAST

fact that they were taking cowries to West Africa from other Western merchants in Zanzibar. Loarer, for example, was told that the cowries were used in porcelain-making and taken to the Baltic,[1] and in all their letters O'Swald and Co. used the word '*kaffee*' instead of 'cowries'.[2] It was probably because the Germans exploited an article not previously taken from East Africa in large quantities that they succeeded in the crowded market of Zanzibar. They did not, however, concentrate exclusively on the cowry trade; they also purchased the staple products of the Swahili Coast. In 1854 a third Hamburg house – Hansing and Co. – entered the Zanzibar trade.[3]

Since the Germans were so secretive about their activities it is difficult to get a correct estimate of the total volume of their trade or of the relative value of its different parts. The French consul, who had to rely on figures reluctantly provided by the German firms, calculated that in 1856 German purchases amounted to $128,712, but this appears to be an undervaluation because either twenty or twenty-one German ships (5,629 or 6,038 tons altogether) visited Zanzibar that year.[4] The following year twenty-three German ships put in to the port. In 1856 the French consul itemized German purchases in the following manner, but the probability that he was making an inaccurate estimate is underlined by the much higher figures provided three years later by Rigby:[5]

	1856	1859
cowries	$46,026	7,800,000 lb. worth $230,000
copal	25,926	210,000 lb. worth $54,000
hides	—	30,000 lb. worth $35,000
ivory	24,074	16,100 lb. worth $25,000
cloves	14,815	280,000 lb. worth $16,000
sesame	12,037	525,000 lb. worth $20,000
tortoise-shell	—	320 lb. worth $1,000
coconut oil	741	—
sundries	5,093	worth $10,000
	$128,712	$391,000

[1] Loarer's Report, Part I, 1849, M.O., O.I. 5/23.
[2] Hieke, *op. cit.*, p. 112.
[3] *Ibid.*, p. 139.
[4] Cochet to Ministry of F.A., no. 6, 15 Jan. 1857, A.N., Aff.Etr. B3/438, for the figure 20, and Rigby to F.O., no. 3, 1 May 1860, F.O. 54/17, for the figure 21.
[5] Cochet and Rigby, as above.

Although the German firms paid for their purchases mainly with specie, they also sold other articles. In 1859 they took the following goods to the Swahili Coast:[1]

	$
specie	350,000
Venetian glass beads	55,000
brass wire	15,000
chinaware	7,000
chintz	5,000
1,200 muskets	4,250
cutlery	3,402
11 bales of broadcloth	825
musket flints	500
wax candles	500
sherbet	500
500 cotton handkerchiefs	500
spirits	400
paint and oil	350
wheaten flour	250
mirrors	200
biscuits	24
sundries	12,000
	455,701

In 1856 Zanzibar's most valuable Western customer was America, whose purchases totalled $565,925. France came a close second with $503,469, and Germany, the exact value of whose purchases is unknown, probably followed in third place.[2] Zanzibar's trade with the Western countries had risen to this level from virtually nothing in a span of thirty years, a development which was to have profound effects on the economic, social, and political organization of the region. The Americans had been the first Western merchants to make a large investment in Swahili Coast commerce, but they were followed closely by the British. However, British trading interests soon came to a virtual end while those of the Americans continued to flourish and expand. Later the French and Germans entered the market.

---

[1] Rigby, as above. See also Hieke, p. 140, for the German use of large quantities of specie.

[2] The figures are those of Cochet, as above.

THE ECONOMIC DEVELOPMENT OF THE COAST

The comparative volume of the trade of the different Western countries and the special characteristics of each nation's activities can best be illustrated by means of tables:[1]

Ships entering Zanzibar

	1855 (Rigby) no.	tonnage	1856 (Rigby) no.	tonnage	1856 (Cochet) no.	tonnage	1857 (Rigby) no.	tonnage
Denmark		nil	1	450	1	450	1	202
Spain	2	460	2	460	1	201	2	680
USA	28	9,142 (incl. whalers)	24	7,215 (incl. whalers)	17	5,105 (excl. whalers)	35	11,481 (incl. whalers)
G. Britain	2	409	2	1,167	2	737	3	770
Metropolitan France	13	5,523	22	10,079	21	9,526	24	8,319
Fr. Colonies					2	59		
Portugal		nil	3	930	2	515	2	94
Prussia		nil	1	600	1	600		nil
Hanseatic towns (Rigby says Hamburg)	15	3,689	20	5,438	19	5,029	22	5,488
Hanover		nil		nil		no fig. given	1	419

These figures give a false picture unless one remembers that German, French and American vessels often put in to Zanzibar more than once on the same voyage because they also went north to the Red Sea and Persian Gulf. In order to obtain a more accurate picture, the shipping of these three nations should be reduced by about half. The figures for American trade provided by Rigby also give a false picture because he did not differentiate between whalers, which called at Zanzibar merely to load provisions, and general merchant vessels. The annual numbers he gave should therefore be reduced by about seven and the tonnage by about 2,000.

The tables on pp. 346 and 347 enable us to see the different characteristics of each country's trade with the Swahili Coast.[2]

The Swahili Coast's trade with the West was of vital importance to the region's economic development. But the expansion of that branch of commerce was accompanied and stimulated by a parallel development which there has been a tendency to ignore – the commercial exchanges between the Swahili Coast and India. The increasing number of Indians taking advantage of the opportunities offered by the East African

[1] The figures are from Rigby and Cochet, as above.   [2] *Idem.*

THE SWAHILI COAST

Exports from the Swahili Coast 1859 (1856 in brackets)

article	measure	GB quant.	GB value $	USA quant.	USA value $	France quant.	France value $	Germany quant.	Germany value $
cloves	frasela	6,860	10,500	24,000	48,000 (5,833)	30,000	60,000	8,000	16,000 (14,815)
copal	frasela	525	6,250	17,000	93,500 (358,704)	—	—	6,000	54,000 (25,926)
ivory	frasela	—	—	6,500	325,000 (175,925)	—	(12,405)	460	25,000 (24,074)
hides	no.	600	800	40,000	50,000 (5,000)	—	(9,321)	30,000	35,000
red pepper	frasela	—	—	2,000	2,600	25,000	30,000 (21,190)	—	—
sesame	bags of 112 lb.	4,903	6,100	—	—	50,000	67,500 (225,850)	15,000	20,000 (12,037)
copra	frasela	—	—	—	—	70,000	60,000 (21,190)	—	—
coconut oil	casks	50	1,400	—	—	—	(7,369)	—	(741)
tortoise-shell	lb.	—	—	—	(4,211)	—	(970)	320	1,000
cowries	bags of 120 lb.	—	—	—	—	—	—	—	—
beeswax		—	—	—	—	—	(38,770)	65,000	30,000 (46,026)
tallow		—	—	—	—	—	(1,368)	—	—
sundries		—	—	15,000	(16,251)	30,000	(23,978)	10,000	(5,093)

THE ECONOMIC DEVELOPMENT OF THE COAST

coast has already been mentioned. Their knowledge of financial dealings and their support by wealthy Indian banking firms enabled them to undertake moneylending, banking and underwriting activities in Zanzibar.[1] Making rapid profits from the high interest rates they charged, they were seldom short of capital. Although there is a record of an interest rate of $4\frac{1}{2}$ per cent being charged, moneylenders sometimes raised their rate as high as 40 per cent.[2] Moneys advanced on landed

Imports by the Swahili Coast from Western Countries

	USA		France		Germany	
	1856	1859	1856	1859	1856	1859
	$	$	$	$	$	$
cottons	529,788	421,850	4,661	—	528	—
arms	10,000	30,000	30,000	21,000	9,630	4,250
powder	12,926	38,150	—	—	—	—
beads	—	—	2,230	41,000	—	55,000
clocks	—	3,600	525	—	—	—
spirits	—	—	5,248	4,240	—	4,640
wheaten flour	1,350	24,000	209	—	—	250
refined sugar	1,037	12,000	116	900	—	—
brass wire	1,650	19,000	—	—	17,182	15,000
glassware	—	—	—	3,950	—	—
chintz	—	—	—	414	—	5,000
chinaware	—	—	—	200	—	7,000
specie	unknown		37,037	400,000	unknown	350,000
fowling pieces	—	—	—	14,000	—	—

security bore interest at 15 to 20 per cent a year.[3] Indians also acquired wealth from the system whereby plantation owners could borrow money by mortgaging their estates to moneylenders who regained the loan by working the plantations.[4] The initial reluctance of the Arabs to accept Indian commercial competition soon lessened when they recognized that without them the capital necessary for economic enterprises would be scarce.

The Indians did not confine themselves to banking pursuits. Their

[1] Journal of Lt Christopher, 1843, encl. in Bombay to Secret Committee, no. 54, 18 July 1843, E.S.L.B. 60; and Burton, *Zanzibar*, II, 407.
[2] Record of a loan by Sanbai of $7,000 to Tara Tupan at $4\frac{1}{2}$ per cent, 9 Sept. 1853, Z.A. Burton, *Zanzibar*, II, 147, for loans at 40 per cent.
[3] Burton, *idem*, p. 407.
[4] Hamerton to Bombay, no. 33, 9 Dec. 1843, B.C. 2034, Dr. 253.

accumulation of capital put them in an excellent position to engage personally in trading ventures. By 1847 they were the almost exclusive purchasers of American cargoes.[1] Various factors contributed to their success. In the first place, they were willing to make only a small profit from their transactions.[2] Secondly, their commercial organization spanned the whole coast, for they kept agents at many littoral ports and were prominent middlemen between the mainland and Zanzibar.[3] Furthermore, their capital allowed them to advance goods to retail vendors and traders bound for the interior and to await payment until the return of the caravans, meanwhile charging a high rate of interest.[4] Another factor in their success was their practice of assuming whatever nationality suited their commercial purpose. Their boats raised the British or Arab flag according to which port they were approaching.[5] As slave traders they preferred to be Zanzibari, but when it came to the payment of customs duties they were treated as Arab rather than British.[6] Although this meant that they paid higher duties, it allowed them to trade on the Mrima, an area forbidden to the Western merchants. The Indians did not pursue maritime activities, generally sending their goods to India on Arab vessels or boats manned by Arabs. They paid a freight rate of about nine dollars a ton for general cargo and thirty dollars a ton for ivory.[7]

The Indians traded in a great variety of articles because they sold not only products from India itself but also British goods which had been exported to India. Prior to the arrival of the Americans in Zanzibar the Indians sold a large amount of cloth and brass wire to the Swahili Coast. Although the Americans rapidly overtook them in sales of cloth, the Indians were able to continue to bring their own and British cottons from India in a profitable quantity because of the great expansion of the East African market. By 1859 $443,851 of Indian cottons were imported by Zanzibar in comparison with $381,850 of American.[8] The Indians also sold a host of other articles in Zanzibar, the most important of which were brass wire, rice, sugar, ghee, copper, and iron goods. Of lesser importance were earthenware, betel, pepper, cardamom, cin-

[1] Ward to Buchanan, no. 16, 7 Mch. 1847, Amer.N.A., Zanz. 2.
[2] Loarer's Report, Part I, 1849, M.O., O.I. 5/23.
[3] Guillain's Report, 1849, A.N., Marine BB4/1036.
[4] Burton, *Zanzibar*, II, 407.
[5] Ward to Buchanan, no. 16, 7 Mch. 1847, Amer.N.A., Zanz. 2.
[6] Guillain, *Côte de Zanguébar*, p. 543.
[7] Loarer's Report, as above, and Guillain's Report, as above.
[8] Rigby to F.O., no. 3, 1 May 1860, F.O. 54/17.

THE ECONOMIC DEVELOPMENT OF THE COAST

namon, ginger, coir rope, cutlery and nails.[1] A list of Zanzibar's imports from India in 1859 gives a good picture of the relative value of various articles:[2]

	$		$
cottons	443,851	sugar-candy	3,500
rice	104,000	opium	3,200
ghee	35,000	Surat caps	2,400
Bengal sugar	16,000	cardamom	2,000
copper utensils	15,000	spun silk	1,600
chintz	10,198	bajree	1,500
anchors	6,000	coffee	1,400
gold lace	6,000	frankincense	1,200
black pepper	5,500	lead	1,200
iron jugs	5,250	molasses	1,000
iron bars	4,880	wooden boxes	1,000
wheat	4,600	pewter	800
oil	4,500	betel nuts	775
cutlery	4,000	chain cables	400
chinaware	4,000	sundries	25,000
cummin seed	3,750		

The size of the Indian trade is evident from the various estimates of its value made at certain dates. In 1843 Kerdudal reckoned Zanzibar's imports from India at $600,000,[3] and the following year the French consul said:

'Si on croirait que le monopole est en faveur des Américains, on serait completement dans l'erreur; les exportations americaines, dans l'année la plus favorable, n'ont pas atteint 400,000 $, tandis que le commerce des Banians ... s'est accru de plus de dix millions de francs [$1,851,851].'[4]

By 1849 British India and the Protected States were sending about thirty-five boats annually to the Swahili Coast,[5] and in 1853 the Bombay Collector of Customs pointed out that sales to Bombay by East Africa were $30\frac{1}{4}$ per cent above those of the previous year and $48\frac{1}{4}$ per cent above the average of the previous five years.[6] In 1859

---

[1] Broquant to Ministry of F.A., 10 Mch. 1845, M.O., O.I. 15/65; Guillain, *Côte de Zanguébar*, pp. 541-2; and Guillain's Report, 1849, A.N., Marine BB4/1036.
[2] Rigby, as above.   [3] Kerdudal to Bazoche, 3 May 1844, M.O., O.I. 15/59.
[4] Broquant to Ministry of F.A., 10 Mch. 1845, M.O., O.I. 15/65.
[5] Guillain's Report, 1849, A.N., Marine BB4/1036.
[6] Acting Collector of Customs, Bombay, to Bombay Council, 30 Sept. 1853, B.C. 2660, Dr. 30.

Zanzibar's imports from British India totalled $284,480 and from Kutch $223,424 – a grand total of $507,904.[1]

Indian purchases on the Swahili Coast were similarly impressive in volume. The following table, for the year 1859, provides information about the major Indian purchases:[2]

Zanzibar's exports to India, 1859
(Exports to Europe and America in brackets)

	$
specie	320,000
ivory	310,000 (350,000)
cloves	100,000 (134,500)
copal	13,500 (153,750)
sandalwood	3,000
coconuts	2,700
hippo teeth	2,000
cowries	1,500 (230,000)
rafters	1,200
rhino-horn	800
beeswax	700
ebony	500
sundries	25,000

The most valuable of their purchases was ivory, of which they bought the best quality, called as a consequence '*bab Kutch*'. The size of their ivory requirements did not seem to vary: in 1848 they took 315,000 lb., worth $315,000, and a similar amount eleven years later, worth $310,000.[3] In Zanzibar they were the sole purchasers of hippo teeth.[4] East African copal, too, always found a ready sale in India, and at the beginning of 1845 a large demand for it in Bombay pushed up the price at Zanzibar from the usual $7½ a *frasela* to $9.[5] In 1845/6 India took 420,000 lb. of copal worth $108,000. In the year between January 1848 and February 1849 the Indians purchased the same amount as in 1845/6 but its value had fallen to $60,000, whereas the American purchase had risen to 700,000 lb., worth $110,000.[6] If Rigby's figures for 1859 are correct, for some reason by that year the copal bought by India had fallen to a mere $13,500.[7] The above table also shows that

---

[1] Rigby to F.O., no. 3, 1 May 1860, F.O. 54/17.   [2] *Idem.*
[3] For 1848, Loarer's Report, Part I, 1849, M.O., O.I. 5/23, and for 1859, Rigby, as above.
[4] Loarer, *idem.*   [5] Guillain's Report, 1849, A.N., Marine BB4/1036.
[6] Loarer, as above.   [7] Rigby, as above.

THE ECONOMIC DEVELOPMENT OF THE COAST

Zanzibar exported a large amount of specie to India. This was a feature of the Indian merchants' practice of treating the Swahili Coast as a temporary residence. None the less the export of specie was less of a drain on the economy of the Swahili Coast than might be imagined because it was offset by the Indians' generous provision of capital for local enterprises. Moreover, by the end of Saiyid Sa'id's reign more Indians were residing permanently in Zanzibar.[1]

Because of their indispensable role in the economic organization of the Swahili Coast the Indians were not squeezed out of its trade when Western merchants arrived. Instead they continued to prosper and came in growing numbers to Zanzibar. Despite the opening of new markets in the West, commerce with India remained an impressive proportion of the entire trade of the Swahili Coast and indeed was larger in volume than Swahili trade with any one Western country. In 1843 Kerdudal reckoned that Indian sales to Zanzibar amounted to $600,000 in comparison with American sales of $200,000 and Arabian of $300,000.[2] By 1859 the relative value of different countries' trade with Zanzibar was thus:[3]

Zanzibar Exports, 1859

	$	£
British India	467,500	(103,889)
Kutch	313,400	(69,644)
Total to India	780,900	(173,533)
Total to Europe and America	967,650	(215,034)
Total to Arabia	105,200	(23,670)

Zanzibar Imports, 1859

	$	£
British India	448,230	(99,607)
Kutch	260,424	(57,872)
Total from India	708,654	(157,479)
Total from Europe and America	1,540,947	(342,487)
Total from Arabia	79,231	(17,827)

How did the traditional merchants from Arabia fare in the face of the new competition from the West and the increased Indian commercial activity? There were three main groups of Arab seafarers – those from

---

[1] See Chapter X, p. 290.
[2] Kerdudal to Bazoche, 3 May 1844, M.O., O.I. 15/59.
[3] Rigby to F.O., no. 3, 1 May 1860, F.O. 54/17.

Oman and the Persian Gulf, those from the south coast of Arabia, and those from the Red Sea. After 1847 about eighty-five vessels came to the Swahili Coast from Arabia each year, of which fifty were from the coast of Oman and the Persian Gulf, twenty-five from the south coast of Arabia, and ten from the Red Sea. These vessels varied in size from 30 to 160 tons, although most of them were from 50 to 60 tons. In addition there arrived 150 smaller boats (*bedeni*) of 15 to 25 tons, mainly from Sur. The total number of vessels had actually been larger before 1847 when more severe measures were applied against the Slave Trade: the decrease can be estimated at about forty boats per annum.[1] By 1856, however, the number had risen again and 300 Arabian and Indian vessels were visiting Zanzibar annually.[2] Overall, however, there was no great increase in Arabian commerce because this was a similar number as had visited the Swahili Coast in the 1820s.[3]

Each of the three groups of Arab seafarers brought different articles to the Swahili Coast. Those from the Red Sea carried Venetian beads, which they obtained from Italy via Egypt, coffee (35,000 lb. a year), aloes, and dragon's blood; those from the south coast of Arabia, having fished on their way southwards, sold dried fish, salt, fish oil, and onions; and those from Oman and the Persian Gulf brought dates and raisins, donkeys and horses, Muscat cloths (in particular lengths for the making of turbans and belts), Persian carpets and silks, nankeen, crude gunpowder, almonds and drugs (mainly saffron and asafoetida). The Arabs also brought, in lesser amounts, honey, waterjugs, made-up clothes, rosewater, and gold and silver thread.[4] The sales of some of these articles were greatly affected by the advent of the Western merchants. Beads were now brought by Western vessels; a variety of European and American cloths was introduced to Zanzibar; and Western gunpowder was of better quality than the Arab equivalent.[5]

It is very difficult to estimate to what extent the Arab merchants were affected by this because so few figures are available to calculate the value of Arab trade and its possible fluctuations. One isolated figure available is that for the Arabs' sale of cloth in 1849 – $150,000.[6] In 1844 Kerdudal

[1] For the shipping figures, Guillain's Report, 1849, A.N., Marine BB4/1036.
[2] Cochet to Ministry of F.A., no. 6, 15 Jan. 1857, A.N., Aff.Etr. B3/438.
[3] Vandries to Philibert, Feb. 1822, M.O., O.I. 17/89.
[4] Guillain, *Côte de Zanguébar*, pp. 536, 540 and 542; Loarer's Report, Part I, 1849, M.O., O.I. 5/23; and Guillain's Report, 1849, A.N., Marine BB4/1036.
[5] Guillain's Report, 1849, as above, and Loarer, as above.
[6] Guillain, *idem*.

estimated that Zanzibar's imports amounted to $300,000.[1] But in 1859 a much lower figure was given by Rigby – $79,231, which was divided in the following manner:[2]

	$
silk and cotton lungis	50,000
frankincense	66
coffee 12,250 lb.	2,410
fish oil	2,000
dates	5,336
dry fruits	6,080
salt 1,840,000 lb.	5,000
Venetian beads	2,459
red dye	440
coarse paper	440
sundries	5,000
	79,231

If Rigby's low estimate is correct, the Arabs sold far less than other countries trading with the Swahili Coast.

The most important Arab purchase from East Africa was slaves. The Slave Trade has been considered in detail in Chapters VIII and IX, where it was shown that the export of slaves from East Africa did not diminish. Apart from slaves, the Arab vessels took cloves, sesame, coconuts, and rafters.[3] By 1849 about 350,000 lb. of cloves were being sent annually to Arabia.[4] Ten years later the Arabs were still buying about the same amount, worth $16,000. That year they also took 200,000 coconuts ($1,200), 12,000 rafters ($3,800), 11,200 lb. of sugar ($1,200), American cottons to the value of $8,000, $50,000 of specie, and sundries worth $25,000.[5] The Arabs were therefore buying both local and foreign products in Zanzibar.

Even though some branches of the Arab trade were affected by the advent of the Europeans, on the whole the Arab merchants benefited from the general economic expansion of the Swahili Coast. In response to the new situation they developed the practice of taking their home-produced goods to Zanzibar where they sold them to Europeans and Americans. The Western merchants were therefore able to avoid having to sail northwards if they did not wish to do so. The Americans,

[1] Kerdudal to Bazoche, 3 May 1844, M.O., O.I. 15/59.
[2] Rigby to F.O., no. 3, 1 May 1860, F.O. 54/17.
[3] Rigby, *idem*; and Guillain, *Côte de Zanguébar*, p. 536.
[4] Loarer's Report, Part I, 1849, M.O., O.I. 5/23.   [5] Rigby, as above.

for example, bought large amounts of Mocha coffee in Zanzibar where it was obtainable at a price which compared favourably with what it would have cost them to go to the Red Sea and buy it there.[1] Western merchants also bought many Arabian drugs at Zanzibar. The effect on Arab traders of Western competition was also less deleterious than it might have been because the Arabs participated in both the Slave Trade and the Indian Ocean carrying trade, neither of which occupations was undertaken by Western vessels. As well as their prominent position in the Swahili coastal trade, the Arabs had a virtual monopoly of the carriage of goods from East Africa to Arabia, the Banadir coast, the Comoro islands, and India. Although some of the vessels which went to India were owned by Indian merchants, they were mainly manned by Arabs. Western ships could not compete in the carrying trade because Arab vessels, which used slave labour, could offer far lower freight rates.[2]

The expanding market had profound effects on the nature and organization of the commercial life of the Swahili Coast. In order to sustain the interest of foreign newcomers it was vitally important for production to rise to meet the new demand and for the provision of goods to be regular, efficient, and dependable. Gradually East African commerce was organized to achieve this end. The provision of ivory, for example, was regularized and supplies increased to meet the new demand. There is no doubt that such a rise took place, although it is difficult to trace the stages at which this increase occurred. The first figure available is that of 1841, when 420,000 lb. were exported.[3] Another source gives a much higher figure for the amount of ivory exported two years later – 750,000 lb.[4] – and it is more likely that a third figure – for 1844 – is nearer the truth: 350,000 lb.[5] In 1849 two widely different estimates of the ivory export were made, an indication of how unwise it is to trust the figures. One source, Loarer, declared that 654,500 lb. were exported, as had been the case each year for the previous twenty years, but the other, Guillain, put the 1848 export at 875,000 lb.[6] By the end of Saiyid Sa'id's reign Burton calculated that

[1] Lists of cargoes in consular returns of American vessels at Zanzibar, Amer.N.A., Zanz. 1, 2, and 3.
[2] Loarer's Report, as above, and Guillain's Report, 1849, A.N., Marine BB4/1036.
[3] Guillain, *Côte de Zanguébar*, p. 535.
[4] Kerdudal to Bazoche, 3 May 1844, M.O., O.I. 15/59.
[5] Broquant to Ministry of F.A., 10 Mch. 1845, M.O., O.I. 15/65.
[6] Loarer, as above, and Guillain's Report, 1849, as above.

between 595,000 and 875,000 lb. of ivory were put on the Zanzibar market every year.[1] Since no figures are available for ivory sales in the 1820s and 1830s, comparisons with the early years of Saiyid Sa'id's reign cannot be made. It is clear, however, that supplies rose later in his reign.

None the less a price rise was fairly inevitable. On the one hand, the seller in the coastal market inflated his prices because the demand for ivory came from a number of different merchants in competition with one another, and on the other, the providers of tusks in the African interior required greater renumeration as their commodity became more desirable and more scarce. In any case the prices of ivory varied widely because there were several different qualities and it was often procured for barter rather than cash. In 1841 at Zanzibar ivory cost $25 to $30 a *frasela*, according to quality. Small or inferior tusks cost less.[2] By 1845 the best quality had risen to $34 a *frasela*, and by 1848 to between $36 and $38.[3] In the latter year the second quality varied between $32 and $34 a *frasela*, and the third between $25 and $28. By 1857 a *frasela* of the best quality was costing between $56 and $70.[4] This type of ivory was bought almost exclusively by Indians to the amount of 315,000 lb. a year, a quantity which was about the same as that which all the Western merchants bought of ivory of any quality. The second and third qualities, mainly purchased by Europeans and Americans, and consequently called '*bab Ulaya*', and the very small teeth, were also bought in small quantities by Hindus to be sent to China and Bengal. The prime quality came from Kilwa, whither it was brought from the Lake Nyasa country. Other regions produced the medium-priced tusks, and ivory of the worst quality generally came from the country behind Lamu.[5]

The expansion of the market meant that ivory had to be supplied regularly and in growing quantities. Previously it had reached the coast either by a relay system or by means of caravans organized by Africans from the interior. Both these methods were inadequate in the

[1] Burton, *Lake Regions*, II, Appendix I, p. 412.
[2] Guillain, *Côte de Zanguébar*, p. 535; and Kerdudal to Bazoche, 9 June 1843, M.O., O.I. 15/63.
[3] For 1845, R. Desfossés to Ministry of Marine, 19 Nov. 1844, A.E., Zanz. C.C.1; and Broquant to Ministry of F.A., 10 Mch. 1845, M.O., O.I. 15/65. For 1848, Guillain's Report, 1849, A.N., Marine BB4/1036.
[4] Burton, *Lake Regions*, II, Appendix I, p. 412.
[5] Guillain's Report, 1849, as above, and Loarer's Report, Part I, 1849, M.O., O.I. 5/23.

new economic situation. It would be more satisfactory if coast merchants themselves went inland to procure ivory. This practice had existed previously to a limited extent, and certainly benefited the participants as far as prices were concerned. Goods were cheaper when merchants went inland to buy them. For example, at Lake Tanganyika in 1831 two *frasela* of beads costing $5 each were exchanged for four *frasela* of ivory.[1]

Gradually the new economic requirements encouraged outsiders to penetrate far into the interior. Probably the first non-Africans to reach Unyamwesi were two Khojas from Surat – Saiyan and Musa Mzuri. They undertook their journey in about 1824, apparently encouraged by the governor of Zanzibar, Sa'id al-Akhbari.[2] In 1828 we hear of the return of elephant-hunters after thirty-day journeys inland.[3] In 1831 a far more ambitious adventure was attempted by Lief ibn Sa'id who travelled through Unyamwesi as far as Lake Tanganyika. He may have got so far because he possibly spoke the Nyamwesi language: his mother appears to have been a Nyamwesi slave in Zanzibar.[4] Thereafter records of journeys to the interior become more frequent. In 1837 Saiyid Sa'id sent one Umar Fumba inland on a trading expedition, in 1839 Waters, the American consul, discussed commercial matters with a man who had been five times far into the interior, and in 1841/2 an Arab caravan crossed Lake Tanganyika to Kazembe.[5] Inland journeys then became so commonplace that ten years later an expedition organized by an Arab trader travelled from the east to the west coast of Africa and back.[6] Traders were stimulated to penetrate deeper from the coast because they constantly had to seek out new markets for the cloth, wire and beads which they exchanged for ivory and slaves and because the products of areas near the coast may have become scarce or too expensive.

---

[1] James Macqueen, 'The Visit of Lief bin Said to the Great African Lake', *J.R.G.S.*, XV (1845), pp. 371-4 (here p. 372).

[2] Burton, *Lake Regions*, II, 223-4.

[3] E. Roberts to L. Woodbury, 26 Dec. 1828, quoted by Sir John Gray, 'Trading expeditions from the Coast to Lakes Tanganyika and Victoria before 1857', *T.N.R.*, no. 49 (Dec. 1957), pp. 226-46 (here p. 228).

[4] As note 1, above.

[5] Journal of R. P. Waters, entries for 23 Mch. and 6 July 1839, printed in Bennett and Brooks, *op. cit.*, pp. 209, 210, and 211; and Burton, *Lake Regions*, II, 151.

[6] 'Notes of a Caravan Journey from the East to the West Coast of Africa, communicated by Vice-consul Brand', *J.R.G.S.*, XXIV (1854), pp. 266-71.

THE ECONOMIC DEVELOPMENT OF THE COAST

The expansion of the coastal market allowed the new system of getting ivory and slaves to the coast and the former system to coexist. There came to be three types of caravans: the traditional ones consisting entirely of interior tribesmen (particularly Nyamwesi), those commissioned by patrons and commanded by Swahilis, and those led by Arabs.[1] Regular routes were followed, along which were established permanent halting places, such as Zungomero, Unyanyembe, and Ujiji.[2] The routes were of course liable to alteration from time to time as the result of political vicissitudes or physical disruption.[3] The most popular routes penetrated the region which lay behind the Mrima coast and extended to the central African lakes. In comparison, the inland area to the north of Mombasa was seldom visited by coastal peoples, although a man from Kao explored the course of the River Ozi.[4] In this latter region exploration was discouraged by the peoples of the interior who preferred to bring their goods to the coast themselves. They used Kao, twelve miles from the mouth of the River Ozi, as their principal market.[5] However, further north, behind the Banadir coast, coastal people did travel inland, taking their goods overland to Ganana, whence they proceeded up the Juba river.[6]

On the Mrima coast the major destinations for caravans were Kilwa Kivinje, Buyuni, Mbwemaji and Pangani, and of lesser importance were the ports of Tongui, Lindi, and Bagamoyo.[7] There was great competition among these coastal towns, particularly Bagamoyo, Mbwemaji and Buyuni, which were close to each other, to persuade the caravans to come to them, so that they would get the best choice of ivory and slaves, receive the benefit of the dues which were payable, and be centres for thriving commercial communities of Indians, who never participated in caravans themselves but would come to the coastal towns and spend months bartering for ivory and slaves.[8]

---

[1] Burton, *Lake Regions*, II, 341.

[2] *Ibid.*, I, 95. See also T. O. Beidelman, 'A History of Ukaguru, 1857-1916', *T.N.R.*, nos 58 and 59 (Mch./Sept. 1962), pp. 11-39.

[3] For incidents, Burton, *Lake Regions*, I, 5 and 303.

[4] Annexe to instructions to Loarer, Jan. 1846, M.O., O.I. 2/10.

[5] Boteler, *op. cit.*, I, 393; Journal of Lt Christopher, 1843, encl. in Bombay to Secret Committee, no. 54, 18 July 1843, E.S.L.B. 60; and Guillain's Report, 1849, A.N., Marine BB4/1036.

[6] Guillain, *idem*.

[7] Loarer's Report, Part II, 1849, M.O., O.I. 2/10.

[8] For a description of the methods of enticement, see Guillain's Report, 1849, A.N., Marine BB4/1036; and Burton, *Lake Regions*, I, 39.

As the littoral towns flourished with the expansion of trade with the African interior, so private traders enriched themselves. Richard Burton, however, considered that the caravan trade did not bring fortunes to its operators. 'Arab merchants', he said, 'gain but little beyond a livelihood in plenty and dignity by their expeditions to the interior.'[1] He calculated that an investment of $1,000 would bring a profit of $1,050, from which had to be subtracted expenses and the cost of goods which were needed for caravanners to bribe their way through hostile regions. Among the expenses was the cost of porterage. This was less onerous when slaves owned or hired by the caravan leaders were used as porters, but became more burdensome when the organizers had to hire free Africans (the Nyamwesi in particular began to undertake this occupation).[2] Burton's view is at variance with other evidence which makes it appear that caravans were a most profitable enterprise. For example, Snai ibn Amir, who had begun life as a confectioner in Muscat, rose in sixteen years to be one of the wealthiest ivory and slave dealers on the East African coast. He travelled three times from the coast to Unyamwesi, besides navigating Lake Tanganyika and visiting Uganda.[3] Had caravanning been unprofitable, the Arabs and Swahilis would not have been so reluctant to let Europeans penetrate the interior lest their source of wealth be usurped. For the same reason, the old Swahili inhabitants resented Arab penetration.[4] The Arabs made substantial profits from their caravans, a fact of great economic significance because those who had led three or four often bought an estate in Zanzibar and planted cloves.[5] Once he had become a plantation owner, the Arab trader could remain in Zanzibar and become a caravan patron. Thus there was no real division between land-owners and caravanners, or indeed ship-owners. By 1856 there were Arab merchants who owned '80,000 clove trees, $100,000 floating capital, a ship or two, and from 1,000 to 2,000 slaves'.[6] Thus the need to maintain a steady supply of ivory to the coast to meet the increased demand had prompted the Arabs to engage in the new profit-making venture of caravanning. This encouraged them to stay in East Africa and to use their resultant prosperity to entrench themselves in Zanzibar as land-owners.

A side-effect of the expansion of the caravan trade was the increased import of firearms, which was ultimately to have momentous implications. Guns and powder, particularly those of British manufacture, had

---

[1] Burton, *ibid.*, II, Appendix I, p. 411.   [2] *Ibid.*, I, 337.   [3] *Ibid.*, p. 323.
[4] *Ibid.*, pp. 16 and 31.   [5] Loarer's Report, Part I, 1849, M.O., O.I. 5/23.
[6] Burton, *Zanzibar*, I, 378.

THE ECONOMIC DEVELOPMENT OF THE COAST

always been imported by the Swahili Coast, but now a greater supply was required, partly in order to arm caravan guards and partly for sale in the interior. Some interior peoples, and particularly the Zigua, acquired a formidable number of firearms.[1] In 1859, 22,780 muskets and fowling pieces and 11,912 barrels of gunpowder were supplied to Zanzibar, of which 8,000 muskets and 11,000 barrels of gunpowder (each of 25 lb.) came from America, 7,000 muskets and 2,000 fowling pieces from France, 1,200 muskets from Germany, and 4,580 muskets and 912 barrels of gunpowder from Singapore.[2]

Just as the demand for East African ivory increased after 1830, so did that for gum copal, widely used in the manufacture of coach varnish. Copal was obtained from the mainland littoral between Mombasa and Cape Delgado, and was of particularly good quality between Kilwa and Pangani.[3] It was a resin which dripped from the copal tree and hardened in the ground, from which it had to be unearthed. Since the digging was an occupation undertaken by local Swahilis, copal was a product not dependent on the caravan trade. After it was dug up, the copal was shipped to Zanzibar in its dirty state and there either cleaned or sold 'raw'. The cleaning process was an industry in itself.[4]

Large quantities of copal had always been sent to Arabia and India but, as with ivory, it was the American demand which initially stimulated the increased supply. The British, too, were soon buying large amounts of copal. In 1841, 105,000 lb. altogether were exported from Zanzibar.[5] Detailed figures exist to illustrate the situation in 1845/6 and 1848/9:[6]

Export of Copal from Zanzibar, 1845/6

				$
America	18,000 *frasela*	at $6	uncleaned	108,000
England	10,000 *frasela*	at $8	cleaned	80,000
France	2,500 *frasela*	at $7½	cleaned	18,250
British India	12,000 *frasela*	at $6½	all types	78,000
	42,500 (1,487,500 lb.)			284,250

---

[1] Burton, *Lake Regions*, I, 125.

[2] Rigby to F.O., no. 3, 1 May 1860, F.O. 54/17. The Singapore trade is not being considered because it began after 1856.

[3] Guillain, *Côte de Zanguébar*, p. 535.

[4] For the digging and processing of copal, see Burton, *Lake Regions*, II, Appendix I, pp. 403-8.

[5] Guillain, *Côte de Zanguébar*, p. 536.

[6] Loarer's Report, Part I, 1849, M.O., O.I. 5/23.

Export of Copal from Zanzibar, Jan. 1848/Feb. 1849

				$
America	20,000 *frasela*	at $5½	uncleaned	110,000
England	8,000 *frasela*	at $7½	cleaned	60,000
France	2,000 *frasela*	at $7½	cleaned	15,000
British India	12,000 *frasela*	at $5	all types	60,000
Arab flag (for England)	2,500 *frasela*	at $6¼	cleaned	16,250
Arab flag (for France)	4,500 *frasela*	at $6½	cleaned	29,250
Hanseatic towns	4,500 *frasela*	at $7	cleaned	31,500
	53,500 (1,872,500 lb.)			322,000

The increase in the quantity of copal sold was therefore about 25 per cent but the increase in the value of the sales only 12 per cent. In 1856 Hamerton estimated that about 800,000 to 1,200,000 lb. were being exported every year.[1]

The price of copal was subject to incessant fluctuations and in any case varied according to its quality and the degree of refinement it had received. Initially the Americans bought large quantities, but when the price in America fell their purchases diminished, stocks built up in Zanzibar and prices collapsed.[2] In the first boom caused by the American purchase and a simultaneous increase in the demand from Bombay, the price of copal rose from about $4 a *frasela* to $9, after which there was a diminution followed by a rise to $9 again by 1856.[3]

The expansion of the ivory and copal trades was a paramount factor in another development: the establishment of centralized control over the littoral ports where these two products were available. The centralization was effected in a number of ways – the extension of political control and the appointment of customs officials (both factors which have already been considered in previous chapters), the imposition of customs dues, the registration of local shipping, and the prohibition of foreign traders from going directly to the littoral ports. This last method, which came to be known as the 'Mrima monopoly', was an important feature of Saiyid Sa'id's policy because his system of government was based on the principle that Zanzibar was at once the political centre and commercial entrepot of the Swahili Coast. Zanzibar's

[1] Burton, *Lake Regions*, II, Appendix I, p. 406.
[2] Loarer's Report, as above; and Ward to Buchanan, no. 14, 1 Jan. 1847, Amer.N.A., Zanz. 2.
[3] Guillain, *Côte de Zanguébar*, p. 535; Loarer, as above; Guillain's Report, 1849, A.N., Marine BB4/1036; and Burton, *Lake Regions*, II, Appendix I, p. 406.

retention of this role would be endangered should rival centres be established. Moreover, without centralized control, Saiyid Sa'id's revenues would be more limited. Since the European and American treaties imposed a duty solely on imports, and none on exports, Westerners trading directly with the Mrima could have by-passed the middlemen who transported goods from the littoral to Zanzibar and who had to pay customs duties. In his treaties with Great Britain and France Sa'id therefore stipulated that ships of those nations were not to buy ivory and gum copal on the littoral between Kilwa and Mtangata.

However, it is possible that the loss of revenue was not Saiyid Sa'id's paramount criterion in imposing this restriction because on the rare occasions when foreign ships did buy articles at mainland ports, the customs officials insisted that the sellers raise the price and pay them the sum they normally would have received if the goods were taken away in local boats.[1] An alternative explanation of the monopoly is offered by Guillain: in 1837 Saiyid Sa'id conceded to one Sa'id ibn Danin, for an annual rent, the monopoly of commerce on the Mrima. Sa'id ibn Danin then ceded his right to Jairam, the customs master at Zanzibar. However, in July 1840, by the general demand of the Sultan's subjects, the commerce became free again for all but Christian traders.[2] This explanation is supported by the fact that no Mrima monopoly was stipulated in the American treaty of 1833. Sa'id later tried to impose the restriction on the Americans, arguing that the treaty had allowed them to trade at any *ports* in his dominions, but as the Mrima villages had no customs officials (which was not true), they could not be classed as regular ports. Although the Sultan approached the State Department several times about the matter, he was unable to prevail on the Americans to change their treaty.[3] It was useful to them in its existing form because, although they did not visit the Mrima to trade, they used the monopoly as a lever to obtain concessions from the Sultan.[4]

[1] Loarer's Report, Part I, 1849, M.O., O.I. 5/23.
[2] Guillain's Report, 1849, A.N., Marine BB4/1036.
[3] Saiyid Sa'id to Palmerston, 11 Mch. 1847, F.O. 54/11; Andrew Ward to State Dept., Jan. 1842, and Sa'id to the President of the USA, n.d. (but end 1842) – Amer.N.A., Zanz. 1; Sa'id to Waters, 30 Nov. 1845, Z.A.; Ward to Buchanan, no. 3, 21 Feb. 1846 and 4 Sept. 1847, Sa'id to Ward, n.d. (1847), and Sa'id to the President of the USA, 11 Mch. 1847 – Amer.N.A., Zanz. 2.
[4] For their disinclination to trade directly with the Mrima, Guillain, *Côte de Zanguébar*, p. 528.

They were able to exert pressure by threatening to trade directly with the Mrima.[1]

The French, too, had arguments with Sa'id about the Mrima after *La Grenouille* had been forbidden to trade at Lindi and Kilwa and after Loarer was not allowed to stay on shore when he visited Kilwa.[2] The governor of Kilwa Kivinje had told the visitors that he had orders to use force if necessary. The French argued that it was only trade in copal and ivory which was forbidden to them, and not all trade. Eventually the French consul at Zanzibar obtained an agreement from Sa'id that the French could trade at Kilwa Kivinje only.[3] As for the British, they were not in such a good position as the French to claim similar concessions because there had been a thorough discussion about the article concerning the Mrima when Cogan had negotiated their treaty in 1839. Cogan had pointed out that the entire abolition of monopolies would be most destructive to Sa'id's revenues, dependent as they were on customs dues. As it was, Saiyid Sa'id would lose $45,000 a year by remitting export duties on British vessels.[4]

Another result of the need to organize trade and centralize it in Zanzibar was the imposition of regular customs duties. Western merchants paid only the 5 per cent duties on imports stipulated in their treaties with the Sultan, but other merchants paid duties on each article according to a fixed scale. These were collected by the customs officials at the different littoral towns who were appointed by the Zanzibar customs master either as his agents or as sub-contractors. Exceptions were the customs posts of Pemba, Mombasa, and the ports to the north, which were independently rented and not sublet by Jairam.[5] In theory the duties which these officials levied were regulated by the Sultan, but in practice Jairam decided what they should be.[6]

Duties were collected by the customs officials at the Swahili ports if

---

[1] Ward to Buchanan, no. 17, 13 Mch. 1847, Amer.N.A., Zanz. 2; and Ward to Shepard, 13 June 1846, printed in Bennett and Brooks, *op. cit.*, p. 365.

[2] Journal of *La Grenouille*, entries from 23 July to 3 Sept., 1848, A.E., Zanz. C.C.1; and Loarer's Report, Part I, 1849, M.O., O.I. 5/23.

[3] Belligny to Ministry of F.A., no. 7, 9 Jan. 1850, A.E., Zanz. C.C.1.

[4] Cogan to Palmerston, 6 May 1839, and Saiyid Sa'id to Palmerston, 2 June 1839, F.O. 54/3.

[5] Hamerton to Bombay, 2 Jan. 1842, encl. in Bombay to Secret Committee, no. 43, 30 Apr. 1842, E.S.L.B. 44; and Belligny to Ministry of F.A., 8 July 1850, A.E., Zanz. C.C.1.

[6] Ward to Buchanan, no. 3, 21 Feb. 1846 and 13 Mch. 1847, Amer.N.A., Zanz. 2; and Guillain's Report, 1849, A.N., Marine BB4/1036.

THE ECONOMIC DEVELOPMENT OF THE COAST

the exported articles were not bound for Zanzibar. But if goods were to be taken to the entrepot they paid no duty when leaving the littoral ports but were instead subject to customs dues on entry to Zanzibar. In the latter case the customs masters were obliged to send a detailed list of the ships' cargoes to the Zanzibar customs master. This system did not come into operation until the 1840s; previously part of the duty was paid on leaving the littoral port and part on entry to Zanzibar.[1] As long as there were different customs officials at each port who separately bought their positions from Saiyid Sa'id, the system had to be thus. But as soon as one man rented the customs collection for the whole area, as Jairam did in the 1830s, the practice could be changed. Preferring to have all the duties paid directly to him, Jairam abolished the payments on goods destined for Zanzibar leaving the littoral ports, and increased the entry duties at Zanzibar.[2] In 1849 these stood at the following level:[3]

Customs Duties on Major Articles, 1849

	origin	
ivory	Mombasa to Rufiji R.	$4 a *frasela*
	Kilwa	2½ a *frasela* (larger tusks)
		2 a *frasela* (smaller tusks)
	Unyamwesi	8 a *frasela*
	Mogadishu to Lamu	2 a *frasela*
	Kisuere to Portuguese possessions	2 a *frasela*
rhino-horn	Unyamwesi	2 a *frasela* (Loarer says $3)
	Mombasa to Rufiji R.	1 a *frasela* (Loarer says $2)
	elsewhere	1 a *frasela*
copal		¾ a *frasela*
hides		5 per cent
tortoise-shell		$⅜ for 3 lb.

There were, of course, attempts to avoid payment of duties, which Jairam tried to limit by ordering that all ivory which entered Zanzibar should be stamped.[4] The regularization and uniform application of customs duties had a beneficial effect on the provision of goods and their collection in one place in amounts large enough to attract foreign buyers. The fact that so many places were under the commercial control of one man – the Zanzibar customs master – encouraged the

[1] Loarer's Report, Part I, 1849, M.O., O.I. 5/23. [2] *Idem.*
[3] Guillain's Report, 1849, A.N., Marine BB4/1036; and Loarer, as above.
[4] Guillain, *idem.*

development of Zanzibar as the major market for the whole coast because it was not to the traders' advantage to go elsewhere to buy and sell.

A further aspect of the regularization of Swahili Coast trade was the more widespread use of money, a development which was valuable to foreign merchants who might have an unfavourable balance of trade. The Maria Theresa dollar and the Spanish piastre were both in use in early nineteenth-century Zanzibar, where they both had the same value,[1] and they continued to be the coins most commonly used in Saiyid Sa'id's reign. In the 1840s the dollar and piastre remained the same value,[2] but in the early 1850s the light weight of some piastres caused dissatisfaction among merchants.[3] However, although in general prices rose, there was little alteration in the exchange rate of the dollar and piastre at Zanzibar, although at changes of season, when specie remittances were made to Muscat, the Red Sea, and India, there were better rates of exchange.[4] Also in use at Zanzibar were Indian rupees and Portuguese gold coins. The latter were the favourite acquisition of all merchants because of their high intrinsic value, but they were not used for ordinary trading.[5] At Zanzibar the usual exchange rate of the Bombay and Company (after 1835) rupee was 214–215 rupees for 100 M.T. dollars.[6] The US dollar, Mexican dollar, and British sovereign were seldom seen in Zanzibar.[7]

So far the expanded market and the impetus it gave to increased production of traditional articles of trade and to the regularization of the commercial mechanism have been considered. The expansion of the market also caused another major development: experimentation in new branches of commerce and the production of new articles for sale. Such experimentation took place in the 1830s and 1840s and had its most startling success in the planting of cloves, a development which made

[1] Albrand's Report, 1819, M.O., Réunion 72/472.

[2] Guillain's Report, 1849, A.N., Marine BB4/1036; and Hamerton to Registrar of Merchant Seamen, London, 10 Aug. 1844, Z.A. The M.T. dollar had a mint par value of £0·2061 or 4s 1½d, and it contained 28·075 grammes of silver.

[3] Ward to Shepard, 20 Jan. 1851, printed in Bennett and Brooks, op. cit., p. 473.

[4] Idem.

[5] Idem; Guillain's Report, 1849, as above; and Loarer's Report, Part I, 1849, M.O., O.I. 5/23.

[6] Guillain, as above; H. P. Marshall to Forsyth, 8 Mch. 1838, Amer.N.A., Zanz. 1; and Hamerton to Bombay, no. 12, 25 Oct. 1849, Z.A.

[7] Ward to Shepard, as note 3. The English sovereign passed at $ M.T. 4¾, but was only in use at times of remittances.

THE ECONOMIC DEVELOPMENT OF THE COAST

the Swahili Coast a yet more attractive market for Western merchants. By 1856 cloves were Zanzibar's third largest export.

The planting of large areas of land with cloves during the late 1820s and the 1830s, and its political and social effects, have already been described in Chapter X.[1] Although figures provided by various observers do not always tally, they all demonstrate the rapid growth of clove exports:[2]

Clove Exports from Zanzibar

	Guillain *frasela*	Kerdudal *frasela*	Ward *frasela*	Loarer *frasela*	Cochet *frasela*	Burton *frasela*
1839-40	9,000	20,000	—	8,000	—	—
1843-4	30,000	20,000	—	—	—	—
1845	—	—	—	30,000	—	—
1846-7	100,000	—	—	30,000	—	—
1847-8	35,000-40,000	—	—	—	—	—
1848-9	120,000-130,000	—	—	70,000	—	—
1850-1	—	—	57,000-85,000	—	—	—
1856	—	—	—	—	46,752	142,857

In 1859 the crop rose to 200,000 *frasela*, worth $250,000.[3] Although the price of cloves fluctuated according to the size of the harvest, the value of the crops of previous years can be calculated roughly by allowing an average price of $5 a *frasela*.[4]

Another product which came on to the Zanzibar market in large quantities was the cowry shell. Before the Germans came to Zanzibar, cowries were only gathered when other trade was dull.[5] In response to their demand in the 1840s there sprung up an important cowry trade in Chole island.[6] By 1856 cowries had become the Swahili Coast's fifth

---

[1] See Chapter X, pp. 283-7.
[2] Guillain's Report, 1849, A.N., Marine BB4/1036; Kerdudal to Bazoche, 3 May 1844, M.O., O.I. 15/59; Ward to Abbot, 13 Mch. 1851, Amer.N.A., Zanz. 3; Loarer's Report, Part I, 1849, M.O., O.I. 5/23; Cochet to Ministry of F.A., no. 6, 15 Jan. 1857, A.N., Aff.Etr. B3/438; and Burton, *Zanzibar*, I, 364. See also Chapter X, p. 284.
[3] Burton, *Zanzibar*, I, 365, for the size of the crop; and Rigby to F.O., no. 3, 1 May 1860, F.O. 54/17, for the value.
[4] For the average price, Guillain's Report, 1849, as above, and Loarer's Report, 1849, as above.
[5] Loarer, as above. [6] Krapf, *op. cit.*, p. 422.

largest export, worth $85,795.[1] In 1859, 8,016,000 lb. worth $245,000 were exported.[2] As in the case of copal, the coastal people were not dependent on the caravan trade to procure cowries.

The Western merchants also stimulated the sale of hides, a trade which in former times had been pursued in only a desultory fashion. The sale of hides boosted the prosperity of Lamu and Brava, where large numbers were obtainable. Since these ports were north of the Mrima and consequently not subject to the restrictions which applied to that area, Western merchants were able to visit them. In 1849 about 28,000 hides were being purchased every year, a number which rose to 35,000 in 1856 (worth $26,190) and to 95,000 in 1859 (worth $115,000).[3]

The products of the coconut palm – oil, copra, coir, and the nut itself – were traditionally exported from the Swahili Coast, but in the 1830s and 1840s attempts were made to manufacture coconut oil on a large scale for sale to Western merchants. In 1841, 18,000 *frasela* were exported and in 1848, 40,000.[4] However, a similar fate befell the production of coconut oil as hit other manufacturing enterprises in Zanzibar, and it was unable to compete with non-manufactured goods as an attractive article for export. By 1856 the export of coconut oil to America, France and Germany was worth only $8,110.[5] Three years later the total export of the oil amounted to only 7,200 *frasela*, worth $18,297.[6] Coconuts themselves went mainly to India, which accepted almost 12,000,000 in 1856.[7] However, the number is deceptive because prises were low; in 1859 the export of nuts was worth only $12,200 to Zanzibar, and that of copra $60,000.[8]

The refinement of sugar and the construction of large ships were other industrial enterprises attempted in Zanzibar. The sugar factories in existence in 1819[9] had not been a success, and in the early 1830s Saiyid Sa'id, at the height of his period of commercial experimentation, established another sugar factory and sent to Bourbon to obtain sugar-cane planters.[10] The attempt to get skilled assistance came to nothing,

---

[1] Cochet to Ministry of F.A., no. 6, 15 Jan. 1857, A.N., Aff.Etr. B3/438.

[2] Rigby to F.O., no. 3, 1 May 1860, F.O. 54/17.

[3] For 1849, Loarer's and Guillain's Reports, as above; for 1856, Cochet, as above; and for 1859, Rigby, as above.

[4] For 1841, Guillain, *Côte de Zanguébar*, p. 538; and for 1848 Loarer, as above.

[5] Cochet, as above.   [6] Rigby, as above.   [7] Burton, *Zanzibar*, I, 220.

[8] Rigby, as above.   [9] See Chapter III, p. 82.

[10] Governor of Bourbon to Ministry of Marine, no. 119, 3 Apr. 1843, M.O., Réunion 86/569.

and the Sultan did not revive his project until the 1840s, when, with the help of Robert Cogan, he imported a steam-driven sugar mill from England.[1] At first the enterprise showed signs of success because in 1844 Hamerton reported that the cultivation of sugar was increasing.[2] By 1847, 250,000 lb. were being produced annually.[3] But the project collapsed when Cogan left Zanzibar and by 1848 Sa'id had to send his sugar to England and America for refining.[4] The following year he tried again to get foreign assistance and came to an arrangement with Classun, an inhabitant of Bourbon. They agreed that Sa'id would provide land and 800 workers while Classun ran the factory.[5] At the same time Sa'id's son, Khalid, ordered an iron sugar mill from England.[6] However, the new project also collapsed, mainly because Classun died of fever.[7] By 1856 all the sugar grown in Zanzibar was consumed on the island and none was exported.[8]

The failure of the sugar projects indicates the difficulty faced by the peoples of the Swahili Coast when they tried to establish manufacturing and industrial processes. Their major problem was their want of specialized knowledge and machinery. At the same time they lacked real impetus because they were able to prosper from the export of non-manufactured goods. Their attempts to construct ships at Zanzibar also failed. A project to build a large vessel in the 1840s was not a success,[9] and by 1856 the American consul reported that there were no facilities for ship repair or construction at Zanzibar to any extent.[10]

Another experiment prompted by the development of new markets was the Omanis' attempt to sell directly to Europe and America by transporting their own goods thither rather than to concentrate on offering articles for sale to Western ships at Zanzibar. This was the grandest of all the commercial experiments of the Omanis. It was only

[1] Hamerton to Aberdeen, 13 Apr. 1844, and Cogan's Diary, entry for 20 Feb. 1844, F.O. 54/6.
[2] Hamerton to Aberdeen, 2 Jan. 1844, F.O. 54/6.
[3] Ward to Buchanan, no. 17, 13 Mch. 1847, Amer.N.A., Zanz. 2.
[4] Ward to Shepard, 14 Dec. 1848, printed in Bennett and Brooks, *op. cit.*, p. 398.
[5] Commander of Réunion and Madagascar to Ministry of Marine, 10 Sept. 1850, M.O., O.I. 15/65.
[6] Khalid to Newman Hunt, 5 Jan. 1849, F.O. 54/8.
[7] Belligny to Ministry of F.A., 17 Aug. 1850, A.E., Zanz. C.C.1.
[8] Burton, *Zanzibar*, I, 222.
[9] Guillain, *Documents*, II, 243; and Loarer's Report, Part I, 1849, M.O., O.I. 5/23.
[10] Mansfield to Mancy, 31 Jan. 1856, Amer.N.A., Zanz. 3.

THE SWAHILI COAST

Saiyid Sa'id himself who was in a position to undertake such enterprises because only he owned the large vessels capable of sailing round the Cape of Good Hope into the Atlantic. Early in his reign Saiyid Sa'id had begun to use his larger warships as commercial vessels, having negotiated for them favourable terms of entry to Bengal and Bourbon.[1] When Western merchants began to trade in Zanzibar, the possibility of sending his vessels to Europe and America caught his imagination.

First to go was the *Sultana* to New York in 1839. She carried 300 carpets (from the Persian Gulf), 1,035 hides, 1,287 sacks of dates (from Arabia), 100 bags of coffee (from Mocha), 108 tusks of ivory, 138 bags of cloves, and 71 boxes of gum copal. The ship returned with guns, gunpowder, cloth, beads and gold leaf.[2] However, this initial voyage was not profitable because it incurred heavy expenses.[3] It may have been for this reason that Saiyid Sa'id changed his intention of sending another vessel to America in 1842/3 and instead despatched one to England.[4] In July 1845 the *Caroline* arrived in London with cloves, coffee, copal, dates, sugar and coconut oil, a cargo altogether worth $100,000.[5] But once again the voyage turned out to be more expensive than the Sultan had envisaged because the duties chargeable on the cargo were £9,000.[6] Unfortunately for the Omanis, the duty of 5 per cent on imports charged to the British at Zanzibar was not reciprocal, and Sa'id merely got most favoured nation treatment by Article I of the 1839 treaty. However, in appreciation of the courageous nature of the Sultan's enterprise, the *Caroline's* repairs, costing £3,484, were done free of charge.[7] Saiyid Sa'id was further discouraged from trading directly with Europe and America by the pressure put upon him by American merchants who thought that they would be adversely affected were he to enter the American market.[8] The Americans were supported by Jairam who feared any diminution in foreign trade at

[1] For his father's negotiations, see Chapter III, p. 97, and for his own, see Chapter VI, p. 137.

[2] Extract from the account book of Ahmad ibn Nahman, who was in charge of the voyage, printed in *T.N.R.*, no. 31 (July 1951), pp. 25-31 (here p. 27).

[3] British agent, Muscat, to Bombay, 4 Apr. 1841, encl. in Bombay to Secret Committee, no. 29, 26 Apr. 1841, E.S.L.B. 31.

[4] R. P. Waters to J. G. Waters, 2 Sept. 1843, and R. P. Waters' notes, 10 Nov. 1842, printed in Bennett and Brooks, *op. cit.*, pp. 246 and 254.

[5] Ward to Buchanan, no. 17, 13 Mch. 1847, Amer.N.A., Zanz. 2; and Fabens to Shepard, 22 Apr. 1845, printed in Bennett and Brooks, *op. cit.*, p. 342.

[6] Newman Hunt to Aberdeen, 25 July 1845, F.O. 54/8.

[7] Admiralty to F.O., 12 Sept. 1845, F.O. 54/8.

[8] Ward to Buchanan, no. 17, 13 Mch. 1847, Amer.N.A., Zanz. 2.

THE ECONOMIC DEVELOPMENT OF THE COAST

Zanzibar; the customs master could not compensate himself for any resultant loss of revenue by exacting duties from the Sultan's ships because Saiyid Sa'id himself paid no export duties.[1] Daunted by such setbacks, in 1847 Sa'id considered ceasing to send his ships to Europe and America, provided he could sell in Zanzibar his own production of cloves and sugar.[2] But when the French began to trade at Zanzibar the Sultan regained his ambition and in 1849 sent the *Caroline* to Marseilles and the *Artemise* to London.[3] The *Caroline* did not face such heavy expenses from customs dues as it had in London in 1845 because the French authorities wanted it to make a more favourable return than the ship which simultaneously arrived in London. They consequently admitted its cargo on the same terms as a French bottom.[4] The *Caroline* therefore made a greater profit than the *Artemise* in London whose expenses exceeded the sum received from the sale of the cargo.[5] However, the prospect of using French ports as a market for Swahili products soon dimmed because the treatment of the *Caroline* in Marseilles as a French ship aroused a great outcry from French merchants interested in the East African trade.[6] Finally, Saiyid Sa'id sent another ship to London in 1852 with 5,000 *frasela* of cloves.[7] No great profits were made from any of these voyages, but this would not have caused the Sultan much distress because he regarded the expeditions as much as prestige operations as commercial ventures. It was indeed somewhat extraordinary for an Arab ruler to be sending his ships round the Cape to Europe and America.

So far the expansion of the Swahili Coast's market and the measures which were taken to increase production and to develop new economic activities have been considered. It yet remains to study the overall effect of this economic upheaval of the first half of the nineteenth century. In the first place, the relative importance of different products altered, and this had an effect on the fortunes of their particular places

---

[1] Ward to Shepard, 13 June 1846, printed in Bennett and Brooks, *op. cit.* p. 365.
[2] Ward to Shepard, 20 Dec. 1847, *ibid.*, p 389.
[3] Ward to Shepard, 26 Jan. 1849, *ibid.*, p. 438.
[4] Ministry of F.A. to Belligny, no. 2, 4 Aug. 1849, A.E., Zanz. C.C.1.
[5] Ward to Shepard, 3 Jan. 1850, printed in Bennett and Brooks, *op. cit.*, p. 451.
[6] Note on the Zanzibar Treaty by Guillain, 20 July 1849, A.E., Zanz. C.C.1.
[7] Webb to Shepard, 27 Jan. 1852, printed in Bennett and Brooks, *op. cit.*, p. 494.

of provenance. The following tables of exports and imports show the alterations from 1843 to 1859 and also the influence of the new demand from the West:

Zanzibar Exports, 1843[1]

	amount	av. price per *frasela*	value
		$	$
coconut oil	40,000 *frasela* (140,000 lb.)	1¼	50,000
cloves	20,000 *frasela* (70,000 lb.)	4¾	95,000
copal	20,000 *frasela* (70,000 lb.)	4	80,000
ivory	20,000 *frasela* (70,000 lb.)	27	540,000

Zanzibar Exports, Jan. 1848 to Feb. 1849[2]

	amount	value
		$
coconut oil	40,000 *frasela* (140,000 lb.)	
cloves	120,000-130,000 *frasela* (420,000-455,000 lb.)	
copal	53,500 *frasela* (1,872,500 lb.)	322,000
ivory	25,000 *frasela* (875,000 lb.)	

Zanzibar Exports, 1859[3]

	amount	value
		$
ivory	488,600 lb.	660,000
cloves	4,860,100 lb.	250,500
cowries	8,016,000 lb.	245,000
copal	875,875 lb.	167,250
hides	95,000 lb.	115,000
sesame	8,388,360 lb.	93,600
copra	2,450,000 lb.	60,000
coconut oil	252,000 lb.	18,297
coconuts	1,750,000 lb.	12,200
red pepper	176,000 lb.	6,400
rafters	20,000 lb.	5,625

[1] Kerdudal to Bazoche, 3 May 1844, M.O., O.I. 15/59.
[2] Loarer's Report, Part I, 1849, M.O., O.I. 5/23.
[3] Rigby to F.O., no. 3, 1 May 1860, F.O. 54/17.

THE ECONOMIC DEVELOPMENT OF THE COAST

Zanzibar Exports to Western Countries, 1859[1]

	amount	value $
ivory	6,960 *frasela* (243,600 lb.)	350,000
copal	23,525 *frasela* (823,375 lb.)	153,750
cloves	68,860 *frasela* (2,410,100 lb.)	134,500
hides	95,000	115,000
sesame	69,903 bags	93,600
copra	70,000 *frasela* (2,450,000 lb.)	60,000
red pepper	2,600 *frasela* (91,000 lb.)	3,400
coconut oil	50 casks	1,400
tortoise-shell	320 lb.	1,000
sundries		55,000

Zanzibar Exports to Western Countries, 1856[2]

	value $
copal	397,031
sesame	237,887
ivory	209,321
copra	113,518
cowries	84,795
cloves	68,630
hides	26,190
coconut oil	8,110
tortoise-shell	5,181
beeswax	1,368
tallow	747
sundries	43,655

Zanzibar Imports, 1859[3]

		amount	value $
bullion			750,000
cottons	American	6,950 bales	421,850
	Indian	204,500 pieces	242,000
	English	150,300 pieces	169,700
rice		18,640,000 lb.	173,000
Venetian beads		868 barrels	98,460
muskets and fowling pieces		22,780	84,781
Muscat silk lungis		200 bales	53,500
salted fish			40,000
gunpowder		11,912 barrels	39,936
sandalwood		700,000 lb.	35,000
ghee		175,000 lb.	35,000

[1] *Idem.*   [2] Cochet to Ministry of F.A., no. 6, 15 Jan. 1857, A.N., Aff.Etr. B3/438.
[3] Rigby, as above.

It is evident from the above tables that by 1859 cowries, hides, and sesame had risen greatly in importance in Zanzibar's export trade. Before the coming of the Germans, cowries had hardly been exported at all. The opening of the Western market was also responsible for the increased importance of hides which formerly had been exported in only limited numbers, and of sesame, which was initially bought by the British – Peters took 400-500 tons a year[1] – and later in great quantities by the French and Germans. The import trade did not alter its nature in such a striking way as the export, but it greatly increased in volume. Although the same articles were sold to Zanzibar as beforehand, they came in greater numbers and from different places. New developments were that cloth from America became more popular than that from India, and that firearms were supplied in larger numbers than before. A new feature of less importance but interesting in a study of the daily life of the region was the introduction of Western luxury goods, such as crockery, glassware, mirrors, clocks, and furniture.

The effect on the people of the Swahili Coast themselves of this increasing volume of trade and of the changing importance of certain articles of export can only be a matter for speculation. We have already seen that the sections of the community which derived the greatest profit from the new situation were the Arab and Indian, and it would be tempting to conclude that this development occurred at the expense of the Swahilis themselves. However, although this is likely to have been the case in Zanzibar, it may not have happened at the mainland ports. At the littoral towns the inhabitants continued to undertake their traditional economic activities, the nature of which was mainly maritime. They derived their major profit from transporting trade goods from one port to another. They may also have profited by participating in a new development which occurred during these years: the despatch by the merchants of the Swahili Coast of their own vessels northwards to Arabia and India. Whereas in the 1770s Morice said that the Swahili Coast sent no ships to those regions because they had none large enough, in 1841 Guillain remarked that the inhabitants of Zanzibar alone had 150 boats, of which eight to sixteen were sent annually to Indian ports, twelve to fifteen to Muscat, thirty to thirty-five to the Arabian coast, and the remainder to the south of Cape Delgado, the Comoro islands and Madagascar.[2] Although these vessels may have

[1] Loarer's Report, Part I, 1849, M.O., O.I. 5/23.
[2] Morice, 'Projet d'un établissement', p. 163; and Guillain, *Côte de Zanguébar*, p. 542.

THE ECONOMIC DEVELOPMENT OF THE COAST

belonged to Indians and Arabs rather than Swahilis, they would have been manned by Swahilis and slaves. The Swahilis were further able to take advantage of the new markets to expand their copal-gathering, their cowry and tortoise-shell collection, and their agriculture. In the northern ports they exploited the new Western demand for hides.

The greatest profits of all were made by Saiyid Sa'id himself. Except perhaps for Jairam, the customs master, he became the richest merchant in Zanzibar.[1] He prospered not only from his personal enterprises – the planting of cloves on the vast estates which he acquired and the caravans he patronized – but also from his revenues – the poll tax from the Hadimu and the customs rentals from Oman and the Swahili Coast.[2] In 1841 the receipts from Oman were $180,000, while those from Zanzibar were $150,000, but by 1848 Oman provided $136,600 and Zanzibar $175,000.[3] By 1856 he received $260,000 from Oman and $222,000 from Zanzibar.[4] Saiyid Sa'id was able to derive a steadily increasing revenue from the Swahili Coast by periodically raising the rent of the customs farm. It rose through these stages: $40,000 (1804), $60,000 (1811), $80,000, $100,000, $105,000, $110,000 (1834), $120,000, $150,000 (1842), $157,000 (1844), $165,000 (1846), $175,000 (1848), $222,000 (1859).[5] Despite his high rental, Jairam was able to enrich himself, not so much from his customs receipts as from the powerful commercial influence which his position allowed him to exercise.[6]

The economic upheaval on the Swahili Coast in the first half of the

---

[1] For the Sultan's wealth, G. J. Abbot to Webster, 12 Mch. 1851, Amer.N.A., Zanz. 3.

[2] For the Sultan as a caravan patron, Journal of R. P. Waters, entry for 24 June 1839, printed in Bennett and Brooks, *op. cit.*, p. 211.

[3] For 1842, Hamerton to Bombay, 29 May 1842, encl. in Bombay to Secret Committee, no. 82, 18 July 1842, E.S.L.B. 48; and for 1848, Guillain, *Documents*, II, 250.

[4] Burton, *Zanzibar*, I, 273.

[5] Dallons, 1803, printed in Freeman-Grenville, *Select Documents*, p. 198; Hardy's Report, 1811, I.O.L., Marine Records Miscellaneous 586; Guillain's Report, 1849, A.N., Marine BB4/1036; Ruschenberger, *op. cit.*, I, 145; Hamerton to Bombay, no. 2, 2 Jan. 1842, encl. in Bombay to Secret Committee, no. 43, 30 Apr. 1842, E.S.L.B. 44; Journal of Lt Christopher, 1843, encl. in Bombay to Secret Committee, no. 54, 18 July 1843, E.S.L.B. 60; Hamerton's 'Report on the Affairs of the Imam of Muscat', 1844, Z.A.; Ward to Buchanan, no. 3, 21 Feb. 1846, Amer.N.A., Zanz. 2; and Loarer's Report, Part I, 1849, M.O., O.I. 5/23.

[6] Burton, *Zanzibar*, I, 271.

nineteenth century had distinctive effects on its several ports. The most detailed descriptions of the economic activities of the littoral towns are those of Loarer and Guillain who voyaged along the East African coast between 1846 and 1849.[1] The adjacent table, which is compiled from their evidence, can be used to compare the situation in the late 1840s with that of the first two decades of the century described in Chapter III.

Comparing the information given by this table with that available for the first two decades of the nineteenth century, it is clear that some of the ports on the southern section of the Swahili Coast, such as Mikindani, Lindi and, in particular, Kilwa Kisiwani, had been hard hit by the decline in European purchases of slaves. Although these towns continued an illegal trade in slaves with European vessels,[2] their economic movement does not reflect a general prosperity. Kilwa Kivinje superseded the other southern ports as the centre for the Slave Trade, as well as becoming the entrepot for the whole southern region. The reasons for this were partly political, stemming from the Omanis' intention to weaken Kilwa Kisiwani, and partly economic. From the economic point of view, the prohibition of Western vessels from trading with the Mrima prevented the littoral towns from providing buyers in large enough numbers to attract caravans from the interior. The caravans, which increased in number during these years, preferred to use as their destination Kilwa Kivinje, where they were guaranteed a market. The Mrima prohibition therefore induced commercial centralization instead of a diversification which the opening of the Swahili Coast's trade to Western merchants might otherwise have caused.

The Mrima prohibition had a second important effect: the ports on the mainland adjacent to Zanzibar had to send their products to the Zanzibar market for sale. As that market expanded, so did the traffic between the mainland and the entrepot. Mbwemaji, Buyuni and Bagamoyo began to develop as popular destinations for caravans. Their geographical position also made them the ideal starting-points for caravans organized by traders residing in Zanzibar. Nearby Pangani, too, prospered as a caravan centre. North of Pangani Zanzibar's commercial influence began to wane because vessels approaching from the north found it convenient to put in to coastal ports before reaching Zanzibar. Mombasa in particular, with its customs master independent

[1] Loarer's Report, Part II, 1849, M.O., O.I. 2/10; and Guillain's Report, 1849, A.N., Marine BB4/1036.
[2] See Chapter VIII, pp. 199-201.

	slaves	ivory	copal	sesame	hides	cowries	rhino-horn	tortoise-shell
Tongui	✓	500–1,000 frasela	500–600 frasela	700–800 tons	a few	✗	✓	—
Mikindani	✓	a little – irregular arrival	1,000–1,200 frasela	200–300 tons	✗	✗	✗	—
Ngao	—	200–300 frasela	2,000 frasela	1,000 tons	✗	✓	—	—
Lindi	1,000–1,200 p.a. Flourished before 1830	700 frasela not good quality	3,000 frasela	✗	✗	✓	✓	—
Kisuere	—	30–40 frasela	2,000 frasela	1,200 tons	✗	✓	—	✓
Kilwa Kisiwani	—	2 tons	✗	100 tons	✗	✓	✗	✓
Kilwa Kivinje	8,000–10,000	4,000–5,000 frasela – ⅓ of best quality	6,000 frasela	✓	✓	—	✗	—
Mafia	✗	✗	✗	✗	✗	✓	150–200 frasela	—
Kwale	—	✗	2,500–3,000 frasela	—	✗	—	—	—
Mbwemaji / Bagamoyo / Buyuni	✓	4,000–5,000 frasela of best quality	12,000–13,000 frasela of best quality	✓	—	✓	200–300 frasela	—
Pemba	✗	✗	✗	✗	✓	✗	—	—
Pangani	—	1,200–1,500 frasela	only a little	✓	✗	✗	—	—
Mombasa	✗	2,500–3,000 frasela	✓	✓	✓	✗	✓	✗
Lamu archipelago	✗	2,000 frasela	✗	✓ (but not important)	500–600	✗	✓	✗

Note: A cross indicates a contrary mention or little likelihood, from other evidence, of the article being exported. A quantity being specified.

...od	hippo teeth	grain	wax	ghee	coconuts and oil	matting	meat	cloves	tallow	number of caravans	number of vessels visiting
✓	—	—	—	—	—	—	×	—	—	✓	30
✓	—	—	—	—	—	—	×	—	—	seldom	unknown
✓	—	—	—	—	—	—	×	—	—	unknown	unknown
✓	✓	—	—	—	—	—	×	—	—	4 or 5 of 400–500 men	unknown
—	✓	2,500 tons millet	—	—	—	—	×	—	—	—	unknown
✓	×	200–300 tons millet	—	—	—	—	—	—	—	×	unknown
—	✓	millet	—	—	—	—	×	—	—	40	unknown, but a large number
—	×	—	✓	✓	✓	✓	✓	—	—	×	unknown
—	—	a little rice	—	—	—	—	—	—	—	×	insignificant
—	—	maize and millet	✓	—	—	—	—	—	—	✓	100 large vessels and many smaller
✓	×	rice	120–150 *frasela*	10,000 *frasela*	✓	—	✓	10,000 *frasela*	✓	×	unknown
—	a few	2,500 tons millet	—	—	—	—	—	—	—	✓	unknown
×	×	3,000 tons maize and rice and millet	✓	—	—	—	—	—	—	✓	unknown
×	×	millet, maize	✓	—	—	—	✓	—	—	×	unknown

dash indicates no particular mention but a possibility that the article was exported. A tick indicates a mention without any

[*to face page 374, 'The Swahili Coast'.*]

THE ECONOMIC DEVELOPMENT OF THE COAST

of the authority of Jairam at Zanzibar, flourished as a small entrepot. Its major misfortune was that it did not offer many slaves for sale. However, there were ample supplies of ivory to compensate the visiting merchant.

The towns of the Lamu archipelago, which were similarly visited by northern vessels on their way southwards, soon had the added advantage of calls by Western ships. They attracted the new traders by exploiting the Western demand for hides, a demand which the Sultan of Zanzibar had not foreseen. By then, however, Zanzibar was so firmly established as the entrepot fot the whole Swahili Coast that its prosperity did not falter at the diversion of some vessels to alternative markets.

In the first half of the nineteenth century the Swahili Coast was able to respond to opportunities for economic development in a manner that would have been impossible for a country like Oman. This response was due in the main to two factors. In the first place, the Swahili Coast had always been a region of great economic potential, possessing desirable natural resources which only required effective exploitation. Among these were ivory, gum copal, coconuts, cowries, and even slaves. Later on, as we have seen, part of the region was successfully transformed into an area of clove plantations. This added yet another item to the list of East African exports. None of these resources required heavy capital investment or large-scale industrialization. From the commercial point of view there was also the advantage that no single one of these products dominated the market; if sales of one article became dull, trade in the others could maintain the economy.

However, it is of little value having a variety of natural resources if they cannot be exploited and if production cannot be organized to meet the realities of a wider market. This was the second main factor in the economic development of the Swahili Coast. The arrival of new personnel in the region brought new organization and commercial drive. One example of this is obviously the part played by Saiyid Saʻid himself who, as a merchant prince, was largely responsible for the development of Zanzibar as the main entrepot on the Swahili Coast. There were also the Omanis who, having come to live on the Swahili Coast, experimented with the caravan trade and the establishment of landed estates. The Indians, too, brought capital and financial expertise to the region. Finally, the prosperity of the Swahili Coast was made possible by the opportunities offered to its commercial classes by the availability of Western markets, access to which was provided by European and American merchants.

CONCLUSION

This book has described the political interaction between two widely separated lands: Oman and the East African coast. Important links had already existed between these two areas in the eighteenth century, but in the first half of the nineteenth century the bonds which connected them were effectively tightened. In 1800 the Arabs already possessed a loose authority over several ports on the Swahili Coast and were more firmly established in Zanzibar. By 1856 the situation had undergone a radical change; Zanzibar was controlled by a resident Omani Sultan, it possessed an elite of land-owning Arabs, it had more than doubled the volume of its exports, and it was host to three Western consuls and several Western firms. The mainland towns had governors and customs officials appointed from Zanzibar and Arabs regularly penetrated the African interior to the Central Lakes and beyond.

A number of factors coincided to stimulate this development, to encourage the Omani Arabs to extend their authority and to arouse Western interest in the region. The Muscat sultanate, itself a new institution, came under pressure from several forces. Some of these were traditional, such as local and factional tensions, and others were less familiar, such as new opportunities presented by the long-established oceanic trade, the territorial advance of the Wahhabis, the attempt to avoid submitting to Muscat's authority by an Omani faction in East Africa, and the pressure of Napoleonic diplomacy. All these forces combined to produce a shift – at first tentative and non-committal, but later definite and permanent – of the Omani Sultan's authority and interest from the Persian Gulf down to the East African littoral.

The growing preoccupation of the Omanis with the affairs of the Swahili Coast in the first two decades of the nineteenth century was thereafter reinforced by the increasing European interest in the area. This caused great concern to the Omanis who envisaged losing their political and commercial pre-eminence to Western competitors. The Europeans' interest had in part been aroused by that of the Omanis whose patrons they were. Both the British and French courted the Omani ruler for diplomatic reasons; it was a genteel prelude to the more aggressive rivalry between European colonial powers which was to overwhelm

CONCLUSION

East Africa in the second half of the nineteenth century. The British considered the ruler's goodwill important because he was the key to their carefully constructed system of influence in the Persian Gulf, a system which had originated in the Napoleonic Wars as a defence against the French. It was continued afterwards owing to a residual suspicion of the French and as part of an attempt to maintain peace in the Persian Gulf, through which passed British despatches to India and where many of their Indian subjects engaged in maritime trade. They therefore wished to preserve the ruler of Muscat's authority and were prepared to achieve this end by giving him naval and military assistance. Indeed, it was the security which the British provided which enabled the ruler of Muscat to spend such a large amount of his time on the Swahili Coast and consolidate his authority there.

British relations with Muscat led to the appointment of a consul who followed its ruler to Zanzibar. The British had also had their attention drawn to East Africa by the Slave Trade, which they were anxious to limit. It was continued pressure about the Slave Trade and the personality of the British consul which contributed to an increase in British influence over the ruler, particularly in his declining years.

The French, too, had ambitions in East Africa which gave the Omanis grounds for concern. Their connexion with Muscat and East Africa had originated in the eighteenth century when they were seeking slaves in East Africa and approached Muscat for more favourable terms of trade. Napoleon, too, had attempted to win the support of Muscat in case any of his Eastern schemes came to fruition. French interest in East Africa was renewed after the Peace of Paris for they had lost Ile de France to the British and were seeking an alternative naval base in the southern Indian Ocean. Various points on the East African coast were proposed. Continuing suspicion of British policy in the Indian Ocean led the French to appoint a consul in Zanzibar and to expand commercial activity on the East African coast.

French and British interest in the Swahili Coast was largely prompted by diplomatic considerations. That of the Americans was commercial in origin. In the early nineteenth century the merchants of Salem, Massachusetts, were extending their commercial activities in the Indian Ocean and their interest in Madagascar led them north to Zanzibar. The availability of gum copal and ivory persuaded them to stay and thus began an expansion of the market for East African products. This in turn provided a further encouragement for the Omanis to consolidate their position on the Swahili Coast.

CONCLUSION

The economic opportunities presented by the East African coast had always been the most potent factor drawing the Omani Arabs towards Zanzibar. When it was realized that the Swahili Coast was attracting European and American traders the Omanis were encouraged to invest more heavily in the region and to settle there in larger numbers. They had far better material prospects in East Africa than in Oman. Their ruler himself began to spend more time in Zanzibar than in Muscat. The Omanis began to organize the East African coastal trade to meet the new Western demand, to penetrate the interior, and to plant estates at the coast. Their exertions were attended with considerable success and the entire region began to be opened up to a wider world.

Apart from economic and political pressures working in favour of Omani expansion on the Swahili Coast there was the personal importance of the ruler Saiyid Sa'id himself. Had the Omanis not possessed a leader of such longevity and ambition, it is possible that their enterprises might not have been so successful. Sa'id showed a considerable degree of skill in his dealings with the Western Powers, many times using his connexion with them to further Omani interests. Quite apart from his more conventional political aptitude he possessed good business sense and himself became the most successful merchant in a mercantile community. He used his political authority to foster trade; the benefits brought by trade in turn helped to strengthen his political position. Towards the end of his reign, however, his leadership became compromised by the fact that he was seen as the client of Western powers whom he had courted for the market they provided and the political protection they seemed to offer him. He also faced the uncomfortable situation that he was playing host to foreigners in his territory who possessed technical knowledge superior to that of his countrymen.

As the Omanis developed an interest in the Swahili Coast so they extended their political control over its peoples. This was necessary for two main reasons. In the first place, the staple articles of trade – ivory, slaves and copal – were brought to several points on the mainland littoral, all of which had to be controlled if that trade was to be fully exploited and Zanzibar become the entrepot for the whole region. Secondly, they faced challenges to their authority from groups of the Swahili population, sometimes supported by governors of Omani origin. In particular, the severe and long-drawn-out struggle for Mombasa involved Saiyid Sa'id in the politics of the Swahili Coast to such an extent that it was afterwards difficult for him to withdraw.

CONCLUSION

The type of control which the Omanis established was loose and patriarchal. It was headed by a merchant prince, a system of government which had recently appeared in Muscat and indeed was not entirely new to the Swahili Coast itself, although there had never been an example of it on such a large scale as that personified by Saiyid Saʻid. Saʻid had his residence in Zanzibar, where the authority of the Omanis was most firmly established. There he presided as patriarch over a small Arab landed elite. At the other towns and villages of the coast the traditional Swahili methods of government were generally retained, with a superimposition of Omani governors, Baluchi garrisons, and Indian customs officials. Nowhere did Omani authority extend very far inland, being confined to the coastal strip.

At most places Omani authority remained light. In the view of sections of the local populace, it was sometimes preferable to accept an alien overlord whose interference was limited than to be controlled by a rival group of compatriots. Although there were many instances of local protest, there was no large-scale Swahili resistance to Omani rule.

The influence of Omanis and Westerners naturally had an effect on the character of Swahili society. To some extent the Swahilis could accept the Omanis because their own culture and society partly derived from Arab and Islamic origins and therefore had certain elements in common with that of the Omanis. Also in many ways the Omanis adapted themselves to the way of life of the Swahili Coast. Within a few years, for example, they had adopted Swahili instead of Arabic as their spoken language. None the less Omani success in establishing their dominion over the Swahili Coast contained the seeds of its own destruction. Taking a long view, the establishment in Zanzibar of rule by a land-owning Omani elite led to new hierarchical arrangements in its society which were an important cause of the 1964 revolution.

As for the Westerners, their coming opened communications between the Swahili Coast and the world outside the Indian Ocean. As yet, however, Western influence was not exerted in any coherent or consistent fashion; by 1856 it was in a transitional stage. Commercially their influence was still limited though of considerable importance; culturally they had as yet made virtually no mark. The heyday of Western imperialism in East Africa would come only in the next half century.

Appendix I
THE MAZRUI GOVERNORS OF MOMBASA

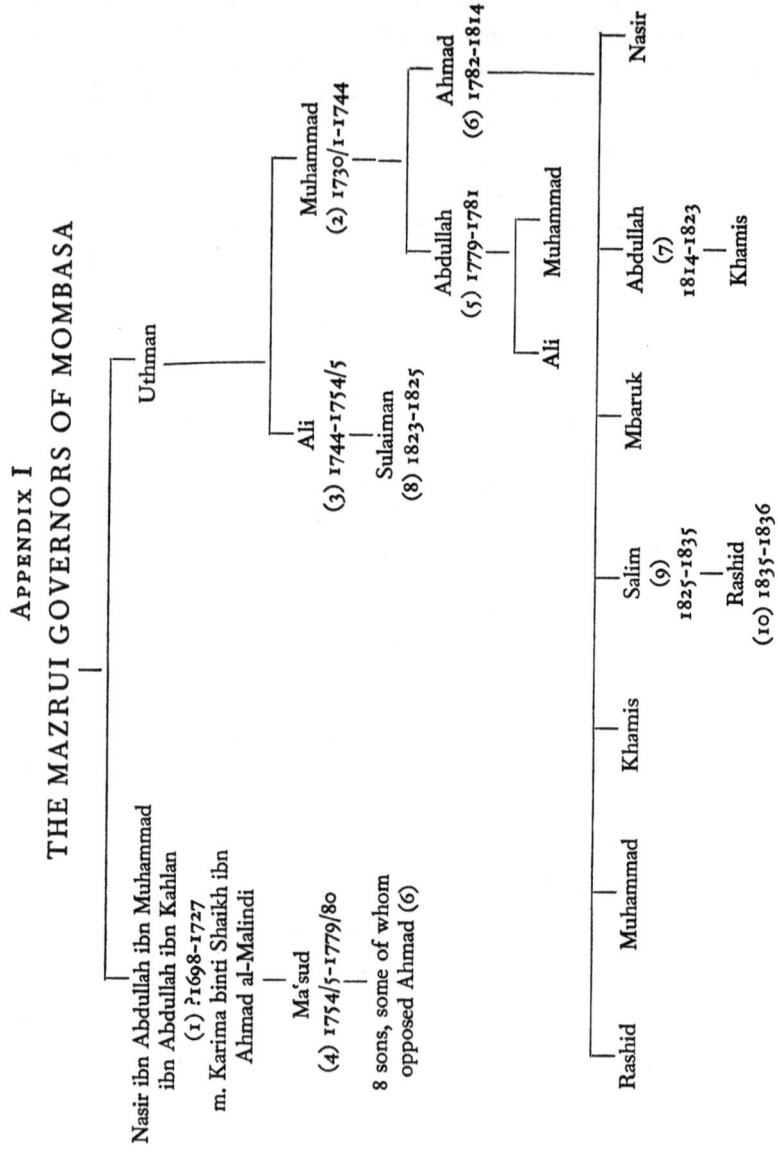

APPENDIX II

SOURCES

The sources which have been used in writing this book fall into four main categories. Firstly, there are the manuscripts in official archives – those of the Zanzibar archives, the American State Department, the British Foreign Office, Colonial Office and Admiralty, the British East India Company, and the French Ministère d'Outremer, Ministère des Affaires Étrangères and Archives Nationales. These archives contain not only official letters and reports, but also useful memoirs and journals. Most important among the latter are the journals of T. Smee and J. B. Emery, and the reports of Albrand, Guillain and Loarer. Smee's reports were actually made in 1811, but it was not until twenty-five years later that his instructions, logs, reports, and enclosures were drawn together into one volume at the request of the Commissioners for the Affairs of India, who were interested in commercial connexions with East Africa (I.O.L., Marine Records Miscellaneous 586).[1] Smee himself is the author of all the reports except those attributed to Lt Hardy, who accompanied him on the voyage. An extract from the reports can also be found in the *Transactions of the Bombay Geographical Society* (1844) and in Burton, *Zanzibar*, II, Appendix III.[2] The journal of Lt Emery, who was in Mombasa from 1824 to 1826, can be found in P.R.O., Adm.52/3940. This is one of the most important eyewitness accounts of life in the region. Many of Emery's letters are also in the R.G.S. archives.

The reports of Albrand, who visited the Swahili Coast in 1819, are particularly rich in detail. Albrand had been well trained in oriental languages in France and was an acute observer.[3] He was appointed interpreter to the French expedition to Kilwa in 1819 and subsequently wrote descriptions of the voyage. Part of his report was printed in the *Bulletin de la Société de Géographie* (1838), but there are some serious misprints in this published version.[4]

[1] For Smee's voyage, see Chapter V, p. 121.
[2] For the full titles and dates of books mentioned in this Appendix, see Bibliography.
[3] Instructions to Albrand by Milius, encl. in Milius to Ministry of Marine, no. 240, 1 Feb. 1819, M.O., Réunion 72/472.
[4] For Albrand's voyage, see Chapter VI, pp. 134-6.

APPENDIX II

Thirty years after Albrand's visit, Guillain and Loarer, together with an interpreter, Vignard,[1] voyaged along the East African coast and reported their findings to the French Government. Guillain, a naval officer stationed at Bourbon, had been sailing in the Indian Ocean since the 1830s and had made several visits to the Swahili Coast before his major expedition of 1846-9. His reports, which he later used as the basis for a three-volume work which was published in 1856, show a keen interest in East African history. He acquired some of his information in 1847 when he went to the library and archives in Goa to research into the old Portuguese establishments on the East African coast.[2] It is also evident from his writings that he had read almost every available printed source dealing with the region. Although it betrays the prejudices of the time, his work is well in advance of mid nineteenth-century historiography, using as it does both these archival and printed sources and a wealth of oral information which he had personally collected. We are also indebted to him for the first photographic record of the peoples and towns of the Swahili Coast because he took a daguerreotype machine with him on the 1846/9 expedition.[3] Lithographs made from the daguerreotypes were produced in an album which accompanied his book. While Guillain studied the northern section of the Swahili Coast, Loarer investigated the southern region. Loarer's reports, which have not been published, are also of great value. They are particularly useful when they deal with commercial and social questions, but his political and historical judgments should be treated with caution. Loarer was somewhat extreme in his opinions and lacked the accuracy of Guillain. The fact that Guillain and Loarer disliked each other[4] has been helpful to the historian because they competed to obtain and relay the best information.

The second category of sources used in writing this book is that of Swahili and Arabic chronicles and literature. The earliest of these is the Mombasa Chronicle, which bears the date 1824. This was first obtained by J. B. Emery when he was at Mombasa in 1824. Emery had the chronicle, which was written in Swahili, translated into Arabic, and then himself translated it into English. His translation was published in

[1] For Vignard, Guillain to Ministry of Marine, 26 Apr. 1849, A.N., Marine BB4/665.
[2] Guillain to Chief of Naval Division at Bourbon, 27 May 1847, A.N., Marine BB4/1036.
[3] Ministry of Marine to Commander of Bourbon, 15 Mch. 1847, M.O., O.I. 2/10.
[4] Guillain to Ministry of Marine, 26 Apr. 1849, A.N., Marine BB4/665.

APPENDIX II

Owen's work of 1833. In 1848 Guillain obtained a very similar document at Mombasa, dated 29 April 1824, which he later published in French translation in his *Documents*. Guillain and Emery's texts have been combined and published by Dr Freeman-Grenville in his *Select Documents*. The early date of the Mombasa Chronicle makes it more reliable than many other local histories in existence. The earliest of these were obtained by German and British officials, explorers and scholars in the late nineteenth and early twentieth centuries. In some cases Africans were encouraged to recount their history, in others traditional poems, songs and stories were written down, and in others again, old documents were discovered.

One of the most important of these traditional histories is the Pate Chronicle, of which various versions exist. The first to be published was that prepared by C. H. Stigand in 1913. Stigand, a British administrative officer, had encouraged Muhammad ibn Fumo Umar al-Nabhani (also known as Bwana Kitini) to recount to him the history of Pate. Bwana Kitini, who was acknowledged as an authority on historical matters, visited Stigand daily for some months and dictated the history from memory.[1] This version of the chronicle is also available in Dr Freeman-Grenville's *Select Documents*. The second version of the chronicle to be published appeared in the *Journal of the African Society* in 1914/15. Prepared by Alice Werner, who conducted research on the Swahili Coast and later became a professor at the School of Oriental and African Studies, London University, this version also appears to have been the work of Bwana Kitini. It purports to have been copied out in 1903 by the order of the then *wali* of Lamu, Abd (Abdullah) ibn Hamad, from a manuscript written by Bwana Kitini, who is said to have received the account from his grandfather, Muhammad ibn Bwana Mkuu, also known as Bwana Simba. The manuscript came into the hands of A. C. Hollis, the Secretary for Native Affairs in the East Africa Protectorate, who passed it to Alice Werner in 1911.[2] Although Bwana Kitini is responsible for both these versions of the Pate Chronicle, they are markedly different. There is very little correlation between them in the dates or succession of the rulers of Pate.

A third version of the Pate Chronicle was published in 1923 by Alfred Voeltzkow, and a fourth in 1928 by M. Heepe. Heepe, who was working under Justus Strandes in the Institute for Oriental Languages at Berlin University, had obtained two texts of the chronicle from Wassmuss,

[1] Stigand, *The Land of Zinj*, p. 29.
[2] *Journal of the African Society*, vol. XIV, no. liv, pp. 148-51.

APPENDIX II

vice-consul at Mombasa. Wassmuss had acquired a version written in Lamu dialect and had part of it translated into Mombasa dialect by Muhammad ibn Saʻid ibn Ahmad Temami. Heepe used both texts for his translation. His version is very similar to Werner's, and indeed once again Bwana Kitini is named as the authority for the chronicle.[1] An interesting study of the relationship between the various versions of the Pate Chronicle has been made by Dr A. H. J. Prins.[2]

Written at about the same time as the Pate Chronicle was the Lamu Chronicle. This manuscript was set down in c. 1897 at the order of Abdullah ibn Hamad, the *wali* of Lamu, and seems to have been copied from one or more earlier documents because it ends with the words: '... the whole of these records we have copied from Shaibu Faraji ibn Hamad al-Bakarij al-Lamuy.'[3] Once again A. C. Hollis was responsible for obtaining the manuscript, which was published, together with a translation by W. Hichens, in 1938.

Hollis collected many other local traditions, the manuscripts of which are in the library of the Royal Anthropological Institute, London. He was able to write a history of Vumba from the stories he was told by Sharif Abukari ibn Qasim ibn Diwan Kikambala al-Masela ba-Alawi and his brother, by the *wali* of Vanga, by Buhuri ibn Nyale, who was chief elder of the Segeju at Pongwe, and by Kalamu Mwacholozi, a leader of the Digo. Hollis also made use of a manuscript history said to have been written in 1721, and of a history of Mombasa by an unknown author.[4]

Also prominent in the collection of local traditions was C. Velten, who was official interpreter to the governor of German East Africa from 1893 to 1896 and who became Professor of Swahili at the Institute of Oriental Languages at Berlin University in 1896. Velten published many local histories in *Prosa und Poesie* (1907), some of which have been translated into English by Dr Freeman-Grenville in *Select Documents*. Velten also obtained information about the Swahili way of life and culture from Mtoro ibn Mwenyi Bakari, Sulaiman ibn Mwenyi Chandi, Salim ibn Abakari and Abdullah ibn Rashid, which he published in *Desturi ẓa Wasuaheli* (1903). This information can be used, with reser-

[1] *Mitteilungen des Seminars für Orientalische Sprachen*, Vol. XXXI (1928), pp. 145-6.
[2] Prins, 'On Swahili Historiography', *Swahili*, no. 28 (1958), pp. 26-41.
[3] *Bantu Studies*, vol. XII, no. 1 (Mch. 1938), p. 33.
[4] Hollis, 'Notes on the History of Vumba', *Journal of the Royal Anthropological Institute*, vol. XXX (1900), p. 275.

APPENDIX II

vations, to apply to an earlier period, particularly where it describes the state of affairs in former days. Some of the material was republished and translated by Lyndon Harries in *Swahili Prose Texts* (1965). Further descriptions of Swahili society and beliefs by Mu'allim Mbaruka ibn Shomari, his brother Mwenyi Hija, who was *akida* in Konduchi, and Muhammad ibn Madigani of Magogoni, were published by Velten in *Sitten und Gebräuche der Suaheli* (1898).

Later collectors of local traditions were Alice Werner and W. Hichens, whose work appears in the *Journals of the Royal Anthropological Institute*, in *Bantu Studies* and in a series of Swahili literature published by the Azania Press at Medstead in the 1930s. Among the latter were the poems *Al-Inkishafi* and *The Advice of Mwana Kupona upon the Wifely Duty*. There are various versions of *Al-Inkishafi*, a poem transmitted orally from generation to generation. Hichens thought it was originally composed after the 1740s, but Stigand dated it far earlier, before 1493. *Mwana Kupona*, also an orally-transmitted poem, can be dated more exactly because it was composed by the wife of Bwana Mataka of Siu, who died *c.* 1860.

Early this century, F. B. Pearce, who was British Resident at Zanzibar, and W. H. Ingrams also collected documents and stories which refer to former times. For example, in Zanzibar, Ingrams found the Ndagoni Chronicle III, dated 13 July 1851, which recounts some events in the history of Pemba.[1] This was placed in the Peace Memorial Museum, Zanzibar, and was published in *Swahili*, no. 30 (1959).

A longer historical chronicle which has been found is the *Kitab al-Zunuj*, of which there are two versions. One of these, which was in the possession of the *qadhi* of Kismayu, was acquired in 1923 by Dr Cerulli from the *qadhi* of Mogadishu. This text, which appears to have been written not long beforehand, makes use of older chronicles and traditions. A second version, which was seen by Dr Cerulli in 1926, was found at Witu in the early 1920s by Alice Werner. Dr Cerulli published the text of the chronicle, together with an Italian translation, in 1957.

Two other local histories found early this century are those written by Amr Umar Sa'adi and Omari bin Stamboul. The latter was *qadhi* of Tanga and died *c.* 1917. A typescript of his work (published in *T.N.R.* [July 1951]) was found by E. C. Baker in the files of the *Bezirksamtmann* of Tanga in 1918 or 1919, but this later disappeared. Baker also collected

[1] Ingrams, *op. cit.*, p. 517. The date of 1750 there quoted is an incorrect calculation of the Christian date from the Muslim date on the chronicle.

APPENDIX II

some other Swahili manuscripts and published articles based on them in *T.N.R.* Amr Umar Sa'adi's 'History of Mafia' was translated by D. W. I. Piggott and printed in *T.N.R.* in 1941. A five-page history of Mombasa, entitled *Asili ya Mvita*, written in Swahili in Arabic script, was obtained by James Kirkman and translated and published by Dr Jan Knappert in *Swahili* (1964). With its muddled chronology and inferior detail, this lacks the authority of the Mombasa Chronicle. The journal *Swahili* also contains many other examples of local history and literature collected by the East African Swahili Committee (now the Institute of Swahili Research, Dar es Salaam).

A more recently written chronicle is the Mazrui MS. Written in Arabic in the early 1940s by Shaikh al-Amin ibn Ali al-Mazrui of Mombasa, this is at present in the possession of Shaikh M. Qasim al-Mazrui of Mombasa, who was kind enough to let me see it. Although this chronicle uses many European sources, it also relies on local historical writings which are not generally accessible. The author usually mentions his sources and remarks when European writings disagree with information derived from local documents and traditions.

A local history which refers to Oman rather than the Swahili Coast is that written by Salil ibn Ruzayq (or Razik) in Arabic *c.* 1840-60. This extensive document was brought to the notice of G. P. Badger in 1860 when he was in Muscat, acting as a member of the Commission of Disputes between Muscat and Zanzibar. Badger's translation of the history – with a detailed introduction – was published in 1871. Ibn Ruzayq is not altogether reliable when he deals with pre-nineteenth-century Omani history, but his treatment of events which occurred during his own lifetime, some of which he would have witnessed, is more accurate.

The third category of sources used in this book is that of eyewitness reports published during or shortly after the period under review, as well as later collections of contemporary records made available by scholars in more recent times. The earliest of these are the descriptions given by Alexander Hamilton (1727) and Austin Bissell (1798). Bissell was first lieutenant on the *Daedalus*, one of the three ships taken by Commodore Blankett up the East coast of Africa to the Red Sea in 1798. In 1806 Bissell published his account of the voyage. The original logs of the three ships are in the P.R.O. Admiralty records.[1]

[1] There is also a description of the voyage in Coupland, *East Africa and its Invaders* (Oxford, 1938), pp. 162-70.

APPENDIX II

Thirteen years after Bissell's voyage, Philip Beaver and James Prior visited the Swahili Coast in the *Nisus* and wrote accounts of their activities. Although Beaver, the captain of the *Nisus*, died at the Cape of Good Hope on the homeward journey, his diary of the voyage was edited by W. H. Smyth and published in 1829. This account had been anticipated in 1819 by a description of the voyage by James Prior, the surgeon of the *Nisus*. Two participants in a British hydrographical survey of the East African coast in the 1820s – Lt Thomas Boteler and Captain W. F. Owen – also published accounts of their voyages. When Owen decided to publish his account of the expedition, Boteler allowed him to use the journal he had kept on the voyage. Owen handed Boteler's journal and his own notes to the publishers, who edited them in a haphazard manner and brought out a book in 1833. Much of this book ascribed to Owen is taken *verbatim* from Boteler's journals, sometimes with acknowledgement, and sometimes without. Boteler's narrative was published in its own right in 1835.

The next descriptions of the Swahili Coast are those written in the 1830s by the merchant Isaacs and the participants in the American expedition to arrange a treaty with the Sultan of Zanzibar – Edmund Roberts (1837) and S. W. Ruschenberger (1838). In the 1840s Guillain and Krapf gathered information which they later used as source material for their books, printed in 1856 and 1858 respectively. Krapf went to East Africa as a Church Missionary Society representative in 1844, reaching his destination at Rabai by travelling down the coast in a dhow. He was joined first by Rebmann and later by Erhardt, who also published descriptions of the region, mostly in the *Church Missionary Intelligencer*. The writings of Krapf, Rebmann and Erhardt are valuable not only as contemporary descriptions but also because the authors possessed a detailed knowledge of the people of the region and had a good command of the Swahili language.

Explorers as well as missionaries provided valuable reports. R. F. Burton and J. H. Speke arrived in Zanzibar late in 1856 to prepare for their expedition to the Central African Lakes sponsored by the R.G.S. Their descriptions were published in 1860, 1863, 1864 and 1871. Those of Burton are fuller than those of Speke, but the latter is often a more reliable commentator in matters which require historical judgment. Burton, always eager to give a flamboyant touch, sometimes goes astray with his historical facts.

An observer who had a more intimate knowledge of the social life of Zanzibar than any European was Salma binti Sa'id (Emily Ruete),

APPENDIX II

the Sultan of Zanzibar's daughter, who published her memoirs in German in 1886. They were translated into English in 1907.[1]

Contemporary descriptions of Oman are more abundant than those of the Swahili Coast. An early observer was Vincenzo Maurizi (known in Oman as Shaikh Mansur), a native of Rome who, after practising as a physician in many parts of the East, became a sort of military adviser to the ruler of Muscat in 1809. Maurizi wrote an account of his activities which ten years later he showed to interested parties in London. The account was then translated into English and published. Buckingham (1828/9) and Wellsted (1838) also published descriptions of life in Oman. Less accessible to the general public were the various reports extracted from the records of the Bombay Presidency and published as *Selections from the Records of the Bombay Government*, no. XXIV (1856). In this volume there are extracts from descriptions of Zanzibar by Hart (1834) and Hamerton (1855).

Eyewitness reports of the Swahili Coast in the late eighteenth and early nineteenth centuries are contained in three volumes – the collection of reports and letters of American merchants and travellers published by Professors Bennett and Brooks, and two books by Dr Freeman-Grenville: *Select Documents* and *The French at Kilwa Island*. *The French at Kilwa Island* contains a translation of the manuscript book entitled 'Projet d'un établissement', the original of which is in Rhodes House Library, Oxford. This manuscript book, which was found by Sir R. Coupland, consists of copies of letters from the French slave-trader, Morice, to the governor of Ile de France, and the governor's replies. Also included in *The French at Kilwa Island* are letters concerning late eighteenth-century East Africa from the French archives and some of the Louis de Curt manuscripts, which are in the Chicago University Rare Books Library. Another eyewitness report available in print is that of C. P. Rigby, composed in 1860. Rigby was appointed British agent in Zanzibar in 1858 and his descriptions are more informative than those of his predecessor, Atkins Hamerton. Finally, the book by Justus Strandes contains much information relating to the Portuguese period on the Swahili Coast. Strandes, who was born in 1859, was for many years the representative of Hansing and Co. in Zanzibar. He made use of the Portuguese archives in Lisbon and Goa, completing his book in 1899. Later on, Strandes continued the tradition of Swahili studies in the University of Berlin. His book was translated into English in 1961.

The fourth category of sources is that of more recent European

[1] For Emily Ruete, see Chapter X, p. 255.

APPENDIX II

writings which contain information relevant to an earlier period. Ingrams, Pearce, Werner, Velten and Hollis have already been mentioned in this respect. It remains to note the work of Miles, Baumann, Prins and Gray. Samuel B. Miles was British Resident at Muscat from 1872 to 1886, with a break as consul in Zanzibar in 1881/2. Of great value are the official reports he compiled and his book, published in 1919. The latter was completed after his death by his wife and contains many mistakes which he would have rectified had he been able to read the completed version. Dr Oskar Baumann, a cartographer and explorer, made a journey to the Swahili Coast in 1895, supported by the Leipzig Exploration Society. He had previously travelled to the Central Lakes for the German Anti-Slavery Society. His books contain valuable descriptions of the way of life on the Swahili Coast at the end of the nineteenth century. The recent anthropological studies by Dr A. H. J. Prins are helpful in forming conclusions about the nature of Swahili society. The late Sir John Gray, who was for many years Chief Justice in Zanzibar, had an opportunity to gather local traditions and documents, which he used in his *History of Zanzibar* (1962).

BIBLIOGRAPHY
MANUSCRIPT SOURCES

1. Foreign Office Records, Public Record Office, London.
   Files F.O. 54 and F.O. 84.
2. Colonial Office Records, Public Record Office, London.
   Only occasional volumes.
3. Admiralty Records, Public Record Office, London.
   Occasional volumes from several sections.
4. India Office Library, London. Series used:
   Proceedings of the Bombay Council.
   Proceedings of the Calcutta Council.
   Letters received from Bombay by London.
   Enclosures to above Letters.
   Letters received from Calcutta by London.
   Home Miscellaneous.
   Marine Miscellaneous.
   Military Records.
   Board's Collections.
5. Ministère des Affaires Étrangères, Paris.
   Zanzibar Commercial Correspondence.
   Zanzibar Political Correspondence.
   Muscat Commercial Correspondence.
   Muscat Political Correspondence.
   Basra Commercial Correspondence.
6. Ministère d'Outremer, Paris.
   Océan Indien files.
   Madagascar files.
   Réunion files.
   Généralités files.
7. Archives Nationales, Paris.
   Marine series.
   Colonies series.
   Affaires Étrangères series.
   Série M.
8. Zanzibar Archives.
9. Records of the Secretariat, Zanzibar.
10. Morice and others. 'Projet d'un établissement'. A manuscript book containing letters and documents relating to East Africa, compiled around the 1780s – in Rhodes House Library, Oxford. This is also printed in translation in Freeman-Grenville, *The French at Kilwa Island* (see below).
11. Records of the Royal Geographical Society, London.
    Emery Correspondence Block 1834-1840.
    Emery MS. File.

BIBLIOGRAPHY

12. British Museum MSS., and charts.
    Van Keulen's collection of charts of various parts of the world.
    Drawings and logs of Capt. Kempthorne, Sloane MS. 3665, 1688-1690.
13. Deeds in the possession of Shaikh M. Qasim Mazrui of Mombasa.
    Deed of 21 Dec. 1836, signed by Sulaiman ibn Muhammad Hamad, governor of Zanzibar.
    Deed of 9 May 1839, signed by Saiyid Sa'id.
14. Mazrui MS. – a history of the Mazrui family at Mombasa until 1835, written by Shaikh al-Amin ibn Ali al-Mazrui in the early 1940s. In the possession of Shaikh M. Qasim al-Mazrui of Mombasa.
15. Mombasa Social Survey (privately typed and bound, 1958; one copy in the possession of Mr Edward Rodwell of Mombasa) containing H. E. Lambert, 'The Twelve Tribes and the Arab Community of Mombasa'.

PRINTED SOURCES

I. PRIMARY SOURCES

Note: Some of the books listed below are not pure primary sources, but contain documents or other primary materials. Also included below are local histories which contain oral or written traditions.

African Institution. *Reports of the Directors of*, vols. 1-21 (London, 1807-27).
Ahmad ibn Nahman. Account book. See Jiddawi.
Aitchison, C. U. *A Collection of Treaties, Engagements and Sanads Relating to India and Neighbouring Countries* (Delhi, 1933).
Albrand, F. 'Extrait d'un Mémoire sur Zanzibar et sur Quiloa', *Bulletin de la Société de Géographie*, vol. X (August 1838), pp. 65-84.
Ali bin Hamed (Shaikh). 'Habari za Mrima', *Mambo Leo* (Dar es Salaam, December 1935), and subsequent numbers.
Al-Inkishafi (a Swahili poem) in Stigand, C. H., *A Grammar of Dialect Changes in the Kiswahili Language* (Cambridge, 1915), and also W. Hichens, *Al-Inkishafi* (Medstead, 1926).
Amr Umar Sa'adi. 'Mafia – its history and traditions', transl. by D. W. I. Piggott, *T.N.R.*, no. 12 (December 1941), pp. 23-7.
Arrowsmith, Aaron. *A Compendium of Ancient and Modern Geography* (London, 1831).
Asili Ya Mvita, printed in *Swahili* (the journal of the East African Swahili Committee), vol. 34/2 (1964), pp. 21-4.
Bennett, Norman R., and Brooks, George E. *New England Merchants in Africa* (Boston, 1965). This is a collection of documents.
Bissell, A. *A Voyage from England to the Red Sea 1798-9* (London, 1806).
Bombay Selections. See *Selections from the Records of the Bombay Government*.
Boteler, Thomas. *Narrative of a Voyage of Discovery to Africa and Arabia*, 2 vols (London, 1835).
Brand. 'Notice of a caravan journey from the East to the West Coast of Africa', *Journal of the Royal Geographical Society*, vol. XXIV (1854), pp. 266-71.

BIBLIOGRAPHY

Browne, J. Ross. *Etchings of a Whaling Cruise* (New York, 1846).
Buckingham, J. S. 'Voyage from Muscat to Bushire', *Oriental Herald*, vol. XIX (October 1828), pp. 39-57; and 'Voyage from Bushire to Muscat', *Oriental Herald*, vol. XXII (July-September 1829), pp. 79-103.
Burton, R. F. *The Lake Regions of Central Africa*, 2 vols (London, 1860).
Burton, R. F. *Zanzibar, City, Island, and Coast*, 2 vols (London, 1872).
Buxton, T. F. *The African Slave Trade and its Remedy* (London, 1840).
Christopher (Lt). 'Extract of a Journal kept on the East Coast of Africa', *Journal of the Royal Geographcial Society*, vol. XIV (1844), pp. 76-103.
Commission of Disputes between the Rulers of Muscat and Zanzibar, Proceedings of (Bombay, 1861).
Dalrymple, Alexander. *General Collection of Nautical Publications*, 9 vols (London, 1772).
D'Après de Mannevillette. *Neptune Oriental* (Paris, 1745).
D'Après de Mannevillette. *Mémoire sur la Navigation de France aux Indes* (Paris, 1768).
Decken, C. C. von der. *Reisen in Ost-Afrika in den Jahren 1859-1865*, 4 vols, ed. by Otto Kersten (Leipzig, 1869-73).
Emery, James Barker. 'A short account of Mombas and the neighbouring Coast of Africa', *Journal of the Royal Geographical Society*, vol. III (1833), pp. 280-3.
Fontanier, V. *Voyage dans l'Inde et dans le Golfe Persique*, 2 vols (Paris, 1844).
Freeman-Grenville, G. S. P. *The East African Coast – Select Documents* (London, 1962).
Freeman-Grenville, G. S. P. *The French at Kilwa Island* (Oxford, 1965). This contains original documents.
Guillain. 'Côte de Zanguébar et Mascate, 1841', *Revue Coloniale* (Paris, 1843), pp. 520-62.
Guillain. *Documents sur l'Histoire, la Géographie, et le Commerce de la Partie Occidentale de Madagascar* (Paris, 1845).
Guillain. *Documents sur l'Histoire, la Géographie et le Commerce de la Côte Orientale d'Afrique*, 3 vols and Album (Paris, 1856).
Hamilton, Alexander. *A New Account of the East Indies*, 2 vols (London, 1727).
Hansard, 1826, New Series XV, pp. 1015-37.
? Hardy, ? Smee, ? Whigham, 'Voyage to the Eastern Shores of Africa, 1811', *Transactions of the Bombay Geographical Society*, vol. VI (1844).
Harries, Lyndon (ed.). *Swahili Prose Texts* (London, 1965).
Hemedi bin Abdulla of Dargube, Tangata. 'A History of Africa', transl. by E. C. Baker in *T.N.R.*, no. 32 (January 1952), pp. 65-82.
Hollis, Sir A. C. 'Notes on the History of Vumba', *Journal of the Royal Anthropological Institute*, vol. XXX (London, 1900), pp. 275-97.
Horsburgh. *The India Directory*, 2 vols (London, 1809). Followed by several revised editions.
Ibn Ruzayq. See Salil ibn Ruzayq.
Isaacs, Nathaniel. *Travels and Adventures in Eastern Africa*, 2 vols. (London, 1836).
Jiddawi, Abdurrahim Mohammed. 'Extracts from an Arab Account Book' [that of Ahmad ibn Nahman], *T.N.R.*, no. 31 (July 1951), pp. 25-31.
Kashf al-Ghummah, transl. by E. C. Ross, *Journal of the Asiatic Society of Bengal* (1874), vol. XLIII, pp. 111-83.

BIBLIOGRAPHY

Kerdudal, Lemauff de. 'Quiloa ou Keloua, 1843', *Revue Coloniale* (Paris, Feb. 1844), pp. 214-23.
Kilwa Chronicle. In J. de Barros, *Da Asia* (Lisbon, 1777-8) Decade I, Book VIII, chapters IV and VI. This is translated into English in G. M. Theal, *Records of South Eastern Africa*, vol. VI (London, 1898).
    See also Guillain, *Documents sur ... l'Afrique orientale* (Paris, 1856), vol. I, pp. 178 et seq.
    For an Arabic version see S. A. Strong, *Journal of the Royal Asiatic Society*, vol. LIV (1895), pp. 385-430. This version was obtained by Kirk from the papers of Muhyi al-Din in 1862, and Kirk made a copy which he presented to the British Museum.
Kisiwani MS. (I) in *Swahili*, no. 31 (September 1960).
Kitab al-Zunuj, printed, with an Italian translation, in E. Cerulli, *Somalia, Scritti vari editi ed inediti*, vol. I (Rome, 1957), pp. 233-92.
Krapf, J. L. 'Les langues et les peuples de la région maritime de l'Afrique australe', *Annales des Voyages*, vol. IV (Paris, 1849).
Krapf, J. L. *Travels, Researches, and Missionary Labours ... in Eastern Africa* (London, 1860). This is a shortened version of the original *Reisen in Ost-Afrika*, 2 vols (Stuttgart, 1858).
Krapf, J. L. *Dictionary of the Swahili Language* (London, 1882).
Lamu Chronicle (Khabari Lamu) by Shaikh Faraji bin Hamed al-Bakarij al-Lamuy, ed. by W. Hichens, *Bantu Studies*, vol. XII (Johannesburg, 1938), pp. 3-33.
'L Ajjemi, A. H. A. *The Kilindi*, ed. by J. W. T. Allen and others (Nairobi, 1963). The *Habari za Wakilindi* was originally published by the U.M.C.A. press, German East Africa, in three parts. The manuscripts of parts II and III are in S.O.A.S. Library, London. A translation of part I by Roland Allen is printed in *T.N.R.*, no. 1 (Mch. 1938), no. 2 (October 1936), and no. 3 (April 1937). See also *Swahili* (1957), pp. 13-66.
Loarer. 'L'Ile de Zanzibar', *Revue de l'Orient*, vol. X (Paris, 1851).
Macqueen, James. 'The Visit of Lief bin Said to the Great African Lake', *Journal of the Royal Geographical Society*, vol. XV (1845), pp. 371-4.
Malte-Brun, Conrad. *Annales des Voyages*, 24 vols (Paris, 1808-14).
Malte-Brun, Conrad. *Nouvelles Annales des Voyages*, 6e series (Paris, 1819-65).
Maurizi, Vincenzo. *History of Seyd Said, Sultan of Muscat* (London, 1819).
Milburn, William. *Oriental Commerce*, 2 vols (London, 1813).
Mombasa Chronicle, in Guillain, *Documents* (see above) I, 614-22, and Owen, *Narrative of Voyages* (see below) I, 414-22. See also G. S. P. Freeman-Grenville, *The East African Coast – Select Documents*, pp. 213-19.
Mondevit, Saulnier de. 'Observations sur la côte de Zanguebar en 1787', in Malte-Brun, *Nouvelles Annales des Voyages*, VI (Paris, 1820), pp. 338-59.
Mwana Kupona. *Advice upon the Wifely Duty*, ed. by Werner, A. and Hichens, W. (Medstead, 1934).
Mwidani bin Mwidadi. 'Usulu wa WaJomvu', in Lambert, H. E., *Chi-Jomvu and Ki-Ngare, Sub-dialects of the Mombasa Area* (Kampala, 1958).
Mwidani bin Mwidadi. 'Khabari za Kale za Jomvu', transl. by L. Harries, *Swahili*, vol. XXXI (1960), pp. 140-9.
Ndagoni MS. (III) in *Swahili*, no. 30 (1959), p. 32.

BIBLIOGRAPHY

Omari bin Stamboul. 'An early history of Mombasa and Tanga', transl. by E. C. Baker, *T.N.R.*, no. 31 (July 1951), pp. 32-6.

Osgood, J. B. F. *Notes on Travel and Recollections of Majunga, Zanzibar ... and other Eastern Ports* (Salem, 1854).

Owen, W. F. *Narrative of Voyages to explore the Eastern Shores of Africa*, 2 vols (London, 1833).

Palgrave, W. G. *Narrative of a Year's Journey through Central and Eastern Arabia, 1862/3* (London, 1865).

Parliamentary Papers, XXV (1829).

Pate Chronicle. Several versions, all stemming from the memory of Bwana Kitini in the 1890s. One version is printed in C. H. Stigand, *The Land of Zinj* (London, 1913). See also M. Heepe, *Suaheli Chronik von Pate, Mitteilungen des Seminars fur Orientalische Sprachen* (Berlin, 1928), vol. XXXI, and A. Werner, 'A Swahili History of Pate', in the *Journal of the African Society*, vol. XIV, no. liv (1914-15), pp. 148-66, no. lv, pp. 278-97, and no. lvi, pp. 392-413. See also A. Voeltzkow, *Reise in Ostafrika* (Stuttgart, 1914-23); and G. S. P. Freeman-Grenville, *The East African Coast – Select Documents* (Oxford, 1962), pp. 241-96.

Petermann, Augustus. *Petermann's Geographische Mitteilungen* 1855. The 1856 volume contains a sketch of a map of part of East and Central Africa by James Erhardt and John Rebmann.

Pimentel, Manoel. *Arte de Navegar* (Lisbon, 1762).

Précis of correspondence regarding the affairs of the Persian Gulf 1801-1853 (Calcutta, 1906).

Prior, James. *Voyage of the Frigate Nisus* (London, 1819).

Rebmann, J. 'Narrative of a Journey to Jagga, the snow country of Eastern Africa', *Church Missionary Intelligencer*, vol. 1, no. 2 (1849).

Rigby, C. P. Report (1860). See Russell, C. E. B.

Roberts, Edmund. *Embassy to the Eastern Courts of Cochin China, Siam and Muscat 1832-4* (New York, 1837).

Ruete, Emily (Salma binti Sa'id). *Memoirs of an Arabian Princess*, transl. by Lionel Strachey (London, 1907). First published in German (Berlin, 1886). Also transl. into French by L. Lindsay as *Mémoires d'une Princesse Arabe* (Paris, 1905).

Ruschenberger, S. W. *Voyage round the World*, 2 vols (Philadelphia, 1838).

Russell, C. E. B. *General Rigby, Zanzibar, and the Slave Trade* (London, 1935). This contains Rigby's Report on Zanzibar of 1860.

Saint-Martin, Vivien de. 'La Côte Orientale d'Afrique, entre le Cap Delgado et le Cap Guardafui', *Annales des Voyages*, vol. III (1845).

Salil ibn Ruzayq (Razik). History of Oman, written 1840-60, printed in G. P. Badger, *History of the Imams and Seyyids of Oman* (London, 1871).

Selections from the Records of the Bombay Government, no. XXIV, New Series (Bombay, 1856).

Senate of the USA, Select Documents of, 1839-40, vol. VII, no. 488.

Smyth, W. H. *The Life and Services of Captain Philip Beaver, late of H.M. Ship Nisus* (London, 1829).

Speke, J. H. *Journal of the Discovery of the Source of the Nile* (London, 1863).

Speke, J. H. *What led to the Discovery of the Source of the Nile* (London, 1864).

BIBLIOGRAPHY

State Papers, vols VIII, X, XI, XIII, XXVIII, XXIX, XXXI, XXXII, XXXIII, XXXIV, XXXV, XL.
Stuhlmann, H. *Die Tagebucher von Dr Emin Pascha*, 5 vols (Hamburg, 1917-27).
Sulivan, G. L. *Dhow Chasing in Zanzibar Waters* (London, 1873).
Sykes, W. H. 'Notes on the possessions of the Imam of Muscat', *Transactions of the Royal Geographical Society*, vol. XXIII (1853), pp. 101-19.
Sylvestre de Sacy. *Chrestomathie Arabe*, 3 vols (Paris, 1806).
Theal, G. M. *Records of Cape Colony*, 34 vols (London, 1897-1905).
Theal, G. M. *Records of South Eastern Africa*, 9 vols (London, 1898-1903).
Velten, C. 'Sitten und Gebräuche der Suaheli', *Mitteilungen des Seminars für Orientalische Sprachen*, vol. I (Berlin, 1898), pp. 9-85.
Velten, C. *Desturi za Wasuaheli* (Göttingen, 1903).
Velten, C. *Prosa und Poesie der Suaheli* (Berlin, 1907).
Wellsted, J. R. *Travels in Arabia*, 2 vols (London, 1838).
Werner, A., and Hichens, W. See Mwana Kupona.

2. SECONDARY SOURCES

Abu Hakima, Ahmad. *History of Eastern Arabia* (Beirut, 1965).
Al-Salimi, Muhammad ibn Abdullah. *Nuhdat al-Ayan* (Cairo, n.d. - c. 1961).
Al-Siyabi. *Is'af al-'a'yan fi ansab ahl 'Uman* (Beirut, 1964).
Amin, Abdul Amir. *British Interests in the Persian Gulf* (Leiden, 1967).
Anderson, J. N. D. *Islamic Law in Africa* (London, 1955).
Arabian American Oil Company (ARAMCO). *Oman and the Southern Shore of the Persian Gulf* (Cairo, 1952).
Auber, Jacques. *Histoire de l'Océan Indien* (Tananarive, 1955).
Badger, G. P. *History of the Imams and Seyyids of Oman*, Hakluyt Society (London, 1871). This contains Salil ibn Ruzayq's work (see above).
Banaji, D. R. *Slavery in British India* (Bombay, 1933).
Baumann, Oskar. *Der Sansibar-Archipel* (Leipzig, 1899). This is part III of *Wissenschaftliche Veröffentlichungen des Vereins für Erdkunde zu Leipzig*.
Beidelman, T. O. *The Matrilineal Peoples of Eastern Tanzania* (London, 1967).
Belgrave, Sir Charles. *The Pirate Coast* (London, 1966).
Boxer, C., and Azevedo, C. de. *Fort Jesus and the Portuguese in Mombasa* (London, 1960).
Brady, C. T. *Commerce and Conquest in East Africa, with particular reference to the Salem trade with Zanzibar* (Salem, 1950).
Corancez. *Histoire des Wahhabis* (Paris, 1810).
Coupland, Sir R. *The British Anti-Slavery Movement* (London, 1933).
Coupland, Sir R. *East Africa and its Invaders* (Oxford, 1938).
Coupland, Sir R. *The Exploitation of East Africa 1856-1890* (London, 1939).
Crofton, R. H. *The Old Consulate at Zanzibar* (Oxford, 1935).
Dale, G. *The Peoples of Zanzibar*, U.M.C.A. (London, 1920).
Das Gupta, A. *Malabar in Asian Trade 1740-1800* (Cambridge, 1967).
Decary, Raymond, *L'Ile Nosy Bé de Madagascar* (Paris, 1960).
Deschamps, Herbert. *Histoire de Madagascar* (Paris, 1965).

BIBLIOGRAPHY

Devic, L. Marcel. *Le Pays des Zendjs* (Paris, 1883).
Fitzgerald, W. W. A. *Travels in East Africa, Zanzibar, and Pemba* (London, 1898).
Freeman-Grenville, G. S. P. *The Mediaeval History of the Coast of Tanganyika* (London, 1962).
Graham, G. S. *Great Britain in the Indian Ocean, 1810-1850* (London, 1967).
Gray, Sir John. *The British in Mombasa 1824-1826* (London, 1957).
Gray, Sir John. *History of Zanzibar from the Middle Ages to 1856* (London, 1962).
Gray, R., and Birmingham, D. (eds). *Pre-colonial African Trade: essays on trade in Central and Eastern Africa before 1900* (London, 1969).
Grottanelli, V. L. *Pescatori dell' Oceano Indiano* (Rome, 1955).
Groves, C. P. *The Planting of Christianity in Africa*, 3 vols (London, 1948-55).
Hardinge, Sir Arthur. *Report on the condition and progress of the East Africa Protectorate* (Parliamentary Command Paper 8683, 1898).
Hichens, W. See *Al-Inkishafi* and *Lamu Chronicle*.
Hieke, Ernst. *Zur Geschichte des Deutschen Handels mit Ostafrika* (Hamburg, 1939).
Hinawi, Mbarak Ali. *Al-Akida and Fort Jesus, Mombasa* (London, 1950).
History of East Africa, 2 vols (Oxford 1963 and 1965); vol. 1 ed. by R. Oliver and G. Mathew; vol. 2 ed. by V. Harlow, E. M. Chilver and A. Smith.
Hoskins, H. L. *British Routes to India* (London, 1928).
Hourani, George. *Arab Seafaring in the Indian Ocean in Ancient and Mediaeval Times* (Princeton, 1951, and Beirut, 1963).
Hoyle, B. S. *The Seaports of East Africa* (Nairobi, 1967).
Ingrams, W. H. *Chronology and Genealogy of Zanzibar Rulers* (Zanzibar, 1926).
Ingrams, W. H. *Zanzibar, its History and Peoples* (London, 1931).
Jackson, Sir Frederick. *Early days in East Africa* (London, 1930).
Jackson Haight, M. V. *European Powers and South East Africa* (London, 1967). This is a revised edition of M. V. Jackson, *European Powers and South East Africa* (London, 1942).
Kelly, J. B. *Sultanate and Imamate in Oman*, Chatham House Memorandum (London, December 1959).
Kelly, J. B. *Eastern Arabian Frontiers* (London, 1964).
Kelly, J. B. *Britain and the Persian Gulf 1795-1880* (Oxford, 1968).
Kersten, Otto. See Decken, C. C. von der.
Kirkman, J. S. *Men and Monuments on the East African Coast* (London, 1964).
Lamphear, J. L. 'The Kamba and the northern Mrima Coast', in Gray and Birmingham (eds) (see above), pp. 75-101.
Landen, R. G. *Oman since 1856* (Princeton, 1967).
Lloyd, Christopher. *The Navy and the Slave Trade* (London, 1949).
Lofchie, Michael F. *Zanzibar: Background to Revolution* (London and Princeton, 1965).
Lorimer. *Gazetteer of the Persian Gulf, Oman, and Central Arabia*, 2 vols (Calcutta, 1908 and 1915).
Lyne, R. N. *Zanzibar in Contemporary Times* (London, 1905).
Marston, T. E. *Britain's Imperial Role in the Red Sea Area 1800-1878* (Connecticut, 1961).

BIBLIOGRAPHY

Mathieson, W. L. *Great Britain and the Slave Trade 1839-1865* (London, 1929).
Middleton, John. *Land Tenure in Zanzibar*, HMSO (1961).
Middleton, John, and Campbell, Jane. *Zanzibar, its Society and Politics* (London, 1965).
Miles, Samuel B. *The Countries and Tribes of the Persian Gulf*, 2 vols (London, 1919). New edition 1965.
Millon-Brunet, Charles. *Les Boutriers de la Mer des Indes* (Paris, 1910).
Moyse-Bartlett, H. *The Pirates of Trucial Oman* (London, 1966).
Ogot, B. A. and Kieran, J. A. (eds). *Zamani – a survey of East African History* (Nairobi, 1968).
Oliver, Roland. *The Missionary Factor in East Africa* (London, 1952).
Pakenham, R. H. W. *Land Tenure among the Wahadimu of Chwaka, Zanzibar Island* (Zanzibar govt. printer, 1947).
Parkinson, C. Northcote. *War in the Eastern Seas 1793-1815* (London, 1954).
Pearce, F. B. *Zanzibar – Island Metropolis* (London, 1920).
Prins, A. H. J. *The Coastal Tribes of the North-Eastern Bantu* (London, 1952).
Prins, A. H. J. *The Swahili-speaking Peoples of Zanzibar and the East African Coast* (London, 1961).
Prins, A. H. J. *Sailing from Lamu* (Assen, 1965).
Pullicino, Philip. *Aulad el Imam* (Zanzibar, 1954). This is a genealogy of the members of Zanzibar's former ruling family.
Reports on the Administration of the Persian Gulf Political Residency and Muscat Political Agency 1875-1884, printed in Calcutta each year. That of 1884 contains a biographical sketch of Saiyid Sa'id by S. B. Miles.
Robinson, R., Gallagher, J., and Denny, A. *Africa and the Victorians* (London, 1961).
Ruete, Rudolph Said. *Said bin Sultan* (London, 1929).
Salem, Elie. *Political Theory and Institutions of the Khawarij* (Baltimore, 1956).
Schramm, Percy E. *Deutschland und Übersee* (Braunschweig, 1950).
Steere, E. *Swahili Tales* (London, 1870).
Stigand, C. H. *The Land of Zinj* (London, 1913). This contains a version of the *Pate Chronicle*.
Strandes, Justus. *The Portuguese Period in East Africa* (Nairobi, 1961). First published under the title *Die Portugiesenzeit von Deutsch- und English-Ost Afrika* (Berlin, 1899).
Strong, S. A. See *Kilwa Chronicle*.
Tew, Mary. *Peoples of the Lake Nyasa Region* (London, 1950).
Thomas, Bertram. *Arab rule under the Al bu Said dynasty of Oman 1741-1937*. Raleigh Lecture (London, 1938).
Toussaint, Auguste. *History of the Indian Ocean* (London, 1966). Originally published in French (Paris, 1961).
Trimingham, J. S. *Islam in East Africa* (Oxford, 1964).
Umberto, Omar. *Il Sultanato di Oman*, no. 10 of Monographs of Italian Foreign Ministry (Rome, 1912).
Webster, Sir C. *The Foreign Policy of Palmerston 1830-1841*, 2 vols (London, 1951).
Wilson, Sir Arnold T. *The Persian Gulf* (Oxford, 1928).
Winder, R. Bayly. *Saudi Arabia in the Nineteenth Century* (London, 1965).

BIBLIOGRAPHY

3. ARTICLES

There are a great many useful and interesting articles in *Tanganyika Notes and Records* (now *Tanzania Notes and Records*) and in *Swahili* (formerly the journal of the East Africa Swahili Committee and now of the Institute of Swahili Research, University College, Dar es Salaam), but only a selection of the most important for this book is given below.

Auzoux, A. 'La France et Mascate aux dixhuitième et dixneuvième siècles', *Revue d'Histoire Diplomatique* XXIII (Paris, 1909), pp. 518-40, and XXIV (1910), pp. 234-65.

Baker, E. C. 'Notes on the Shirazi of East Africa', *T.N.R.*, no. 11 (April 1941), pp. 1-10.

Baker, E. C. 'Notes on the History of the Wasegeju', *T.N.R.*, no. 27 (June 1949), pp. 16-39.

Baumann, Oskar. 'Mafia Island', *T.N.R.*, no. 46 (January 1957), pp. 5-24.

Baxter, H. C. 'Pangani – the Trade Centre of Ancient History', *T.N.R.*, no. 17 (June 1944), pp. 15-25.

Beachey, R. W. 'The East African Ivory Trade in the 19th Century', *Journal of African History*, vol. VIII, no. 2 (London, 1967).

Becker, G. H. 'Materialien zur Kenntnis des Islam in Ost-Afrika', *Der Islam*, vol. II (1911), pp. 1-48. Also ed. and transl. by Martin, B. G., *T.N.R.*, no. 68 (1968), pp. 31-61.

Beidelman, T. O. 'The Baraguyu', *T.N.R.*, no. 55 (September 1960), pp. 245-78.

Beidelman, T. O. 'A History of Ukaguru, 1857-1916', *T.N.R.*, nos. 58 and 59 (March/September 1962), pp. 11-39.

Bennett, Norman R. 'Americans in Zanzibar 1825-1845', in both *Essex Institute Historical Collections*, vol. XCV (July 1959), pp. 239-62, and *T.N.R.*, no. 56 (March 1961), pp. 93-108.

Bennett, Norman R. 'Americans in Zanzibar 1845-1865', in both *Essex Institute Historical Collections*, vol. XCVII (1961), pp. 31-56, and *T.N.R.*, no. 57 (1961), pp. 121-38.

Berg, F. J. 'The Swahili Community of Mombasa 1500-1900', *Journal of African History*, vol. IX, no. 1 (1968), pp. 35-56.

Bouvat, L. 'L'Islam dans l'Afrique nègre (Souahili)', *Revue du Monde Mussulman*, II (Paris, 1907), pp. 10-27.

Chiragdin, Shihabuddin. 'Sheikh Mbaruk bin Rashid bin Salim bin Hemed al-Mazrui', *Swahili*, no. 31 (1960).

Chittick, N. 'A new look at the history of Pate', *Journal of African History*, vol. X, no. 3 (London, 1969), pp. 375-91.

Cornell, P. G. 'W. F. Owen, Naval Surveyor', *Collections of the Nova Scotia Historical Society*, vol. 32 (1959), pp. 169-82.

Eccles, G. J. 'The Sultanate of Muscat and Oman', *Asiatic Review*, vol. XXIV (October 1928), pp. 571-5.

Edinburgh Review, vol. XXXII (1819), 'A Voyage up the Persian Gulf ...'.

Edinburgh Review, vol. XLVII (1828), 'Narrative of a Journey from India to England'.

BIBLIOGRAPHY

Edinburgh Review, vol. LXI (1835), Review of Boteler's 'Voyage'.
Edinburgh Review, vol. LXVIII (1839), Review of Ruschenberger.
Eilts, Hermann Frederick. 'Ahmad bin Na'aman's Mission to the United States in 1840. The Voyage of Al-Sultanah to New York City', *Essex Institute Historical Collections*, vol. XCVIII (1962), pp. 219-77.
Freeman-Grenville, G. S. P. 'Some Problems of East African coinage', *T.N.R.*, no. 52 (October 1959), pp. 250-60.
Freeman-Grenville, G. S. P. 'The Historiography of the East African Coast', *T.N.R.*, no. 55 (September 1960), pp. 279-89.
Furber, Holden. 'The Overland Route to India', *Journal of Indian History* (August 1951), pp. 106-33.
Gavin, R. J. 'Sayyid Sa'id', *Tarikh*, I (Nigeria, November 1952), pp. 16-29.
Gray, Sir John. 'Early Connections between the United States and East Africa', *T.N.R.*, no. 22 (December 1946), pp. 55-86.
Gray, Sir John. 'A History of Kilwa', part I in *T.N.R.*, no. 31 (July 1951), pp. 1-24, and part II in *T.N.R.*, no. 37 (1952), pp. 11-37.
Gray, Sir John. 'The French at Kilwa, 1776-1784', *T.N.R.*, no. 44 (September 1956), pp. 28-49.
Gray, Sir John. 'Trading expeditions from the Coast to Lakes Tanganyika and Victoria', *T.N.R.*, no. 49 (December 1957), pp. 226-46.
Gray, Sir John. 'The recovery of Kilwa by the Arabs in 1785', *T.N.R.*, no. 62 (March 1964).
Hieke, Ernst. 'Die erst feste deutsche Niederlassung in Ostafrika', *Deutsch Kolonial Zeitung*, vol. XLVIII (1936), p. 86.
Mathew, Gervase. 'The Culture of the East African Coast in the 17th and 18th centuries', *Man*, vol. LVI, pp. 65-8.
Northway, Philip. 'Salem and the Zanzibar – East African Trade', *Essex Institute Historical Collections*, vol. XC (April 1954).
Prins, A. H. J. 'On Swahili Historiography', *Swahili*, no. 28 (1958), pp. 26-41.
Revington, T. M. 'Some Notes on the Mafia Island Group', *T.N.R.*, no. 1 (March 1926), pp. 34-7.
Robinson, A. E. 'The Shirazi Colonization of East Africa: Vumba', *T.N.R.*, no. 7 (June 1939), pp. 92-112.
Ruete, Rudolph Said. 'Dates and references of the history of the Al bu Sa'idi dynasty', *Journal of the Central Asian Society*, vol. XVIII (April 1931), pp. 1-23.
Sachau, E. 'Ueber die religiösen Anschauungen der Ibaditischen Muhammedaner in Oman und Ostafrika', *Mitteilungen des Seminars für Orientalische Sprachen*, vol. II (1899), pp. 47-82.
Schefer, Christian. 'L'Expansion française dans la Monarchie de Juillet', *Revue des Deux Mondes*, 6ᵉ période, no. 11 (1 September 1912), p. 161.
'Some notes on Kilwa', *T.N.R.*, no. 2 (October 1936), pp. 94-5.
Stride, H. G. 'The Maria Theresa Thaler', *Numismatic Chronicle* (1956), 6th series, vol. XVI, pp. 339-43.
Veccia Vaglieri, Laura. 'L'Imamato ibedita dell "Oman"', *Annali Istituto Orientale di Napoli*, new series III (1949), pp. 245-82.

BIBLIOGRAPHY

Werner, A. The Bantu Coast Tribes of the East African Protectorate', *Journal of the Royal Anthropological Institute*, vol. XLV (London, 1915), pp. 326-54.

Werner, A. 'The Wahadimu of Zanzibar', *Journal of the African Society*, vol XV, no. lx (July 1916), pp. 356-60.

THESES

Al-Akkad, Salah. 'La Rivalité Franco-Britannique dans le Golfe Persique et les Dependances de l'Oman 1798-1862', University of Paris, thesis for Faculté des Lettres (1956).

Bathurst, R. D. 'The Ya'rubi Dynasty of Oman', Oxford University D.Phil. thesis (1967).

Bridges, R. C. 'The British Exploration of East Africa 1788-1885', London University Ph.D. thesis (1963).

Glyn-Jones, Eleanor M. 'Britain and the End of Slavery in East Africa', Oxford University B.Litt. thesis (1956).

Jones, M. K. 'The Slave Trade at Mauritius, 1810-1829', Oxford University B.Litt. thesis (1936).

Qasim, Jemal Zakariyya – a thesis on the Al bu Sa'idis in Oman and Zanzibar, Cairo University (1959).

Spray, W. A. 'Surveying and Charting the Indian Ocean: the British contribution 1750-1838', London University Ph.D. thesis (1966).

Yapp, M. E. 'British Policy in Central Asia 1830-1843', London University Ph.D. thesis (1960).

INDEX

Abbas Mirza, 148
Abd al-Rahman ibn Nur al-Din, 123
Abdul Aziz, 81
Abdullah ibn Ahmad al-Mazrui, governor of Mombasa, 50; marriage, 59; as leader in Pate, 123; and Lamu archipelago, 125-6; and Saiyid Sa'id, 125-6; asks British for help, 132
Abdullah ibn Hafithi, 63
Abdullah ibn Jad, governor of Zanzibar, 26
Abdullah ibn Jum'ah al-Barvani Al Harthi, 131, 138, 222, 266, 271-2
Abdullah ibn Muhammad al-Mazrui, governor of Mombasa, 50; and Three Tribes, 53; and Pate, 55
Abdullah ibn Salim Al Harthi, 267
Abdullah ibn Sulaiyim, 129, 297
Aberdeen, George Hamilton Gordon, Earl of, and French consul at Zanzibar, 181; 184-5; orders Hamerton's removal, 193; and Omani envoy, 236-7
Abji Sewji, 292
Abubakr, ruler of Pate, 63
Abyssinia, 97, 155, 169
Adawini, 268
Aden, 155, 169
Adza binti Saif, 280
African Institution, 220-1
Africans, definition of, 24-5
Ahmad (Sultan Ahmad), ruler of Pate, 63, 65, 122, 123, 124
Ahmad the Younger, ruler of Pate, 124
Ahmad ibn Muhammad al-Mazrui, governor of Mombasa, 30; rebellion against, 53; and Tanga, 59

Ahmad ibn Nahman, 179, 180, 271
Ahmad ibn Sa'id Al Bu Sa'idi, Imam, accession, 22, 26; revolts against, 36; and Kilwa, 31; and Mombasa, 48-9
Ahmad ibn Saif, governor of Zanzibar, 272
Ahmad ibn Shaikh al-Malindi, 54-5
Ahmad ibn Sultan Al Bu Sa'idi, 137
Al Abriyin, 268
Al-Amin ibn Ali al-Mazrui (Shaikh), 386
Alawi, 71
Albrand, Fortuné, 135-6, 200, 295, 381
Al Bu Sa'idis, become Imams, 48; as a clan in Zanzibar, 268; as governors, 272-3
Al Harthi, 72, 130-1, 266-9
Al-Hasa, 98
Ali ibn Mansur, governor of Mombasa, 309
Ali ibn Muhammad, governor of Mogadishu, 299
Ali ibn Muhyi al-Din, 71
Ali ibn Nasir, envoy to England, 176, 178, 181, 236, 151, 267, 271; as governor of Mombasa, 309
Ali ibn Saif, governor of Lamu, 303
Ali ibn Uthman al-Mazrui, governor of Mombasa, 50, 58
Al Masakira, 269
Almonds, 352
Aloes, 333, 352
Ambar, governor of Zanzibar, 271, 288
Amber, 20
Amir ibn Sa'id, 158

401

INDEX

Amiri, on Mrima, 38-41; at Mombasa 55; at Pate, 62
Antakara, 168
Antimony, 336
Anti-Slavery Society, 228
Army, of Muscat, 101, 257; of Saiyid Sa'id, 255-60, 282
Arrowroot, 334
Asafoetida, 334, 352
Athmani of Pemba, 127
Auckland, George Eden, Earl of, Governor-General of India, 230

Baba Khan, Shah of Persia, 106
Badger, G. P., 386
Badr ibn Saif, 107, 110-1, 121
Bagamoyo, 86, 315-6; and caravans, 357, 374; exports from, 374 (table)
Bahrain, and Sultan ibn Ahmad, 102; attacked by Saiyid Sa'id, 144; Saiyid Sa'id's plans for, 164-5, 193, 236-8; and Muhammad Ali, 164, 172; and 1839 treaty, 181, 230
Bajun, 61, 64
Bajun tribe at Mombasa, 52
Baker, E. C., 385-6
Baluchis, *See* Army
Banadir coast, and Bajun, 61; and Saiyid Sa'id, 296-300; and caravans, 76, 357; commerce of, 64, 88, 92-3, 354. *See also* Mogadishu, Marka and Brava
Bandar Abbas, 102, 113
Bani Ali, 268
Bani Bu Ali, 116-17, 222, 269
Bani Bu Hasan, 258, 168, 298
Bani Jabir, 47, 258
Bani Kibanda, section of Kilifi tribe, 53
Bani Kilban, 268
Bani Lamk, 268
Bani Qitab, 269
Bani Riyam, 269

Bani Ruwaihah, 258
Bani Wahib, 268
Bani Yas, and Mazruis, 47; in Zanzibar, 268
Barghash ibn Sa'id, 267, 277
Barqa, 111
Barrow, 2nd Secretary to Admiralty, 139
Basra, French Resident at, 103; and Saiyid Sa'id, 144, 150
Batavia, 98
Batias, 290, 311
Battash, 268
Baudais, Captain, 187, 188
Baumann, Oskar, 389
Bazoche, governor of Bourbon, 180
Beads, imported by Zanzibar, 82, 368, 371, by Mombasa, 87; exchanged for slaves, 210, 356; and caravans, 356; sold by Red Sea Arabs, 352, by French, 340-1, 347, by Americans, 330, 347, by British 336, by Germans, 344, 347
Beauchamp, Abbé, 104
Beaver, Captain Philip, 121, 387
Beeswax, exported from Zanzibar, 82, 371, from Kilwa Kisiwani, 84, 374 (table), from Mombasa, 87, 374 (table), from elsewhere, 374 (table); bought by Americans, 333, 346, by French, 341, 346, by British, 337, by Indians, 350
Belligny, French consul at Zanzibar, 190, 191
Bengal, trade with Persian Gulf, 98
Bentinck, Lord William Cavendish, Governor-General of India, 148, 152
Berbera, 296-7
Betel, 348-9
Betsimisaraka, 130, 258 n. 7
Bhavnagar, 98
Bhoras, 290
Bissell, Austin, 386

402

INDEX

Blane, Resident in Persian Gulf, 147
Blankett, Commodore, 70, 75, 94, 106, 120, 386
Bogle, Archibald H., Resident at Muscat, 107
Bombay, trade with East Africa, 75, 349-51, with Persian Gulf, 98; people from living in Zanzibar, 290. *See also* Indians.
Bombay Marine, 93-4, 154
Bombetok, 200, 321
Bondei, 56, 60
Boriti poles. *See* Rafters
Boteler, Lt Thomas, 96, 130, 387
Bourbon, policy in 1819, 134-8; proposed treaty with Zanzibar, 153-6, 338; and Americans, 150; and taking of Nossi Bé, 171; ceases to be naval station, 190; commerce of, 137, 138, 142-3, 338, 345; and free labourers, 180, 237; and Slave Trade, 84, 153, 197-200, 223
Brava, and Sultan Omari, 63; and Omanis, 129, 296-300; and French plans, 168, 188, 298; and British, 297; and Hamad ibn Ahmad, 297; commerce of, 75, 92, 366
Broquant, French consul at Zanzibar, early career, 184; becomes consul, 185; and Swahili commerce, 187; lack of influence, 189; friendship with Hamerton, 189; death, 190
Bruce, James, 121
Bruce, Captain William, Resident in Persian Gulf, 221
Buckingham, J. S., 388
Bumbwini, 284
Buraimi, 102, 164-5, 171, 192
Burton, Sir Richard, 387; visits Chogwe, 315; view of French trade, 342; view of caravan trade, 358

Bushire, 144, 150
Buxton, T. F., 228
Buyuni, 86, 315; and caravans, 357, 374; exports of, 374 (table)
Bwana Bakari wa Bwana Mkuu of Pate, 65
Bwana Mataka. *See* Mataka ibn Mubarak
Bwana Mkuu of Pate, 58, 65
Bwana Mkuu, chief elder of Pate, 124
Bwana Tamu the Younger, 66, 68
Bweni, 38

Camphor, 333
Caravans, routes, 76, 356-7, 374; and Slave Trade, 208-9; costs and profits of, 215, 358; types and number of, 355-6, 357, 374 (table); and porters, 216, 288, 358; and ivory, 355-6
Cardamom, 348-9
Caroline, 189, 235, 261-2, 336, 368-9
Carpets, 352, 368
Cavaignac, 108, 111
Cerulli, Dr E., 385
Chagga, 213, 215
Chahbar, 101
Chak Chak, 86
Changamwe tribe, 52, 53, 310
Chogwe, 315
Chole, 36, 37, 365
Chonyi, 56
Christian, Commodore, 143
Chwaka, 29, 30
Cinnamon, 82, 348
Classun, 367
Cloth, imported by Zanzibar, 82, 368, 371-2, by Mombasa, 87; and caravans, 356; exchanged for slaves, 210-11; sold by Indians, 78, 330, 348-9, by British, 330, 336-7, by French, 340-1, 347, by Germans, 344, 347, by Arabs, 352

INDEX

Cloves, introduced to Zanzibar, 82, 203, 248, 268, 283-7, 322, 324-5, 365, 375; grown by Saiyid Sa'id, 286-7, 322; exported from Zanzibar, 368-9, 370-1, from Pemba, 374 (table), from Bourbon, 142-3, 153; quantity and price of, 365; bought by British, 336, 356, by Americans, 326, 333, 346, by French, 341, 346, by Indians, 350, by Arabs, 353. *See also* Plantations

Cochet, L., French consul at Zanzibar, 190

Cochin China, 151

Coconut oil, quantity, 366; from Zanzibar, 83, 366, 368, 370-1, from elsewhere, 374 (table); bought by Germans, 343, 346 by French, 341, 346, by Americans, 333, 346, by British, 336, 346

Coconuts, 30, 375; exported from Zanzibar, 82, 366, 370-1, from Mombasa, 87, 374 (table), from Lamu archipelago, 374 (table), from elsewhere, 374 (table); bought by Indians, 350, 366, by Arabs, 353

Coffee, planted in Zanzibar, 82; exported by Zanzibar, 368; sold by Red Sea Arabs, 352, 354, by Indians, 345

Cogan, Captain Robert, and the *Liverpool*, 157; as Saiyid Sa'id's agent, 159, 176, 237; and Slave Trade, 207; and British treaty, 159-60, 228-30, 362; and Hamerton, 174, 176-7, 193; and Latham's Island, 285, 335; commercial dealings of, 177, 335, 367

Coir, 30, 82, 333, 349, 366, 374 (table)

Cole, Sir Lowry, governor of Mauritius, 140

Comarond, slave trader, 103, 198, 201

Comoro islands, and Slave Trade, 219; and Saiyid Sa'id, 311; trade with East Africa, 354, 372; people of in Zanzibar, 293. *See also* Grand Comore, Johanna, Mayotte and Mohelli

Cooley, W. D., 157

Copal. *See* Gum copal

Copper, 348-9. *See also* Wire

Copra, 341, 346, 366, 370-1

Coromandel coast, 98

Corvée, 20-1, 282

Coupland, Sir Reginald, 231, 388

Cowry shells, 20, 375; exported from Zanzibar, 82, 370-1, from Kilwa Kisiwani, 84, 374 (table), from Mombasa, 87, 374 (table), from Lamu archipelago, 91, 96, 374 (table), from elsewhere, 374 (table); collection of, 373; quantity, 365-6; bought by Americans, 333, 346, by French, 341, 346, by Germans, 342-3, 346, 365, 372, by Indians, 350

Cram, merchant, 335

Cummin seed, 349

Customs collection, at Zanzibar, 78, 292-3, 362-3; at Kilwa Kisiwani, 85, 317; at Muscat, 97, 99-100; at Pemba, 362; at Mombasa, 309, 362, 374-5; at Lindi, 320; on Mrima, 314, 362; and Indians, 348; Al Bu Sa'idis exempt from, 204-5, 369; dues, 360, 362

Dalrymple, Alexander, 94
D'Après de Mannevillette, 94
Dates, 82, 352-3, 368
Debassyns, Vicomte, 142, 143
De Cossigny, 119
De Hell, governor of Bourbon, 167, 182-3

De Lagiène, 183
Denmark, trade with East Africa, 345
Dhafrah, 47
Digo, 42, 56; as fighting men, 56, 59; as inhabitants of Zanzibar, 293; and Shambala, 314
Diu, 3, 223
Diwani, on Mrima, 38-42, 313-14, 322; at Pemba, 59, 312
Doe, 42, 43, 213, 316
Donkeys, 352
Dragon's blood, 352
Drugs, 333, 337, 352-3
Dubai, 146, 258
Dumont, French interpreter at Zanzibar, 189
Duncan, J., governor of Bombay, 120
Dunga, 282, 285
Duperré, Admiral, Minister of Marine, 183
Duruma, 56, 311
Dyes, 333, 352-3

East India Company, and 1833 Act of Parliament, 148; and consul in Zanzibar, 157-61, 190-1, 176-7
Ebony, 350
Egypt, and the French, 104, 113; advance across Arabia, 163-4. *See also* Muhammad Ali
Elphinstone, Hon. Mountstuart, governor of Bombay, 116, 132, 140-1, 150, 225-6
Emery, Lt J. B., at Mazrui councils, 54; and Pemba, 128; and Slave Trade, 214; reports on East Africa, 325, 381; and *Mombasa Chronicle*, 382
Erhardt, J. J., 387

Faisal ibn Turki, Wahhabi leader, 182, 238

Famao, 65
Farquhar, Sir Robert, governor of Mauritius, and Slave Trade, 219-221, 223, 226
Faza, 61, 63, 64; commerce, 88, 90
Firearms and gunpowder, and Zigua, 214, 359; and Nyika, 311; used by slaves, 289; possessed by Saiyid Sa'id, 259-60; imported by Swahili Coast, 260, 358-9, 368, 371; sold by Americans, 326, 330-331, 333, 347, 359, by British, 333, 336-7, 359, by French, 340-1, 347, 359, by Germans, 344, 347, 359, by Arabs, 352
Fish, in Zanzibar waters, 30; imported by Zanzibar, 82, 352-3, 371; exported by Lamu archipelago, 91
Fuga, 42
Fumobakari ibn Shaikh, 301-3
Fumoluti (preceded Fumomadi in Pate), 64, 68
Fumoluti ibn Shaikh, 122; ? the same man, 124, 300-01
Fumoluti (different from above?), 124
Fumomadi of Pate, 62-4; and Lamu, 66; and Mazruis, 68, 122
Fontanier, French consul in Basra, 155, 156
Forbes, Captain, 326
Fort Dauphin, Madagascar, 137
Fort Jesus, Omani siege of, 21, 46; Mazrui garrison of, 55; and W. F. Owen, 132; and Saiyid Sa'id, 306-308
France, early connexion with Zanzibar, 96, 135-8; establishes consul in Zanzibar, 155-6, 166-9, 180-5, 377; influence in Zanzibar, 178-9, 190-1; 1844 treaty with Zanzibar, 184-5, 253, 339, 361; and Guillain's expedition, 187-9, 338-40;

405

INDEX

France—*continued*
  and Mrima monopoly, 361, 362; visited by Saiyid Sa'id's ships, 369; trade, 338-42, 344-7; connexion with Muscat, 103-04, 136-137, 155-6, 166, with Red Sea, 113-14, 155, 169, 186. *See also* Ile de France and Bourbon
Frankincense, 349, 353
Freeman-Grenville, Dr G. S. P., 383, 384
Freycinet, governor of Bourbon, 138

Galla, 56; and Nyika, 57, 88, 214; and Slave Trade, 214-15; and Mazruis, 60; at Pate, 62; commerce of, 91-2
Gangarra. *See* Majengera
Gazi, 312-13
Germany, trade with East Africa, 342-5, 365
Ghafiri, 22, 48, 268-9
Ghee, imported by Zanzibar, 82, 371; exported from Mombasa, 87, 374 (table), from elsewhere, 374 (table); sold by Indians, 348-9
Ginger, 348
Giriama, 56
Gold leaf and gold thread, 352, 368
Grand Comore, 186, 295, 320
Gray, Sir John, 389
Guillain, Commander C., expedition of 1838, 154-6, 166, 338, of 1840, 166, 180, of 1846-9, 187-9, 339, 374; and Broquant's death, 190; reports by, 381-3, 387; plans for Banadir coast, 295-6, 298; and Mombasa Chronicle, 383
Guirard, 104-05
Guizot, François, and French consul at Zanzibar, 180, 184; policy in Indian Ocean, 183, 185-6, 187, 188; Saiyid Sa'id's protests to, 186, 254; and British, 236

Gum copal, 20, 375, 378; collection of, 373; duties on, 363; quantity and price, 359-60; exported from Zanzibar, 82, 359-60, 368, 370-1, from Kilwa Kisiwani, 359, 374 (table), from Mombasa, 87, 374 (table), from elsewhere, 359, 374 (table); bought by Americans, 326, 333, 346, 359-60, 377, by British, 336, 346, 359, by French, 341-2, 346, 359, by Germans, 344, 345, 359, by Indians, 350, 359
Gunpowder, *See* Firearms
Gwadur, 101, 255

Hadimu, 28-9, 31, 373
Hadramaut, mercenaries from, 256, 289; people living in Zanzibar, 265, 293; trade with East Africa, 294, 351-2
Hajar mts, 102
Hajariyin, 258, 268
Hajji Dervish, 188-90
Hamad ibn Ahmad Al Bu Sa'idi, 124, 129, 297; ? the same man, 302
Hamad ibn Sa'id Al Bu Sa'idi, 22
Hamburg, trade with East Africa, 342-5
Hamerton, Atkins, British consul in Zanzibar, early career, 165-6; at Muscat, 167, 171; goes to Zanzibar, 171-3; made consul, 176-7; illness of, 69; character, 174-6, 377; unpopularity, 178-9, 254; and Cogan, 176-8; and free labourers, 180, 237; view of British policy, 187; friendship with French consul, 189; plans for removal of, 193-4, 237; leaves Zanzibar in 1852, 205; view of Saiyid Sa'id, 250-1, 296; reports by, 388; and commerce, 338; and Slave Trade, 207, 232, 233-4, 237-8, 239, 240, 242-3

406

INDEX

Hamilton, Alexander, 94, 386
Hamud ibn Azzan, 145-6, 164, 192 n. 1
Hanjam, 101
Hansing and Co., 343, 388
Haramili ibn Salih, 82
Hardware, 330, 348
Hardy, Lt, 121, 208, 213-14, 381
Harries, Lyndon, 385
Hart, Captain, 152, 156, 158, 248-9, 388
Hasan, Sultan on the Mrima, 318
Hasan ibn Ibrahim, Captain, 151, 264
Hasham, 258
Hastings, Earl of, Governor-General of India, 116
Heepe, M., 383-4
Hehe, 213
Henderson, merchant, 335
Hennell, Samuel, Resident in Persian Gulf, 167, 171, 231
Hertz, 342-4
Hichens, W., 385
Hides, exported from Zanzibar, 82, 368, 370-1, from Mombasa, 87, 374 (table), from Lamu archipelago, 91, 366, 374 (table), 375, from Banadir coast, 93, 366, from elsewhere, 374 (table); quantity, 366; duties on, 363; bought by Americans, 333, 339-40, 346, by British, 337, 346, by French, 339, 341, 346, by Germans, 343, 346
Hilal ibn Sa'id, birth, 273; and Wahhabis, 149; quarrel with father, 273-5; goes to Lamu, 303-4
Hinawi, 22, 48, 268
Hippo teeth, 84, 350, 374 (table)
Holland (Dutch), and Omanis, 21; trade, 105
Hollis, A. C., 383-4
Honey, 352
Hormuz, 101

Horsburgh, 94
Horses, sold by Arabs, 352
Household goods, imported by Zanzibar, 330-1, 336, 340-1, 344, 347-8, 372
Hova of Madagascar, 167
Hunt, Robert Newman. *See* Newman Hunt

Ibadhis, 22, 69; *qadhi* in Zanzibar, 277
Ibn Khalfan. *See* Sa'id ibn Khalfan
Ibn Ruzayq (Razik). *See* Salil ibn Ruzayq
Ibo, 198
Ibrahim ibn Isa, ruler of Lindi, 320
Ile de France, purchase of slaves, 80, 84, 103-4, 119, 197-9; other trade, 96; and Sultan ibn Ahmad, 107-8; and Saiyid Sa'id, 112; loss by French, 115, 134, 199, 377. *See also* Mauritius
Imamate of Oman, office, 22, 101, 109, 117, 192, 277
Indian Navy, 93-4, 154
Indians, trade of, 75, 77, 78-9, 81, 97, 217, 347-51, 372 (*see also* Cloth); sell British goods, 337-8, 348; commercial organization of, 347-348; and caravan trade, 357; provision of capital by, 209, 212, 291, 347-8, 351, 375; living in Zanzibar, 78-9, 290-2, 351, in Mombasa, 89, 310-11, in Lamu archipelago, 92; number of, 209, 291
Indigo, 251
Ingrams, W. H., 385
Iron, 82, 348-9
Isaacs, Nathaniel, 325-6, 387
Ivory, 20, 21, 375, 378; exported from Zanzibar, 82, 368, 370-1, from Kilwa, 84, 355, 374 (table), from Mombasa, 88, 374 (table),

INDEX

Ivory—*continued*
375, from Lamu archipelago, 91-2, 355, 374 (table), from Banadir coast, 93, from elsewhere, 374 (table); quantity and price, 210, 334, 354-5; duties on, 363; freight charges for, 348; connexion with Slave Trade, 216; bought by French, 341-2, 346, by Americans, 326, 333, 334, 346, 355, 377, by British, 336-7, 346, by Germans, 343, 346

Ja'alan, 98
Jabir, 47
Jairam Sewji, customs master at Zanzibar, 292-3; leases customs collections, 320, 362-3; his rental, 373; his wealth, 217, 373; his powerful position, 328; and Mrima monopoly, 361; and Slave Trade, 234; his slaves, 204, 242, 292; and American consul, 194, 327; and direct trade with Europe, 368-9
Janaba, 269
Jibana, 56
Jibondo, 36
Johanna, commerce of, 92; and Pate, 120; and Mombasa, 132; and French, 138, 186; and British consul, 186
Jomvu tribe at Mombasa, 52, 56
Jomvu village, 55, 57; commerce of, 88, 89
Juani, 36
Juba River, 45, 95, 357
Jukes, surgeon Andrew, 221
Jumbe, system of government on Mrima coast, 38-43

Kamba, 56; and caravans, 76, 88; and Nyika, 90, and Slave Trade, 214
Kambe, 56

Kao, 357
Kaole, 315, 316
Karagwe, 210
Kathiawar, and Slave Trade, 231
Katwa, 52
Kauma, 56
Kazembe, 356
Keir, Major-General Sir William Grant, 230-1
Kemball, Arnold, Assistant Resident in Persian Gulf, 193
Kerdudal, Lemauff de, 179-82, 318
Kergarion de Loemaria, 198
Kerimba, 198
Khaduj binti Sa'id, 274
Khalfan (sons of), 99
Khalid ibn Sa'id, birth, 273; as regent in Zanzibar, 274; and judiciary, 278; and French, 171, 177, 191; and Hamerton, 174; and war with Pate, 302; commercial pursuits, 269, 275, 367; death, 250, 267, 275
Khamis ibn Uthman, visits England, 157; and French, 179, 190; and Newman Hunt, 327; position in Zanzibar, 271, 281
Kharaq, 113, 182
Khasa binti Ahmad al-Mazrui, 312
Khasab, 102
Khazair, 268
Khojas, 290
Khorasan, 148
Khurshid Pasha, 163-4, 172, 182
Kichwele, 284
Kikoneni, 39, 42
Kilifi River, 60
Kilifi tribe, 52, 53, 56
Kilindini tribe, 52, 56, 308
Kilindini village, 46, 307-8
Kilwa Kisiwani, 94; Omani governor and garrison at, 25, 31-2, 49, 84, 120, 130, 199; sultanate of, 33-4, 121, 317-18; customs dues and

408

revenue of, 33-4; influence of, 34-5; inhabitants of, 35-6; harbours of, 83-4; and French, 96, 131, 134-8, 198-201, 222; exports from, 84, 374 (table); imports to, 84; decline of, 35-6, 85, 317-18, 374; and slaves – *see* Slavery
Kilwa Kivinje, 85-6; origin and growth, 318-19, 374; Omani governor at, 85, 130, 318-19, 322; and Slave Trade, 213; and caravans, 357, 374; and Mrima monopoly, 362, 374; exports from, 374 (table)
Kimwere, 71, 302, 314-15
Kinamte, 65
Kipumbwe, 38
Kisabengo, Zigua leader, 214
Kisimani Mafia, 36
Kisuere, 320, 374 (table)
Kitini, Bwana, 383
Kizimbani, 284
Knappert, Dr Jan, 386
Koma, 36
Krapf, J. L., at Kilwa Kisiwani, 213; at Kisuere, 320; and Mombasa mission, 252, 387; and Duruma, 311, view of Saiyid Sa'id's authority, 296, 315
Kua, 36
Kutch, trade with East Africa, 75, 78, 79, 88, 350-1; trade with Persian Gulf, 98; and Slave Trade, 206, 230-1; people from, living in Zanzibar, 290
Kwale, near Mafia, 36, 374 (table)
Kwale, near Tanga, 59, 130
Kwavi, 56

Laccadive islands, 342
Ladha Damji, 292
Lamu, 37, 61; relations with Pate, 64-5; type of government, 65; schools, 70; asks Saiyid Sa'id for help, 122, 124; and Omani garrison, 301, 303; and French agent, 339-40; customs dues at, 362; and Slave Trade, 215; trade of, 75, 88, 91-2, 374 (table), 375
Latham's Island (Fungu), 84, 177, 285, 335
Lead, 341, 349
Leveson-Gower, Granville, Baron, 233
Lief ibn Sa'id, 356
Likoni, 59
Lindi, 36; Omani governor at, 130, 320; and Slave Trade, 213, 374; and caravans, 357; and Mrima monopoly, 362; commerce of, 88, 374 (table)
Liverpool, 156-7, 159, 251, 261
Loarer, view of Hamerton, 174; view of Saiyid Sa'id, 250-1, 254-5; plans for Banadir coast, 188; at Kilwa Kisiwani, 318-19, 362; and Guillain's expedition, 339, 374; view of German trade, 343; reports by, 381-2

Mackenzie, Dr, 233
Madagascar, and French, 137, 167-8, 183, 185-6; and Saiyid Sa'id, 168, 256-7, 321; and Slave Trade, 199-200, 219-20, 228; and Americans, 150, 377; and Swahili trade, 372; people of, in Zanzibar, 293
Madinah, 172
Mafia, 27, 36, 94; inhabitants of, 36-8; arrival of Zanzibaris at, 36-7, 283; and the French, 135 raids; on, 130-1, 258; exports from, 84, 374 (table); and Omani governor, 130, 319
Magubiko, 40
Maizan, French explorer, 189, 253, 317
Maize, 374 (table)

409

INDEX

Majengera (Gangarra), 36
Majid ibn Sa'id, and French influence, 191; succeeds father, 250, 267, 276
Makran, 98, 101
Malabar coast, 98, 107, 136
Malay islands, 98
Maldive islands, 342
Malindane, 33-4
Malindi, 90
Malindi family at Mombasa, 52, 53-4, 56
Milius, governor of Bourbon, 136-7
Manasir, 268
Manda, 61, 90
Mangapwani, 284
Marakatos, 64
Maria Theresa dollar. *See* specie
Marka, trade of, 75, 92; and Saiyid Sa'id, 129, 297-300; French plans for, 188
Marshall, American consul at Muscat, 194
Marungu, 210
Masai, raids on Nyika, 311-12
Mascarene islands. *See* Ile de France and Bourbon
Massieu, Captain, 224
Massieu, French slave trader, 198
Ma'sud ibn Nasir al-Mazrui, governor of Mombasa, 50, 58
Mataka ibn Mubarak (Bwana Mataka), 301-4, 385
Matrah, 111
Mauritius, and Americans, 150; and free labourers, 178, 234; and Slave Trade, 199-200, 219-20, 224, 228, 231. *See also* Ile de France
Maurizi, Vincenzo, 257, 388
Mayotte, 18-23, 188
Mazruis, in Oman, 46-7; become governors of Mombasa, 45, 47-50; system of government, 53-5; influence along coast, 59, 60, 64, 126; and Pemba, 58, 127-9; and Pate, 68, 122-6; and French, 132, 143; and British Establishment, 132, 139-42; send delegation to Bombay, 139-40; war against Saiyid Sa'id, 261, 301, 305-8, 378; and Saiyid Sa'id's proposed treaty, 305; number of, 307; at Gazi, 312, 313; at Takaungu, 60, 308, 312; family tree, 380
Mbwemaji, 38, 86, 315-16; and caravans, 357, 374; exports from, 374 (table)
Mbwera, 38
McMullan, American consul in Zanzibar, 180
Meat, 374 (table)
Mehdi Ali Khan, 105
Melbourne, William Lamb, Viscount, 173
Mikindani, 34, 88, 374 (table)
Miles, S. B., 389
Milius, governor of Bourbon, 136-7
Millet, 374 (table)
Minab, 102
Minto, Lord, Governor-General of India, 170
Missionaries, 252
Mocha, 99; British bombardment of, 138; and British agent, 170
Mogadishu, commerce of, 92; and Europeans, 95; French plans for, 168, 188, 290; and Saiyid Sa'id, 130, 295-300
Mohelli, Saiyid Sa'id's claims to, 295, 320-1; assists Saiyid Sa'id with troops, 256
Molasses, 349
Mombasa, Omani capture of, 25, 46; in 1720s, 46, 53; in 1740s, 26, 120; attacks Zanzibar, 49, 55, 59; harbours, 45-6; taxes, 51; inhabitants, 51-2; system of government, 53-5; commerce, 87-90, 374

(table), 374-5; British Establishment at, 132, 139-42, 225, 247; Saiyid Saʻid's plans for, 144, 150, 247; at war with Saiyid Saʻid, 261, 301, 305-8, 378; and Nasir ibn Sulaiman, 306, 312; town wall of, 307; plague at, 308; ruled by Saiyid Saʻid, 309-10; and Slave Trade, 214-15, 375; and Indians, 310-11; and customs collection, 309, 362, 374-5
Mondevit, Saulnier de, 198, 201
Money. *See* Specie
Mongallo. *See* Ngao
Monsoon winds, 20, 74-5
Moors, 24, 27
Moorsom, Captain, 142
Moresby, Captain Fairfax, 139, 199, 200, 221, 222-3, 225
Morice, 94, 119, 198, 208, 318, 388
Mother-of-pearl, 334
Mozambique, and Omanis, 20, 21; commerce of, 92; and Slave Trade, 200, 320; and French trade, 198; and Saiyid Saʻid, 226-7, 320
Mrima, system of government at, 38-43, 313-14, 322; and Omanis, 130; trade of, 80; inhabitants as slaves, 213
Mrima monopoly, 185, 189, 190, 313-14, 360-2, 374
Msene, 210
Mshirazi, Shaikh of Three Tribes, 310
Mtangata, 38, 41, 361; and Portuguese, 59
Mtoni, 247
Mtwapa tribe, 52, 56
Mubarak ibn Ahmad al-Mazrui, 51, 124, 127, 140
Muhammad, last sultan of Kilwa, 318
Muhammad Ali of Egypt, 113, 115, 155, 163-4, 169, 172

Muhammad ibn Isa, ruler of Lindi, 320
Muhammad ibn Jumʻah al-Barvani Al Harthi, governor of Mafia, 130
Muhammad ibn Khamis, 157, 236 n. 2, 264, 271
Muhammad ibn Mataka, 304
Muhammad ibn Nasir, envoy to Banadir coast, 298-9
Muhammad ibn Nasir, governor of Pemba, 312
Muhammad ibn Saʻid, 277
Muhammad ibn Salim, 145-6
Muhammad ibn Shahali, leader of Changamwe, 351
Muhammad ibn Uthman al-Mazrui, 48-50, 52-3
Muhyi al-Din, 71, 281, 283; negotiates with Pate, 303; goes to Tanga, 313
Mukalla, 79, 255, 312
Murshid, 142-3
Musa binti Ahmad, 280
Musa Mzuri, 356
Muscat, rise of, 22; revenue of, 99-100, 373; commerce of, 76, 97-9, 351-4, 372; British agent at, 169-171; relations with French, 103-4, 155-6, 166; relations with Americans, 151, 194-5, 329
Mutlaq al-Mutairi, 115
Mvita tribe, 52, 56
Mwana Darini of Pate, 72
Mwana Khadija, 63, 68, 72
Mwenyi mkubwa, on Mrima coast, 38-41
Mwenyi mkuu, at Zanzibar, 27-8, 31, 281-3, 285; on Mrima coast, 38-41
Mysore, 106

Nabhani clan of Pate, 62, 72, 123
Najd, 148

411

INDEX

Nakhl, 115
Napoleonic Wars, 97, 113-14, 117, 120, 377
Nasir ibn Abdullah al-Mazrui, 47-8
Nasir ibn Hamad, governor of Zanzibar, 272
Nasir ibn Khalaf, governor of Pemba, 312
Nasir ibn Muhammad, governor of Mafia, 130
Nasir ibn Sulaiman of Pemba, 127; and Banadir coast, 297; occupies Mombasa, 306; death, 312
Naval stores, 330, 333
Navigation Laws, 98
Nayayira, 268
Ndege islands, 34
Nepean, Sir Evan, governor of Bombay, 219-20
Newman Hunt and Christopher, 157-8, 325-6, 327-8, 335
Ngao (Mongallo?), 35, 36, 214, 227 n. 3, 247, 266, 320; exports from, 374 (table)
Nguru, as slaves, 213
Nguru hills, 214
Ngwachani of Pemba, 127
Nine Tribes of Mombasa, 52-4, 309-310
Noel, 166-7, 180
Norsworthy, R. B., goes to East Africa, 325; and Newman Hunt, 327-8, 335; complains about British position, 158-9, 160, 328; and Slave Trade, 242; and Brava, 299; and Mrima, 318
Nossi Bé, and Passot, 167; acquired by French, 171-3, 182, 254; and Slave Trade, 200. *See also* Sakalava
Nossi Cumba, 182
Nossi Mitsou, 182
Nourse, Commodore, 224
Nutmeg, 82

Nyamwesi, as slaves, 213; and caravans, 216, 356-8
Nyasa, Lake, and caravans, 318; and ivory, 355
Nyika peoples, 55-7; commerce of, 88-9; as slave-owners, 204, 214; and Saiyid Sa'id, 311-12

Omani Arabs, settlement on Swahili Coast, 20-1, 24, 25-6, 265-9, 377-378; appearance of, 279; assimilation with Swahilis, 279-81, 379; and Portuguese, 21, 31; capture Mombasa 1698, 25, 46; clan system of, 270; as plantation owners, 82-3, 269, 279, 283-7, 324, 358, 375, 378; as slave-owners, 279; and caravans, 357-8, 375, 378; commerce of, 20-1, 96-100, 348, 351-4, 377-8 and *see also* Slaves, Ivory, Gum copal. *See also* Sa'id ibn Sultan, Ships, Imamate, Saiyidship and Muscat
Omari (Sultan Omari), ruler of Pate, 63, 68
Opium, 349
O'Swald, 342-4
Otondo (Utondwe), 38
Ottoman Empire, 110; and Napoleon, 113; British support of, 164, 169
Owen, W. F., 95; and Pemba, 128-9, 140; and Mombasa, 132, 139-42; and Khamis ibn Uthman, 157-8, 327; and British treaty, 158, 160; at Mozambique, 200; and Slave Trade, 225, 226, 228, 244; and Banadir coast, 297; and Ozi, 300-01; reports on East Africa, 325, 387; and *Mombasa Chronicle*, 382-3
Ozi, 92; and Pate, 63; and Fumoluti, 300-01; commerce of, 88; and African exploration, 357
Ozi tribe at Mombasa, 52

INDEX

Page, Captain, 180
Palmerston, Henry John Temple, Viscount, and Owen's proposals, 158, 228; and British treaty, 160; and French consul in Zanzibar, 167, 169; and British consul at Zanzibar, 170; and Hamerton's removal, 193; and Omani envoys, 175; and Slave Trade, 229-30, 231; loses position, 236
Pangani, 38, 41; and Portuguese, 59; and Kimwere, 314-15; and caravans, 357, 374; copal at, 359; exports from, 374 (table)
Pangani River, 76
Parker, merchant, 335-6
Parsees, 291
Pasni, and Slave Trade, 231
Passot, 167, 318
Pate, inhabitants, 61-2; type of government, 62; taxation, 63; regalia, 63-4; town and harbour, 66; influence on mainland, 64; raids Mombasa, 53; and Mazruis, 58, 68, 122-6, 128; early dealings with Omanis, 67, 95, and French, 96; and British, 120; and Johanna, 120; asks Saiyid Sa'id for help, 123; at war with Saiyid Sa'id, 187, 249, 256-61, 300-05; customs duties, 362; and Slave Trade, 215; commerce of, 75, 88, 91-2, 95-6, 374 (table), 375, and *see also* Hides
Pate tribe at Mombasa, 52
Paza tribe at Mombasa, 52
Pearce, F. B., 385
Peel, Sir Robert, 173
Pemba, 95; inhabitants, 58-9; Omani garrison at, 25, 58; Mombasa's claim to, 57-8, 312; and French, 135; commerce of, 86-7, 374 (table); plantations on, 203, 322; customs duties at, 362. *See also* Nasir ibn Sulaiman

Pepper and peppers, 333, 346, 348-9, 370-1
Persian Gulf, as British route, 102-3, 118, 377; and British in 1830s, 145, 148-9, in 1840s, 169, 186; trade of, 98, 351-3. *See also* Slavery
Peters, Francis, 159, 335, 336, 372
Pewter, 349
Philips, midshipman George, 300-1
Piggott, D. W. I., 386
Pimentel, Manoel, 94
Pingree and West, American firm, 329
Plantations, on Zanzibar and Pemba, 29, 82-3, 203, 283-7, 322; capital for 208-9; mortgage, 347; Arab owners of, 358, 378
Pollock, merchant, 335
Pokomo, 56, 92
Porte, *See* Ottoman Empire
Porterage, 216, 358
Portuguese, in 16th century, 20, 24; in Oman, 21; treaty of 1637, 64; and Swahili rebellion, 21; in 1720s, 25-6, 31, 46, 58, 59, 67; and Saiyid Sa'id, 150; and Slave Trade, 197-8, 199-200, 206; trade with East Africa, 345
Powell, Frank, American consul at Muscat, 195
Prince Regent yacht, 159
Prins, Dr A. H. J., 389
Prior, James, surgeon, 387

Qadhis, in Zanzibar, 277-8, 283; in Mombasa, 310-11
Qais ibn Ahmad, 109, 110-11
Qatif, 98
Qawasim, and Sultan, 102; and Badr, 109-10; piracy of, 109, 114; and British truce, 111; expeditions against, 115-16, 133, 222; forbidden to enter Zanzibar, 236
Qishm, 101, 222

INDEX

Qurun, 268
Quseir, 170

Rabai, Nyika group, 56
Rabai village, 387
Rabaud Bros., French firm, 339
Radama, ruler of Madagascar, 219, 220, 321
Rafters, 350, 353, 370
Ranavalano, queen of Madagascar, 321
Ras al-Hadd, 78
Ras al-Khaima, 102, 116
Ras Hafun, 75, 296
Ras Musandam, 98, 102, 103
Ras Ngomeni, 59, 60
Rashid ibn Ahmad al-Mazrui, 297
Rashid ibn Salim al-Mazrui, 308
Rastaq, 47
Rebmann, Johann, 387
Red Sea, trade with East Africa, 75, 294, 352-3; and American trade, 329; and slaves, 204-5; and French plans, 113, 155, 169, 186
Régis Bros., French firm, 340
Rensha Ramji, 292
Rhino-horn, exported from Zanzibar, 20, 82, from Mombasa, 87, 88, 374 (table), from elsewhere, 374 (table); duty on, 363; bought by British, 337, by Indians, 350
Ribe, 56
Rice, grown at Zanzibar, 30, 82, at Pemba, 86, 374 (table), elsewhere, 374 (table); sold by Indians, 348-349; imported by Zanzibar, 371
Rigby, C. P., 388
Roberts, Edmund, 150-1, 152, 248, 326, 387
Romain Desfossés, governor of Bourbon, 184
Rontaunay, French firm, 338
Rosewater, 352
Rosilly, 103, 198, 199

Rovuma River, 76
Ruete, Emily. *See* Salma binti Sa'id
Rufiji River, 76
Rufu River, 76
Rufus Greene and Co., American firm, 329
Ruga, *diwani* of Vumba, 59
Ruschenberger, S. W., 387

Sabaki River, 64
Sadani, 38, 315
Sahdad ibn Sahdi, 48
Saffron, 352
Sa'id ibn Ahmad Al Bu Sa'idi, Imam, 22, 26, 109; death, 22
Sa'id ibn Danin, 361
Sa'id ibn Khalfan, 151, 155-6, 166, 170
Sa'id ibn Muhammad al-Akhbari, governor of Zanzibar, 272, 356
Sa'id ibn Sultan, Saiyid of Muscat and Sultan of Zanzibar, youth, 109; rise to power, 43, 111-18; appearance and personality, 250-2, 254-5; wives, 280; children, 273-7; system of government and judiciary, 269-73, 277-9, 322-3, 378-9; and *mwenyi mkuu*, 281; revenue, 234-5, 248-9, 281-2, 362, 373; plantations of, 203, 248, 268, 269, 286-7, 324, 369, 373; commercial dealings, 251-2, 335, 366-7, 378; encourage caravans, 356, 373; sends ships to Europe and America, 336, 337, 368-9; slaves of, 204, 215, 287; and Slave Trade, *see* Slavery; moves to Zanzibar, 226-227, 246-9; plans for succession and will, 249-50, 276, 289; and Lamu archipelago, 122-6, 187, 300-05; and Mombasa, *see* Mazruis and Mombasa; and Pemba, 127-9; and Banadir coast, 296-300; and Kimwere, 314-15; and Kilwa

INDEX

Kisiwani, 317-18; and Kilwa Kivinje, 318-19; and Egypt, 164; Omani rebellions against, 145-9, 151-2, 192, 277; and French plans, 134-8, 142-4; and French treaty, 152-4; and French consulate, 155-156, 166-9, 181-5, 377; and Maizan 189; and British in 1820s, 139-49, 247; and 1839 British treaty, 160-1; and British consulate, 156-61, 169-73, 176-7, 249, 328; attitude to East India Co. and F.O., 175-7; and Al Harthi, 266-7; and Sakalava, 167-8, 172-3, 321

Saif ibn Abdullah, Omani governor of Pate, 124
Saif ibn Ahmad Al Bu Sa'idi, 26, 32, 49
Saif ibn Ahmad, governor of Lamu, 300
Saif ibn Muhammad, 99
Sainte Marie, Madagascar, 137
Saiyan, 356
Saiyidship of Muscat, 101, 109, 376, 379
Sakalava, raids on Swahili Coast, 35, 258; and Saiyid Sa'id, 167-8, 172, 321
Salahima, 268
Salih ibn Haramili al-Abri, 267-8
Salil ibn Ruzayq (or Razik), 386
Salim ibn Abdullah, 279
Salim ibn Ahmad al-Mazrui, 51, 305-8
Salim ibn Nasir Al Bu Sa'idi, 316
Salim ibn Sultan, 109
Salma binti Sa'id (Emily Ruete), 255, 280, 387-8
Salt, 352
Salt, Henry, 121
Samayil, 47
Sa'ud, leader of Wahhabis, 115
Sausse, 82, 134-6
Schmeisser, 342

Segeju, 42, 56; as fighting men, 59; living in Zanzibar, 293; and Shambala, 314
Selem, 284
Senna, 333
Sesame, exported from Zanzibar, 370-1, from Mombasa, 87, 374 (table), from elsewhere, 374 (table); bought by Americans, 334, 346, by British, 337, 346, 370-1, by French, 341-2, 346, 370-1, by Germans, 343, 346, 370-371, by Arabs, 353
Seton, Captain David, Resident at Muscat, 108, 199
Sewji, Jairam. *See* Jairam
Shafi'i, 69, 283
Shaha, on Mrima, 38-40; at Mombasa, 54
Shaka tribe at Mombasa, 52
Sham ibn Misham, 52
Shambala, 42, 56, 314-15; and Mazruis, 60; as slaves, 213. *See also* Kimwere
Shatri family, 37, 72, 319
Shela, battle of, 55, 122, 123, 125; village of, 61, 91
Shepard and Bertram, American firm, 329
Shimba hills, 289
Ships, Sultan ibn Ahmad's fleet, 101; number at Muscat, 21, 98; types of, 75-6, 77, 78, 352; construction at Zanzibar, 83, 262-3, 367; construction at Lamu archipelago, 92; registration of, 253, 360; Saiyid Sa'id's fleet, 248, 260-4, 368-9; European use of to impress Arabs, 179-80
Shiraz, 97
Shirazis, 24-5, 27, 33; at Zanzibar, 283; at Mombasa, 52
Shomwi, on Mrima, 38-43
Shurshit, 274

415

INDEX

Siam, 151
Silver thread, 352
Sind, 79, 97, 98, 155; and Slave Trade, 206
Singapore, 359
Siu, 61-3; relationship with Pate, 64-5; blockaded by Saiyid Sa'id, 261; Bwana Mataka of, 301-4; trade of, 88, 91
Skinner, Lt, 104
Slaves, slavery, Slave Trade, 20, 378; import and export by Zanzibar, 82, 198-9, 204-07, 212-13; export by Kilwa Kisiwani, 32, 35, 84, 96, 198-201, 206, 209-10, 212-13, 222, 243, 374, 374 (table), by Kisuere, 320, by Banadir coast, 93, from elsewhere, 213-15, 374, 374 (table); at Mombasa, 214-15; bought by Portuguese, 200, 206, 320, by Spanish, 200-01, by Ile de France (Mauritius) and Bourbon – *see* those headings; by Arabians, 201, 204-06, 353, by India, 201, 204-06, 224, 230-2; British campaign against, 139, 199, 219, 243-244; and African Institution, 220-221; and Anti-Slavery Society, 228; and W. F. Owen, 139-40, 142; and Farquhar, 219-21, 223, 226; British approaches to Saiyid Sa'id about, 219-20, 221; Moresby and his treaty, 221, 222-4, 237, 247; and 1839 treaty, 228-30; compensation for Saiyid Sa'id, 226, 235; British treaties with Persian Gulf shaikhs, 230-1; 1845 treaty, 231-41, 352; French measures against, 153, 199; numbers involved, 199, 204-07, 216, 221, 233, 241, 287-8; prices and profits, 201-02, 209-11, 216-17; duties on, 202, 211, 215, 234; used on plantations, 25, 203, 288
289; and caravans, 208-09, 216; and ivory, 216; and Indian merchants, 209, 211-12, 242-3, 253, 291-2; owned on Swahili Coast, 204; and northern Arabs, 240, 294; slave stealing, 293; prohibition of public sale of, 239; and ship registration, 253; slave revolts in Zanzibar, 256, 289; slaves as soldiers, 259, 282, 288; living in Zanzibar, 287-8; manumission of, 289
Smee, Lt Thomas, 94, 95, 99, 121, 122, 213, 381
Snai ibn Amir, 358
Socotra, 155, 223
Sohar, 164, 192
Somali, culture, 45; people, 61; as slaves, 93
Songo Songo, 36
Spain, demand for slaves, 200-01; trade with East Africa, 345
Specie, types of money and rates of exchange, 364; 5-franc piece, 340, brought to Zanzibar by French, 340-1, 347, by Germans, 344, 347, by Americans, 326, 331, 347; imported by Zanzibar, 371; exported from Zanzibar by Indians, 350-1, 364, by Arabs, 353, 364
Speke, J. H., 387
Spirits, sold by Americans, 330, 347, by Germans, 344, 347, by British, 336, by French, 340-1, 347
Stambuli ibn Kombo, governor of Banadir coast, 300
Stigand, C. H., 383
Strandes, Justus, 383, 388
Suez, 170, 186
Sugar and sugar cane, imported by Zanzibar, 82, 331; grown in Zanzibar, 30, 83, 153, 369; factories in Zanzibar, 251-2, 335, 366-7; exported from Zanzibar,

368, from Mombasa, 87; grown in Pemba, 86; sold by French, 341, 347, by Americans, 347, by Indians, 348-9; bought by Arabs, 353

Sulaiman ibn Ali al-Mazrui, governor of Mombasa, 50-1, 54, 305

Sulaiman ibn Hamad (Muhammad), governor of Zanzibar, becomes governor, 272; and French, 179, 191; commercial pursuits, 269, 272-3; leases land, 286; and judiciary, 278; goes to Tanga, 313

Sur, 78, 88, 98, 352

Surat, trade with East Africa, 76, 78; trade with Persian Gulf, 97, 98-9; and British, 107; people from living in Zanzibar, 290

Sultan ibn Ahmad, ruler of Muscat, comes to power, 101; and British, 104-09, 120-1; and French, 104-09; commerce, 97; death, 109

Sultan ibn Saqr, 146

Sultana, 178, 261, 264, 368

Suʻudi party in Lamu, 65

Swahili, peoples, 19, 24-5, 95; location, 19; religion, 20, 69-70, 283; language, 25, 71, 280, 379; literature, 71; education, 70-1; marriage, 72; women, 72; calendar 72-3; commercial activities, 19-20, 83, 85, 89, 92, 372-3; caravans, 357-8; inhabitants of Zanzibar, 283-4, 285, 287; rebellion against Portuguese, 21; 1720s rebellion, 25; flee to Mafia, 27, 37, 283; resentment towards Arabs, 280, 287, 358, 378-9

Tajura, 169

Takaungu, 56; and Mazruis, 60, 308, 312

Tallow, exported from Zanzibar, 371, from Pangani, 374 (table); bought by Americans, 333, 346, by French, 341, 346

Tana River, 52

Tanga, 38, 41; and Portuguese, 59; and Omanis, 313, 322; attacked by Gazi, 312; and Kimwere, 314

Tangana tribe, 52

Tanganyika, Lake, 213, 214, 356-8

Tangui ibn Chenbe, 309

Tengweni, 288

Thompson, T. P., 116-17, 231, 244

Thorn, merchant, 328

Three Tribes of Mombasa, 52-3, 309-10

Thuwaini ibn Saʻid, birth, 273; and Wahhabis, 184; and Sohar, 192 n. 1, 192; becomes regent, 273, 276; as Saiyid Saʻid's successor, 250; and father's death, 191

Tipu Sultan, 106, 107

Tobacco, 331, 333

Tomkinson, Lt, 121

Tongwe, 315

Topan Tajir, 292

Tortoiseshell, 20; exported from Zanzibar, 371, from Kilwa Kisiwani, 84, 374 (table), from elsewhere, 374 (table); duties on, 363; Swahili collection of, 373; bought by Americans, 333, 346, by British, 336, 346, by French, 341, 346, by Germans, 343, 346

Tostain, 198

Treaties and engagements, 1776 Ile de France and Kilwa, 198; 1785 Ile de France and Kilwa, 201; 1785 and 1786 Ile de France and Oman, 198; 1798 Britain and Muscat, 105, 112, 176; 1800 Britain and Muscat, 107, 110, 112, 176; 1807 Muscat and Ile de France, 113; 1807 France and Persia, 113; 1815 Treaty of Paris, 134; 1817 Britain and Madagascar, 219, 220; 1819

Treaties—*continued*
 Bourbon and Kilwa Kisiwani, 131, 135-6; 1820 Britain and Spain, 200; 1820 Britain and Persian Gulf shaikhs, 230; 1822 Bourbon and Muscat, 137, 138, 142-3, 185, 338; 1822 Britain and Zanzibar (Moresby Treaty), 139, 200, 222-224, 237; 1827 Muscat and Bourbon, 142-3, 338; 1828 Saiyid Sa'id and Mazruis, 306; 1833 America and Zanzibar, 150-2, 253, 260, 298, 326; 1836 Saiyid Sa'id and Twelve Tribes, 309-10; 1838 Britain and Persian Gulf shaikhs, 231; 1838 Saiyid Sa'id and Sakalava, 167-8, 172, 321; 1839 Britain and Zanzibar, 159-61, 229, 253, 335, 361, 362, 368; 1844 France and Zanzibar, 184-5, 253, 339, 361; 1845 Britain and Zanzibar, 205, 238-9, 241; 1847 Britain and Persian Gulf shaikhs, 241
Tumbatu, 28, 72, 73
Turki ibn Abdullah Al Sa'ud, leader of Wahhabis, 147, 149, 182
Turki ibn Sa'id, 277

Ubena, 210
Uganda, 214, 358
Ujiji, 210, 357
Ujipa, 210
Umar Fumba, 356
United States of America, arrival on Swahili Coast, 149-51, 326, 377; establishes consul in Zanzibar, 151, 194; trade with Zanzibar, 212, 326-34, 344-5, 346, with Banadir coast, 298, with Red Sea, 354; 1833 treaty with Zanzibar, 150-2, 253, 260, 298, 326; correspondence with Saiyid Sa'id, 195
Unyamwesi, 76, 315, 356. *See also* Nyamwesi

Unyanyembe, 357
Usagara hills, 214, 316
Utondwe. *See* Otondo
Uvira, 210
Uwais, shaikh of Brava, 299

Vailhen, Captain, 153-4, 156, 338
Vandries, 131
Van Keulen, 94
Velten, Carl, 384
Victoria, Queen, and Omani envoy, 175; and Saiyid Sa'id, 178, 218, 255 n. 2
Victoria Nyanza, Lake, 213
Vidal Bros., French firm, 339, 342
Vignard, 382
Vijana, 39
Villèle, 142
Voeltzkow, Alfred, 383
Vumba, 41; and Segeju, 42; and Portuguese, 59; and Mazruis, 59

Wahhabis, 99-100, 102, 376; truce with Sultan, 102; and Badr, 109-111; and Qawasim, 109, 114; retreat, 115, 133; revival, 147-8; decline, 149; 2nd revival, 182, 184, 192
Walker, William, 139
Wami River, 76, 208
Ward, Charles, American consul in Zanzibar, becomes consul, 195; as agent for American firms, 329; and American navy, 179; and Hamerton, 187, 194; and Saiyid Sa'id, 195, 254; and Slave Trade, 243
Warden, Francis, 116, 141
Warshaikh, 75
Wasin, 38; inhabitants, 56; *diwani* of, 39, 41; and Portuguese, 59; and Omanis, 130, 313; and Mazruis, 59 60

INDEX

Wassmuss, German consul at Mombasa, 383-4

Waters, Richard, American consul in Zanzibar, and French consul, 166; and Hamerton, 174-5, 178; and customs master, 178, 194, 327; influence in Zanzibar, 178; Unpopularity with Sultan, 195, 254; tries to lease land, 286; and caravanners, 356

Wax. *See* Beeswax

Wayunbili, 65

Waziri, on Mrima, 38-42; at Mombasa, 54; at Pate, 62

Wellsted, J. R., 388

Werner, Alice B., 383-5

Wheat, 349

Willoughby, J. P., 228, 244

Wilson, merchant, 335

Wilson, Major David, Resident in Persian Gulf, 145-6

Wire, imported by Mombasa, 87; and caravans, 210, 356; sold by Americans, 330-1, 347, by British, 336, by Germans, 344, 347, by Indians, 348

Wood, 20; imported by Zanzibar, 371; bought by Indians, 350; exported from Kilwa Kisiwani, 84, 374 (table); from elsewhere, 374 (table)

Woodbury, Senator Levi, 150

Yao, 216

Yaqut, governor of Zanzibar, 27, 271, 288

Yusuf of Banadir coast, 188, 299, 302

Zaila, 155

Zanzibar, as centre of Omani power, 25, 50, 83, 246, 360-1; as an entrepot, 77-8, 79-80, 81, 84, 296, 360-361, 363-4, 374-5, 378; fort at, 26, 256; governors of and their monopoly, 26-7, 80-1, 271-3; administration, 27-8, 269-73; judicial system, 277-9; schools, 70; size of population, 30, 265, 287; Arab inhabitants, 265-9; Swahili inhabitants, 283, 285, 287; Indian inhabitants, 290-3; slave inhabitants, 287-90; European inhabitants, 252; and northern Arabs, 293-4; Saiyid Sa'id's move to, 226-7, 246-9; revenue, 30, 202, 248-9, 281-2, 373; plantations, 29, 203, 283-7, 322, 324; land law, 285-6; Mombasa's attack on 1753/1754, 49, 55, 59; capture of Pemba, 127-8; and Wasin, 130; and Mafia, 130-1; American arrival at, 149-52, 160; French consulate at, 155-61, 166-9, 181-5, 377; pro-French party at, 178-9, 190-1; and British consulate, 156-61, 169-73, 176-7, 232, 249, 328

Zaramo, 42, 316-17

Zena, party at Lamu, 65

Zevaco, French doctor in Zanzibar, 190

Zigua, 42; and Mazruis, 60; living in Zanzibar, 293; and slaves, 213, 289; and Shambala, 314; raid caravans, 315; and littoral villages, 316

Zungomero, 357

For Product Safety Concerns and Information please contact our EU
representative GPSR@taylorandfrancis.com
Taylor & Francis Verlag GmbH, Kaufingerstraße 24, 80331 München, Germany

www.ingramcontent.com/pod-product-compliance
Lightning Source LLC
Chambersburg PA
CBHW052138300426
44115CB00011B/1430